Triumph Bonneville
T100, Speedmaster, America, Thruxton and Scrambler
Service and Repair Manual

by Matthew Coombs, Phil Mather & Penny Cox

Models covered

(4364-304-3AL3)

Bonneville. 790cc. 2001 to 2006
Bonneville. 865cc. 2007 to 2012
Bonneville SE. 865cc. 2009 to 2012
T100. 790cc. 2002 to 2004
T100. 865cc. 2005 to 2012
America. 790cc. 2002 to 2006
America. 865cc. 2007 to 2012
Speedmaster. 790cc. 2003 to 2004
Speedmaster. 865cc. 2005 to 2012
Thruxton. 865cc. 2004 to 2012
Scrambler. 865cc 2006 to 2012

ABCDE
FGHIJ
KL

© Haynes Publishing 2012

A book in the **Haynes Service and Repair Manual Series**

ISBN **978 1 84425 917 5**

British Library Cataloguing in Publication Data
A catalogue record for this book is available from the British Library

Library of Congress Control Number 2011944401

Printed in the USA

Haynes Publishing
Sparkford, Yeovil, Somerset BA22 7JJ, England

Haynes North America, Inc
861 Lawrence Drive, Newbury Park, California 91320, USA

Haynes Publishing Nordiska AB
Box 1504, 751 45 UPPSALA, Sweden

Contents

LIVING WITH YOUR TRIUMPH

Introduction

Pre-ride checks

Bike spec

MAINTENANCE

Routine maintenance and servicing

Contents

REPAIRS AND OVERHAUL

Engine, transmission and associated systems

Chassis and bodywork components

Electrical system

Wiring diagrams

REFERENCE

Index

A Phoenix from the ashes

by Julian Ryder

Where is the most modern motorcycle factory in the World? Tokyo? Berlin? Turin, maybe? No, it's in Hinckley, Leicestershire. Improbable as it may seem, the Triumph factory in the Midlands of England is a more advanced production facility than anything the mighty Japanese industry, German efficiency or Italian flair can boast. Still more amazingly, the first motorcycle rolled off the brand new production line in July 1991, nine years after the last of the old Triumphs had trickled out of the old Meriden factory.

It's important to realise that the new Triumph company has very little to do with the company that was a giant on the world stage in the post-war years when British motorcycle makers dominated the global markets. It is true that new owner John Bloor bought the patents, manufacturing rights and, most importantly, trademarks when the old factory's assets were sold in 1983, but the products of the old and new companies bear no relation at all to one another. Apart, of course, from the name on the tanks. Bloor's research-and-development team started work in Collier Street, Coventry and in 1985 work started on the ten-acre green-field factory site which was occupied for the first time the following year.

The R & D team soon dispensed with the old Meriden factory's project for a modern DOHC, eight-valve twin known within the factory as the Diana project (after Princess Di) but shown at the NEC International Bike Show in 1982 as the Phoenix. The world got to see the new Triumphs for the first time at the Cologne Show in late 1990. The company was obviously anxious to distance itself from the old, leaky, unreliable image of the traditional British motorcycle, but it was equally anxious not to engage in a head-on technology war with the big four Japanese factories. The new motto was 'proven technology', the new engines were in-line threes and fours with double overhead camshafts and four valves per cylinder. They were all housed in a universal steel chassis with a large-diameter tubular backbone, and interestingly the new bikes would all carry famous model names from Triumph's past.

If you were looking to compare the technology level with an established machine, you'd have to point to the Kawasaki GPZ900R launched back in '84. Do not take this as a suggestion, current in '91, that the new Triumphs were in some way Kawasakis in disguise because the cam chain was sited on the right-hand side of the motor rather than between the middle cylinders. Yes, of course Triumph had looked at the technology and manufacturing of the Japanese companies and naturally found that an in-line multi-cylinder motor was the most economical way to go. It's just the same in the car world, the straight four is cheaper than the V6 because it uses fewer, simpler parts. In fact the layout of the new motor would seem to indicate that designers from the car world had been brought in by John Bloor. If anyone still harbours the belief that Triumph copied or co-operated with Kawasaki, try and find a contemporary Kawasaki that uses wet liners (cylinder liners in direct contact with coolant as opposed to sleeves fitted into the barrels).

But if Triumph's technology wasn't exactly path-breaking it was certainly very clever. The key concept was the modular design of the motor based around long and short-throw crankshafts in three and four-cylinder configurations. Every engine used the common 76

Bonneville

mm bore with either 55 or 65 mm throw cranks so that the short-stroke engine would be 750 cc in three-cylinder form and 1000 cc as a four. Put the long-stroke crank in and you get a 900 cc triple and a 1200 cc four. The first bike to hit the shops was the 1200 Trophy, a four-cylinder sports tourer which was immediately competitive in a very strong class. There was also a 900 cc, three-cylinder Trophy. The 750 and 1000 Daytonas used the short-stroke motor in three and four-cylinder forms in what were intended to be the sportsters of the range. The other two models, 750 and 900 cc three-cylinder Tridents, cashed in on the early-'90s fad for naked retro bikes that followed the world-wide success of the Kawasaki Zephyr.

The reborn Triumphs were received with acclaim from the motorcycle press – tinged with not a little surprise. They really were very good motorcycles, the big Trophy was a match for the Japanese opposition in a class full of very accomplished machinery. The fact it could live with a modern day classic like the Yamaha FJ1200 straight off the drawing board was a tribute to John Bloor's designers and production engineers. The bike was big, fast, heavy and quite high, but it worked and worked well. And it didn't leak oil or break down, it was obvious that whatever else people were going to say about Triumphs they weren't going to able to resurrect the old jokes about British bangers leaving puddles of lubricant under them. As the rest of the range arrived and tests of them got into print, the star of the show emerged; it was the long-stroke, three-cylinder, 900 cc motor. It didn't matter how it was dressed up, the big triple had that indefinable quality – character. It was the motor the Japanese would never have made, very torquey but with a hint of vibration that endears rather than annoys. Somewhere among the modern, water-cooled, multi-valve technology, the 900-triple had the genes of the old air-cooled OHV Triumph Tridents that appeared in 1969 and stayed in production until '75.

The range stayed basically unchanged for two years, until the Cologne Show of '92. Looking back at the first range it is now easy to see – hindsight again – that the identity of all the models was far too close. The sports tourer Trophy models were reckoned to be a little too sporting, the basic Tridents still had the handlebar and footrest positions of faired bikes. Triumph management later agreed that the first range evinced a certain lack of confidence, that was certainly not the case with the revamped 1993 range.

Visitors to the Cologne Show in September '92 agreed that the Triumphs were the stars, any lack of confidence there may have been two years earlier was completely gone. Any shyness the management may have felt about the Triumph name's past was shaken off as the new Tridents went retro style. Overall, the identities of the original bikes became more individual and more obviously separated; the Trophy models became more touring oriented, the Daytona

T100

more sporty looking and the Trident models more traditional. The factory even had the confidence to put small Union Flag emblems on the side panels of each model, no more apologising for the imagined shortcomings of British engineering. Despite this spreading of the range's appeal, all these bikes were still built on the original modular concept.

There was, however, an exception to this rule of uniformity in the shape of a brand new bike, the Tiger 900. This model was in the enduro/desert-racer style much favoured on Continental Europe but not at all popular in the UK. Here was a Triumph with a 19-inch front tyre, wire wheels and a lower power output than the other 900s. Judging their market as cleverly as ever, the factory held back another new model for the International Bike Show at the Birmingham NEC. This was the Daytona 1200, an out and out speed machine with a hidden political agenda. Its high-compression, 147 PS engine gave it brutal straight-line performance in much the same way as the big Kawasakis of the mid-'80s, and like them it wasn't too clever in the corners because of its weight and length. The bike was built as much to show that Triumph could do it as to sell in big numbers, it also had the secondary function of thumbing the corporate nose at the UK importers' gentlemen's agreement not to bring in bikes of over 125 PS.

Next year's NEC show saw two more new Triumphs, both reworkings of what was now regarded as a modern classic, the 900 triple. The Speed Triple was a clever reincarnation of the British cafe racer style, complete with clip-on handlebars and rear-set footrests. The other newcomer was a more radical project, the Daytona Super III. Externally the motor looked like the usual 900 cc three with 115 PS as opposed to the standard 900 Daytona's 98 PS.

Triumph's next big step was into the US market, where the old company was so strong in the post-war years when the only competition was Harley-Davidson and where there is considerable affection for the marque. The name Triumph chose to spearhead this new challenge was Thunderbird, a trademark sourced in Native American mythology. This time the famous name adorned yet another version of the 900 triple but this time heavily restyled and in a retro package. Dummy cooling fins give it the look of an air-cooled motor, the logo was cast into the clutch cover, and there were soft edges and large expanses of polished alloy. Inside those restyled cases, the motor was retuned even more than the Tiger's for a very user-friendly dose of low-down punch and mid-range power. The cycle parts were given an equally radical redesign, although the retro style stopped short of giving the Thunderbird twin rear shock absorbers. But everything else, the shape of the tank, the chrome headlight and countless other details, harks back to the original Thunderbird and nothing does so as shamelessly as the 'mouth-organ' tank badge, a classic icon if ever there was one.

The first Thunderbird derivative, the Adventurer, appeared for 1996 with a different rear subframe and rear-end styling including a

America

Speedmaster

sissy bar and single seat. That same year, the short-stroke 750 cc motor bowed out of the range, but it went with a bang not a whimper not in a final batch of Tridents but in a limited-edition run of 750 Speed Triples. The bigger Speed Triple's motor was inserted in the Sprint and the result called the Sprint Sport. The reason for using up all those motors was the advent of the new range of fuel-injected and heavily revised three-cylinder engines that first powered the T509 Speed Triple and T595 Daytona of 1997.

The first fuel-injected Triumph, the Daytona T595, was a major milestone for the Factory. It represented a change of policy, the first time Triumph would venture to confront their opposition on the cutting edge of technology. In early 1997, the Honda FireBlade and Ducati 916 ruled. The T595 was able to play in the same ball park. Only on a race track could the Japanese and Italian machines be shown to be better. In the real world the T595 was at least as good a bike. The old long stroke of 65 mm was retained but everything else was new, it was a radical departure from the modular concept that had dominated production until now. You could see how the new motor was a lightened version of the old triple, but fuel injection was new and the frame was a radical departure from previous practice. Serpentine tubing ran from steering head to swingarm pivot and it was aluminium. Bodywork looked tasty too. Despite what Triumph had said about not taking on the Japanese back in 1991, the T595 came out of comparative tests with the 'Blade and 916 on equal terms. The new bike was also given the Speed Triple treatment and adorned with bug-eyed twin headlights in the fashionable 'streetfighter' style. You liked it or loathed it, but you couldn't ignore it.

The trouble with the Supersports end of the market is that the goal posts keep moving, so Triumph hedged their bets by softening the 955i's nominal 128 PS to 108, housing it in a simpler twin-beam frame and calling the result the Sprint ST. This continuation of the original Sprint concept was one of the hits of 1999. As a sports tourer, the fuel-injected Sprint ST was right up there with Honda's class leader, the VFR. Some magazines even preferred the British bike. High praise. The Tiger got the fuel-injected 855 cc motor in '99. Not that development of the carburetted bikes was neglected. Triumph got a Thunderbird derivative right in 1998 with the Thunderbird Sport. The Legend TT is the same bike with a different exhaust system and graphics.

Up to 1999 Triumph concentrated on big bikes but then they took another giant step towards the big time by taking on the Japanese in the most competitive market sector of them all, Supersports 600, with the TT600. For 2001 the most famous name of all was bought out of retirement: Bonneville. The new Bonneville shared the name, engine configuration and style of its predecessors, the T120 and T140, but that was where the similarity ended. It used a 360° carburetted air-cooled twin engine in a utterly non-traditional capacity of 790 cc. The nostalgic picture was completed by wire

Scrambler

wheels and a paint scheme harking back to the 1960s. A factory custom version, the America, followed in 2002.

From a standing start in 1991, the Hinckley factory was competing in all the major motorcycle market sectors. Much bigger production volumes meant the original modular concept was no longer a necessity. By the dawn of the 21st Century Triumph had sold over 100,000 motorcycles. Then the factory was struck by one of the biggest fires ever at a British industrial site. In March 2002 the production line, moulding shop and stores were destroyed and many other parts of the plant severely damaged. Just six months later the rebuilt factory was running at full capacity. The first new product out of the doors was the Daytona 600, a replacement for the TT600. Where the first Supersports 600 Triumph had failed to compete with the Japanese this one was good enough to win an Isle of Man TT.

Development of the Bonneville family continued, with derivatives in the form of the T100 and the custom styled Speedmaster being introduced for the 2003 model year. With the introduction of the Thruxton in 2004, the original 790 cc engine got a 4 mm overbore to increase its capacity to 865 cc. The Thruxton, named after the small 1965 run of hot Bonnies for production race homologation, is styled along the lines of a modern café racer. The Speedmaster and T100 benefitted from the 865 cc engine from 2005. Next on Hinckley's resurrection list was the Scrambler which harks back to the models originally designed for the US market with both pipes sweeping at high level down the right-hand side of the bike and high, off-road style 'bars.

The nicely differentiated range was now well established: Triumph call the Daytonas, Sprints and Tiger 'Urban Sports' while the Bonneville and its derivatives are billed as 'Modern

Thruxton

Classics'. With an eye on America Triumph then unleashed their most audacious bike yet: the Rocket III. (Whisper it, but Rocket III was actually a BSA model name back in the 1970s.) They call it a cruiser but behemoth would be a better description, it's the first production bike to boast a capacity of over two litres and the only thing on the roads that can make a Harley V-Rod look shy and retiring.

Triumph has gone from hesitant newcomer (or should that be returnee?) to a player on the world motorcycling stage. To anyone who remembers the state of the British industry when the original Triumph factory closed its doors, that is nothing short of a miracle.

Acknowledgements

Our thanks are due to Fowlers of Bristol who supplied the machines featured in the illustrations throughout this manual. We would also like to thank NGK Spark Plugs (UK) Ltd for supplying the colour spark plug condition photographs, the Avon Rubber Company for supplying information on tyre fitting and Draper Tools Ltd for some of the workshop tools shown.

Thanks are also due to Julian Ryder who wrote the introduction 'A Phoenix from the Ashes' and to Triumph Motorcycles, Hinckley, for permission to use model pictures of the Triumph models. Triumph Motorcycles Limited bears no responsibility for the content of this book, having had no part in its origination or preparation.

About this manual

The aim of this manual is to help you get the best value from your motorcycle. It can do so in several ways. It can help you decide what work must be done, even if you choose to have it done by a dealer; it provides information and procedures for routine maintenance and servicing; and it offers diagnostic and repair procedures to follow when trouble occurs.

We hope you use the manual to tackle the work yourself. For many simpler jobs, doing it yourself may be quicker than arranging an appointment to get the motorcycle into a dealer and making the trips to leave it and pick it up. More importantly, a lot of money can be saved by avoiding the expense the shop must pass on to you to cover its labour and overhead costs. An added benefit is the sense of satisfaction and accomplishment that you feel after doing the job yourself.

References to the left or right side of the motorcycle assume you are sitting on the seat, facing forward.

We take great pride in the accuracy of information given in this manual, but motorcycle manufacturers make alterations and design changes during the production run of a particular motorcycle of which they do not inform us. No liability can be accepted by the authors or publishers for loss, damage or injury caused by any errors in, or omissions from, the information given.

Illegal copying

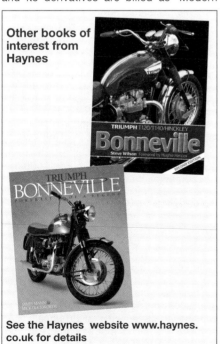

Bonneville

The first model in this new parallel twin range, the Bonneville, was launched in November 2000 for the 2001 model year. It combined the styling and character derived from the most popular of the original Meriden models with the technology of modern design and technology.

The Bonneville used a 790 cc parallel twin air- and oil-cooled unit engine. Its 360° crank meant the pistons rose and fell simultaneously, but were set to fire on alternate strokes. Twin balancer shafts ran off a gear on the right-hand end of the crankshaft to eliminate most of the vibration, leaving enough to provide some essential character. A central cam chain drove the double overhead camshafts actuating the four valves per cylinder.

The cable-operated clutch was a wet, multi-plate unit with conventional springs. The five-speed constant-mesh transmission drove the rear wheel via chain and sprockets that run unconventionally down the right-hand side of the bike, allowing the looks of the original design engine covers to be retained.

The engine had a wet-sump lubrication system incorporating two pumps. The rear pump drew oil from the sump via a strainer and distributed it, via the filter, to the crankshaft's main and big-end bearings, the camshafts, and to the transmission output shaft. The front pump drew oil in the same way and circulated it around the cylinder block and head to cool them before sending it to the oil cooler at the front. The cooled oil then returned to the sump. The front pump also fed a lubrication circuit for the transmission input shaft and the clutch.

Fuel was fed by gravity to the two 36 mm CV carburettors. The carburettors were electrically heated to prevent icing and incorporated a throttle position sensor that transmitted information on throttle angle and rate of change to the ignition control unit (ICU).

The ignition system was fully digital electronic. A pick-up coil mounted on the right-hand side of the engine received signals from projections on the alternator rotor and sent information on crankshaft position and speed to the ICU. This, together with information from the throttle position sensor, was used to determine the ideal firing point. A primary voltage was sent to the single ignition coil which provided the HT voltage to each spark plug simultaneously on a 'wasted spark' system.

The engine sat in a tubular steel, twin-cradle frame with removable sections. Front suspension was by 41 mm oil-damped telescopic forks. Rear suspension was by tubular steel swingarm pivoting through the crankcase and acting on twin shock absorbers that were adjustable for spring pre-load.

The front brake had an hydraulic, twin-piston sliding caliper acting on a single 310 mm disc, and the rear brake had an hydraulic, twin-piston sliding caliper acting on a 255 mm disc. The wheels were steel-spoked and ran tubed tyres.

In 2007 the Bonneville was given the new, larger capacity 865 cc engine originally fitted to the Thruxton. The engine was all-black with polished covers.

A major mechanical change took place in 2008 with the introduction of electronic fuel injection, ensuring the 865cc twin kept within Euro 3 legislation. The throttle bodies were cleverly designed to give the appearance of carburettors and thus retain the bike's traditional look.

The year 2009 was significant because it marked the 50th anniversary of the Bonneville name. There were no mechanical changes for 2009, but the bike's styling reflected many features of the 1970s T140D. Cast wheels replaced the wire-spoked items of the 2008 models, the mudguards were smaller and neater, the shorter silencers were borrowed from the Thruxton, the front brake master cylinder had a remote reservoir and decals replaced the chromed fuel tank badges of the earlier model.

For 2010, new electronic instruments were fitted and the speedometer was activated by a pick-up off the gearbox rather than via a cable off the front wheel.

Bonneville SE

A slightly higher spec Special Edition Bonneville was introduced for 2009. It was as the regular model (including its 2009 improvements), but with a tachometer included in the instruments, brushed alloy engine covers and a chrome tank badge. The SE model received uprated electronic instruments in 2010.

T100

Launched initially as a centennial edition of the Bonneville for the 2002 model year, the T100 was then incorporated into the Triumph range in its own right the following year.

From 2002 to 2004 it used the same engine, frame and suspension as the Bonneville, but with added styling cues reminiscent of the sixties machine. Differences included the addition of a tachometer, rubber knee pads mounted on the fuel tank, alternative colour schemes and polished engine covers.

In November 2004, for the 2005 model year, the T100 was given a slightly de-tuned version of the new 865 cc engine first used in the Thruxton.

Apart from receiving electronic fuel injection in 2008, changes to the T100 have amounted to the addition of fork gaiters in 2009 and electronic instruments in 2010. In celebration of the Bonneville's 50th, an anniversary model was produced for 2009 only with a special logo on the side panels, two-tone paintwork and chromed valve cover. A Steve McQueen edition T100 was released in 2012 in the style of the TR6 Trophy he rode in the film *The Great Escape*; it differed from the standard model in having a single seat, bash plate, khaki paintwork and special graphics. Also in 2012, a special edition T100 was launched to celebrate 110 years of Triumph motorcycles and is recognisable by its two-tone silver and Brooklands

green paintwork, black mudguards, chromed valve cover, chainguard and grabrail and its tank-mounted jubilee crest.

America

The Bonneville America was launched in 2002 and was designed to compete directly with the cruisers and low-riders so popular in America.

It used the 790 cc engine of the Bonneville but with a different crankshaft throw, giving it a firing interval between the cylinders of 270°, and a resultant off-beat feel and sound. Combined with slightly taller gearing achieved by changing the final drive ratio, it mimicked the traditional V-twin cruiser characteristics of the bikes against which it was designed to compete.

While the core of the bike remained the same as the Bonneville, with shared frame, suspension and braking components, a number of design features such as the forward-mounted foot-controls, low-slung seat, raked-back handlebars and raked-out forks, and instruments mounted on the fuel tank, gave it an entirely different character and establish it as a significantly different machine.

In 2007 the America was given the new, larger capacity 865 cc engine originally fitted to the Thruxton. The engine was all-black with polished covers. Additional changes included newly styled cast alloy wheels, and re-designed pillion footrest brackets, fork shrouds drive sprocket cover and front fork shrouds.

In 2008 the America received electronic fuel injection and a new fuel tank with increased capacity. Electronic instruments were fitted in 2010, then for the following year the America received a make-over with changes to riding position and steering geometry. The front wheel diameter was reduced by two inches to 16", the front turn signals were repositioned from the handlebars to the bottom yoke and the separate rider and passenger seats were replaced by the dualseat already fitted to Speedmaster models.

Speedmaster

The Speedmaster was launched in 2003 and was designed to be a Bonneville America with attitude.

For 2003 and 2004 it used the 790 cc engine of the America but with shorter gearing, achieved by altering the final drive ratio, to give it more acceleration. For 2005 the Speedmaster was given the new, larger capacity 865 cc engine, further detuned than the 2005 T100, giving it more torque at lower engine speeds, and again utilising the 270° crankshaft of the original America to retain the off-beat firing pattern.

The Speedmaster had twin front brake calipers and discs, different handlebars, controls and seat, and cast alloy wheels which ran tubeless tyres.

In 2007 the Speedmaster was equipped with newly styled cast alloy wheels, and re-designed pillion footrest brackets, fork shrouds and drive sprocket cover.

Apart from receiving electronic fuel injection in 2008 and electronic instruments and restyled front discs in 2010, changes to the Speedmaster were not outwardly obvious. In 2011, however, the deletion of the metal shrouds fitted to the front forks of earlier Speedmasters, a single front disc brake, new design wheels and a host of detail styling refinements gave the Speedmaster a fresh new look.

Thruxton

The Thruxton was launched in November 2003 for the 2004 model year, and was the first machine to be equipped with the new 865 cc version of the parallel twin engine.

The new engine featured a traditional 360° crankshaft and was tuned to a higher level than those used later in the other machines in Triumph's line-up, establishing the Thruxton as the 'sports' bike of the range.

The Thruxton had drop handlebars and adjustable spring pre-load for the front suspension, with a steeper steering angle for more agile handling and longer rear shock absorbers.

In addition to electronic fuel injection, a number of other changes were made to the Thruxton in 2008; the original clip-on drop handlebars were replaced by a one-piece handlebar, an integral front brake master cylinder and fluid reservoir replaced the separate items of earlier models, and handlebar end mirrors were fitted. In 2010 electronic instruments were fitted and a special edition model with flyscreen, special paint finish and black-painted engine casings was available.

Scrambler

The Scrambler was launched in 2006, styled after the dual-purpose street scramblers that were produced in the 1960s for the American market.

The engine was the same 865 cc unit fitted to the America and Speedmaster, with a 270° crankshaft and mild state of tune. However, in keeping with the off-road theme, steering geometry was altered and ground clearance raised.

The Scrambler was equipped with dual-purpose tyres and high level exhaust pipes as standard, with solo seat and luggage rack, headlight grille, handlebar brace and sump guard available from a range of accessories.

Changes to the Scrambler have been few. It was fitted with electronic fuel injection from 2008 and electronic instruments from 2010.

Identification numbers

Frame and engine numbers

The frame serial number is stamped into the right-hand side of the steering head. The engine number is stamped into the top of the crankcase on the right-hand side. Both of these numbers should be recorded and kept in a safe place so they can be furnished to law enforcement officials in the event of a theft.

The frame and engine serial numbers should also be kept in a handy place (such as with your driver's licence) so they are always available when purchasing or ordering parts for your machine.

Buying spare parts

Once you have found the identification numbers, record them for reference when buying parts. Since the manufacturers change specifications, parts and vendors (companies that manufacture various components on the machine), providing the ID numbers is the only way to be reasonably sure that you are buying the correct parts.

Whenever possible, take the worn part to the dealer so direct comparison with the new component can be made. Along the trail from the manufacturer to the parts shelf, there are numerous places that the part can end up with the wrong number or be listed incorrectly.

The two places to purchase new parts for your motorcycle – the franchised or main dealer and the parts/accessories store – differ in the type of parts they carry. While dealers can obtain every single genuine part for your motorcycle, the accessory store is usually limited to normal high wear items such as chains and sprockets, brake pads, spark plugs and cables, and to tune-up parts and various engine gaskets, etc.

Used parts can be obtained from a breaker for roughly half the price of new ones, but you can't always be sure of what you're getting. Once again, take your worn part to the breaker for direct comparison, or when ordering by mail order make sure that you can return it if you are not happy.

Whether buying new or used parts, the best course is to deal directly with someone who specialises in your particular make.

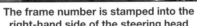

The engine number is stamped into the top of the crankcase on the right-hand side of the engine

The frame number is stamped into the right-hand side of the steering head

The VIN plate (arrowed) is riveted to the frame behind the steering head on the left-hand side

Professional mechanics are trained in safe working procedures. However enthusiastic you may be about getting on with the job at hand, take the time to ensure that your safety is not put at risk. A moment's lack of attention can result in an accident, as can failure to observe simple precautions.

There will always be new ways of having accidents, and the following is not a comprehensive list of all dangers; it is intended rather to make you aware of the risks and to encourage a safe approach to all work you carry out on your bike.

Asbestos

● Certain friction, insulating, sealing and other products - such as brake pads, clutch linings, gaskets, etc. - contain asbestos. Extreme care must be taken to avoid inhalation of dust from such products since it is hazardous to health. If in doubt, assume that they do contain asbestos.

Fire

● Remember at all times that petrol is highly flammable. Never smoke or have any kind of naked flame around, when working on the vehicle. But the risk does not end there - a spark caused by an electrical short-circuit, by two metal surfaces contacting each other, by careless use of tools, or even by static electricity built up in your body under certain conditions, can ignite petrol vapour, which in a confined space is highly explosive. Never use petrol as a cleaning solvent. Use an approved safety solvent.

● Always disconnect the battery earth terminal before working on any part of the fuel or electrical system, and never risk spilling fuel on to a hot engine or exhaust.

● It is recommended that a fire extinguisher of a type suitable for fuel and electrical fires is kept handy in the garage or workplace at all times. Never try to extinguish a fuel or electrical fire with water.

Fumes

● Certain fumes are highly toxic and can quickly cause unconsciousness and even death if inhaled to any extent. Petrol vapour comes into this category, as do the vapours from certain solvents such as trichloro-ethylene. Any draining or pouring of such volatile fluids should be done in a well ventilated area.

● When using cleaning fluids and solvents, read the instructions carefully. Never use materials from unmarked containers - they may give off poisonous vapours.

● Never run the engine of a motor vehicle in an enclosed space such as a garage. Exhaust fumes contain carbon monoxide which is extremely poisonous; if you need to run the engine, always do so in the open air or at least have the rear of the vehicle outside the workplace.

The battery

● Never cause a spark, or allow a naked light near the vehicle's battery. It will normally be giving off a certain amount of hydrogen gas, which is highly explosive.

● Always disconnect the battery ground (earth) terminal before working on the fuel or electrical systems (except where noted).

● If possible, loosen the filler plugs or cover when charging the battery from an external source. Do not charge at an excessive rate or the battery may burst.

● Take care when topping up, cleaning or carrying the battery. The acid electrolyte, evenwhen diluted, is very corrosive and should not be allowed to contact the eyes or skin. Always wear rubber gloves and goggles or a face shield. If you ever need to prepare electrolyte yourself, always add the acid slowly to the water; never add the water to the acid.

Electricity

● When using an electric power tool, inspection light etc., always ensure that the appliance is correctly connected to its plug and that, where necessary, it is properly grounded (earthed). Do not use such appliances in damp conditions and, again, beware of creating a spark or applying excessive heat in the vicinity of fuel or fuel vapour. Also ensure that the appliances meet national safety standards.

● A severe electric shock can result from touching certain parts of the electrical system, such as the spark plug wires (HT leads), when the engine is running or being cranked, particularly if components are damp or the insulation is defective. Where an electronic ignition system is used, the secondary (HT) voltage is much higher and could prove fatal.

Remember...

✗ **Don't** start the engine without first ascertaining that the transmission is in neutral.

✗ **Don't** suddenly remove the pressure cap from a hot cooling system - cover it with a cloth and release the pressure gradually first, or you may get scalded by escaping coolant.

✗ **Don't** attempt to drain oil until you are sure it has cooled sufficiently to avoid scalding you.

✗ **Don't** grasp any part of the engine or exhaust system without first ascertaining that it is cool enough not to burn you.

✗ **Don't** allow brake fluid or antifreeze to contact the machine's paintwork or plastic components.

✗ **Don't** siphon toxic liquids such as fuel, hydraulic fluid or antifreeze by mouth, or allow them to remain on your skin.

✗ **Don't** inhale dust - it may be injurious to health (see Asbestos heading).

✗ **Don't** allow any spilled oil or grease to remain on the floor - wipe it up right away, before someone slips on it.

✗ **Don't** use ill-fitting spanners or other tools which may slip and cause injury.

✗ **Don't** lift a heavy component which may be beyond your capability - get assistance.

✗ **Don't** rush to finish a job or take unverified short cuts.

✗ **Don't** allow children or animals in or around an unattended vehicle.

✗ **Don't** inflate a tyre above the recommended pressure. Apart from over-stressing the carcass, in extreme cases the tyre may blow off forcibly.

✔ **Do** ensure that the machine is supported securely at all times. This is especially important when the machine is blocked up to aid wheel or fork removal.

✔ **Do** take care when attempting to loosen a stubborn nut or bolt. It is generally better to pull on a spanner, rather than push, so that if you slip, you fall away from the machine rather than onto it.

✔ **Do** wear eye protection when using power tools such as drill, sander, bench grinder etc.

✔ **Do** use a barrier cream on your hands prior to undertaking dirty jobs - it will protect your skin from infection as well as making the dirt easier to remove afterwards; but make sure your hands aren't left slippery. Note that long-term contact with used engine oil can be a health hazard.

✔ **Do** keep loose clothing (cuffs, ties etc. and long hair) well out of the way of moving mechanical parts.

✔ **Do** remove rings, wristwatch etc., before working on the vehicle - especially the electrical system.

✔ **Do** keep your work area tidy - it is only too easy to fall over articles left lying around.

✔ **Do** exercise caution when compressing springs for removal or installation. Ensure that the tension is applied and released in a controlled manner, using suitable tools which preclude the possibility of the spring escaping violently.

✔ **Do** ensure that any lifting tackle used has a safe working load rating adequate for the job.

✔ **Do** get someone to check periodically that all is well, when working alone on the vehicle.

✔ **Do** carry out work in a logical sequence and check that everything is correctly assembled and tightened afterwards.

✔ **Do** remember that your vehicle's safety affects that of yourself and others. If in doubt on any point, get professional advice.

● If in spite of following these precautions, you are unfortunate enough to injure yourself, seek medical attention as soon as possible.

Note: *The daily safety checks outlined in the owners handbook covers those items which should be inspected on a daily basis or every time you use the machine.*

Engine oil level

Before you start:

✔ The engine oil is checked after the engine has been running. Triumph recommend running the engine at idle for five minutes, then stop the engine and allow it to stand for three minutes to allow the oil to settle.
✔ Hold the motorcycle upright on a level surface when checking the level.
✔ On Scrambler models, take extreme care when topping-up the oil if the engine has been running – the hot exhaust pipes can cause severe burns.

Bike care:

● If you have to add oil frequently, check whether you have any leaks from the engine

The correct oil

● Modern engines place great demands on their oil. It is very important that you always top up with a good quality oil of the specified type and viscosity. Do not overfill the engine. Any excess oil must be drained off.

Oil type	Semi-synthetic or fully-synthetic motorcycle engine oil. Triumph recommend Castrol Power 1 Racing 4T (Power RS Racing 4T in the US)
Oil viscosity	SAE 10W/40 or 15W/50 to API grade SH or higher, JASO MA spec

joints, oil seals and gaskets, or the cooler and its pipes. If not, the engine could be burning oil, in which case there will be white smoke coming out of the exhaust – (see *Fault Finding*).

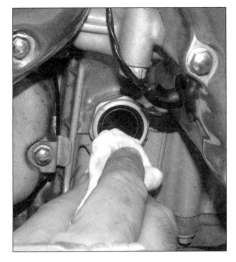

1 The oil level inspection window is located on the right-hand side of the engine between the alternator and front sprocket covers. Wipe the window clean if necessary.

2 With the motorcycle vertical and level, the oil should lie between the upper and lower level lines (arrowed) next to the window.

3 If the level is close to, on or below the lower line, unscrew the oil filler cap from the crankcase – a coin is useful for this. On Scrambler models, where access is restricted, use a long reach screwdriver.

4 Using a suitable funnel if necessary, top up the engine with the recommended grade and type of oil to bring the level mid-way between the lines. Do not overfill – if the level goes above the upper level line drain the excess off (see Chapter 1).

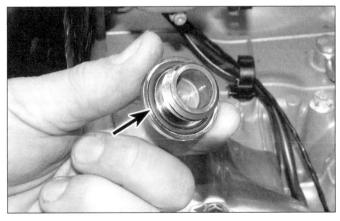

5 Check the condition of the O-ring (arrowed) and replace it with a new one if it is damaged, deformed or deteriorated. Make sure it is correctly fitted then screw the filler cap into the crankcase.

Brake fluid levels

Before you start:

✔ Make sure you have a supply of DOT 4 hydraulic fluid. It should be from a sealed container, not one which has been standing around open to the air.

✔ Wrap a rag around the reservoir being worked on to ensure that any spillage does not come into contact with painted surfaces.

✔ When checking the fluid in the front reservoir turn the handlebars as required so the reservoir is level. When checking the fluid in the rear reservoir support the motorcycle so it is upright and level.

 Warning: Brake hydraulic fluid can harm your eyes and damage painted surfaces, so use extreme caution when handling and pouring it and cover surrounding surfaces with rag. Do not use fluid that has been standing open for some time, as it is hygroscopic (absorbs moisture from the air) which can cause a dangerous loss of braking effectiveness.

Bike care:

● The fluid in the front and rear brake master cylinder reservoirs will gradually drop as the brake pads wear down. If the fluid level is low check the brake pads for wear (see Chapter 1).

● If either fluid reservoir requires repeated topping-up there could be a leak somewhere in the system, which must be investigated immediately.

● Check for signs of fluid leakage from the hydraulic hoses and/or brake system components – if found, rectify immediately (see Chapter 6).

● Check the operation of both brakes before taking the machine on the road; if there is evidence of air in the system (spongy feel to lever or pedal), it must be bled (see Chapter 6).

FRONT – INTEGRAL RESERVOIR TYPE

Fitted to Bonneville up to VIN 380776, T100, Thruxton with one-piece handlebars, America and Speedmaster models

1 The front brake fluid level is visible in the window in the reservoir body and must lie above the LOWER level line (arrowed).

2 If the level is on or below the LOWER line, undo the reservoir cover screws and remove the cover, diaphragm plate and rubber diaphragm.

3 Top the reservoir up with new clean DOT 4 hydraulic fluid . . .

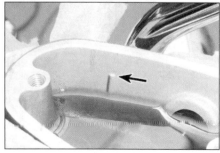

4 . . . until the level is almost up to the top of the upper level mark (arrowed) on the inside of the reservoir. Do not overfill and take care to avoid spills (see **Warning**).

5 Wipe any moisture drops off the rubber diaphragm using an absorbent lint-free cloth.

6 Ensure that the diaphragm is correctly seated before fitting the plate and cover. Secure the cover with the screws.

FRONT –
ROUND RESERVOIR TYPE

Fitted to Bonneville from VIN 380777, Thruxton with clip-on handlebars and Scrambler models

1 The front brake fluid level is visible through the reservoir body and must lie between the UPPER and LOWER level lines (arrowed).

2 If the level is on or below the LOWER line, undo the reservoir cap clamp bolt and remove the clamp, then unscrew the cap and remove the diaphragm plate and rubber diaphragm.

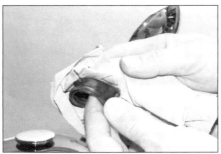

3 Top the reservoir up with new clean DOT 4 hydraulic fluid, until the level is almost up to the UPPER level line on the reservoir. Do not overfill and take care to avoid spills (see **Warning**).

4 Wipe any moisture drops off the rubber diaphragm using an absorbent lint-free cloth.

5 Ensure that the diaphragm is correctly seated before installing the plate and cap. Secure the cap with its clamp.

REAR –
Bonneville, T100 and
Thruxton

1 Remove the right-hand side panel (see Chapter 7). The rear brake fluid level is visible through the reservoir body and must lie between the UPPER and LOWER level lines (arrowed).

2 If the level is on or below the LOWER line, wrap a rag round the reservoir then, undo the cover screws and remove the cover, diaphragm plate and rubber diaphragm. If an angled screwdriver is not available remove the seat to improve access (see Chapter 7).

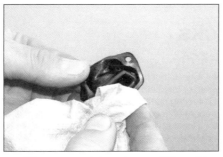

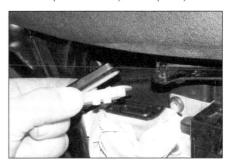

3 Top the reservoir up with new clean DOT 4 hydraulic fluid until the level is almost up to the UPPER level line. Do not overfill and take care to avoid spills (see **Warning**).

4 Wipe any moisture drops off the rubber diaphragm using an absorbent lint-free cloth.

5 Ensure that the diaphragm is correctly seated before installing the plate and cover. Install the side panel.

REAR – America, Speedmaster and Scrambler

1 On America and Speedmaster models, the rear brake fluid level is visible through the reservoir body and must lie between the UPPER and LOWER level lines (arrowed).

2 If the level is on or below the LOWER line, slacken the reservoir mounting bolt to free the shroud then lift it off the reservoir.

3 On Scrambler models, the rear brake fluid level is visible through the reservoir body and must lie between the UPPER and LOWER level lines (arrowed).

4 If the level is on or below the LOWER line, undo the bolts securing the reservoir cover and lift the cover off.

5 On all models, wrap a rag round the reservoir then unscrew the cap and remove the diaphragm plate and rubber diaphragm.

6 Top the reservoir up with new clean DOT 4 hydraulic fluid until the level is almost up to the UPPER level line. Do not overfill and take care to avoid spills (see **Warning**).

7 Wipe any moisture drops off the rubber diaphragm using an absorbent lint-free cloth.

8 Ensure that the diaphragm is correctly seated before installing the plate and cap. On America and Speedmaster models, fit the shroud and tighten the reservoir mounting bolt. On Scrambler models, fit the reservoir cover.

Legal and safety checks

Lighting and signalling
● Take a minute to check that the headlight, tail light, brake light, instrument lights and turn signals all work correctly.
● Check that the horn sounds when the button is pressed.
● A working speedometer, graduated in mph, is a statutory requirement in the UK.

Safety
● Check that the throttle grip rotates smoothly when opened and snaps shut when released, in all steering positions. Also check for the correct amount of freeplay (see Chapter 1).
● Check that the steering moves freely from lock-to-lock.
● Check that the brake lever and pedal, clutch lever and gearchange lever operate smoothly. Lubricate them at the specified intervals or when necessary (see Chapter 1).

● Check that the engine shuts off when the kill switch is operated.
● Check that the stand return springs hold the sidestand up securely when retracted.

Fuel
● This may seem obvious, but check that you have enough fuel to complete your journey. If you notice signs of fuel leakage – rectify the cause immediately.
● Ensure you use the correct grade fuel – see Chapter 1 Specifications.

Tyres

The correct pressures
● Tyre pressures change with changes in air temperature and atmospheric pressure, therefore any change in the weather will affect the pressure in the tyre.
● The tyres must be checked when **cold**, not immediately after riding. Note that incorrect tyre pressures will cause abnormal tread wear and unsafe handling. In extreme cases very low tyre pressures may cause the tyre to slip on the rim or come off.
● Use an accurate pressure gauge. Many forecourt gauges are wildly inaccurate. If you buy your own, spend as much as you can justify on a quality gauge.
● Proper air pressure will increase tyre life and provide maximum stability and ride comfort.

Tyre care
● Check the tyres carefully for cuts, tears, embedded nails or other sharp objects and excessive wear. Operation of the motorcycle with excessively worn tyres is extremely hazardous, as traction and handling are directly affected.

● Check the condition of the tyre valve and ensure the dust cap is in place.
● Pick out any stones or nails which may have become embedded in the tyre tread. If left, they will eventually penetrate through the casing and cause a puncture.
● If tyre damage is apparent, or unexplained loss of pressure is experienced, seek the advice of a tyre fitting specialist without delay.

Tyre tread depth
● At the time of writing UK law requires that tread depth must be at least 1 mm over 3/4 of the tread breadth all the way around the tyre, with no bald patches. Many riders, however, consider 2 mm tread depth minimum to be a safer limit. Triumph recommend a minimum of 2 mm for general use, and 3 mm on the rear if the bike is ridden at speeds in excess of 80 mph (130 km/h).
● All tyres now incorporate wear indicators in the tread. Identify the location marking on the tyre sidewall to locate the indicator bar and replace the tyre if the tread has worn down to the bar – some tyres have wear bars near the edge as well as in the centre.

1 Unscrew the dust cap from the valve. Air shouldn't escape unless the valve core is depressed; if it does, use a valve core key to tighten the core – some pressure gauges incorporate a key.

2 Check the tyre pressures when **cold**. Do not forget to fit the cap after checking the pressure.

3 Measure tread depth at the centre of the tyre using a depth gauge.

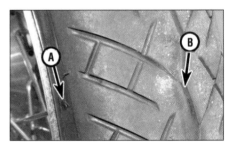

4 Tyre tread wear indicator bar (A) and its location marking (B – usually either an arrow, a triangle or the letters TWI) on the sidewall.

Carburettor models

Model	Front	Rear
Bonneville, T100		
Solo	33 psi (2.3 Bar)	38 psi (2.6 Bar)
Pillion	33 psi (2.3 Bar)	41 psi (2.8 Bar)
Thruxton		
Solo	33 psi (2.3 Bar)	33 psi (2.3 Bar)
Pillion	33 psi (2.3 Bar)	41 psi (2.8 Bar)
Scrambler		
Solo	30 psi (2.1 Bar)	34 psi (2.34 Bar)
Pillion	30 psi (2.1 Bar)	41 psi (2.8 Bar)
America (spoked wheels)		
Solo	30 psi (2.1 Bar)	31 psi (2.1 Bar)
Pillion	31 psi (2.13 Bar)	36 psi (2.5 Bar)
America (cast wheels), Speedmaster	36 psi (2.5 Bar)	42 psi (2.9 Bar)

EFI models
Pressures are for solo and pillion use

Model	Front	Rear
Bonneville, T100, Thruxton	33 psi (2.3 Bar)	41 psi (2.8 Bar)
America (spoked wheels)		
Solo	30 psi (2.1 Bar)	31 psi (2.1 Bar)
Pillion	31 psi (2.1 Bar)	36 psi (2.5 Bar)
America (cast wheels)		
Up to 2010	36 psi (2.5 Bar)	42 psi (2.9 Bar)
From 2011	30 psi (2.1 Bar)	42 psi (2.9 Bar)
Speedmaster	36 psi (2.5 Bar)	42 psi (2.9 Bar)
Scrambler	30 psi (2.1 Bar)	41 psi (2.8 Bar)

Suspension, steering and drive chain

Suspension and Steering
● Check that the front and rear suspension operates smoothly without binding (see Chapter 1).
● Check that the suspension is adjusted as required, where applicable (see Chapter 5).
● Check that the steering moves smoothly from lock-to-lock, and that there is no freeplay.

Drive chain
● Check that the chain isn't too loose or too tight, and adjust it if necessary (see Chapter 1).
● If the chain looks dry, lubricate it (see Chapter 1).

Dimensions and weights

Bonneville and T100
Overall length
  2001 to 2004 . . . . .2250 mm
  2005   . . . . .2243 mm
  2006 to 2008. . . . . .2230 mm
  2009-on . . . . .2130 mm
Overall width
  2001 to 2005. . . . . .860 mm
  2006 to 2008. . . . . .840 mm
  2009-on . . . . .765 mm
Overall height
  2001 to 2005. . . . . .1105 mm
  2006-on . . . . .1100 mm
Wheelbase
  2001 to 2004. . . . . .1493 mm
  2005   . . . . .1484 mm
  2006 to 2008. . . . . .1500 mm
  2009-on . . . . .1490 mm
Seat height
  2001 to 2008. . . . . .775 mm
  2009-on . . . . .750 mm
Weight (dry) .205 kg

Scrambler
Overall length . . . . .2213 mm
Overall width. . . . . .865 mm
Overall height . . . . .1202 mm
Wheelbase . . . . .1500 mm
Seat height . . . . .825 mm
Weight (dry) .205 kg

Thruxton
Overall length
  2004 and 2005 . . . . 2212 mm
  2006-on . . . . .2150 mm
Overall width
  2004 and 2005 . . . . 714 mm
  2006-on . . . . 695 mm clip-on bars, 950 mm high bars
Overall height
  2004 and 2005 . . . . 1170 mm
  2006-on . . . . 1095 mm clip-on bars, 1120 mm high bars
Wheelbase
  2004 and 2005 . . . . 1477 mm
  2006 and 2007 . . . . 1490 mm
  2008-on . . . . 1510 mm
Seat height . . . . 790 mm
Weight (dry) . . . . 205 kg

America
Overall length
  2002 to 2005. . . . . .2424 mm
  2006-on . . . . .2420 mm
Overall width
  2002 to 2006. . . . . .955 mm
  2007 to 2010. . . . . .960 mm
  2011-on . . . . .821 mm
Overall height
  2002 to 2006. . . . . .1184 mm
  2007 to 2010. . . . . .1170 mm
  2011-on . . . . .1175 mm
Wheelbase
  2002 to 2010. . . . . .1655 mm
  2011-on . . . . .1610 mm
Seat height
  2002 to 2010. . . . . .720 mm
  2011-on . . . . .690 mm
Weight
  2002 to 2010. . . . . .226 kg (dry)
  2011-on . . . . .250 kg (wet)

Speedmaster
Overall length
  2003 to 2005. . . . . .2424 mm
  2006 to 2010. . . . . .2420 mm
  2011-on . . . . .2370 mm
Overall width
  2003 to 2005. . . . . .955 mm
  2006-on . . . . .830 mm
Overall height
  2003 to 2005. . . . . .1184 mm
  2006 to 2010. . . . . .1160 mm
  2011-on . . . . .1170 mm
Wheelbase
  2003 to 2010. . . . . .1655 mm
  2011-on . . . . .1610 mm
Seat height
  2002 to 2010. . . . . .720 mm
  2011-on . . . . .700 mm
Weight
  2003 to 2010. . . . . .229 kg (dry)
  2011-on . . . . .250 kg (wet)

Engine

Type . . . . Four-stroke parallel twin
Capacity
  Bonneville and America
    2001 to 2006. . . . . 790 cc
    2007-on . . . . 865 cc
  T100
    2003 and 2004 . . . . 790 cc
    2005-on . . . . 865 cc
  Speedmaster
    2003 and 2004 . . . . 790 cc
    2005-on . . . . 865 cc
  Thruxton and Scrambler. . . . . 865 cc
Bore
  790 cc engine. . . . . 86.0 mm
  865 cc engine. . . . . 90.0 mm
Stroke . . . . 68 mm
Compression ratio . . . . 9.2 to 1
Firing interval
  Bonneville, T100 and Thruxton. . . . . 360°
  America, Speedmaster and Scrambler . . . . 270°
Cooling system. . . . . Air/oil cooled
Clutch . . . . Wet multi-plate with cable release
Transmission. . . . . Five-speed constant mesh
Final drive. . . . . Chain and sprockets
Camshafts . . . . DOHC, chain and gear-driven
Fuel system
  2001 to 2007 models . . . . Twin CVK Keihin carburettors
  2008-on models . . . . Multipoint sequential electronic fuel injection (EFI)
Exhaust system . . . . Two-into-two
Ignition system . . . . Digital electronic

Chassis

Bonneville and T100

Frame type. . . . . Tubular steel twin cradle with box-section spine
Rake and Trail
  2001 to 2004. . . . . 29°, 117 mm
  2005 to 2008. . . . . 28°, 110 mm
  2009-on . . . . 27.5°, 117 mm

1 gal = 3.785 ll

Fuel tank capacity
  Total (inc. reserve)
    2001 to 2004. . . . . 16.0 litres
    2005-on . . . . 16.6 litres
  Reserve. . . . . 3.0 litres (3.5 litres EFI models)
Front suspension
  Type . . . . Oil-damped, coil sprung 41 mm telescopic forks
  Travel . . . . 120 mm
Rear suspension
  Type . . . . Tubular steel double-sided swingarm and twin coil sprung shock absorbers with adjustable pre-load
  Travel . . . . 105 mm
Wheels
  Bonneville 2001 to 2008, all T100 . . . . Steel spoke, front 2.5 x 19 inch, rear 3.5 x 17 inch
  Bonneville 2009-on. . . . . Cast alloy, front 3.0 x 17 inch, rear 3.5 x 17 inch

Tyres

	Front	Rear
Bonneville 2001 to 2008, all T100	100/90-19, tubed	130/80-17, tubed
Bonneville 2009-on.	110/70 R17, tubeless	130/80 R17, tubeless

Front brake . . . . Single 310 mm disc with twin piston sliding caliper
Rear brake . . . . Single 255 mm disc with twin piston sliding caliper

America and Speedmaster

Frame type. . . . . Tubular steel twin cradle with box-section spine
Rake and Trail
  2002 to 2010. . . . . 33.3°, 153 mm
  2011-on America . . . . 33.4°, 155 mm
  2011-on Speedmaster . . . . 33.4°, 168 mm
Fuel tank capacity
  Total (inc. reserve) – 2002 to 2007 . . . . 16.6 litres
  Total (inc. reserve) – 2008-on . . . . 19.5 litres
  Reserve. . . . . 3.5 litres

Chassis (continued)

America and Speedmaster (continued)

Front suspension
Type .... Oil-damped, coil sprung 41 mm telescopic forks
Travel .... 130 mm
Rear suspension
Type .... Tubular steel double-sided swingarm and twin coil sprung shock absorbers with adjustable pre-load
Travel .... 96 mm
Wheels
America
2002 to 2006............................... Steel spoke, front 2.5 x 18 inch, rear 3.5 x 15 inch
2007 to 2010............................... Cast alloy, front 2.5 x 18 inch, rear 3.5 x 15 inch
2011-on .... Cast alloy, front 3.0 x 16 inch, rear 4.0 x 15 inch
Speedmaster
2003 to 2010............................... Cast alloy, front 2.5 x 18 inch, rear 3.5 x 15 inch
2011-on .... Cast alloy, front 2.5 x 19 inch, rear 4.0 x 15 inch

Tyres

	Front	Rear
America 2002 to 2006	110/90 18, tubed	170/80 15, tubed
America 2007 to 2010	110/90 18, tubeless	170/80 15, tubeless
America 2011-on	130/90 R16, tubeless	170/80 B15, tubeless
Speedmaster 2003 to 2010	110/90 18, tubeless	170/80 15, tubeless
Speedmaster 2011-on	100/90 R19, tubeless	170/80 B15, tubeless

Front brake
America and 2011-on Speedmaster .... Single 310 mm disc with twin piston sliding caliper
Speedmaster 2003 to 2010 .... Twin 310 mm discs with twin piston sliding calipers
Rear brake
2002 to 2005.. Single 255 mm disc with twin piston sliding caliper
2006-on .... Single 285 mm disc with twin piston sliding caliper

Thruxton

Frame type.. Tubular steel twin cradle with box-section spine
Rake and Trail... 27°, 97 mm
Fuel tank capacity
Total (inc. reserve)
2004 to 2005... 16.0 litres
2006-on... 16.6 litres
Reserve... 3.0 litres (3.5 litres on EFI model)
Front suspension
Type .... Oil-damped, coil sprung 41 mm telescopic forks with adjustable pre-load
Travel .... 120 mm
Rear suspension
Type .... Tubular steel double-sided swingarm and twin coil sprung shock absorbers with adjustable pre-load
Travel .... 105 mm
Wheels .... Steel spoke, front 2.5 x 18 inch, rear 3.5 x 17 inch
Tyres
Front .... 100/90-18, tubed
Rear .... 130/80-R17, tubed
Front brake .... Single 320 mm floating disc with twin piston sliding caliper
Rear brake .... Single 255 mm disc with twin piston sliding caliper

Scrambler

Frame type.. Tubular steel twin cradle with box-section spine
Rake and Trail... 27.8°, 105 mm
Fuel tank capacity
Total (inc. reserve).. 16.6 litres
Reserve... 3.0 litres (3.5 litres on EFI model)
Front suspension
Type .... Oil-damped, coil sprung 41 mm telescopic forks with adjustable pre-load
Travel .... 120 mm
Rear suspension
Type .... Tubular steel double-sided swingarm and twin coil sprung shock absorbers with adjustable pre-load
Travel .... 105 mm
Wheels .... Steel spoke, front 2.5 x 19 inch, rear 3.5 x 17 inch
Tyres
Front .... 100/90-19, tubed
Rear .... 130/80-17, tubed
Front brake .... Single 310 mm disc with twin piston sliding caliper
Rear brake .... Single 255 mm disc with twin piston sliding caliper

Chapter 1
Routine maintenance and servicing

Contents

Degrees of difficulty

| Easy, suitable for novice with little experience | | Fairly easy, suitable for beginner with some experience | | Fairly difficult, suitable for competent DIY mechanic | | Difficult, suitable for experienced DIY mechanic | | Very difficult, suitable for expert DIY or professional | |

Engine

Engine idle speed	1000 ± 50 rpm
Spark plugs	
Type	NGK DPR8EA-9
Electrode gap	0.8 to 0.9 mm
Valve clearances (COLD engine)	
Intake valves	0.15 to 0.20 mm
Exhaust valves	0.25 to 0.30 mm
Cylinder compression	see Section 32

Miscellaneous

Drive chain	
Slack (with bike on sidestand)	
Bonneville and T100	20 to 30 mm *(handwritten: ⇒ 1" → 1.3")*
Thruxton and Scrambler	30 to 40 mm
America and Speedmaster	35 to 45 mm
Stretch limit (21 pin length – see text)	321 mm *(handwritten: → 12.63)*
Throttle twistgrip freeplay	2 to 3 mm
Clutch cable freeplay	2 to 3 mm
Tyre pressures (cold)	see *Pre-ride checks*
Brake pad friction material minimum thickness	1.5 mm

Lubricants and fluids

Fuel grade – carburettor models	
Europe	Unleaded, minimum 95 RON (Research Octane Number)
US and Canada	Unleaded, minimum 89 (CLC or AKI (R+M) / 2 method)
Fuel grade – EFI models	
Europe	Unleaded, minimum 91 RON (Research Octane Number)
US and Canada	Unleaded, minimum 87 (CLC or AKI (R+M) / 2 method)
Engine oil type	Semi-synthetic or fully-synthetic motorcycle engine oil
Engine oil viscosity	SAE 10W/40 or 15W/50 to API grade SH or higher, JASO MA spec
Engine oil capacity	
Oil change	3.3 litres
Oil and filter change	3.8 litres
Dry fill (following rebuild)	4.5 litres
Front fork oil	10W (Kayaba G10)
Brake fluid	DOT 4
Drive chain	aerosol chain lubricant suitable for sealed chains
Steering head bearings	multi-purpose grease
Swingarm pivot bearings	multi-purpose grease
Bearing seal lips	multi-purpose grease
Gearchange lever/rear brake pedal/footrest pivots	multi-purpose grease
Brake and clutch lever pivots	multi-purpose grease
Sidestand pivot	multi-purpose grease
Throttle grip	engine oil
Front brake lever piston tip	silicone grease
Cables	aerosol cable lubricant

Torque settings

Alternator cover bolts	9 Nm
Chainguard screws	7 Nm
Engine oil drain bolt	25 Nm
Handlebar positioning bolts – Thruxton wth separate handlebars	11 Nm
Handlebar clamp bolts – Thruxton wth separate handlebars	27 Nm
Headlight mounting bolts – Bonneville, T100, Thruxton and Scrambler	10 Nm
Headlight bracket mounting bolt – America and Speedmaster	27 Nm
Headlight bracket pinch bolt – America and Speedmaster	27 Nm
Engine oil filter	10 Nm
Rear axle nut	
Bonneville, T100, Thruxton and Scrambler	85 Nm
America and Speedmaster	110 Nm
Spark plugs	20 Nm
Sprocket cover bolts	9 Nm
Steering head bearing adjuster nut pre-load (with service tool)	40 Nm
Steering head bearing locknut (with service tool)	40 Nm
Steering stem nut	90 Nm
Top yoke fork clamp bolts	
Bonneville, T100, Thruxton and Scrambler	27 Nm
America and Speedmaster	20 Nm

Note: *The daily safety checks outlined in the owner's manual cover those items which should be inspected on a daily basis or every time you ride. Always perform the pre-ride inspection at every maintenance interval (in addition to the procedures listed). The intervals listed below are the intervals recommended by the manufacturer.*

Pre-ride

See *'Pre-ride checks'* at the beginning of this manual.

After the initial 500 miles (800 km)

Note: *The first service is performed by a Triumph dealer after the first 500 miles (800 km) from new. Thereafter, maintenance is carried out according to the following intervals of the schedule.*

Every 200 miles (300 km)

☐ Clean and lubricate the drive chain (Section 1)

Every 500 miles (800 km)

☐ Check and adjust drive chain slack (Section 2)
☐ Check for drive chain and sprockets wear (Section 3)

Every 6000 miles (10,000 km) or 12 months

Carry out all the items under the Pre-ride checks and the 200 and 500 mile (300 and 800 km) checks, plus the following:
☐ Check the spark plugs (Section 4)
☐ Check the fuel hoses and fuel system components (Section 5)
☐ Change the engine oil and filter (Section 6)
☐ Check and clean the air filter element (Section 7)
☐ Check carburettor synchronisation (Section 8)
☐ Check and adjust the engine idle speed (Section 9)
☐ Check throttle cable operation and freeplay (Section 10)
☐ Check the operation of the clutch and its cable (Section 11)
☐ Check the brake pads for wear (Section 12)
☐ Check the operation of the brakes, and for fluid leakage (Section 13)
☐ Check and lubricate the sidestand, lever pivots and cables (Section 14)
☐ Check the tightness of all nuts and bolts (Section 15)

Every 6000 miles (10,000 km) or 12 months (continued)

☐ Check the steering head bearing freeplay (Section 16)
☐ Check the front and rear suspension (Section 17)
☐ Check the tyre and wheel condition (Section 18)
☐ Check the wheel bearings (Section 19)
☐ Check the sidestand and the starter interlock circuit operation (Section 20)
☐ Check the battery (Section 21)
☐ Check and adjust the headlight aim (Section 22)

Every 12,000 miles (20,000 km) or two years

Carry out all the items under the 6000 mile (10,000 km) or 12 months check, plus the following:
☐ Replace the spark plugs with new ones (Section 23)
☐ Check the valve clearances (Section 24)
☐ Replace the air filter element with a new one (Section 25)
☐ Lubricate the steering head bearings (Section 16)
☐ Check the secondary air injection system (Section 26)
☐ Clean the fuel strainer if signs of fuel starvation are apparent (Section 27)

Every two years

☐ Change the brake fluid (Section 28)

Every 24,000 miles (40,000 km) or four years

Carry out all the items under the 12,000 mile (20,000 km) or two years checks, plus the following:
☐ Change the front fork oil (Section 29)
☐ Replace the fuel system hoses with new ones (Section 30)

Every four years

☐ Replace the brake hoses with new ones (Section 31)

Non-scheduled maintenance

☐ Check the cylinder compression (Section 32)

Note: *The safety checks outlined in the owner's manual, and described in detail at the front of this manual, covers those items which should be inspected on a daily basis or every time you ride. Always perform the pre-ride inspection at every maintenance interval (in addition to the procedures listed). The intervals listed below are the intervals recommended by the manufacturer.*

Pre-ride

☐ See *Pre-ride checks* at the beginning of this manual.

After the initial 500 miles (800 km)

Note: *This check is usually performed by a Triumph dealer after the first 500 miles (800 km) from new. Thereafter, maintenance is carried out according to the following intervals of the schedule.*

Every 200 miles (300 km)

☐ Lubricate the drive chain (Section 1)

Every 500 miles (800 km)

☐ Check and adjust drive chain slack (Section 2)
☐ Check for drive chain and sprockets wear (Section 3)

Every 6000 miles (10,000 km) or 12 months

Carry out all the items under the Pre-ride checks and the 200 and 500 mile (300 and 800 km) checks, plus the following:

☐ Check the spark plugs (Section 4)
☐ Check the fuel hoses and fuel system components (Section 5)
☐ Change the engine oil and filter and check the oil cooler (Section 6)
☐ Check and clean the air filter element (Section 7)
☐ Check throttle body synchronisation (Section 8)
☐ Check the engine management system for stored fault codes – either a dealer operation using the Triumph diagnostic tool or using an aftermarket fault code reader.
☐ Check throttle cable operation and freeplay (Section 10)
☐ Check the operation of the clutch and its cable (Section 11)
☐ Check the brake pads for wear (Section 12)
☐ Check the operation of the brakes, and for fluid leakage (Section 13)

Every 6000 miles (10,000 km) or 12 months (continued)

☐ Check and lubricate the sidestand, lever pivots and cables (Section 14)
☐ Check the tightness of all nuts and bolts (Section 15)
☐ Check the steering head bearing freeplay (Section 16)
☐ Check the suspension (Section 17)
☐ Check the tyre and wheel condition (Section 18)
☐ Check the wheel bearings (Section 19)
☐ Check the sidestand and the starter interlock circuit operation (Section 20)
☐ Check the battery (Section 21)
☐ Check the headlight aim (Section 22)

Every 12,000 miles (20,000 km) or two years

Carry out all the items under the 6000 mile (10,000 km) check, plus the following:

☐ Fit new spark plugs (Section 23)
☐ Check and adjust the valve clearances (Section 24)
☐ Renew the air filter element (Section 25)
☐ Fit a new fuel filter (Section 5)
☐ Lubricate the steering head bearings (Section 16)
☐ Check the secondary air injection system (Section 26)
☐ Change the fuel filter (Section 27)

Every two years

☐ Change the brake fluid (Section 28)

Every 24,000 miles (40,000 km) or four years

Carry out all the items under the 12,000 mile (20,000 km) check, plus the following:

☐ Change the front fork oil (Section 29)
☐ Fit new fuel hoses (Section 30)

Every four years

☐ Fit new brake hoses (Section 31)

Component locations on right side – Bonneville (T100, Thruxton and Scrambler similar)

1 Battery
2 Spark plug
3 SAIS reed valves
4 Throttle cable upper adjuster
5 Front brake fluid reservoir
6 Front fork seal
7 Oil filler cap
8 Oil level inspection window
9 EVAP canister (California)
10 Rear brake fluid reservoir
11 Rear shock pre-load adjuster
12 Drive chain adjuster

Component locations on left side – Bonneville (T100, Thruxton and Scrambler similar)

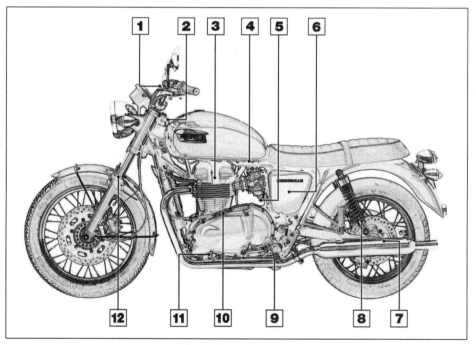

1 Clutch cable upper adjuster
2 Steering head bearing adjuster
3 Spark plug
4 Fuel filter*
5 Idle speed adjuster
6 Air filter
7 Drive chain adjuster
8 Rear shock pre-load adjuster
9 Oil filter
10 Clutch cable lower adjuster
11 Oil drain plug
12 Front fork seal
*Fuel filter is integral with tap on
carburettor models and integral with fuel
pump on EFI models

Component locations on right side – America (Speedmaster similar)

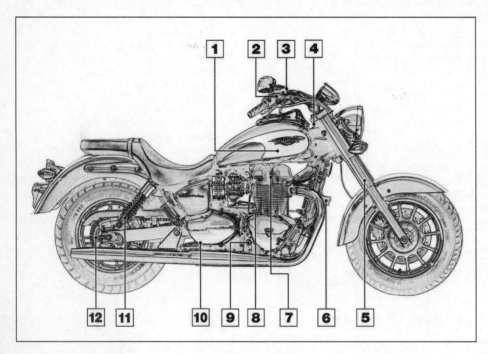

1 SAIS reed valves
2 Throttle cable upper adjuster
3 Front brake fluid reservoir
4 Steering head bearing adjuster
5 Front fork seal
6 Rear brake fluid reservoir
7 Spark plug
8 Oil filler cap
9 Oil level inspection window
10 EVAP canister (California)
11 Rear shock pre-load adjuster
12 Drive chain adjuster

Component locations on left side – Speedmaster (America similar)

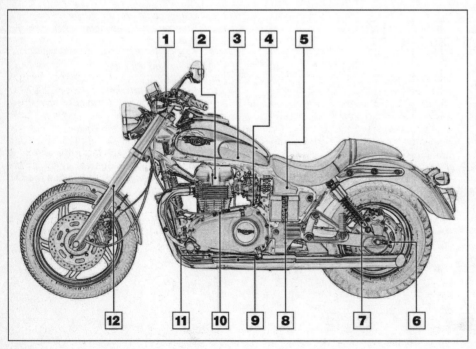

1 Clutch cable upper adjuster
2 Spark plug
3 Fuel filter*
4 Idle speed adjuster
5 Air filter
6 Drive chain adjuster
7 Rear shock pre-load adjuster
8 Battery
9 Oil filter
10 Clutch cable lower adjuster
11 Oil drain plug
12 Front fork seal
*Fuel filter is integral with tap on carburettor models and integral with fuel pump on EFI models

1 This Chapter is designed to help the home mechanic maintain his/her motorcycle for safety, economy, long life and peak performance.

2 Deciding where to start or plug into the routine maintenance schedule depends on several factors. If your motorcycle has been maintained according to the warranty standards and has just come out of warranty, start routine maintenance as it coincides with the next mileage or calendar interval. If you have owned the machine for some time but have never performed any maintenance on it, start at the nearest interval and include some additional procedures to ensure that nothing important is overlooked. If you have just had a major engine overhaul, then start the maintenance routine from the beginning. If you have a used machine and have no knowledge of its history or maintenance record, combine all the checks into one large service initially and then settle into the specified maintenance schedule.

3 Before beginning any maintenance or repair, the machine should be cleaned thoroughly, especially around the oil filter, spark plugs, valve cover, body panels, carburettors etc. Cleaning will help ensure that dirt does not contaminate the engine and will allow you to detect wear and damage that could otherwise easily go unnoticed.

4 Certain maintenance information is sometimes printed on labels attached to the motorcycle. If the information on the labels differs from that included here, use the information on the label.

Every 200 miles (300 km)

1 Drive chain cleaning and lubrication

1 If required, clean the chain using a dedicated aerosol chain cleaner, or wash it in paraffin or a suitable non-flammable or high flash-point solvent that will not damage the sealing O-rings or X-rings, using a soft brush to work any dirt out if necessary. Wipe the cleaner off the chain and allow it to dry, using compressed air if available. If the chain is excessively dirty remove it (see Chapter 5) and soak it for a while in the paraffin or solvent before cleaning it as described.

Caution: Don't use petrol (gasoline), an unsuitable solvent or other cleaning fluids which might damage the internal sealing properties of the chain. Don't use high-pressure water to clean the chain.

The entire process shouldn't take longer than ten minutes, otherwise the sealing rings could be damaged.

2 The best time to lubricate the chain is after the motorcycle has been ridden. When the chain is warm, the lubricant will penetrate the joints between the sideplates better than when cold. **Note:** *Triumph specifies an aerosol chain lube that it is suitable for sealed chains; do not use any other chain lubricants – the solvents could damage the chain's sealing rings. Apply the oil to the area where the sideplates overlap – not the middle of the rollers* **(see illustration)**.

HAYNES HiNT *Apply the lubricant to the top of the lower chain run, so centrifugal force will work the oil into the chain when the bike is moving. After applying the lubricant, let it soak in a few minutes before wiping off any excess.*

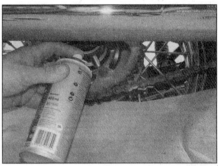

1.2 Apply the specified lubricant to the overlap between the sideplates

 Warning: Take care not to get any lubricant on the tyre or brake disc. If any of the lubricant inadvertently contacts them, clean it off thoroughly using a suitable solvent or dedicated brake cleaner before riding the machine.

Every 500 miles (800 km)

2 Drive chain slack check and adjustment

Check

1 A neglected drive chain won't last long and will quickly damage the sprockets. Routine chain adjustment and lubrication isn't difficult and will ensure maximum chain and sprocket life.

2 To check the chain, place the bike on its sidestand and make sure the transmission is in neutral. Make sure the ignition switch is OFF.

3 Push up on the bottom run of the chain midway between the two sprockets and measure the amount of slack, then compare your measurement to that listed in this Chapter's Specifications **(see illustration)**. As the chain stretches with wear, adjustment will be necessary (see below). Since the chain will rarely wear evenly, move the bike so that another section of chain can be checked; do this several times to check the entire length of chain, and mark the tightest spot.

Caution: Riding the bike with excess slack in the chain could lead to damage.

4 In some cases where lubrication has been neglected, corrosion and galling may cause the links to bind and kink, which effectively shortens the chain's length and makes it tight. Thoroughly clean and work free any such links, then highlight them with a marker pen or paint. After the bike has been ridden repeat the measurement for slack in the highlighted area. If the chain has kinked again and is still tight, replace it with a new one. A rusty, kinked or worn chain will damage the sprockets and can damage transmission bearings. If in any doubt as to the condition of a chain, it is far better to install a new one than risk damage to other components and possibly yourself (see Chapter 5).

5 Check the entire length of the chain for damaged rollers, loose links and pins, and missing O-rings, and replace it with a new one if necessary. **Note:** *Never install a new chain on old sprockets, and never use the old chain if you install new sprockets – replace the chain and sprockets as a set. Refer to Section 3 for sprocket checks and chain stretch checks.*

Adjustment

6 Move the bike so that the chain is positioned with the tightest point at the centre of its bottom run, then place it on its sidestand.

2.3 Measuring drive chain slack

2.7 Slacken the axle nut

[handwritten] 19 mm on left   24 on right

2.8 Turn the adjuster bolt as required

[handwritten] 8 mm

2.9 Make sure the back of the swingarm aligns with the same index line on each adjustment marker

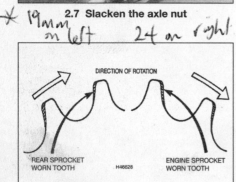

DIRECTION OF ROTATION

REAR SPROCKET WORN TOOTH   H46628   ENGINE SPROCKET WORN TOOTH

3.3 Check the sprockets in the areas indicated to see if they are worn

3.6 Undo the screws (arrowed) and remove the chainguard

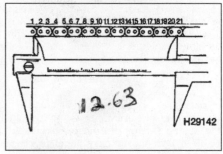

[handwritten] 12.63   H29142

3.7 Measure the distance between the 1st and 21st pins to determine chain stretch

7 Slacken the rear axle nut **(see illustration)**.
8 Turn the adjuster bolt on each side evenly until the amount of freeplay specified at the beginning of the Chapter is obtained at the centre of the bottom run of the chain **(see illustration)**. Turn the bolts anti-clockwise to reduce chain slack and clockwise to create it.
9 Following adjustment, check that the rear edge of the swingarm is in the same position in relation to the index lines on each chain adjuster **(see illustration)**. It is important the same index line on each side aligns with the rear edge of the swingarm; if not, the rear wheel will be out of alignment with the front. If there is a difference in the positions, adjust one of them so that its position is exactly the same as the other. Check the chain freeplay as described above and readjust if necessary.
10 Tighten the axle nut, preferably to the torque setting specified at the beginning of the Chapter if you have the tools, and noting that on Bonneville and T100 you will have to remove the silencer (see Chapter 3) to get the wrench on the nut **(see illustration 2.7)**. Recheck the adjustment as above, then check that the wheel runs freely. Now turn

each adjuster bolt anti-clockwise slightly so its shoulder is tight against the adjuster.

3 Drive chain and sprocket wear and chain stretch check

1 To check the chain, place the bike on its sidestand and make sure the transmission is in neutral. Make sure the ignition switch is OFF.
2 Check the entire length of the chain for damaged rollers, loose links and pins, and missing sealing rings. Fit a new chain if damage is found (see Chapter 5). **Note:** *Never install a new chain on old sprockets, and never use the old chain if you install new sprockets – replace the chain and sprockets as a set.*
3 Undo the front sprocket cover bolts and remove the cover. Check the teeth on the front sprocket and the rear sprocket for wear **(see illustration)**. If the sprocket teeth are worn excessively, replace the chain and both sprockets with a new set (see Chapter 5). Install the sprocket cover and tighten its bolts to the torque setting specified at the beginning of the Chapter.

4 Inspect the drive chain slider on the front of the swingarm for excessive wear and damage and replace it with a new one if necessary (see Chapter 5).
5 Measure the amount of chain stretch as follows:
6 Undo the chainguard screws and remove the guard **(see illustration)**. Obtain a weight of between 10 and 20 kg and hang it from the centre of the bottom run of the chain so that the top run becomes taut.
7 Measure along the top run the length of 21 pins (from the centre of the 1st pin to the centre of the 21st pin) and compare the result to the stretch limit specified at the beginning of the Chapter **(see illustration)**. Rotate the rear wheel so that several sections of the chain can be measured, then calculate the average. If the chain stretch measurement exceeds the service limit the chain must be replaced with a new one (see Chapter 5). **Note:** *Never install a new chain on old sprockets, and never use the old chain if you install new sprockets – replace the chain and sprockets as a set..*
8 If the chain is good, remove the weight and install the chainguard.

Every 6000 miles (10,000 km) or 12 months

Carry out all the items under the Pre-ride checks and the 200 and 500 mile (300 and 800 km) checks, plus the following:

4 Spark plug check

⚠️ *Warning: Make sure the engine is cool before removing the spark plugs.*
Caution: Do not interchange the spark plug caps on each head – each cap must be fitted to its correct plug.

1 Make sure your spark plug socket or wrench is the correct size (18 mm hex) before attempting to remove the plugs. Access to the plugs is restricted by the secondary air injection system pipes – to improve access remove the fuel tank (see Chapter 3A or 3B).

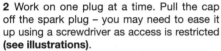

4.2a Ease the cap up using a screwdriver . . .

4.2b . . . then lift it off the plug by hand

4.3 Unscrew and remove the plug

2 Work on one plug at a time. Pull the cap off the spark plug – you may need to ease it up using a screwdriver as access is restricted **(see illustrations)**.

3 Clean the area around the base of the plug to prevent any dirt dropping into the engine. Using a deep socket or a suitable plug wrench, unscrew and remove the plug from the cylinder head **(see illustration)**.

4 Inspect the electrodes for wear. Both the centre and side electrodes should have square edges and the side electrode should be of uniform thickness – if not, they are worn. Look for excessive deposits and evidence of a cracked or chipped insulator around the centre electrode. Compare the spark plugs to the colour chart at the end of this manual. Check the threads, the washer and the ceramic insulator body for cracks and other damage.

5 If the electrodes are not excessively worn, and if the deposits can be removed easily with a wire brush, and there are no cracks or chips visible in the insulator, the plugs can be re-used. If in doubt concerning the condition of the plugs, replace them with new ones, as the expense is minimal. Note that the spark plugs should be replaced with new ones at every second service interval, i.e. every 12,000 miles (20,000 km).

6 Cleaning spark plugs by sandblasting is permitted, provided you clean the plugs with a high flash-point solvent afterwards.

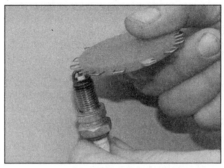

4.7a A wire type gauge is recommended to measure the spark plug electrode gap

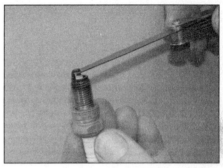

4.7b A blade type feeler gauge can also be used

7 Before installing the plug, make sure it is the correct type and heat range and check the gap between the electrodes **(see illustrations)**. Compare the gap to that specified and adjust as necessary. If the gap must be adjusted, bend the side electrodes only and be very careful not to chip or crack the insulator nose **(see illustration)**. Make sure the sealing washer is in place on the plug before installing it.

8 Fit the plug into the end of the tool (but see Haynes Hint), then use the tool to insert the plug **(see illustration)**. If a torque wrench can be applied, tighten the spark plugs to the torque setting specified at the beginning of

the Chapter. Otherwise, tighten them according the instructions on the box – generally if new plugs are being used, tighten

HAYNES HINT *You can slip a short length of hose over the end of the plug to use as a tool to thread it into place, or there are commercially available rubber tools as shown (see illustration 4.8). The hose will grip the plug well enough to turn it, but will start to slip if the plug begins to cross-thread in the hole – this will prevent damaged threads.*

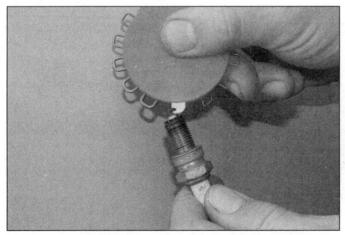

4.7c Adjust the gap by bending the side electrode

4.8 Thread the plug as far as possible by hand

them by 1/2 a turn after the washer has seated, and if the old plugs are being reused, tighten them by 1/8 to 1/4 turn after they have seated. Do not over-tighten them.

9 Fit the spark plug cap, making sure it locates correctly onto the plug **(see illustration 4.2b)**.

 HAYNES HiNT *Stripped plug threads in the cylinder head can be repaired with a thread insert – see 'Tools and Workshop Tips' in the Reference section.*

5 Fuel system check

⚠️ *Warning: Petrol (gasoline) is extremely flammable, so take extra precautions when you work on any part of the fuel system. Don't smoke or allow open flames or bare light bulbs near the work area, and don't work in a garage where a natural gas-type appliance is present. If you spill any fuel on your skin, rinse it off immediately with soap and water. When you perform any kind of work on the fuel system, wear safety glasses and have a fire extinguisher suitable for a Class B type fire (flammable liquids) on hand.*

Fuel system check – carburettor models

1 Remove the fuel tank (see Chapter 3A). Check the tank, fuel tap and fuel supply hose for signs of leakage, deterioration or damage; in particular check that there is no leakage from the tap and fuel hose. Also check the fuel tank and air filter housing drain and breather hoses and the crankcase breather hose **(see illustration)**. Replace any hoses which are cracked or have deteriorated with new ones (see Chapter 3A).

2 If the tap has been leaking from the face, tightening the assembly screw on the bottom may help **(see illustration)**. If leakage persists, fit a new tap. If the tap has been leaking from the base, tightening the mounting bolts may help. Otherwise, remove the tap and fit new seals (see Chapter 3). Remove any corrosion or paint bubbles before installing the tap.

3 If there is evidence of fuel leakage from any of the carburettors, first locate the source – if it is from the bottom, tighten the float chamber drain screw – otherwise refer to Chapter 3A.

4 On California models, check the EVAP system hoses for loose connections, cracks and deterioration and replace them with new ones if necessary.

Fuel system check – EFI models

5 Remove the fuel tank (see Chapter 3B). Check the condition of the fuel hose and

the tank breather hose (Chapter 3B) and the crankcase breather hose **(see illustration 5.1)**.

6 On California models, check the EVAP system hoses for loose connections, cracks and deterioration and replace them with new ones if necessary.

6 Engine oil and filter change

⚠️ *Warning: Be careful when draining the oil, as the exhaust pipes, the engine, and the oil itself can cause severe burns. Engine oil, particularly used oil, is harmful to the skin so protective gloves should be worn – latex medical gloves are ideal, and are cheap and readily available from medical suppliers.*

1 Consistent routine oil and filter changes are the single most important maintenance procedure you can perform on a motorcycle. The oil not only lubricates the internal parts of the engine, transmission and clutch, but it also acts as a coolant, a cleaner, a sealant, and a protector. Because of these demands, the oil takes a terrific amount of abuse and should be replaced often with new oil of the recommended grade and type. Saving a little money on the difference in cost between good oil and cheap oil won't pay off if the engine is damaged. The oil filter should be changed with every oil change.

2 Before changing the oil, warm up the engine so the oil will drain easily. Make sure the bike is on level ground. Allow the oil to settle for ten minutes after stopping the engine.

3 Position a clean drain tray below front of the engine. Unscrew the filler cap from the crankcase to vent it and to act as a reminder that there is no oil in the engine **(see illustration)**. On Scrambler models, access to the filler cap is restricted by the exhaust system – use a large, long reach screwdriver to unscrew the cap **(see illustration)**.

4 Unscrew the drain bolt from the front of the sump and allow the oil to flow into the drain

5.1 Crankcase breather hose (arrowed)

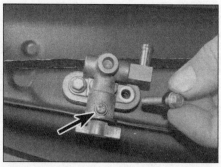
5.2 Fuel tap assembly screw (arrowed) and mounting bolts

6.3a Unscrew the oil filler cap – a coin is useful for doing this

6.3b Use a long reach screwdriver to unscrew the filler cap (arrowed) on Scrambler models

6.4a Unscrew the oil drain bolt . . .

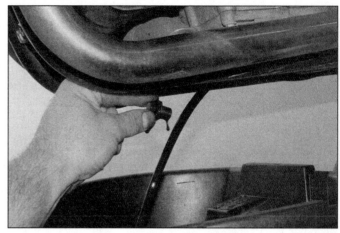

6.4b . . . and allow the oil to drain

tray – hold the bike upright to allow complete drainage **(see illustrations)**. Discard the sealing washer on the drain bolt and replace it with a new one **(see illustration)**.

5 When the oil has completely drained, fit the bolt into the sump using a new sealing washer, and tighten it to the torque setting specified at the beginning of the Chapter **(see illustration)**. Avoid overtightening, as it is quite easy to damage the threads in the tank.

6 Now place the drain tray below the oil filter, which is at the back of the engine. Unscrew the oil filter using either the Triumph service tool (part No. T3880313) or a commercially available filter removing wrench and socket extension or a strap or chain-type removing tool, and tip any residual oil into the drain tray **(see illustrations)**. Be very careful not to touch the exhaust if it is still hot or warm – it is best to let it cool down first. Wipe any oil off the exhaust pipes to prevent too much smoke when you start it. Discard the old filter – it should never be reused.

7 Clean the filter mating surface on the crankcase. Fill the new filter with the recommended type of new engine oil and smear some onto the rubber seal **(see illustration)**. Manoeuvre it into position and screw it onto the engine until the seal just seats **(see illustration)**. If the filter wrench is being used, tighten the filter to the torque setting

6.4c Remove the old sealing washer and discard it

6.5 Fit a new sealing washer and tighten the bolt to the specified torque

6.6a Unscrew the filter using a filter wrench . . .

6.6b . . . or a strap type removing tool . . .

6.6c . . . then remove and drain the filter

6.7a Fill the filter with oil and smear its sealing ring . . .

6.7b . . . then thread it onto the engine

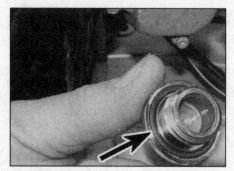

6.8 Make sure the O-ring (arrowed) is in its groove under the cap

specified at the beginning of the Chapter **(see illustration 6.6a)**. Otherwise, tighten the filter as tight as possible by hand, or by the number of turns specified on the filter or its packaging. **Note:** *Do not use a strap or chain tool to tighten the filter as you will damage it.*

8 Refill the engine to the proper level using the recommended type and amount of oil (see *Pre-ride checks*). Install the filler cap, using a new O-ring if necessary **(see illustration)**. Start the engine and let it run for two or three minutes (make sure that the oil pressure warning light extinguishes after a few seconds). Shut it off, wait a few minutes, then check the oil level (see *Pre-ride checks*). If necessary, add more oil to bring the level in the window between the lines. Check around the drain bolt and the oil filter for leaks.

9 Refer to Chapter 2, Section 6, and check the oil cooler and its braided steel hoses for damage and leaks. Replace any components as necessary with new ones.

10 The old oil drained from the engine cannot be re-used and should be disposed of properly. Check with your local refuse disposal company, disposal facility or environmental agency to see whether they will accept the used oil for recycling. Don't pour used oil into drains or onto the ground.

> **HAYNES HINT** *Check the old oil carefully – if it is very metallic coloured, then the engine is experiencing wear from break-in (new engine) or from insufficient lubrication. If there are flakes or chips of metal in the oil, then something is drastically wrong internally and the engine will have to be disassembled for inspection and repair. If there are pieces of fibre-like material in the oil, the clutch is experiencing excessive wear and should be checked.*

7 Air filter check and cleaning

Bonneville, T100, Thruxton and Scrambler

1 Remove the left-hand side panel (see Chapter 7). Carefully displace the relays from their mounts **(see illustration)**.

2 Undo the screws securing the air filter cover and remove it, noting the wiring clip held by one of the screws **(see illustrations)**.

3 Remove the filter from the housing, noting how it fits **(see illustration)**.

4 Tap the filter on a hard surface to dislodge any large particles of dirt. If compressed air is available, use it to blow through the element, directing it in the opposite direction of normal airflow, i.e. from the outside towards the inside **(see illustration)**.

> **HAYNES HINT** *If using compressed air to clean the filter, place either your hand, a rag, or a piece of card on the inside to prevent any dust and debris being blown from one side of the element into the other.*

Caution: If the machine is continually ridden in dusty conditions, the filter should be cleaned more frequently.

5 Check the filter for signs of damage. If the element is torn or cannot be cleaned, or is obviously beyond further use, replace it with a new one. Do not use petrol (gasoline) or solvents to clean the element. Do not run the engine without a filter.

6 Fit the filter in the housing, making sure it is correctly seated **(see illustration 7.3)**.

7 Check the condition of the rubber seal in the groove in the cover and replace it with a new one if it is damaged, deformed or deteriorated. Make sure the seal is correctly seated in its groove. Fit the cover and secure it with its screws, not forgetting the clip **(see illustrations)**.

7.1 Displace the relays from their mounts

7.2a Unscrew the bolts (arrowed) . . .

7.2b . . . then remove the cover . . .

7.3 . . . and withdraw the filter

7.4 Blow the filter through with compressed air if available

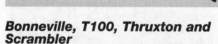

7.7a Fit the cover . . .

7.7b ... not forgetting the wiring clip with the upper front bolt

7.8 Check the tube (arrowed) for residue and empty it if necessary

8 Carburettor/throttle body synchronisation

Carburettor models

8 Check the drain tube on the bottom of the air filter housing for a build up of residue and if necessary release the clip, pull the tube off its union and drain it **(see illustration)**. Refit the tube once all residue has gone.

9 Install the side panel (see Chapter 7).

America and Speedmaster

10 Remove the seat(s) (see Chapter 7).

11 On EFI models, detach the diagnostic plug from the air filter cover and disconnect the ambient air pressure sensor wiring **(see illustration)**. On all models, undo the screw securing the wiring connector cover and lift if off the air filter housing **(see illustration)**.

12 Unscrew the bolts securing the air filter cover and remove it **(see illustration)**.

13 Remove the filter from the housing, noting how it fits **(see illustration)**.

14 Clean and check the filter as described in Steps 4 and 5.

15 Fit the filter in the housing, making sure it is correctly seated **(see illustration 7.13)**.

16 Check the condition of the rubber seal in the groove in the cover and replace it with a new one if it is damaged, deformed or deteriorated. Make sure the seal is correctly seated in its groove. Fit the cover and secure it with its screws **(see illustration 7.12)**.

17 Install the wiring connector cover, making sure the tab at the back locates correctly in the slot in the frame cross-piece **(see illustration)**.

18 Pull the bungs out of the bottom of the air filter housing drain tubes and allow any residue to drain. Refit the bungs once all residue has gone.

19 Install all disturbed components.

> **Warning: Petrol (gasoline) is extremely flammable, so take extra precautions when you work on any part of the fuel system. Don't smoke or allow open flames or bare light bulbs near the work area, and don't work in a garage where a natural gas-type appliance is present. If you spill any fuel on your skin, rinse it off immediately with soap and water. When you perform any kind of work on the fuel system, wear safety glasses and have a fire extinguisher suitable for a Class B type fire (flammable liquids) on hand.**

> **Warning: Take great care not to burn your hand on the hot engine unit when accessing the gauge take-off points on the intake manifolds. Do not allow exhaust gases to build up in the work area; either perform the check outside or use an exhaust gas extraction system.**

1 Carburettor synchronisation (or balancing) is simply the process of adjusting the carburettors so that they pass the same amount of fuel/air mixture to each cylinder. This is done by measuring the vacuum produced in each intake duct. Carburettors that are out of synchronisation will result in increased fuel consumption, increased engine temperature, erratic idling, less than ideal throttle response and higher vibration levels. If a valve clearance check is part of the service you are performing, do that first (see Section 24).

2 To properly synchronise the carburettors you will need a set of vacuum gauges or a manometer. These instruments measure engine vacuum, and can be obtained from motorcycle dealers or mail order parts suppliers. The equipment used should be suitable for a twin cylinder engine and come complete with the necessary adapters and hoses to fit the take off points on the intake ducts.

3 Start the engine and let it run until it reaches normal operating temperature, then check that the idle speed is correctly set, and adjust it if necessary (see Section 9).

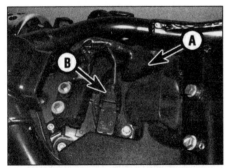

7.11a Diagnostic plug (A) and AP sensor wiring connector (B) – EFI models

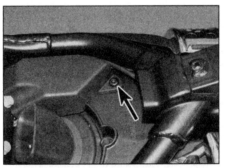

7.11b Undo the screw (arrowed) and remove the wiring cover

7.12 Unscrew the bolts (arrowed) ...

7.13 ... and remove the cover and filter

7.17 Fit the tab into the slot in the frame (arrowed)

8.4a Pull the SAIS hose off the union . . .

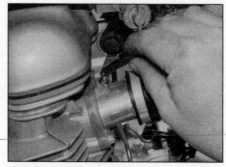

8.4b . . . and fit the gauge hose in its place

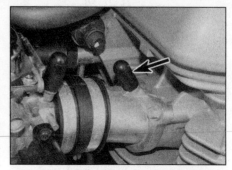

8.6 Remove the blanking cap (arrowed) and fit the other gauge hose

8.7a Carburettor synchronisation screw (arrowed)

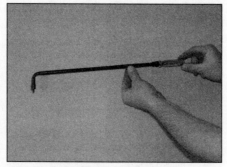

8.7b An angled screwdriver makes access and adjustment much easier

4 Detach the secondary air injection system vacuum hose from the take-off union on the left-hand cylinder intake adapter and attach the left-hand gauge or manometer hose in its place **(see illustrations)**.
5 On California models detach the EVAP system hose from the take-off union on the right-hand cylinder intake adapter and attach right-hand gauge or manometer hose in its place.
6 On all other models remove the blanking cap from the take-off point on the right-hand cylinder intake adapter and attach the right-hand gauge or manometer hose in is place **(see illustrations)**. Make sure the left-hand gauge is attached to the left-hand cylinder, and so for the right-hand.
7 Visually identify the synchronisation screw which is situated in between the carburettors and is best accessed using an angled screwdriver as shown **(see illustrations)**.

8 Start the engine and let it idle. If the gauges are fitted with damping adjustment, set this so that the needle flutter is just eliminated but so that they can still respond to small changes in pressure. Open the throttle slightly a couple of times then let the engine settle at idle.
9 The vacuum readings for both cylinders should be the same. If the vacuum readings differ, synchronise the carburettors by turning the synchronisation screw until the readings are the same **(see illustration)**. **Note:** *Do not press on the screw whilst adjusting it, otherwise a false reading will be obtained.* Turn the screw a small amount at a time and allow the readings to stabilise before making further adjustments. When the carburettors are synchronised, open and close the throttle quickly to settle the linkage, and recheck the gauge readings, readjusting if necessary.
10 When the adjustment is complete adjust

the idle speed (see Section 9), and check the throttle cable freeplay (see Section 10). Remove the gauges and refit the blanking cap or EVAP hose and the SAIS hose, making sure they are fully pushed onto their unions **(see illustrations 8.6 and 8.4a)**.

EFI models

11 The throttle bodies cannot be synchronised in the normal way by measuring the vacuum present in each throttle body using a set of vacuum gauges or a manometer. They can only be synchronised using the Triumph engine management system diagnostic tool. Take the bike to a Triumph dealer. Adjustment is made via the synchronisation screw set in the throttle linkage between the two throttle bodies **(see illustration)**.

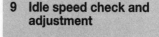

9 Idle speed check and adjustment

Carburettor models

1 The idle speed should be checked and adjusted before and after the carburettors are synchronised (balanced), after checking the valve clearances, and when it is obviously too high or too low. Before adjusting the idle speed, make sure the spark plugs are clean and the gaps correct, and the air filter is clean. If a valve clearance check is part of the service you are performing, do that first (see Section 24). Also, turn the handlebars from side-to-side and check the idle speed does not change as you do. If it does, the throttle cables may not be adjusted or routed correctly, or may be worn out. This is a dangerous condition that can cause loss of control of the bike. Be sure to correct this problem before proceeding.
2 Start the engine and let it run until it reaches normal operating temperature. Place the motorcycle on its sidestand, and make sure the transmission is in neutral.
3 The idle speed adjuster is a knurled knob located on the left-hand side of the

8.9 Checking and adjusting carburettor synchronisation (balance)

8.11 Throttle body synchronisation screw (arrowed) – EFI models

9.3 Idle speed adjuster knob (arrowed) – carburettor models

9.6 Idle speed adjuster knob (arrowed) – EFI model

10.3 Twist the throttle and measure the amount of free rotation

carburettors **(see illustration)**. With the engine idling, adjust the speed by turning the knob until the idle speed listed in this Chapter's Specifications is obtained. Turn the knob clockwise to increase idle speed, and anti-clockwise to decrease it.

4 Snap the throttle open and shut a few times, then recheck the idle speed. If necessary, repeat the adjustment procedure.

5 If a smooth, steady idle cannot be achieved, the fuel/air mixture may be incorrect (check the pilot screw settings – see Chapter 3A Specifications) or the carburettors may need synchronising (see Section 8), or the secondary air injection system may be faulty. Also check the intake duct rubbers for cracks which will cause an air leak, resulting in a weak mixture.

EFI models

6 The idle speed adjuster knob can be found under the left-hand side of the throttle bodies **(see illustration)**. If, with the engine warmed up to normal operating temperature, the idle speed is incorrect according to the figure in the Specifications at the beginning of this Chapter, it can be adjusted by turning the screw clockwise to increase idle speed and anti-clockwise to reduce it.

7 Note that Triumph advise the use of the tachometer function of their diagnostic tester or an auxiliary tachometer to set the idle speed accurately, rather than relying on the motorcycle's tachometer reading. Care must be taken not to set the idle speed below 1000

rpm otherwise battery charge problems may be experienced.

10 Throttle cable check

1 Make sure the throttle grip rotates smoothly and freely from fully closed to fully open with the front wheel turned at various angles. The grip should return automatically from fully open to fully closed when released.

2 If the throttle sticks, this is probably due to a cable fault. Disconnect the cables at their upper ends (see Chapter 3A or 3B) and lubricate them (see Section 14). Check that the inner cables slide freely and easily in the outer cables. If not, replace the cables with new ones. Note that in very rare cases the fault could lie in the carburettors/throttle bodies rather than the cables, necessitating their removal and inspection (see Chapter 3A or 3B).

3 With the throttle operating smoothly, check for a small amount of freeplay in the cables, measured in terms of the amount of twistgrip rotation before the throttle opens, and compare the amount to that listed in this Chapter's Specifications **(see illustration)**. If it's incorrect, adjust the cables to correct it as follows.

4 Where fitted, pull the rubber boot off the adjuster at the handlebar end of the opening cable **(see illustration)**.

5 Loosen the locknut on the opening cable

then turn the adjuster until the specified amount of freeplay is obtained (see this Chapter's Specifications) **(see illustration)**. Retighten the locknut. Fit the rubber boot.

6 If the adjuster has reached its limit, or if major adjustment is required, reset the adjuster so that the freeplay is at a maximum (i.e. the adjuster is fully turned in), then remove the fuel tank if required for best access (see Chapter 3A or 3B), and adjust the cables at the carburettor/throttle body end. Fully slacken the top nut on the opening cable and adjust the position of the cable elbow in the bracket by repositioning the lower nut as required, then tighten the top nut **(see illustration)**. Any fine alteration can be made at the handlebar end as in Step 5. If the cables cannot be adjusted as specified, install new ones (see Chapter 3A or 3B).

> **⚠ Warning:** *Turn the handlebars all the way through their travel with the engine idling. Idle speed should not change. If it does, the cables may be routed incorrectly. Correct this condition before riding the bike.*

7 Install the fuel tank (see Chapter 3). Check that the throttle twistgrip operates smoothly and snaps shut quickly when released.

11 Clutch check and adjustment

1 Check that the clutch lever operates smoothly and easily.

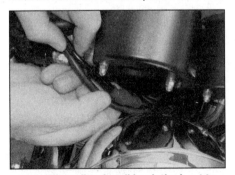

10.4 Where fitted, pull back the boot to access the adjuster

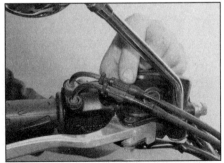

10.5 Slacken the adjuster lock ring or nut and turn the adjuster as described

10.6 Slacken the nut (arrowed) and reset the position of the cable in the bracket as described

2 If the lever action is heavy or stiff, disconnect the cable at its upper end (see Chapter 2) and lubricate it (see Section 14). If the inner cable still does not run smoothly in the outer cable, replace it with a new one. If the action is still stiff, remove the lever and check for damage or distortion, or any other cause, and remedy as necessary (see Chapter 5). Clean and lubricate the pivot and contact areas (see Section 14). If the lever is good, refer to Chapter 2 and check the release mechanism in the cover and the clutch itself.

3 With the cable operating smoothly, check that the clutch cable is correctly adjusted. Periodic adjustment is necessary to compensate for wear in the clutch plates and stretch of the cable. Check that the amount of freeplay at the clutch lever is within the specifications listed at the beginning of the Chapter **(see illustration)**.

4 If adjustment is required, first slacken the adjuster locking ring. Turn the adjuster in or out until the required amount of freeplay is obtained **(see illustration)**. To increase freeplay, turn the adjuster clockwise (into the lever bracket). To reduce freeplay, turn the adjuster anti-clockwise (out of the lever bracket). Tighten the locking ring securely.

5 If all the adjustment has been taken up at the lever, reset the adjuster to give the maximum amount of freeplay, then set the correct amount of freeplay by repositioning the threaded section of the cable in the bracket on the left-hand side of the engine. Slacken the nuts securing the cable in its bracket and adjust them as required until the cable is positioned to give the correct freeplay **(see illustration)**. To increase freeplay, thread the nuts up the cable (towards the handlebar end). To reduce freeplay, thread them down the cable. Tighten the nuts against the bracket. Subsequent adjustments can now be made using the lever adjuster only.

6 On Thruxton and Scrambler models the clutch lever has a span adjuster that alters the distance of the lever from the handlebar **(see illustration)**. Each setting is identified by a number on the adjuster, which must align with the arrow on the lever. Pull the lever away from the handlebar and turn the adjuster ring

11.3 Clutch freeplay is measured in the gap between the inner end of the lever and its bracket

11.5 Slacken the nuts (arrowed) and adjust the cable position as described

until the setting that best suits the rider is obtained. There are four settings – setting 1 gives the largest span, and setting 4 the smallest.

12 Brake pad wear check

1 Visually check the amount of friction material remaining on each brake pad in each caliper **(see illustrations)**. Grooves in the friction material indicate the state of wear – when the grooves are no longer visible, replace the pads with new ones.

2 The thickness of friction material remaining is the definitive way of judging wear, and there

11.4 Back the lockring (arrowed) off the bracket and turn the adjuster as required

11.6 Clutch lever span adjuster – align the required setting number with the triangle on the lever

should never be less than 1.5 mm (the groove base is set at this thickness). If necessary remove the pads from the caliper (see Chapter 6) and measure the thickness of material. Also check that the material is worn evenly across the pad – if not one of the pistons is sticking or has seized.

3 If the pads are worn they must be replaced with new ones. If the pads are excessively worn, check the brake discs (see Chapter 6).

4 Refer to Chapter 6 for details of pad removal and installation.

13 Brake system check

1 A routine general check of the brake system will ensure that any problems are discovered and remedied before the rider's safety is jeopardised.

2 Check the brake lever and pedal for loose mountings, improper or rough action, excessive play, bends, and other damage. Lubricate the lever and pedal at the specified interval or as required (see Section 14). Replace any damaged parts with new ones (see Chapter 5).

3 Make sure all brake component fasteners are tight. Check the brake pads for wear (see Section 12) and make sure the fluid level in the reservoirs is correct (see *Pre-ride checks*). Look for leaks at the hose connections

12.1a Visually check the amount of friction material in the calipers

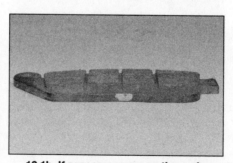

12.1b If necessary remove the pads and measure the thickness of remaining material or check the depth of the grooves

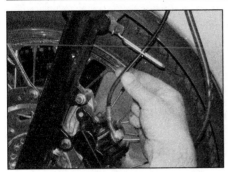

13.3 Check the hoses, pipe and all connections for leaks

13.6a Clevis locknut (arrowed) – Bonneville

13.6b Clevis locknut (arrowed) – America and Speedmaster

and check for cracks in the hoses **(see illustration)**. If the lever or pedal is spongy, bleed the brakes (see Chapter 6).

4 Make sure the brake light operates when the brake lever or pedal is applied. Neither the front brake light switch, mounted on the underside of the master cylinder, nor the rear brake light switch, mounted on the inside of the pedal, are adjustable. If they fail to operate properly, check them (see Chapter 8).

5 The front brake lever has a span adjuster that alters the distance of the lever from the handlebar **(see illustration 11.6)**. Each setting is identified by a number on the adjuster, which must align with the arrow on the lever. Pull the lever away from the handlebar and turn the adjuster ring until the setting that best suits the rider is obtained. There are four settings – setting 1 gives the largest span, and setting 4 the smallest.

6 Check that the locknut on the rear brake master cylinder pushrod clevis is tight **(see illustrations)**. The pushrod length should be set correctly to ensure safe operation of the brake – if required, measure the pushrod length and adjust it accordingly (see Chapter 6, Section 9).

14 Stand, lever pivot and cable lubrication

1 Since the controls, cables and various other components of a motorcycle are exposed to the elements, they should be checked and lubricated periodically to ensure safe and trouble-free operation.

2 The footrests, clutch and brake levers, brake pedal, and sidestand pivot should be lubricated frequently. In order for the lubricant to be applied where it will do the most good, the component should be disassembled. The lubricant recommended by Triumph for each application is listed at the beginning of the Chapter. If chain or cable lubricant is being used, it can be applied to the pivot joint gaps and will usually work its way into the areas where friction occurs, so less disassembly of the

component is needed (however it is always better to do so and clean off all corrosion, dirt and old lubricant first). If motor oil or light grease is being used, apply it sparingly as it may attract dirt (which could cause the controls to bind or wear at an accelerated rate).

3 To lubricate the cables, disconnect the relevant cable at its upper end (see Chapter 2 for the clutch cable and 3 for the throttle cables), then lubricate it with a pressure adapter (but note they don't fit well on flanged cable ends) and aerosol lubricant **(see illustration)**.

15 Nut and bolt tightness check

1 Since vibration of the machine tends to loosen fasteners, all nuts, bolts, screws, etc. should be checked for proper tightness.

2 Pay particular attention to the following:
Spark plugs (Section 4)
Engine oil drain bolt and filter (Section 6)
Lever and pedal bolts (Chapter 5)
Footrest and sidestand bolts (Chapter 5)
Engine mounting bolts (Chapter 2)
Shock absorber bolts; swingarm pivot bolt and nut (Chapter 5)
Handlebar bolts (Chapter 5)
Front fork clamp bolts (top and bottom yoke) and fork top bolts (Chapter 5)
Steering stem nut (Section 16)

14.3 Lubricating a cable with a pressure lubricator. Make sure the tool seals around the inner cable

Front axle nut and axle clamp bolts (Chapter 6)
Rear axle nut (Chapter 6)
Front sprocket nut and rear sprocket nuts (Chapter 5)
Brake caliper and master cylinder mounting bolts (Chapter 6)
Brake hose banjo bolts and caliper bleed valves (Chapter 6)
Brake disc bolts (Chapter 6)
Exhaust system bolts/nuts (Chapter 3A or 3B)

3 If a torque wrench is available, use it along with the torque specifications at the beginning of this and other Chapters.

16 Steering head bearing freeplay check and adjustment

1 Steering head bearings can become dented, rough or loose during normal use of the machine, particularly if the bike is ridden hard or used regularly on poor road surfaces. Worn, loose or tight steering head bearings can cause severe handling problems, a condition that is potentially dangerous.

Check

2 Support the motorcycle on an auxiliary stand, and raise the front wheel off the ground using a jack with a block of wood between the jack head and the engine.

3 Point the front wheel straight-ahead and slowly move the handlebars from side-to-side. Any dents or roughness in the bearing races will be felt and the bars will not move smoothly and freely. Again point the wheel straight-ahead, and tap the front of the wheel to one side. The wheel should 'fall' under its own weight to the limit of its lock, indicating that the bearings are not too tight. Check for similar movement to the other side. If the steering doesn't perform as described, and it's not due to the resistance of cables or hoses, then the bearings should be adjusted as described below.

4 Next, grasp the bottom of the forks and gently pull and push them forward and

> **HAYNES HiNT** *Make sure you are not mistaking any movement between the bike and stand or jack, or between the stand or jack and the ground, for freeplay in the bearings. Do not pull and push the forks too hard – a gentle movement is all that is needed. Freeplay in the forks themselves due to worn bushes can also be misinterpreted as steering head bearing play – do not confuse the two.*

backward **(see illustration)**. Any looseness or freeplay in the steering head bearings will be felt as front-to-rear movement of the forks. If play is felt, adjust the bearings as described below.

Adjustment

Note: *Two thin 38 mm spanners are required (Triumph Part No. 3880140-T0301) which have an offset square cut into them to accept a torque wrench. This will enable the bearings to be pre-loaded to a specific torque and the locknut to be tightened to the specified torque.*

5 Cover the fuel tank in plenty of rag to prevent damage should a tool slip, or to be absolutely certain remove it (see Chapter 3A or 3B).

6 Slacken the fork clamp bolts in the top yoke **(see illustration)**. On Thruxton models with separate (clip-on) handlebars, slacken the handlebar clamp bolts and remove the handlebar positioning bolts **(see illustrations)**.

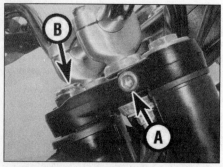

16.6a Slacken the fork clamp bolt (A) on each side and the steering stem nut (B)

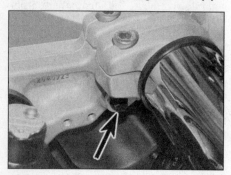

16.6c ... and unscrew the positioning bolt (arrowed)

16.4 Checking for play in the steering head bearings

7 Unscrew and remove the steering stem nut and its washer **(see illustration 16.6a)**. Ease the top yoke up slightly (but not off the steering stem) to expose the adjuster nut and its locknut **(see illustration)**.

8 Slacken off the locknut **(see illustration 16.7)**. Check that the threads of the steering stem are completely free of grease as this will affect the torque setting applied during the following procedure, wipe the threads clean if necessary.

9 If you have the Triumph spanner, slacken the adjuster nut slightly until pressure is just released, then fit a torque wrench to the spanner (at a 90° angle to the spanner) and tighten the nut to the torque setting specified at the beginning of the Chapter to pre-load the bearings. Remove the torque wrench, then turn the handlebars from side to side to settle the bearings, then slacken the adjuster nut again. If you do not have the Triumph spanner,

16.6b On Thruxtons with clip-ons also slacken the handlebar clamp bolt (arrowed) . . .

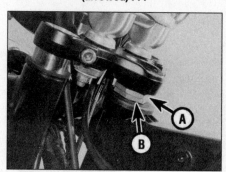

16.7 Ease the yoke up to reveal the locknut (A) and adjuster nut (B)

follow the same procedure using the available spanner and pre-load the bearings according to feel, then slacken the adjuster nut.

10 Now tighten the adjuster nut to 3 Nm using the Triumph spanner. This will remove all freeplay, yet enable the steering to move freely. If this spanner is not available, tighten the adjuster nut by hand until all freeplay is removed yet the steering is able to move freely. The object is to set the adjuster nut so that the bearings are under a very light loading, just enough to remove any freeplay, but not so much that the steering does not move freely from side to side as described in the check procedure.

11 If the bearings cannot be correctly adjusted, disassemble the steering head and check the bearings and races (see Chapter 5). *Caution: Take great care not to apply excessive pressure because this will cause premature failure of the bearings.*

12 With the bearings correctly adjusted, counter-hold the adjuster nut and tighten the locknut against it, also to the specified torque setting if the special tool is available. Make sure the adjuster nut does not turn with the locknut – if it does repeat the adjustment procedure.

13 Push the top yoke down to seat it. Install the steering stem nut with its washer and tighten it to the torque setting specified at the beginning of the Chapter **(see illustration 18.6a)**. Now tighten both the top yoke fork clamp bolts to the specified torque.

14 On Thruxton models with separate handlebars, install the handlebar positioning bolts and tighten them to the specified torque **(see illustration 18.6c)**. Now tighten the handlebar clamp bolts to the specified torque **(see illustration 18.6b)**.

15 Check the bearing adjustment as described above and re-adjust if necessary.

16 Install the fuel tank if removed (see Chapter 3A or 3B).

Steering head bearing lubrication

(Every 12,000 miles (20,000 km) or 24 months)

17 Over a period of time the grease will harden or may be washed out of the bearings by incorrect use of jet washes.

18 Refer to Chapter 6 and disassemble the steering head for re-greasing of the bearings.

17 Suspension check

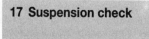

1 The suspension components must be maintained in top operating condition to ensure rider safety. Loose, worn or damaged suspension parts decrease the motorcycle's stability and control.

Front suspension

2 While standing alongside the motorcycle, and with it off the stand and upright, apply the front brake and push on the handlebars to compress the forks several times. See if they move up-and-down smoothly without binding. If binding is felt, the forks should be disassembled and inspected (see Chapter 5).

3 On Bonneville, T100 and Thruxton models, inspect the area above and around each dust seal for signs of oil leakage, pitting and corrosion. Carefully ease the fork protector and dust seal off the fork slider using a flat-bladed screwdriver and inspect the area around the fork seal **(see illustration)**. On Scrambler and 2009-on T100 models, ease the gaiter up to check for oil leaks and to inspect the fork tubes for pitting **(see illustration)**. If leakage is evident, the seals in each fork must be replaced with new ones (see Chapter 5). If there is pitting in the chrome tubes within the extent of fork travel, you should consider replacing them with new ones as it will eventually cause the seals to fail. Press the dust seal and fork protector back into place on completion. On America and 2003 to 2010 Speedmaster models the shrouded design of their forks fully protects the fork tubes from stone chips – all that is necessary is to ensure there is no sign of oil leakage from the fork seals.

4 Check the tightness of all suspension nuts and bolts to be sure none have worked loose, applying the torque settings at the beginning of Chapter 5.

Rear suspension

5 Inspect the rear shock absorbers for damage and fluid leakage and tightness of their mountings. If leakage is found on either shock, the shocks must be renewed as a pair (see Chapter 5).

6 With the aid of an assistant to support the bike, compress the rear suspension several times. It should move up and down freely without binding. If any binding is felt, the worn or faulty component must be identified and checked (see Chapter 5). The problem could be due to one or both shock absorbers or the swingarm components.

7 Support the motorcycle on an auxiliary stand so that the rear wheel is off the ground. Grab the swingarm ends feel for any side-to-side

17.3a Check for oil leakage and pitting on the fork tube (arrowed)

freeplay – there should be no discernible movement **(see illustration)**. If there's a little movement or a slight clicking can be heard, inspect the tightness of all the swingarm and rear suspension mounting bolts and nuts, referring to the procedures and torque settings specified at the beginning of Chapter 5, and re-check for movement.

8 Next, grasp the top of the rear wheel and pull it upwards – there should be no discernible freeplay before the shock absorbers begin to compress **(see illustration)**. Any freeplay felt in either check indicates worn bearings in the swingarm or worn suspension mountings. The worn components must be identified and replaced with new ones (see Chapter 5).

9 To make an accurate assessment of the swingarm bearings, remove the rear wheel (see Chapter 6) and disconnect the shock absorbers from their mountings on the swingarm (see Chapter 5). Grasp the rear of the swingarm with one hand and place your other hand at the junction of the swingarm and the engine. Try to move the rear of the swingarm from side-to-side. Any wear (play) in the bearings should be felt as forward and backward (not side-to-side) movement between the swingarm and the engine at the front. Next, move the swingarm up and down through its full travel. It should move freely, without any binding or rough spots. If there is any play in the swingarm or if it does not move freely, remove the bearings for inspection (see Chapter 5).

17.3b Displace the gaiter on Scrambler models to check the seals and fork tubes

Swingarm bearing lubrication

10 Over a period of time the grease will harden or may be washed out of the bearings by incorrect use of jet washes or dirt will penetrate the bearings due to failed seals.

11 Triumph do not specify a particular service interval for this procedure, but every so often, and particularly if jet washes have been used or the bike has been ridden in wet weather often, you should remove the swingarm as described in Chapter 5 for inspection and greasing or replacement of the bearings. The suspension is not equipped with grease nipples.

18 Tyre and wheel check

Tyres

1 Check the tyre condition and tread depth thoroughly – see *Pre-ride checks*.

Wheels

2 The cast wheels fitted on Speedmaster models are virtually maintenance free, but they should be kept clean and checked periodically for cracks and other damage. Also check the wheel runout and alignment (see Chapter 6). Never attempt to repair damaged cast wheels; they must be replaced with new ones. Check

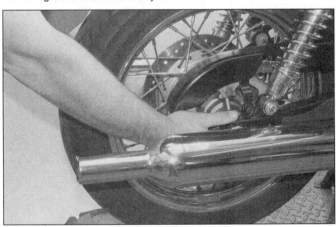

17.7 Checking for play in the swingarm bearings

17.8 Checking for play in the rear suspension mountings

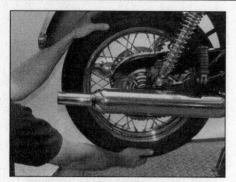

19.2 Checking for play in the wheel bearings

the valve rubber for signs of damage or deterioration and have it replaced if necessary. Also, make sure the valve stem cap is in place and tight.

3 On all other models, visually check the spokes for damage, breakage or corrosion. A broken or bent spoke must be replaced with a new one immediately because the load taken by it will be transferred to adjacent spokes, which may in turn fail.

4 If you suspect that any of the spokes are incorrectly tensioned, tap each one lightly with a screwdriver and note the sound produced. Properly tensioned spokes will make a sharp pinging sound, loose ones will produce a lower pitch, and overtightened ones will be higher pitched. A spoke wrench will be needed if any of the spokes require adjustment. Unevenly tensioned spokes will promote rim misalignment – check the wheel runout and alignment (see Chapter 6) and seek the help of a wheel building expert if this is suspected.

19 Wheel bearing check

1 Wheel bearings will wear over a period of time and result in handling problems.
2 Support the motorcycle upright using an auxiliary stand, and support it so that the wheel being checked is off the ground. Check for any play in the bearings by pushing and pulling the wheel against the axle – turn the steering to full lock to keep it steady when checking the front wheel **(see illustration)**. Also spin the wheel and check that it rotates smoothly.
3 If any play is detected in the hub, or if the wheel does not rotate smoothly and freely (and this is not due to brake or chain drag), remove the wheel and check the bearings for wear or damage (see Chapter 6). If in doubt replace them with new ones.

20 Sidestand and starter lockout circuit

1 Check the stand springs for damage and distortion. The springs must be capable of retracting the stand fully and holding it retracted when the motorcycle is in use. If a spring is sagged or broken it must be replaced with a new one.
2 Lubricate the stand pivots regularly (see Section 14).
3 Check the stand and its mount for bends and cracks, and that the bolts and nut are tightened to the correct torque settings (see Chapter 5). If necessary stands can often be repaired by welding.
4 Check the operation of the starter lockout circuit by shifting the transmission into neutral, retracting the stand, pulling in the clutch lever on EFI models, and starting the engine. With the engine idling, pull in the clutch lever and select a gear. Extend the sidestand. The engine should stop as the sidestand is extended. Also check that the engine cannot be started when the sidestand is down and the engine is in gear, irrespective of the clutch position.
5 If the circuit does not operate as described, check the various switches (sidestand, neutral and clutch) and the diodes in the circuit (see Chapter 8).

21 Battery check

1 All models are fitted with a sealed MF (maintenance free) battery. **Note:** *Do not attempt to remove the battery caps to check the electrolyte level or battery specific gravity. Removal will damage the caps, resulting in electrolyte leakage and battery damage.* The only maintenance required is to check that the terminals are clean and tight and that the casing is not damaged or leaking. See Chapter 9 for further details.
2 If the machine is not in regular use, remove the battery and give it a refresher charge every month to six weeks (see Chapter 8).

22 Headlight aim check and adjustment

Note: *An improperly adjusted headlight may cause problems for oncoming traffic or provide poor, unsafe illumination of the road ahead. Before adjusting the headlight aim, be sure to consult with local traffic laws and regulations – for UK models refer to MOT Test Checks in the Reference section.*
1 The headlight beam can adjusted both horizontally and vertically. Before making any adjustment, check that the tyre pressures are correct and the suspension is adjusted as required. Make any adjustments to the headlight aim with the machine on level ground, with the fuel tank half full, with an assistant sitting on the seat, and at night with the headlight switched to low beam. If the bike is usually ridden with a passenger on the back, have a second assistant to do this.

Bonneville, T100, Thruxton and Scrambler

2 Horizontal adjustment is made by turning the adjuster screw in the headlight rim using a

22.2 Turn the screw in the rim to alter horizontal alignment

22.3 Slacken the bolt (arrowed) on each side and tilt the headlight

Phillips screwdriver. Turn the screw clockwise to move the beam to the left, and anti-clockwise to move it to the right **(see illustration)**.

3 Vertical adjustment is made by slackening the headlight mounting bolts and tilting the headlight up or down to the correct height, then retightening the bolts to the torque setting specified at the beginning of the Chapter **(see illustration)**.

America and Speedmaster

4 Horizontal adjustment is made by slackening the headlight bracket mounting bolt on the underside of the bottom yoke and turning the headlight to the left or right as required, then tightening the bolt to the torque setting specified at the beginning of the Chapter **(see illustration)**.

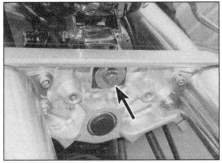

22.4 Slacken the bolt (arrowed) and swivel the headlight

5 Vertical adjustment is made by slackening the headlight bracket pinch bolt and tilting the headlight up or down to the correct height,

22.5 Slacken the nut (arrowed) and tilt the headlight

then tightening the bolt to the torque setting specified at the beginning of the Chapter **(see illustration)**.

Every 12,000 miles (20,000 km) or two years

Carry out all the items under the 6000 mile (10,000 km) or 12 months check, plus the following:

23 Spark plug renewal

1 Remove the old spark plugs as described in Section 4 and install new ones.

24 Valve clearance check and adjustment

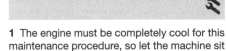

1 The engine must be completely cool for this maintenance procedure, so let the machine sit overnight before beginning.
2 Drain the engine oil (see Section 6). Remove the spark plugs to allow the engine to be turned over easier (see Section 4).
3 Remove the valve cover (see Chapter 2).
4 Remove the alternator cover (see Chapter 8).

5 Make a chart or sketch of all valve positions so that a note of each clearance can be made against the relevant valve.
6 Turn the engine **clockwise** using a 10 mm hex bit on the alternator rotor bolt until the camshaft lobes for the right-hand cylinder are pointing away from their valves **(see illustration)**.
7 With the engine in this position, check the clearances on both the inlet and exhaust valves for that cylinder. Insert a feeler gauge of the same thickness as the correct valve clearance (see Specifications, noting that there is a difference between inlet and exhaust) between the base of each camshaft lobe and the top of the cam follower on each valve and check that it is a firm sliding fit – you should feel a slight drag when the you pull the gauge out **(see illustration)**. If not, use the feeler gauges to obtain the exact clearance. Record the measured clearance on the chart.
8 Now do the left-hand cylinder. Turn the

engine clockwise until the camshaft lobes are pointing away from the valves as before. Check the valve clearances as described in Step 7.
9 When all clearances have been measured and charted, identify whether the clearance on any valve falls outside the specified range. If any do, the shim on that valve must be replaced with one of a thickness which will restore the correct clearance.
10 If a shim needs replacing remove the camshaft(s) (see Chapter 2). There is no need to remove both camshafts if shims from only one side (i.e. inlet or exhaust) of the engine need replacing. Place rags over the spark plug holes and the cam chain tunnel to prevent a shim from dropping into the engine on removal. Work on one valve at a time. If you want to remove more than one shim at a time, store them in a marked container or bag, denoting which cylinder and which valve they are from, so that they do not get mixed up.

24.6 Turn the alternator rotor clockwise until the camshaft lobes are positioned as shown

24.7 Insert the feeler gauge between the base of the lobe and the top of the follower as shown

24.11a Carefully lift out the follower . . .

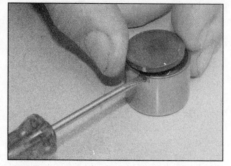

24.11b . . . then remove the shim from the top as shown

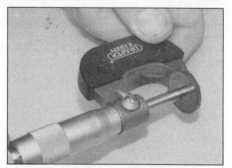

24.12 The size should be marked on the shim but check its thickness using a micrometer anyway

11 With the camshaft removed, lift the cam follower of the valve in question out of the cylinder head, using either a magnet or the suction created by a valve lapping tool if you can't grip it with your fingers, or long nosed pliers can be used with care – do not grip the follower tightly as you could score it **(see illustration)**. Remove the shim from the top of the cam follower using a small screwdriver inserted in one of the cut-outs in the follower **(see illustration)**.

12 A size mark should be stamped on one face of the shim – a shim marked 230 is 2.30 mm thick. If the mark is not visible measure the shim thickness using a micrometer **(see illustration)**. It is recommended that the shim be measured anyway to check whether it has worn. Shims are available in 0.025 mm increments from 2.025 to 3.200 mm. If the shim thickness is less than its denomination, this must be taken into account when selecting a new shim.

13 Calculate the required replacement shim size using the formula $a = (b - c) + d$, where a is the required shim size, b is the measured valve clearance, c is the specified valve clearance, and d is the existing shim thickness. For example:

The measured clearance of an inlet valve is 0.23 mm, so $b = 0.23$.

The specified clearance range for an inlet valve is 0.15 to 0.20 mm, the mid-point being 0.175 mm, so $c = 0.175$.

The thickness of the existing shim is 2.475 mm, so $d = 2.475$.

Therefore, the required replacement shim $a = 0.23 - 0.175 + 2.475$, which is 2.530 mm. The nearest available shim size is therefore 2.525. Using this shim restores the valve clearance within the specified range at 0.18 mm.

Note: *If the required replacement shim is greater than 3.200 mm (the largest available), the valve is probably not seating correctly due to a build-up of carbon deposits and should be checked and cleaned or resurfaced as required (see Chapter 2).*

14 Obtain the replacement shim, then lubricate it with molybdenum disulphide oil (a 50/50 mixture of molybdenum disulphide grease and engine oil) and fit it into the recess in the top of the cam follower with the size mark facing down **(see illustration 24.11b)**. Check that the shim is correctly seated. Lubricate the follower with molybdenum disulphide oil (a 50/50 mixture of molybdenum disulphide grease and engine oil) and fit it onto its valve, making sure it fits squarely in its bore **(see illustration 24.11a)**.

15 Repeat the process for any other valves until the clearances are correct, then install the camshafts (see Chapter 2).

16 Rotate the crankshaft clockwise several turns to seat the new shim(s), then check the clearances again.

17 Install the alternator cover (see Chapter 8).

18 Install the valve cover (see Chapter 2). Install the spark plugs (see Section 4).

19 Refill the engine with the correct quantity of oil (see Section 6).

25 Air filter renewal

Caution: If the machine is continually ridden in wet or dusty conditions, the filter should be replaced more frequently.

1 Refer to the procedure in Section 7 and replace the air filter with a new one.

26 Secondary air induction system (SAIS)

Carburettor models

Note: *Later Bonneville, T100 and Scrambler models (from VIN 317247) are fitted with an electronically controlled valve unit.*

1 If the valve clearances are all correct and the carburettors have been synchronised, and have no other faults, yet the idle speed cannot be set properly, it is possible that the secondary air induction system (SAIS) is faulty. Further information on the function of the system can be found in Chapter 3A.

2 Remove the fuel tank (see Chapter 3A). Check the air cut-off valve and reed valve unit for signs of physical damage **(see illustration)** and replace it with a new one if necessary (see Chapter 3A).

3 Check the SAIS hoses and pipes for signs of deterioration or damage, and check that they are all securely connected with the hoses clamped at each end. Replace any hoses which are cracked or deteriorated with new ones.

4 Check that the valve unit only allows air to pass through it via the union for the air filter housing hose and exiting the unions for the hoses to the cylinder head when a vacuum is applied to the air cut-off diaphragm valve union on the front. If air can flow when no vacuum is applied the cut-off valve is stuck open and the unit must be replaced with a new one (see Chapter 3A). If air cannot flow when a vacuum is applied first check that the reed valves are not stuck closed (see Step 6). If they are good the cut-off valve is stuck closed or the vacuum diaphragm has a hole

26.2 Check the valve unit (arrowed) and the hoses and pipes to and from it

26.4 Check the valve using a pencil (arrowed)

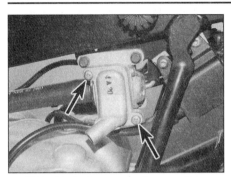

26.6a Undo the screws (arrowed) . . .

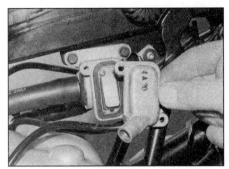

26.6b . . . and remove the cover . . .

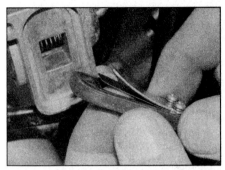

26.6c . . . then remove and check the reed valve

in it. The valve can be checked by removing the reed valve cover (see Step 6), and with the hose detached pressing on the valve with a pencil to see if it opens and closes **(see illustration)**. The diaphragm can be checked by removing the front cover on the valve. The reed valves and their covers, and all the hoses and pipes are available as individual parts. The air cut-off valve and diaphragm assembly is integral with the valve unit body.

5 Check that no air can pass through via either of the unions for the hoses to the cylinder head at any time – if it can the reed valve for the relevant union is not seating properly and needs to be inspected, cleaned, and if necessary replaced with a new one (See Step 6).

6 Remove the fuel tank (see Chapter 3A). Undo the screws securing the reed valve cover and remove it – there is no need to detach the hose from its union but do so if necessary **(see illustrations)**. Remove the reed valve **(see illustration)**. Check the reeds for cracks, warpage and any other damage or deterioration, and for signs of exhaust gases blowing past the valve. Also check the contact areas between the reeds and the reed holders, and the holders themselves, for any signs of damage or deterioration. Clean off any carbon deposits or other foreign particles using a high flash-point solvent.

EFI models

7 The system consists of an electrically actuated control valve and two reed valves contained in a separate housing. To access both components and their hoses, remove the fuel tank (see Chapter 3B).

8 Check the condition of the hose from the air filter housing to the control valve, the hose from the control valve to the reed valve housing and two short hoses which link the reed valve housing to the metal pipes on the engine. Check that the wiring connector to the control valve is secure.

9 Unbolt the reed valve housing from the frame and remove the two screws from each side to free the individual reed valve covers **(see illustration)**. Carefully remove the reed valves **(see illustration)**. Check the reeds

26.9a Remove the two screws (arrowed) to free each reed valve cover . . .

26.9b . . . and lift out the valve – EFI models

for cracks, warpage (the reed must lay flat against its seat) or other signs of damage. Check that there is no sign of exhaust gases having blown past the reeds. Carefully clean off any carbon deposits using a high flash-point solvent.

27 Fuel strainer/fuel filter

Carburettor models

1 A fuel strainer is mounted in the tank and it integral with the fuel tap. Cleaning of the strainer is advised after a high mileage

has been covered or if fuel **starvation is** suspected.

2 Remove the fuel tank and unbolt the fuel tap (see Chapter 3A). Clean the gauze strainer to remove all traces of dirt and fuel sediment **(see illustrations)**. Check the gauze for holes. If any are found, an new tap should be fitted – the strainer is not available separately. If the strainer is dirty, check the condition of the inside of the tank – if there is evidence of rust, drain and clean the tank.

EFI models

3 A fuel filter is incorporated in the fuel pump assembly inside the tank. The filter should be renewed every 12,000 miles.

4 Refer to Chapter 3B, Section 3 for pump removal and filter access details.

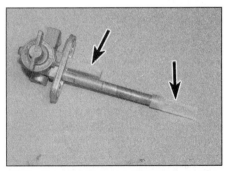

27.2a Two strainers are fitted, one for the main supply circuit and one for the reserve

27.2b Carefully pull the strainer off so it can be flushed through from the inside if necessary

Every two years

28 Brake fluid change

1 The brake fluid should be renewed every two years or whenever a master cylinder or caliper overhaul is carried out. Refer to the brake bleeding section in Chapter 6, noting that all old fluid must be pumped from the fluid reservoir and hydraulic hoses before filling with new fluid.

Every 24,000 miles (40,000 km) or four years

Carry out all the items under the 12,000 mile (20,000 km) or two years checks, plus the following:

29 Front fork oil change

1 Fork oil degrades over a period of time and loses its damping qualities. Refer to the fork oil change procedure in Chapter 5. The forks do not need to be completely disassembled.

30 Fuel system hose renewal

 Warning: Petrol (gasoline) is extremely flammable, so take extra precautions when you work on any part of the fuel system. Don't smoke or allow open flames or bare light bulbs near the work area, and don't work in a garage where a natural gas-type appliance is present. If you spill any fuel on your skin, rinse it off immediately with soap and water. When you perform any kind of work on the fuel system, wear safety glasses and have a fire extinguisher suitable for a Class B type fire (flammable liquids) on hand.

1 The fuel system hoses should be replaced with new ones at the first signs of cracking or hardening, or at the specified interval regardless of their apparent condition. This includes all the vent and drain hoses, the vacuum hoses, the crankcase breather hose **(see illustration 5.1)**, and the SAIS system hoses (see Section 26). On California models you should also replace the EVAP system hoses with new ones (see Chapter 4).

2 Remove the fuel tank (see Chapter 3A or 3B). Disconnect the hoses, noting the routing of each hose and where and how it connects (see Chapter 3A or 3B, referring to the relevant Section). It is advisable to make a sketch of the various hoses before removing them to ensure they are correctly installed.

3 Secure each new hose to its unions using new clamps or sealing washers where fitted. Run the engine and check for leaks before taking the machine out on the road.

Every four years

31 Brake hose renewal

1 The hoses deteriorate with age and should be replaced with new ones regardless of their apparent condition. Refer to Chapter 6 and disconnect the brake hoses from the master cylinders and calipers. Always replace the banjo union sealing washers with new ones.

Non-scheduled maintenance

32 Cylinder compression check

1 Poor engine performance can be caused by many things, including leaking valves, incorrect valve clearances, a leaking head gasket, or worn pistons, rings and/or cylinder walls. A cylinder compression check will help pinpoint these conditions and can also indicate the presence of excessive carbon deposits in the cylinder heads.

2 The only tools required are a compression gauge with 12 mm thread size adaptor and a spark plug wrench. Depending on the outcome of the initial test, a squirt-type oil can may also be needed.

3 Make sure the valve clearances are correctly set (see Section 24) and that the cylinder head fasteners are tightened to the correct torque setting (see Chapter 2).

4 Refer to *Fault Finding Equipment* in the Reference section for details of the compression test. Triumph do not provide any figures for standard and minimum running compression, however an engine in good condition should show 150 to 180 psi, and anything less than 120 psi is in need of attention. Also look for large differences between the cylinders, even if neither is too low in itself. If in doubt refer to a Triumph dealer.

Chapter 2
Engine, clutch and transmission

Contents

Degrees of difficulty

Easy, suitable for novice with little experience	**Fairly easy,** suitable for beginner with some experience	**Fairly difficult,** suitable for competent DIY mechanic	**Difficult,** suitable for experienced DIY mechanic	**Very difficult,** suitable for expert DIY or professional

Specifications

General

Type	Four-stroke parallel twin
Capacity	
Bonneville – 2001 to 2006	790 cc
Bonneville – 2007-on	865 cc
America – 2002 to 2006	790 cc
America – 2007-on	865 cc
T100 and Speedmaster – 2003 to 2004.	790 cc
T100 and Speedmaster – 2005-on.	865 cc
Thruxton and Scrambler.	865 cc
Bore	
790 cc engine.	86.0 mm
865 cc engine.	90.0 mm
Stroke	68 mm
Compression ratio	9.2 to 1
Cylinder identification.	No. 1 left cylinder, No. 2 right cylinder
Firing interval	
Bonneville, T100 and Thruxton.	360°
America, Speedmaster and Scrambler	270°
Cooling system.	Air/oil cooled
Camshafts	DOHC, chain and gear-driven
Clutch	Wet multi-plate with cable release
Transmission.	Five-speed constant mesh
Final drive.	Chain and sprockets

Camshafts and followers

Camshaft bearing oil clearance
  Bonneville, T100 and Thruxton
    Standard . . . . 0.040 to 0.091 mm
    Service limit (max) . . . . 0.12 mm
  America and Speedmaster
    Standard . . . . 0.030 to 0.070 mm
    Service limit (max) . . . . 0.12 mm
Camshaft journal diameter . . . . 22.930 to 22.960 mm
Camshaft journal holder internal diameter . . . . 23.000 to 23.021 mm
Camshaft end-float (max) . . . . 0.20 mm
Camshaft run-out (max) . . . . 0.05 mm
Follower diameter
  Standard . . . . 27.978 to 27.993 mm
  Service limit (min) . . . . 27.970 mm
Follower bore diameter
  Standard . . . . 28.015 to 28.035 mm
  Service limit (max) . . . . 28.050 mm
Cam chain stretch limit . . . . 149.48 mm

Valves, guides and springs

Valve size
  Intake valve . . . . 31.0 mm
  Exhaust valve . . . . 26.0 mm
Valve clearances . . . . see Chapter 1
Valve lift
  Intake valve . . . . 9.5 mm
  Exhaust valve . . . . 9.4 mm
Stem diameter
  Intake valve
    Standard . . . . 5.463 to 5.478 mm
    Service limit (min) . . . . 5.453 mm
  Exhaust valve
    Standard . . . . 5.451 to 5.466 mm
    Service limit (min) . . . . 5.441 mm
Guide bore diameter
  Standard . . . . 5.500 to 5.515 mm
  Service limit (max) . . . . 5.543 mm
Seat width in head
  Standard . . . . 0.9 to 1.1 mm
  Service limit (max) . . . . 1.5 mm
Seat width on valve
  Standard . . . . 1.27 to 1.56 mm
  Service limit (max) . . . . 1.56 mm
Spring free length (min)
  Standard . . . . 42.4 mm
  Service limit (max) . . . . 41.7 mm

Pistons

Piston diameter (max – measured 13 mm up from skirt, at 90° to piston pin axis)
  790 cc engine
    Standard . . . . 85.975 to 85.990 mm
    Service limit (min) . . . . 85.935 mm
  865 cc engine
    Standard . . . . 89.972 to 89.988 mm
    Service limit (min) . . . . 89.933 mm
Piston pin diameter
  Standard . . . . 18.995 to 19.000 mm
  Service limit (min) . . . . 18.985 mm
Piston pin bore diameter (in piston)
  Standard . . . . 19.002 to 19.008 mm
  Service limit (max)
    790 cc engines . . . . 19.036 mm
    865 cc engines . . . . 19.030 mm
Connecting rod small-end internal diameter
  Standard . . . . 19.016 to 19.034 mm
  Service limit (max) . . . . 19.040 mm

Piston rings

Ring-to-groove clearance

Standard... 0.02 to 0.06 mm

Service limit (max).. 0.075 mm

Piston ring groove width

Top and 2nd rings... 1.01 to 1.03 mm

Oil ring.. 2.01 to 2.03 mm

Ring installed end gap	**790 cc engine**	**865 cc engine**
Top ring...	0.12 to 0.33 mm	0.17 to 0.33 mm
2nd ring..	0.27 to 0.48 mm	0.32 to 0.48 mm
Oil ring..	0.17 to 0.73 mm	0.17 to 0.73 mm

Cylinder head

Warpage

Standard... 0.03 mm max

Service limit (max).. 0.07 mm

Cylinders

Bore diameter

790 cc engine

Standard... 85.991 to 86.009 mm

Service limit (max)..................................... 86.034 mm

865 cc engine

Standard... 89.991 to 90.009 mm

Service limit (max)..................................... 90.034 mm

Clutch – Bonneville and T100 models up to engine no. 211132

Friction plate

Quantity

Type A.. 5

Type B (innermost).................................. 1

Type C (outermost).................................. 1

Thickness (min)

Standard.. 3.22 to 3.38 mm

Service limit (min)................................... 3.1 mm

Plain plate

Quantity

Type A.. 5

Type B (outermost).................................. 1

Warpage (max)... 0.15 mm

Clutch – Bonneville and T100 models from engine no. 211133 onwards, Thruxton, America, Speedmaster and Scrambler

Friction plate

Quantity

Type A.. 5

Type B (innermost and outermost).................... 2

Thickness (min)

Standard.. 3.22 to 3.38 mm

Service limit (min)................................... 3.1 mm

Plain plate

Quantity... 6

Warpage (max)... 0.15 mm

Lubrication system

Oil type, viscosity and capacity............................... see Chapter 1

Oil pressure.. 40 psi (0.5 Bar) at 4000 rpm with engine at normal operating temperature

Oil pump

Inner rotor tip-to-outer rotor clearance

Standard.. 0.15 mm

Service limit (max)................................... 0.20 mm

Outer rotor-to-housing clearance (max)

Standard.. 0.15 to 0.22 mm

Service limit (max)................................... 0.35 mm

Rotor end-float (max)

Standard.. 0.02 to 0.07 mm

Service limit (max)................................... 0.10 mm

Crankshaft and main bearings

Main bearing oil clearance
    Standard. . . . . 0.019 to 0.044 mm
    Service limit (max) . . . . 0.10 mm
Main journal diameter
    Standard. . . . . 37.960 to 37.976 mm
    Service limit (min) . . . . 37.936 mm
End-float
    Standard. . . . . 0.05 to 0.20 mm
    Service limit (max) . . . . 0.40 mm

Connecting rods and big-end bearings

Big-end side clearance
    Standard. . . . . 0.15 to 0.30 mm
    Service limit (max) . . . . 0.50 mm
Crankpin diameter – up to engine no. 520266
    Standard. . . . . 40.946 to 40.960 mm
    Service limit (min) . . . . 40.932 mm
Crankpin diameter – from engine no. 520267 onwards
    Standard. . . . . 40.968 to 40.982 mm
    Service limit . . . . 40.954 mm
Big-end bearing oil clearance
    Standard. . . . . 0.036 to 0.066 mm
    Service limit (max) . . . . 0.10 mm
For connecting rod small-end specifications see under 'Pistons'.

Gearchange mechanism, selector drum and forks

Selector fork end thickness (min)
    Standard. . . . . 5.8 to 5.9 mm
    Service limit (min) . . . . 5.7 mm
Pinion groove width (max)
    Standard. . . . . 6.0 to 6.1 mm
    Service limit (max) . . . . 6.2 mm

Transmission

Primary reduction. 1.740:1 (62/108)
Final reduction (no. of teeth)
    Bonneville and T100 – 790 cc engine. 2.530:1 (43/17T)
    Bonneville and T100 – 865 cc engine. 2.390:1 (43/18T)
    Thruxton and Scrambler. 2.390:1 (43/18T)
    America. 2.470:1 (42/17T)
    Speedmaster – 790 cc engine 2.625:1 (42/16T)
    Speedmaster – 865 cc engine 2.687:1 (43/16T)
1st gear 2.730:1 (41/15T)
2nd gear 1.950:1 (37/19T)
3rd gear 1.550:1 (34/22T)
4th gear 1.290:1 (31/24T)
5th gear 1.070:1 (29/27T)

Torque settings

Alternator cover bolts. . . . . 10 Nm
Balancer shaft retainer screws. . . . . 12 Nm
Breather rotor screws. . . . . 12 Nm
Cam chain guide blade bolts . . . . 10 Nm
Cam chain tensioner blade nut . . . . 10 Nm
Cam chain tensioner cap bolt . . . . 20 Nm
Cam chain tensioner mounting bolts . . . . 9 Nm
Camshaft drive gear shaft bolt
    Engine number up to 186916. . . . . 10 Nm
    Engine number from 186917-on. . . . . 28 Nm
Camshaft holder bolts . . . . 10 Nm
Camshaft oil feed pipe bolts . . . . 8 Nm
Clutch cover bolts . . . . 10 Nm
Clutch nut. . . . . 105 Nm
Clutch spring bolts. . . . . 9 Nm
Connecting rods – caps with nuts and bolts
    First stage. . . . . 22 Nm
    Second stage . . . . minus 140°
    Third stage . . . . 10 Nm
    Fourth stage . . . . 14 Nm
    Fifth stage. . . . . plus 120°

Torque settings (continued)

Connecting rods – caps with bolts only
    First stage . . . . 14 Nm
    Second stage . . . . plus 120°
Crankcase bolts – Bonneville and T100 up to engine number 307173, Thruxton, Scrambler, America and Speedmaster up to engine number 326093
    Initial setting – all bolts . . . . 10 Nm
    Final setting
        M10 x 118.5 mm silver bolts . . . . 40 Nm
        M10 x 118.5 mm green bolts . . . . 75°
        M8 bolts . . . . 32 Nm
Crankcase bolts – Bonneville and T100 from engine number 307174, Thruxton, Scrambler, America and Speedmaster from engine number 326094
    Initial setting – all bolts . . . . 10 Nm
    Final setting
        M10 x 120.5 mm bolts . . . . 75°
        M8 bolts . . . . 32 Nm
Cylinder head intake adapters . . . . 12 Nm
Cylinder head 10 mm nuts
    Stage 1 . . . . 20 Nm
    Stage 2 . . . . 26 Nm
    Stage 3 . . . . 28 Nm
    Stage 4 . . . . 120°
Engine earth lead . . . . 28 Nm
Engine mounting bolts
    Bonneville, T100, Thruxton and Scrambler
        Frame cradle section bolts
            up to VIN 333839 (black bolts) . . . . 45 Nm
            from VIN 333840 (silver bolts) . . . . 40 Nm
        Upper and lower rear mounting bolt nuts . . . . 80 Nm
        Upper and lower front mounting bolt nuts . . . . 80 Nm
        Bracket-to-cylinder head bolt nut . . . . 80 Nm
        Bracket-to-frame bolt nut . . . . 22 Nm
        Cradle brace bolts . . . . 22 Nm
    America and Speedmaster
        Rear mounting bolt nut . . . . 80 Nm
        Cylinder head to bracket bolt nut . . . . 80 Nm
        Upper and lower front mounting bolt nuts . . . . 80 Nm
        Frame cradle section bolts
            up to VIN 333839 (black bolts) . . . . 55 Nm
            from VIN 333840 (silver bolts) . . . . 40 Nm
        Swingarm pivot bolt nut . . . . 110 Nm
        Swingarm pivot clamp bolts . . . . 45 Nm
Front footrest mounting bracket bolts – America and Speedmaster . . . 30 Nm
Gearchange mechanism cover bolts . . . . 8 Nm
Gearchange shaft centralising spring pin . . . . 23 Nm
Gearchange stopper arm bolt . . . . 12 Nm
Oil cooler fittings
    Feed pipe banjo bolts to cylinder head . . . . 30 Nm
    Feed pipe banjo bolts to cooler . . . . 45 Nm
    Return pipe banjo bolt to sump (early Bonneville and T100) . . . . . . 45 Nm
    Return pipe flare nut to joint piece . . . . 15 Nm
    Joint piece to sump . . . . 45 Nm
    Return pipe banjo bolt to cooler . . . . 45 Nm
    Cooler mounting bolts . . . . 8 Nm
Oil pipe (external) to crankcase banjo bolt . . . . 30 Nm
Oil pipe (internal) banjo bolts . . . . 8 Nm
Oil pressure relief valve . . . . 15 Nm
Oil pressure switch . . . . 13 Nm
Oil pump bolts . . . . 12 Nm
Oil strainer bolts . . . . 6 Nm
Selector drum cam plate bolt . . . . 12 Nm
Selector fork shaft retainer screw . . . . 12 Nm
Sump bolts . . . . 12 Nm
Starter clutch housing bolts . . . . 16 Nm
Valve cover bolts . . . . 14 Nm

1 General information

The engine/transmission unit is a 790 cc or 865 cc (according to model) parallel-twin air- and oil-cooled unit engine. Bonneville, T100 and Thruxton models have a 360° crank which means the pistons rise and fall simultaneously, though they fire on alternate strokes. America, Speedmaster and Scrambler models have a 270° crank which means their motion is offset and the firing order uneven.

The engine/transmission unit is constructed in aluminium alloy and the crankcase is divided horizontally. The one-piece crankshaft runs in four main bearings. The right-hand end of the crankshaft carries the alternator rotor. Twin balancer shafts run off a gear on the right-hand end of the crankshaft. The ignition timing triggers are incorporated in the alternator rotor.

A central cam chain drives the double overhead camshafts via sprockets and gears. There are the four valves per cylinder.

Primary drive to the clutch is via gears on the left-hand side of the engine. The cable-operated clutch is a wet multi-plate unit with conventional springs. The five-speed constant-mesh transmission drives the rear wheel via chain and sprockets that run unconventionally down the right-hand side of the bike.

The engine has a wet-sump lubrication system incorporating two pumps. The rear pump draws oil from the sump via a strainer and distributes it via the filter to the crankshaft main and big-end bearings, the camshafts, and to the transmission output shaft. The front pump draws oil in the same way and circulates it around the cylinder block and head to cool them before sending it to the oil cooler at the front. The cooled oil returns to the sump. The front pump also feeds a lubrication circuit for the transmission input shaft and the clutch.

2 Component access

Operations possible with the engine in the frame

The components and assemblies listed below can be removed without having to remove the engine from the frame. If however, a number of areas require attention at the same time, removal of the engine is recommended.

Valve cover
Cam chain tensioner
Camshafts
Cylinder head
Cylinder block
Pistons
Clutch
Oil pumps
Sump and oil strainer

Alternator
Starter clutch and gears
Gearchange mechanism
Starter motor
Oil pressure switch
Neutral switch

Operations requiring engine removal

It is necessary to remove the engine from the frame and separate the crankcase halves to gain access to the following components:

Cam chain
Connecting rods
Crankshaft
Balancer shafts
Transmission shafts
Selector drum and forks
Oil pressure relief valve

3 Major engine repair general note

1 It is not always easy to determine when or if an engine should be completely overhauled, as a number of factors must be considered.

2 High mileage is not necessarily an indication that an overhaul is needed, while low mileage, on the other hand, does not preclude the need for an overhaul. Frequency of servicing is probably the single most important consideration. An engine that has regular and frequent oil and filter changes, as well as other required maintenance, will most likely give many miles of reliable service. Conversely, a neglected engine, or one which has not been run in properly, may require an overhaul very early in its life.

3 Exhaust smoke and excessive oil consumption are both indications that piston rings and/or valve guides are in need of attention, although make sure that the fault is not due to oil leakage.

4 If the engine is making obvious knocking or rumbling noises, the connecting rods and/or main bearings are probably at fault.

5 Loss of power, rough running, excessive valve train noise and high fuel consumption may also point to the need for an overhaul, especially if they are all present at the same time. If a complete tune-up does not remedy the situation, major mechanical work is the only solution.

6 An engine overhaul generally involves restoring the internal parts to the specifications of a new engine. The piston rings and main and connecting rod bearings are usually renewed during a major overhaul. Generally the valve seats are re-ground, since they are usually in less than perfect condition at this point. The end result should be a like new engine that will give as many trouble-free miles as the original.

7 Before beginning the engine overhaul, read through the related procedures to familiarise yourself with the scope and requirements of the job. Overhauling an engine is not all that difficult,

but it is time consuming. Plan on the motorcycle being tied up for a minimum of two weeks. Check on the availability of parts and make sure that any necessary special tools, equipment and supplies are obtained in advance.

8 Most work can be done with typical workshop hand tools, although a number of precision measuring tools are required for inspecting parts to determine the extent of wear. Often a dealer will handle the inspection of parts and offer advice concerning reconditioning and renewal. As a general rule, time is the primary cost of an overhaul so it does not pay to install worn or substandard parts.

9 As a final note, to ensure maximum life and minimum trouble from a rebuilt engine, everything must be assembled with care in a spotlessly clean environment.

4 Engine removal and installation

Caution: The engine is very heavy. Engine removal and installation should be carried out with the aid of at least one assistant; personal injury or damage could occur if the engine falls or is dropped. An hydraulic or mechanical floor jack should be used to support and lower or raise the engine – an hydraulic trolley jack is advised because its wheels enable easy movement of the engine while it is still supported.

Bonneville, T100, Thruxton and Scrambler

Removal

Note: *Give any exposed or corroded nuts and bolts a spray with some penetrating fluid/lubricant (such as WD40) before trying to undo them.*

1 Give some thought to how to support the motorcycle during engine removal (see Step 6). Note that work can be made easier by raising the machine to a suitable working height on an hydraulic ramp or other suitable platform. Make sure the motorcycle is secure and will not topple over (also see *Tools and Workshop Tips* in the Reference section).

2 If the engine is dirty, particularly around its mountings, wash it thoroughly before starting. This makes working on the engine much easier and rules out the possibility of caked on lumps of dirt falling into some vital component.

3 Disconnect the battery leads (see Chapter 8).

4 Drain the engine oil and remove the oil filter (see Chapter 1).

5 Remove the fuel tank and carburettors (Chapter 3A) or fuel tank and throttle bodies (Chapter 3B). Plug the engine intake ducts with clean rag.

6 Remove the exhaust system (Chapter 3A or 3B). It is suggested that you place an axle stand under each passenger footrest mount or under the frame rear downtube sections, avoiding the removable cradle sections, using

4.8 Unscrew the crankcase bolt and detach the earth lead

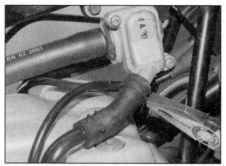

4.11 Release the clamp and detach the hose from each side

4.13 Unscrew the bolt and remove the lever

some rag between them to prevent scratches **(see illustration 4.22)**.

7 Remove the front sprocket (see Chapter 5).

8 Remove the swingarm (see Chapter 5), then remove the drive chain. Unscrew the crankcase bolt securing the earth lead to the back of the engine and detach the lead, then thread the bolt back into the engine **(see illustration)**. Secure it clear, noting its routing.

9 On California models remove the EVAP system canisters (see Chapter 3A or 3B).

10 Pull the spark plug caps off the plugs and secure the leads clear of the engine.

11 Release the clamps and detach the SAIS system outlet hoses from the valve unit **(see illustration)**.

12 Remove the oil cooler along with its feed and return pipes (see Section 6).

13 Note the alignment of the gearchange lever with the punch mark on the shaft, then slacken the pinch bolt and slide the lever off **(see illustration)**. On Thruxton models, follow the above procedure and slide the gearchange linkage arm off the gearchange shaft (see Chapter 5, Section 3).

14 Refer to Chapter 1, Section 11 and create slack in the clutch cable using the adjuster at the lever on the handlebar. Refer to Section 17 and detach the clutch cable from the engine. Either release the cable clips from the left-hand frame cradle section, or thread the front nut off the end of the cable, then draw the cable through the clips **(see illustration)**.

15 Release the crankcase breather hose clamp and pull the hose off its union on the engine **(see illustration)**.

16 If you are performing a full engine strip or a procedure that involves removing the alternator rotor, it is worth doing so now as the bolt is tight and the rotor can be difficult to get off the shaft – doing so with the engine still in the frame means you don't have to hold and support it. Refer to Chapter 8 to remove it.

17 If you have not removed the alternator, trace the wiring from the cover and disconnect the alternator and ignition pick-up coil (crankshaft position sensor on EFI models) wiring connectors. On EFI models also disconnect the speed sensor wire connector under the right-hand side panel, or if access to the connector is difficult, unbolt the coil/sensor itself.

18 Pull back the rubber boot covering the

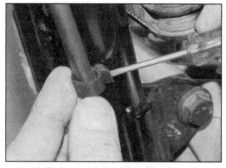

4.14 Release the cable clips from the frame if required

starter motor terminal, then unscrew the nut and detach the lead **(see illustration)**. Release the clips from the inside of the right-hand frame cradle by carefully levering them out with a screwdriver and secure the lead clear, noting its routing **(see illustration)**. Remove the starter

4.18a Unscrew the nut (arrowed) and detach the starter motor lead

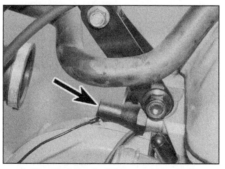

4.19a Pull the boot (arrowed) off the switch . . .

4.15 Detach the crankcase breather hose

motor now if required (see Chapter 8), or do so after the engine has been removed if necessary.

19 Pull the rubber boot off the oil pressure switch, then undo the screw and detach the wire from the terminal **(see illustrations)**. Secure it clear, noting its routing.

4.18b Release the lead from the frame

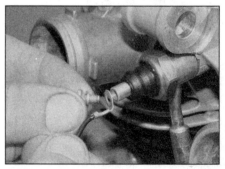

4.19b . . . then undo the screw and detach the wire

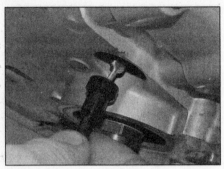

4.20 Detach the wire from the neutral switch

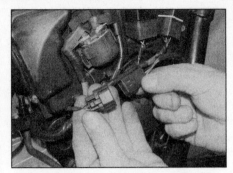

4.21 Sidestand switch wiring connector

4.22 Place a jack under the engine to support it

20 Pull the rubber boot off the neutral switch then pull the wiring connector off the terminal (see illustration). Secure it clear, noting its routing.

21 Disconnect the sidestand switch wiring connector (see illustration). Release the wiring from any clips or ties, ignoring those on the left-hand frame cradle section as the switch will come away with that.

22 At this point, position an hydraulic or mechanical jack under the engine with a block of wood between them (see illustration). Make sure the jack is centrally positioned so the engine will not topple in any direction when the last mounting bolt is removed. Raise the jack to take the weight of the engine, but make sure it is not lifting the bike and taking the weight of that as well. The idea is to support the engine so that there is no pressure on any of the mounting bolts once they have been slackened, so they

can be easily withdrawn. Note that it may be necessary to adjust the jack as some of the bolts are removed to relieve the stress transferred to the other bolts.

> **HAYNES HINT** *After removing each engine mounting bolt, make a note of its location and fit any locknut, nut, washer or spacer that goes with the bolt back onto it, in the correct order and way round – this ensures that everything can be reassembled with ease later on.*

23 Unscrew the nut on the lower front mounting bolt then remove the bolt (see illustrations). If the bolt is tight do not drift it out as you could damage the threads – wait until the cradle sections are loose then withdraw it.

24 Unscrew the bolts securing the brace between the frame cradle sections and remove the brace (see illustration). Unscrew the bolts securing each cradle section to the main frame and remove the cradles, noting the plates the bolts thread into and the oil cooler mounting bracket (see illustrations).

25 Unscrew the nuts and withdraw the bolts securing the brackets between the rear of the cylinder head and the frame and remove the brackets (see illustration). As they are shaped, mark each bracket as to its location and orientation as an aid to installation.

26 Unscrew the nut on the upper front mounting bolt then remove the bolt (see illustration).

27 Make sure the engine is supported by the jack, and have an assistant hold it.

28 Unscrew the nuts on the upper and lower rear mounting bolts then remove the bolts

4.23a Unscrew the nut . . .

4.23b . . . and withdraw the bolt

4.24a Unscrew the bolts and remove the brace

4.24b Unscrew the bolts at the top of the cradle . . .

4.24c . . . and the bolts (arrowed) at the back . . .

4.24d . . . and remove the cradle

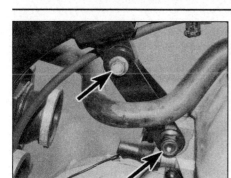

4.25 Unscrew the nuts (arrowed), withdraw the bolts and remove the brackets

4.26 Unscrew the nut and withdraw the bolt

4.28a Remove the upper rear bolt . . .

(see illustrations). Unscrew the bolts and remove the lower rear mounting bolt bracket on the right-hand side along with the plate the bolts thread into **(see illustration)**.

29 Check that all wiring, cables and hoses are disconnected and well clear. Carefully lift the front of the engine slightly to release the upper rear mounting from the frame, then lower the engine and manoeuvre it out from the right-hand side. If using a trolley jack make sure it does not slide away as you manoeuvre the engine – have an assistant ready for this. If using a mechanical jack make sure it does not topple over.

Installation

Note: *The upper front mounting bolt (illustration 4.26), lower front mounting bolt (illustration 4.23b) and cylinder head mounting bolts (illustration 4.25) can be fitted from the right-hand side rather than from the left as shown in the procedure.*

30 Manoeuvre the engine into position under the frame and lift it onto the jack **(see illustration 4.22)**. Raise the engine, taking care not to catch any part on the frame. Raise and move the engine in a reverse of the way it was removed. When the mounting bolt holes are aligned fit the lower rear mounting bolt bracket and its threaded plate and tighten the bolts **(see illustration 4.28c)**. Now slide the lower rear mounting bolt through from the right-hand side and the upper rear mounting bolt through from the left-hand side **(see illustrations 4.28b and a)**. Fit the nut onto the end of each bolt and tighten them finger-tight.

31 Slide the upper front mounting bolt

through from the left-hand side then thread the nut onto its end and tighten it finger-tight **(see illustration 4.26)**.

32 Fit the brackets between the rear of the cylinder head and the frame, making sure each is correctly positioned **(see illustration)**. Slide the bolts through from the left-hand side and tighten their nuts finger-tight – make sure the bracket-to-frame nut is tightened hard enough to prevent the brackets twisting when the bracket-to-cylinder head nut is fully tightened later.

33 Fit the frame cradle sections to each side then fit the bolts with their plates and the oil cooler bracket and tighten the bolts finger-tight **(see illustrations 4.24d, c and b)**. Fit the brace between the cradles and tighten its bolts finger-tight **(see illustration 4.24a)**.

34 Slide the lower front mounting bolt through from the left-hand side then thread the nut onto its end and tighten it finger-tight **(see illustration 4.23b and a)**.

35 Now tighten the bolts in the following order to the torque settings specified at the beginning of the Chapter.
● First tighten the cradle section bolts.
● Second tighten the upper and lower rear mounting bolt nuts.
● Third tighten the upper and lower front mounting bolt nuts.
● Fourth tighten the bracket-to-cylinder head bolt nut, then tighten the bracket-to-frame bolt nut, noting the difference in their torque settings.
● Lastly tighten the cradle brace bolts.

36 The remainder of the installation procedure is the reverse of removal, noting the following points:

● Make sure all wires, cables and hoses are correctly routed and connected, and secured by any clips or ties.
● Secure the earth lead to the engine and tighten the bolt to the torque setting specified at the beginning of the Chapter before installing the swingarm **(see illustration 4.8)**.
● Use new gaskets on the exhaust pipe connections.
● When fitting the gearchange lever or linkage arm onto the shaft, align the punch mark as noted on removal, and tighten the pinch bolt securely **(see illustration 4.13)**.
● Refer to Section 6 for installation of the oil cooler.
● Do not forget to connect the crankcase breather hose to the engine **(see illustration 4.15)**.
● Refill the engine with the specified quantity of oil (see Chapter 1).
● Adjust throttle and clutch cable freeplay (see Chapter 1).
● Adjust the drive chain (see Chapter 1).
● If the engine has been disassembled refer to the final Section of this Chapter for initial starting and running procedures. Adjust the idle speed (see Chapter 1).

America and Speedmaster
Removal

Note: *Give any exposed or corroded nuts and bolts a spray with some penetrating fluid/lubricant (such as WD40) before trying to undo them.*

37 Give some thought to how to support the motorcycle during engine removal (see Step 43). Note that work can be made easier

4.28b . . . and the lower rear bolt . . .

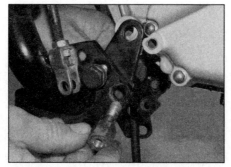

4.28c . . . then unscrew the bolts and remove the bracket

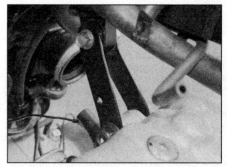

4.32 Make sure the brackets are the correct way round

4.47 Unscrew the bolt (arrowed) and slide the arm off the shaft

4.48 Unscrew the bolts (arrowed) on each side

4.57 Sidestand switch wiring connector (arrowed)

by raising the machine to a suitable working height on an hydraulic ramp or other suitable platform. Make sure the motorcycle is secure and will not topple over (also see *Tools and Workshop Tips* in the Reference section).

38 If the engine is dirty, particularly around its mountings, wash it thoroughly before starting. This makes working on the engine much easier and rules out the possibility of caked on lumps of dirt falling into some vital component.

39 Remove the seat(s) (see Chapter 7).

40 Remove the battery and its holder (see Chapter 8).

41 Drain the engine oil and remove the oil filter (see Chapter 1).

42 Remove the fuel tank and carburettors (Chapter 3A) or fuel tank and throttle bodies (Chapter 3B). Plug the engine intake ducts with clean rag.

43 Remove the exhaust system (Chapter 4). It is suggested that you place an axle stand under each passenger footrest plate/silencer mount or under the frame rear downtube sections, avoiding the removable cradle sections, using some rag between them to prevent scratches **(see illustration 4.22)**.

44 On California models remove the EVAP system canisters (see Chapter 3).

45 Pull the spark plug caps off the plugs and secure the leads clear of the engine.

46 Release the clamps and detach the SAIS system hoses from the valve unit **(see illustration 4.11)**.

47 Note the alignment of the gearchange linkage arm with the punch mark on the shaft, then slacken the pinch bolt and slide the arm off **(see illustration)**.

48 Unscrew the bolts securing the front footrest mounting bracket assembly to the frame **(see illustration)**.

49 Remove the front sprocket (see Chapter 5). Make sure the drive chain is not looped around the end of the shaft.

50 Refer to Chapter 1, Section 11 and create slack in the clutch cable using the adjuster at the lever on the handlebar. Refer to Section 17 and detach the clutch cable from the engine.

51 Release the crankcase breather hose clamp and pull the hose off its union on the engine **(see illustration 4.15)**.

52 If you are performing a full engine strip or a procedure that involves removing the alternator rotor, it is worth doing so now as the bolt is tight and the rotor can be difficult to get

off the shaft – doing so with the engine still in the frame means you don't have to hold and support it. Refer to Chapter 8 to remove it.

53 If you have not removed the alternator, trace the wiring from the cover and disconnect the alternator and ignition pick-up coil wiring connectors.

54 Pull back the rubber boot covering the starter motor terminal, then unscrew the nut and detach the lead **(see illustration 4.18a)**. Release the clips from the inside of the right-hand frame cradle by carefully levering them out with a screwdriver and secure the lead clear, noting its routing **(see illustration 4.18b)**. Remove the starter motor now if required (see Chapter 8), or do so after the engine has been removed if necessary.

55 Pull the rubber boot off the oil pressure switch, then undo the screw and detach the wire from the terminal **(see illustrations 4.19a and b)**. Secure it clear, noting its routing.

56 Pull the rubber boot off the neutral switch then pull the wiring connector off the terminal **(see illustration 4.20)**. Secure it clear, noting its routing.

57 Disconnect the sidestand switch wiring connector **(see illustration)**. Release the wiring from any clips or ties, ignoring those on the left-hand frame cradle section as the switch will come away with that.

58 Displace the rear brake fluid reservoir and tie it to another part of the bike so it is upright and above the level of the master cylinder but is not in the way of engine removal **(see illustration)**.

59 Remove the oil cooler along with its feed and return pipes (see Section 6).

60 At this point, position an hydraulic or

mechanical jack under the engine with a block of wood between them **(see illustration 4.22)**. Make sure the jack is centrally positioned so the engine will not topple in any direction when the last mounting bolt is removed. Raise the jack to take the weight of the engine, but make sure it is not lifting the bike and taking the weight of that as well. The idea is to support the engine so that there is no pressure on any of the mounting bolts once they have been slackened, so they can be easily withdrawn. Note that it may be necessary to adjust the jack as some of the bolts are removed to relieve the stress transferred to the other bolts.

> **HAYNES HiNT**
> *After removing each engine mounting bolt, make a note of its location and fit any locknut, nut, washer or spacer that goes with the bolt back onto it, in the correct order and way round – this ensures that everything can be reassembled with ease later on.*

61 Unscrew the nut on the lower front mounting bolt then remove the bolt, collecting the spacer that fits between the engine and the left-hand frame cradle section as you do **(see illustration)**. If the bolt is tight do not drift it out as you could damage the threads – wait until the cradle sections are loose then withdraw it.

62 Unscrew the bolts securing each cradle section to the main frame and remove the cradles, noting the plates the bolts thread into and the oil cooler and horn mounting brackets **(see illustrations 4.24b, c and d)**.

63 Slacken the swingarm pivot clamp bolts

4.58 Displace the reservoir and secure it clear

4.61 Note the spacer (arrowed) between the engine and frame

4.63a Slacken the clamp bolt (arrowed) on each side, then remove the cap and unscrew the nut

4.63b Retrieve the spacers (arrowed) as you withdraw the bolt

4.64 Unscrew the nut (arrowed) and withdraw the bolt

(see illustration). Unscrew the nut on the swingarm pivot bolt. Carefully drive the swingarm pivot through the engine, removing the left-hand spacers as you do, until it clears the crankcase but is still located in both the swingarm and the frame, thus keeping the swingarm supported **(see illustration)**. Bear in mind that this leaves the pivot bolt sticking out, which will cause much grief when you walk into it or trip over it.

64 Unscrew the nut and withdraw the bolt securing the rear of the cylinder head to the frame bracket **(see illustration)**.

65 Unscrew the nut on the rear mounting bolt then remove the bolt **(see illustrations 4.28a)**.

66 Check that all wiring (with the exception of the engine earth lead), cables and hoses are disconnected and well clear. Carefully lower the engine on the jack, allowing it to pivot on the upper front mounting bolt. When it becomes accessible unscrew the bolt securing the earth lead to the back of the engine and detach the lead **(see illustration 4.8)**. If using a mechanical jack make sure it does not topple over. When the jack is fully lowered, unscrew the nut on the upper front mounting bolt and remove the bolt, keeping the engine supported as you do **(see illustration 4.26)**. Lift the engine off the jack, remove it, and manoeuvre the engine out of the side of the frame. If using a trolley jack make sure it does not slide away as you manoeuvre the engine – have an assistant ready for this.

Installation

Note: *The upper front mounting bolt (illustration 4.26), lower front mounting bolt (illustration 4.61) and cylinder head mounting bolts (illustration 4.64) can be fitted from the right-hand side rather than from the left as shown in the procedure.*

67 Manoeuvre the engine into position under the frame and lift it onto the jack **(see illustration 4.22)**. Raise the front of the engine, taking care not to catch any part of it on the frame, and move it in a reverse of the way it was removed. When the upper front mounting bolt hole is aligned slide the bolt through from the left-hand side **(see illustration 4.26)**. Fit the nut onto the end of the bolt and tighten it finger-tight.

68 Secure the earth lead to the engine and tighten the bolt to the torque setting specified at the beginning of the Chapter **(see illustration 4.8)**.

69 Raise the engine so it pivots up on the front bolt, making sure it fits correctly between the swingarm ends, and taking care not to catch any part on the frame, and when the mounting bolt holes are aligned slide the rear mounting bolt through from the left-hand side **(see illustration 4.28a)**. Fit the nut onto the end of the bolt and tighten it finger-tight. Also fit the bolt securing the rear of the cylinder head to its bracket and tighten the nut finger-tight **(see illustration 4.64)**.

70 Slide the swingarm pivot bolt through the engine and the left-hand side of the swingarm, then fit the spacers and slide it through the frame **(see illustration 4.63b)**. Make sure the spacers are correctly engaged between the frame and the swingarm. Fit the nut onto the end of the pivot bolt and tighten it finger-tight **(see illustration 4.63a)**.

71 Fit the frame cradle sections to each side then fit the bolts with their plates and the oil cooler bracket on the right-hand side and the horn bracket on the left-hand side and tighten the bolts finger-tight **(see illustrations 4.24d, c and b)**.

72 Slide the lower front mounting bolt through from the left-hand side, not forgetting the spacer between the engine and the left-hand frame cradle, then thread the nut onto its end and tighten it finger-tight **(see illustration 4.61)**.

73 Remove the jack. Now tighten the bolts in the following order to the torque settings specified at the beginning of the Chapter.

● First tighten the rear mounting bolt nut and the cylinder head to bracket bolt nut.
● Second tighten the upper and lower front mounting bolt nuts.
● Third tighten the cradle section bolts.
● Fourth tighten the swingarm pivot bolt nut.
● Lastly tighten the swingarm pivot clamp bolts.

74 The remainder of the installation procedure is the reverse of removal, noting the following points:

● Use new gaskets on the exhaust pipe connections.
● When fitting the gearchange linkage arm onto the shaft, align the punch mark as noted on removal, and tighten the pinch bolt securely **(see illustration 4.47)**.
● Make sure all wires, cables and hoses

are correctly routed and connected, and secured by any clips or ties.
● Refer to Section 6 for installation of the oil cooler.
● Tighten the front footrest mounting bracket assembly bolts to the specified torque **(see illustration 4.48)**.
● Do not forget to connect the crankcase breather hose to the engine **(see illustration 4.15)**.
● Refill the engine with the specified quantity of oil (see Chapter 1).
● Adjust throttle and clutch cable freeplay (see Chapter 1).
● Adjust the drive chain (see Chapter 1).
● If the engine has been disassembled refer to the final Section of this Chapter for initial starting and running procedures. Adjust the idle speed (see Chapter 1).

---

5 Engine disassembly and reassembly general information

Disassembly

1 Before disassembling the engine, thoroughly clean and degrease its external surfaces. This will prevent contamination of the engine internals, and will also make working a lot easier and cleaner. A high flash-point solvent, such as paraffin (kerosene) can be used, or better still, a proprietary engine degreaser such as Gunk. Use old paintbrushes and toothbrushes to work the solvent into the various recesses of the casings. Take care to exclude solvent or water from the electrical components and intake and exhaust ports.

 Warning: The use of petrol (gasoline) as a cleaning agent should be avoided because of the risk of fire.

2 When clean and dry, position the engine on the workbench, leaving suitable clear area for working. Make sure the engine is stable – some strategically placed blocks of wood under the crankcase or engine covers will help support it and keep it stable while you work. Gather a selection of small containers, plastic bags and some labels so that parts can be grouped together in an easily identifiable manner. Also get some paper and a pen so that notes can be taken. You will also need a supply of clean rag, which should be as absorbent as possible.

3 Before commencing work, read through the appropriate section so that some idea of the necessary procedure can be gained. When removing components note that great force is seldom required, unless specified (checking the specified torque setting of the particular bolt being removed will indicate how tight it is, and therefore how much force should be needed). In many cases, a component's reluctance to be removed is indicative of an incorrect approach or removal method – if in any doubt, re-check with the text.

4 When disassembling the engine, keep 'mated' parts together (including gears, cylinder bores, pistons, connecting rods, valves, etc. that have been in contact with each other during engine operation). These 'mated' parts must be reused or replaced as an assembly. It is worth obtaining a large sheet of card and marking it according to the layout of the engine so that parts can be placed on it and stored in relation to their position in the engine as they are removed.

5 A complete engine/transmission disassembly should be done in the following general order with reference to the appropriate Sections.

Remove the starter motor (see Chapter 8)
Remove the valve cover and camshafts
Remove the cylinder head and block
Remove the pistons
Remove the alternator rotor (see Chapter 8)
Remove the clutch and starter clutch
Remove the oil pumps
Remove the gearchange mechanism
Separate the crankcase halves
Remove the balancer shafts
Remove the crankshaft and the connecting rods
Remove the selector drum and forks and the transmission shafts/gears

Reassembly

6 Reassembly is accomplished by reversing the general disassembly sequence. Make sure all components are spotlessly clean and lubricated as directed in the text. Where fitted, O-rings, oil seals, gaskets and sealing washers must always be replaced with new ones. Refer to any notes you have made and take your time – rebuilding an engine can be very satisfying, but not if it all goes wrong when you start it up. If you are unsure about something stop and work it out, starting again and re-reading the procedure as many times as necessary. Leaving uncertainties in your mind will give you sleepless nights.

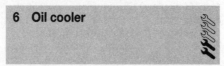

6 Oil cooler

Note: *The oil cooler can be removed with the engine in the frame. If the engine has been removed, ignore the steps which do not apply.*

Removal

1 The cooler is located on the front of the engine. Drain the engine oil (see Chapter 1). Remove the horn (see Chapter 8). If you are removing the cooler with its feed and return pipes, remove the complete exhaust system (see Chapter 3A or 3B). If you are removing the cooler without its feed and return pipes, remove the right-hand silencer and downpipe only (see Chapter 3A or 3B). After the oil has drained place the container below the cooler to catch any that remains.

2 To remove the cooler without its feed and return pipes, first clean around the pipe unions on the cooler to prevent dirt getting into the system. On EFI models the oil temperature sensor threads in the top of the oil cooler; refer to Chapter 3B, Section 10, and remove the sensor. Counter-hold the union hex using an open-ended spanner and unscrew the banjo bolt on each pipe (see illustration). Discard the sealing washers as new ones must be used (see illustration). On Bonneville, T100, Thruxton and Scrambler models unscrew the bolts securing the oil cooler, noting the collars in the mounting grommets, and manoeuvre the cooler out (see illustrations). On America and Speedmaster models unscrew the bolt(s) securing the oil cooler, noting the washer and the collar in the grommet and how it also secures the rear brake fluid reservoir, then lift the reservoir so the pegs on the bottom clear their grommets, and manoeuvre the cooler out.

3 To remove the cooler with its feed and return hoses, first clean around the pipe unions on the engine to prevent dirt getting into the system. On EFI models the oil temperature sensor threads into the top of the oil cooler; refer to Chapter 3B, Section 10, and remove the sensor. Unscrew the banjo bolts securing the oil feed pipes to the cylinder head **(see**

6.2a Counter-hold the union hex when unscrewing each banjo bolt

6.2b Discard the sealing washers and obtain new ones

6.2c Unscrew the bolts (arrowed) . . .

6.2d . . . and remove the cooler

6.2e Take care not to lose the collars in the grommets

6.3a Unscrew the banjo bolt (arrowed) on each side

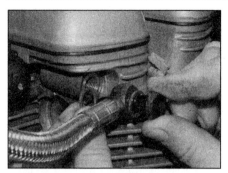

6.3b Discard the sealing washers and obtain new ones

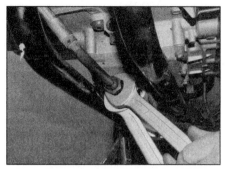

6.3c Counter-hold the joint piece and unscrew the flare nut . . .

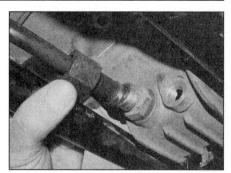

6.3d . . . then detach the pipe . . .

illustration). Detach the pipes and discard the sealing washers **(see illustration)**. On early Bonneville and T100 models with a banjo fitting for the return pipe on the sump, unscrew the bolt, detach the pipe and discard the sealing washers. On all other models counter-hold the joint piece on the sump using an open-ended spanner and unscrew the flare nut securing the pipe to the joint piece, then detach the pipe and discard the O-ring **(see illustrations)**. If required then unscrew the joint piece from the sump and discard the sealing washer **(see illustration)**. On Bonneville, T100, Thruxton and Scrambler models unscrew the bolts securing the oil cooler to its brackets, noting the collars in the mounting grommets, and manoeuvre the cooler out with its pipes **(see illustration 4.2c, d and e)**. On America and Speedmaster models unscrew the bolt securing the oil cooler, noting the washer and the collar in the grommet and how it also secures the rear brake fluid reservoir, then lift the reservoir so the pegs on the bottom clear their grommets, and manoeuvre the cooler out with its pipes.

4 To remove the hoses but leave the cooler in place, first clean around the pipe unions on the cooler and engine to prevent dirt getting into the system. To detach the pipes from the cooler counter-hold the union hex using an open-ended spanner and unscrew the banjo bolt on each pipe **(see illustration 6.2a)**. Discard the sealing washers as new ones must be used **(see illustration 6.2b)**. To detach the pipes from the engine first unscrew the banjo bolts securing the oil feed pipes to the cylinder head **(see illustration 6.3a)**. Detach the pipes and discard the

sealing washers **(see illustration 6.3b)**. On early Bonneville and T100 models with a banjo fitting for the return pipe on the sump, unscrew the bolt, detach the pipe and discard the sealing washers. On all other models counter-hold the joint piece on the sump using an open-ended spanner and unscrew the flare nut securing the pipe to the joint piece, then detach the pipe and discard the O-ring **(see illustrations 6.3c, d and e)**. If required then unscrew the joint piece from the sump and discard the sealing washer **(see illustration 6.3f)**.

Inspection

5 Check the cooler fins for mud, dirt and insects which may impede the flow of air through it. If the fins are dirty, clean them using water or low pressure compressed air directed from the inner side. If the fins are bent or distorted, straighten them carefully with a screwdriver. If the air flow is restricted by bent or damaged fins over more than 20% of the surface area, replace the cooler with a new one.

6 Check the condition of the pipes and replace them with new ones if they are damaged, deformed or show signs of cracking.

Installation

7 Installation is the reverse of removal, noting the following:

● Check the condition of the cooler mounting grommets and replace them with new ones if they are damaged, deformed or deteriorated. Make sure the collars are

in the mounting grommets **(see illustration 6.2e)**.

● Use new sealing washers on each side of each pipe union with a banjo fitting **(see illustrations 6.2b and 6.3b)**. On all models except early Bonneville and T100 use a new O-ring between the return pipe end and the joint piece on the sump **(see illustration 6.3e)**.

● Tighten the banjo bolts, the joint piece and the pipe flare nut to the torque settings specified at the beginning of the Chapter, noting the difference in setting for the banjo bolts to the cylinder head and those to the cooler and sump (where fitted). Also tighten the cooler mounting bolt(s) to the specified torque.

● Fill the engine with the specified quantity of oil (see Chapter 1).

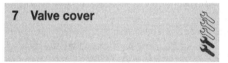

7 Valve cover

Note: *The valve cover can be removed with the engine in the frame. If the engine has been removed, ignore the steps which do not apply.*

Removal

1 Remove the fuel tank and the SAIS (Secondary Air Injection System) control valve along with its hoses and pipes – you can leave the pipe unions on the cylinder head (see Chapter 3A or 3B).

2 Unscrew the valve cover bolts **(see illustration)**.

6.3e . . . and discard the O-ring

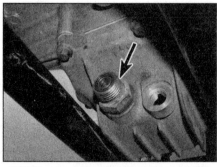

6.3f Unscrew the joint piece (arrowed) if required

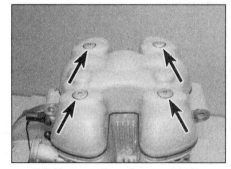

7.2 Unscrew the valve cover bolts (arrowed) . . .

7.3 . . . and lift the cover off the head

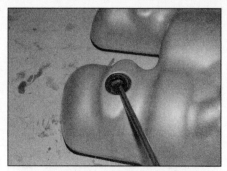

7.4 Check the condition of the sealing washers

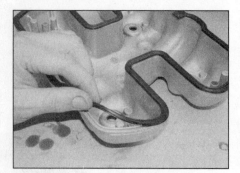

7.6 Fit the gasket into the groove

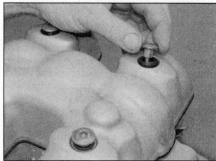

7.7 Fit the washers and bolts and tighten the bolts

3 Lift the valve cover off the cylinder head **(see illustration)** If it is stuck, do not try to lever it off with a screwdriver. Tap it gently around the sides with a rubber hammer or block of wood to dislodge it.
4 Check the condition of the sealing washers

on the bolts and replace them with new ones if necessary **(see illustration)**. The cover gasket is reusable as long as it is not damaged, deformed or deteriorated, but note that it is always advisable to use a new one.

Installation

5 Clean the mating surface of the cylinder head with solvent, removing any traces of old sealant.
6 Fit the cover gasket into the groove, using a smear of grease to help stick it in place **(see illustration)**. If the old gasket is being reused, make sure its mating surface is clean and sound.
7 Position the valve cover on the cylinder head, making sure the gasket stays in place **(see illustration 7.3)**. Install the cover bolts, making sure the sealing washers are fitted with their steel side uppermost and using new ones if necessary, and tighten them evenly and in a diagonal sequence to the torque setting specified at the beginning of the Chapter **(see illustration)**.
8 Install the SAIS control valve and the fuel tank (see Chapter 3A or 3B).

8 Camshafts, shims and followers

Note: *The camshafts and followers can be removed with the engine in the frame.*

Removal

1 Drain the engine oil (see Chapter 1). Remove the spark plugs to allow the engine to be turned over easier (see Chapter 1).
2 Remove the valve cover (see Section 7).
3 Remove the alternator cover (see Chapter 8).
4 Turn the engine **clockwise** using a 10 mm hex bit on the alternator rotor bolt until the camshaft lobes for the right-hand cylinder are positioned as shown for your model and the TOP mark on the camshaft drive gear is at the top **(see illustrations and 10.12)**. Now make a fine adjustment to the engine position so that on Bonneville, T100 and Thruxton models the line on the alternator rotor (marked R on EFI models) is in line with the crankcase mating surfaces at the front, and on America, Speedmaster and Scrambler models the line marked L on the alternator rotor is in line with crankcase mating surfaces at the front **(see illustrations)**. Also check that the marks on the left-hand side of the camshaft driven gears are aligned with those on the drive gear as shown with the line on the drive gear positioned between the two lines on the exhaust camshaft driven gear and the dot on the drive gear positioned between the two dots on the intake camshaft driven gear **(see illustration)**.

8.4a Camshaft lobe position – Bonneville, T100 and Thruxton

8.4b Camshaft lobe position – America, Speedmaster and Scrambler

8.4c Alternator timing mark alignment – Bonneville, T100 and Thruxton

8.4d Alternator timing mark alignment – America, Speedmaster and Scrambler

8.4e Make sure the lines and dots on the relative gears are aligned as shown

8.5 Unscrew the bolts (arrowed) and remove the pipe

8.6a Insert the locking pin in the holes in the gears, using a screwdriver to twist the gear teeth to align the holes if necessary

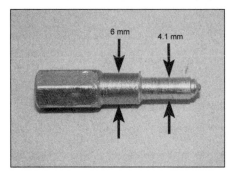

8.6b This is the stepped pin we made to ensure a good fit

5 Unscrew the camshaft oil feed pipe banjo bolts and remove the sealing washers **(see illustration)**. Ease the pipe side arm out of its bore and lift the pipe off the camshaft holders. Remove the O-ring. Discard the O-ring and washers as new ones must be used.

6 The driven gear on each camshaft has a sprung gear to prevent backlash. To keep their teeth aligned when disengaged from the drive gear insert a suitable locking pin through the holes **(see illustration)** – use of the Triumph special tool set (part No. T3880330) is advised for this purpose. The set includes two stepped pins (one for each camshaft) and a holding tool for gear alignment on installation (if the pins have been removed). The pins are stepped to locate in the different sized holes of the main and sprung gears and thus hold them in exact alignment. A suitable pin can be fabricated **(see illustration)** if you have access to a lathe. Beware of using a single diameter pin which locates in the smaller hole because the tension of the spring will twist the pin in the larger hole when the camshaft is removed, making installation extremely difficult. The other advantage of the Triumph tool set is that one of the pieces is used for aligning the gears so the pin can be inserted when the camshaft is out, though this will only be necessary if the pin is removed for disassembly of the sprung gear – otherwise the pin can stay in place so the gears do not need aligning on installation.

7 Mark each camshaft according to its location (i.e. intake or exhaust) so they cannot be inadvertently interchanged – the

intake camshaft has a groove in its centre to distinguish it from the exhaust camshaft **(see illustration)**. If you are going to detach the sprung gears from the driven gears also mark them according to location.

8 Before removing the camshaft holders, make a note of which fits where, as they must be installed in the same place. The holders are numbered 1 to 6 and the numbers are marked on the cap, though not that clearly **(see illustrations)**. For clarity mark each holder with its number using a suitable permanent marker, and when removed store them in correct order. Also note the arrow on each holder which points to the front of the engine. It is essential that they are returned to their original locations on installation.

9 Unscrew the camshaft holder bolts for the camshaft being worked on, slackening them

evenly and a little at a time in a criss-cross pattern, starting with the bolts above the right-hand cylinder valves first so that the pressure from the open valves on the left-hand cylinder cannot cause the camshaft to bend **(see illustration)**.

Caution: A camshaft could break if the holder bolts are not slackened as described and the pressure from a depressed valve causes the shaft to bend. Also, if the holder does not come squarely away from the head, the holder is likely to break. If this happens the cylinder head must be replaced with a new one; the holders are matched to the head and cannot be obtained separately.

10 Remove the bolts, then lift off the camshaft holders, noting how they fit **(see illustration)**. Retrieve the dowels from either

8.7 Note the groove (arrowed) in the intake camshaft

8.8a Camshaft holder identification numbering

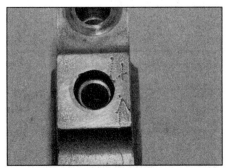

8.8b The number and an arrow (which points to the front of the engine) is marked on each cap

8.9 Unscrew the camshaft holder bolts as described . . .

8.10 . . . and remove the holders, noting the dowels

8.11 Lift the camshaft out, noting how it engages with the drive gear

8.12a Carefully lift out the follower . . .

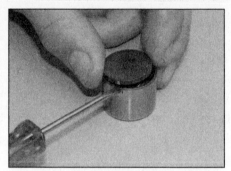

8.12b . . . and remove the shim from the top if necessary

the holder or the cylinder head, if they are loose.

11 Remove the camshaft **(see illustration)**. Keep all 'mated' parts together. Note that unless you are going to remove the sprung gear from the driven gear you should leave the locking pin in place to avoid having to realign them on installation.

12 If you are removing the shims and followers, obtain a container which is divided into eight compartments (or two containers divided into four), and label each compartment with the identity of a valve location in the cylinder head, for example the No. 1 (left-hand) cylinder, intake camshaft, left-hand valve could be marked 1-I-L. If a container is not available, use labelled plastic bags. Lift each cam follower out of the cylinder head using either a magnet or the suction created by a valve lapping tool, though fingers may suffice, and long nosed pliers can be used with care – do not grip the follower tightly as you could score it **(see illustration)**. Store the follower and its shim in its correct compartment in the container, or in its labelled bag. If required remove the shim from the top of each cam follower using a small screwdriver inserted in one of the cut-outs in the follower, but note that to prevent any possible mix-up it is best to leave the shim in the follower **(see illustration)**.

13 On completion cover the top of the cylinder head with a rag to prevent anything falling into the engine.

Inspection

Note: *Before discarding the camshafts or the cylinder head and camshaft holders because of wear or damage, check with local machine shops specialising in motorcycle engineering work. In the case of the camshafts, it may be possible for cam lobes to be welded, reground and hardened, at a cost far lower than that of a new camshaft. Due to the cost of a new cylinder head, it is recommended that all options be explored.*

14 Inspect the bearing surfaces in the camshaft holders and cylinder head and the corresponding journals on the camshafts. Look for score marks, deep scratches and evidence of spalling (a pitted appearance). Check the oil passages for clogging.

15 Check the camshaft lobes for heat discoloration (blue appearance), score marks, chipped areas, flat spots and spalling. Also check the lobe contact surfaces on the shims. If damage is noted or wear is excessive, the camshaft must be replaced with a new one.

16 Next, check the camshaft journal oil clearances preferably using Plastigauge (but note that if none is available the oil clearance can be obtained by measuring the journal diameter and holder/head bore as described in Step 20, then calculating the difference, though this method is not as accurate). Note that Plastigauge comes in two different sizes, graded according to a range of clearances it can measure – make sure you order the correct one according to the oil clearance figure specified. Follow any instructions regarding the use of the product in conjunction with the instructions below.

HAYNES HiNT *Refer to Tools and Workshop Tips in the Reference section for details of how to read a micrometer and dial gauge.*

17 Check one camshaft at a time. Clean the camshaft and the bearing surfaces in the cylinder head and camshaft holders with a clean lint-free cloth, then lay the camshaft in its correct location in the head, making sure that the lobes are not contacting the shims/followers (if not removed) or valve stem ends – if they are the shaft will turn as the holder bolts are tightened which will disturb the Plastigauge and lead to a false reading.

8.20 Measure the diameter of the journal with a micrometer

18 Cut strips of Plastigauge and lay one piece on each journal, parallel with the camshaft centreline. Make sure the camshaft holder dowels are installed. Fit the holders onto their correct journal according to the marks made earlier and with the arrow pointing to the front of the engine (see Step 8). Lubricate the bolt threads with oil and tighten them evenly and a little at a time in a criss-cross sequence, making sure the holders are pulled down squarely onto the dowels, to the torque setting specified at the beginning of the Chapter. While doing this, don't let the camshaft rotate, or the Plastigauge will be disturbed and you will have to start again.

19 Now unscrew the camshaft holder bolts evenly and a little at a time in a criss-cross sequence, and lift off the holders.

20 To determine the oil clearance, compare the crushed Plastigauge (at its widest point) on each journal to the scale printed on the Plastigauge container. Compare the results to this Chapter's Specifications. If the oil clearance is greater than specified, measure the diameter of the camshaft journal with a micrometer **(see illustration)**. If the journal diameter is less than the specified limit, replace the camshaft with a new one and recheck the clearance. If the clearance is still too great, or if the camshaft journal is within its limit, replace the cylinder head and holders as a set with new ones. If required the holder/cylinder head bore sizes can be measured with the camshafts removed and the holders tightened down, using a small bore gauge and micrometer, comparing the results to the specifications.

21 Inspect the outer surfaces of the cam followers for evidence of scoring or other damage. If a follower is in poor condition, it is probable that the bore in which it works is also damaged. Check for clearance between the followers and their bores. If the bores are seriously out-of-round or tapered, a new cylinder head is needed.

22 Check the drive and driven gears for cracks, broken or chipped teeth, and wear or other damage. Also check the sprocket teeth on the drive gear. If they are worn, check the cam chain and its sprocket on the crankshaft. If wear this severe is apparent, the entire engine should be disassembled

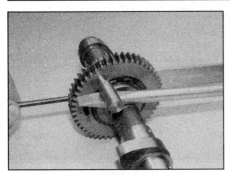

8.23a Remove the locking pin as described

8.23b Remove the circlip . . .

8.23c . . . the wave washer . . .

8.23d . . . the sprung gear . . .

8.23e . . . and the spring

for inspection. The drive gear and the sprung gears are available separately, but the driven gears are not, and so if these are damaged new camshafts must be fitted. Refer to Section 10 for removal of the drive gear/ sprocket and the cam chain, and Step 23 for the sprung gear.

23 To remove the sprung gear, first remove the locking pin – the gears will turn one tooth in opposite directions when you do. Use the Triumph holding tool to take the tension off the pin as you remove it, or alternatively hold the camshaft using an open-ended spanner on the flats and lever against a second pin inserted in one of the large holes in the sprung

gear **(see illustration)**. Remove the circlip securing the gear and lift off the wave washer **(see illustrations)**. Lift the sprung gear off the driven gear, noting how they fit together, and retrieve the spring from inside the driven gear, noting how it fits **(see illustration)**. Reassemble the gears in a reverse method – locate the spring in the driven gear with its ends on the either side of the pin **(see illustration)**. Fit the sprung gear onto the driven gear so that the pin on the sprung gear is to the right of that in the driven gear when positioned as shown **(see illustration)**. Lock the camshaft in a vice equipped with soft jaws using some rag as further protection

then turn the sprung gear one tooth against spring pressure and insert the locking pin – turn the gear using either the Triumph holding tool (part of the set) or a suitable commercially available equivalent with pins that locate in the holes in the sprung gear inserted in one of the large holes in the sprung gear, or by clamping the teeth in alignment using mole grips or similar or by levering them using a large screwdriver and a pin, making sure the teeth are not marked. Alternatively hold the camshaft using an open-ended spanner on the flats and lever against a pin inserted in one of the large holes in the sprung gear as shown **(see illustration 8.23a)**.

Installation

24 Lubricate the shim with molybdenum disulphide oil and fit it into its recess in the follower with the size mark facing down **(see illustration 8.12b)**. Check that the shim is correctly seated. Lubricate the follower with molybdenum disulphide oil (a 50/50 mixture of molybdenum disulphide grease and engine oil) and fit it onto its valve, making sure it fits squarely in its bore **(see illustration 8.12a)**. Repeat the process for all other valves.

25 Make sure that on Bonneville, T100 and Thruxton models the line on the alternator rotor (marked R on EFI models) is in line with the crankcase mating surfaces at the front,

8.23f Position the spring ends as shown . . .

8.23g . . . and locate the pin on the sprung gear against the right-hand spring end

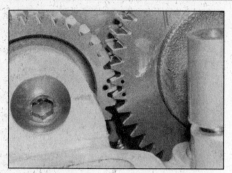

8.27a When fitting the intake camshaft align the dots between the gears as shown

8.27b When fitting the exhaust camshaft . . .

8.27c . . . align the lines between the gears as shown

and on America, Speedmaster and Scrambler models the line marked L on the alternator rotor is in line with crankcase mating surfaces at the front, turning the engine as required **(see illustration 8.4c or d)**. Check that the TOP marking on the camshaft drive gear is at the top **(see illustration 10.12a)**.

26 Make sure the bearing surfaces on the camshafts and in the cylinder head are clean, then apply molybdenum disulphide oil (a 50/50 mixture of molybdenum disulphide grease and engine oil) to each of them. Also apply it to the camshaft lobes.

27 If the locking pin has been removed from the camshaft driven gear, fit it as described in Step 23. Lay each camshaft onto the cylinder head, making sure each is returned to its original position according to the markings made on removal, engaging its driven gear teeth with those on the drive gear and aligning

it so that all the marks described in Step 4 are in exact alignment **(see illustrations)**.

28 Fit the camshaft holder dowels into the cylinder head or holders if removed. Make sure the bearing surfaces in the holders are clean, then apply molybdenum disulphide oil (a 50/50 mixture of molybdenum disulphide grease and engine oil) to them. Fit the holders onto their correct journal according to the marks and with the arrow pointing to the front of the engine (see Step 8) **(see illustrations 8.10 and 8.8a and b)**.

29 Lubricate the threads of the holder bolts with engine oil, then locate them in the holders and tighten them all finger-tight **(see illustration 8.9)**. Make sure the thrust faces on caps numbered 4 and 6 locate correctly between the thrust faces on the camshafts **(see illustration)**. Tighten the bolts evenly

and a little at a time in a criss-cross pattern, starting with the bolts that are above the left-hand cylinder valves that will be opened as the camshaft is tightened down, until the holders are seated on the head. Whilst tightening the bolts, make sure the holders are being pulled squarely down and are not binding on the dowels and that the thrust faces on caps numbered 4 and 6 locate correctly between the thrust faces on the camshafts. Once the holders are seated tighten the bolts in the sequence shown to the torque setting specified at the beginning of the Chapter **(see illustration)**.

30 Make sure all marks are correctly aligned as described in Step 4.

31 Install the camshaft oil feed pipe using a new O-ring and sealing washers and tighten the banjo bolts to the specified torque setting **(see illustrations)**.

32 Remove the driven gear locking pins **(see illustration 8.6a)**.

33 Rotate the engine clockwise through two full turns (720°) and re-check that the valve timing marks are correctly aligned (see Step 4).

34 Check the valve clearances (Chapter 1), especially if any of the valve components have been renewed.

35 Install the alternator cover (see Chapter 8).

36 Install the valve cover (see Section 7).

37 Install the spark plugs (see Chapter 1). Refill the engine with the specified quantity of oil (see Chapter 1).

8.29a Make sure the thrust faces seat together properly (arrow)

8.29b Tighten the bolts for the camshaft holders in the sequence shown

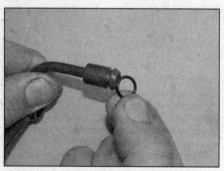

8.31a Fit a new O-ring onto the pipe . . .

8.31b . . . then seat it in its hole

8.31c Use a new sealing washer with each bolt

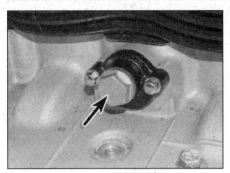

9.5 Unscrew the cap bolt (arrowed) and withdraw the spring

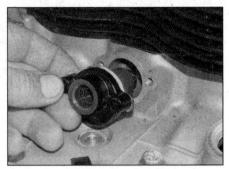

9.6 Unscrew the mounting bolts (arrowed) and withdraw the tensioner

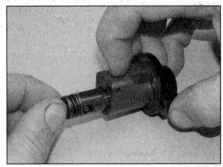

9.8 Release the ratchet and check the action of the tensioner

9 Cam chain tensioner and blades

Note: *The cam chain tensioner and blades can be removed with the engine in the frame. If the engine has been removed, ignore the steps that do not apply.*

Tensioner

Caution: The tensioner plunger is spring-loaded and has a non-return mechanism. Once you start to remove the tensioner mounting bolts, you must remove the tensioner all the way and reset the plunger before tightening the bolts. Failure to do so will result in an over-tensioned cam chain and the tensioner and/or chain and sprockets will be damaged.
Caution: Do not turn the engine with the tensioner removed as the chain could easily jump teeth on a sprocket and the valve timing will be incorrect.

Removal

1 Drain the engine oil (See Chapter 1). Remove the spark plugs to allow the engine to be turned over easier (see Chapter 1).
2 Remove the valve cover (see Section 7).
3 Remove the alternator cover (see Chapter 8).
4 If the camshafts have not been removed, align the engine as described in Section 8, Step 4.
5 Unscrew the tensioner cap bolt, noting that it is under spring pressure, and remove the sealing washer **(see illustration)**. Withdraw the spring. Discard the sealing washer as a new one must be used on installation.
6 Unscrew the tensioner mounting bolts and withdraw the tensioner from the engine, noting which way up it fits **(see illustration)**. Remove the gasket and discard it – a new one must be used. Do not rotate the engine with the tensioner removed.

Inspection

7 Examine the tensioner components for signs of wear and damage.
8 Release the ratchet mechanism and check that the plunger moves freely in and out of the tensioner body **(see illustration)**. As the plunger extends make sure the ratchet

clicks into each groove in the plunger. Check that when engaged the ratchet prevents the plunger being pushed in.
9 If the tensioner or any of its components are worn or damaged, or if the plunger is seized in the body, the tensioner must be replaced with a new one.

Installation

10 Remove all traces of old gasket from the cylinder block and tensioner body mating surfaces and make sure they are clean and dry.
11 If you are refitting the old tensioner, release the ratchet mechanism and press the tensioner plunger all the way into the tensioner body, then draw it out so the ratchet locates in the first notch in the plunger **(see illustration 9.8)**.
12 If you are fitting a new tensioner it comes assembled with the plunger locked in place by the cap bolt. To unlock it, thread the cap

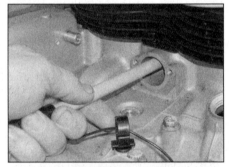

9.13 Push on the tensioner blade to take up any slack in the chain

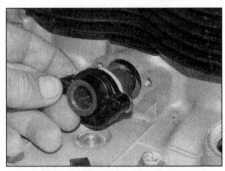

9.14b . . . then install the tensioner

bolt into the tensioner – as you do so the bolt threads itself off the plunger and the plunger will spring out, clicking over the ratchet mechanism. Fully unscrew the cap bolt and remove the spring, then set the plunger into the tensioner as in Step 11.
13 Take up any slack in the camchain by inserting a screwdriver or rod in the tensioner bore and pushing on the tensioner blade **(see illustration)**. Make sure all timing marks are still correctly aligned (see Section 8, Step 4).
14 Fit a new gasket onto the tensioner body, then fit the tensioner into the engine, making sure it is the correct way round **(see illustrations)**. Tighten the mounting bolts to the torque setting specified at the beginning of the Chapter.
15 Insert the spring then install the cap bolt with a new sealing washer and tighten it to the torque setting specified at the beginning of the Chapter **(see illustration)**. While you

9.14a Fit a new gasket . . .

9.15 Fit the spring and the cap bolt with a new sealing washer

9.21a Unscrew the bolts (arrowed) . . .

9.21b . . . and lift the blade out

9.22a Unscrew the nut . . .

are compressing the spring and tightening the bolt you should hear the plunger being forced out and clicking over the ratchet mechanism.

16 Rotate the engine clockwise through four complete turns and check the timing marks are correctly aligned (see Section 8, step 4).

17 Install the alternator cover (see Chapter 8).

18 Install the valve cover (see Section 7).

19 Install the spark plugs (see Chapter 1). Refill the engine with the specified quantity of oil (see Chapter 1).

Blades

Removal

20 Remove the camshaft drive gear/sprocket (see Section 10).

21 To remove the guide blade from the front of the cylinder head block the air tube orifice to prevent a bolt dropping down, then unscrew the blade plate bolts and draw the blade out of the tunnel (see illustrations).

22 To remove the tensioner blade from the rear of the cylinder head unscrew the nut and remove the washer on the back of the head then lift the blade out of the tunnel (see illustrations).

Inspection

23 Examine the blades for signs of wear and damage, and replace them with new ones if necessary.

Installation

24 Installation is the reverse of removal. Do not forget the washer with the tensioner blade nut. Apply a drop of thread locking compound

(ThreeBond 1305) to the threads of the nut before installing it, then tighten the nut and the bolts to the torque setting specified at the beginning of the Chapter.

10 Camshaft drive gear/ sprocket and camchain

Note 1: *The camshaft drive gear/sprocket can be removed with the engine in the frame. If the engine has been removed and/or partially stripped ignore the Steps which do not apply.*
Note 2: *To remove the camchain the engine must be removed from the frame, the crankcases must be separated and the crankshaft must be removed.*

Camshaft drive gear/sprocket

Removal

1 Remove the secondary air intake system (SAIS) pipes and unions from the cylinder head (see Chapter 3A or 3B).

2 Remove the camshafts (see Section 8).

3 Remove the cam chain tensioner (see Section 9).

4 Stuff some rag down the cam chain tunnel – there are washers that need to be retrieved as you withdraw the gear shaft, and it is easy to drop them, so the rag prevents them going all the way to the bottom of the crankcase (see illustration).

5 On models with an engine number up to 186916 unscrew the drive gear shaft bolt from the top of the shaft housing. Support the drive gear and begin to withdraw the shaft, noting that there is a thrust washer

9.22b . . . and lift the blade out

on each side of the gear/sprocket, and on engine Nos. 173085-on a spring washer on the right-hand side, which will be free to drop into the bottom of the engine once the shaft is withdrawn – make sure you retrieve the washers as you withdraw the shaft and do not allow them to drop – using a magnet is a good way of removing them. Once the shaft is withdrawn slip the gear/sprocket out of the chain and remove it. Do not allow the chain to drop down the tunnel – use a rod through the shaft housing or a piece of wire to secure the chain.

6 On models with an engine number from 186917-on counter-hold the shaft using a hex key in its right-hand end and unscrew the drive gear shaft bolt almost all the way out of the left-hand end (see illustrations). On the engine photographed, however, it was found that the shaft itself unscrewed from the bolt. Support the drive gear and start to push the shaft out with the bolt, removing the bolt once the shaft is free enough to be pulled out, or withdraw the shaft

10.4 Stuff some rag under the gear to block the tunnel

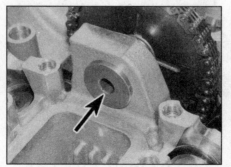

10.6a Use a hex key in the shaft end (arrowed) to counter-hold it . . .

10.6b . . . then unscrew the bolt

10.6c Push the shaft out . . .

10.6d . . . and retrieve the washer . . .

10.6e . . . then fully withdraw the shaft and remove the gear

if it has unscrewed from the bolt, noting that there is a thick thrust washer on the left-hand side of the gear/sprocket which is free to drop into the bottom of the engine once the shaft is withdrawn – make sure you retrieve the washer as you withdraw the shaft and do not allow it to drop **(see illustrations)**. Once the shaft is withdrawn slip the gear/sprocket out of the chain and remove it. Do not allow the chain to drop down the tunnel – use a rod through the shaft housing or a piece of wire to secure the chain.

Caution: If a washer is dropped into the engine it MUST be retrieved, even if it means splitting the crankcase halves. A telescopic magnet is a very useful tool, and often a washer can be found and retrieved easily, though it may be necessary to remove the sump. DO NOT RUN THE ENGINE IF A WASHER HAS NOT BEEN FOUND.

Inspection

7 Check the sprocket and gear teeth for wear and damage. If the sprocket is worn or damaged, replace the gear/sprocket with a new one, and carefully check the cam chain for wear. If the chain is worn it is also worth checking the drive sprocket on the crankshaft, though this involves a lot more work. If the gear teeth are worn or damaged check the driven gears on the camshafts.

8 Check the chain for binding, kinks and any obvious damage and replace it with a new one if necessary.

9 Check that the needle bearing(s), and on engine Nos. 186917-on the ball bearing, rotate freely and smoothly and without excessive freeplay between the shaft and the gear/sprocket **(see illustration)**. Also

check the shaft contact surfaces for wear and damage. Replace the bearings and/or shaft with new ones if necessary. Refer to *Tools and Workshop Tips* in the Reference Section for information on bearings and their removal and installation if required.

Installation

10 Make sure that on Bonneville, T100 and Thruxton models the line on the alternator rotor is in line with the crankcase mating surfaces at the front, and on America, Speedmaster and Scrambler models the line marked L on the alternator rotor is in line with crankcase mating surfaces at the front, turning the engine as required **(see illustration 8.4c or d)**.

11 Lubricate the bearings with clean engine oil. Smear some molybdenum disulphide oil (a 50/50 mixture of molybdenum disulphide grease and engine oil) onto the shaft contact surfaces. Stuff some rag down the cam chain tunnel.

12 Position the drive gear/sprocket, making sure the TOP marking is on the right-hand side and at the top, and the lines on the right-hand face are parallel with the cylinder head-to-camshaft holder mating surface, and slip the chain round the sprocket **(see illustration)**. Keep hold of the gear and slide the shaft through, fitting the spring washer (engine Nos. 173085 to 186916), right-hand thrust washer (engine Nos. up to 186916) and left-hand thrust washer (all models) as you slide the shaft through, and taking great care not to drop the washer(s) into the engine, using a magnet as on removal if available (see *Caution* above) **(see illustrations 10.6d and c)**.

13 With the shaft installed take up any slack in the cam chain by inserting a screwdriver or

rod in the tensioner bore and pushing on the tensioner blade **(see illustration 9.13)**. Make sure all timing marks are still correctly aligned (see Section 8, Step 4).

14 On models with an engine number up to 186916 align the bolt holes between the shaft and the housing then install the bolt and tighten it to the torque setting specified at the beginning of the Chapter.

15 On models with an engine number from 186917-on install the bolt in the end of the shaft and tighten it to the torque setting specified at the beginning of the Chapter, counter-holding the shaft end as before **(see illustrations 10.6b and a)**.

16 Remove the rag from the cam chain tunnel. Install the cam chain tensioner (see Section 9).

17 Install the camshafts (see Section 8).

18 Install the secondary air intake system (SAIS) pipes and unions (see Chapter 3).

Cam chain

19 Remove the engine from the frame and separate the crankcase halves (see Sections 4 and 22).

20 Mark the chain so that it can be installed so that it runs in the same direction as before.

21 Remove the crankshaft (see Section 25).

22 Slip the chain off its sprocket **(see illustration)**. Check the chain for binding, kinks and any obvious damage and replace it with a new one if necessary.

23 If the chain appears to be in good condition, check it for stretch as follows. Hang the chain from a hook and attach a 13kg (28lb) weight from its lower end.

10.9 Check the bearings (arrowed)

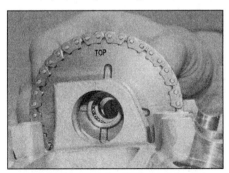

10.12 Make sure the TOP mark is at the top and facing the right-hand side

10.22 Disengage the chain and remove it

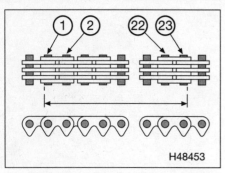

10.24 Measuring cam chain stretch

11.1 Intake adapter bolts (arrowed)

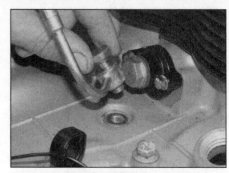

11.4 Unscrew the bolt and remove the oil pipe

24 Measure the length of 23 pins (from the outer edge of the 1st pin to the outer edge of the 23rd pin) and compare the result to the stretch limit specified at the beginning of the Chapter **(see illustration)**. If the chain has stretched beyond the limit it must be renewed.
25 Installation is the reverse of removal.

11 Cylinder head removal and installation

Caution: The engine must be completely cool before beginning this procedure or the cylinder head may become warped.
Note 1: *The cylinder head can be removed with the engine in the frame. If the engine has been removed, ignore the steps that don't apply.*
Note 2: *Triumph recommend that when the cylinder head is removed the block also be removed and a new gasket fitted (see Section 13). This is because the release of pressure on the base gasket when the cylinder head nuts are unscrewed could lead to the seal between the block and the crankcase being broken, even though it may not be apparent that the block has lifted. You will only know when the engine is run and if there is leakage.*

Removal

1 Remove the carburettors/throttle bodies and the exhaust system (see Chapter 3A or 3B). If required unscrew the bolts securing the intake adapters to the cylinder head and remove them **(see illustration)**. Discard the O-rings as new ones must be used.
2 Remove the camshafts, the cam chain

tensioner and blades, and the camshaft drive gear/sprocket (see Sections 8, 9 and 10). If no work is to be carried out on the cylinder head and it will stay upright you can leave the shims and followers in place, otherwise remove them with the camshafts.
3 Remove the spark plugs (see Chapter 1).
4 Remove the oil pressure switch (see Chapter 8). Unscrew the banjo bolt securing the oil pipe to the crankcase and remove the pipe **(see illustration)**. Discard the sealing washers as new ones must be used.
5 On Bonneville, T100, Thruxton and Scrambler models unscrew the nuts and withdraw the bolts securing the brackets between the rear of the cylinder head and the frame and remove the brackets **(see illustration 4.25)**.
6 On America and Speedmaster models unscrew the nut and withdraw the bolt securing the rear of the cylinder head to the frame bracket **(see illustration 4.64)**.
7 Unscrew the nut on the upper front mounting bolt then remove the bolt **(see illustration 4.26)**.
8 The cylinder head is secured by eight 10 mm nuts **(see illustration)**. Unscrew the nuts, slackening them evenly and a little at a time in the numerical sequence shown until they are all loose. Remove the nuts, taking care not to drop any of them down the cam chain tunnel.
Caution: If a nut is dropped into the engine it MUST be retrieved, even if it means splitting the crankcase halves. A telescopic magnet is a very useful tool, and often a nut can be found and retrieved easily, though it may be necessary to remove the sump. DO NOT RUN THE ENGINE IF A NUT HAS NOT BEEN FOUND.

9 Carefully pull the cylinder head up off the cylinder block, making sure the block stays in place **(see illustration)**. If an assistant is available have them hold the block while you lift the head – this is not so important if the block is being removed anyway, but in any event you don't want them lifting together. If the seal between the block and the crankcase breaks the block will have to be removed as well and a new gasket fitted (but see **Note 2** above). If the head is stuck, tap around it with a soft-faced mallet to break the seal, but avoid striking the cooling fins as these are easily broken. Do not try to free the head by inserting a screwdriver between it and the block – you'll damage the sealing surfaces. Protrusions from the head (but not the fins) can be used as leverage points with care if necessary. Pass the cam chain down through the tunnel as you lift the head and drape it over the front of the block – try not to let the chain fall into the crankcase – secure it with a piece of wire or metal bar to prevent it from slipping back if necessary.
10 Pull the breather tube out of the crankcase or the cylinder head, noting which way round it fits **(see illustration)**. Discard the O-rings as new ones must be used.
11 Remove the old gasket and discard it **(see illustration 11.16b)**. Remove the two dowels from either the block or the underside of the head if they are loose **(see illustration 11.16a)**. Cover the cylinder block with some clean rag.
12 Check the cylinder head gasket and the mating surfaces on the cylinder head and block for signs of leakage, which could indicate warpage.
13 Refer to Section 12 to check the cylinder

11.8 Cylinder head nuts (arrowed) and slackening sequence

11.9 Carefully lift the head up off the block

11.10 Remove the breather tube and discard its O-rings

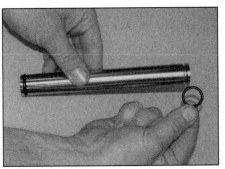

11.16 Fit a new O-ring onto each end of the tube

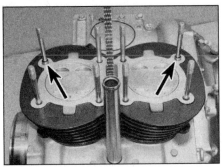

11.17a Fit the two dowels (arrowed) . . .

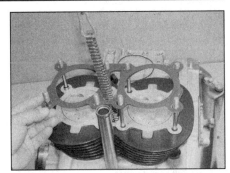

11.17b . . . then lay the gasket on . . .

head and valves, and to Section 13 to check the block.

Installation

14 Clean all traces of old gasket material from the cylinder head and block. If a scraper is used, take care not to scratch or gouge the soft aluminium. Be careful not to let any of the gasket material drop into the crankcase.

15 Check that the cylinder head studs are tight in the crankcase. If any are loose, remove them, then clean their threads and apply a suitable non-permanent thread locking compound before retightening them. Refer to Section 2 'Fasteners' of *Tools and Workshop Tips* in the Reference section at the end of this manual for details of how to slacken and tighten studs using two nuts locked together.

16 Fit a new O-ring onto each end of the breather tube and smear them with oil **(see illustration)**. Fit the tube into the crankcase **(see illustration 11.10)**.

17 Fit the two dowels into the block if removed and push them firmly home **(see illustration)**. Ensure both cylinder head and block mating surfaces are clean then lay a new gasket onto the dowels with the TOP mark facing up and at the back **(see illustrations)**. Never re-use the old gasket.

18 Fit the head onto the studs and carefully lower it onto the block, passing the cam chain up through the tunnel as you do – it is helpful to have an assistant to pass the chain up and slip a piece of wire through it to prevent it falling back into the engine **(see illustration 11.9)**. Keep the chain taut to prevent it becoming disengaged from the drive sprocket. Make

11.17c . . . with the TOP mark facing up

sure the breather tube locates then press the cylinder head down onto the gasket, making sure the dowels locate **(see illustration)**.

19 Fit the cylinder head nuts, taking great care not to drop any into the engine (see *Caution* above), and tighten them finger-tight **(see illustration)**.

20 Now tighten the nuts in a reverse of the slackening sequence shown in illustration 11.8 to the stage 1 torque setting specified at the beginning of the chapter. Repeat the sequence to the stage 2 torque setting, then repeat the sequence again to the stage 3 torque setting. Finally attach a degree disc to the wrench and angle-tighten each nut 120° following the same sequence **(see illustration)**.

21 Slide the upper front engine mounting bolt through from the left-hand side and tighten its nut to the specified torque **(see illustration 4.26)**.

22 On Bonneville, T100, Thruxton and Scrambler models fit the brackets between the rear of the cylinder head and the frame,

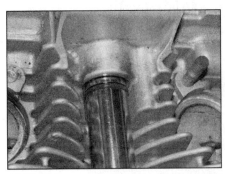

11.18 Make sure the pipe locates correctly in the head

making sure each is correctly positioned **(see illustration 4.32)**. Slide the bolts through from the left-hand side and tighten their nuts to the specified torque.

23 On America and Speedmaster models fit the bolt securing the rear of the cylinder head to its bracket and tighten the nut to the specified torque **(see illustration 4.64)**.

24 Install the oil pipe using new sealing washers and tighten the banjo bolt and the oil pressure switch initially finger-tight only to ensure correct alignment of the pipe **(see illustration 11.4)**. Now tighten the switch and the bolt to the specified torque settings. Connect the wiring connector to the switch and fit the rubber boot.

25 Install the spark plugs (see Chapter 1).

26 Install the camshaft drive gear/sprocket, the cam chain tensioner and blades, and the camshafts (see Sections 10, 9 and 8).

27 If removed fit the intake adapters to the cylinder using new O-rings – make sure the O-rings seat properly in their grooves and stay in place while tightening the bolts. Tighten the bolts evenly to the torque setting specified at the beginning of the Chapter. Install the carburettors/throttle bodies and the exhaust system (see Chapter 3A or 3B).

12 Cylinder head and valve overhaul

1 Because of the complex nature of this job and the special tools and equipment required, most owners leave servicing of the valves, valve seats and valve guides to a

11.19 Fit the head nuts . . .

11.20 . . . and tighten them as described

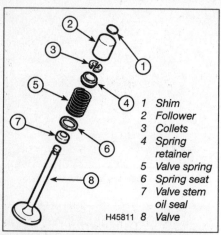

1 Shim
2 Follower
3 Collets
4 Spring retainer
5 Valve spring
6 Spring seat
7 Valve stem oil seal
H45811 8 Valve

12.5 Valve components

professional. However, you can make an initial assessment of whether the valves are seating correctly, and therefore sealing, by pouring a small amount of solvent into each of the valve ports. If the solvent leaks past any valve into the combustion chamber area the valve is not seating correctly and sealing.

2 With the correct tools (a valve spring compressor is essential – make sure it is suitable for motorcycle work), you can also remove the valves and associated components from the cylinder head, clean them and check them for wear to assess the extent of the work needed, and, unless seat cutting or guide replacement is required, grind in the valves and reassemble them in the head.

3 A dealer service department or specialist can replace the guides and re-cut the valve seats.

4 After the valve service has been performed, be sure to clean it very thoroughly before installation on the engine to remove any metal particles or abrasive grit that may still be present from the valve service operations. Use compressed air, if available, to blow out all the holes and passages.

Disassembly

5 Before proceeding, arrange to label and store the valves along with their related

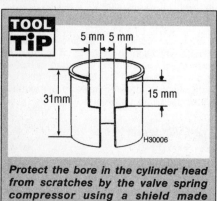

TOOL TiP

Protect the bore in the cylinder head from scratches by the valve spring compressor using a shield made from a 35mm film canister cut to the dimensions shown

12.7a Fit the valve spring compressor . . .

components in such a way that they can be returned to their original locations without getting mixed up **(see illustration)**. A good way to do this is to use the same containers as the followers and shims are stored in (see Section 8), or to obtain two separate containers (one for each cylinder), each divided into four compartments, and label each compartment with the location of a valve, i.e. intake or exhaust camshaft, left or right valve. If a container is not available, use labelled plastic bags (egg cartons also do very well!).

6 Remove the cylinder head (see Section 11). Clean off all traces of old gasket material from the mating surface. If a scraper is used, take care not to scratch or gouge the soft aluminium; refer to Tools and Workshop Tips for details of gasket removal methods.

7 Locate the valve spring compressor on each end of the first valve assembly to be removed, **(see illustration)**. Make sure the compressor is the correct size – on the underside of the head the plate must only contact the valve and not the soft aluminium of the head; if the plate is too big for the valve, you can use a spacer between them **(see illustration)**. On the top of the valve the adaptor needs to be about the same size as the spring retainer – if it is too big it will contact the follower bore and mark it, and if it is too small it will be difficult to remove and install the collets **(see illustration)**. If your adaptor is too big or small, change it for one that is a good fit.

8 Compress the spring on the first valve

12.8a Remove the collets as described

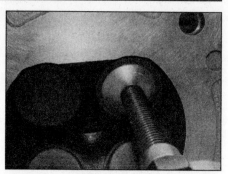

12.7b . . . making sure it locates correctly on the valve . . .

12.7c . . . and on the spring retainer

– do not compress it any more than is necessary to free the collets. Remove the collets, using either needle-nose pliers, tweezers, a mechanic's telescopic magnet, or a screwdriver with a dab of grease on it **(see illustration)**. Carefully release the valve spring compressor and remove it. Remove the spring retainer, noting which way up it fits **(see illustration 12.32b)**. Remove the spring **(see illustration 12.32a)**. Press down on the top of the valve stem and draw the valve out from the underside of the head **(see illustration 12.30)**. If the valve binds in the guide (won't pull through), push it back into the head and deburr the area around the collet groove with a very fine file or whetstone **(see illustration)**.

9 Once the valve has been removed pull the valve stem seal off the top of the valve guide with pliers or a dedicated tool and discard it

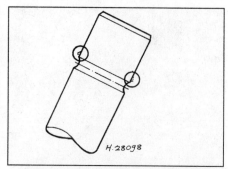

12.8b Remove any burrs (circled) if the valve stem won't pull through the guide

– never reuse the old seal **(see illustration)**. Remove the spring seat using a mechanic's telescopic magnet, or turn the head upside down and tip it out, taking care not to lose it **(see illustration)**.

10 Repeat the procedure for the remaining valves. Remember to keep the parts for each valve together and in order so they can be reinstalled in the same location.

11 Next, clean the cylinder head with solvent and dry it thoroughly. Compressed air will speed the drying process and ensure that all holes and recessed areas are reached.

12 Clean all of the valve springs, collets, retainers and spring seats with solvent and dry them thoroughly. Do the parts from one valve at a time so they don't get mixed up.

13 Scrape off any deposits that may have formed on the valve, then use a motorised wire brush to remove deposits from the valve heads and stems. Again, make sure the valves do not get mixed up.

Inspection

14 Inspect the head very carefully for cracks and other damage. If cracks are found, a new head will be required. Check the camshaft bearing surfaces for wear and evidence of seizure. Check the camshafts and holders for wear as well (see Section 8).

15 Using a precision straight-edge and a feeler gauge set to the warpage limit listed in the specifications at the beginning of the Chapter, check the head gasket mating surface for warpage. Refer to *Tools and Workshop Tips* in the Reference section for details of how to use the straight-edge. If the head shows no signs of warpage but there is evidence of leakage from the gasket, check the top of the cylinder block as well.

16 Examine the valve seats in the combustion chamber. If they are pitted, cracked or burned, the head will require work beyond the scope of the home mechanic. Measure the valve seat width in both the head and on the valve and compare them to this Chapter's Specifications **(see illustrations)**. If either or both exceed the service limit, or if they vary around the circumference, overhaul is required.

17 Clean the valve guide to remove any carbon build-up, then measure the inside diameter of the guide with a small hole gauge and micrometer **(see illustration)**. Measure

12.9a Pull the oil seal off the top of the guide . . .

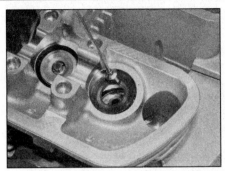
12.9b . . . then remove the spring seat

12.16a Measure the valve seat width (between the arrows) in the head . . .

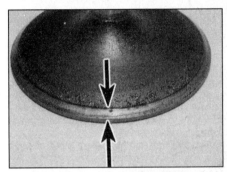
12.16b . . . and on the valve

the guide at the ends and at the centre to determine if it is worn in a bell-mouth pattern (more wear at the ends). Also measure the valve stem diameter **(see illustration)**. Replace whichever component is worn beyond its specifications with a new one. If the valve guide is within specifications, but is worn unevenly, replace it with a new one.

18 Carefully inspect each valve face, stem and collet groove area for cracks, pits and burned spots.

19 Rotate the valve and check for any obvious indication that it is bent, in which case it must be replaced with a new one.

20 Check the end of the stem for pitting and excessive wear and replace the valve with a new one if necessary. The stem end can be ground down slightly, provided that the amount of stem above the collet groove after grinding is sufficient.

21 Check the end of each valve spring for wear and pitting. Measure the spring free

length and compare it to the specifications **(see illustration)**. If the spring is shorter than specified it has sagged and must be replaced with a new one. Also place the spring upright on a flat surface and check it for bend by placing a ruler against it, or alternatively lay it against a set square. If the bend in any spring is excessive, it must be replaced with a new one.

22 Check the spring seats, retainers and collets for obvious wear and cracks. Any questionable parts should not be reused, as extensive damage will occur in the event of failure during engine operation.

23 If the inspection indicates that no overhaul work is required, the valve components can be reinstalled in the head.

Reassembly

24 Unless a valve service has been performed, before installing the valves in the head they should be ground in (lapped) to ensure a positive seal between the valves and seats.

12.17a Measure the guide bore diameter . . .

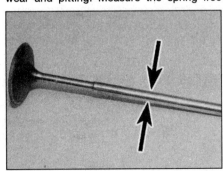
12.17b . . . and the valve stem diameter

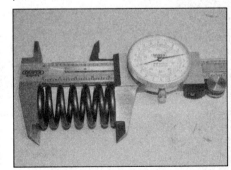
12.21 Measure the free length of the valve springs and check them for tilt

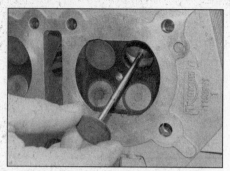

12.30 Lubricate the stem and insert the valve in the guide

12.31a Fit a new valve stem seal ...

12.31b ... using a deep socket to press it into place

This procedure requires coarse and fine valve grinding compound and a valve grinding tool (either hand-held or drill driven – note that some drill-driven tools specify using only a fine grinding compound). If a grinding tool is not available, a piece of rubber or plastic hose can be slipped over the valve stem (after the valve has been installed in the guide) and used to turn the valve.

25 Apply a small amount of coarse grinding compound to the valve face. Smear some molybdenum disulphide oil (a 50/50 mixture of molybdenum disulphide grease and engine oil) to the valve stem, then slip the valve into the guide (see illustration 12.30). Note: *Make sure each valve is installed in its correct guide and be careful not to get any grinding compound on the valve stem.* Attach the grinding tool to the valve.

26 If a hand tool is being used rotate the tool between the palms of your hands. Use a back-and-forth motion (as though rubbing your hands together) rather than a circular

motion (i.e. so that the valve rotates alternately clockwise and anti-clockwise rather than in one direction only). If a motorised tool is being used, follow its instructions for use and take note of the correct drive speed for it – if your drill runs too fast and is not variable, use a hand tool instead. Lift the valve off the seat and turn it at regular intervals to distribute the grinding compound properly. Continue the grinding procedure until the valve face and seat contact area is of uniform width, and unbroken around the entire circumference.

27 Carefully remove the valve and wipe off all traces of grinding compound, making sure none gets in the guide. Use solvent to clean the valve and wipe the seat area thoroughly with a solvent soaked cloth.

28 Repeat the procedure with fine valve grinding compound, then use solvent to clean the valve and flush the guide, and wipe the seat area thoroughly with a solvent soaked cloth. Repeat the entire procedure for the

remaining valves. On completion thoroughly clean the entire head again, then blow through all passages with compressed air. Make sure all traces of the grinding compound have been removed before assembling the head.

29 Working on one valve at a time, lay the spring seat in place in the cylinder head (see illustration 12.9b).

30 Coat the valve stem with molybdenum disulphide oil (a 50/50 mixture of molybdenum disulphide grease and engine oil), then slide the valve into its guide (see illustration). Check that it moves up and down freely.

31 Hold the valve against the underside of the head to prevent it dropping out, then fit a new oil seal onto the valve stem, rotating it slightly as you do (see illustration). Slide the seal down the stem and press it onto the top of the guide using an appropriately sized deep socket – finger pressure is sufficient to get it to clip into place (see illustration). Don't remove the seal again or it will be damaged. Having the valve in place when you fit the seal allows the stem to be used as a guide and negates the possibility of twisting or cocking and damaging it as you press it onto the guide.

32 Fit the spring (see illustration). Fit the spring retainer, with its shouldered side facing down so that it locates in the top of the spring (see illustration).

33 Compress the valve spring with the spring compressor, making sure it is correctly located onto each end of the valve assembly (see Step 7) (see illustrations 12.7a, b and c). Do not compress the spring any more than is necessary to slip the collets into place. The collets must be installed with the wider end at the top. Apply a small amount of grease to the collets to help hold them in place. Locate each collet in turn onto the valve stem, locating the ridge on its inside into the groove in the stem (see illustration 12.8a), then carefully release the compressor, making sure the collets seat and lock as you do. Check that the collets are securely locked in the retaining groove (see illustration).

34 Support the cylinder head on blocks so the valves can't contact the workbench top, then tap the top of the valve stem using a brass drift and hammer (see illustration). This will help seat the collets in the groove. If you don't have a brass drift, use a soft-faced hammer and a piece of hard wood as an interface.

12.32a Fit the valve spring ...

12.32b ... then fit the spring retainer

12.33 Check the collets are correctly seated ...

12.34 ... and tap the stem end to make sure they are locked into the groove

13.2 Pull the cylinder block up off the crankcase

13.7a Use a bore gauge . . .

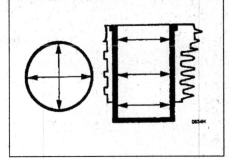

13.7b . . . and measure at the points shown

Check for proper sealing of the valves by pouring a small amount of solvent into each of the valve ports. If the solvent leaks past any valve into the combustion chamber area the valve grinding operation on that valve should be repeated.

35 Repeat the procedure for the remaining valves. Remember to keep the parts for each valve together, and separate from the other valves, so they can be reinstalled in the same location. After the cylinder head and camshafts have been installed, check and adjust the valve clearances as required (see Chapter 1).

13 Cylinder block

Note: *The cylinder block can be removed with the engine in the frame.*

Removal

1 Remove the cylinder head (see Section 11).
2 Carefully pull the cylinder block up off the crankcase **(see illustration)**. If it is stuck, tap around it with a soft-faced mallet, but avoid striking the cooling fins as these are easily broken. Do not try to free it by inserting a screwdriver between it and the crankcase – you'll damage the sealing surfaces. Protrusions from the block (but not the fins) can be used as leverage points with care if necessary. Pass

the cam chain down through the tunnel as you lift the head and drape it over the front of the engine, and take care not to allow the pistons or connecting rods to knock against the crankcase once the pistons are free. Try not to let the chain fall into the crankcase – secure it with a piece of wire or metal bar to prevent it from slipping back if necessary.
3 Remove the old gasket and discard it **(see illustration 11.11b)**. Stuff some rag around each connecting rod under the piston to support them and prevent anything falling into the crankcase. Remove the two dowels if they are loose **(see illustration 11.11a)**. If either appears to be missing it is probably stuck in the underside of the block.
4 Check the mating surfaces on the block and crankcase for signs of leakage, which could indicate warpage.
5 Clean all traces of old gasket material from the cylinder head and block and crankcase. If a scraper is used, take care not to scratch or gouge the soft aluminium. Be careful not to let any of the gasket material drop into the crankcase.

Inspection

6 Check the bore walls carefully for scratches and score marks (but do not confuse them with the fine cross-hatch lines produced by the cylinder honing process, which are normal, unless they have been worn away).
7 Using a telescoping bore gauge and a micrometer (see *Tools and Workshop Tips*), check the dimensions of each bore to assess the amount of wear, taper and ovality. Measure near the top (but below the level of the top piston ring at TDC), centre and bottom (but

above the level of the oil ring at BDC) of the bore, both parallel to and across the crankshaft axis **(see illustrations)**. Compare the results to the specifications at the beginning of the Chapter. If the bores are worn, oval or tapered beyond the service limit the block must be replaced with a new one (oversize sets of pistons and rings are not available), and a new set of pistons and rings fitted.
8 If the precision measuring tools are not available, take the cylinders to an Triumph dealer or specialist motorcycle repair shop for assessment and advice.

Installation

9 Check that none of the cylinder head studs are loose and tighten them if necessary, referring to Section 2 'Fasteners' of *Tools and Workshop Tips* in the Reference section at the end of this manual for details of how to slacken and tighten studs using two nuts locked together.
10 On Bonneville, T100 and Thruxton models position the crankshaft so that both pistons are at their highest point. On America, Speedmaster and Scrambler models position the crankshaft so that both pistons are level with each other.
11 Fit the two dowels into the crankcase if removed and push them firmly home **(see illustration)**. Remove the rags from around the pistons, taking care not to let the connecting rods fall against the rim of the crankcase. Ensure both cylinder block and crankcase mating surfaces are clean then lay a new base gasket onto the crankcase, making sure the TOP mark is facing up and it locates over the dowels **(see illustration)**.

13.11a Fit the two dowels (arrowed) . . .

13.11b . . . then lay the gasket on . . .

13.11c . . . with the TOP mark facing up

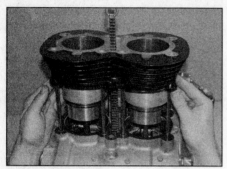

13.13a Carefully lower the block onto the pistons . . .

The gasket can only fit one way, so if the holes do not line up properly the gasket is upside down. Never re-use the old gasket.

12 Ensure the piston ring end gaps are positioned correctly before fitting the cylinder block (see Section 15). Lubricate the cylinder walls, pistons and piston rings with clean engine oil. If possible have an assistant to support the cylinder block while the pistons and rings are fed into the bores.

13 Carefully lower the block onto the pistons so the crowns fit into the bores **(see illustration)**. Support the block so the weight is off the top rings then feed the cam chain up the tunnel and slip a piece of wire through it to prevent it falling back into the engine. Keep the chain taut to prevent it becoming disengaged from the drive sprocket. Carefully compress and feed each ring into the bore as the cylinder is lowered, making sure the pistons enter the bores squarely and do not get cocked sideways – there is a good lead-in for the rings, enabling them to be quite easily hand-fed into the bore **(see illustration)**. Do not use force on the block if it appears to be stuck as the piston and/or rings will be damaged – rings are easily broken and broken pieces of ring can all too easily fall into the bottom of the crankcase. Lift the block slightly, check the rings are in their grooves and try again.

14 When the pistons and rings are correctly fitted in the bore and the chain is routed up the tunnel, press the cylinder block down onto the base gasket, making sure the dowels locate. Hold the block down and turn the crankshaft to check that the pistons move

13.13b . . . and feed the rings into the bore

up and down freely. If it does not turn easily remove the block and check the rings – do not force the crankshaft to turn.

15 Install the cylinder head (see Section 11).

14 Pistons

Removal

1 Remove the cylinder block (see Section 13).

2 Before removing the pistons from the connecting rods, use a permanent felt marker pen to write the cylinder identity on the crown of each piston (or on the skirt if the piston is dirty and going to be cleaned). Note the triangle on each crown that points to the front of the engine – it is very important that each piston is returned to its original cylinder, and is the correct way round **(see illustration)**. Turn the crankshaft to position the piston being removed at its highest point. Stuff clean rag around the connecting rods to prevent a dropped circlip falling into the crankcase.

3 Carefully prise out the circlip from the outer side of the piston using needle-nose pliers or a small flat-bladed screwdriver inserted into the notch **(see illustration)**. Push the piston pin out from the inner side to free the piston from the connecting rod **(see illustration)**. Remove the other circlip and discard them both as new ones must be used. When the piston has been removed, slide its pin back into its bore so that related parts do not get mixed up.

Inspection

4 Using your thumbs or a piston ring removal and installation tool, carefully remove the rings from the pistons **(see illustrations 15.11, 10b, and 8c, b and a)**. Do not nick or gouge the pistons in the process. Carefully note which way up each ring fits and in which groove as they must be installed in their original positions if being re-used – the top and middle rings can be identified by their different profiles **(see illustration 15.10a)**.

5 Scrape all traces of carbon from the tops of the pistons. A hand-held wire brush or a piece of fine emery cloth can be used once most of the deposits have been scraped away. Do not, under any circumstances, use a wire brush mounted in a drill motor to remove deposits from the pistons; the piston material is soft and will be eroded away by the wire brush.

6 Use a piston ring groove cleaning tool to remove any carbon deposits from the ring grooves. If a tool is not available, a piece broken off an old ring will do the job. Be very careful to remove only the carbon deposits. Do not remove any metal and do not nick or gouge the sides of the ring grooves.

7 Once the deposits have been removed, clean the pistons with solvent and dry them thoroughly. If the identification previously marked on the piston is cleaned off, be sure to re-mark it with the correct identity and orientation. Make sure the oil return holes below the oil ring groove are clear.

8 Carefully inspect each piston for cracks around the skirt, at the pin bosses and at the ring lands. Normal piston wear appears as even, vertical wear on the thrust surfaces of the piston and slight looseness of the top ring

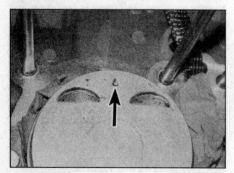

14.2 Note the triangle (arrowed) which must be at the front of the engine

14.3a Prise the circlip out from one side of the piston

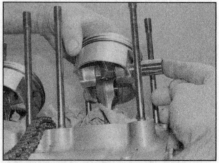

14.3b Push the piston pin out from the other side then withdraw it and remove the piston

14.10 Fit the ring into the groove and measure clearance with a feeler gauge

14.11 Measure the piston diameter with a micrometer

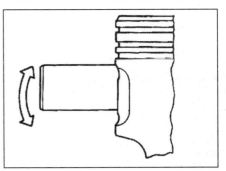

14.12a Slip the pin into the piston and check for freeplay between them

in its groove. If the skirt is scored or scuffed, the engine may have been suffering from overheating and/or abnormal combustion, which caused excessively high operating temperatures. Check that the circlip grooves are not damaged.

9 A hole in the piston crown, an extreme to be sure, is an indication that abnormal combustion (pre-ignition) was occurring. Burned areas at the edge of the piston crown are usually evidence of spark knock (detonation). If any of the above problems exist, the causes must be corrected or the damage will occur again. Obviously the piston must be replaced with a new one (see Step 13).

10 Measure the piston ring-to-groove clearance by laying each piston ring in its groove and slipping a feeler gauge in underneath it **(see illustration)**. Make sure you have the correct ring for the groove. Check the clearance at three or four locations around the groove. If new rings are being used, measure the clearance using the new rings. If the clearance is greater than specified with the old rings, replace them with new ones, then check the clearance again. If the clearance is greater than that specified with new rings, the piston is worn and must be replaced with a new one. If you are fitting new pistons, fit the new rings that come with them – do not use the old ones.

11 Check the piston diameter by measuring 13 mm up from the bottom of the skirt and at 90° to the piston pin axis **(see illustration)**.

Replace the pistons with new ones if worn below the service limit specified.

12 Apply clean engine oil to the piston pin, insert it into the piston and check for any freeplay between the two **(see illustration)**. Measure the pin external diameter at each end and the pin bore in the piston **(see illustrations)**. Compare the results to the specifications at the beginning of the Chapter and replace components that are worn beyond their specified limits with new ones. If not already done, repeat the measurements between the pin and the connecting rod small-end (see Section 26).

Installation

13 Inspect and install the piston rings (see Section 15).

14 When installing the pistons onto the connecting rods, make sure you have the correct piston for the cylinder being worked on, and that it is the correct way round with the triangle at the front **(see illustration 14.2)**. Stuff clean rag around the connecting rods to prevent a dropped circlip falling into the crankcase.

15 Working on one piston at a time, lubricate the piston pin, the piston pin bore and the connecting rod small-end bore with molybdenum disulphide oil (a 50/50 mixture of molybdenum disulphide grease and clean engine oil).

16 Install a **new** circlip in the inner side of the piston (do not re-use old circlips).

Compress the circlip only just enough to fit it and make sure it is properly seated in its groove. Line up the piston on its correct connecting rod, and insert the piston pin from the outer side **(see illustration 14.3b)**. Secure the pin with the other **new** circlip **(see illustration)**.

17 Repeat for the other piston, then remove the rag from the crankcase.

18 Install the cylinder block (see Section 13).

15 Piston rings

1 It is good practice to fit new piston rings when an engine is overhauled. Before installing the rings (new or old), check their installed end gaps as follows.

2 If new rings are being used, lay out each piston with a new ring set and keep them together so the rings will be matched with the same piston and bore during the end gap measurement procedure and engine assembly. If the old rings are being reused, make sure they are matched with their correct piston and cylinder.

3 Insert the ring being checked into the top of its bore and square it up with the bore walls by pushing it in with the **top** of the piston, pushing the piston down until the bottom groove in the piston is level with the

14.12b Measure the external diameter of the pin . . .

14.12c . . . and the internal diameter of the bore in the piston

14.16 Make sure each circlip locates correctly in its groove

15.3a Fit the ring into the bore then square it up using the piston . . .

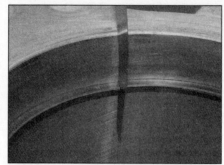

15.3b . . . and measure the installed end gap

15.9a Pull the oil ring expander ends apart and fit it in its groove . . .

15.9b . . . then fit the lower side rail . . .

15.9c . . . and the upper side rail

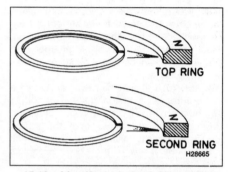

15.10a Identify each ring by its profile

top of the bore **(see illustration)**. Slip a feeler gauge between the ends of the ring and measure the gap **(see illustration)**. Compare the measurements to the specifications at the beginning of the Chapter.

4 If the gap is larger or smaller than specified, double check to make sure that you have the correct rings before proceeding.

5 If the gap is too small, the ring ends may come in contact with each other during engine operation, which can cause serious damage.

6 Excess end gap is not critical unless it exceeds the service limit. Again, double-check to make sure you have the correct rings for your engine and check that the bore is not worn (see Section 13).

7 Repeat the procedure for the other rings. Remember to keep the rings, pistons and bores matched up.

8 Once the ring end gaps have been checked, the rings can be installed on the pistons.

9 Install the oil control ring (lowest on the piston) first. It is composed of three separate components, namely the expander and the upper and lower side rails, which are interchangeable and can be fitted either way up. Slip the expander into its groove – pull the ends apart enough to slip it in and make sure the ends sit against each other correctly once in **(see illustration)**. Next, install the side rails **(see illustrations)**. Do not use a piston ring installation tool on the oil ring side rails as they may be damaged. Instead, place one end of the side rail into the groove between the expander and the ring land. Hold it firmly in place and slide a finger around the piston while pushing the rail into the groove. Make

sure the ends of the expander do not overlap and that the side rails can be turned freely.

10 The top and middle rings can be identified by their different profiles **(see illustration)**. Install the second (middle) ring next. Make sure it is the correct way up with the N or 2N mark at the top **(see illustration)**. Fit the 2nd ring into the middle groove in the piston **(see illustration)**. Do not expand the ring any more than is necessary to slide it into place. To avoid breaking the ring, use a piston ring installation tool, or alternatively pieces of old feeler gauge blades can be used as shown **(see illustration)**.

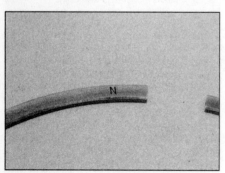

15.10b Fit the ring with the N mark at the top

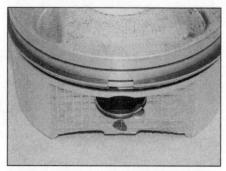

15.10c Fit the middle ring into its groove

15.10d Use the pieces of feeler gauge as shown to guide the rings onto the piston

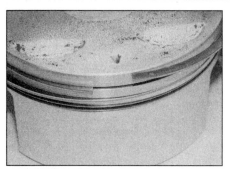

15.11 Fit the top ring into its groove

11 Finally, install the top ring in the same manner into the top groove in the piston with its N mark at the top **(see illustration)**.

12 Once the rings are correctly installed, check they move freely without snagging and stagger their end gaps as shown **(see illustration)**.

16 Clutch

Note 1: *The clutch can be removed with the engine in the frame. If the engine has already been removed, ignore the preliminary steps which don't apply.*

Note 2: *Triumph recommend the use of an alignment mandrel (Pt. No. T3880014) for use when rebuilding the clutch. The tool is used to align the lifter plate with the hole in the transmission input shaft, thus enabling the pushrod seat to move freely in the shaft when the clutch lever is operated. The tool is not*

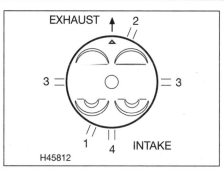

15.12 Stagger the ring end gaps as shown

1 Top ring
2 Second (middle) ring
3 Oil control ring side rails
4 Oil control ring expander

essential, although the installation procedure can take some time without it.

Removal

1 Drain the engine oil (see Chapter 1).

2 Note the alignment of the gearchange lever or linkage arm (according to model) with the punch mark on the shaft, then slacken the pinch bolt and slide the lever or arm off the shaft **(see illustration 4.13 or 4.47)**.

3 On America and Speedmaster models remove the left-hand exhaust silencer (see Chapter 3A or 3B). Unscrew the bolts securing the front footrest bracket assembly to the frame then displace it upwards so it is clear of the clutch cover and tie it to the frame using cable ties **(see illustration 4.48)**.

4 Detach the clutch cable from the release mechanism arm (see Section 17).

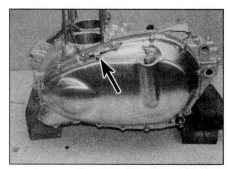

16.6a Unscrew the bolts, noting the cable bracket (arrowed) . . .

5 Detach the breather hose from the crankcase **(see illustration 4.15)**.

6 Unscrew the clutch cover bolts, noting the cable bracket, and remove the cover, noting how it fits **(see illustration)**. Remove the gasket and discard it. Remove the four dowels if they are loose **(see illustration 16.34)**. Note the wave washer on the starter idle/reduction gear shaft and remove it for safekeeping – if it is not on the shaft it will be stuck to the shaft bore rim in the cover **(see illustration)**. Remove the release mechanism pushrod from the cover for safekeeping, noting which way round it fits **(see illustration)**.

7 If the clutch housing is being removed, withdraw the starter idle/reduction gear shaft and remove the gear **(see illustration)**. On models up to engine no. 221607, unscrew the breather rotor bolts and remove the rotor and its plate **(see illustration)**. Remove the starter driven gear from the starter clutch, turning it clockwise as you do to release it from the sprags **(see illustration)**.

16.6b . . . and remove the cover

16.6c Remove the wave washer . . .

16.6d . . . and the pushrod

16.7a Withdraw the shaft and remove the gear

16.7b Unscrew the bolts (arrowed) and remove the breather and its plate . . .

16.7c . . . then remove the starter driven gear

16.8a Withdraw the pushrod seat . . .

16.8b . . . then unscrew the bolts and remove the plate . . .

16.8c . . . and the springs

8 Remove the pushrod seat from the centre of the lifter plate (see illustration). Working in a criss-cross pattern, and holding the clutch housing to prevent it turning, gradually slacken the lifter plate bolts until spring

16.9a Using a home-made holding tool located against the clutch centre walls . . .

pressure is released, then remove the bolts, the plate and the springs (see illustrations).
9 To remove the clutch nut the transmission input shaft must be counter-held to prevent it turning. This can be done in several ways.

16.9b . . . to prevent rotation while unscrewing the clutch nut

If the engine is in the frame, engage 5th gear and have an assistant hold the rear brake on hard with the rear tyre in firm contact with the ground. Alternatively, the Triumph service tool (Pt. No. T3880360), which consists of a plate that bolts onto the pressure plate and is held using a suitable socket drive bar, or a suitable commercially available or home-made holding tool that locates against the wall sections in the clutch centre as shown, can be used (see illustration). With the shaft locked, unscrew the clutch nut, then remove the spring washer (see illustration).
10 Grasp the pressure plate lugs and remove the complete clutch centre, clutch plate assembly and pressure plate as one (see illustration). If required, place the clutch centre face down on a bench, then remove the pressure plate (see illustration 16.27). Remove the clutch friction and plain plates one by one, keeping them in order even if you are replacing them with new ones as there are different types – the old ones can be used as a guide to installing the new ones (see illustration 16.26d).
11 Slide the clutch housing off the shaft (see illustration).
12 Remove the oil pump drive gear then slide the shouldered bush off the shaft (see illustrations).

Inspection

13 After an extended period of service the clutch friction plates will wear and promote clutch slip. Measure the thickness of each friction plate using a Vernier caliper (see illustration). If the thickness is less than

16.10 Grasp the pressure plate lugs and draw the assembly off the shaft

16.11 Slide the clutch housing off the shaft

16.12a Remove the oil pump gear . . .

16.12b . . . and slide the bush off the shaft

16.13 Measure the thickness of each friction plate

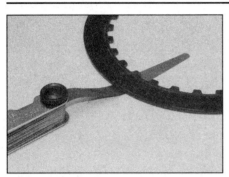

16.14 Check the plain plates for warpage

16.16a Check the friction plate tabs and clutch housing slots as described

16.16b Check the plain plate tongues and the clutch centre slots as described

the service limit given in the Specifications at the beginning of the Chapter, the friction plates must be replaced with new ones as a set. Also, if any of the plates smell burnt or are glazed, they must be replaced as a set.

14 The plain plates should not show any signs of excess heating (bluing). Check for warpage using a flat surface and feeler gauges **(see illustration)**. If any plate exceeds the maximum amount of warpage, or shows signs of bluing, all plain plates must be renewed as a set.

15 Check all the clutch springs for cracks, sag and bend and replace all the springs with new ones as a set if necessary – Triumph provide no figures for spring free length, but if the springs are a different length it shows sag in the shorter ones.

16 Inspect the edges of the tabs on the friction plates and the corresponding slots in the clutch housing for burrs and indentations **(see illustration)**. Similarly check for wear between the inner teeth of the plain plates and the slots in the clutch centre **(see illustration)**. Wear of this nature will cause clutch drag and slow disengagement during gear changes as the plates will snag when the pressure plate is lifted. With care a small amount of wear can be corrected by dressing with a fine file, but if wear is excessive (greater than 0.3 mm) new components should be installed.

17 Check the needle bearings in the clutch housing and oil pump drive gear and the

shouldered bush they run on for signs of wear, damage or scoring, and freeplay between them when fitted together, and replace them with new ones if necessary **(see illustrations)**.

18 Check the lifter plate and the bearing for signs of wear or damage, and replace any parts with new ones as necessary **(see illustration)**. Check the pushrod and pushrod seat for wear. Refer to Section 17 and check the release mechanism components in the cover.

19 Check the teeth of the primary driven gear on the back of the clutch housing and the corresponding teeth of the primary drive gear on the crankshaft. Replace the clutch housing and/or crankshaft with new ones if worn or chipped teeth are discovered. Similarly check the oil pump drive gear on the back of the housing and its driven gears on the pumps **(see illustration 16.23)**.

Installation

20 Remove all traces of old gasket from the crankcase and clutch cover mating surfaces.

21 Smear the input shaft, the inside and outside of the shouldered spacer, and the needle bearings in the clutch housing and oil pump drive gear with molybdenum disulphide oil (50% molybdenum grease and 50% engine oil).

22 Slide the shouldered bush onto the shaft

with the shouldered end innermost **(see illustration 16.12b)**.

23 Slide the oil pump drive gear onto the bush **(see illustration 16.12a)**, making sure the pins are on the outside and the teeth engage with those on the driven gears on the pumps **(see illustration)**.

24 Slide the clutch housing onto the bush, making sure the teeth on the primary driven gear engage with those on the primary drive gear on the crankshaft and that the holes in the back of the primary driven gear locate over the pins on the oil pump drive gear so they are locked together **(see illustration 16.11)**. Try to turn the oil pump driven gears while holding the clutch housing – if they turn, the pins have not located in the holes, but will do if

16.17a Check the clutch housing bearing (arrowed) . . .

16.17b . . . the oil pump gear bearing and the bush

16.18 Check the pushrod seat and the bearing for wear

16.23 Make sure all the gears are engaged correctly

16.24 Make sure the housing has located onto the drive gear pins by turning the driven gears

16.26a Fit the outermost dark friction plate . . .

16.26b . . . then the dark plain plate . . .

you continue turning the driven gears while pushing the clutch housing in **(see illustration)**.

25 Place the clutch centre face down on the work bench. If new plates are being fitted, identify the two friction plates and one plain plate that are darker in colour than the rest.

If you are fitting the old plates they should already be in the correct order. Coat each clutch plate with engine oil before installing it.

26 First fit the outermost dark friction plate, followed by the dark plain plate **(see illustrations)**. Now alternate standard colour friction and plain plates until all are installed,

then finally fit the innermost dark friction plate **(see illustrations)**. Align the tabs of the friction plates as you install them.

27 Fit the pressure plate into the clutch centre, making sure the castellations with the slots in the centre **(see illustration)**.

28 Grasp the complete clutch centre, clutch plate assembly and pressure plate as one and slide it onto the shaft and into the housing with the pressure plate innermost, aligning the splines between the shaft and the centre and the tabs on the friction plates with the slots in the housing **(see illustration)**.

29 Slide the spring washer onto the shaft with the OUT mark on the outside **(see illustration)**. Fit the clutch nut, then using the method employed on removal to prevent the clutch turning, tighten the nut to the torque setting specified at the beginning of the Chapter **(see illustrations)**. **Note:** *Check that the clutch centre rotates freely after tightening the clutch nut.*

16.26c . . . then normal friction plates . . . .

16.26d . . . and plain plates . . .

16.26e . . . finishing with the innermost dark friction plate

16.27 Fit the pressure plate into the clutch centre, making sure it engages correctly

16.28 Slide the complete assembly onto the shaft

16.29a Slide the washer onto the shaft with the OUT mark facing out . . .

16.29b . . . then fit the clutch nut . . .

16.29c . . . and tighten it to the specified torque

16.31 The seat should slide easily in and out of the bearing and shaft

16.32 Locate the breather rotor plate then fit the rotor

16.34a Where fitted, smear the O-ring and the oil seal (arrowed) with grease

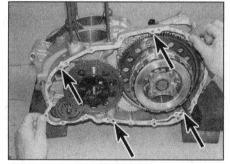

16.34b Lay a new gasket onto the dowels (arrowed)

16.35a Install the cover, making sure everything locates correctly

16.35b Do not forget the cable bracket

30 Fit the clutch springs over their posts (see illustration 16.8c). Make sure the bearing is seated in the lifter plate. Lubricate the bearing and the pushrod seat with molybdenum disulphide oil (50% molybdenum grease and 50% engine oil) (see illustration 16.18).

31 If the Triumph alignment mandrel (see **Note 2** on page 2•31) is not being used, locate the lifter plate and fit the bolts, and tighten them lightly until the springs just start to compress (see illustration 16.8b). Slide the pushrod seat through the bearing in the lifter plate and into the input shaft (see illustration 16.8a). The pushrod seat should slide easily in and out of the shaft and bearing, indicating their holes are centred. If the seat is tight, centre the lifter plate by moving it around until the seat moves easily. This centralisation must be maintained while the clutch spring bolts are tightened. To do this, tighten them evenly and only a little at a time and in a criss-cross sequence, until the torque setting specified at the beginning of the Chapter is reached. When the bolts are tightened, check that the seat is still free to move in and out (see illustration) – if it is tight slacken the bolts and repeat the procedure until the seat is free when all bolts are tight. Be prepared for this procedure to take some time – you may achieve it first time or it could take many attempts! If you find it just won't align, order the alignment mandrel tool from a Triumph dealer.

32 If removed, lubricate the starter driven gear hub, the starter clutch sprags and the idle/reduction gear shaft with engine oil. Fit the starter driven gear into the starter clutch, turning it clockwise as you do to spread the

sprags (see illustration 16.7c). On models up to engine no. 221607, fit the breather rotor plate and rotor, then apply a suitable thread locking compound to its screws and tighten them to the specified torque setting (see illustration). Position the starter idle/reduction gear so the teeth on the smaller gear engage with those on the driven gear and insert the shaft (see illustration 16.7a).

33 Check the condition of the gearchange shaft oil seal and bearing in the cover and replace them with new ones if necessary (see Section 19, Step 11). Check the release mechanism components are correctly installed (see Section 17).

34 Fit the release mechanism pushrod into the cover with the rounded end facing out (see illustration 16.6d). Fit the wave washer onto the starter idle/reduction gear shaft (see illustration 16.6c). Make sure the four dowels are in the crankcase or cover. On bikes with engine numbers up to 221607, smear the breather pipe O-ring and oil seal with grease (see illustration). On all models, smear the gearchange shaft oil seal with grease. Lay a new gasket onto the dowels, using dabs of grease to keep it in place if required (see illustration).

35 Fit the cover, keeping the mating surfaces parallel and making sure the breather rotor and idle/reduction gear shaft ends and the breather pipe locate in their bores, and making sure the dowels locate correctly and the gasket stays in place (see illustration). Install the cover bolts, not forgetting the cable bracket, and tighten them finger-tight (see illustration). Now tighten the cover bolts in a criss-cross sequence to the specified torque setting.

36 Install all remaining components (see Steps 5 to 1). On America and Speedmaster models tighten the front footrest bracket assembly bolts to the specified torque setting. On all models, make sure the gearchange lever or linkage arm is correctly aligned.

37 Refill the engine with the specified quantity of oil (see Chapter 1).

38 Check the action of the clutch.

17 Clutch cable and release mechanism

Cable

1 Slacken the adjuster lockring at the lever end of the cable (see illustration). Screw the adjuster fully into the lever bracket, then turn it out to align the slot in the adjuster with that in the lever bracket.

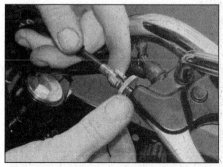

17.1 Slacken the lockring then thread the adjuster in and align the slots

17.2a Slacken the locknuts . . .

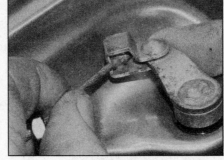

17.2b . . . then release the cable end from the arm . . .

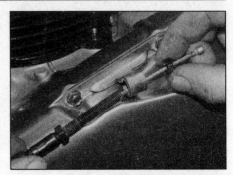

17.2c . . . and draw the cable out of the bracket

2 Slacken the locknuts securing the cable in the bracket on the engine (**see illustration**). Thread the front nut fully up the cable and the rear nut off the end. Push the release arm forward and slip the inner cable end out of the arm (**see illustration**). Draw the cable out of the bracket (**see illustration**).
3 At the lever end pull the outer cable end from the socket in the adjuster and release the inner cable from the lever (**see illustrations**).
4 Thread the front nut off the lower end of the cable, then draw the cable through its clips on the left-hand frame cradle section. Remove the cable from the machine, noting its routing.

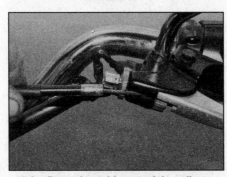

17.3a Draw the cable out of the adjuster and bracket . . .

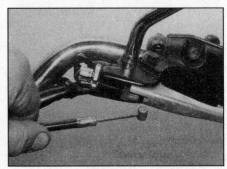

17.3b . . . and free the end from the lever

HAYNES HiNT *Before removing the cable from the bike, tape the lower end of the new cable to the upper end of the old cable. Slowly pull the lower end of the old cable out, guiding the new cable down into position. Using this method will ensure the cable is routed correctly. If you don't yet have the new cable, do the same thing with a piece of string, then use the string later to draw the new cable through.*

5 Before fitting the new cable check the clutch release mechanism arm in the clutch cover for smooth operation and any signs of wear or damage. Remove it for cleaning and re-greasing if required (see below).
6 Installation is the reverse of removal. Apply

grease to the cable ends. Make sure the cable is correctly routed and secured in its clips. Turn the adjuster on the lever bracket so that the slots are not aligned. Adjust the clutch lever freeplay (see Chapter 1). Tighten the lockring against the adjuster.

Release mechanism

7 Remove the clutch cover (see Section 16, Steps 1 to 6).
8 Withdraw the shaft from the cover and tip the spring out (**see illustrations**).
9 Clean all old grease off the shaft and its oil seal and needle bearings using solvent.
10 Check the condition of the seal and the bearings and replace them with new ones if necessary – lever the seal out using a seal hook or screwdriver, then pull the bearings out, referring to *Tools and Workshop Tips* in the Reference Section for removal and

installation methods (**see illustration**). Lubricate the new bearings and seal with molybdenum disulphide grease then press them into place. If the bearings were rusted or worn check the section of the shaft they run on.
11 Check the return spring for damaged ends and fatigued coil and replace it with a new one if necessary.
12 Check the pushrod and its seat in the lifter plate for wear damage and replace them with new ones if necessary.
13 If not already done smear molybdenum disulphide grease over the seal lips and push it in so it will spread over the bearings when the shaft is inserted. Fit the return spring end into the hole in the bottom of the shaft, then with the cover angled up insert the shaft, making sure the spring remains in place and that its other end locates in the hole in the cover (**see**

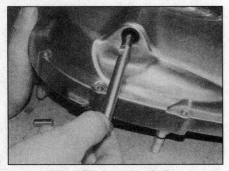

17.8a Withdraw the shaft . . .

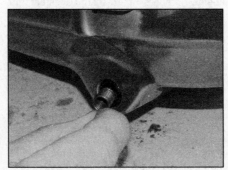

17.8b . . . and tip the spring out

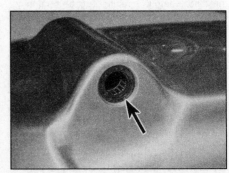

17.10 Check the seal and bearing (arrowed)

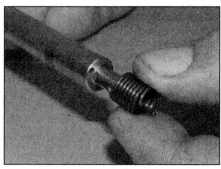

17.13 Locate the spring end in the hole in the shaft

illustration). Check the spring has located correctly by turning the shaft – it should come under spring pressure and return when released.

14 Smear the pushrod with molybdenum disulphide grease then fit it into its bore with the rounded end facing out **(see illustration 16.6d)**. Check that the pushrod moves in and out when the arm is turned **(see illustration)**.

15 Install the clutch cover (see Section 16, Steps 33 to 38).

18 Oil pumps

Note: *The oil pumps can be removed with the engine in the frame.*

Removal

1 Remove the clutch (see Section 16).
2 Remove the circlips securing the oil pump

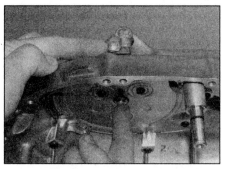

17.14 Check the action of the arm and pushrod

driven gears **(see illustration)**. Pull the gears off the shafts, noting that the bigger one is for the front pump.

3 To remove the front pump unscrew its bolts and remove it from the crankcase, noting that on later models a thin metal gasket may be

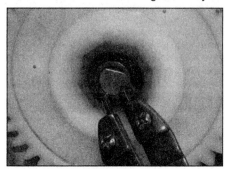

18.2 Release the circlip on each gear and remove the gears

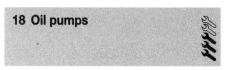

fitted between the pump and crankcase (see illustrations).

4 To remove the rear pump unscrew the oil pipe bolt and remove the pipe, noting the sealing washer and O-ring **(see illustration)**. Unscrew the remaining bolts and remove the pump from the crankcase **(see illustration)**. Discard the pipe sealing washer as a new one must be used, but retain the O-ring as for some reason it is not listed as being available separately from the pipe. If it is damaged and a new one is needed you should be able to source an identical O-ring from a motor factor.

Disassembly

5 Work on one pump at a time to avoid the possibility of interchanging components.
6 Unscrew the bolt and remove the inner cover **(see illustrations)**. Remove the washer from the end of the shaft **(see illustration)**. Remove the dowel for safekeeping if it is loose.

18.3a Unscrew the bolts . . .

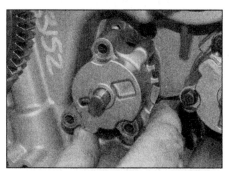

18.3b . . . and remove the front pump

18.4a Unscrew the bolt (arrowed) and remove the pipe

18.4b Unscrew the two remaining bolts and remove the pump

18.6a Unscrew the bolt . . .

18.6b . . . and remove the inner cover

18.6c Remove the washer and the dowel (arrowed) if loose

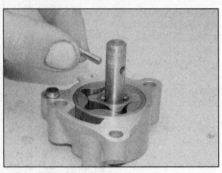

18.7a Withdraw the shaft and remove the drive pin . . .

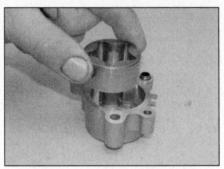

18.7b . . . then remove the rotors

18.11a Measuring the inner rotor tip–to-outer rotor clearance

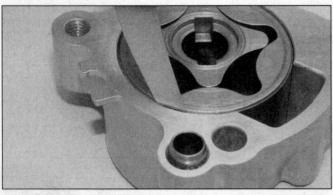

18.11b Measuring the outer rotor-to-housing clearance

18.11c Measuring rotor end-float

7 Withdraw the shaft and remove the drive pin from it **(see illustration)**. Remove the inner and outer rotors from the pump body and keep them together so they can be installed the same way round **(see illustration)**.

Inspection

8 Clean all components in solvent and dry them using compressed air or lint-free cloth.
9 Check the pump body and cover for cracks and other damage.
10 Inspect the rotors, body, and cover for scoring and wear. If any damage, scoring or uneven or excessive wear is evident, replace the pump with a new one – individual components are not available.
11 Fit the outer rotor back into the pump then fit the inner rotor into the outer rotor with

the drive pin slot facing out **(see illustration 18.13a)**. With the rotors positioned as shown measure the clearance between the inner rotor tip and the outer rotor with a feeler gauge and compare it to the service limit listed in the specifications at the beginning of the Chapter **(see illustration)**. Also measure the clearance between the outer rotor and the rotor housing with a feeler gauge **(see illustration)**. If possible lay a straight-edge across the rotors and the crankcase and measure the clearance (rotor end-float) using feeler gauges **(see illustration)**. If any clearance measured is greater than the maximum listed, replace the pump with a new one.

Assembly and installation

12 Lubricate the rotors with clean oil.

13 Fit the outer rotor into the pump, then fit the inner rotor into the outer rotor with the drive pin slot facing out **(see illustration)**. Fit the drive pin into its hole in the shaft then slide the shaft into the rotor and pump body, locating the pin in its slot **(see illustration)**.
14 Fit the dowel into the pump body if removed **(see illustration 18.6c)**. Fit the washer onto the end of the shaft. Fit the inner cover onto the pump and secure it with its bolt **(see illustrations 18.6b and a)**.
15 Locate the rear pump in the crankcase then install the two lower bolts and tighten them finger-tight **(see illustration 18.4b)**. Make sure the O-ring is fitted into its groove in the pipe end and smear it with oil **(see illustration)**. Locate the pipe in its bore and against the pump, then install the remaining

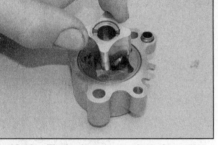

18.13a Fit the inner rotor into the outer rotor with the drive pin slot facing out

18.13b Locate the drive pin in the slot as shown

18.15a Fit a new O-ring onto the pipe . . .

18.15b . . . then locate the pipe . . .

18.15c . . . using a new sealing washer with the bolt

18.17 Align the flats when fitting the gears on the shafts

bolt with a new sealing washer and tighten all three bolts to the torque setting specified at the beginning of the Chapter **(see illustrations)**.

16 Locate the front pump in the crankcase, together with the metal gasket if originally fitted. Install the bolts and tighten them to the torque setting specified at the beginning of the Chapter **(see illustrations 18.3b and a)**.

17 Slide the driven gears onto the shafts, aligning the flats and fitting the larger gear to the front pump **(see illustration)**. Secure the gears with the circlips, making sure they locate in their grooves **(see illustration 18.2)**.

18 Install the clutch (see Section 16).

---

19 Gearchange mechanism

Note: The gearchange mechanism can be removed with the engine in the frame. If the engine has already been removed, ignore the preliminary steps.

Removal

1 Remove the clutch (see Section 16).
2 Remove the front sprocket (see Chapter 5). Clean the area around the gearchange mechanism cover.

3 Unscrew the bolts and remove the cover, noting the wiring clamp **(see illustration)**. Discard the gasket. Remove the locating pins if loose.

4 Remove the E-clip and washer from the left-hand end of the shaft **(see illustration)**.

5 Note how the gearchange selector arm locates over the selector drum cam plate, and how the shaft centralising spring ends locate on either side of the pin. Withdraw the gearchange shaft from the engine, noting the washer **(see illustration and 19.13)**.

6 Note how the stopper arm spring ends locate and how the roller on the arm locates in the neutral detent on the selector drum cam, then unscrew the stopper arm bolt

and remove the plain washer, the arm, the shouldered washer, and the spring, noting how they fit **(see illustration)**.

Inspection

7 Inspect the stopper arm and selector arm return springs and the shaft centralising spring **(see illustration)**. If they are fatigued, worn or damaged they must be replaced with new ones – the selector arm return spring is part of the shaft assembly and not available separately. Remove the E-clip to release the centralising spring. Make sure the centralising spring pin is tight in the crankcase – if necessary tighten it to the torque setting specified at the beginning of the Chapter.

19.3 Unscrew the bolts, noting the wiring clamp (arrowed), and remove the cover

19.4 Remove the E-clip and washer from the shaft

19.5 Withdraw the shaft, noting how it locates

19.6 Note the fitting of the spring ends and the roller, then unscrew the bolt (arrowed) and remove the arm

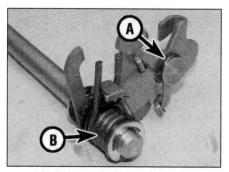

19.7 Selector arm return spring (A) and shaft centralising spring (B)

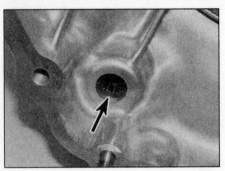

19.11a Check the oil seal and the bearing (arrowed)

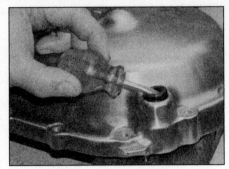

19.11b Lever out the seal . . .

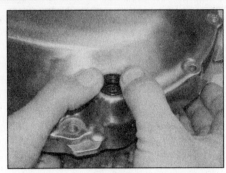

19.11c . . . and press the new one into place

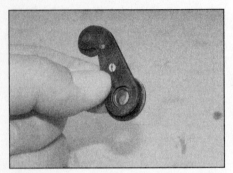

19.12a Fit the shouldered washer into the arm . . .

19.12b . . . then fit the bolt with its washer and the return spring

19.12c Locate the assembly on the crankcase and against the cam plate and tighten the bolt . . .

8 Inspect the selector arm pawls and the cam plate for wear.
9 Check the stopper arm roller and the cam plate detents for wear. Check that the roller spins freely.
10 Check the gearchange shaft for distortion and damage to the splines. If the shaft is bent you can attempt to straighten it, but if the splines are damaged the shaft must be replaced with a new one.
11 Check the condition of the shaft oil seal and bearing in the clutch cover and replace them with new ones if necessary (see illustration) – lever the seal out using a seal hook or screwdriver, then pull the bearing out, referring to *Tools and Workshop Tips* in the Reference Section for removal and installation

methods (see illustration). Lubricate the new bearing and seal with molybdenum disulphide grease then press them into place (see illustration). If the bearing was rusted or worn check the section of the shaft it runs on.

Installation

12 Fit the shouldered washer into the inside of the stopper arm (see illustration). Apply threadlock to the threads of the stopper arm bolt. Fit the bolt with its washer through the arm and shouldered washer, then locate the return spring (see illustration). Fit the stopper arm assembly, making sure the spring ends locate correctly over the arm and against the crankcase, using a screwdriver to position the roller in the neutral detent in the cam plate

as you tighten the bolt to the torque setting specified at the beginning of the Chapter (see illustrations). Make sure the stopper arm is free to move and is returned by the pressure of the spring.
13 Smear some grease onto the lips of the shaft oil seal in the crankcase. Make sure the washer is fitted against the E-clip on the inner face of the selector arm, and the centralising spring ends are correctly located on each side of the tab (see illustration and 19.7). Slide the shaft into its hole in the engine (see illustration 19.5), making sure the centralising spring ends locate correctly each side of the locating pin in the crankcase (see illustration).
14 Slide the washer onto the left-hand end

19.12d . . . making sure the spring ends (arrowed) are correctly positioned

19.13a Make sure the washer (arrowed) is on the shaft

19.13b Make sure everything is correctly positioned

of the shaft, then fit the E-clip into its groove **(see illustrations)**.

15 Fit the gearchange mechanism cover locating pins if removed, then install the cover using a new gasket. Tighten the bolts evenly in a criss-cross sequence to the torque setting specified at the beginning of the Chapter, not forgetting to fit the wiring clamp **(see illustrations and 19.3)**.

16 Install the front sprocket (see Chapter 5).

17 Install the clutch (see Section 16).

---

20 Starter clutch

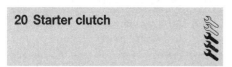

Note: *The starter clutch can be removed with the engine in the frame. If the engine has been removed, ignore the steps which do not apply.*

Check

1 The operation of the starter clutch can be checked while it is in situ. Remove the starter motor (see Chapter 8). Check that the idle/reduction gear is able to rotate freely clockwise as you look at it via the starter motor aperture, but locks when rotated anti-clockwise. If not, the starter clutch is faulty and should be removed for inspection. As a double check, after removing the clutch cover and the idle/reduction gear, see if the starter driven gear rotates freely in a clockwise direction and locks against the rotor in an anti-clockwise direction – if not the starter clutch is faulty.

Removal

2 Remove the clutch cover (see Section 16, Steps 1 to 6).

3 Withdraw the starter idle/reduction gear shaft and remove the gear **(see illustration 16.7a)**. Unscrew the breather rotor bolts and remove the rotor and its plate **(see illustration 16.7b)**. Remove the starter driven gear from

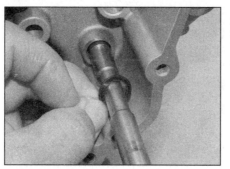

19.14a Slide on the washer . . .

19.14b . . . then fit the E-clip

19.15a Lay a new gasket onto the pins (arrowed) . . .

19.15b . . . then fit the cover

the starter clutch, turning it clockwise as you do to release it from the sprags **(see illustration 16.7c)**.

4 Unscrew the starter clutch housing bolts and remove it from the end of the crankshaft **(see illustrations)**.

Inspection

5 Check the condition of the sprags inside the clutch housing and the corresponding surface on the driven gear hub. If they are damaged, marked or flattened at any point, or if the sprags are not securely held in their housing by their retaining springs, new components should be obtained – the sprag assembly and housing come as a set

and the starter driven gear is available separately.

6 Check the bush in the starter driven gear hub and its corresponding surface on the crankshaft **(see illustration)**. If the bush surfaces show signs of excessive wear (i.e. the oil retaining holes in its surface are not visible) replace the driven gear with a new one.

7 Check the teeth on the starter motor drive shaft, idle/reduction gear and starter driven gear. If worn or chipped teeth are discovered on related gears replace the relevant components with new ones. Check the idle/reduction gear shaft for damage, and check that the gear is not a loose fit.

20.4a Unscrew the bolts (arrowed) . . .

20.4b . . . and remove the starter clutch

20.6 Check the bush (arrowed) and its bearing surface on the crankshaft

21.7 Unscrew the bolts (arrowed) and remove the sump

21.8 Unscrew the bolts (arrowed) and remove the strainer

Installation

8 Wipe the mating surfaces of the inner face of the starter clutch housing and the primary drive gear on the crankshaft. Clean the threads of the starter clutch housing bolts and apply a suitable non-permanent thread locking compound, then fit the starter clutch onto the crankshaft and tighten the bolts evenly and a little at a time in a criss-cross sequence to the torque setting specified at the beginning of the Chapter (see illustrations 20.4b and a).

9 Lubricate the starter driven gear hub, the starter clutch sprags and the idle/reduction gear shaft with engine oil. Fit the starter driven gear into the starter clutch, turning it clockwise as you do to spread the sprags (see illustration 16.7c). Fit the breather rotor plate and rotor, then apply a suitable thread locking compound to its screws and tighten them to the specified torque setting (see illustration 16.32). Position the starter idle/reduction gear so the teeth on the smaller gear engage with those on the driven gear and insert the shaft (see illustration 16.7a).

10 Install the clutch cover (see Section 16, Steps 33 to 38).

21 Sump and oil strainer

Note: The sump and oil strainer can be removed with the engine in the frame, but it is necessary to remove the cradle sections. If the engine has been removed, ignore the Steps that do not apply. To remove the oil pressure

relief valve the engine must be removed from the frame and the crankcase halves separated.

Removal

1 Support the motorcycle on an auxiliary stand so that it is upright.

2 Drain the engine oil and remove the filter (see Chapter 1). Remove the oil cooler with its feed and return pipes (see Section 6). Remove the exhaust system on all models except the Scrambler (see Chapter 3A or 3B).

3 On America, Speedmaster and Thruxton models note the alignment of the gearchange linkage arm with the punch mark on the shaft, then slacken the pinch bolt and slide the arm off (see illustration 4.47). On America and Speedmaster models, unscrew the bolts securing the front footrest bracket assembly to the frame then displace it upwards so it is clear of the clutch cover and tie it to the frame using cable ties (see illustration 4.48).

4 Release the starter motor cable clips from the inside of the right-hand frame cradle by carefully levering them out with a screwdriver (see illustration 4.18b).

5 On Bonneville, T100, Thruxton and Scrambler models unscrew the nut on the lower front mounting bolt then remove the bolt (see illustrations 4.23a and b). Unscrew the bolts securing the brace between the frame cradle sections and remove the brace (see illustration 4.24a). Unscrew the bolts securing each cradle section to the main frame and remove the cradles, noting the plates the bolts thread into and the oil cooler mounting bracket (see illustrations 4.24b, c and d).

6 On America and Speedmaster models

unscrew the nut on the lower front mounting bolt then remove the bolt, collecting the spacer that fits between the engine and the left-hand frame cradle section as you do (see illustration 4.61). Unscrew the bolts securing each cradle section to the main frame and remove the cradles, noting the plates the bolts thread into and the oil cooler and horn mounting brackets (see illustrations 4.24b, c and d).

7 Unscrew the sump bolts, slackening them evenly in a criss-cross sequence to prevent distortion, and remove the sump (see illustration). Discard the gasket as a new one must be used. Note the positions of the dowels and remove them if they are loose.

8 Unscrew the oil strainer bolts and remove the strainer (see illustration). Discard the O-ring.

9 If required, for example if a full engine strip is being done, unscrew the bolts securing the internal oil pipe and remove it (see illustration). Discard the sealing washers and obtain new ones.

Inspection

10 Remove all traces of gasket from the sump and crankcase mating surfaces, and clean the inside of the sump with solvent.

11 Clean the oil strainer in solvent and remove any debris caught in the strainer mesh (see illustration). Inspect the strainer for any signs of wear or damage and replace it with a new one, if necessary.

Installation

12 If removed install the internal oil pipe using new sealing washers between the pipe and the bolt heads and tighten the bolts to

21.9 Unscrew the bolts (arrowed) and remove the pipe

21.11 Make sure the strainer mesh is clear

21.12 Fit the pipe using new sealing washers on the bolts

21.13 Install the strainer using a new O-ring

21.14 Lay a new gasket in place . . .

21.15 . . . then install the sump

the torque setting specified at the beginning of the Chapter (see illustration).

13 Fit a new O-ring into the groove in the base of the strainer (see illustration). Clean the threads of the bolts and apply a suitable non-permanent thread locking compound. Install the oil strainer and tighten the bolts to the specified torque setting.

14 Lay a new gasket onto the sump (if the engine is in the frame) or onto the crankcase (if the engine has been removed and is positioned upside down on the work surface) (see illustration). Make sure the holes in the gasket align correctly with the bolt holes.

15 Position the sump on the crankcase, then install the bolts and tighten them evenly and a little at a time in a criss-cross pattern to the specified torque setting (see illustration).

16 On Bonneville, T100, Thruxton and Scrambler models fit the frame cradle sections to each side then fit the bolts with their plates and the oil cooler bracket and tighten the bolts finger-tight (see illustrations 4.24d, c and b). Fit the brace between the cradles and tighten its bolts finger-tight (see illustration 4.24a). Slide the lower front mounting bolt through from the left-hand side then thread the nut onto its end and tighten it finger-tight (see illustration 4.23b and a). Now go round and tighten the bolts and nut to the torque settings specified at the beginning of the Chapter.

17 On America and Speedmaster models fit the frame cradle sections to each side then fit the bolts with their plates and the oil cooler bracket on the right-hand side and the horn bracket on the left-hand side and tighten the bolts finger-tight (see illustrations 4.24d, c and b). Slide the lower front mounting bolt through from the left-hand side, not forgetting the spacer between the engine and the left-hand frame cradle, then thread the nut onto its end and tighten it finger-tight (see illustration 4.61). Now go round and tighten the bolts and nut to the torque settings specified at the beginning of the Chapter.

18 Press the starter motor lead clips into the holes in the right-hand frame cradle (see illustration 4.18b).

19 Install the remaining components (see Steps 3 and 2). On America and Speedmaster models tighten the front footrest bracket

assembly bolts to the specified torque setting (see illustration 4.48). On all models, make sure the gearchange lever or linkage arm is correctly aligned (see illustration 4.47).

20 Fit a new oil filter then fill the engine with the correct type and quantity of oil (see Chapter 1).

21 Start the engine and check that there are no leaks around the sump.

22 Crankcase separation and reassembly

Note: *Where an option to remove a component is given (i.e. if required, remove the neutral switch), it should be removed if a full engine strip, overhaul and rebuild is being carried out. However if the crankcases are being split solely to correct an isolated problem with a component or assembly not related to the optional component, then it can remain in place.*

Note: *To separate the crankcase halves, the engine must be removed from the frame.*

Separation

1 To access the connecting rods, crankshaft, balancer shafts, main and big-end bearings, transmission shafts, selector drum and forks and oil pressure relief valve, the crankcase must be split into two parts.

2 To enable the crankcases to be separated, the engine must be removed from the frame (see Section 4).

3 If the crankcases are being separated as part of a complete engine overhaul, remove the following components:

a) *Cylinder head and all associated components (Sections 7 to 11)*
b) *Cylinder block and pistons (Sections 13 and 14)*
c) *Clutch (Section 16).*
d) *Oil pumps (Section 18).*
e) *Gearchange mechanism (Section 19).*
f) *Starter clutch (Section 20).*
g) *Oil sump and strainer (Section 21).*
h) *Neutral switch (Chapter 8).*
i) *Pick-up coil (Chapter 4).*
j) *Alternator rotor (Chapter 8).*
k) *Starter motor (Chapter 8).*

4 If the crankcases are being separated

to inspect or access the transmission components only, or to inspect the crankshaft without removing it, the engine top-end components (cam chain tensioner, camshafts, cylinder head, cylinder block etc) can remain in situ. The crankshaft can be removed leaving the connecting rods in place, in which case the top-end need only be stripped as far as the camshaft drive gear, leaving the cylinder head, block and pistons in place. However, if removal of the crankshaft and connecting rods is intended, full disassembly of the top-end is necessary.

5 The crankcases are joined by ten 8 mm bolts on the upper crankcase half, eleven 8 mm bolts and eight 10 mm bolts on the lower crankcase half. Make a cardboard template of each crankcase half and punch a hole for each bolt location. This will ensure all bolts are installed correctly on reassembly – this is important, as many of them are of slightly differing length.

6 With the engine the correct way up unscrew the upper crankcase bolts evenly and a little at a time in the numerical sequence shown until they are finger-tight, then remove them (see illustration). **Note:** *As each bolt is*

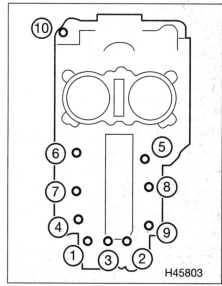

22.6 Upper crankcase bolt loosening sequence

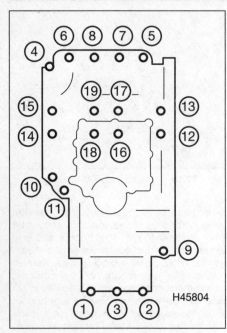

22.7 Lower crankcase bolt loosening sequence

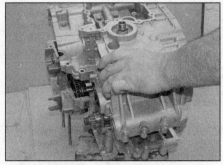

22.8 Carefully separate the crankcase halves

22.9 Remove the dowels (arrowed) if loose

removed, store it in its relative position in the cardboard template of the crankcase half.

7 Carefully turn the engine over. Unscrew the lower crankcase bolts evenly and a little at a time in the numerical sequence shown until they are finger-tight, then remove them **(see illustration)**. **Note:** *As each bolt is removed, store it in its relative position in the cardboard template of the crankcase half.*

8 Carefully lift the lower crankcase half off the upper half, using a soft-faced hammer to tap around the joint to initially separate the halves, if necessary **(see illustration)**. **Note:** *If the halves do not separate easily, make sure all fasteners have been removed. Do not try and separate the halves by levering against the crankcase mating surfaces as they are easily scored and will leak oil. Tap around the joint faces with a soft-faced mallet.* The transmission shafts, balancer shafts and crankshaft will remain in the upper crankcase

half. The selector drum and forks will come away with the lower half.

9 Remove the locating dowels from the crankcase (they could be in either half) **(see illustration)**.

10 Refer to Sections 25 to 30 for the removal and installation of the components housed within the crankcases, then refer to Section 23.

Reassembly

11 Remove all traces of sealant from the crankcase mating surfaces. Clean all the crankcase bolts.

12 Ensure that the crankshaft, connecting rods, balancer shafts, transmission shafts and all related bearings are correctly installed in the upper crankcase half, and the selector drum and forks and oil pressure relief valve are correctly installed in the lower

crankcase half. If the transmission shafts have not been removed, check the condition of the oil seal on the left-hand end of the output shaft and replace it with a new one if it is damaged, deformed or deteriorated – it is advisable to fit a new one whatever the condition of the old **(see illustrations 28.5b and c)**. Make sure that the transmission shafts and selector drum are in the neutral position.

13 Generously lubricate the crankshaft, balancer shaft gears, transmission shafts and selector drum and forks, particularly around the bearings and mated parts, with molybdenum disulphide oil (50% molybdenum grease and 50% engine oil). Wipe over the mating surfaces of both crankcase halves using a rag soaked in high flash-point solvent to remove all traces of oil.

14 Apply a small amount of suitable sealant (such as Three Bond 1216) to the mating surface of the lower crankcase half as shown **(see illustrations)**.

Caution: Do not apply an excessive amount of sealant as it will ooze out when the case halves are assembled and may obstruct oil passages. Do not apply the sealant on or too close (within 2 to 3 mm) to any of the bearing shells or surfaces.

15 If removed, fit the locating dowels into the crankcase **(see illustration 22.9)**. Check again that all components are in position, particularly that the bearing shells are still correctly located in the lower crankcase half.

16 Carefully fit the lower crankcase half onto the upper crankcase half, making sure the dowels locate correctly **(see illustration 22.8)**. Check that the lower crankcase half is correctly seated. **Note:** *The crankcase halves should fit together without being forced. If the casings are not correctly seated, remove the lower crankcase half and investigate the problem. Do not attempt to pull them together using the crankcase bolts as the casing will crack and be ruined.* Make sure the output shaft oil seal is correctly seated.

17 Insert all the lower crankcase bolts in their correct positions and tighten them finger-tight

22.14a Apply a suitable sealant . . .

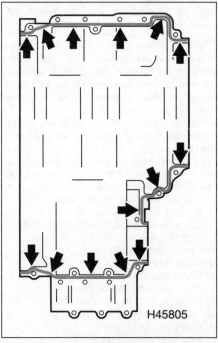

22.14b . . . to the shaded area of the lower crankcase half

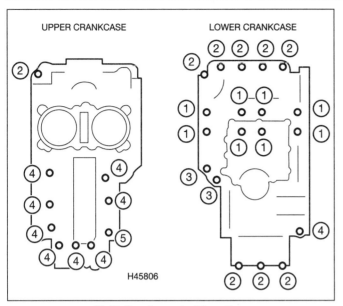

22.17 Crankcase bolt locations

1 M10 bolts
2 M8 x 35 mm bolts
3 M8 x 43 mm bolts
4 M8 x 80 mm bolts
5 M8 x 105 mm bolt

22.18 Crankcase bolt tightening sequence

(see illustration). Check the colour of the 10 mm bolts – they will be either silver or green; this information is important in order that the correct torque setting can be applied (see Specifications). Check also that the 8 mm bolts are in the correct positions because their lengths differ. Turn the engine over. Insert all the upper crankcase bolts in their correct positions and tighten them finger-tight. Turn the engine over.

18 Tighten the lower crankcase bolts in the correct numerical sequence to the initial torque setting specified at the beginning of the Chapter **(see illustration)**. Turn the engine over. Tighten the upper crankcase bolts in the correct numerical sequence to the initial torque setting specified at the beginning of the Chapter. Turn the engine over. Tighten the lower crankcase 10 mm bolts (numbered 1 to 8) in the correct numerical sequence to the final torque setting specified (according to colour) at the beginning of the Chapter. Now tighten the lower crankcase 8 mm bolts (numbered 9 to 19) in the correct numerical sequence to the final torque setting specified at the beginning of the Chapter. Turn the engine over. Tighten the upper crankcase bolts in the correct numerical sequence to the final torque setting specified at the beginning of the Chapter. Go round all the bolts once again in the correct sequence to their specified final torque.

19 With all crankcase fasteners tightened, check that the crankshaft, balancer shafts and transmission shafts rotate smoothly and easily. Check that the transmission shafts rotate freely and independently in neutral, then rotate the selector drum by hand and select each gear in turn whilst rotating the input shaft. Check that all gears can be selected and that the shafts

rotate freely in every gear. If there are any signs of undue stiffness, tight or rough spots, or of any other problem, the fault must be rectified before proceeding further.

20 Install all other removed assemblies in the reverse of the sequences given in Steps 2 to 4, according to your procedure.

23 Crankcase inspection and servicing

1 After the crankcases have been separated, remove the crankshaft and bearings, balancer shafts, transmission shafts, selector drum and forks, and any other components or assemblies not already removed, referring to the relevant Sections of this and other Chapters.

2 Clean the crankcases thoroughly with new solvent and dry them with compressed air. Blow out all oil passages and pipes with compressed air.

3 Remove all traces of old gasket sealant from the mating surfaces. Minor damage to the surfaces can be cleaned up with a fine sharpening stone or grindstone.

Caution: Be very careful not to nick or gouge the crankcase mating surfaces, or oil leaks will result. Check both crankcase halves very carefully for cracks and other damage.

4 Small cracks or holes in aluminium castings can be repaired with an epoxy resin adhesive as a temporary measure. Permanent repairs can be made by argon-arc welding, but this is a job for a specialist who will also be able to advise on the economy or practical aspect of such a repair. DIY low temperature welding kits, such as Lumiweld or Technoweld, are

also available for small repairs. If any damage is found that can't be repaired, renew the crankcase halves as a set.

5 Damaged threads can be economically reclaimed by using a diamond section wire insert, of the Heli-Coil type, which is easily fitted after drilling and re-tapping the affected thread.

6 Sheared studs or screws can be removed with stud or screw extractors, and they usually succeed in dislodging the most stubborn of them.

HAYNES HINT *Refer to Tools and Workshop Tips (Section 2) in the Reference section for details of installing a thread insert and using screw extractors.*

7 Install all components before reassembling the crankcase halves.

Oil pressure relief valve

8 Unscrew the valve from the lower crankcase half **(see illustration)**.

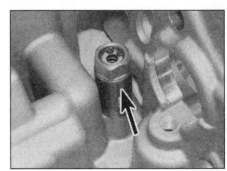

23.8 Oil pressure relief valve (arrowed)

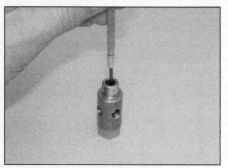

23.9 Check the action of the valve as described

23.10 Apply a threadlock to the valve threads

9 Check the plunger moves smoothly when pushed into the body and returns under spring pressure **(see illustration)**. If not, replace the valve with a new one.

10 Apply a thread locking compound to the valve threads, making sure none enters the valve itself **(see illustration)**. Thread the valve into the crankcase and tighten it to the torque setting specified at the beginning of the Chapter.

24 Crankshaft and connecting rod bearing information

1 Even though the crankshaft (main) and connecting rod (big-end) bearings are generally replaced with new ones during the engine overhaul, the old bearings should be retained for close examination as they may reveal valuable information about the condition of the engine.

2 Bearing failure occurs mainly because of lack of lubrication, the presence of dirt or other foreign particles, overloading the engine and/or corrosion. Regardless of the cause of bearing failure, it must be corrected before the engine is reassembled to prevent it from happening again.

3 When examining the main and connecting rod bearings keep them all in order to enable you to match any noted bearing problems with the corresponding crankshaft journal.

4 Dirt and other foreign particles get into the engine in a variety of ways. It may be left in the engine during assembly or it may pass through

25.3 Carefully lift the crankshaft out

filters or breathers. It may get into the oil and from there into the bearings. Metal chips from machining operations and normal engine wear are often present. Abrasives are sometimes left in engine components after reconditioning operations, especially when parts are not thoroughly cleaned using the proper cleaning methods. Whatever the source, these foreign objects often end up imbedded in the soft bearing material and are easily recognised. Large particles will not imbed in the bearing and will score or gouge the bearing and journal. The best prevention for this cause of bearing failure is to clean all parts thoroughly and keep everything spotlessly clean during engine reassembly. Frequent and regular oil and filter changes are also recommended.

5 Lack of lubrication or lubrication breakdown has a number of interrelated causes. Excessive heat (which thins the oil), overloading (which squeezes the oil from the bearing face) and oil leakage or throw off (from excessive bearing clearances, worn oil pump or high engine speeds) all contribute to lubrication breakdown. Blocked oil passages will also starve a bearing and destroy it. When lack of lubrication is the cause of bearing failure, the bearing material is wiped or extruded from the steel backing of the bearing. Temperatures may increase to the point where the steel backing and the journal turn blue from overheating.

HAYNES HiNT *Refer to Tools and Workshop Tips for bearing fault finding.*

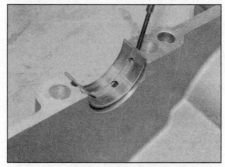

25.5 Remove the main bearing shells if required

6 Riding habits can have a definite effect on bearing life. Full throttle low speed operation, or labouring the engine, puts very high loads on bearings, which tend to squeeze out the oil film. These loads cause the bearings to flex, which produces fine cracks in the bearing face (fatigue failure). Eventually the bearing material will loosen in pieces and tear away from the steel backing. Short trip riding leads to corrosion of bearings, as insufficient engine heat is produced to drive off the condensed water and corrosive gases produced. These products collect in the engine oil, forming acid and sludge. As the oil is carried to the engine bearings, the acid attacks and corrodes the bearing material.

7 Incorrect bearing installation during engine assembly will lead to bearing failure as well. Tight fitting bearings that leave insufficient bearing oil clearances result in oil starvation. Dirt or foreign particles trapped behind a bearing insert result in high spots on the bearing that lead to failure.

8 To avoid bearing problems, clean all parts thoroughly before reassembly, double check all bearing clearance measurements and lubricate the new bearings with clean engine oil during installation.

25 Crankshaft and main bearings

Removal

1 Separate the crankcase halves (see Section 22). Remove the rear balancer shaft (see Section 27).

2 If the cylinder block and pistons have not been removed, separate the connecting rods from the crankshaft (see Section 26, Steps 3 and 4), then push the rods and pistons up the bores so they are clear. Do not pull the rods and pistons back down the bores – they cannot be removed this way.

3 Lift the crankshaft, connecting rods (if attached) and cam chain out of the upper crankcase half **(see illustration)**. If it appears stuck, tap it gently using a soft-faced mallet.

4 If required, remove the cam chain, and if attached separate the connecting rods from the crankshaft (see Section 26).

5 If required, remove the bearing shells from the crankcase halves by pushing their centres to the side, then lifting them out **(see illustration)**. Keep the shells in order.

Inspection

6 Clean the crankshaft with solvent, squirting through all the oil passages. If available, blow the crank dry with compressed air, and also blow through the oil passages.

7 Refer to Section 24 and examine the main bearings. If they are scored, badly scuffed or appear to have been seized, new bearing shells must be installed (see below). Always renew the shells as a set. If they are

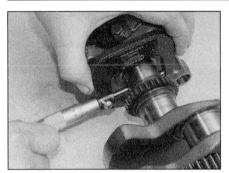

25.21a Measure the diameter of each journal . . .

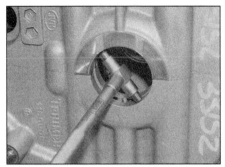

25.21b . . . and diameter of the journal housing

25.24 Make sure the tab locates in its notch (arrow)

badly damaged, check the corresponding crankshaft journal. Evidence of extreme heat, such as discoloration, indicates that lubrication failure has occurred. Be sure to thoroughly check the oil pumps and pressure relief valve as well as all oil holes and passages before reassembling the engine.

8 Inspect the crankshaft journals, paying particular attention where damaged bearings have been discovered. If the journals are scored or pitted in any way a new crankshaft will be required.

Oil clearance check

9 Whether new bearing shells are being fitted or the original ones are being re-used, the main bearing oil clearance should be checked before the engine is reassembled. Main bearing oil clearance is measured with a product known as Plastigauge.

10 If not already done, remove the bearing shells from the crankcase halves (see Step 5). Clean the backs of the shells and the bearing housings in both crankcase halves, and the main bearing journals on the crankshaft.

11 Press the bearing shells into their cut-outs, ensuring that the tab on each shell engages in the notch in the crankcase **(see illustration 25.24)**. Make sure the bearings are fitted in the correct locations and take care not to touch any shell's bearing surface with your fingers.

12 Ensure the shells and crankshaft are clean and dry. Lay the crankshaft in position in the upper crankcase **(see illustration 25.3)**.

13 Cut several lengths of the appropriate size Plastigauge (they should be slightly shorter than the width of the crankshaft journals). Place a strand of Plastigauge on each journal, making sure it will be clear of the oil holes in the shells when the lower crankcase is installed. Make sure the crankshaft is not rotated.

14 If removed, fit the dowels into the crankcase **(see illustration 22.9)**. Carefully fit the lower crankcase half onto the upper half, making sure the dowels locate correctly and the Plastigauge is not disturbed **(see illustration 22.8)**. Check that the lower crankcase half is correctly seated. **Note:** *Do not tighten the crankcase bolts if the casing is not correctly seated.*

15 Clean the threads of the 10 mm lower crankcase bolts (Nos. 1 to 8) **(see illustration 22.18a or b)**. Insert them in their original locations **(see illustration 22.17)**. Secure the bolts finger-tight at first, then tighten them evenly and a little at a time in the correct numerical sequence to the final torque setting specified (according to their colour code) at the beginning of the Chapter, making sure the crankshaft does not rotate. Go round the bolts once again to the same torque.

16 Now unscrew the bolts evenly and a little at a time in the correct numerical sequence until they are finger-tight, then remove them **(see illustration 22.7)**. **Note:** *As each bolt is removed store it in its relative position in the cardboard template of the lower crankcase half.* Carefully lift off the lower crankcase half, making sure the Plastigauge is not disturbed.

17 Compare the width of the crushed Plastigauge on each crankshaft journal to the scale printed on the Plastigauge envelope to obtain the main bearing oil clearance. Compare the reading to the specifications at the beginning of the Chapter.

18 On completion carefully scrape away all traces of the Plastigauge material from the crankshaft journal and bearing shells; use a fingernail or other object which is unlikely to score them.

19 If the oil clearance on all journals falls into the specified range, new bearing shells are not required (provided they are in good condition). If the clearance is beyond the service limit, refer to Steps 21 and 22 and select new bearing shells. Install the new shells and check the oil clearance once again (the new shells may bring bearing clearance within the specified range). Always replace all of the shells at the same time.

20 If the clearance is still greater than the service limit listed in this Chapter's

Specifications measure the diameter of the journal. If any journal is less than the service limit specified replace the crankshaft with a new one.

Main bearing shell selection

21 Replacement bearing shells for the main bearings are supplied on a selective fit basis. Measurements of the crankshaft journal diameters and the journal housing bore sizes need to be taken to identify the correct replacement bearings. Measure and note the diameter of each journal **(see illustration)**. With the crankshaft and the old shells removed assemble the crankcase halves and tighten the 10 mm bolts to the specified final torque setting according to their colour code (see Step 15). Using a bore gauge measure the diameter of each housing **(see illustration)**.

22 A range of bearing shells is available. Using the measurements for the each journal and its bore, select the colour of replacement shell required for each bearing according to the table below. The colour code is marked on the side of the shell **(see illustration 26.17)**.

Installation

23 If not already done, remove the bearing shells from the crankcase halves (see Step 5). Clean the backs of the shells and the bearing cut-outs in both crankcase halves, and the main bearing journals on the crankshaft. If new shells are being fitted, ensure that all traces of the protective grease are cleaned off using paraffin (kerosene). Wipe the shells and crankcase halves dry with a lint-free cloth. Make sure all the oil passages and holes are clear, and blow them through with compressed air if it is available.

24 Press the bearing shells into their locations. Make sure the tab on each shell

Journal housing diameter	Crankshaft journal diameter	
	37.960 to 37.968 mm	37.969 to 37.976 mm
41.104 to 41.112 mm	RED	WHITE
41.113 to 41.121 mm	BLUE	RED
41.122 to 41.130 mm	GREEN	BLUE

25.26 Make sure the punch marks on the drive and driven gears align as shown

26.2 Measure the connecting rod side clearance

26.3a The oil hole (arrowed) faces the back of the engine . . .

engages in the notch in the casing **(see illustration)**. Make sure the bearings are fitted in the correct locations and take care not to touch any shell's bearing surface with your fingers. Lubricate each shell with clean engine oil.

25 If removed from the engine, fit the connecting rods onto the crankshaft (see Section 26).

26 Fit the cam chain onto its sprocket **(see illustration 10.22)**. Turn the front balancer shaft as required so the punch mark on its gear is facing to the back of the engine. Locate the corresponding punch mark on the drive gear on the crankshaft and align it so it faces forwards. The punch marks are stamped into both the inner and outer face of each gear. Lower the crankshaft into position in the upper crankcase, feeding the cam chain and if installed the connecting rods into position, and making sure all bearings remain in place, and engaging it with the front balancer shaft gear so the punch marks align **(see illustration)**.

27 If detached and left in the engine, pull the connecting rods and pistons down the bores, then refer to Section 26, Steps 18 to 22, and fit the connecting rods onto the crankshaft.

28 Install the rear balancer shaft (see Section 27). Make sure all balancer shaft and crankshaft alignment marks are correctly positioned.

29 Check that the crankshaft rotates smoothly and freely. If there are any signs of roughness or tightness, detach the rods and recheck the assembly, and if that is good,

recheck the main bearing oil clearances (see above). Sometimes tapping the bottom of the connecting rod cap will relieve tightness.

30 Reassemble the crankcase halves (see Section 22).

26 Connecting rods

Note: *Two types of connecting rod are used, the first type is available in two size ranges and the cap is secured by bolts and nuts; this type is fitted to all engines up to No. 197182, eng nos. 253372 to 292625 and from 296931 onwards. The second type of connecting rod has a fracture-type joint with the cap and is secured by bolts; this type is fitted to eng nos. 197183 to 253371 and 292626 to 296930. If the rod caps are disturbed it is important to renew the nuts on the first type of rod and to renew the bolts on the second type (fracture) rod. Also follow the correct tightening sequence because it differs according to the rod type fitted.*

Removal

1 Remove the crankshaft (see Section 25).

2 Before removing the rods from the crankshaft, measure the side clearance between the rods and the crank web with a feeler gauge **(see illustration)**. If the clearance is greater than the service limit listed in this Chapter's Specifications, replace the rods with new ones.

3 Using paint or a felt marker pen, mark the

relevant cylinder identity on each connecting rod. Mark across the cap-to-connecting rod join to ensure that the cap is fitted the correct way around on reassembly. Note that the oil hole in each rod faces the back of the engine. There is a weight grade marked on one side of the rod and a size grade marked on one side of the cap – these marks should be on the same side when assembled **(see illustrations)**.

4 Turn the crankshaft so the connecting rod cap nuts or bolts are conveniently positioned. Unscrew the nuts or bolts and separate the connecting rod and cap from the crankpin – the bearing shells should come away with the rod and cap **(see illustrations)**. When the nuts or bolts are partially unscrewed tap their heads with a soft-faced hammer to separate the rod and cap if required. Keep the rod, cap, nuts/bolts and (if they are to be re-used) the bearing shells together in their correct positions to ensure correct installation. Note that on installation new nuts or bolts must be used according to connecting rod type, but the old ones can be used for checking the oil clearance.

Inspection

5 Check the connecting rods for cracks and other obvious damage.

6 Apply clean engine oil to the piston pin, insert it into the connecting rod small-end and check for any freeplay between the two. Measure the pin OD in the middle and the small-end bore ID and compare the measurements to the specifications at the

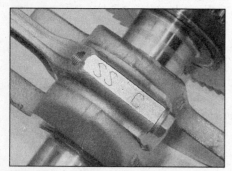

26.3b . . . and the size and weight grade marks must be on the same side

26.4a Unscrew the connecting rod big-end cap nuts or bolts (arrowed) . . .

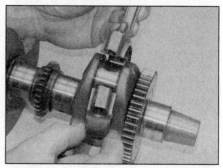

26.4b . . . and separate the rods from the shaft

26.6a Measure the external diameter of the pin . . .

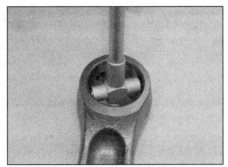

26.6b . . . and the internal diameter of the connecting rod small-end

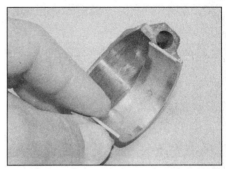

26.10 Remove the shells from the rod and cap

beginning of the Chapter (see illustrations). Replace components that are worn beyond the specified limits with new ones.

7 Refer to Section 24 and examine the connecting rod bearing shells. If they are scored, badly scuffed or appear to have seized, new shells must be installed. Always renew the shells in the connecting rods as a set. If they are badly damaged, check the corresponding crankpin. Evidence of extreme heat, such as discoloration, indicates that lubrication failure has occurred. Be sure to thoroughly check the oil pump and pressure relief valve as well as all oil holes and passages before reassembling the engine.

8 Have the rods checked for twist and bend by a Triumph dealer if you are in doubt about their straightness.

Oil clearance check

9 Whether new bearing shells are being fitted or the original ones are being re-used, check the connecting rod bearing oil clearance prior to reassembly. Check one rod at a time and make sure the rod does not turn on the crankshaft as this will distort the Plastigauge. If possible position or clamp the crankshaft and rod so they are stable and cannot move.

10 Remove the bearing shells from the connecting rod and cap (see illustration). Clean the backs of the shells and their

housing in the rod and cap. Clean the crankpins.

11 Press the bearing shells into place, making sure they are in their original position if checking the original shells, and ensuring that the tab on each shell engages the notch in the rod or cap (see illustration). Take care not to touch any shell's bearing surface with your fingers.

12 Fit the connecting rod onto the crankshaft. Cut a length of the Plastigauge (it should be slightly shorter than the width of the crankpin) and place it on the exposed part of the crankpin journal away from the oil holes. Fit the connecting rod cap. Make sure the rods and caps are fitted the correct way around so the previously made markings align (see Step 3), and tighten the bearing cap nuts or bolts as described in Step 20 or 21 according to connecting rod type whilst ensuring that the rod does not rotate. Now slacken the nuts or bolts and remove the connecting rod cap, again taking great care not to rotate the connecting rod.

13 Compare the width of the crushed Plastigauge at its widest point to the scale printed on the Plastigauge envelope to obtain the connecting rod bearing oil clearance.

14 If the oil clearance falls into the specified range, new bearing shells are not required (provided they are in good condition). If the

clearance is beyond the service limit, refer to Steps 16 and 17 and select new bearing shells. Install the new shells and check the oil clearance once again (the new shells may bring bearing clearance within the specified range). Always replace all of the shells at the same time. If the clearance is excessive, even with new shells, measure the diameter of the crankpin and compare it to the specifications (see illustration). If it is worn beyond the specified range, replace the crankshaft with a new one.

15 On completion carefully clean off all traces of the Plastigauge material from the crankpin and bearing shells.

Bearing shell selection

16 Replacement bearing shells for the connecting rods are supplied on a selective fit basis. Measurements of the crankpin journal diameters need to be taken, and on con-rods with nuts securing the caps, the size code letter (or big-end bore diameter measurement) will be required; this information is essential to identify the correct replacement bearings. On all models measure and note the diameter of each journal (see illustration 26.14). On con-rods with nuts securing the caps, identify the size code letter on the connecting rod cap (either an A or B); note that on later engines (from no. 520267 onwards) it is necessary

26.11 Fit the shell into its housing making sure the tab locates in the notch (arrowed)

26.14 Measure the diameter of the crankpin to see if it is worn

26.17 Shell colour code mark (arrowed)

to measure the connecting rod big-end bore inside diameter with the cap and rod assembled.

17 A range of bearing shells is available. Using the measurements for each crankpin, and on con-rods with nuts also the size code letter or big-end bore measurement, select the colour of replacement shell required for each journal according to the table above for your engine. The colour code is marked on the side of the shell **(see illustration)**.

Installation

18 Work on one rod at a time, and make sure it is installed the correct way round (see Step 3). Clean the backs of the shells and their housing in the rod and cap. If new shells are being fitted, ensure that all traces of any protective grease are cleaned off using paraffin (kerosene). Wipe the shells, cap and rod dry with a clean lint free cloth. Fit the bearing shells in the connecting rod and cap,

Connecting rods with nuts and bolts – up to engine no. 197182, 253372 to 292625, 296931 to 520266

	Crankpin journal diameter	
Connecting rod code	40.946 to 40.953 mm	40.954 to 40.960 mm
A	RED	WHITE
B	BLUE	RED

Connecting rods with nuts and bolts – from engine no. 520267

	Crankpin journal diameter	
Connecting rod big-end ID	40.968 to 40.975 mm	40.976 to 40.982 mm
44.000 to 44.009 mm	RED	WHITE
44.010 to 44.018 mm	BLUE	RED

Connecting rods with bolts only – engine nos. 197183 to 253371 and 292626 to 296930

Crankpin journal diameter	
40.946 to 40.953 mm	40.954 to 40.960 mm
RED	WHITE

making sure the tab on each shell engages the notch **(see illustration 26.11)**.

19 Lubricate each shell's bearing surface with molybdenum disulphide oil (a 50/50 mixture of molybdenum disulphide grease and clean engine oil). Fit the connecting rod onto the crankpin so that its oil hole will face the back of the engine **(see illustration 26.3a)**. Fit the connecting rod cap, making sure it is the correct way round and that it seats cleanly against the rod **(see illustration 26.4b)** – the caps are sheared off and so have a very close fit. Check to make sure that all components

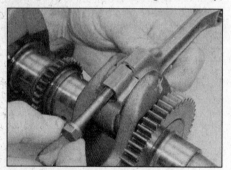

26.21a Fit the bolts and tighten them as described . . .

26.21c . . . and then through the specified angle

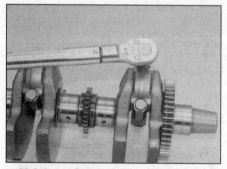

26.21b . . . first to the specified torque setting . . .

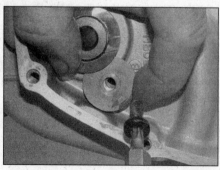

27.2a Undo the screw and remove the retainer . . .

have been returned to their original locations using the marks made on disassembly.

20 On engines with nuts to secure the connecting rod caps, apply molybdenum disulphide grease under the heads and to the threads of the **new** nuts. Fit the nuts and tighten them in five stages as follows: tighten each nut in one go to the first stage torque setting specified at the beginning of the Chapter; **slacken** each nut through 140°; tighten each nut in one go to the third stage torque setting; tighten each nut in one go to the fourth stage torque setting; tighten each nut in one go through 120° using a degree disc **(see illustration 26.21c)**.

21 On engines with bolts to secure the connecting rod caps, apply molybdenum disulphide grease under the heads and to the threads of the **new** bolts. Fit the bolts and tighten them in two stages as follows: tighten each bolt in one go to the first stage torque setting specified at the beginning of the Chapter; tighten each bolt in one go through 120° using a degree disc **(see illustrations)**.

22 Check that the rod rotates smoothly and freely on the crankpin. If there are any signs of roughness or tightness, remove the rod and investigate the cause. Note that you will again need new nuts or bolts according to rod type.

23 Install the crankshaft (see Section 25).

27 Balancer shafts

Removal

1 Separate the crankcase halves (see Section 22).

2 Undo the screw and remove the front balancer shaft retainer, noting how it locates **(see illustration)**. Hold the balancer and withdraw the shaft, then lift the balancer out of the crankcase (see illustration).

3 On engines from number 139643, if the pick-up coil has not been removed free its wiring from the guide, noting how the guide also acts as the rear balancer shaft retainer plate (see illustration). On engines up to number 139642 the retainer is a disc the same as for the front balancer (see illustration 27.2a). Undo the screw and remove the rear balancer shaft retainer, noting how it locates. Hold the balancer and withdraw the shaft, then lift the balancer out of the crankcase (see illustration).

Inspection

4 Check the gear on each shaft and the drive gear on the crankshaft for worn or chipped teeth and replace the shafts with new ones if necessary.

5 Check the condition of the needle bearings in the end of each balancer and replace them with new ones if necessary (see illustration). Also check the section of the shaft they run on for wear. Refer to *Tools and Workshop Tips* in the Reference Section for details on needle bearing checks and removal and installation methods.

Installation

6 The shafts are not interchangeable – make sure you install them correctly. Identify each shaft according to the letter marked on one of its weights – the shaft marked F is the front and the one marked R is the rear (see illustrations). Apply molybdenum disulphide oil (a mixture of 50% molybdenum disulphide grease and 50% engine oil) to the bearings. If only one shaft has been removed make sure the other is correctly timed with the crankshaft as described in the following Steps before installing the shaft.

7 To install the rear balancer, turn the crankshaft as required so the balancer timing punch mark on the drive gear is facing the back of the engine. Locate the corresponding punch mark on the driven gear on the rear balancer and align it so it faces forwards. The punch marks are stamped into both the inner and outer face of each gear. Lower the balancer into position in the upper crankcase, engaging it with the drive gear on the crankshaft so the punch marks align (see illustration), then slide the shaft in, aligning the slot in the shaft end for the retainer

27.2b ... then withdraw the shaft and remove the balancer

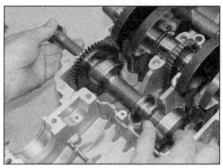

27.3b ... then withdraw the shaft and remove the balancer

with the retainer screw hole (see illustration 27.3a). Clean the threads of the retainer screw and apply a suitable thread locking compound. Fit the retainer, locating its rim in the slot, and tighten the screw to the torque setting specified at the beginning of the Chapter (see illustration 27.3b). On engines from number 139643, if the pick-up coil has not been removed feed the wiring round its guide.

8 To install the front balancer, turn the crankshaft as required so the balancer timing punch mark on the drive gear is facing the front of the engine. Locate the corresponding punch mark on the driven gear on the front balancer and align it so it faces backwards. The punch marks are stamped into both the inner and outer face of each gear. Lower the balancer into position in the upper crankcase, engaging it with the drive gear on the crankshaft so the punch marks align (see illustration 27.7), then slide the shaft in, aligning the slot in the shaft

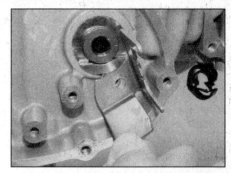

27.3a Undo the screw and remove the retainer ...

27.5 Check the bearings (arrowed) in each balancer

end for the retainer with the retainer screw hole (see illustration 27.3b). Clean the threads of the retainer screw and apply a suitable thread locking compound. Fit the retainer, locating its rim in the slot, and tighten the screw to the torque setting specified at the beginning of the Chapter (see illustration 27.3a).

9 Reassemble the crankcase halves (see Section 22).

28 Transmission shaft removal and installation

Note: *To access the transmission shafts the engine must be removed from the frame and the crankcases separated. References to the right- and left-hand ends of the transmission shafts are made as though the engine is the correct way up.*

27.6a The front balancer is marked with an F

27.6b The rear balancer is marked with an R

27.7 Make sure the punch mark on the drive gear on the crankshaft aligns with the driven gear on the balancer as shown

28.2 Remove the input shaft. . .

28.3 . . . then the output shaft

28.5a Locate the retainer against the bearing

Removal

1 Separate the crankcase halves (Section 22).
2 Lift the input shaft out of the upper crankcase half, noting how it locates and engages with the output shaft **(see illustration)**. Remove the half-ring bearing retainer from either the crankcase or the bearing itself on the left-hand end of the shaft **(see illustration 28.6a)**.
3 Lift the output shaft out of the upper crankcase half, noting how it locates **(see illustration)**. Remove the oil seal from the right-hand end of the shaft, then remove the bearing retainer **(see illustrations 28.5a and c)**.
4 If necessary, disassemble the transmission shafts and inspect them for wear or damage, and check the bearings (see Section 29).

Installation

5 Fit the bearing retainer onto the right-hand end of the output shaft **(see illustration)**. Smear clean engine oil onto the lips of a new

oil seal and slide it onto the shaft end **(see illustrations)**. Make sure the needle bearing sleeve on the left-hand end of the shaft is fitted with its chamfered edge outermost **(see illustration 29.34b)**. Lay the shaft in the upper crankcase, making sure the locating the pin on the needle bearing sleeve fits into its hole and the retainer on the right-hand end locates in its slot **(see illustrations)**.
6 Fit the input shaft bearing half-ring retainer into its slot in the crankcase **(see illustration)**. Make sure the needle bearing sleeve on the right-hand end of the shaft is fitted with its chamfered edge outermost **(see illustration 29.19b)**. Lay the input shaft in the upper crankcase, engaging its gears with those on the output shaft, and making sure the locating the pin on the needle bearing sleeve fits into its hole and the groove in the bearing on the left-hand end engages correctly with the half-ring retainer **(see illustration and 28.2)**.

7 Make sure both transmission shafts are correctly seated and their related pinions are correctly engaged.
Caution: If the retainers are not correctly engaged, the crankcase halves will not seat correctly.
8 Position the gears in the neutral position and check the shafts are free to rotate easily and independently (i.e. the input shaft can turn whilst the output shaft is held stationary) before proceeding further.
9 Join the crankcase halves (Section 22).

29 Transmission shaft disassembly, inspection and reassembly

Note: *References to the right- and left-hand ends of the transmission shafts are made as though they are installed in the engine and the engine is the correct way up.*

28.5b Lubricate the oil seal . . .

28.5c . . . then slide it onto the shaft

28.5d Locate the pin in its hole . . .

28.5e . . . and the retainer in its slot (arrowed)

28.6a Fit the retainer into its slot

28.6b Locate the pin in its hole

HAYNES HiNT *When disassembling the transmission shafts, place the parts on a long rod or thread a wire through them to keep them in order and facing the proper direction.*

1 Remove the transmission shafts from the crankcase (see Section 28). Always disassemble the transmission shafts separately to avoid mixing up the components **(see illustrations)**.

Input shaft disassembly

2 Remove the needle bearing sleeve from the right-hand end of the shaft **(see illustration 29.19c)**. Remove the bearing retaining ring, then slide the bearing off the shaft **(see illustrations 29.19b and a)**.
3 Slide the thrust washer and the 2nd gear pinion off the shaft **(see illustrations 29.18b and a)**.
4 Remove the circlip securing the 5th gear pinion, then slide the splined washer, the pinion and its splined bush, and the splined washer off the shaft **(see illustrations 29.17e, d, c, b and a)**.
5 Remove the circlip securing the combined 3rd/4th gear pinion, then slide the pinion off the shaft **(see illustrations 29.16b and a)**.

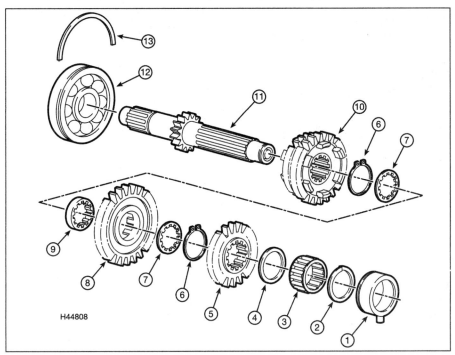

H44808

29.1a Transmission input shaft components

1 Needle bearing sleeve	6 Circlip	11 Input shaft/1st gear pinion
2 Retaining ring	7 Splined washer	12 Ball bearing
3 Needle bearing	8 5th gear pinion	13 Bearing retainer
4 Thrust washer	9 Splined bush	
5 2nd gear pinion	10 3rd/4th gear pinion	

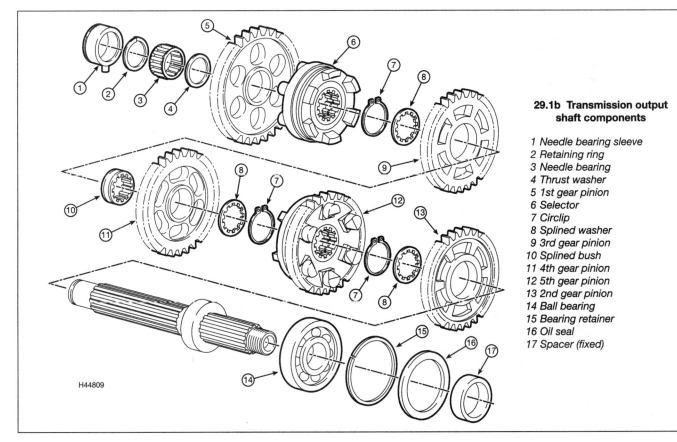

H44809

29.1b Transmission output shaft components

1 Needle bearing sleeve
2 Retaining ring
3 Needle bearing
4 Thrust washer
5 1st gear pinion
6 Selector
7 Circlip
8 Splined washer
9 3rd gear pinion
10 Splined bush
11 4th gear pinion
12 5th gear pinion
13 2nd gear pinion
14 Ball bearing
15 Bearing retainer
16 Oil seal
17 Spacer (fixed)

29.6 The 1st gear pinion (arrowed) is part of the shaft

29.11 Where fitted check the bush (arrowed) in the pinion for wear

6 The 1st gear pinion is integral with the shaft **(see illustration)**.

Input shaft inspection

7 Wash all of the components in clean solvent and dry them off.
8 Check the gear teeth for cracking chipping, pitting and other obvious wear or damage. Any pinion that is damaged as such must be replaced with a new one.
9 Inspect the dogs and the dog holes in the gears for cracks, chips, and excessive wear especially in the form of rounded edges. Make sure mating gears engage properly. Replace paired gears as a set if necessary.
10 Check for signs of scoring or bluing on the pinions and shaft. This could be caused by overheating due to inadequate lubrication. Check that all the oil holes and passages are clear. Replace any damaged pinions with new ones.
11 Check that each pinion moves freely on the shaft or its bush but without undue

freeplay. If a pinion is fitted with a bush **(see illustration)**, check it for wear – if the oil retaining holes are shallow or barely visible a new pinion must be fitted.
12 The shaft is unlikely to sustain damage unless the engine has seized, placing an unusually high loading on the transmission, or the machine has covered a very high mileage. Check the surface of the shaft, especially where a pinion turns on it, and replace it with a new one if it has scored or picked up, or if there are any cracks.
13 Check that the transmission shaft bearings rotate freely and smoothly and the ball bearings are tight on the shaft. Remove the old bearings and fit new ones if necessary. A press is needed to remove the ball bearings – see *Tools and Workshop Tips* in the Reference Section.
14 Discard all the circlips as new ones must be used.

Input shaft reassembly

15 During reassembly, apply molybdenum

disulphide oil (a 50/50 mixture of molybdenum disulphide grease and clean engine oil) to the mating surfaces of the shaft, pinions and bushes. When installing the circlips, do not expand the ends any further than is necessary and locate them as shown, i.e. against a spline wall, not in the spline trenches. Install the stamped circlips so that their chamfered side faces the pinion it secures, i.e. so that its sharp edge faces the direction of thrust load (see *correct fitting of a stamped circlip* illustration in Tools and Workshop Tips of the Reference section).
16 Slide the combined 3rd/4th gear pinion onto the shaft, so that the smaller (3rd gear) pinion faces the 1st gear pinion, and making sure the oil hole in the groove does not align with those on the shaft **(see illustration)**. Fit the circlip, making sure that it locates correctly in its groove **(see illustration)**.
17 Slide the splined washer onto the shaft

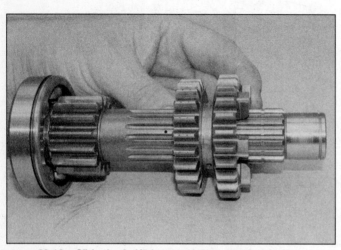

29.16a Slide the 3rd/4th gear pinion onto the shaft . . .

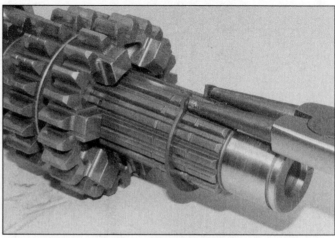

29.16b . . . then fit the circlip

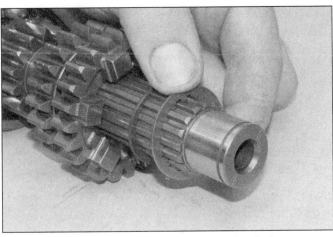

29.17a Slide the splined washer onto the shaft . . .

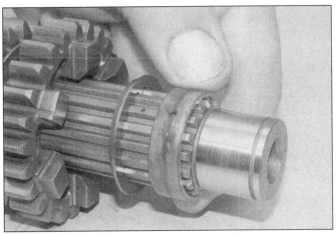

29.17b . . . followed by the bush . . .

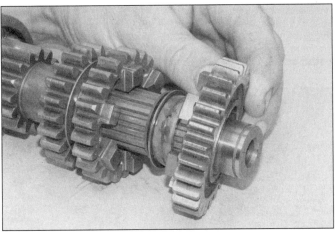

29.17c . . . then fit the 5th gear pinion onto the bush

29.17d Slide the splined washer onto the shaft . . .

(see illustration). Slide the 5th gear pinion splined bush onto the shaft, aligning the oil hole in the bush with that in the shaft, then slide the pinion onto the bush, with its dogs facing the 4th gear pinion (see illustrations). Slide the splined washer onto the shaft then fit the circlip, making sure that it locates correctly in its groove (see illustrations).

29.17e . . . then fit the circlip . . .

29.17f . . . locating it in its groove

29.18a Slide the 2nd gear pinion onto the shaft . . .

29.18b . . . followed by the thrust washer

18 Slide the 2nd gear pinion onto the shaft with its lipped side facing out, then slide the thrust washer on **(see illustrations)**.
19 Slide the needle bearing onto the end of the shaft and secure it with the retaining ring, making sure it locates in its groove **(see illustrations)**. Fit the sleeve over the bearing with its chamfered end outermost **(see illustration)**.
20 Check that all components have been correctly installed **(see illustration)**.

Output shaft disassembly

21 Remove the needle bearing sleeve from the left-hand end of the shaft. Remove the bearing retaining ring, then slide the bearing off the shaft.

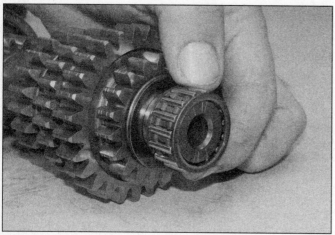

29.19a Slide the needle bearing on . . .

29.19b . . . and secure it with the retaining ring

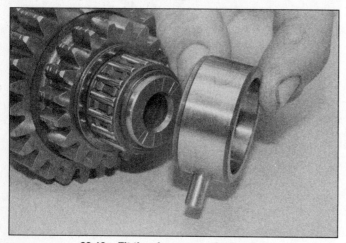

29.19c Fit the sleeve over the bearing

29.20 The assembled input shaft should look like this

29.28a Slide the 2nd gear pinion onto the shaft . . .

29.28b . . . followed by the splined washer . . .

22 Remove the thrust washer then slide the 1st gear pinion and the selector wheel off the shaft **(see illustrations 29.33b and a and 29.32).**

23 Remove the circlip securing the 3rd gear pinion, then slide the splined washer, the 3rd gear pinion, the 4th gear pinion, their splined bush, and the splined washer off the shaft **(see illustrations 29.31b and a and 29.30d, c, b and a).**

24 Remove the circlip securing the 5th gear pinion, then slide the pinion off the shaft **(see illustrations 29.29b and a).**

25 Remove the circlip securing the 2nd gear pinion, then slide the splined washer and the pinion off the shaft **(see illustrations 29.28c, b and a).**

Output shaft inspection

26 Refer to Steps 7 to 14 above.

Output shaft reassembly

27 During reassembly, apply molybdenum disulphide oil (a 50/50 mixture of molybdenum disulphide grease and clean engine oil) to the mating surfaces of the shaft, pinions and bushes. When installing the circlips, do not expand the ends any further than is necessary

and locate them as shown, i.e. against a spline wall, not in the spline trenches. Install the stamped circlips so that their chamfered side faces the pinion it secures, i.e. so that its sharp edge faces the direction of thrust load (see *correct fitting of a stamped circlip* illustration in Tools and Workshop Tips of the Reference section). Use new needle bearings and do not expand their ends any more than necessary when installing them.

28 Slide the 2nd gear pinion onto the shaft with its recessed side facing away from the bearing **(see illustration)**. Slide the splined washer onto the shaft **(see illustration)**.

Secure them in place with the circlip, making sure it is properly seated in its groove **(see illustrations)**.

29 Slide the 5th gear pinion onto the shaft with its selector fork groove facing away from the 2nd gear pinion, aligning it so the oil hole in the groove does **not** align with those in the shaft **(see illustration)**. Secure it in place with the circlip, making sure it is properly seated in its groove **(see illustrations)**.

30 Slide the splined washer onto the shaft, followed by the 4th and 3rd gear pinion bush, aligning the oil holes in the bush with

29.28c . . . then fit the circlip . . .

29.28d . . . locating it in its groove

29.29a Slide the 5th gear pinion onto the shaft . . .

29.29b . . . then fit the circlip . . .

29.29c . . . locating it in its groove

29.30a Slide the splined washer onto the shaft . . .

29.30b . . . then fit the bush

29.30c Slide the 4th gear pinion onto the bush . . .

29.30d . . . followed by the 3rd gear pinion

those on the shaft, **(see illustrations)**. Slide the 4th gear pinion onto the bush with its recessed side facing the 5th gear pinion **(see illustration)**. Slide the 3rd gear pinion onto the bush with its raised centre section facing the similar section on the 4th gear pinion **(see illustration)**.

31 Slide the splined washer onto the shaft, then fit the circlip, making sure it is properly seated in its groove **(see illustrations)**.

32 Slide the selector wheel onto the shaft with its groove facing the 3rd gear pinion,

29.31a Slide the splined washer onto the shaft . . .

29.31b . . . then fit the circlip . . .

29.31c . . . locating it in its groove

29.32 Slide the selector onto the shaft

29.33a Slide the 1st gear pinion onto the shaft . . .

29.33b . . . then fit the thrust washer

and aligning it so the oil hole in the groove does not align with that in the shaft (see illustration).

33 Slide the 1st gear pinion onto the shaft with its recessed side facing in (see illustration). Slide the thrust washer against the 1st gear pinion (see illustration).

34 Slide the needle bearing onto the end of the shaft and secure it with the retaining ring, making sure it locates in its groove (see illustrations). Fit the sleeve over the bearing with its chamfered end outermost (see illustration).

35 Check that all components have been correctly installed (see illustration).

29.34a Slide the needle bearing on . . .

29.34b . . . and secure it with the retaining ring

30 Selector drum and forks

Note: *To access the selector drum and forks the engine must be removed from the frame and the crankcases separated.*

Removal

1 Separate the crankcase halves (Section 22). Remove the neutral switch (see Chapter 8) if not already done.

2 On engine up to number 128236 the selector forks are numbered 1 to 3 from left to right with the numbers facing the right-hand side for identification – if the numbers are not clearly visible mark them yourself before removal using a felt pen according to where they fit and which way round. On all later engines the forks are not marked in the same way, so mark them yourself before removal using a felt pen according to where they fit and which way round. On the model photographed we found that the manufacturing marks were usable for identification – the forks were marked 00, 01 and 02 from right to left with the marks facing the left-hand side – you can check

29.34c Fit the sleeve over the bearing

29.35 The assembled output shaft should look like this

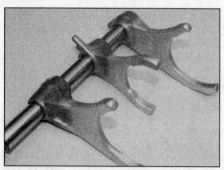

30.2 Check for existing usable identification markings or make some of your own

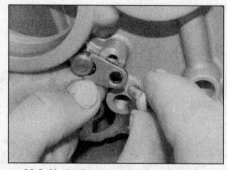

30.3 Undo the screw and remove the retainer

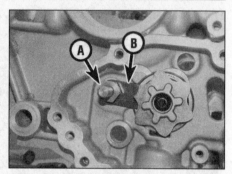

30.4a Unscrew the pin (A) and remove the retainer (B)

30.4b Counter-hold the drum and unscrew the bolt

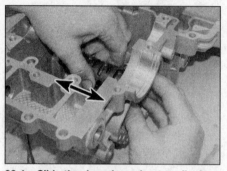

30.4c Slide the drum in and out to displace the cam plate and bearing

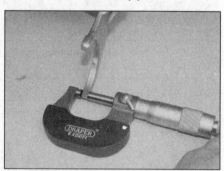

30.6a Measure the fork end thickness . . .

for such marks on your forks and note them accordingly **(see illustration)**.

3 Undo the selector fork shaft retainer screw and remove the retainer **(see illustration)**. Withdraw the shaft and remove the forks as they are released, noting how they locate in the selector drum tracks **(see illustrations 30.13c, b and a)**. Once removed, slide the forks back onto the shaft in their correct order and way round **(see illustration 30.2)**.

4 Unscrew the gearchange shaft centralising spring pin and remove the selector drum retainer **(see illustration)**. Counter-hold the drum using a screwdriver or rod passed through its centre and unscrew the cam plate bolt **(see illustration)**. Slide the drum back and forth in the crankcase until the cam plate

and bearing are displaced, then remove the drum **(see illustration)**.

Inspection

5 Inspect the selector forks for any signs of wear or damage, especially around the fork ends where they engage with the groove in the gear pinion. Check closely to see if the forks are bent. If the forks are in any way damaged they must be replaced with new ones.

6 Measure the thickness of the fork ends and the width of the groove and compare the readings to the specifications **(see illustrations)**. Replace whichever components that are worn beyond their specifications with new ones.

7 Check that the forks fit correctly on their

shaft. They should move freely with a light fit but no appreciable freeplay. Replace the forks and/or shafts with new ones if they are worn. Check that the fork shaft holes in the casing are neither worn nor damaged.

8 Check the selector fork shaft is straight by rolling it along a flat surface, or check for runout using V-blocks and a dial gauge. A bent shaft will cause difficulty in selecting gears and make the gearchange action heavy. Replace the shaft with a new one if bent.

9 Inspect the selector drum grooves and selector fork guide pins for signs of wear or damage and replace them with new ones if necessary **(see illustration)**.

10 Check that the selector drum bearing rotates freely and smoothly **(see illustration)**.

30.6b . . . and the width of its groove

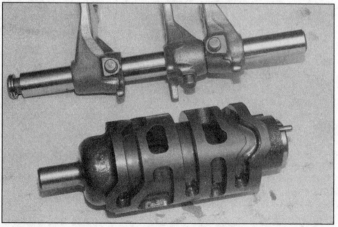

30.9 Check the grooves in the drum and the pins on the forks

30.10 Check the bearing

30.11a Fit the drum into the crankcase . . .

30.11b . . . then fit the cam plate with the bearing, locating the cut-out over the pin

30.11c Secure the plate with its bolt

30.12 Locate the retainer and tighten the pin to the specified torque

30.13a Slide the shaft in and fit the left-hand fork . . .

Remove the old bearing and fit a new one if necessary (see *Tools and Workshop Tips* in the Reference Section). Check the drum shaft end and its bush in the crankcase for wear.

Installation

11 Position the selector drum in the crankcase aligning the neutral switch contact with the switch hole in the crankcase **(see illustration)**. Fit the bearing and cam plate, locating the pin in the drum end in the cut-out in the back of the plate **(see illustration)**. Clean the threads of the cam plate bolt and apply a suitable thread locking compound, then tighten it to the torque setting specified at the beginning of the Chapter, counter-holding the drum as on removal **(see illustration)**.

12 Clean the threads of the centralising spring pin and apply a suitable thread locking compound. Locate the drum retainer and tighten the pin to the specified torque setting **(see illustration)**.

13 Apply molybdenum disulphide oil (a 50/50 mixture of molybdenum disulphide grease and clean engine oil) to the selector fork shaft. Slide the shaft into the crankcase with its slotted end outermost, and fit the forks as you do, locating their guide pins in the selector drum tracks **(see illustrations)**. Make sure you have the forks correctly positioned according to their marks or ones you have made yourself on removal – see Step 2. The forks are all different and not interchangeable.

14 Clean the threads of the shaft retainer

screw and apply a suitable thread locking compound. Locate the retainer in the groove in the shaft end and tighten the screw to the specified torque setting **(see illustration 30.3)**.

15 Install the neutral switch (see Chapter 8). Reassemble the crankcase halves (see Section 22).

31 Running-in procedure

1 Make sure the engine oil level is correct (see *Pre-ride checks*). Make sure there is fuel in the tank.

2 Start the engine in the normal way – set the

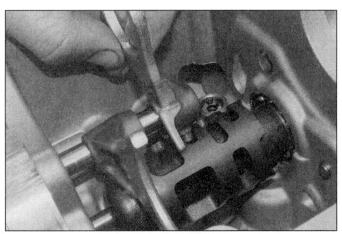

30.13b . . . the centre fork . . .

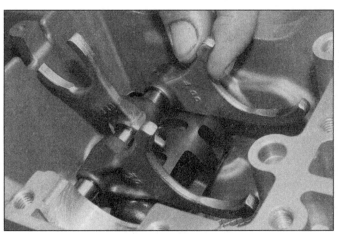

30.13c . . . and the right-hand fork as you do

choke enough to encourage the bike to start, but not so much as to allow it to race. Allow the engine to run at a moderately fast idle until it reaches operating temperature. Check carefully that there are no oil leaks.

 Warning: If the oil pressure warning light doesn't go off, or it comes on while the engine is running, stop the engine immediately.

3 Check the engine oil level. Also check carburettor synchronisation (where applicable) and idle speed (see Chapter 1).

4 Make sure the transmission and controls, especially the brakes, function properly before road testing the machine.

5 If a lubrication failure is suspected, stop the engine immediately and try to find the cause. If an engine is run without oil, even for a short period of time, severe damage will occur.

6 Treat the machine gently for the first few miles to make sure oil has circulated throughout the engine and any new parts installed have started to seat.

7 Even greater care is necessary if new main and big-end bearings have been fitted. This means greater use of the transmission and a restraining hand on the throttle until at least 500 miles (800 km) have been covered. There's no point in keeping to any set speed limit – the main idea is to keep from labouring the engine and to gradually increase performance up to the 500 mile (800 km) mark. These recommendations can be lessened to an extent according to what new parts have been fitted. Experience is the best guide, since it's easy to tell when an engine is running freely. The following maximum engine speed limitations, which Triumph provide for new motorcycles, which can be used as a guide.

8 Upon completion of the road test, and after the engine has cooled down completely, recheck the valve clearances (see Chapter 1) and check the engine oil level (see *Pre-ride checks*).

Up to 500 miles (800 km)	Do not use full throttle. Do not exceed 75% of maximum engine speed. Vary throttle position/engine speed. Do not labour the engine – use a lower gear
500 to 1000 miles (800 to 1500 km)	Vary throttle position/speed. Use full throttle for short bursts only
Over 1000 miles (1500 km)	Do not exceed tachometer red line

Chapter 3A
Fuel and exhaust systems – carburettor models

Contents

Degrees of difficulty

| **Easy,** suitable for novice with little experience | | **Fairly easy,** suitable for beginner with some experience | | **Fairly difficult,** suitable for competent DIY mechanic | | **Difficult,** suitable for experienced DIY mechanic | | **Very difficult,** suitable for expert DIY or professional | |

Specifications

Fuel

Grade
  European models . . . . Unleaded, minimum 95 RON (Research Octane Number)
  US and Canadian models. . . . . Unleaded, minimum 89 (CLC or AKI (R+M) /2 method)
Fuel tank capacity
  Bonneville and T100
    Total (inc. reserve)
      2001 to 2004 models . . . . 16.0 litres
      2005-on models . . . . 16.6 litres
    Reserve. . . . . 3.0 litres
  America and Speedmaster
    Total (inc. reserve). . . . . 16.6 litres
    Reserve. . . . . 3.5 litres
  Thruxton
    Total (inc. reserve)
      2004 to 2005. . . . . 16.0 litres
      2006-on. . . . . 16.6 litres
    Reserve – all years . . . . 3.0 litres
  Scrambler
    Total (inc. reserve). . . . . 16.6 litres
    Reserve. . . . . 3.0 litres

Carburettors

Type	2 x Keihin CVK 36
Fuel level	1.0 to 3.0 mm above float chamber mating surface
Float height.	16.0 to 18.0 mm
Idle speed.	see Chapter 1
Pilot screw base setting (no. of turns out)	
Bonneville, T100 and Thruxton.	2.5
America and Scrambler	1.5
Speedmaster	2.0
Main jet	
Bonneville, T100 and Thruxton	110
America, Speedmaster and Scrambler	120
Main air jet	
Bonneville, T100 and Thruxton	80
America and 790 cc Speedmaster	80
865 cc Speedmaster and Scrambler	100
Needle	
Bonneville and 790 cc T100	NAGB
865 cc T100 and Thruxton	NBZT
America and 790 cc Speedmaster	NBAD
865 cc Speedmaster	NBZY
Scrambler	N3RL
Pilot jet	
America and 790 cc Speedmaster.	42
All other models	40
Starter jet	
790 cc engines	52
865 cc engines	55

Torque wrench settings

Cylinder head intake adapters	12 Nm
Exhaust system – Bonneville, T100 and Thruxton	
Downpipe flange nuts.	19 Nm
Downpipe rear bolts.	22 Nm
Front sprocket cover bolts	9 Nm
Joint pipe clamp bolt	22 Nm
Passenger footrest holder nut/silencer mount	27 Nm
Rider's footrest bracket mounting bolts.	27 Nm
Rider's footrest bracket clamp bolt	45 Nm
Silencer clamp bolt.	22 Nm
Exhaust system – America and Speedmaster	
Downpipe flange nuts.	19 Nm
Downpipe rear bolts.	15 Nm
Joint pipe clamp bolt	22 Nm
Passenger footrest plate bolts/silencer mount.	27 Nm
Silencer clamp bolt.	22 Nm
Exhaust system – Scrambler	
Exhaust pipe flange nuts	19 Nm
Exhaust pipe assembly mounting bolt	19 Nm
Exhaust pipe and silencer clamp bolts.	10 Nm
Silencer to bracket bolts.	15 Nm
Silencer bracket bolt.	15 Nm
Fuel tank mounting bolt(s)	
Bonneville, T100, Thruxton and Scrambler	9 Nm
America and Speedmaster.	19 Nm
Throttle cable housing/master cylinder clamp bolts	12 Nm

---

1 General information and precautions

General information

The fuel system consists of the fuel tank, the fuel tap with integral strainer, fuel hoses, carburettors and control cables.

The carburettors used are CV types. There is a carburettor for each cylinder. For cold starting, a choke knob is mounted on the left-hand side of the carburettor assembly.

Air is drawn into the carburettors via an air filter, which is housed under the seat.

The exhaust is a two-into-two design. A secondary air induction system (SAIS) reduces harmful emissions.

Many of the fuel system service procedures are considered routine maintenance items and for that reason are included in Chapter 1.

Precautions

 Warning: Petrol (gasoline) is extremely flammable, so take extra precautions when you work on any part of the fuel system. Don't smoke or allow open flames or bare light bulbs near the work area, and don't work in a garage where a natural gas-type appliance is present. If you spill any fuel on your skin, rinse it off immediately with

soap and water. When you perform any kind of work on the fuel system, wear safety glasses and have a fire extinguisher suitable for a class B type fire (flammable liquids) on hand.

Always perform service procedures in a well-ventilated area to prevent a build-up of fumes.

Never work in a building containing a gas appliance with a pilot light, or any other form of naked flame. Ensure that there are no naked light bulbs or any sources of flame or sparks nearby.

Do not smoke (or allow anyone else to smoke) while in the vicinity of petrol (gasoline), or of components containing petrol. Remember the possible presence of vapour from these sources and move well clear before smoking.

Check all electrical equipment belonging to the house, garage or workshop where work is being undertaken (see the *Safety First!* section of this manual). Remember that certain electrical appliances such as drills, cutters etc. create sparks in the normal course of operation and must not be used near petrol (gasoline) or any component containing it. Again, remember the possible presence of fumes before using electrical equipment.

Always mop up any spilt fuel and safely dispose of the rag used.

Any stored fuel that is drained off during servicing work must be kept in sealed containers that are suitable for holding petrol (gasoline), and clearly marked as such; the containers themselves should be kept in a safe place. Note that this last point applies equally to the fuel tank if it is removed from the machine; also remember to keep its filler cap closed at all times.

Read the *Safety first!* section of this manual carefully before starting work.

2 Fuel tank and fuel tap

⚠️ **Warning: Refer to the precautions given in Section 1 before starting work.**

Fuel tank

Removal

1 Make sure the fuel filler cap is secure. Turn the fuel tap off.

2.4 Release the clamp and pull the hose off the tap

2 Remove the seat (see Chapter 7).
3 On America and Speedmaster remove the tank-mounted instrument panel (see Chapter 8).
4 Have a rag ready to catch any residual fuel from the fuel hose and tap, then release the clamp and detach the hose from the tap **(see illustration)**.
5 Unscrew the fuel tank mounting bolt(s) **(see illustrations)**.
6 Lift the tank and detach the breather hose (on California models the EVAP system hose) from its union on the right-hand side **(see illustrations)**.

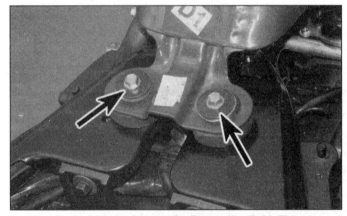

2.5a Fuel tank bolts (arrowed) – Bonneville, T100, Thruxton and Scrambler

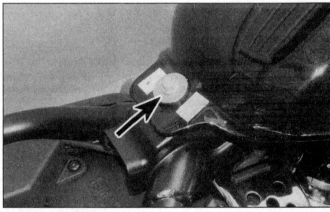

2.5b Fuel tank bolt (arrowed) – America and Speedmaster

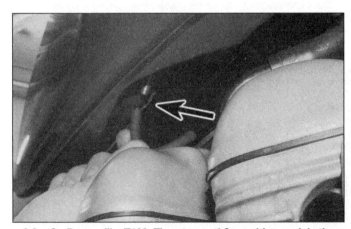

2.6a On Bonneville, T100, Thruxton and Scrambler models the hose (arrowed) is towards the back of the tank

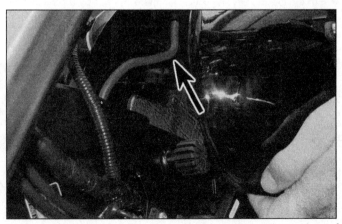

2.6b On America and Speedmaster the hose (arrowed) is at the front

2.7 Carefully lift the tank away

2.13a Unscrew the bolts . . .

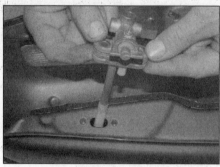

2.13b . . . and remove the tap

7 Carefully lift the rear of the tank and draw it back to free it from the frame **(see illustration)**.

8 Inspect the tank mounting rubbers for signs of damage or deterioration and replace them with new ones if necessary.

Draining

9 Remove the fuel tank as described above.
10 Connect a drain hose to the fuel outlet union on the tap and insert its end in a container suitable and large enough for storing the fuel. Turn the fuel tap to the 'ON' position and allow the tank to drain. When the tank has drained, turn the tap to the 'OFF' position.

Installation

11 Installation is the reverse of removal, noting the following:
● Make sure the tank rubbers are correctly fitted and the collar(s) is/are fitted with the mounting bolt(s).
● Take care not to trap and block the fuel tank breather hose when installing the tank.
● Make sure the hoses are fully pushed onto their unions, and the fuel hose is secured by its clamp.
● Tighten the mounting bolt(s) to the torque setting specified at the beginning of the chapter.
● Turn the fuel tap ON and check that there is no sign of fuel leakage, then turn if off.

Fuel tap

Removal

12 Remove the fuel tank and drain it as described in Steps 1 to 10, then turn it over and rest it on some rag.
13 Unscrew the bolts securing the tap to the tank and withdraw the tap **(see illustrations)**. Note the washers with the screws. Remove the upper O-ring, the tap spacer and the lower O-ring **(see illustrations 2.14c, b and a)**. Discard the O-rings as new one must be used.

Installation

14 Fit a new O-ring into the groove in the tap, with the flat side uppermost so its ribbed side fits into the groove **(see illustration)**. Fit the spacer with its flat side facing down onto the O-ring **(see illustration)**. Fit a new O-ring into the groove in the spacer, with the flat side uppermost so its ribbed side fits into the groove **(see illustration)**.
15 Install the tap, making sure the O-rings and spacer stay in place, and secure it with its bolts, not forgetting the washers **(see illustrations 2.13b and a)**.
16 Install the fuel tank (see above).

Cleaning and repair

17 All repairs to the fuel tank should be carried out by a professional who has experience in this critical and potentially dangerous work.

Even after cleaning and flushing of the fuel system, explosive fumes can remain and ignite during repair of the tank.
18 If the fuel tank is removed from the bike, it should not be placed in an area where sparks or open flames could ignite the fumes coming out of the tank. Be especially careful inside garages where a natural gas-type appliance is located, because the pilot light could cause an explosion.

3 Air/fuel mixture adjustment

1 If the engine runs extremely rough at idle or continually stalls, and if carburettor synchronisation (see Chapter 1) or an overhaul does not cure the problem (and it definitely is a carburation problem – see Section 4), the pilot screws may require adjustment. It is worth noting at this point that unless you have the experience to carry this out it is best to entrust the task to a motorcycle dealer, tuner or fuel systems specialist. Also, due to the increased emphasis on controlling exhaust emissions in certain world markets, regulations have been formulated which prevent adjustment of the air/fuel mixture. On such models the pilot screws may have an anti-tamper plug fitted to prevent adjustment; if a new pilot screw is fitted it should be set-up in conjunction

2.14a Fit the lower O-ring . . .

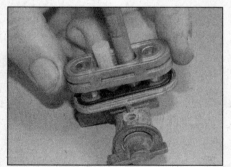

2.14b . . . the spacer . . .

2.14c . . . and the upper O-ring as described

3.2a Access to the pilot screws (arrowed) . . .

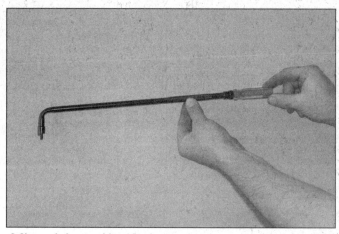

3.2b . . . is best achieved using a purpose-made tool such as the one shown

with an exhaust gas analyser to ensure that the machine does not exceed emissions regulations. The exhaust CO content on all models should be 0.48 to 3.0% with the engine oil temperature at 75°C, choke OFF, SAIS hoses clamped, and idling at 1000 rpm; it is measured at the silencer ends.

2 The pilot screws are located underneath the carburettors, between the float bowl and the intake duct on the cylinder head, and are best accessed using a purpose-made angled screwdriver, available from any good accessory dealer **(see illustrations)**. Make sure the valve clearances are correct and the carburettors are synchronised before adjusting the pilot screws (see Chapter 1).

3 Warm the engine up to normal working temperature, then stop it. Screw in the pilot screw on each carburettor until they seat lightly, then back them out to the number of turns specified (see this Chapter's Specifications). This is the base position for adjustment.

4 Start the engine and reset the idle speed to the correct level (see Chapter 1). Working on one carburettor at a time, turn the pilot screw by a small amount either side of this position to find the point at which the highest consistent idle speed is obtained. When you've reached this position, reset the idle speed to the specified amount (see Chapter 1). Repeat on the other carburettor.

4 Carburettor overhaul

1 Poor engine performance, hesitation, hard starting, stalling, flooding and backfiring are all signs that major carburettor maintenance may be required.

2 Keep in mind that many so-called carburettor problems are really not carburettor problems at all, but mechanical problems within the engine, or ignition system malfunctions. Try to establish for certain that the carburettors are in need of maintenance before beginning a major overhaul.

3 Check the fuel tap, strainer, the fuel hose, the intake ducts on the cylinder head and their joint clamps, the air filter, the ignition system, the spark plugs, valve clearances and carburettor synchronisation before assuming that a carburettor overhaul is required.

4 Most carburettor problems are caused by dirt particles, varnish and other deposits which build up in and block the fuel and air passages. Also, in time, gaskets and O-rings shrink or deteriorate and cause fuel and air leaks which lead to poor performance.

5 When overhauling the carburettors, disassemble them completely and clean the parts thoroughly with a carburettor cleaning solvent and dry them with filtered, unlubricated

compressed air. Blow through the fuel and air passages with compressed air to force out any dirt that may have been loosened but not removed by the solvent. Once the cleaning process is complete, reassemble the carburettor using new gaskets and O-rings.

6 Before disassembling the carburettors, make sure you have all the necessary parts, some carburettor cleaner, a supply of clean rags, some means of blowing out the carburettor passages and a clean place to work. It is recommended that only one carburettor be overhauled at a time to avoid mixing up parts.

5 Carburettor removal and installation

> ⚠ **Warning: Refer to the precautions given in Section 1 before starting work.**

Removal

1 Remove the fuel tank (see Section 2). Remove the side panels (see Chapter 7).

2 Disconnect the carburettor heater system wiring connectors **(see illustration)**.

3 Disconnect the throttle position sensor wiring connector, and on America and Speedmaster free the wiring from its clip **(see illustrations)**.

5.2 Pull the four heater connectors (arrowed) off their terminals

5.3a TPS wiring connector – Bonneville, T100, Thruxton and Scrambler

5.3b TPS wiring connector (arrowed) – America and Speedmaster

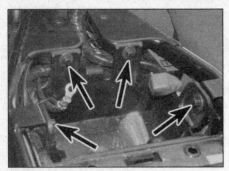

5.5a Air filter housing bolts (arrowed) – Bonneville, T100, Thruxton and Scrambler

5.5b On America and Speedmaster unscrew the bolt (arrowed) on each side

5.6a Fully slacken the clamp screw (arrowed) on each side . . .

4 On California models detach the EVAP system hoses from their unions on the carburettors.

5 On Bonneville, T100, Thruxton and Scrambler models remove the battery (see Chapter 8). On all models remove the air filter housing mounting bolts (see illustrations).

6 Fully slacken the clamp screws securing the air intake rubbers to the back of the carburettors – note the orientation of the clamps (see illustration). Slide the air filter housing back off the carburettors as far as it will go (see illustration).

7 Fully slacken the clamps securing the carburettors to the cylinder head intake rubbers and the clamp securing the left-hand intake rubber to the cylinder head, as above noting the orientation of the clamps (see illustration). Ease the carburettors back out of the intake rubbers and draw them to the left-hand side, removing the left-hand intake rubber when possible to make room for the right-hand carburettor (see illustrations). Note: Keep the carburettors level to prevent fuel spillage from the float chambers.

8 Detach the throttle cables, noting which fits where (see Section 9).

Caution: Stuff clean rag into each cylinder head intake after removing the carburettors, to prevent anything from falling in.

9 Place a suitable container below the float chambers, then slacken the drain bolt on each chamber in turn and drain all the fuel from the carburettors (see illustration). Tighten the bolts once all the fuel has been drained.

10 If required unscrew the bolts securing the intake adapters to the cylinder head and remove them, on 865cc engines along with the insulators that fit between them (see illustration). Discard the O-rings as new ones must be used – on 865cc engine the insulators and adapters both have O-rings.

5.6b . . . then draw the housing back

5.7a Slacken the clamp screw (A) on each side and the screw (B) on the left-hand side

5.7b Draw the carburettors half-way out . . .

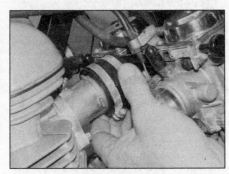

5.7c . . . then remove the left-hand intake rubber . . .

5.7d . . . to make room for the right-hand carburettor

5.9 Slacken the bolt (arrowed) on each float chamber to drain the carburettors

5.10 Intake adapter bolts (arrowed)

Installation

11 Installation is the reverse of removal, noting the following.

● If removed fit the intake adapters along with their insulators on 865 cc engines to the cylinder head using new O-rings – make sure the O-rings seat properly in their grooves and stay in place while tightening the bolts. Tighten the bolts evenly to the torque setting specified at the beginning of the Chapter.

● Check for cracks or splits in the air intake rubbers and the cylinder head intake rubbers, and replace them with new ones if necessary.

● Refer to Section 9 for installation of the throttle cables. Check the operation of the cables and adjust them as necessary (see Chapter 1).

● Make sure the carburettors are fully engaged with the cylinder head intake rubbers – they can be difficult to engage, so a squirt of WD40 or a smear of grease will ease entry. Make sure the clamps are positioned correctly. Do not forget to install and tighten the air filter housing bolts.

● Make sure all hoses are correctly routed and secured and not trapped or kinked.

● Do not forget to connect the throttle position sensor and heater system wiring connectors.

● Check idle speed and carburettor synchronisation and adjust as necessary (see Chapter 1).

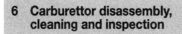

6 Carburettor disassembly, cleaning and inspection

Warning: Refer to the precautions given in Section 1 before starting work.

Disassembly

1 Remove the carburettors from the machine as described in the previous Section. **Note:** *Do not separate the carburettors – individual bodies are not available, so if one needs replacing a new pair must be obtained. Each carburettor can be dismantled sufficiently for all normal cleaning and adjustments while joined together. Dismantle the carburettors separately to avoid interchanging parts.*

2 Check the operation of the choke plungers by pulling on the knob then letting it go. It should pull out smoothly and return home easily under spring pressure. If required remove the blanking caps from their unions, then undo the two screws securing the choke linkage bar to the carburettors, noting the plastic washers **(see illustrations)**. Lift off the bar, noting how it fits, taking care not to lose the plunger springs and the detent ball and its spring – remove these and the inner plastic washers **(see illustrations)**. Unscrew the choke plunger nut, using a pair of thin-nosed pliers if access is too restricted for a spanner, and withdraw the plunger from the carburettor body being disassembled **(see illustration)**.

3 Unscrew and remove the top cover retaining screws and remove the cover **(see illustration)**.

6.2a Remove the blanking caps . . .

6.2b . . . then undo the screws . . .

6.2c . . . lift off the linkage bar . . .

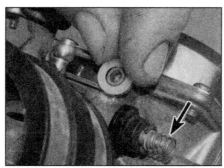

6.2d . . . and remove the inner plastic washers and plunger springs (arrowed) . . .

6.2e . . . and the detent ball (arrowed) . . .

6.2f . . . and its spring . . .

6.2g . . . then unscrew the choke plunger nut

6.3 Undo the screws (arrowed) and remove the top cover

6.4a Remove the spring . . .

6.4b . . . and the piston/diaphragm assembly

6.4c Push the needle up . . .

4 Remove the spring from inside the piston **(see illustration)**. Carefully peel the diaphragm away from its sealing groove in the carburettor and withdraw the diaphragm/ piston assembly **(see illustration)**. Carefully push the needle up from the bottom of the piston and remove the holder, noting how

it locates, and the needle from the top **(see illustrations)**.
Caution: Do not use a sharp instrument to displace the diaphragm, as it is easily damaged.
5 Undo the screws securing the float chamber to the base of the carburettor and remove it,

on the left-hand carburettor noting how two of the screws secure the idle speed adjuster holder **(see illustration)**. Remove the rubber gasket and discard it, as a new one must be used.
6 Withdraw the float pivot pin and remove the float assembly, noting how it fits **(see illustrations 7.6c and b)**. Unhook the needle valve from the tab on the float, noting how it fits **(see illustration 7.6a)**.
7 Unscrew and remove the main jet **(see illustration)**.
8 Unscrew and remove the needle jet holder **(see illustration)**. Tip the needle jet out of the carburettor, noting which way round it fits **(see illustration)**.
9 Unscrew and remove the pilot jet **(see illustration)**.
10 The pilot screw can be removed from the carburettor, but note that its setting will be disturbed **(see Haynes Hint)**. Where fitted remove the anti-tamper plug. Unscrew and remove the pilot screw along with its spring, washer and O-ring **(see illustration 3.2a)**. Discard the O-ring, as a new one must be used.

6.4d . . . and remove the needle holder . . .

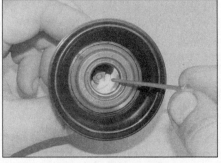

6.4e . . . and the needle

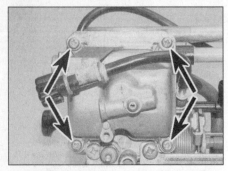

6.5 Float chamber screws (arrowed)

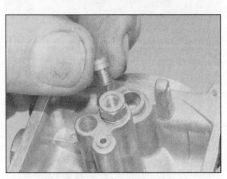

6.7 Remove the main jet . . .

> **HAYNES HINT** *To record the pilot screw's current setting, turn the screw in until it seats lightly, counting the number of turns necessary to achieve this, then fully unscrew it. On installation, the screw is simply backed out the number of turns you've recorded.*

6.8a . . . and the needle jet holder . . .

6.8b . . . then tip the needle jet (arrowed) out

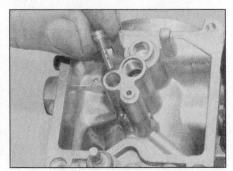

6.9 Remove the pilot jet

11 On the left-hand carburettor undo the air cut-off valve cover screws and remove the spring, the small O-ring, and the diaphragm noting how they fit **(see illustrations)**.

12 A throttle position sensor is mounted on the outside of the right-hand carburettor **(see illustration)**. Do not remove the sensor from the carburettor – it is an integral part and is not available separately. The manufacturer does not provide tests or set up data for the sensor.

Cleaning

Caution: Use only a dedicated carburettor cleaner or petroleum-based solvent for carburettor cleaning. Do not use caustic cleaners.

13 Submerge the carburettor body and individual metal components in the solvent for approximately thirty minutes (or longer, if the directions recommend it).

14 After the carburettor has soaked long enough for the cleaner to loosen and dissolve most of the varnish and other deposits, use a nylon-bristle brush to remove any stubborn deposits. Rinse it again, then dry it with compressed air.

15 Use a jet of compressed air to blow out all of the fuel and air passages in the main and upper body.

Caution: Never clean the jets or passages with a piece of wire or a drill bit, as they will be enlarged, causing the fuel and air metering rates to be upset.

Inspection

16 Inspect the needle on the end of the choke plunger, the spring and the plunger linkage bar **(see illustration)**. Replace any component that is worn, damaged or bent.

17 If removed from the carburettor, check the tapered portion of the pilot screw and the spring and O-ring for wear or damage. Replace any worn or damaged component with a new one if necessary.

18 Check the carburettor body, float chamber and top cover for cracks, distorted sealing surfaces and other damage. If any defects are found, replace the faulty component with a new one, although replacement of the entire carburettor may be necessary (check with a dealer on the availability of separate components).

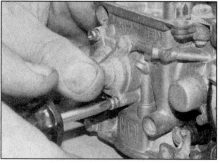

6.11a Undo the screws . . .

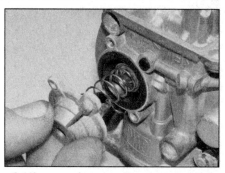

6.11b . . . and remove the cover and the spring . . .

6.11c . . . the small O-ring (arrowed) . . .

6.11d . . . and the diaphragm

19 Check the piston diaphragm for splits, holes, creases and general deterioration. Holding it up to a light will help to reveal problems of this nature. Replace it with a new one if necessary – it is available separately from the piston.

20 Insert the piston in the carburettor body and check that it moves up and down smoothly. Check the surface of the piston for wear. If it is worn excessively or doesn't move smoothly in the guide, replace the components with new ones as necessary. Make sure the spring is not distorted.

21 Check the needle is straight by rolling it on a flat surface such as a piece of glass. Replace it with a new one if it is bent, or if the tip is worn.

22 Check the tip of the float needle valve and the valve seat in the carburettor **(see illustration)**. If the valve is worn replace it with a new one. If the seat is worn a new

carburettor must be obtained. Check the spring-loaded rod in the valve operates correctly.

23 Operate the throttle shaft to make sure the throttle butterfly valve opens and closes smoothly. If it doesn't, clean the throttle linkage, and also check the butterfly for distortion, or for any debris caught between its edge and the carburettor. Also check that the butterfly is central on the shaft – if the screws securing it to the shaft have come loose it may be catching.

24 Check the float for damage. This will usually be apparent by the presence of fuel inside the float. If it is damaged, replace it with a new one.

25 Check the air cut-off valve diaphragm for splits, holes, creases and general deterioration. Holding it up to a light will help to reveal problems of this nature. Replace it with a new one if necessary. Check the tip of

6.12 Throttle position sensor (arrowed)

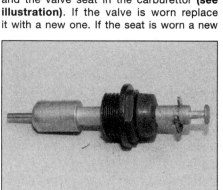

6.16 Choke plunger assembly

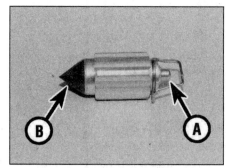

6.22 Check the valve's spring loaded rod (A) and tip (B) for wear or damage

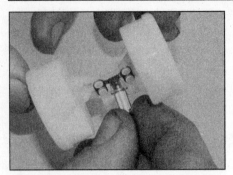

7.6a Hook the needle valve onto the tab on the float . . .

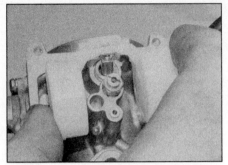

7.6b . . . then install the float assembly, locating the valve in the seat . . .

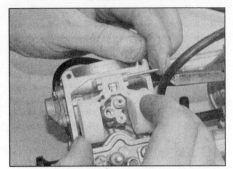

7.6c . . . and slide the pivot pin through

the peg in the centre of the inner face of the diaphragm for wear **(see illustration 6.11d)**. Make sure the hose from the valve housing to the right-hand carburettor is in good condition and securely connected at each end. Make sure the spring is good.

---

7 Carburettor reassembly and fuel level check

⚠ **Warning: Refer to the precautions given in Section 1 before proceeding.**
Note: *When reassembling the carburettors, be sure to use the new O-rings, seals and other parts supplied in the rebuild kit. Do not*

overtighten the carburettor jets and screws, as they are easily damaged.

Reassembly

1 Fit the air cut-off valve diaphragm into the carburettor **(see illustration 6.11d)**. Fit a new O-ring into the air passage **(see illustration 6.11c)**. Locate the spring then fit the cover and tighten its screws **(see illustrations 6.11b and a)**.
2 Install the pilot screw (if removed) along with its spring, washer and O-ring, turning it in until it seats lightly **(see illustration 3.2a)**. Now, turn the screw out the number of turns previously recorded, or as specified at the beginning of the Chapter. Fit a new anti-tamper plug (where necessary) after the carburettors have been installed and the pilot screws set-up with the engine running.

3 Screw the pilot jet into the carburettor **(see illustration 6.9)**.
4 Fit the needle jet into the carburettor making sure it is the correct way round and so seats correctly **(see illustration 6.8b)**. Screw the needle jet holder into the carburettor **(see illustration 6.8a)**.
5 Screw the main jet into the needle jet holder **(see illustration 6.7)**.
6 Hook the float needle valve onto the tab on the float assembly **(see illustration)**. Position the float assembly onto the carburettor, making sure the needle valve locates in the seat **(see illustration)**. Install the pivot pin **(see illustration)**.
7 To check the float height, hold the carburettor so the float hangs down, then tilt it back until the needle valve is just seated, but not so far that the needle's spring-loaded rod is compressed. Measure the height of the float above the chamber mating surface with an accurate ruler **(see illustration)**. The height should be as specified at the beginning of the Chapter. If not, adjust the float height by carefully bending the float tab a little at a time until the correct height is obtained. **Note:** *With the float held the same way up as it is when installed, bending the tab up lowers the fuel level - bending it down raises the fuel level.*
8 Fit a new rubber seal onto the float chamber, making sure it is seated properly in its groove, then fit the chamber onto the carburettor, not forgetting the idle speed adjuster holder on the left-hand carburettor, and tighten its screws **(see illustrations)**.
9 Fit the needle into the piston, then fit the needle holder, making sure it locates correctly and does not block the air hole in the piston **(see illustrations 6.4e and d)**.
10 Fit the piston/diaphragm assembly into the carburettor (it only fits one way) and lightly push the piston down, making sure the needle is correctly aligned with the needle jet **(see illustration)**. Press the rim of the diaphragm into its groove, making sure it is correctly seated. Fit the spring into the piston, making sure it locates correctly onto the needle holder **(see illustration 6.4a)**.
11 Fit the top cover onto the carburettor, locating the centre peg into the top of the spring and the outer pegs into the holes in

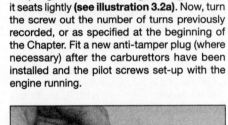

FLOAT HEIGHT

H45810

7.7 Measuring float height

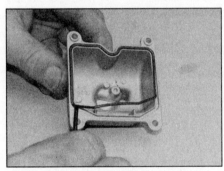

7.8a Fit a new seal into the groove . . .

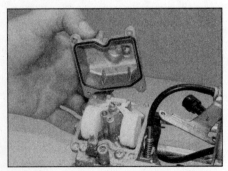

7.8b . . . and install the float chamber

7.10 Slide the piston down into the carburettor and locate the diaphragm rim

the carburettor body, and tighten its screws **(see illustration)**. Check that the piston moves smoothly in the guide by pushing it up with your finger. Note that the piston should descend slowly and smoothly as the diaphragm draws air into the chamber – it should not drop sharply under spring pressure.

12 Fit the choke plunger into the carburettor body and tighten the nut to secure it **(see illustration 6.2g)**. Make sure the E-clip is secure on the plunger shaft, then fit the spring over the shaft and against the clip **(see illustration)**. Fit the detent ball spring into its hole **(see illustration 6.2f)**, then push grease in to help the ball stay in place and fit the ball **(see illustration and 6.2e)**. Fit the inner plastic washers, then fit the choke linkage bar onto the plungers, making sure the slots locate correctly in between the spring ends and the nipple on the end of each choke plunger **(see illustrations 6.2d and c)**, and the detent ball stays in place and locates in its hole in the bar **(see illustration)**. Fit the outer plastic washers and secure the linkage bar in place with the screws **(see illustration 6.2b)**. Fit the blanking caps onto their unions **(see illustration 6.2a)**.

13 Install the carburettors (see Section 5).

Fuel level check

Note: *The fuel level is checked with the carburettors installed.*

14 To check the fuel level, position the motorcycle on level ground and support it so that it is vertical.

15 Turn the fuel tap OFF. Attach some clear tubing (suitable for holding petrol (gasoline) and long enough to reach to the top of the carburettors) to the drain hose union on the bottom of the float chamber on the first carburettor and position its open end in a suitable container **(see illustration 5.9)**. Slacken the drain screw and allow the carburettor to drain, then tighten the screw.

16 Now position the open end of the tubing vertically alongside the carburettor being checked and use tape to fix in position.

17 Turn the fuel tap ON. Slacken the drain screw and allow the fuel to flow into the tubing. The level at which the fuel stabilises in the tubing indicates the level of the fuel in the float chamber. Refer to the Specifications at the beginning of the Chapter and measure the level relative to the mating surface of the float chamber with the carburettor body. Tighten the drain screw, then detach the tubing, catching the residual fuel with a rag. Repeat the procedure for the other carburettor.

18 If the level was incorrect, remove the carburettors, then remove the float from the chamber (see Section 7), and adjust the float height by carefully bending the float tab a little at a time until the correct height is obtained. **Note:** *With the float held the same way up as it is when installed, bending the tab up lowers the fuel level - bending it down raises the fuel level.*

7.11 Insert the spring and fit the cover

7.12b Push grease into the hole to help keep the ball in place

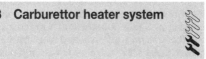

8 Carburettor heater system

Check

1 Each carburettor has a heater element threaded into its body to prevent carburettor icing under certain conditions **(see illustration 5.2)**. The elements are controlled by a thermo-switch mounted on the air filter housing behind the right-hand side panel **(see illustration)**. The switch is set to turn on at temperatures below 10°C.

2 No test details are provided for the switch or heating elements. If neither element gets hot when the temperature is below 10°C it is likely that the switch or its input or earth wiring is faulty. If one of the elements gets hot but the other is cold either that element or

7.12a Fit the spring over the shaft

7.12c Locate the hole in the bar over the detent ball (arrowed)

its individual wiring from the switch is faulty.

3 First make sure that all the wiring and connectors in the relevant switch or element circuit are good, continuity testing each wire and checking for voltage into the switch or element – refer to the wiring diagrams at the end of Chapter 8 and to *Fault Finding Equipment* in the Reference Section. Also check that each heater element is tight in its carburettor. If all is good replace the faulty component with a new one.

Removal and installation

4 To remove a heater element, disconnect its wiring connectors, then unscrew it from the carburettor body **(see illustration 5.2)**.

5 To access the thermo-switch, remove the right-hand side panel (see Chapter 7) **(see illustration 8.1)**. Release the switch from its clips and disconnect its wiring connector **(see illustration)**.

6 Installation is the reverse of removal.

8.1 Carburettor heater switch (arrowed) and its wiring connector

8.5 Use a small screwdriver to free the thermo-switch

9.3a Slip the closing cable out of the bracket . . .

9.3b . . . and detach its end from the cam

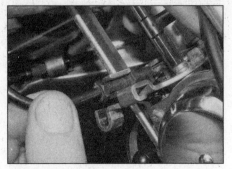

9.3c Slip the opening cable out of the bracket . . .

9 Throttle cables

> *Warning: Refer to the precautions given in Section 1 before proceeding.*

Removal

1 Displace the carburettors (see Section 5).
2 Mark each cable according to its location at both ends. If new cables are being fitted, match them to the old cables to ensure they are correctly installed.
3 Slacken the cable top locknuts and thread them up the elbow **(see illustration)**. Slip the cables out of the bracket and detach the cable ends from the throttle cam **(see illustrations)**.
4 Withdraw the cables from the machine, carefully noting their correct routing – you can tie string to their ends which can be drawn

through with the cables and used as a guide to draw the new cables in when installing them.
5 On Bonneville, T100, America and Speedmaster models unscrew the throttle opening cable elbow retaining plate screw and the closing cable retaining nut on the right-hand switch housing **(see illustration)**. Detach the switch housing front by undoing the screws **(see illustrations)**. Remove the two screws to free the master cylinder/housing and its clamp from the handlebar. Detach the cable ends from the pulley, then remove the cable elbows from the housing **(see illustration)**.
6 On Thruxton and Scrambler models pull the rubber boot off the cables at the throttle housing end **(see illustration)**. Unscrew the throttle housing screws and separate the halves. Detach the cable ends from the pulley in the housing, then remove the cable elbows from the housing.

Installation

7 On Thruxton and Scrambler models lubricate the cable nipples with multi-purpose grease and fit them into the throttle pulley at the handlebar, making sure they are the correct way round. Fit the cable elbows into the housing, making sure they locate correctly. Join the housing halves and tighten the screws **(see illustration 9.6)**. Fit the rubber boot.
8 On Bonneville, T100, America and Speedmaster models lubricate the cable nipples with multi-purpose grease, fit them through the housing and engage them in the throttle pulley **(see illustration 9.5d)**. The opening cable has the retaining plate. Fit the cable elbows into the housing and secure with the retaining plate and screw (opening cable) and with the nut (closing cable). Mount the master cylinder/housing on the handlebar and fit the clamp so that the joint aligns with the punch mark in the bar. Tighten the upper bolt fully, then tighten the lower bolt

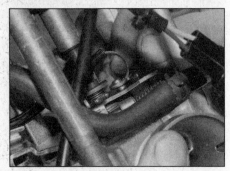

9.3d . . . and detach its end from the cam

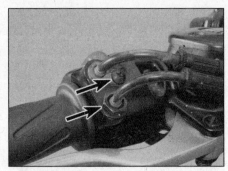

9.5a Undo the screw and the nut (arrowed)

9.5b Undo the screws (arrowed) . . .

9.5c . . . and detach the switch housing . . .

9.5d . . . then free the cable ends from the pulley

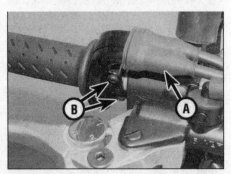

9.6 Pull back the boot (A) then undo the screws (B)

10.1 Slacken the clamp bolt (arrowed)

10.2a Unscrew the nut . . .

10.2b . . . and withdraw the footrest . . .

(there will be a gap at the lower joint), both to the specified torque setting. Install the switch housing **(see illustrations 19.5c and b)**. Tighten the closing cable retaining nut and fit the opening cable retaining plate and screw **(see illustration 9.5a)**.

9 Feed the cables through to the carburettors, making sure they are correctly routed. The cables must not interfere with any other component and should not be kinked or bent sharply.

10 Fit the carburettors part-way between the engine and air filter housing (see Section 6). Lubricate the cable ends with multi-purpose grease.

11 The throttle opening cable fits into the rear section of the bracket. Fit the cable ends into the throttle cam then locate the cables in the bracket and draw them up so that the lower nut becomes captive against the small lug **(see illustrations 9.3d, c, b and a)**. Tighten the top nuts down onto the bracket.

12 Fully install the carburettors (see Section 5). Adjust the cable freeplay (see Chapter 1). Operate the throttle to check that it opens and closes freely. Turn the handlebars back and forth to make sure the cable doesn't cause the steering to bind.

13 Start the engine and check that the idle speed does not rise as the handlebars are turned. If it does, the throttle cables are routed incorrectly. Correct the problem before riding the motorcycle.

10 Exhaust system

⚠ **Warning: If the engine has been running the exhaust system will be very hot. Allow the system to cool before carrying out any work.**

Note: *Before starting work on the exhaust system spray all the nuts, mounting bolts and clamp bolts with penetrating fluid – many of them are exposed and are prone to corrosion.*

Silencers – Bonneville, T100 and Thruxton

Removal

1 Slacken the clamp bolt securing the

10.2c . . . then remove the silencer

silencer to the downpipe **(see illustration)**. On Thruxton models note the shield secured by the clamp.

2 Unscrew the nut from the passenger footrest holder and remove the metal washer, which might stick to the rubber washer **(see illustration)**. Withdraw the footrest assembly from the silencer bracket and frame **(see illustration)**. Release the silencer from the downpipe assembly **(see illustration)**. Remove the washers, and where fitted the spacer, from the inner side of the bracket **(see illustration 10.3c)**. Remove the collar and rubber mounting bush from the outer side **(see illustrations 10.3b and a)**. Check the condition of the rubber bush and washer and replace them with new ones if damaged, deformed or deteriorated.

Installation

3 Fit the rubber bush into the outer side of the bracket, then fit the collar into the bush **(see**

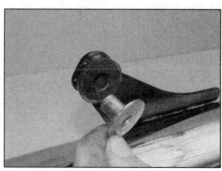

10.3b . . . and the collar into the bush

10.2d Remove the metal washer and rubber washer

illustrations). Fit the spacer (where fitted), and the rubber washer over their protruding ends on the outside of the bracket **(see illustration)**. Smear a small amount (4 cc) of clear silicone sealant around the end of the downpipe.

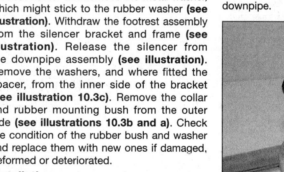

10.3a Fit the rubber bush into the bracket . . .

10.3c Fit the rubber washer over the end of the bush

10.4 Make sure the pegs on the holder locate in the holes in the frame

4 Fit the silencer onto the downpipe assembly, making sure it is pushed fully home **(see illustration 10.2c)**. Align the silencer mounting bracket at the rear and install the footrest assembly, making sure the pegs on its flange locate in the holes in the frame **(see illustration)**. Fit the washer and tighten the nut to the torque setting specified at the beginning of the Chapter **(see illustration 10.2a)**. Tighten the clamp bolt to the specified

torque setting, on Thruxton models making sure the shield is correctly fitted **(see illustration 10.1)**.
5 Run the engine and check the system for leaks.

Silencers – America and Speedmaster

Removal

6 Slacken the clamp bolt securing the silencer to the downpipe **(see illustration)**.
7 Unscrew the passenger footrest plate bolts and remove the footrest assembly, noting the washer on the inside for the lower bolt **(see illustration)**.
8 Twist the silencer so the bracket moves away from the frame. Release the silencer from the downpipe assembly. Remove the rubber mounting bushes. Check the condition of the rubber bushes and replace them with new ones if damaged, deformed or deteriorated.

Installation

9 Fit the rubber bushes into the bracket.

Smear a small amount (4 cc) of clear silicone sealant around the end of the downpipe.
10 Fit the silencer onto the downpipe assembly, making sure it is pushed fully home. Twist the silencer mounting bracket onto its spigot at the rear. Install the footrest plate assembly, not forgetting the inner washer with the rear bolt, and tighten the bolts to the torque setting specified at the beginning of the Chapter **(see illustration)**. Tighten the clamp bolt to the specified torque setting **(see illustration 10.6)**.
11 Run the engine and check the system for leaks.

Downpipes – Bonneville, T100 and Thruxton

Removal

12 Remove the silencers (see above).
13 Remove the right-hand side panel (see Chapter 7).
14 Undo the front sprocket cover bolts and remove the cover **(see illustration)**.
15 Remove the clip and withdraw the pin securing the rear brake master cylinder pushrod

10.6 Slacken the clamp bolt (arrowed)

10.7 Unscrew the bolts (arrowed) and remove the footrest plate

10.10 Do not forget the washer on the lower bolt

10.14 Unscrew the bolts (arrowed) and remove the cover

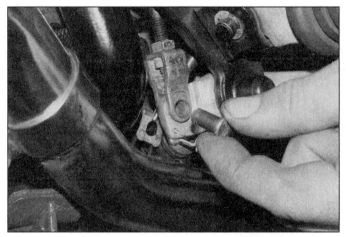

10.15a Remove the clip and withdraw the pin

10.15b Slacken the clamp bolt (A), then unscrew the bolts (B) . . .

to the brake pedal **(see illustration)**. Slacken the swingarm pivot clamp bolt in the rider's right-hand footrest bracket **(see illustration)**. Unscrew the footrest bracket bolts, then detach the pushrod from the pedal and draw the bracket off the pivot, manoeuvring it around the rod **(see illustration)**.

16 Slacken the downpipe joint clamp bolt **(see illustration)**.

17 Unscrew the bolt securing the rear of each downpipe to the frame **(see illustration)**.

18 Unscrew the downpipe flange nuts – on the machine photographed, on one side the nuts were corroded to the studs and the studs themselves threaded out of the cylinder head **(see illustration)**.

19 Detach the downpipes from the cylinder head as a pair and move them forwards, then pull them apart at the joint pipe under the engine and remove them separately **(see illustration)**.

20 Remove the gasket from each port in the cylinder head and discard it, as a new one must be fitted. Note the rubber bushes in each rear bracket and replace them with new ones if they are damaged, deformed or deteriorated **(see illustration)**.

Installation

21 Make sure the rubber bushes are fitted into each rear mount and that they are in good condition **(see illustration 10.20)**. Fit a new gasket into each of the cylinder head ports **(see illustration)**. If necessary, apply a

10.15c . . . and remove the bracket assembly

10.16 Slacken the clamp bolt (arrowed)

10.17 Unscrew the mounting bolt (arrowed) for each downpipe

10.18 Unscrew the downpipe flange nuts (arrowed)

10.19 Detach the pipes from the head then pull them apart at the joint

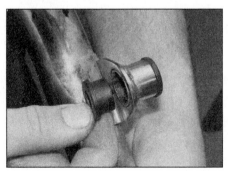

10.20 Check the bushes in each bracket

10.21 Fit a new gasket into each port

10.22a Locate the right-hand pipe . . .

10.22b . . . fitting the flange over the studs . . .

10.22c . . . and secure it with the rear bolt

smear of grease to the gaskets to keep them in place whilst fitting the downpipe. Make sure the joint pipe clamp is in place.

22 Manoeuvre the right-hand downpipe into position and locate the head in its port in the cylinder head, then fit the rear mounting bolt and the flange nuts/studs and tighten them lightly to keep it in place **(see illustrations)**. Manoeuvre the left-hand downpipe into position, engaging the joint pipes, and pulling the downpipes together to make sure the joint pipes are fully engaged **(see illustrations)**. Install the rear mounting bolt and the flange nuts/studs again tightening them lightly.

23 First tighten the rear mounting bolts to the torque setting specified at the beginning of the Chapter, then tighten the downpipe flange nuts/studs evenly and a bit at a time to the torque setting specified at the beginning of the Chapter. Finally tighten the joint pipe clamp bolt to the specified torque.

24 Fit the rider's right-hand footrest bracket and tighten the mounting bolts and the clamp bolt to the specified torque settings **(see illustrations 10.15c and b)**. Locate the master cylinder pushrod over the brake pedal then insert the pin and secure it with the clip **(see illustration 10.15a)**.

25 Install the sprocket cover and tighten its bolts to the torque setting specified at the beginning of the Chapter **(see illustration)**.

26 Install the silencers (see above), then run the engine and check that there are no exhaust gas leaks.

Downpipes – America and Speedmaster

Removal

27 Remove the silencers (see above).

28 Slacken the downpipe joint clamp bolt **(see illustration 10.16)**.

29 Unscrew the bolt securing the rear of each downpipe to the frame **(see illustration)**.

30 Unscrew the downpipe flange nuts **(see illustration 10.18)**.

31 Detach the downpipes from the cylinder head as a pair and move them forwards, then pull them apart at the joint pipe under the engine and remove them separately.

32 Remove the gasket from each port in the cylinder head and discard it, as a new one must be fitted. Note the rubber bushes in each rear bracket and replace them with new ones if they are damaged, deformed or deteriorated.

Installation

33 Make sure the rubber bushes are fitted into each rear mount and that they are in good condition. Fit a new gasket into each of the cylinder head ports **(see illustration 10.21)**. If necessary, apply a smear of grease to the gaskets to keep them in place whilst fitting the downpipe. Make sure the joint pipe clamp is in place.

34 Manoeuvre the downpipes into position

10.22d Locate the left-hand pipe . . .

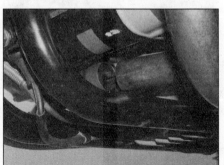

10.22e . . . fitting the joint pipes together

10.25 Install the sprocket cover

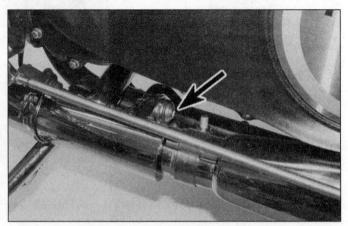

10.29 Unscrew the mounting bolt (arrowed) for each downpipe

10.37 Location of the upper silencer clamp bolt (arrowed)

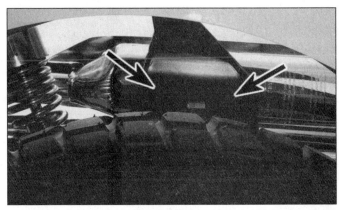

10.38a Undo the bolts (arrowed) on the back of the support bracket . . .

and fit the joint pipes together in a reverse of the way they were removed, then fit the head of each downpipe in its port in the cylinder head. Install the rear mounting bolts and tighten them enough to support the pipes **(see illustration 10.29)**.

35 Fit the downpipe flange nuts and tighten them evenly and a bit at a time to the torque setting specified at the beginning of the Chapter. Now tighten the rear bolts to the specified torque. Finally tighten the joint pipe clamp bolt to the specified torque.

36 Install the silencers (see above), then run the engine and check that there are no exhaust gas leaks.

Silencers – Scrambler

Removal

37 To remove the upper silencer, first slacken the clamp bolt securing the silencer to the exhaust pipe **(see illustration)**.

38 Unscrew the bolts securing the silencer to the support bracket, then draw the silencer off the pipe, noting the location of the seal **(see illustrations)**.

39 If required, undo the screws securing the heat shield and lift it off.

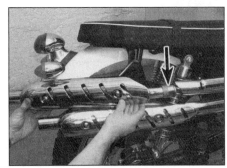

10.38b . . . and remove the silencer. Note the seal (arrowed)

40 Follow the same procedure to remove the lower silencer.

Installation

41 Installation is the reverse of removal. Check the condition of the exhaust seals and fit new ones if they are damaged or there is evidence that the joints between the pipes and the silencers have been leaking **(see illustration)**. Tighten the silencer mounting bolts and the clamp bolts to the torque settings specified at the beginning of the Chapter.

10.41 Fit new exhaust seals if the old ones have been leaking

42 Run the engine and check that there are no exhaust gas leaks.

Exhaust pipes – Scrambler

Removal

43 Remove the silencers (see above).

44 Unscrew the right-hand exhaust pipe flange nuts and ease the flange off the fixing studs **(see illustration)**.

45 Undo the screws securing the heat shield and lift it off **(see illustration)**.

46 Slacken the exhaust pipe joint clamp bolt,

10.44 Unscrew the right-hand exhaust pipe flange nuts (arrowed)

10.45 Heat shield is secured by two screws (arrowed)

10.46a Location of the exhaust pipe joint clamp bolt

10.46b Remove the right-hand pipe, noting the seal (arrowed)

10.47 Unscrew the left-hand exhaust pipe flange nuts (arrowed)

then draw the right-hand pipe off the exhaust assembly, noting the location of the seal **(see illustrations)**.

47 Unscrew the left-hand exhaust pipe flange nuts and ease the flange off the fixing studs **(see illustration)**.

48 Loosen the exhaust assembly mounting bolt **(see illustration)**. Support the assembly and remove the bolt, then manoeuvre the exhaust pipes off **(see illustration)**.

49 Remove the gasket from each port in the cylinder head and discard it, as a new one must be fitted **(see illustration 10.21)**. Note the collar and rubber bush in the exhaust assembly mounting bracket and renew the bush if it is damaged, deformed or deteriorated **(see illustrations 10.3b and a)**.

Installation

50 Make sure the rubber bush and collar are fitted into the exhaust assembly mounting bracket. Fit a new gasket into each of the cylinder head ports.

51 Manoeuvre the assembly into position and locate the left-hand pipe its port in the cylinder head, then install the assembly mounting bolt finger-tight. Ensure that the left-hand exhaust flange is correctly located on the fixing studs **(see illustration)**.

52 Tighten the mounting bolt to the torque setting specified at the beginning of the Chapter, then tighten the flange nuts to the specified torque.

53 Make sure the right-hand pipe joint clamp and seal are in place, then install the pipe pushing it all the way onto the assembly and into the cylinder head port **(see illustration**

10.46b). Locate the flange on the fixing studs, then tighten the flange nuts to the specified torque.

54 Tighten the exhaust pipe joint clamp bolt to the specified torque **(see illustration 10.46a)**. Install the heat shield and tighten the screws securely.

55 Install the silencers (see above), then run the engine and check that there are no exhaust gas leaks.

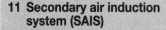

11 Secondary air induction system (SAIS)

Function

1 The air induction system uses negative exhaust gas pulses to suck fresh air from the filter housing into the exhaust ports, where it mixes with hot combustion gases. The extra oxygen causes continued combustion, allowing unburnt hydrocarbons to burn off, thereby reducing emissions. A control valve regulates the flow of fresh air into the

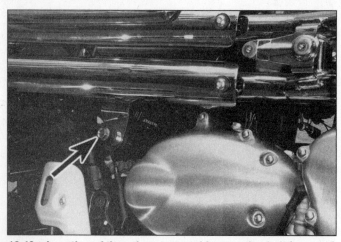

10.48a Location of the exhaust assembly mounting bolt (arrowed)

10.48b Lift the exhaust pipe assembly off

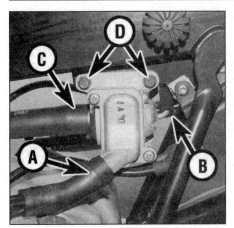

11.4 Detach the outlet hose (A) from each side, the vacuum hose (B) and intake hose (C), then unscrew the bolts (D) – early models

unit. Opening of the valve is actuated by vacuum taken from the intake duct adaptor to the left-hand cylinder on early models, and electronically by the ignition control unit on the very last of the carburettor engined Bonneville, T100, Thruxton and Scrambler models.

2 Reed valves control the flow of air into the ports, opening when there is negative pressure and closing to prevent exhaust gases passing back into the air filter housing. The reed valves and system hoses require periodic inspection to ensure the system is function correctly; refer to Chapter 1, Section 26 for further information.

Removal and Installation

3 Remove the fuel tank (see Section 2).
4 To remove the SAIS valve assembly on early models, release the clamps securing the outlet

hoses and detach them from their unions on the valve **(see illustration)**. Pull the vacuum hose off its union on the front. Pull the air intake hose off its union on the back. Unscrew the bolts securing the unit to the frame and remove it.

5 To remove the SAIS control valve and reed valve housing on late models, release the clamps securing each outlet hose and pull the hoses off their unions on the reed valve housing **(see illustrations in Chapter 3B, Section 13)**. Disconnect the wire connector to the control valve and pull the air intake hose off the back of the valve. Remove the two bolts, noting the wire harness guide, and remove the SAIS components from the machine. Refer to Chapter 3B, Section 13 for control valve testing.

6 The pipe elbows between the hoses and the cylinder head unions are secured to the unions by a clamp which can be released using a screwdriver but is difficult to re-fit without a special tool **(see illustration)**. If necessary replace the clamp with a jubilee-type. Remove the sealing collars and replace them with new ones if they are deformed or damaged **(see illustration)**.

7 To remove the unions from the cylinder head unscrew them after detaching the hoses and/or pipe elbows **(see illustration)**. On installation use new sealing washers if necessary.

12 EVAP system (California models)

1 This system prevents the escape of fuel vapour into the atmosphere by storing it in a charcoal-filled canister.
2 When the engine is not running, excess

fuel vapour from the tank and carburettors passes into the canister. When the engine is started, intake manifold depression draws the vapour back from the canister into the engine to be burned during the normal combustion process.

3 The system is not adjustable and can only be properly tested and serviced by a Triumph dealer. However the owner can check that all the hoses are in good condition and are securely connected at each end. Replace any hoses that are cracked, split or generally deteriorated with new ones.

13 Catalytic converter

1 Models sold in certain markets have a catalytic converter located in each silencer to minimise the amount of pollutants which escape into the atmosphere. It is an open-loop system, which has no link with the fuel and ignition systems.
2 The catalytic converter is a simple device in operation and one which requires no routine maintenance.
3 Note the following points:
a) *Always use unleaded fuel – the use of leaded or LRP fuel will destroy the converter.*
b) *Do not use any fuel or oil additives.*
c) *Keep the fuel and ignition systems in good order – if the fuel/air mixture is suspected of being incorrect have it checked on an exhaust gas analyser.*
d) *Handle the silencers carefully and do not drop them otherwise the catalysts might be damaged.*

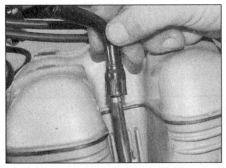

11.5a Release the clamp and pull the pipe off the union

11.5b Remove the sealing collar and fit a new one if necessary

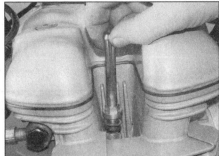

11.6 Unscrew the union and remove the sealing washer

Notes

Chapter 3B
Fuel and exhaust systems – EFI models

Contents

Degrees of difficulty

Easy, suitable for novice with little experience		**Fairly easy,** suitable for beginner with some experience		**Fairly difficult,** suitable for competent DIY mechanic		**Difficult,** suitable for experienced DIY mechanic		**Very difficult,** suitable for expert DIY or professional	

Specifications

Fuel

Grade	
Europe	Unleaded, minimum 91 RON (Europe Research Octane Number)
US	Unleaded, minimum 87 (R+M)/2 (US CLC or AKI Octane rating)
Fuel tank capacity	
Bonneville, T100, Thruxton and Scrambler	16.6 litres
America and Speedmaster.	19.5 litres
Fuel quantity remaining when low level warning light comes on	3.5 litres

Fuel injection system

Operating pressure (nominal).	43.5 psi (3 Bar) @ idle
Fuel injector resistance.	9.5 to 11.5 ohms
Oil temperature sensor resistance	
Warm engine.	200 to 400 ohms
At 20°C (68°F).	2.35 to 2.65 K-ohms
At -10°C (14°F).	8.50 to 10.25 K-ohms
Intake air temperature (IAT) sensor resistance	
At 80°C (176°F).	290 to 390 ohms
At 20°C (68°F).	2.35 to 2.65 K-ohms
At -10°C (14°F).	8.50 to 10.25 K-ohms
Secondary air induction system control valve resistance	18 to 25 ohms
EVAP system purge valve resistance (California models)	22 to 30 ohms

Torque settings

Fuel pump mounting plate bolts . . . . 9 Nm
Fuel tank mounting bolts . . . . 9 Nm
Intake stub screws . . . . 12 Nm
Oil temperature sensor . . . . 18 Nm
Oxygen sensors . . . . 25 Nm
Throttle body joining bolt nuts . . . . 6 Nm
Throttle cable housing/master cylinder clamp bolts
    Bonneville up to VIN 380776, T100 and Thruxton . . . . 12 Nm
    America and Speedmaster . . . . 15 Nm
Exhaust system
    Silencer to frame bolt – 2011-on America and Speedmaster . . . . . . 15 Nm
    All other fasteners . . . . refer to Chapter 3A Specifications

1 General information and precautions

General information

From 2008 all 865cc models were fitted with electronic fuel injection (EFI). Fuel and ignition system operations are controlled by an electronic control module, or ECM. The ECM receives information from various sensors around the motorcycle, which it uses to determine the optimum fuel requirements for the fuel injection system and the optimum timing for the ignition system for all engine speeds and loads.

The sensors used are for atmospheric pressure, crankshaft position, engine oil temperature, manifold absolute pressure, intake air temperature, oxygen (lambda), road speed, throttle position, and tip-over.

The fuel system consists of the fuel tank, the fuel pump with integral filter, pressure regulator and level sensor, the fuel hose, fuel rail and injectors, the throttle bodies and throttle control cables. The fuel pump is housed inside the tank. There is an injector for each cylinder, housed inside the throttle bodies, which are cleverly designed to have the appearance of carburettors. The low fuel warning circuit is operated by a level sensor that is an integral part of the fuel pump. A two-stage manual choke system is fitted to assist cold starting.

The exhaust system is a two-into-two design, incorporating a catalytic converter and oxygen sensors. An air induction system (SAIS) is fitted and is controlled by the ECM.

The ignition system, whilst covered fully in Chapter 4, is referred to here because of its association with the EFI system. The ECM controls both fuelling and ignition.

The EFI system has an in-built two-stage diagnostic function. The initial stage is fault detection, whereupon the system notes the fault and counts the occurrences, looking for repetition. If the fault was a temporary glitch that does not reoccur, no DTC (diagnostic trouble code, or fault code) is registered. If the fault continues a DTC is registered, and the ECM records and stores all engine and system data at that moment, and the malfunction indicator lamp (MIL) in the instrument cluster illuminates. Recorded faults can then be downloaded using Triumph's diagnostic tool or an aftermarket fault code reader, which reads the data and lists a P-code to indicate the exact fault. If this happens, the system in most cases switches itself into 'limp home' mode, so that in theory you should not be left stranded, or in some cases switches itself off, in which case you will be left stranded, depending on the severity of the fault – with minor faults it is possible that you will notice no difference in the running of the motorcycle. If after the DTC has been logged and the MIL comes on the fault clears itself, the MIL will remain on until the engine has been through three engine warm-up and system power-down cycles without the fault recurring, and the DTC will self-erase after forty such cycles. If the fault does not clear itself but is repaired the DTC can be erased using the diagnostic tool or code reader and the MIL will turn itself off.

Because of their nature, the individual system components can be checked but not repaired. If system troubles occur, and the faulty component can be isolated, the only cure for the problem is to replace the part with a new one. Keep in mind that most electrical parts, once purchased, cannot be returned. To avoid unnecessary expense, make very sure the faulty component has been positively identified before buying a new part.

Many of the bolts used on Triumph motorcycles are of the Torx type. Unless you are already equipped with a good range of Torx bits, you are advised to obtain a set. Make sure you get bits that can be used in conjunction with a socket set so that a torque wrench can be applied – a Torx key set will not be adequate on its own, though will be useful in addition to the bits.

Precautions

⚠️ *Warning: Petrol (gasoline) is extremely flammable, so take extra precautions when you work on any part of the fuel system. Don't smoke or allow open flames or bare light bulbs near the work area, and don't work in a garage where a natural gas-type appliance is present. If you spill any fuel on your skin, rinse it off immediately with soap and water. When you perform any kind of work on the fuel system, wear safety glasses and have a fire extinguisher suitable for a class B type fire (flammable liquids) on hand.*

● Always perform fuel-related procedures in a well-ventilated area to prevent a build-up of fumes.

● Never work in a building containing a gas appliance with a pilot light, or any other form of naked flame. Ensure that there are no naked light bulbs or any sources of flame or sparks nearby.

● Do not smoke (or allow anyone else to smoke) while in the vicinity of petrol (gasoline) or of components containing it. Remember the possible presence of vapour from these sources and move well clear before smoking.

● Check all electrical equipment belonging to the house, garage or workshop where work is being undertaken (see the *Safety first!* section of this manual). Remember that certain electrical appliances such as drills, cutters etc. create sparks in the normal course of operation and must not be used near petrol (gasoline) or any component containing it. Again, remember the possible presence of fumes before using electrical equipment.

● Always mop up any spilt fuel and safely dispose of the rag used.

● Any stored fuel that is drained off during servicing work must be kept in sealed containers that are suitable for holding petrol (gasoline), and clearly marked as such; the containers themselves should be kept in a safe place. Note that this last point applies equally to the fuel tank if it is removed from the machine; also remember to keep its filler cap closed at all times.

● Read the *Safety first!* section of this manual carefully before starting work.

● Owners of machines used in the US, particularly California, should note that their machines must comply at all times with Federal or State legislation governing the permissible levels of noise and of pollutants such as unburnt hydrocarbons, carbon monoxide etc. that can be emitted by those machines. All vehicles offered for sale must comply with legislation in force at the date of manufacture and must not subsequently be altered in any way which will affect their emission of noise or of pollutants.

● In practice, this means that adjustments may not be made to any part of the fuel, ignition or exhaust systems by anyone who is not authorised or mechanically qualified to do so, or who does not have the tools, equipment and data necessary to properly carry out the task. Also if any part of these systems is to be replaced it must be replaced with only genuine Triumph components or by components which are approved under the relevant legislation. The machine must never be used with any part of these systems removed, modified or damaged.

2 Fuel tank

> ⚠ Warning: Refer to the precautions given in Section 1 before starting work.

Removal

Note: *If the tank is full of fuel it will be quite heavy, and supporting it while disconnecting the hoses and wiring connectors will be more difficult – it is advisable to have an assistant on hand to help.*

1 Remove the seat (Chapter 7) and disconnect the battery negative lead (see Chapter 8). On America and Speedmaster models, refer to Chapter 8, Section 16, step 14 and remove the warning light panel from the top of the fuel tank.

2 Remove the two mounting bolts from the rear of the tank, then lift it at the rear to identify the fuel pump/level sensor wire connector and disconnect it **(see illustrations)**.

3 Ease the tank rearwards off its mounting rubbers and have your assistant support it so that it is tilted to gain access to the right underside.

4 Slide the orange fuel hose connector cover back to reveal the clips, then press the

2.2a Fuel tank is secured at the rear by two bolts

2.4a Fuel pipe being disconnected from the pump stub

clips in and pull the hose off its union **(see illustration)**. The connector is self-sealing so there shouldn't be any fuel loss. Disconnect the breather hose from the right-hand side (EVAP vent hose on California models) **(see illustration)**; on California models seal the EVAP hose end with a plug whilst it is disconnected.

5 Lift the tank free **(see illustration)**. Inspect the tank support rubbers and the mounting bolt rubbers for signs of damage or deterioration and replace them with new ones if necessary – note the collars fitted in the mounting bolt rubbers.

Installation

6 Installation is the reverse of removal, noting the following:

● Check that the tank mounting rubbers are in place on the frame and that the tank

2.2b Disconnect the pump/level sensor wiring at the 4-pin connector

2.4b Breather pipe is a push fit on the tank stub (arrowed)

engages them when it is fitted back into place **(see illustration)**.

● When reconnecting the fuel hose, make sure the connector is fully pushed onto the union until the clips locate, then slide the connector cover in to cover the clips – if the cover won't push in the connector is not properly located **(see illustration)**.

● Make sure the mounting bolt collars and sleeve are correctly fitted. Tighten the fuel tank mounting bolts to the torque setting specified at the beginning of the Chapter.

● Before installing the seat, switch the ignition ON and check that there are no leaks around the hose unions as the pump pressurises the system.

Cleaning and repair

7 All repairs to the fuel tank should be carried out by a professional who has experience in

2.5 Lifting the tank free of the bike

2.6a Tank channel (A) fits over mounting rubber (B) on each side

2.6b Press in the orange cover once the fuel pipe is in place

this critical and potentially dangerous work. Even after cleaning and flushing of the fuel system, explosive fumes can remain and ignite during repair of the tank.

8 If the fuel tank is removed from the bike, it should not be placed in an area where sparks or open flames could ignite the fumes coming out of the tank. Be especially careful inside garages where a natural gas-type appliance is located, because the pilot light could cause an explosion.

3 Fuel pump assembly and relay

3.6 Manoeuvre the pump assembly out of the tank

3.8a Unbolt the fuel pipe . . .

⚠️ *Warning: Refer to the precautions given in Section 1 before starting work.*

Fuel pump check

1 The fuel pump is located inside the fuel tank.

2 The fuel pump runs for a few seconds when the ignition is switched ON, then cuts out when the system is up to operating pressure, and cuts in again when the engine is started. If you can't hear anything, first check the fuse (see Wiring Diagrams). Next check the wiring and wiring connectors in the fuel pump and relay circuit, referring to *Electrical system fault finding* at the beginning of Chapter 8 and to the Wiring Diagram for your model at the end of it. Next, check the relay (see below). If they are all good, remove the pump (see below) and check the internal connections.

3 Using a fully charged 12 volt battery and two insulated jumper wires, connect the negative (-) lead to the black wire terminal, then briefly touch the positive (+) lead to the purple/white wire terminal – the pump should operate. If the pump does not operate, replace it with a new one. The pump is controlled by the ECM, so if the pump, its relay and the wiring are all good, it is possible the ECM is faulty.

4 If the pump operates but is thought to be delivering an insufficient amount of fuel, first check that the fuel tank breather hose is unobstructed, and that the fuel hose is in good condition and not pinched or trapped. If all is good, check the fuel pressure (see Section 4).

3.8b . . . and draw the pipe clamp back

3.9 Fuel filter must be fitted in correct direction

Fuel pump removal

5 Make sure the ignition is switched OFF. Using a siphon pump, drain the fuel from the tank into a suitable container. Remove the fuel tank (see Section 2). Turn the tank upside down and rest it on some rag.

6 Note the orientation of the fuel pump and its mounting plate. Unscrew the 12 bolts evenly in a criss-cross sequence, then remove the plate and withdraw the pump assembly **(see illustration)**. Remove the pump seal, and discard it as a new one must be used.

7 The pump assembly can be dismantled and all parts are available, including the filter.

Filter

8 Remove the bolt which retains the fuel pipe to the bracket **(see illustration)**. Using pliers, squeeze the ears of the pipe clamp together and move the clamp away from the filter stub

at each end of the filter **(see illustration)**. Please a wad of rag or tissue paper under the filter to catch the fuel which will be held in the filter, then pull off the pipes to free the filter.

9 Fit the new filter so that the arrow on its body points towards the pressure regulator side (this end of the filter also has an OUT marking) **(see illustration)**.

Pump and strainer

10 Detach the pump's wire connector **(see illustration)**.

11 Using pliers, squeeze the ears of the pipe clamp together and move the clamp away from the pump stub **(see illustration)**. Pull the pipe off the pump stub.

12 Release the fuel baffle from the end of the pump after slackening its clamp **(see illustration)**. Inspect the gauze fuel strainer which is fixed to the end of the pump and

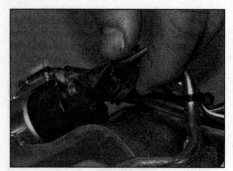
3.10 Release the pump wire connector

3.11 Free the fuel pipe clamp and pull the pipe off the stub

3.12a Fuel baffle is retained by a clamp

remove any fuel sediment or dirt from it using a soft bristled brush **(see illustration)**.

13 To release the pump from its bracket, undo the screw and separate the bracket halves **(see illustrations)**. When refitting the pump check that its rubber seat is correctly engaged in the bracket **(see illustration)**.

Fuel level sensor

14 To remove the sensor, cut the cable-tie and disconnect the wire connector **(see illustration)**. Slip the sensor out of its holder **(see illustration)**.

Pressure regulator

15 Pull off the fuel hose and remove the screw which retains the pressure regulator **(see illustration)**. Pull off the regulator noting its O-ring.

Fuel pump installation

16 Installation is the reverse of removal, noting the following:
- Use a new O-ring on the pressure regulator connection.
- Fit the fuel filter (it's recommended to fit a new one) so that its arrow points towards the pressure regulator.
- Make sure the fuel tank and pump mounting plate mating surfaces are clean.
- Fit a new seal onto the tank **(see illustration)**. Manoeuvre the pump into the tank, making sure the seal remains in place and seats correctly.
- Make sure everything is correctly aligned and seated, then tighten the mounting plate bolts evenly and a little at a time to the torque setting specified at the beginning of the Chapter.
- On completion, start the engine and check carefully that there is no leakage from around the pump mounting plate and from the hose connection.

Fuel pump relay

Note: *Refer to the Wiring Diagrams at the end of Chapter 8 for relay terminal identification.*

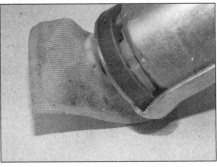

3.12b Any sign of dirt, as on this strainer, should be carefully brushed off

3.13a Undo the pump bracket clamp screw . . .

3.13b . . . and separate the clamp

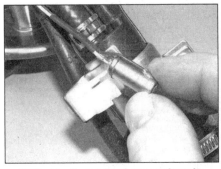

3.13c Lugs on rubber seat fit into slots in bracket

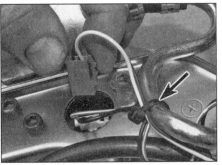

3.14a Disconnecting the level sensor wiring. Cut the cable-tie (arrowed)

3.15 Fuel pressure regulator

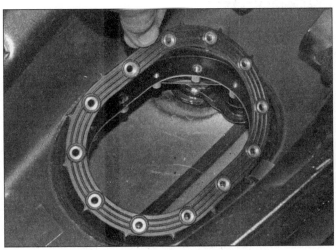

3.14b Unclip the level sensor from its holder

3.16 Seat the new seal on the tank surface

3.17a Fuel pump relay is a push fit – Bonneville, T100, Thruxton and Scrambler

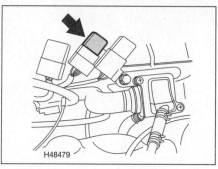

3.17b Fuel pump relay location – America and Speedmaster

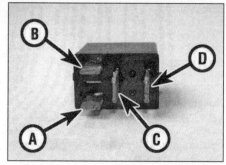

3.18 Fuel pump relay test terminals

17 The fuel pump relay is located under the fuel tank. Disconnect the relay from its connector block **(see illustrations)**. Check the terminals and sockets for damage and corrosion.

18 Using a fully-charged 12 volt battery and two insulated jumper wires, connect the battery across the relay coil terminals (A and B) on the relay; at this point the relay should be heard to click and there should be continuity or zero resistance indicated when a meter is connected across terminals C and D **(see illustration)**. If this is the case the relay is proved good. If the relay does not click when battery voltage is applied and the meter indicates no continuity or infinite resistance, the relay is faulty and must be replaced with a new one. If the relay is good, test the pump (see above).

> **Warning: Refer to the precautions given in Section 1 before starting work.**

1 To check the fuel pressure, the Triumph tool (Pt. No. T3880001) is needed. The tool comprises a gauge and two adapter hoses, one marked A, the other marked B – use adapter hose B. A commercial pressure gauge will not be of any use.

2 Make sure the ignition switch is in the OFF position. Refer to Section 2 and raise the fuel

tank sufficiently to detach the fuel hose from the fuel pump mounting plate and rest the fuel tank on the frame. Note that the battery must remain connected and that the fuel pump wiring must be connected for this test.

3 Connect adapter hose B between the bike's fuel hose and the fuel pump union on the underside of the tank. Press each connector onto its union until it is felt and heard to click into place. Fit the pressure gauge into its union, again until it is felt to click into place.

4 Turn the ignition switch ON, start the engine and allow it to idle. The pressure should be as specified at the beginning of the Chapter.

5 Turn the ignition OFF. Have some rag ready to catch residual fuel in the adapter hose. Release the pressure gauge by sliding its outer ferrule down – the gauge will spring out of the union. Release the adapter hose by pressing the clips on the connectors in. Install the fuel tank (see Section 2).

6 If the pressure is too low, either the pressure regulator is stuck open, the fuel pump is faulty, the filter is blocked, or there is a leak in the system, probably from a hose joint. Firstly check the system for leaks. If none are found, fit a new fuel pump.

7 If the pressure is too high, there could be a blockage somewhere in the system, and/or the pressure regulator could be stuck closed, or the fuel pump check valve could be faulty. First check the fuel rail and injectors for a blockage (see Section 7). Next fit a new fuel hose. If the pressure is still too high fit a new fuel pump.

> **Warning: Refer to the precautions given in Section 1 before starting work.**

1 The low fuel level warning light should come on when there is 3.5 litres of fuel remaining in the tank. It will also come on when the ignition is first turned on, as a check of the warning light.

2 If the warning light fails to come on, first check the level sensor and instrument cluster wiring connectors (see Section 2 and Chapter 8 respectively), then check the black/green wire between the sensor and the ECM for continuity, referring to 'Electrical system fault finding' at the beginning of Chapter 8 and to the wiring diagrams at the end of it.

3 The sensor is located on the fuel pump bracket inside the fuel tank and is available separately from the pump. Refer to Section 3 for removal and installation details.

> **Warning: Refer to the precautions given in Section 1 before starting work.**

Removal

1 Remove both side panels (see Chapter 7).

2 Remove the fuel tank (see Section 2).

3 Disconnect the fuel injector wiring and throttle position sensor (TPS) connectors **(see illustrations)**.

4 Pull the large-bore hose off the back of the SAIS control valve and pivot it around to the rear about its stub on the air filter housing **(see illustration 13.6a)**.

5 Slacken the clamps securing the throttle body to the air filter housing adaptors and the intake stubs on each side, noting that it may help to remove the clamps completely **(see illustration)**. Carefully ease the throttle body out of the rubber adaptors

6.3a Release the injector . . .

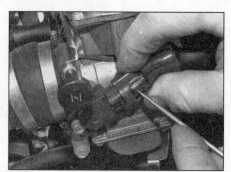

6.3b . . . and TPS wiring

6.5a Fully unscrew the adaptor clamp screws (arrowed)

6.5b Withdraw the throttle bodies from the left side

6.6a Slacken off the throttle cable adjuster nuts . . .

6.6b . . . slip the adjusters out of the bracket . . .

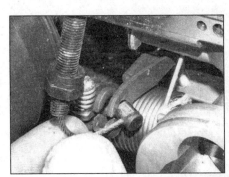

6.6c . . . and withdraw each cable end from the cam

towards the left-hand side of the frame **(see illustration)**.

6 When free of the adaptors, slacken off the throttle cable bracket nuts, slip the cables out of the bracket and detach the cable ends from the cam **(see illustrations)**.

7 If required undo the screws securing each intake stub to the cylinder head and remove them. Discard the O-rings – new ones must be used. Plug the intakes in the cylinder head with clean rag.

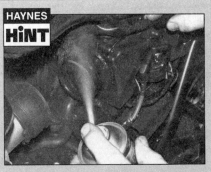

Use of a silicone spray on the air intake rubbers will aid installation of the throttle bodies.

Inspection

8 Spray injector cleaner over the throttle bodies to remove any dirt and grime, paying particular attention to the throttle cam assembly and spring. Use a nylon brush if required, but be careful not to embed dirt particles into the cam assembly as this could cause the throttle to stick.

Caution: Use only a dedicated spray cleaner (such as a carburettor and injector cleaner) for throttle body cleaning.

9 If you have removed the intake stubs clean them and their mating surfaces on the cylinder head.

6.14 Ease the edge of the intake rubber over the throttle body with a small screwdriver

10 Check the throttle bodies for cracks or any other damage which may result in air getting in.

11 Check that the throttle butterflies move smoothly and freely in the bodies, and make sure that the inside of each body is completely clean.

12 Check that the throttle cable cam moves smoothly and freely, taking into account spring pressure. Clean any grit and dirt from around the cam. Check the spring for signs of damage and distortion.

13 Dismantling of the throttle body and removal of the injectors is covered in Section 7.

Installation

14 Installation is the reverse of removal, noting the following:

● Do not forget to remove the rag from the intakes.

● If removed, fit the intake stubs using new O-rings and tighten the screws to the torque setting specified at the beginning of the Chapter.

● Ensure that the throttle bodies are fully engaged with the intake stubs before tightening the clamps. Use a small flat-bladed screwdriver to carefully ease the air intake rubbers into place **(see illustration)**.

● Make sure the wiring connectors are reconnected.

● Check the operation of the throttle cables and adjust as necessary (see Chapter 1).

7.1 Injector operation can be checked 'by ear'

7.3 Measuring injector resistance

7.5 Disconnecting the fuel hose from the fuel rail

7.6a Remove the top cover . . .

7.6b . . . and the blanking plate . . .

7.6c . . . and disconnect the wiring

7 Fuel injectors and throttle body components

⚠️ **Warning: Refer to the precautions given in Section 1 before proceeding.**

Check

1 The operation of the injectors can be checked with a sounding rod, stethoscope or even a screwdriver held to the ear. Start the engine and allow it to idle, then place the rod against the top of the throttle body; the injector will emit a clicking noise if functioning correctly **(see illustration)**. If either injector is silent, the injector or its wiring harness could be faulty.

2 If the MIL warning light has come on, use a fault code reader as described in Section 8 to download the P-code.

3 The resistance of the injectors can be checked and compared to the value given in the Specifications at the beginning of this Chapter. Disconnect the 3-pin wiring connector from the injector sub-harness **(see illustration 6.3a)**. Connect an ohmmeter between the yellow/pink and brown/pink terminals of the connector and measure the resistance for cyl No. 1 injector **(see illustration)**. Now connector between the yellow/purple and brown/pink and measure the resistance for cyl No. 2 injector. If the resistance of any injector differs greatly from that specified replace it with a new one.

4 If the injectors are good check for continuity in the wiring from each injector to the ECM and the EMS (engine management system) relay, referring to *Electrical System Fault Finding* at the beginning of Chapter 8 and to the wiring diagram for your model at the end of it. If all is good check the EMS fuse (see Chapter 8), the EMS relay (Section 9), then the ECM (Section 8).

Removal

Note: *New injectors are supplied complete with new seals – the seals are not available separately. Because of this, removal of the injectors is not advised unless they are being renewed.*

5 Remove the throttle body assembly (see Section 6). Disconnect the fuel hose from its union on the fuel rail **(see illustration)**.

6 Remove the four screws retaining each top cover, slide out the blanking plates then disconnect the wiring from the injector **(see illustrations)**.

7 Undo the choke rod screws, noting their nylon washers **(see illustration)**. Ease the rod away from the throttle body and catch the detent ball and spring as the rod is disengaged from the choke valves **(see illustrations)**. There are also two more nylon washers behind the choke rod and springs on each choke valve.

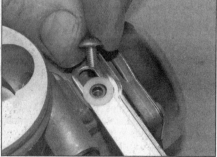

7.7a Note the nylon washer under the choke rod screws

7.7b Free the choke rod from the plungers

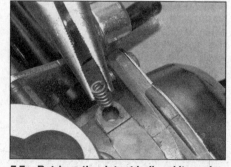

7.7c Retrieve the detent ball and its spring from the left body

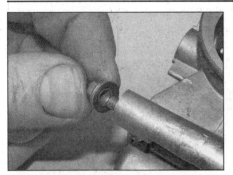

7.8a Throttle bodies are held together by two nuts . . .

7.8b . . . and long bolts

7.9a Injector holder screw

7.9b Remove injector and holder together

7.9c Seal on front end of injector may be fitted to its seat in the body or on the injector

7.13 Note the shoulder (arrowed) on the joining bolt spacers

8 The individual throttle bodies are joined by two long bolts. Remove the nut from the end of each bolt and extract the bolts (see illustrations). Gently ease the two throttle bodies apart, noting that the two springs in the throttle linkage and the long spacers will be freed. Ease the fuel rail out of one throttle body (see illustration 7.14a). At this stage it is important to take careful note of the position of all components as an aid to correct reassembly.

9 Remove the screw from the injector holder, then ease the holder and injector out of the throttle body (see illustrations). Pull the injector and holder apart to separate them. Note the seal on the front end of the injector

which may remain on its seat in the body, and the seal between the injector and holder (see illustration).

10 Modern fuels contain detergents which should keep the rail injectors clean and free of gum or varnish from residue fuel. Clean the rail in a dedicated cleaner and blow it through with compressed air. If an injector is suspected of being blocked, flush it through with injector cleaner.

Installation

11 Assemble the holder and injector. Push each injector into its socket in the throttle body and secure with the screw.

12 Fit a new O-ring to each end of the fuel rail and install the rail in the throttle body, engaging the hex shaped end of the rail in the holder (see illustration 7.14a). Smear the rail O-ring with oil to help it engage.

13 Install the long bolts from the left side and pass them through the spacers; the spacers have a shoulder on one end which engages a recess in the throttle body (see illustration).

14 Now offer up the other throttle body and press the fuel rail into place, aligning its hex in the injector holder (see illustration). At the same time ensure that the throttle mechanism engages correctly and the spring is inserted as the two are pushed

7.14a Fit a new O-ring (A) to each end of rail and engage hex (B) correctly

7.14b Engage the throttle mechanism . . .

7.14c Insert the large spring . . .

7.14d . . . and the small spring

7.14e Throttle valves should be closed and throttle mechanism positioned as shown

7.15 Wiring with grey sleeve connects to left body (A), and with black sleeve to the right (B)

7.16 When the fuel hose is in place, push the cover in to lock it

home; note that both throttle valves must be closed (see illustrations). Insert the small spring in the synchronising screw location (see illustrations). Once all components are correctly located secure the long bolts with their nuts, tightening them to the specified torque setting.

15 Reconnect the wiring to the injectors – the wiring with the grey sleeve goes to the left-hand throttle body (see illustration).

Slide the blanking plates into position. Fit the throttle body tops.

16 Push the fuel hose back onto the fuel rail stub and slide the cover across to lock it on (see illustration).

17 Ensure each choke plunger is pushed into the throttle body then fit the spring to the end of each plunger (see illustration). Insert the detent spring and ball. Fit a nylon washer over each choke rod mounting boss, offer up the

rod and engage it with choke plungers, then fit the rod over the mountings and secure with the screws (complete with nylon washers). Check that the choke rod is able to slide freely into its two detent position.

18 Install the throttle body (see Section 6).

19 Note that if the throttle bodies were separated or the throttle cam disturbed in any way, the throttle synchronisation should be checked afterwards. This must be carried out using the diagnostic tester.

8 Fault codes and ECM

⚠️ **Warning: Refer to the precautions given in Section 1 before starting work.**

1 For a general description of the system, see Section 1.

Diagnostic tool and fault codes

2 To diagnose the exact cause of a failure in the system, either the Triumph diagnostic tool or an EOBD (OBD2) fault code reader is essential (see illustration).

7.17 Small spring fits over the end of each choke plunger before installing the choke rod

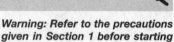

8.2 A typical fault code reader with OBD2 fitting

**8.4a Diagnostic connector (arrowed) –
Bonneville, T100, Thruxton and Scrambler**

**8.4b Diagnostic connector (arrowed) –
America and Speedmaster**

**8.4c Fault code reader in use and
displaying a P-code**

3 The ECM has in-built diagnostic functions which record and store all data should a permanent fault occur. Diagnostic trouble codes (DTCs) can then be read using the diagnostic tool, which lists a P-code to indicate the exact fault. Should a fault occur, the malfunction indicator light or symbol (MIL) in the speedometer illuminates. If this happens, the management system switches itself into 'limp home' mode, so that in theory you should not be left stranded. Depending on the problem, it is possible that you will notice no difference in the running of the motorcycle.

4 The socket for the diagnostic tool is located under the seat **(see illustrations)**. With the ignition off, plug the code reader into the socket. Turn the ignition on and allow the code reader to process any stored fault codes – these will be displayed as a four digit number prefixed by the letter P **(see illustration)**. Turn off the ignition and disconnect the code reader once the P-code has been noted. Refer to the accompanying table to link the code with the faulty circuit. Once the fault has been rectified the code reader can be used to delete the stored code from the ECM's memory.

5 If you don't have access to a code reader it is possible to perform certain tests and checks to identify a particular fault, but the difficulty is knowing in which part of the system the fault has occurred, and therefore where to start checking. Further details on the functions of and checks that can be made to the individual sensors and components and the wiring between them are detailed below and in other Sections of this Chapter.

P-code	Circuit affected
P0201	Injector cyl 1 circuit fault – misfire = open circuit, flooding = short circuit
P0202	Injector cyl 2 circuit fault – misfire = open circuit, flooding = short circuit
P0335	Crankshaft position sensor circuit fault
P0032	Oxygen sensor heater cyl 1 – short circuit to battery
P0031	Oxygen sensor heater cyl 1 – open circuit to battery/short to earth
P0130	Oxygen sensor cyl 1 circuit fault
P0052	Oxygen sensor heater cyl 2 – short circuit to battery
P0051	Oxygen sensor heater cyl 2 – open circuit to battery/short to earth
P0150	Oxygen sensor cyl 1 circuit fault
P1131	Oxygen sensor wiring inadvertently swapped
P0122	Throttle position sensor low input – short to earth or open circuit
P0123	Throttle position sensor high input – short to sensor supply
P0351	Ignition coil circuit fault (single coil models) or ignition coil cyl 1 circuit fault (models with two coils)
P0352	Ignition coil cyl 2 circuit fault (models with two coils)
P0107	MAP sensor cyl 1 low voltage

P-code	Circuit affected
P0108	MAP sensor cyl 1 high voltage
P1105	MAP sensor cyl 1 vacuum hose fault
P1687	MAP sensor cyl 2 low voltage
P1688	MAP sensor cyl 2 high voltage
P1106	MAP sensor cyl 2 vacuum hose fault
P1111	MAP sensor vacuum pipes inadvertently swapped
P1107	Ambient air pressure sensor circuit low voltage
P1108	Ambient air pressure sensor circuit high voltage
P0112	Intake air temperature too high
P0113	Intake air temperature too low
P0117	Engine oil temperature too high – sensor short circuit to earth
P0118	Engine oil temperature too low – sensor open circuit or short circuit to battery+
P560	Motorcycle voltage system fault
P1231	Fuel pump short circuit to earth or open circuit
P1232	Fuel pump relay short circuit to battery+
P0444	EVAP purge control valve short circuit to earth or open circuit
P0445	EVAP purge control valve short circuit to battery
P0414	SAIS control valve short circuit to battery

P-code	Circuit affected
P0413	SAIS control valve short circuit to earth or open circuit
P0500	Speed sensor fault (models with electronic speedometer)
P0616	Headlight cut-out relay coil short circuit to earth or open circuit
P0617	Headlight cut-out relay short circuit to battery+
P0654	Tachometer fault (models with cable driven speedometer)
P1685	EMS relay circuit fault
P1659	EMS ignition voltage input circuit fault
P1631	Tip-over sensor circuit low voltage
P1632	Tip-over sensor circuit high voltage
P0560	System voltage problem – battery circuit fault
P1610	Fuel level warning light circuit fault
P0603	EEPROM fault
P1690	CAN-bus network communication fault between ECM and instruments (models with electronic speedometer – 2010-on)
P1696	5 volt sensor supply circuit – short circuit to earth
P1697	5 volt sensor supply circuit – short circuit to Vbat (battery voltage)
P1698	5 volt sensor supply circuit fault
P1602	Tunelock fault. Motorcycle cannot be operated. MIL flashes

Fault tracing

Note: *Refer to 'Electrical system fault finding' at the beginning of Chapter 8 and to the wiring diagram for your model at the end of it.*

6 If a fault is indicated, check the wiring and connectors to and from the ECM (electronic control module) and the various sensors and all their related components. It may be that a connector is dirty or corroded or has come loose – a dirty or corroded terminal or connector will affect the resistance in that circuit, which will upset the information going to the ECM, and therefore affect the decisions it makes in controlling the system. Electrical contact cleaners are available in aerosol cans from good suppliers.

7 A wire could be pinched and is shorting out – a continuity test of all wires from connector to connector will locate this. Albeit a fiddly and

laborious task, the only way to determine any wiring faults is to systematically work through the Wiring Diagram (at the end of Chapter 8) and test each individual wire and connector for continuity – all wires are colour-coded.

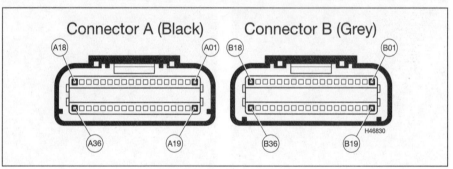

8.7 ECM terminal pin identification

When making continuity checks, isolate the wire being tested by disconnecting the wiring connectors at each end. The Wiring Diagrams show the terminal identification for each wire on the ECM with the letter given on the wiring diagram indicating the relevant ECM connector, and the number referring to the terminal within that connector, as shown **(see illustration)** – match these to the terminals on the ECM connectors when making the tests.

8 If all the wiring and connectors appear good, remove the relevant sensor and make sure its sensing tip or head is clean and undamaged, as this can often be the cause of inaccurate signals being sent to the ECM.

ECM (electronic control module)

Note: *Before removing the ECM, make sure the ignition has been switched OFF for at least one minute to allow the system to power down.*

9 On Bonneville, T100, Thruxton and Scrambler models the ECM is under the seat directly behind the battery. Disconnect the battery leads, negative lead first **(see illustrations)**. Release the battery retaining strap, pull out the wedge at the front of the battery and lift off the cover from the rear of the battery **(see illustrations)**. Lift the battery out of its holder **(see illustration)**. Lift out the ECM, peel back the wire connector sleeves, then press in the tabs and disconnect the grey and black connectors from the ECM **(see illustration)**.

10 On America and Speedmaster models up to 2010 the ECM is under the left-hand side panel behind the battery. Refer to Chapter 8,

8.9a On Bonneville, T100, Thruxton and Scrambler models, disconnect the battery negative . . .

8.9b . . . and positive leads . . .

8.9c . . . release the retaining strap (arrowed) . . .

8.9d . . . pull out the wedge . . .

8.9e . . . remove the rear cover . . .

8.9f . . . and lift out the battery

8.9g Peel back the connector covers then disconnect the ECM connectors

8.11 ECM location – 2011-on America and Speedmaster

9.2a EMS relay location (arrowed) – Bonneville, T100, Thruxton and Scrambler

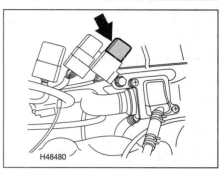

9.2b EMS relay location (arrowed) – America and Speedmaster

Section 3 and remove the battery. Free the rubber cover from the ECM, then press in the tabs and disconnect the grey and black connectors (see illustration 8.9g).

11 On America and Speedmaster models from 2011 the ECM is under the right-hand side panel (see illustration). Remove the retaining bracket screw, then release the bracket. Peel back the ECM's wire connector sleeves, then press in the tabs and disconnect the grey and black connectors (see illustration 8.9g).

12 Installation is the reverse of removal. Check the terminal pins and connectors for damage and corrosion. The connectors are colour-coded black and grey and shaped so they cannot be re-connected the wrong way round (see illustration 8.7).

9 EMS relay

Note: Before disconnecting the relay, make sure the ignition has been switched OFF for at least one minute to allow the system to power down, then disconnect the battery (see Chapter 8). Refer to the Wiring Diagrams at the end of Chapter 8 for relay terminal identification.

1 The engine management system (EMS) has its own power relay which is designed to provide a steady voltage supply to the ECM. The ECM holds the relay open after the ignition is switched off to enable it perform various power-down functions, such as writing data to the memory.

2 The EMS relay is located under the seat on Bonneville, T100, Thruxton and Scrambler models and under the fuel tank on America and Speedmaster models (see illustrations). Disconnect the relay from its connector block. Check the terminals and sockets for damage and corrosion.

3 Using a fully-charged 12 volt battery and two insulated jumper wires, connect the battery across the relay coil terminals (A and B) on the relay; at this point the relay should be heard to click and there should be continuity or zero resistance indicated when a meter is connected across terminals C and D (see illustration). If this is the case the relay is proved good. If the relay does not click when battery voltage is applied and the meter indicates no continuity or infinite resistance, the relay is faulty and must be replaced with a new one.

10 Sensors

Note: Before disconnecting the wiring connector from any sensor, make sure the ignition is switched OFF, and disconnect the battery (see Chapter 8).

Ambient air pressure (AP) sensor

1 The AP sensor reads the pressure of the atmospheric (barometric) pressure (i.e. air density). The ECM combines this with other information to determine fuelling requirements.

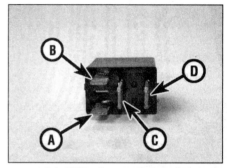

9.3 EMS relay test terminals

2 The sensor is located under the seat (see illustrations). Disconnect the wiring connector from the sensor, then unscrew the bolt securing it. Installation is the reverse of removal.

Crankshaft position (CKP) sensor

3 The CKP sensor reads the position of the crankshaft and how fast it is turning; this information is used by the ECM to determine which cylinder is on its ignition stroke and when it should fire. The ECM combines engine speed with information from other sensors to determine fuelling and ignition requirements.

4 The sensor is mounted to the right-hand side of the upper crankcase (see illustration 4.8 in Chapter 4). Its wire connector is located on the right-hand side of the frame, above the air filter housing (see illustration); remove the side panel for access. Note that

10.2a Ambient air pressure sensor (arrowed) – Bonneville, T100, Thruxton and Scrambler

10.2b Ambient air pressure sensor – America and Speedmaster

10.4 Crankshaft position sensor wire connector (arrowed)

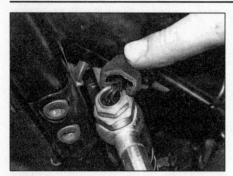

10.5a Oil temperature sensor – Bonneville shown

10.5b Oil temperature sensor – America shown

10.6 Oil temperature sensor resistance test

in certain cases, removal of the air filter housing may be required for full access to the connector.

Oil temperature sensor

5 The sensor reads the temperature of the engine oil, and the ECM uses the information to determine fuelling requirements, particularly for hot and cold starting. It is screwed into the banjo union bolt at the top left side (Bonneville, T100, Thruxton and Scrambler) or top right side (America and Speedmaster) of the oil cooler (see illustrations).

6 A fault with the sensor will cause the MIL to come on – refer to Section 8 for details of how to download fault codes. The sensor's resistance can be measured across the two pins in the wiring connector and the reading compared to the base value at 20°C (68°F)

given in the Specifications. Make sure the ignition is switched OFF before conducting the test. Trace the wiring up to the connector which is under the fuel tank, disconnect it and make the tests on the sensor side of the connector (see illustration).

7 Refer to Chapter 2, Section 6 for details of sensor removal and installation.

Intake air temperature (IAT) sensor

8 The sensor reads the temperature of the air in the air filter housing. As changes in temperature affect air density, the ECM uses the information to determine fuelling requirements.

9 The sensor is located in the right-hand side of the air filter housing on Bonneville, T100, Thruxton and Scrambler models and can be

accessed by removing the right-hand side panel. On America and Speedmaster models, the sensor is located in the top of the air filter housing; remove the seat for access. A single screw retains the sensor (see illustrations).

10 A fault with the sensor will cause the MIL to come on – refer to Section 8 for details of how to download fault codes. To test the sensor, make sure the ignition is switched OFF then remove the right-hand side panel and disconnect the sensor's wire connector. Using a multimeter set to the K-ohms range, measure the resistance across the sensor's two terminals and compare it with the value given for 20°C (68°F) in the Specifications (see illustration).

Manifold absolute pressure (MAP) sensors

11 Individual MAP sensors read the pressure of the air in each throttle body.

12 The sensors are mounted under the fuel tank alongside the frame top tube; on the right-hand side on Bonneville, T100, Thruxton and Scrambler models and on the left-hand side on America and Speedmaster models. A bolt retains each MAP sensor. It is important that the sensors, their wiring and vacuum hoses are not mixed up. Note that the wiring to the left-hand cylinder sensor is marked 'cylinder 1' and the wiring and sensor itself for the right-hand cylinder are marked with a dab of red paint (see illustrations). The vacuum pipes which link the sensors to the intake manifolds, have two dots of paint on their

10.9a Remove the screw to free the IAT sensor on Bonneville, T100, Thruxton and Scrambler

10.9b IAT sensor (arrowed) on America and Speedmaster

10.10 IAT sensor resistance test

10.12a Left-hand MAP sensor wiring label

10.12b Right-hand MAP sensor wiring marking (arrowed)

10.12c Vacuum pipe links the MAP sensor to the stub (arrowed) on the intake manifold

10.16a Note the oxygen sensor wiring route behind the oil cooler mounting and through the frame clip (arrowed) . . .

upper ends – white dots on the left pipe and red dots on the right **(see illustration)**.

13 No testing is possible, apart from checking that the wiring and hoses are in good order. A fault with either sensor will cause the MIL to come on – refer to Section 8 for details of how to download fault codes.

Oxygen (lambda) sensors

14 An oxygen sensor is located in each exhaust downpipe. The sensors measure oxygen left in the unburnt exhaust gases and generate a signal voltage which is fed back to the ECM. In this way the ECM can correct the mixture supplied to the engine to ensure that the oxygen content of the exhaust gases remains within a narrow range and suitable for the operation of the catalytic converter. This type of system is called closed-loop control. Each sensor contains a heater element to enable the sensor to reach its operating temperature quickly upon start-up.

15 A fault with either sensor will cause the MIL to come on – refer to Section 8 for details of how to download fault codes.

16 Remove the fuel tank to access the sensor wiring connectors. Trace the wiring from the sensor, freeing it from its guides and any ties on the frame downtubes, and disconnect it at

the wiring connector **(see illustrations)**. Feed the wiring back down to the sensor, noting its routing.

17 Unscrew and remove the sensor – the sensor is fragile so care must be taken not to apply undue force. If the sensor is difficult to unscrew or the area around it is badly corroded, apply a penetrating fluid **(see illustration)**.

18 When installing the sensor, apply copper grease to the sensor threads. A torque setting is specified at the beginning of the Chapter, but note not only is a special cut-away socket required to accommodate the sensor wiring, but that the exhaust downpipe will require removal to provide access. Reconnect the sensor wiring connector, making sure the wiring is correctly routed and secured; note that the wiring to the right-hand sensor has red tape around the sleeve at its upper end **(see illustration)**.

Throttle position (TP) sensor

19 The sensor reads the amount of throttle being used.

20 The sensor is located on the left-hand end of the throttle body **(see illustration)**. Do not remove the throttle position sensor unless you know it is faulty and are replacing it with a new

one, or unless you are replacing the throttle body with a new one. If you do remove it, it must be set up using the Triumph diagnostic tool. Failure to set the sensor position correctly could cause a sticking throttle and loss of throttle control.

21 Disconnect the wiring to the TP sensor. Undo the sensor's retaining screw and ease the sensor out of the throttle body, rotating it slightly anticlockwise to free its O-ring.

22 Locate the new O-ring and sensor into the throttle body, engaging it with the throttle shaft, then secure it with the retaining screw.

10.16b . . . up to the sensor wiring connectors near the frame headstock

10.17 A ring spanner with cut-out to accept the wiring being used to unscrew the oxygen sensor

10.18 Wiring from right-hand oxygen sensor is marked with red tape (arrowed)

10.20 Throttle position sensor

10.25a Tip-over sensor – Bonneville, T100, Thruxton and Scrambler

10.25b Tip-over sensor – America and Speedmaster

of the O-ring and replace it with a new one if it is deformed or has deteriorated, or there is evidence of oil leakage from it **(see illustration)**.

11 Throttle cables

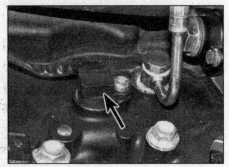

10.28a Speed sensor (arrowed)

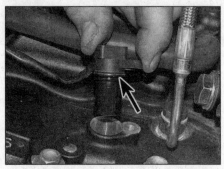

10.28b Note sensor O-ring (arrowed)

⚠ *Warning: Refer to the precautions given in Section 1 before proceeding.*

Removal

1 Displace the throttle bodies (see Section 6). This will involve detaching the lower ends of the cables from the throttle cam.

2 Mark each cable according to its location at both ends. If new cables are being fitted, match them to the old cables to ensure they are correctly installed.

3 On Bonneville models up to VIN 380776, T100, Thruxton, America and Speedmaster models, unscrew the throttle opening cable elbow retaining plate screw and the closing cable retaining nut on the right-hand switch housing **(see illustration)**. Detach the switch housing front by undoing the screws **(see illustrations)**. Remove the two screws to free the master cylinder/housing and its clamp from the handlebar. Detach the cable ends from the pulley, then remove the cable elbows from the housing **(see illustration)**.

4 On Bonneville models from VIN 380777 and Scrambler models, pull the rubber boot off the cables at the throttle housing

23 The sensor must now be set up correctly using the Triumph diagnostic tool.

Tip-over (TO) sensor

24 The sensor is basically a safety switch that tells the ECM if the bike has fallen over, in which case the ECM will shut down the fuel pump and stop the engine. The switch can be reset by picking the bike up and turning the ignition off, then on again. A fault with the sensor will cause the MIL to come on – refer to Section 8 for details of how to download fault codes.

25 The sensor is mounted underneath the seat **(see illustrations)**. Disconnect its wiring connector. Unscrew the bolts and remove the sensor.

26 Install the sensor with the UP mark at the top.

Speed sensor – models with electronic speedometer

27 The sensor reads the road speed of the bike by counting the rate at which the transmission output shaft is turning. This information is used by the ECM in conjunction with engine speed information to determine which gear the bike is in, and controls fuelling and ignition accordingly. A fault with the sensor will cause the MIL to come on – refer to Section 8 for details of how to download fault codes.

28 The speed sensor is located in the top of the crankcase **(see illustration)**. Make sure the ignition is switched OFF. Remove the right-hand side panel to access the wiring connector –

trace the wiring from the sensor to locate it. Disconnect the wiring connector, then unscrew the bolt and remove the sensor. Installation is the reverse of removal – check the condition

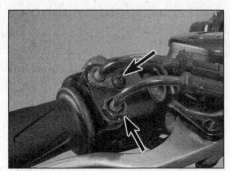

11.3a Undo the screw and nut (arrowed)

11.3c . . . and detach the switch housing . . .

11.3b Undo the screws (arrowed) . . .

11.3d . . . then free the cable ends from the pulley

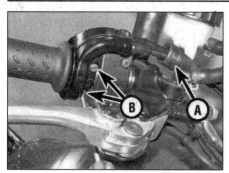

11.4a Pull back the cable boot (A) and remove the two screws (B) . . .

11.4b . . . separate the housing halves . . .

11.4c . . . and disconnect the cables

end **(see illustration)**. Unscrew the throttle housing screws and separate the halves **(see illustration)**. Detach the cable ends from the pulley in the housing **(see illustration)**.

Installation

5 On Bonneville models from VIN 380777 and Scrambler models, lubricate the cable nipples with multi-purpose grease and fit them into the cable pulley at the handlebar, making sure they are the correct way round. Fit the cable elbows into the housing, making sure they locate correctly. Join the housing halves and tighten the screws **(see illustration 11.4a)**. Fit the rubber boot.

6 On Bonneville models up to VIN 380776, T100, Thruxton, America and Speedmaster models, lubricate the cable nipples with multi-purpose grease, fit them through the housing and engage them in the throttle pulley **(see illustration 11.3d)**. The opening cable has the retaining plate. Fit the cable elbows into the housing and secure with the retaining plate and screw (opening cable) and with the nut (closing cable). Mount the master cylinder/housing on the handlebar and fit the clamp so that the joint aligns with the punch mark in the bar. Tighten the upper bolt fully, then tighten the lower bolt (there will be a gap at the lower joint), both to the specified torque setting. Install the switch housing **(see illustrations 11.3c and b)**. Tighten the closing cable retaining nut and fit the opening cable retaining plate and screw **(see illustration 11.3a)**.

7 Feed the cables through to the throttle bodies, making sure they are correctly routed. The cables must not interfere with any other component and should not be kinked or bent sharply.

8 Fit the throttle bodes partway between the engine and air filter housing (see Section 6). Lubricate the cable ends with multi-purpose grease.

9 The throttle opening cable fits into the rear section of the bracket. Fit the cable ends into the throttle cam then locate the cables in the bracket and draw them up so that the lower nut becomes captive against the small lug. Tighten the top nuts down onto the bracket.

10 Fully install the throttle bodies (see Section 6). Adjust the cable freeplay (see Chapter 1). Operate the throttle to check that it opens and closes freely. Turn the handlebars back and

forth to make sure the cables don't cause the steering to bind.

11 Start the engine and check that the idle speed does not rise as the handlebars are turned. If it does, the throttle cables are routed incorrectly. Correct the problem before riding the motorcycle.

12 Exhaust system

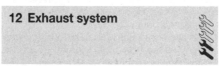

Silencers

1 Refer to Chapter 3A, Section 10, noting the following.
● Later Bonneville models (from VIN 380777) are fitted with the Thruxton style silencers.
● On 2011 and later America and Speedmaster models, the silencer rear mounting bolts directly to the frame **(see illustration)** unlike on earlier models where it is held by the passenger footrest plate lower bolt.

Exhaust pipes

2 Refer to Chapter 3A, Section 10, noting that the oxygen sensor wiring must be disconnected at the wire connectors under the fuel tank **(see illustration 10.16b)**. It is important when reconnecting the sensor wiring not to inadvertently swap over the left and right sensor wire connections – the right-hand sensor wiring and connector have a red marking. If the wire connections are inadvertently swapped, engine damage could occur and a fault code will be registered.

12.1 Silencer bolts directly to frame on 2011-on America and Speedmaster

13 Secondary air induction system (SAIS)

1 The system consists of an electrically actuated control valve and two reed valves, with a hose system supplying air from the air filter housing via the control valve to the reed valves. At certain engine speeds, the electronic control module (ECM) opens the control valve and air is drawn into the exhaust ports via the reed valves. The introduced air promotes further combustion of the exhaust gases, reducing the level of pollutants. The reed valves prevent exhaust gases blowing back into the air filter housing.

Control valve and hoses

2 Remove the fuel tank (see Section 2).

3 Check the system hoses for loose connections, cracks and deterioration, and replace them with new ones if necessary.

4 A control valve fault should be indicated by the MIL (Malfunction Indicator Light) in the speedometer and it is possible to download the fault code with the Triumph diagnostic tool or a fault code reader (see Section 8).

5 If a fault is indicated trace the wiring from the valve and disconnect it at the connector **(see illustration)**. Check for continuity in the wiring between the loom side of the connector and the ECM. Measure the resistance of the control valve windings using an ohmmeter connected across the terminals in the valve side of the connector – it should be as

13.5a Disconnect the control valve wiring

13.5b Testing the control valve resistance

13.6a Pull off the air inlet hose . . .

13.6b . . . and the air outlet hose

specified at the beginning of the Chapter; note that the test can be made with the valve in situ or on the bench **(see illustration)**.

6 Release the clip and disconnect the air inlet and outlet hoses **(see illustrations)**. Remove the control valve, noting how it locates.

7 Blow into the valve inlet union – air should flow through the valve and out the outlet union **(see illustration)**. Now, using a fully charged 12 volt battery and two insulated jumper wires, connect the battery across the two wire terminals; the valve should be heard to close **(see illustration)**. Check that the valve has closed by again blowing into the inlet union – no air should flow through the valve. If the valve does not function as described, replace it with a new one.

8 Installation is the reverse of removal. Note that the control valve locates over two studs **(see illustration)**. Ensure that the wiring connector terminals are clean and that the connector is secure.

Reed valves

9 Refer to Chapter 1, Section 26 for information on the reed valves.

14 EVAP system – California market models

1 This system prevents the escape of fuel vapour into the atmosphere by storing it in a charcoal-filled canister located beneath the swingarm. The purge control valve is also located next to the canister.

2 When the engine is stopped, fuel vapour from the tank is directed into the canister via the vent hose where it is absorbed and stored

whilst the motorcycle is standing. When the engine is started, the purge control valve opens, thus drawing vapours which are stored in the canister into the throttle body to be burned during the normal combustion process.

3 The canister incorporates a one-way valve which prevents fuel vapour returning to the tank. The tank filler cap also has a one-way valve which allows air into the tank as the volume of fuel decreases, but prevents any fuel vapour from escaping.

4 The system is not adjustable and can be properly tested only by a Triumph dealer, as the diagnostic tool is required. However the owner can check that all the hoses are in good condition and are securely connected at each end. Replace any hoses that are cracked, split or generally deteriorated with new ones.

5 You can also check the purge valve by disconnecting the wiring connector and measuring the resistance of the valve using an ohmmeter. If the result is not as specified at the beginning of the Chapter, in particular if there is infinite or no resistance, replace the valve with a new one.

15 Catalytic converter

General information

1 The catalytic converter minimises the level of exhaust pollutants released into the atmosphere. It consists of a canister containing a fine mesh impregnated with a catalyst material, over which the hot exhaust gases pass. The catalyst speeds up the oxidation

of harmful carbon monoxide, unburned hydrocarbons and soot, effectively reducing the quantity of harmful products released into the atmosphere via the exhaust gases.

2 The catalytic converter is housed in the exhaust downpipe assembly.

3 It operates under closed-loop control with an oxygen (Lambda) sensor in each silencer feeding back gas oxygen content information to the ECM; information on the sensor can be found in Section 10.

Precautions

4 The catalytic converter is a reliable and simple device which needs no maintenance in itself, but there are some precautions the owner should note if the converter is to function properly for its full service life.

● DO NOT use leaded or lead replacement petrol (gasoline) – the additives will coat the precious metals, reducing their converting efficiency and will eventually destroy the catalytic converter.

● Always keep the ignition and fuel systems well-maintained in accordance with the manufacturer's schedule.

● If the engine develops a misfire, do not ride the bike at all (or at least as little as possible) until the fault is cured.

● DO NOT use fuel or engine oil additives – these may contain substances harmful to the catalytic converter.

● DO NOT continue to use the bike if the engine burns oil to the extent of leaving a visible trail of blue smoke.

● Remember that the catalytic converter is FRAGILE – do not strike it with tools during servicing work.

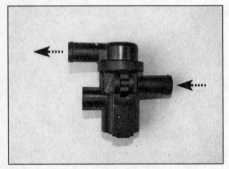

13.7a Air should flow freely through the valve . . .

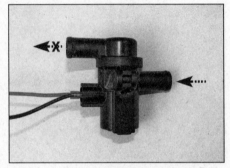

13.7b . . . except when battery voltage is applied

13.8 Locate the control valve mounting holes over the two studs (arrowed)

Chapter 4
Ignition system

Contents

Degrees of difficulty

| Easy, suitable for novice with little experience | | Fairly easy, suitable for beginner with some experience | | Fairly difficult, suitable for competent DIY mechanic |  | Difficult, suitable for experienced DIY mechanic | | Very difficult, suitable for expert DIY or professional | |

Specifications

General information

Spark plugs	see Chapter 1

Ignition HT coil(s)

Primary winding resistance	
Carburettor models	approx. 6 ohms
EFI models	1.3 to 1.9 ohms
Secondary winding resistance	approx. 15 K-ohms @ 20°C
Spark plug cap resistance	approx. 5 K-ohms @ 20°C

Pick-up coil/CKP sensor

Air gap	0.8 to 0.9 mm

Torque settings

Alternator cover bolts.	9 Nm
Front footrest mounting bracket bolts – America and Speedmaster . . .	30 Nm
Pick-up coil/CKP sensor screws	10 Nm

1 General information

All models are fitted with a digital inductive ignition system, which due to its lack of mechanical parts is totally maintenance free. On carburettor models, the system comprises triggers on the alternator rotor, a pick-up coil, ignition control unit and ignition HT coils(s). On EFI models, ignition and fuel system management is controlled by the engine control module (ECM); the ignition element of the system comprises the triggers on the alternator rotor, a crankshaft position (CKP) sensor, the ECM and ignition HT coil(s).

Bonneville, T100 and Thruxton models are fitted with one HT coil which serves both cylinder spark plugs using the wasted spark principal. America, Speedmaster and Scrambler models have two HT coils due to the engine's 270° firing pattern.

The ignition triggers, which are on the alternator rotor on the right-hand end of the crankshaft, magnetically operate the pick-up coil (CKP sensor on EFI models) as the crankshaft rotates. The coil/sensor provides the ignition control unit (ECM on EFI models) with engine speed and piston position. The ignition timing is then determined by the control unit/ECM, which compares the signals it receives from the coil/sensor and also the throttle position sensor to stored data in the form of ignition maps in its ROM – there is no provision for adjusting the ignition timing. The ignition control unit/ECM then supplies the HT coil(s) with the power necessary to produce a spark at the plugs at the optimum time.

A rev limiter cuts in at 7400 rpm on 790 cc engines and at 8000 rpm on 865 cc engines.

The system also incorporates a starter lockout circuit which will cut the ignition if the sidestand is extended whilst the engine is running and in gear, or if a gear is selected whilst the engine is running and the sidestand is extended. It also prevents the engine from being started if the engine is in gear while the sidestand is down. The engine can be started with the sidestand down as long as it is in neutral.

Because of their nature, the individual ignition system components can be checked but not repaired. If ignition system troubles occur, and the faulty component can be isolated, the only cure for the problem is to replace the part with a new one. Keep in mind that most electrical parts, once purchased, cannot be returned. To avoid unnecessary expense, make very sure the faulty component has been positively identified before buying a replacement part.

2 Ignition system check

⚠️ **Warning: The energy levels in electronic systems can be very high. On no account should the ignition be switched on whilst the plugs or plug caps are being held. Shocks from the HT circuit can be most unpleasant.**

2.2a Ease the cap up using a
screwdriver . . .

2.2b . . . then lift it off the plug by hand

3.2 Ignition coil (arrowed) –
Bonneville, T100 and Thruxton

**Secondly, it is vital that the engine is not
turned over or run with any of the plug caps
removed, and that the plugs are soundly
earthed (grounded) when the system is
checked for sparking. The ignition system
components can be seriously damaged if
the HT circuit becomes isolated.**

1 As no means of adjustment is available, any
failure of the system can be traced to failure of
a system component or a simple wiring fault. Of
the two possibilities, the latter is by far the most
likely. In the event of failure, check the system in
a logical fashion, as described below.

2 Work on one cylinder at a time. Pull the cap
off the spark plug – you may need to ease it
up using a screwdriver as access is restricted
(see illustrations). Fit a spare spark plug that
is known to be good into the cap and lay the
plug against the cylinder head with the threads
contacting it. If necessary, hold the spark plug
with an insulated tool.

 **Warning: Do not remove either of
the spark plugs from the engine
to perform this check – atomised
fuel being pumped out of the
open spark plug hole could ignite, causing
severe injury! Make sure the test plug is
securely held against the engine – otherwise
when the engine is turned over, the ignition
control unit/ECM could be damaged.**

3 Check that the kill switch is in the 'RUN'
position and the transmission is in neutral,
then turn the ignition switch ON, and turn the
engine over on the starter motor. If the system
is in good condition a regular, fat blue spark
should be evident at the plug electrodes.

If the spark appears thin or yellowish, or is
non-existent, further investigation will be
necessary. Turn the ignition off and repeat the
test for the other spark plug.

4 The ignition system must be able to
produce a spark which is capable of jumping
a particular size gap. A healthy system should
produce a spark capable of jumping at least
8 mm. Simple ignition spark gap testing tools
are available, some of which are adjustable to
set the exact gap – follow the manufacturer's
instructions, and check each spark plug.

5 If the test results are good the entire ignition
system can be considered good. If the spark
appears thin or yellowish, or is non-existent,
further investigation is necessary.

6 Ignition faults can be divided into two
categories, namely those where the ignition
system has failed completely, and those
which are due to a partial failure. The likely
faults are listed below, starting with the most
probable source of failure. Work through the
list systematically, referring to the subsequent
sections for full details of the necessary checks
and tests, and to the *Wiring Diagrams* at the
end of Chapter 8. **Note:** *Before checking
the following items ensure that the battery is
fully charged and that all fuses are in good
condition.*

● Loose, corroded or damaged wiring
connections, broken or shorted wiring
between any of the component parts of the
ignition system (see Chapter 8, Section 2).
● Faulty HT lead or spark plug cap, faulty spark
plug, dirty, worn or corroded plug electrodes,
or incorrect gap between electrodes.

● Faulty ignition (main) switch or engine kill
switch (see Chapter 8).
● Faulty neutral, clutch or sidestand switch,
or diode unit (see Chapter 8).
● Faulty pick-up coil/CKP sensor or damaged
trigger.
● Faulty ignition HT coil(s).
● Faulty ignition control unit/ECM.

7 If the above checks don't reveal the cause
of the problem, have the ignition system
tested by a Triumph dealer.

3 Ignition HT coil(s)

Check

Bonneville, T100 and Thruxton

1 Make sure the ignition is switched OFF.
Remove the seat (see Chapter 7). Disconnect
the battery (see Chapter 8).

2 The coil is mounted below the main frame
spar under the fuel tank **(see illustration)**.
Remove the fuel tank for access (see Chapter 3). Check the coil visually for cracks,
loose wiring connectors and leads, and other
damage.

3 The coil can be tested in situ. Pull the caps
off the spark plugs **(see illustration)**.

4 Measure the primary circuit resistance
with an ohmmeter or multimeter as follows:
disconnect the primary circuit wiring
connectors from the coil, noting which fits
where – the red wire goes to the positive (+)

3.3 Pull the cap off each plug

3.4a Disconnect the primary
wiring connectors

3.4b To test the coil primary resistance,
connect the multimeter leads between the
primary circuit connector terminals

3.5 To test the coil secondary resistance, connect the probes to the spark plug cap sockets

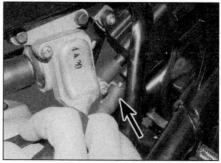

3.6a Pull the lead (arrowed) out of the coil . . .

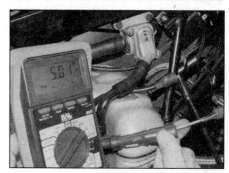

3.6b . . . and check the resistance of the lead and plug cap as shown

terminal on the coil **(see illustration)**. Set the meter to the ohms x 1 scale and measure the resistance between the terminals on the coil **(see illustration)**. If the reading obtained is not within the range shown in the Specifications, it is possible that the coil is defective.

5 Measure the secondary circuit resistance with a multimeter as follows: set the meter to the K-ohm scale. Connect the meter probes to the contacts in the spark plug caps **(see illustration)**. If the reading obtained is not within the range shown in the Specifications, it is possible that the coil is defective.

6 Before buying a new coil, pull the HT lead out of its socket on the coil and measure the resistance of the lead and cap by connecting the meter probes between the HT lead end and the spark plug socket in the cap **(see illustrations)**. If the reading obtained is not as specified, replace the spark plug cap with a new one. If the coil is still suspect, substitute it with one that is known to be good before condemning it. If the problem still exists, then the fault is probably in the primary wiring circuit – refer to Wiring Diagrams at the end of Chapter 8 and check the wiring and connectors in the circuit.

7 If the coil is confirmed to be faulty, it must be replaced with a new one: it is a sealed unit and cannot therefore be repaired.

America, Speedmaster and Scrambler

8 Make sure the ignition is switched OFF. Remove the seat (see Chapter 7). Disconnect the battery (see Chapter 8).

9 The coils are mounted below the main frame spar under the fuel tank **(see illustration)**.

3.9 Ignition coil (arrowed) – America and Speedmaster

Remove the fuel tank for access (see Chapter 3A or 3B). The left-hand coil is for the left-hand cylinder. Check the coils visually for cracks, loose wiring connectors and leads, and other damage.

10 The coils can be tested in situ. Pull the cap off the spark plug for the coil being tested **(see illustration 3.3)**.

11 Measure the primary circuit resistance with an ohmmeter or multimeter as follows: disconnect the primary circuit wiring connectors, noting which fits where – the red wire goes to the positive (+) terminal on the coil **(see illustration 3.4a)**. Set the meter to the ohms x 1 scale and measure the resistance between the terminals on the coil **(see illustration 3.4b)**. If the reading obtained is not within the range shown in the Specifications, it is possible that the coil is defective.

12 Measure the secondary circuit resistance with a multimeter as follows: set the meter to the K-ohm scale. Connect the positive (+) meter probe to the contact in the spark plug and the negative (-) probe to the primary circuit terminal for the red wire. If the reading obtained is not within the range shown in the Specifications, it is possible that the coil is defective.

13 Before buying a new coil, pull the HT lead out of its socket on the coil and measure the resistance of the lead and cap by connecting the meter probes between the HT lead end and the spark plug socket in the cap **(see illustrations 3.6a and b)**. If the reading obtained is not as specified, replace the spark plug cap with a new one. If the coil is still suspect, substitute it with one that is known to be good before condemning it. If the problem still exists, then the fault is probably

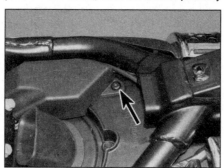

4.2 Undo the screw (arrowed) and remove the wiring cover

in the primary wiring circuit – refer to Wiring Diagrams at the end of Chapter 8 and check the wiring and connectors in the circuit.

14 If a coil is confirmed to be faulty, it must be replaced with a new one: the coils are sealed units and cannot therefore be repaired.

Removal and installation

15 Make sure the ignition is switched OFF. Remove the seat (see Chapter 7). Disconnect the battery (see Chapter 8).

16 The coil(s) is/are mounted below the main frame spar under the fuel tank **(see illustration 3.2 or 3.9)**. Remove the fuel tank for access (see Chapter 3A or 3B).

17 Pull the cap(s) off the spark plug(s) **(see illustration 3.3)**. Feed the lead(s) through to the coil(s), noting its routing.

18 Disconnect the primary circuit wiring connectors from the coil, making a careful note of which fits where **(see illustration 3.4a)**. Unscrew the bolts securing the coil and remove it.

19 Installation is the reverse of removal. Make sure the wiring connectors and HT leads are correctly routed and securely connected.

4 Pick-up coil/crankshaft position sensor

Check – carburettor models

1 Disconnect the battery negative (–) lead (see Chapter 8).

2 On Bonneville, T100, Thruxton and Scrambler remove the right-hand side panel (see Chapter 7). On America and Speedmaster remove the seat(s) (see Chapter 7), then undo the screw and release the wiring connector bundle cover.

3 If the pick-up coil is thought to be faulty, first check that it is not due to a damaged or broken wire or terminal: pinched or broken wires can usually be repaired.

4 Trace the wiring from the alternator cover on the right-hand side of the engine and disconnect it at the 2-pin connector. Using a multimeter set to the ohms x 100 scale, check for a resistance between the terminals on the pick-up coil side of the connector.

4.8 Undo the screws (arrowed) and remove the pick-up coil/CKP sensor

5 Triumph do not give a specification for the coil resistance, but if the meter indicates a short circuit (no measurable resistance) or an open circuit (infinite, or very high resistance) the pick-up coil should be substituted with one that is known to be good to see if the problem is cured.

Check – EFI models

6 Refer to Chapter 3B, Section 10 for the crankshaft position (CKP) sensor checking procedures.

Removal and installation – all models

7 Remove the alternator cover (see Chapter 8). Trace the wiring from the pick-up coil (CKP sensor) on the right-hand side of the engine and disconnect it at the 2-pin connector. Feed the wiring back to the coil, noting its routing and releasing it from any clips or ties.

8 Undo the screws securing the coil/sensor, then free its wiring from the rear balancer shaft retainer plate, noting its routing, and the grommet from the cut-out, and remove the coil/sensor from the engine **(see illustration)**.

9 Apply a suitable non-permanent thread locking compound to the coil/sensor screws. Fit it onto the engine and tighten its screws finger-tight **(see illustration)**. Route the wiring around the retainer plate and locate the wiring grommet in its cut-out **(see illustrations)**. Align one of the triggers on the alternator rotor with the coil/sensor pick-up tip and set the air gap between them as specified at the beginning of the Chapter using a feeler gauge **(see illustration)**. When it is correct tighten the screws to the torque setting specified at the beginning of the chapter, making

5.3a Ignition control unit (arrowed) – Bonneville, T100, Thruxton and Scrambler

4.9a Apply thread lock to the screws

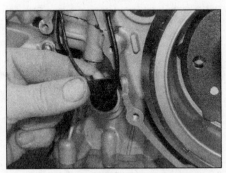

4.9c ... then fit the grommet into its cut-out

sure the coil/sensor does not move – check the air gap again to be sure. Feed the wiring through to the connector, securing it with any clips or ties and making sure it is correctly routed, and reconnect it.

10 Install the alternator cover.

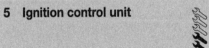

5 Ignition control unit

Check

1 If the tests shown in the preceding or following Sections have failed to isolate the cause of an ignition fault, it is possible that the ignition control unit itself is faulty. No test details are available with which the unit can be tested. If a fault is suspected seek the advice of a Triumph dealer.

5.3b Ignition control unit (arrowed) – America and Speedmaster

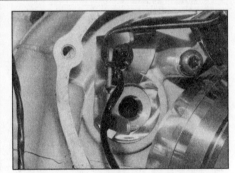

4.9b Route the wiring correctly ...

4.9d Check the air gap as described

Removal

2 Remove the seat (see Chapter 7). Make sure the ignition is OFF. Disconnect the battery negative lead (see Chapter 8). On America and Speedmaster remove the fuel tank (see Chapter 3A).

3 Disconnect the wiring connector from the unit **(see illustrations)**.

4 On Bonneville, T100, Thruxton and Scrambler models, unscrew the nut securing the unit and remove it.

5 On America and Speedmaster models, unscrew the bolts securing the unit and remove it.

Installation

6 Installation is the reverse of removal. Make sure the wiring connector is correctly and securely connected.

6 Ignition timing

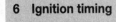

Since it is not possible to adjust the ignition timing and since no component is subject to mechanical wear, there is no provision for any checks. While in theory it is possible to check the timing dynamically (engine running) using a stroboscopic lamp, the firing point at idle is not actually marked on the alternator rotor. If the timing is suspected of being out or not advancing properly, the fault may lie with the pick-up coil/CKP sensor and its wiring and connectors (see Section 4) or the ignition control unit/ECM.

Chapter 5
Frame, suspension and final drive

Contents

Degrees of difficulty

Easy, suitable for novice with little experience	**Fairly easy,** suitable for beginner with some experience	**Fairly difficult,** suitable for competent DIY mechanic	**Difficult,** suitable for experienced DIY mechanic	**Very difficult,** suitable for expert DIY or professional

Specifications

Front forks
Fork oil type	10W (Kayaba G10)
Fork oil capacity	
Bonneville 2001 to 2008 (up to VIN 380776) and all T100	484 cc
Bonneville 2009-on (from VIN 380777).	499 cc
America and Speedmaster 2002 to 2007.	484 cc
America and Speedmaster 2008 to 2010.	552 cc
America 2011-on	561 cc
Speedmaster 2011-on	555 cc
Thruxton.	466 cc
Scrambler.	517 cc
Fork oil level*	
Bonneville 2001 to 2008 (up to VIN 380776) and all T100	120 mm
Bonneville 2009-on (from VIN 380777).	106 mm
America and Speedmaster 2002 to 2007.	166 mm
America and Speedmaster 2008 to 2010.	161 mm
America and Speedmaster 2011-on	135 mm
Thruxton.	143 mm
Scrambler.	123 mm

*Oil level is measured from the top of the tube with the spring removed and the leg fully compressed.

Final drive
Drive chain slack, lubricant and chain stretch limit	see Chapter 1
Drive chain type	
Bonneville and T100.	DID 525 VM2, 102 link
Thruxton.	DID 525 VM2, 104 link
America and Speedmaster.	DID 525 VM2, 112 link
Scrambler.	DID 525 VM2, 106 link

Final drive (continued)

Sprocket sizes	Front (engine)	Rear (wheel)
Bonneville and T100		
with 790 cc engine	17T	43T
with 865 cc engine	18T	43T
Thruxton and Scrambler	18T	43T
Speedmaster		
with 790 cc engine up to VIN 179828	16T	42T
with 790 cc engine from VIN 179829 and all 865 cc engines	18T	42T
America		
with 790 cc engine	17T	42T
with 865 cc engine up to VIN 282963 (Factory 2)		
or up to VIN 273654 (Factory 4)	17T	42T
with 865 cc engine from VIN 282964 (Factory 2)		
or from VIN 273655 (Factory 4)	18T	42T

Torque settings

Clutch lever bracket clamp bolts	15 Nm
Brake pedal pivot bolt	
Bonneville and T100	15 Nm
America and Speedmaster	30 Nm
Thruxton	22 Nm
Scrambler	27 Nm
Footrest mounting nut	17 Nm
Fork clamp bolts	
Bonneville, T100, Thruxton and Scrambler	
Top and bottom yokes	27 Nm
America and Speedmaster	
Top yoke – up to 2010	26 Nm
Top yoke – 2011-on	24 Nm
Bottom yoke	45 Nm
Fork damper rod bolt	
Bonneville, T100, Thruxton and Scrambler	30 Nm
America and Speedmaster	43 Nm
Fork top bolt	23 Nm
Front brake master cylinder clamp bolts	15 Nm
Front sprocket cover bolts	9 Nm
Front sprocket nut	132 Nm
Handlebar end-weights	5 Nm
Handlebar clamp bolts – Bonneville, T100, America, Speedmaster	
and Scrambler	26 Nm
Handlebar clamp bolts – Thruxton	27 Nm
Handlebar positioning bolts – Thruxton	11 Nm
Handlebar holder nuts (holder-to-top yoke)	
Bonneville, T100, Scrambler and Thruxton with high handlebars	35 Nm
America and Speedmaster up to 2010	45 Nm
America 2011-on	35 Nm
Handlebar holder bolts (holder-to-top yoke) – 2011-on Speedmaster	62 Nm
Rear shock absorber mounting bolts	28 Nm
Rear sprocket carrier studs	30 Nm
Rear sprocket nuts	
Bonneville, T100, Thruxton and Scrambler	55 Nm
America and Speedmaster	85 Nm
Rider's footrest bracket mounting bolts – Bonneville, T100	
and Thruxton	27 Nm
Sidestand pivot bolt	20 Nm
Sidestand pivot bolt nut	25 Nm
Steering head bearing adjuster nut pre-load (with service tool)	40 Nm
Steering head bearing locknut (with service tool)	40 Nm
Steering stem nut	90 Nm
Swingarm pivot clamp bolts – Bonneville, T100, Thruxton and Scrambler	
Up to VIN 333839	45 Nm
From VIN 333840	40 Nm
Swingarm pivot clamp bolts – America and Speedmaster	40 Nm
Swingarm pivot bolt nut	110 Nm

3.1a Remove the E-clip . . .

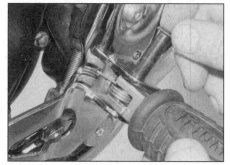

3.1b . . . and withdraw the pivot pin, noting the spring ends

3.2 Remove the E-clip (arrowed) and withdraw the pivot pin

1 General information

All models have a twin cradle steel frame. The main spine of the frame is in box section, while the rest is tubular and with removable cradle sections.

Front suspension is by a pair of oil-damped telescopic forks. On Thruxton models the forks have adjustable spring pre-load.

At the rear, a box-section steel swingarm acts on twin shock absorbers. The shock absorbers are adjustable for spring pre-load on all models.

Drive to the rear wheel is by chain and sprockets.

2 Frame inspection and repair

1 The frame should not require attention unless accident damage has occurred. In most cases, fitting a new frame is the only satisfactory remedy for such damage. A few frame specialists have the jigs and other

equipment necessary for straightening a frame to the required standard of accuracy, but even then there is no simple way of assessing to what extent the frame may have been over stressed.

2 After the machine has accumulated a lot of miles, examine the frame closely for signs of cracking or splitting at the welded joints. Loose engine mount bolts can cause ovaling or fracturing of the mounting tabs. Minor damage can often be repaired by welding, depending on the extent and nature of the damage.

3 Remember that a frame which is out of alignment will cause handling problems. If misalignment is suspected as the result of an accident, it will be necessary to strip the machine completely so the frame can be thoroughly checked.

3 Footrests, brake pedal and gearchange lever

Footrests

1 To remove the front footrests, remove the E-clip from the bottom of the pivot pin, then

withdraw the pin and remove the footrest, noting how the return spring ends locate **(see illustrations)**.

2 To remove the rear footrests, remove the E-clip from the bottom of the pivot pin, then withdraw the pin and remove the footrest, noting how the detent ball and spring are fitted **(see illustration)**. Take care not to let the ball and spring ping out.

3 On Thruxton models the footrest rubbers can be removed and replaced with new ones by undoing the screws on the underside **(see illustration)**.

4 Installation is the reverse of removal. Apply grease to the pivot pin, and to the mating surfaces of the footrest and its holder.

Brake pedal

Removal

5 On Bonneville and T100 models first check to see if the pivot bolt head is accessed from the outside of the bracket or the inside – on the model photographed it was accessed from the inside, but on others it may be on the outside. If accessed from the inside, undo the front sprocket cover bolts and remove the cover **(see illustration)**. Remove the clip and withdraw the pin securing the rear brake master

3.3 Undo the screws (arrowed) to release the rubber

3.5a Unscrew the bolts (arrowed) and remove the cover

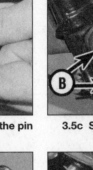
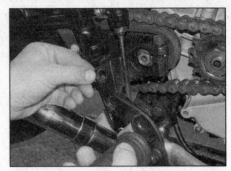

3.5b Remove the clip and withdraw the pin

3.5c Slacken the clamp bolt (A), then unscrew the bolts (B) . . .

3.5d . . . and remove the bracket assembly

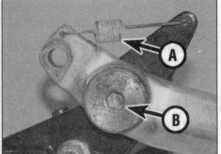
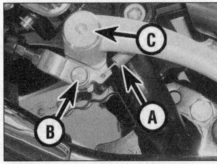
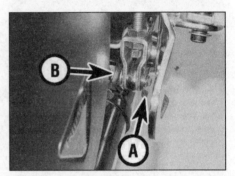

3.5e Unhook the spring (A) then unscrew the pivot bolt (B)

3.6 Unhook the spring (A), remove the pin (B) and unscrew the bolt (C)

3.7a Remove the clip (A) and withdraw the pin (B)

cylinder pushrod to the brake pedal (see illustration). Slacken the swingarm pivot clamp bolt in the rider's right-hand footrest bracket (see illustration). Unscrew the footrest bracket bolts, then detach the pushrod from the pedal and draw the bracket off the pivot, manoeuvring it around the rod (see illustration). On all models unhook the brake pedal return spring from the pedal (see illustration). Unscrew the pedal pivot bolt and remove the pedal. Note the bush fitted in the pedal.

6 On Thruxton models, unhook the brake pedal return spring from the pedal (see illustration). Remove the clip and withdraw the pin securing the rear brake master cylinder pushrod to the brake pedal. Unscrew the pedal pivot bolt and remove the pedal. Note the bush fitted in the pedal.

7 On America and Speedmaster models, remove the clip and withdraw the pin securing the rear brake master cylinder pushrod to the

brake pedal (see illustration). Unscrew the pedal pivot bolt and remove the pedal, noting how the return spring fits (see illustration). Note the bush fitted in the pedal.

8 On Scrambler models, unhook the brake light switch and pedal return springs from the pedal (see illustration). Remove the clip and withdraw the pin securing the rear brake master cylinder pushrod to the brake pedal. Unscrew the pedal pivot bolt on the inside of the footrest bracket and remove the pedal. Note the bush fitted in the pedal.

Installation

9 Installation is the reverse of removal, noting the following:
● Apply grease to the pivot section of the bolt and to the bush.
● Apply threadlock to the pivot bolt threads and tighten the bolt to the torque setting specified at the beginning of the Chapter.

● On Bonneville and T100 models where the bolt was accessed from the inside, tighten the rider's right-hand footrest bracket bolts, the clamp bolt and the sprocket cover bolts to the torque settings specified at the beginning of the Chapter.
● Check that the locknut on the rear brake master cylinder pushrod clevis is tight. The pushrod length should be set correctly to ensure safe operation of the brake – if required, measure the pushrod length and adjust it accordingly (see Chapter 6, Section 9).

Gearchange lever
Removal

10 On Bonneville, T100 and Scrambler models, note the alignment of the punch mark on the gearchange shaft end with the slit in the lever clamp, then unscrew the pinch bolt and slide the lever off the shaft (see illustration).

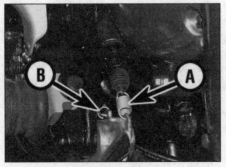

3.7b Brake pedal pivot bolt (arrowed)

3.8 Rear brake light switch (A) and pedal (B) return springs

3.10 Unscrew the pinch bolt and slide the lever off

11 On Thruxton models, slacken the gearchange lever linkage rod locknuts, then unscrew the rod and separate it from the lever and the arm (the rod is reverse-threaded on one end, so will unscrew from both lever and arm simultaneously when turned in the one direction) **(see illustration)**. Note how far the rod is threaded into the lever and arm, as this determines the height of the lever relative to the footrest. Unscrew the lever pivot bolt and remove the lever **(see illustration)**.

12 On America and Speedmaster models first remove the footrest (see Step 1). Slacken the gearchange lever linkage rod locknuts, then unscrew the rod and separate it from the lever and the arm (the rod is reverse-threaded on one end, so will unscrew from both lever and arm simultaneously when turned in the one direction) **(see illustration)**. Note how far the rod is threaded into the lever and arm, as this determines the height of the lever relative to the footrest. Unscrew the lever pivot bolt and remove the lever, noting the bush and the wave washer **(see illustration)**.

Installation

13 Installation is the reverse of removal, noting the following:

● On Thruxton, America and Speedmaster models, apply grease to the pivot section of the bolt and apply threadlock to the pivot bolt threads. Thread the linkage rod simultaneously into the lever and arm. Set lever gear lever height as noted on removal, then tighten the locknuts securely **(see illustration 3.12a)**. To adjust the lever height, slacken the locknuts and thread the rod in or out as required, then retighten the nuts.

● On Bonneville, T100 and Scrambler models, align the slit in the clamp with the punch mark on the end of the gearchange shaft as noted on removal **(see illustration)**.

● Check the operation of the gear lever.

4 Sidestand removal and installation

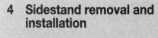

Removal

1 The sidestand is attached to a bracket on the frame. Two springs (one inside the other)

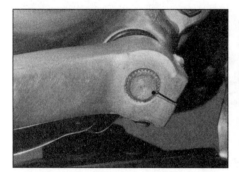

3.13 Align the punch mark with the slit in the clamp

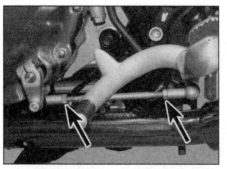

3.11a Slacken the nuts (arrowed) and unscrew the linkage rod . . .

3.12a Slacken the nuts (arrowed) and unscrew the linkage rod . . .

ensure the stand is held in the retracted or extended position.

2 Support the bike on an auxiliary stand.

3 Unhook the stand springs from the post on the frame **(see illustration)**.

4 Unscrew the nut from the pivot bolt. Unscrew the pivot bolt and remove the stand.

Installation

5 Installation is the reverse of removal, noting the following:

● Apply grease to the pivot bolt shank and the mating surfaces of the stand and the frame.

● Tighten the pivot bolt to the torque setting specified at the beginning of the Chapter, then fit the nut and tighten that to the specified torque **(see illustration 4.3)**.

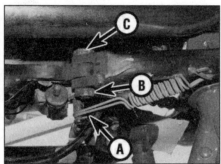

4.3 Unhook the springs (A), then unscrew the nut (B) then the pivot bolt (C)

3.11b . . . then unscrew the pivot bolt (arrowed) and remove the lever

3.12b . . . then unscrew the pivot bolt (arrowed) and remove the lever

● Reconnect the springs and check that they hold the stand securely up when not in use – an accident is almost certain to occur if the stand extends while the machine is in motion.

● Check the operation of the sidestand switch (see Chapter 1, Section 20).

5 Handlebars and levers

Handlebars – Bonneville 2001 to 2008, T100, Thruxton with high handlebars, America and Speedmaster

Removal

Note: *Note that the handlebars can be displaced from the top yoke without removing the individual assemblies from them. Follow Step 8 only if this is required and cover the instrument cluster with rag so that the handlebar assembly can be laid on it.*

1 The mirrors on Bonneville, T100, America and Speedmaster models can be removed if desired (see Chapter 7). The bar-end mirrors on Thruxton models will require removal in order to slide off the throttle grip or remove the left-hand grip; remove the bolt and washer to free each mirror, noting the bush and spacer.

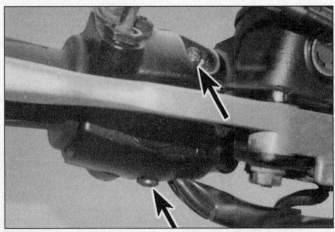

5.2a Undo the screws (arrowed) . . .

5.2b . . . and detach the switch housing

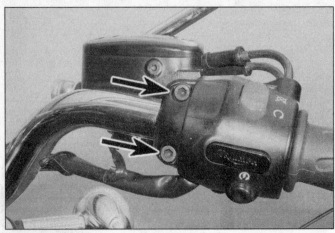

5.3 Master cylinder clamp bolts (arrowed)

5.4 Clutch lever bracket clamp bolts (arrowed)

2 Undo the switch housing screws and displace the housings from each side (see illustrations). Free the wiring clips from the handlebars.

3 Unscrew the clamp bolts to free the front brake master cylinder from the handlebar, leaving it attached by the throttle cable to the twistgrip (see illustration).

4 Unscrew the clamp bolts and displace the clutch lever bracket assembly, leaving it attached to the cable (see illustration).

5 Unscrew the handlebar end-weight retaining screw and remove the weight from the right-hand end of the handlebar (see illustration).

6 Unscrew the handlebar end-weight retaining screw and remove the weight from the left-hand end of the handlebar. If required slide the grip off the handlebar – you will probably have to slide a screwdriver or inject aerosol lubricant between the grip and the handlebar to release it. If the grip has been glued on, you will probably have to slit it with a knife.

7 If the handlebar holders are being removed from the top yoke, slacken the nuts (bolts on 2011-on Speedmaster) securing them on the underside of the yoke now (see illustration).

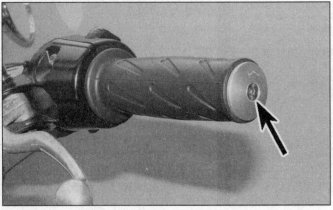

5.5 Undo the screw (arrowed) and remove the end-weight

5.7 If required slacken each holder nut (arrowed)

8 Carefully prise the blanking caps out of the handlebar clamp bolts **(see illustration)**. Note how the punch mark(s) on the handlebar aligns with the mating surface of the holder(s). Support the handlebars, then unscrew the bolts and remove the clamps, then draw the handlebar out of the throttle twistgrip **(see illustration)**. Make sure the master cylinder/throttle assembly is supported or tied so no strain is placed on the brake hose or cables.

9 If required, unscrew the nuts on the handlebar holder bolts, then draw the holders out of the top yoke, on Bonneville, T100 and Thruxton models noting the arrangement of the washers, dampers and sleeves. On 2011-on Speedmaster models, the holder bolts thread directly into the holders from the underside.

Installation

10 Installation is the reverse of removal, noting the following.

● If removed, tighten the handlebar holder nuts (bolts on 2011-on Speedmaster) after the handlebars are installed, and tighten them to the torque setting specified at the beginning of the Chapter.

● Apply engine oil to the clamp bolt threads. Apply some grease to the throttle twistgrip section of the handlebar.

● Slide the right-hand end of the handlebar into the throttle twistgrip before positioning the handlebar on the holder(s).

● Fit the handlebar clamp(s) and tighten the bolts enough to prevent the handlebars rotating but not so much as to restrict all movement for alignment.

● On Bonneville and T100 models, align the punch marks on the front with the mating surfaces of the holder and clamp, and make sure the bars are central **(see illustration)**.

● On America and Speedmaster models, align the punch mark on the rear with the mating surfaces of the left-hand holder and clamp, and make sure the bars are central.

● When the handlebars are correctly positioned tighten the clamp bolts evenly to the torque setting specified at the beginning of the Chapter.

● Align the mating surfaces of the master cylinder and clutch lever bracket assemblies and their clamps with the punch marks on the handlebar (either top or bottom, depending on model), then tighten the bolts evenly to the specified torque setting.

● Tighten the handlebar end-weights to the specified torque setting. If new grips are being fitted, secure them using a suitable adhesive.

● Check and adjust the throttle cable and clutch lever freeplay (see Chapter 1). Check the operation of the throttle and clutch cable, and the front brake before riding the machine.

Handlebars – Thruxton with clip-ons

Right handlebar removal

11 If required remove the rear view mirror to avoid the possibility of damage (see Chap-

5.8a Prise the blanking caps out . . .

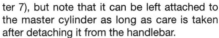

ter 7), but note that it can be left attached to the master cylinder as long as care is taken after detaching it from the handlebar.

12 Displace the front brake master cylinder and reservoir (see Chapter 6). Keep the master cylinder reservoir upright to prevent fluid leakage – wrap it in some rag just in case.

13 Displace the handlebar switch housing (see Chapter 8).

14 Detach the throttle cables (See Chapter 3A) or slacken the cable housing screws then slide the twistgrip and cable housing off the end of the handlebar with the cables still attached after the handlebar has been displaced from the fork **(see illustration)**.

15 Unscrew the handlebar end-weight retaining screw and remove the weight from the end of the handlebar **(see illustration 5.5)**. If the throttle cables have been detached, slide the twistgrip off the handlebar.

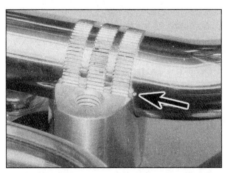

5.10 Align the punch mark (arrowed) with the clamp mating surfaces

5.16a Unscrew the positioning bolt (arrowed) on each side . . .

5.8b . . . then unscrew the bolts

16 Unscrew the handlebar positioning bolt for each handlebar on the underside of the yoke **(see illustration)**. Slacken the fork clamp bolts in the top yoke **(see illustration)**. Unscrew the steering stem nut and remove the washer. Gently ease the top yoke up and off the forks and position it clear, using a rag to protect other components.

17 Slacken the handlebar clamp bolt **(see illustration 5.16b)**, then ease the handlebar up and off the fork. If required, slide the throttle twistgrip off the handlebar.

Left handlebar removal

18 If required remove the rear view mirror to avoid the possibility of damage (see Chapter 7), but note that it can be left attached to the clutch lever bracket as long as care is taken after detaching it from the handlebar.

5.14 Slacken the cable housing screws (arrowed)

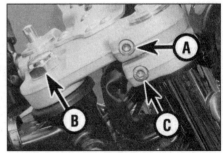

5.16b . . . then slacken the fork clamp bolt (A) on each side and unscrew the steering stem nut (B). Handlebar clamp bolt (C)

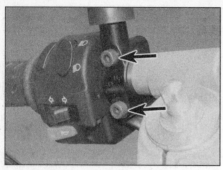

5.19 Clutch lever bracket clamp bolts (arrowed)

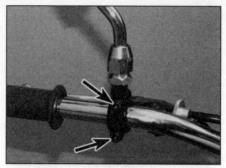

5.27 Undo the clamp bolts (arrowed) to free the clutch lever from the handlebar

19 Unscrew the clamp bolts and displace the clutch lever bracket assembly (see illustration).

20 Displace the handlebar switch housing (see Chapter 8).

21 Unscrew the handlebar end-weight retaining screw and remove the weight from the end of the handlebar (see illustration 5.5). If required slide the grip off the handlebar – you will probably have to slide a screwdriver or inject aerosol lubricant between the grip and the handlebar to release it. If the grip has been glued on, you will probably have to slit it with a knife.

22 Unscrew the handlebar positioning bolt for each handlebar on the underside of the yoke (see illustration 5.16a). Slacken the fork clamp bolts in the top yoke (see illustration 5.16b). Unscrew the steering stem nut and remove the washer (see illustration 5.16b). Gently ease the top yoke up and off the forks and position it clear, using a rag to protect other components.

23 Slacken the handlebar clamp bolt (see illustration 5.16b), then ease the handlebar up and off the fork.

Installation

24 Installation is the reverse of removal, noting the following.
● Apply some grease to the throttle twistgrip section of the handlebar.
● If the throttle cables were not detached slide the twistgrip and cable housing onto the handlebar before fitting the bar onto the fork.
● Tighten the steering stem nut first, then

the fork clamp bolts in the top yoke, then the handlebar positioning bolts, then the handlebar clamp bolts, tightening them all to the torque settings specified at the beginning of the Chapter.
● Align the master cylinder and clamp mating surfaces with the punch mark on the top of the handlebar, and tighten the clamp bolts evenly to the specified torque setting.
● Align the clutch lever bracket and clamp mating surfaces with the punch mark on the top of the handlebar, ensuring that the UP mark on the clamp is positioned correctly. Tighten the clamp bolts evenly to the specified torque setting (see illustration 5.19).
● Make sure the pin in one half of each switch housing locates in its hole in the handlebar.
● Make sure the throttle opens freely and snaps shut when released.
● Check and adjust the throttle cables and clutch cable (see Chapter 1). Check the operation of the throttle and clutch, and the front brake before riding the machine.

Handlebars – Scrambler and 2009-on Bonneville

Removal

Note: *Note that once the instrument panel has been displaced, the handlebars can be displaced from the top yoke without removing the individual assemblies from them. Follow Step 35 only if this is required and cover the fuel tank with rag so that the handlebar assembly can be laid on it.*

25 If required remove the rear view mirrors to

avoid the possibility of damage (see Chapter 7), but note that they can be left attached to the master cylinder and clutch lever bracket assemblies as long as care is taken after detaching them from the handlebars.

26 Undo the switch housing screws and displace the left and right-hand switch housings (see Chapter 8). Free the wiring clips from the handlebars.

27 Unscrew the clamp bolts and displace the clutch lever bracket assembly, leaving it attached to the cable (see illustration).

28 Detach the throttle cables (see Chapter 3) or slacken the twistgrip housing screws, then slide the housing off the end of the handlebars with the cables still attached after the handlebars have been displaced from the fork (see illustration 5.14).

29 Displace the front brake master cylinder and reservoir (see Chapter 6). Keep the master cylinder reservoir upright to prevent fluid leakage – wrap it in some rag just in case.

30 Unscrew the right-hand handlebar end-weight retaining screw and remove the weight (see illustration 5.5). If the throttle cables have been detached, slide the twistgrip housing off the handlebar.

31 Unscrew the left-hand handlebar end-weight retaining screw and remove the weight. If required, slide the grip off the handlebar – you will probably have to slide a screwdriver or inject aerosol lubricant between the grip and the handlebar to release it. If the grip has been glued on, you will probably have to slit it with a knife.

32 If the handlebar holders are being removed from the top yoke, slacken the nuts securing them on the underside of the yoke now (see illustration 5.7).

33 On early Scrambler models (with a one-piece handlebar holder), unscrew the instrument panel and manoeuvre the instrument forwards (see illustrations); there's no need to disconnect the speedometer cable or wiring.

34 Note how the punch mark on the handlebars aligns with the rear mating surface of the left-hand holder.

35 Support the handlebars, then unscrew the bolts and remove the holder (early Scrambler) or two holders (later Scrambler and Bonneville) (see illustrations). If not

5.33a Undo the bolts (arrowed) . . .

5.33b . . . and displace the instrument panel – early Scrambler shown

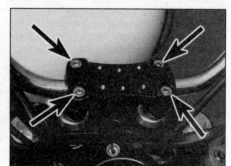

5.35a Four bolts secure the one-piece handlebar holder on the early Scrambler

already done, slide the twistgrip housing off the handlebar.

36 If required, unscrew the nuts securing the handlebar holders, then draw the holders out of the top yoke, noting the arrangement of the washers, dampers and sleeves.

Installation

37 Installation is the reverse of removal, noting the following.

● If removed, first tighten the handlebar holder nuts finger-tight, then tighten the nuts to the torque setting specified at the beginning of the Chapter after the handlebars are installed.

● Apply a smear of grease to the throttle twistgrip end of the handlebar.

● If the throttle cables have not been detached, slide the twistgrip housing onto the end of the handlebar before positioning them on the holders.

● On early Scramblers (with the one-piece holder), position the handlebars, then install the holder and tighten its bolts finger-tight; the arrow on the top surface of the holder should point forwards. Align the punch mark on the handlebar with the holder joint then tighten the front bolts to the specified torque setting. Now tighten the rear bolts – this will leave a gap at the rear of the holder.

● On later Scramblers and Bonnevilles (with separate holders), install each clamp so that the mounting hole with the punched dot faces forwards. Align the punch mark on the handlebar with the holder joint then tighten the front bolt on each holder to the specified torque setting. Now tighten the rear bolt on each holder – this will leave a gap at the rear of each holder.

● Align the mating surfaces of the master cylinder and clutch lever bracket assemblies with the punch marks on the top of the handlebars, then tighten the clamp bolts evenly to the specified torque setting.

● Align the tabs on the switch housings with the holes in the handlebars, then install the housings (see Chapter 8).

● If a new left-hand grip is being fitted, secure it using a suitable adhesive.

5.35b Prise out caps to reveal bolts on separate holders fitted to later Scrambler and Bonneville models

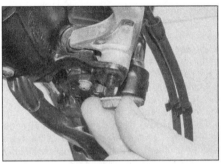
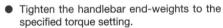

5.38a Unscrew the nut . . .

● Tighten the handlebar end-weights to the specified torque setting.

● Check that the brake hose, clutch cable and wiring are correctly aligned inside the guide on the fork yoke **(see illustration)**.

● Install the instrument panel on early Scramblers and tighten the bolts to the specified torque setting.

● Check and adjust the throttle cable and clutch lever freeplay (see Chapter 1). Check the operation of the throttle and clutch cables, and the front brake before riding the machine.

Front brake lever

38 Unscrew the nut on the underside of the lever bracket **(see illustration)**. Unscrew the

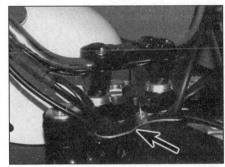

5.37 Ensure all the wiring, cables and hose are inside the guide (arrowed)

5.38b . . . then unscrew the pivot bolt and remove the lever

pivot bolt and remove the lever **(see illustration)**.

39 Installation is the reverse of removal. Apply grease to the pivot bolt shaft and the contact areas between the lever and its bracket. Apply silicone grease to the contact surfaces of the lever tip and master cylinder pushrod.

Clutch lever

40 Slacken the clutch cable adjuster locking ring then thread the adjuster fully into the bracket to provide maximum freeplay in the cable **(see illustration)**.

41 On models without a span adjuster, unscrew the nut on the underside of the lever bracket **(see illustration)**. Unscrew the pivot

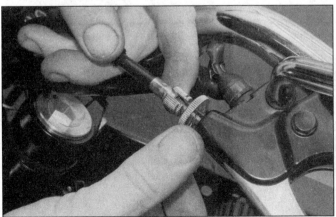

5.40 Back the locking ring off the bracket and thread the adjuster in

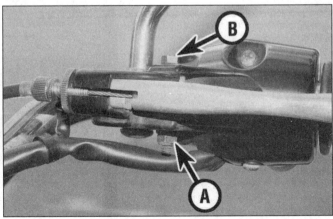

5.41 Unscrew the nut (A), then unscrew the pivot bolt (B)

5.42a Unscrew the nut (arrowed) . . .

5.42b . . . then push the pivot up from the bottom and withdraw it, noting how the flats engage

5.42c Remove the pivot collar from the lever

bolt and slip the lever out, detaching the cable nipple as you do.

42 On models with a span adjuster, unscrew the lever pivot nut then remove the pivot and slip the lever out, detaching the cable nipple as you do **(see illustrations)**. Note the collar in the lever pivot bore, and how the flats on the underside of the pivot head engage with those in the lever bracket **(see illustrations)**.

43 Installation is the reverse of removal. Apply grease to the pivot bolt shaft and the contact areas between the lever and its bracket, and to the clutch cable nipple. Adjust the clutch cable freeplay (see Chapter 1).

6 Fork removal and installation

Removal

Note: *On Bonneville, T100, Thruxton and Scrambler models, installation of the forks is much easier if they are worked on one at a time. If both forks are removed it may be difficult to align the headlight mounting tubes on installation.*

1 Remove the front wheel (see Chapter 6). Tie the front brake caliper(s) back out of the way.

2 Remove the front mudguard (see Chapter 7).

3 On Thruxton models with clip-on handlebars, slacken the handlebar clamp bolt for the fork being removed **(see illustration 5.16b)**.

4 On America and 2003 to 2010 Speedmaster models, unscrew the bolts securing the lower fork shroud to the underside of the bottom yoke **(see illustration)**. Slide the shroud down and allow it to rest on the mudguard mounting lugs, using rag or tape to protect them.

5 Mark each fork as to which side is fitted on. Note the amount of protrusion (if any) of the fork tube above the top surface of the top yoke and record this information as a guide to refitting – as standard the top of the tube should be flush with the top yoke with only the top bolt rim protruding above it.

6 Working on one fork at a time, slacken the fork clamp bolt in the top yoke **(see illustration)**. If the fork is to be disassembled, or if the fork oil is being changed, slacken the fork top bolt now **(see illustration)**.

7 Slacken the fork clamp bolt in the bottom yoke, and remove the fork by twisting it

and pulling it downwards, noting the routing of all cables, hoses and wiring **(see illustrations)**.

8 On Bonneville, T100, Thruxton and Scrambler models note how the forks pass through the headlight mounting tubes. If both forks are being removed secure the headlight assembly so that it remains between the yokes. If the yokes are being removed to access the steering head bearings displace the headlight assembly and collect the rubber spacer from the top and bottom of each tube.

9 On America and 2003 to 2010 Speedmaster models, note how the forks pass through the upper fork shrouds between the yokes – the shrouds should stay in place. If the yokes are being removed to access the steering head bearings displace the shrouds and collect the rubber spacer from the top and bottom of each. If required, slide the lower shroud up and off the top of the fork.

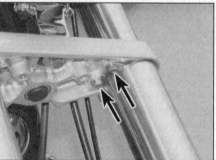

6.4 Unscrew the bolts (arrowed) and slide the shroud down

6.6a Slacken the fork clamp bolt (arrowed) . . .

6.6b . . . and if required the fork top bolt

6.7a Slacken the clamp bolt (arrowed) in the bottom yoke . . .

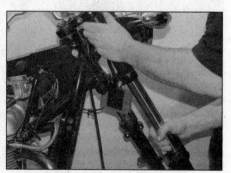

6.7b . . . and remove the fork

HAYNES HINT *If the fork legs are seized in the yokes, spray the area with penetrating oil and allow time for it to soak in before trying again. If necessary lever the clamp open by using a large flat-bladed screwdriver, taking care not to scratch anything.*

6.11 Make sure the rubber spacers locate correctly and stay in place

6.12 Slide the fork up through the yokes and tubes or shrouds according to model

Installation

10 On America and 2003 to 2010 Speedmaster models, if removed slide the lower shroud onto the fork – make sure the correct side shroud is fitted onto the correct fork. When installing each fork make sure the rubber spacer is correctly fitted and stays in place in the top and bottom of each upper shroud, and that the shroud is correctly positioned between the yokes so that the fork fits through it.

11 On Bonneville, T100, Thruxton and Scrambler models, when installing each fork make sure the rubber spacer is correctly fitted and stays in place in the top and bottom of each headlight mounting tube, and that the tube is correctly positioned between the yokes so that the fork fits through it **(see illustration)**. On Scrambler and 2009-on T100 models, ensure that the fork gaiters are installed on each fork before installation.

12 Remove all traces of corrosion from the fork tube and the yokes. Make sure you fit the correct fork onto the correct side of the bike, as noted on removal. Slide the fork up through the bottom yoke, on Bonneville, T100, Thruxton and Scrambler models through the headlight mounting tube, on America and 2003 to 2010 Speedmaster models through the upper shroud, and on Thruxton models through the handlebar clamp, and into the top yoke, making sure all cables, hoses and wiring are routed on the correct side of the fork, and that the rubber spacers in the tube/shroud stay in place **(see illustration)**. Note that the top rubber is easily dislodged as the fork passes through it, and can be difficult to reseat, especially on Bonneville, T100, Thruxton and Scrambler models where the weight of the headlight assembly makes things more difficult, and more so if both forks have been removed and you are installing the first fork. If necessary, slacken the steering stem nut

enough to allow the top yoke to be raised, and push the fork up so it protrudes from the top of the tube/shroud, then fit the top rubber over the fork and into place. Draw the fork down slightly to help seat the rubber, then press the yoke down and tighten the steering stem nut lightly to keep it in place and finish positioning the fork. On completion do not forget to tighten the steering stem nut to the specified torque setting.

13 Set the amount of protrusion of the fork above the top yoke as noted on removal – as standard the top of the tube should be flush with the top yoke with only the top bolt rim protruding above it. Make sure it is the same for each fork.

14 Tighten the fork clamp bolt in the bottom yoke to the torque setting specified at the beginning of the Chapter **(see illustration 6.7a)**. If the fork has been dismantled or if the fork oil was changed, and if not already done, now tighten the fork top bolt to the specified torque setting **(see illustration 6.6b)**. Now tighten the fork clamp bolt in the top yoke to the specified torque **(see illustration 6.6a)**.

15 On Thruxton models with clip-on handlebars, tighten the handlebar clamp bolt to the specified torque setting **(see illustration 5.16b)**. Check that the handlebar positioning bolt is secured to its specified torque **(see illustration 5.16a)**. On all Thruxton models adjust the suspension as required (see Section 12).

16 On America and 2003 to 2010 Speedmaster

models slide the lower shroud up against the bottom yoke and tighten its bolts **(see illustration 6.4)**. On Scrambler models, ensure that the fork gaiters are positioned up against the underside of the bottom yoke and that the clips are tightened securely.

17 Install the front mudguard (see Chapter 7), and the front wheel (see Chapter 6).

18 Check the operation of the front forks and brake before riding the machine.

7 Fork oil change

1 Remove the forks (see Section 6). Always work on the fork legs separately to avoid interchanging parts and thus causing an accelerated rate of wear.

2 On Thruxton models note the amount of spring pre-load, then set the adjuster to its minimum setting (see Section 12).

3 Unscrew the fork top bolt from the top of the fork tube, noting that it is under some pressure from the spring **(see illustration)**. Use a ratchet type tool so you can maintain downward pressure on the bolt against the spring, then release it slowly once the bolt is unscrewed. Alternatively hold the top bolt still and turn the fork tube itself so it threads off the bolt.

4 On Thruxton models remove the pre-load adjuster plate. On all models remove the spacer, the washer and the spring **(see illustrations)**.

5 Invert the fork over a suitable container and

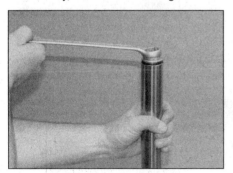

7.3 Unscrew the top bolt

7.4a Remove the spacer . . .

7.4b . . . and the washer and spring

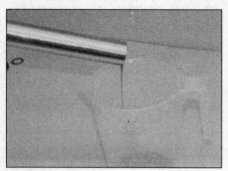

7.5a Invert the fork over a container . . .

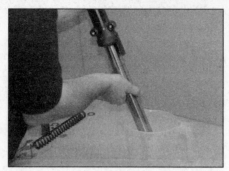

7.5b . . . and pump the fork to expel the oil

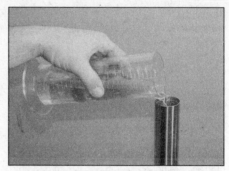

7.6a Pour the oil into the top of the tube

7.6b Measure the oil level and adjust if necessary

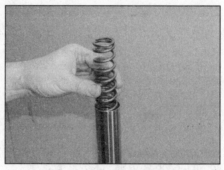

7.7a Install the spring . . .

7.7b . . . the washer . . .

pump the fork tube to expel as much oil as possible **(see illustrations)**. Support the fork upside down in the container for a while to allow as much oil as possible to drain, and pump the fork again.

6 Slowly pour in the specified quantity and grade of fork oil, then pump the fork tube slowly at least ten times to distribute it evenly **(see illustration)**. Allow the oil to settle and any air bubbles to disperse for about ten minutes – support the fork upright to do so. Fully compress the fork tube into the slider and measure the oil level from the top of the tube; make any adjustment by adding more or tipping some out until the oil is at the level specified at the beginning of the Chapter **(see illustration)**.

7 Pull the fork tube out of the slider as far as possible then install the spring **(see illustration)**. Fit the washer and the spacer, and on Thruxton models the pre-load adjuster plate **(see illustrations)**.

8 Check the condition of the top bolt O-ring and replace it with a new one if necessary. Smear the O-ring with fork oil.

9 Extend the fork tube and screw the top bolt into it, making sure it is not cross-threaded, and maintaining some downward pressure against the spring until a few threads have caught – using a ratchet tool will make this easier **(see illustration)**. If a ratchet tool is not available keep the top bolt counter-held with a spanner and turn the fork tube so it threads onto the bolt **(see illustration 7.3)**. **Note:** *The top bolt can be tightened to the specified torque setting at this stage if the tube is held between the padded jaws of a vice, but do not risk distorting the tube by doing so. A*

better method is to tighten the top bolt when the fork has been installed in the bike and is securely held in the bottom yoke (Section 6, Step 14).

TOOL TiP *Use a ratchet-type tool when removing and installing the fork top bolt. This makes it unnecessary to remove the tool from the bolt whilst threading it in making it easier to maintain a downward pressure on the spring.*

10 Install the forks (see Section 6). On Thruxton models reset the amount of spring pre-load (see Section 12).

8 Fork disassembly, inspection and reassembly

Disassembly

Note: *Always work on the fork legs separately to avoid interchanging parts and thus causing an accelerated rate of wear.*

1 Remove the forks (see Section 6). On Scrambler models, draw the gaiters off the fork tubes. If the gaiters are cracked, perished or torn, fit new ones on reassembly.

2 Remove the axle clamp bolt(s) from the bottom of the slider, where fitted **(see**

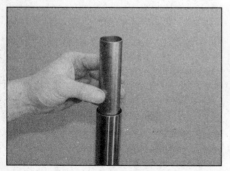

7.7c . . . and the spacer

7.9 Thread the top bolt into the tube

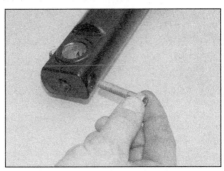

8.2a Remove the axle clamp bolt . . .

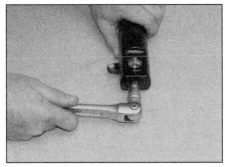

8.2b . . . then slacken the damper rod bolt

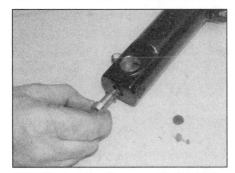

8.4a Remove the damper rod bolt with its washer

8.4b Tip the damper rod out of the fork

8.5 Remove the protector

8.6 Prise out the dust seal using a flat-bladed screwdriver

illustration). Slacken the damper rod bolt in the base of the fork slider **(see illustration)**. If an assistant is not available to hold the fork, clamp the brake caliper lugs between the padded jaws of a vice. If the bolt won't undo (usually because the damper rod turns with it), have your assistant compress the fork, or use an air wrench if available, or wait until the spring has been removed, then use a holding tool to prevent the damper rod turning with the bolt.

3 Refer to Section 7, Steps 2 to 5, and drain the fork oil.

4 Remove the previously slackened damper rod bolt and its copper sealing washer from the bottom of the slider **(see illustration)**. Discard the sealing washer as a new one must be used on reassembly. Tip the damper rod and its spring out of the tube **(see illustration)**.

5 On Bonneville, T100 and Thruxton models, if required remove the fork protector from the top of the slider, noting how it fits – though this is not essential removing it gives better clearance for installing the top bush and oil seal **(see illustration)**. On some models the protector is clamped in place by a bolt, on others it clips into place over a detent. On 2011-on Speedmaster models, remove the chromed seal protector from the top of the fork slider.

6 Carefully prise out the dust seal from the top of the slider to gain access to the oil seal retaining clip **(see illustration)**. Discard the dust seal as a new one must be used.

7 Carefully remove the retaining clip, taking care not to scratch the surface of the tube **(see illustration)**.

8 To separate the tube from the slider it is necessary to displace the oil seal and top bush. The bottom bush on the tube does not pass through the top bush in the slider, and this can be used to good effect. Push the tube gently inwards until it stops against the damper seat. Take care not to do this forcibly or the seat may be damaged. Now pull the tube sharply outwards until the bottom bush strikes the top bush **(see illustration)**. Repeat this operation until the oil seal and top bush are tapped out of the slider.

9 Tip the damper rod seat out of the slider – you may have to push it from the bottom via the damper bolt hole **(see illustration)**.

10 Slide the oil seal, washer and top bush off the tube, noting which way up they fit **(see**

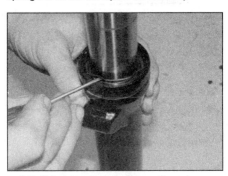

8.7 Prise out the retaining clip using a flat-bladed screwdriver

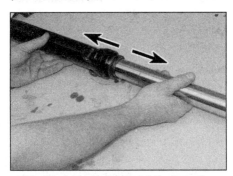

8.8 To separate the fork tube from the slider, pull them apart firmly several times - the slide hammer effect will displace the oil seal and outer bush

8.9 Tip the damper rod seat out of the slider

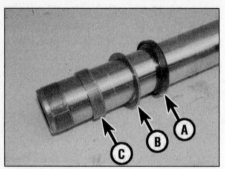

8.10 Slide the oil seal (A), washer (B) and top bush (C) off the tube

8.14 Lever the ends apart and slide the bush off

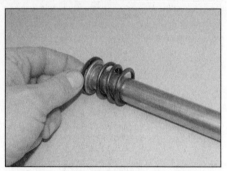

8.15 Check the ring on the top of the rod for wear

illustration). Discard the oil seal as a new one must be used.

Caution: Do not remove the bottom bush from the tube unless it is to be replaced with a new one (Step 14).

Inspection

11 Clean all parts in solvent and blow them dry with compressed air, if available. Check the fork tube for score marks, scratches, flaking of the chrome finish and excessive or abnormal wear. Replace the inner tubes in both forks with new ones if any dents are found. Check the fork seal seat in the top of the slider for nicks, gouges and scratches. If damage is evident, leaks will occur. Also check the oil seal washer for damage or distortion, and replace it with a new one if necessary.

12 Check the fork tube for run-out (bending)

using V-blocks and a dial gauge, or have it done by a Triumph dealer or suspension specialist. Triumph do not specify a run-out limit, but if the tube is bent beyond the generally accepted limit of 0.2 mm seek the advice of a suspension specialist.

⚠️ *Warning: If the fork tube is bent, it should not be straightened; replace it with a new one.*

13 Check the spring for cracks and other damage. Compare the free length of the spring from each fork. Replace both springs with new ones if damage or unequal sag is evident. Never replace only one spring. Also check the rebound spring on the damper rod.

14 Examine the working (sliding) surfaces of the two bushes; if worn or scuffed they must be replaced with new ones – they are worn if the grey Teflon coating has rubbed off to reveal the copper surface. To remove the

bottom bush from the fork tube, prise it apart at the slit using a flat-bladed screwdriver and slide it off **(see illustration)**. Make sure the new one seats properly.

15 Check the damper rod and its piston ring for damage and wear, and replace the rod with a new one if necessary **(see illustration)**.

Reassembly

16 Smear fork oil onto the damper rod piston ring, and make sure it is correctly seated in its groove in the top of the rod **(see illustration 8.15)**. If removed fit the rebound spring onto the rod. Insert the damper rod into the top of the fork tube and slide it down so that it projects fully from the bottom of the tube **(see illustration)**. Fit the damper rod seat onto the bottom of the rod, then push them both up into the bottom of the tube **(see illustrations)**.

17 Oil the fork tube and bottom bush with the specified fork oil and insert the assembly into the slider **(see illustration)**. Fit a new copper sealing washer onto the damper rod bolt and apply a few drops of a suitable non-permanent thread locking compound, then insert the bolt into the bottom of the slider and thread it into the rod **(see illustration)**. Tighten the bolt to the specified torque setting. If the damper rod rotates inside the tube, use a holding tool passed down through the tube and fitted into the top of the rod or wait until the fork is fully reassembled before tightening the bolt.

18 Push the fork tube fully into the slider, then oil the top bush and slide it down over the tube **(see illustration)**. Press the bush

8.16a Fit the damper rod into the tube

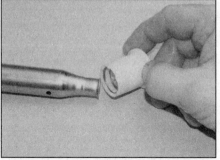

8.16b Fit the seat onto the bottom of the rod . . .

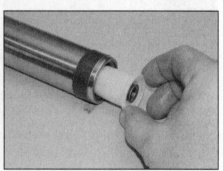

8.16c . . . then push them up into the tube

8.17a Fit the tube into the slider

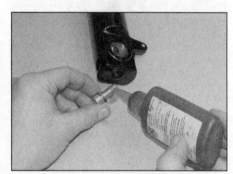

8.17b Apply threadlock to the bolt and use a new sealing washer

8.18a Press the outer bush in . . .

8.18b . . . then lay the washer on top of the bush . . .

8.18c . . . to protect it as you drive the bush in . . .

8.19 . . . until its top rim is flush with the washer seat

8.20 Press the oil seal into the tube and drive it fully into place

8.21 Install the retaining clip . . .

squarely into its recess in the slider as far as possible, then fit the oil seal washer **(see illustration)**. Using a suitable drift covered in insulating tape, carefully drive the bush fully into its recess using the oil seal washer to prevent damaging the edges of the bush **(see illustration)**. Make sure the bush enters the recess squarely, and take care not to scratch or gouge the inner tube – it pays to wrap some insulating tape around it as well as the drift.

19 Remove the washer to check the bush is seated fully and squarely in its recess in the slider, then wipe the recess clean and refit the washer **(see illustration)**.

20 Smear the new oil seal's lips with fork oil and slide it over the tube so that its markings face upwards **(see illustration)**. Press the seal into the slider, then drive it fully into place as described in Step 18 until the retaining clip groove is visible above it.

21 Once the seal is correctly seated, fit the retaining clip, making sure it is correctly located in its groove **(see illustration)**.

22 Lubricate the lips of the new dust seal then slide it down the fork tube and press it into position **(see illustration)**.

23 On Bonneville, T100 and Thruxton models, if removed fit the fork protector onto the top of the slider **(see illustration)**. On 2011-on Speedmaster models, seat the seal protector down onto the top of the fork slider ensuring that the vent hole is towards the rear.

24 Refer to Section 7, Steps 6 to 9, and refill the fork with oil.

25 If necessary now tighten the damper rod bolt to the specified torque setting **(see illustration 8.2b)**. Install the axle clamp bolt(s) in the bottom of the slider, where removed **(see illustration 8.2a)**.

26 On Scrambler and 2009-on T100 models install the fork gaiters, ensuring they are correctly located over the tops of the sliders.

27 Install the forks (see Section 6). On Thruxton models reset the amount of spring pre-load (see Section 12).

9 Steering stem and head bearings

Note: *Two thin 38 mm spanners are required (Triumph Part No. 3880140-T0301) which have an offset square cut into them to accept a torque wrench. This will enable the bearings to be pre-loaded to a specific torque and the locknut to be tightened to the specified torque.*

Removal

1 Remove the fuel tank (see Chapter 3A or 3B) – this will prevent the possibility of damage should a tool slip.

2 On Bonneville, T100, Thruxton and Scrambler models, unscrew the regulator/ rectifier mounting bolts and displace the unit **(see illustration)**. On Thruxton, Scrambler and 2011-on America models, displace both front turn signal assemblies from the bottom

8.22 . . . followed by the dust seal

8.23 Fit the ridge on the protector into the cut-out in the top of the slider (arrowed)

9.2 Unscrew the bolts displace the regulator/rectifier

9.3 Unscrew the bolt (arrowed) and displace the headlight assembly

9.4 Unscrew the bolt (arrowed) to release the brake hose

9.7a Unscrew the nut and remove the washer

yoke. Support the components using wire or cable-ties to avoid straining the wiring.

3 On America and Speedmaster models unscrew the headlight assembly mounting bolt on the underside of the bottom yoke **(see illustration)**. Secure it to one side using rag to protect other components.

4 Unscrew the bolt securing the front brake hose guide to the bottom yoke **(see illustration)**.

5 Remove the front forks (see Section 6). On Bonneville, T100, Thruxton and Scrambler models displace the headlight assembly from between the yokes, retrieving the rubber spacers from the top and bottom of each tube, and secure it to one side using rag to protect other components.

6 Displace the handlebars (see Section 5) and the instrument panel (see Chapter 8) from the top yoke if required, but note that they can remain attached to the yoke and be lifted off with it and the whole assembly placed aside.

7 Unscrew the steering stem nut and remove the washer **(see illustration)**. Ease the top yoke and handlebars (if not displaced) up and off the steering stem and position the assembly clear, using rag to protect other components, and securing it as required **(see illustration)** – on the machine photographed the whole assembly was tied to a roof rafter **(see illustration)**. Take care not to strain the cables, brake hose and wiring, and if possible keep the master cylinder reservoir upright, and in any event cover it in rag.

8 Unscrew and remove the adjuster locknut **(see illustration)**.

9 Support the bottom yoke, then unscrew the adjuster nut and remove it with the bearing cover **(see illustration)**.

10 Gently lower the bottom yoke and steering stem out of the frame **(see illustration)**.

11 Remove the inner race and bearing from the top of the steering head **(see illustration**

9.13). Remove the bearing from the base of the steering stem **(see illustration 9.12)**. Remove all traces of old grease from the bearings and races and check them for wear or damage as described in Section 10. **Note:** *Do not attempt to remove the outer races from the steering head or the inner race from the steering stem unless they are to be replaced with new ones.*

Installation

12 Smear a liberal quantity of multi-purpose grease onto the bearing races, and work some grease well into both the upper and lower bearings. Also smear the grease seal on the base of the steering stem. Fit the lower bearing onto the steering stem **(see illustration)**.

13 Carefully lift the steering stem/bottom yoke up through the steering head **(see illustration 9.10)**. Fit the upper bearing and its inner race into the top of the steering head

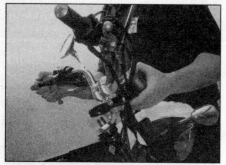

9.7b Lift the yoke (and handlebars if attached) off the stem and place it aside . . .

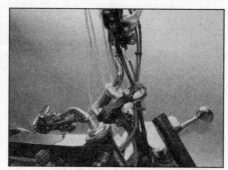

9.7c . . . tying it up or supporting it as required

9.8 Unscrew the locknut

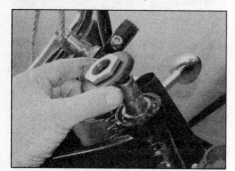

9.9 Unscrew the adjuster nut . . .

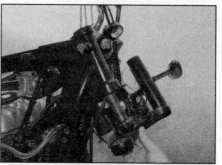

9.10 . . . and draw the bottom yoke/ steering stem out of the steering head

9.12 Fit the lower bearing onto the inner race on the base of the stem

9.13 Fit the upper bearing (arrowed) and the inner race

9.15 Using the spanner to set the adjuster nut

9.14 Using the Triumph spanner in conjunction with a torque wrench to pre-load the bearings

9.17 Counter-hold the adjuster nut and tighten the locknut to the specified torque

(see illustration). Clean any grease off the steering stem threads as its presence will affect the torque setting applied during the following procedure. Now fit the bearing cover and adjuster nut, securing the nut finger-tight at this stage (see illustration 9.9).

14 If you have the Triumph service tool (see Note), fit a torque wrench to the spanner (at a 90° angle to the spanner) and tighten the nut to the torque setting specified at the beginning of the Chapter to pre-load the bearings (see illustration). Remove the torque wrench, then turn the bottom yoke from side to side to settle the bearings, then slacken the adjuster nut again. If you do not have the Triumph spanner, follow the same procedure using the available spanner and pre-load the bearings according to feel.

15 Now tighten the adjuster nut to 3 Nm using the Triumph spanner (see illustration). This will remove all freeplay, yet enable the

steering to move freely. If this spanner is not available, tighten the adjuster nut by hand until all freeplay is removed yet the steering is able to move freely. The object is to set the adjuster nut so that the bearings are under a very light loading, just enough to remove any freeplay, but not so much that the steering does not move freely from side to side as described in the check procedure in Chapter 1.

16 Now install all remaining components except the fuel tank, referring to the relevant Sections of this Chapter where necessary and to the torque settings specified at the beginning of the Chapter, and leaving the top yoke on the steering stem and forks but without the steering stem nut and with the clamp bolts loose and with the yoke raised above the adjuster nut and locknut so they are exposed for further adjustment. All components must be in place for an accurate setting of the head bearings to be made so their inertia can be

taken into account. Re-check and finely adjust the amount of freeplay.

Caution: Take great care not to apply excessive pressure because this will cause premature failure of the bearings.

17 With the bearings correctly adjusted, counter-hold the adjuster nut and tighten the locknut against it, also to the specified torque setting if the special tool is available (see illustration). Make sure the adjuster nut does not turn with the locknut – if it does repeat the adjustment procedure.

18 Install the top yoke and tighten the steering stem nut and the fork clamp bolts in the top yoke, and on Thruxton models with clip-on handlebars if necessary the handlebar positioning bolts and then tighten the clamp bolts, to the torque settings specified at the beginning of the Chapter.

19 Install the remaining components in a reverse of the removal procedure.

20 Carry out a final check of the steering head bearing freeplay as described in Chapter 1, and if necessary re-adjust.

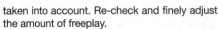

10 Steering head bearing replacement

Inspection

1 Remove the steering stem (see Section 9).

2 Remove all traces of old grease from the bearings and races and check them for wear or damage.

3 The inner and outer races should be polished and free from indentations (see illustration). Inspect the bearing balls for signs of wear, damage or discoloration, and examine the ball retainer cage for signs of cracks or splits. If there are any signs of wear on any of the above components both upper and lower bearing assemblies must be replaced with new ones as a set. Only remove the outer races in the steering head and the lower bearing inner race on the steering stem if new ones are needed – do not re-use them once they have been removed.

Removal and installation

4 The outer races are an interference fit in the steering head and can be tapped from position with a suitable drift (see illustrations). Tap

10.3 Checking the inner races for wear

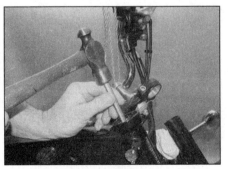

10.4a Drive the bearing races out with a brass drift . . .

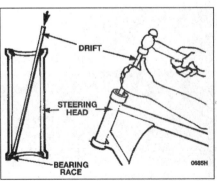

10.4b . . . locating it as shown

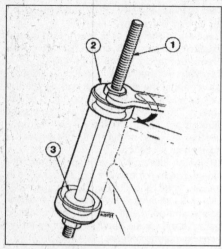

10.6 Drawbolt arrangement for fitting steering stem bearing races

1 Long bolt or threaded bar
2 Thick washer
3 Guide for lower race

firmly and evenly around each race to ensure that it is driven out squarely. It may prove advantageous to curve the end of the drift slightly to improve access.

5 Alternatively, the races can be removed using a slide-hammer type bearing extractor; these can often be hired from tool shops.

6 The new outer races can be pressed into the head using a drawbolt arrangement **(see illustration)**, or by using a large diameter

11.3 Unscrew the lower then upper mounting bolts and remove the washers . . .

11.5 . . . then draw the shock absorber off its mounts

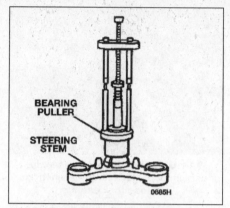

10.7 Remove the lower bearing inner race using a puller if necessary

tubular drift. Ensure that the drawbolt washer or drift (as applicable) bears only on the outer edge of the race and does not contact the working surface. Alternatively, have the races installed by a Triumph dealer equipped with the bearing race installation tools.

 Installation of new bearing outer races is made much easier if the races are left overnight in the freezer. This causes them to contract slightly making them a looser fit. Alternatively, use a freeze spray.

7 The lower bearing inner race should only be removed from the steering stem if a new one is being fitted. To remove the race, use two screwdrivers placed on opposite sides to work it free, using blocks of wood to improve leverage and protect the yoke, or tap under it using a cold chisel. If the steering stem is placed on its side on a hard surface, thread a suitable nut onto the top to prevent the threads being damaged. If the race is firmly in place it will be necessary to use a puller **(see illustration)**. Take the steering stem to a Triumph dealer if required.

8 Remove the seal from the bottom of the stem and replace it with a new one. Smear the new one with grease.

9 Fit the new lower race onto the steering

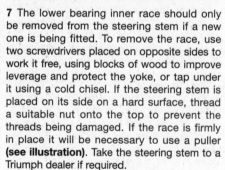

11.7 Check for pitting and oil on the rod

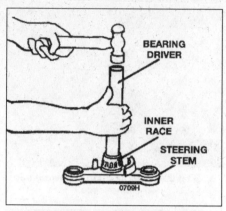

10.9 Drive the new race on using a suitable driver or a length of pipe

stem. A length of tubing with an internal diameter slightly larger than the steering stem will be needed to tap the new race into position – make sure the drift contacts the inner rim of the race only and not the bearing's working surface **(see illustration)**.

10 Install the steering stem (see Section 9).

11 Rear shock absorbers

1 It is advisable to remove one shock absorber at a time. If you need to remove both of them at the same time, for example if removing the swingarm, support the motorcycle on an auxiliary stand that does not take the weight through any part of the rear suspension, or by using a hoist. Position a support under the rear wheel or swingarm so that they do not drop when the second shock absorber is removed, but also making sure that the weight of the machine is off the rear suspension so that the shocks are not compressed. Make a note of which way round the shock absorbers fit.

2 On Thruxton models remove the exhaust silencers. On Scrambler models, remove both exhaust silencers to allow removal of the right-hand rear shock absorber. Refer to Chapter 3A or 3B for details of silencer removal.

3 Unscrew the shock absorber lower mounting bolt and remove the washer **(see illustration)**.

4 Unscrew the shock absorber upper mounting bolt and remove the washer.

5 Draw the shock absorber off its mounts **(see illustration)**.

Inspection

6 Inspect the shock absorber for obvious physical damage and the coil spring for looseness, cracks or signs of fatigue.

7 Inspect the rod for signs of bending, pitting and oil leakage **(see illustration)**.

11.8 Check the bush in each mount

8 Inspect the pivot bushes at the top and bottom for wear or damage **(see illustration)**.
9 With the exception of the mounting bolts and washers, Triumph do not supply individual shock absorber components. It may, however, be possible to have the shocks rebuilt by a suspension specialist – do not attempt to dismantle them at home.

Installation

10 Installation is the reverse of removal, noting the following points.
● Apply multi-purpose grease to the shock absorber bushes and mounts.
● Clean the threads of the bolts and apply a suitable thread locking compound.
● Tighten the bolts to the torque setting specified at the beginning of the Chapter.

12 Suspension adjustment

Front suspension – Thruxton only

1 The front forks are adjustable for spring pre-load only. Use a suitable spanner on the adjuster flats on the top of the forks **(see illustration)**, noting that the amount of pre-load is indicated by lines on the adjuster. Turn the adjuster clockwise to increase pre-load and anti-clockwise to decrease it. Always make sure both adjusters are set equally. The standard pre-load setting is with 4 lines visible.

13.4 Displace the caliper bracket, noting how it locates

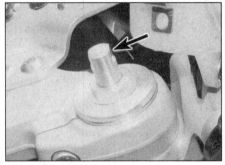

12.1 Spring pre-load adjuster (arrowed)

Rear suspension – all models

2 The shock absorbers are adjustable for spring pre-load only. They are adjusted by turning the spring seat on the bottom of the shock absorber using a suitable tool such as an Allen key, screwdriver or rod located in the circular lug **(see illustration)**. There are five positions. The highest notch (1) for the stopper is the softest setting and the lower notch (5) is the hardest setting. Align the notch required with the adjustment stopper. Turn the spring seat clockwise to increase pre-load and anti-clockwise to decrease it. The standard setting for Bonneville models up to VIN 380776, T100, Thruxton, Scrambler, America and Speedmaster models is notch 2. The standard setting for Bonneville models from VIN 380777 is notch 1.
3 Always make sure that both shock absorbers are set to the same position, otherwise handling of the bike will be adversely affected.

13 Swingarm removal and installation

Bonneville, T100, Thruxton and Scrambler

Removal

1 Support the motorcycle on an auxiliary stand that does not take the weight through any part of the rear suspension, or by using a hoist.
2 Remove the exhaust silencers (see Chapter 3A or 3B).

13.6 Undo the screws (arrowed) and remove the guard

12.2 Turn the spring seat using a suitable tool in the hole (arrowed)

3 Unscrew the bolt securing the brake hose guide to the top of the swingarm and detach the guide **(see illustration)** – if the bolt is corroded or seized spray it liberally with penetrating fluid, then tap it smartly on the head with a hammer, otherwise it may shear off.
4 Remove the rear wheel (see Chapter 6). Remove the brake caliper bracket from the swingarm, noting how it locates **(see illustration)**.
5 Undo the front sprocket cover bolts and remove the cover **(see illustration 3.5a)**.
6 If required, undo the screws securing the chainguard, bearing in mind the information in Step 3 regarding seized bolts/screws **(see illustration)**. Remove the guard, noting how it fits.
7 On Thruxton models, note the alignment of the punch mark in the end of the gearchange shaft with that on the linkage arm, then unscrew the pinch bolt and slide the arm off the shaft **(see illustration)**.

13.3 Unscrew the bolt (arrowed) and detach the guide

13.7 Note the alignment of the punch marks, then unscrew the bolt (arrowed) and slide the arm off

13.8a Remove the cap

13.8b Unscrew the bolts (arrowed) . . .

13.8c . . . and remove the bracket

13.9 Swingarm pivot clamp bolt in the right-hand side (arrowed)

13.10a Unscrew the nut and remove the washer . . .

13.10b . . . and the bush

8 Remove the cap from the left-hand end of the swingarm pivot bolt (see illustration). Unscrew the swingarm pivot clamp bolt in the rider's left-hand footrest bracket, noting how it secures the wiring guide (see illustration).

If required free the wiring from the guide and remove the guide. Unscrew the footrest bracket bolts and draw the bracket off the pivot (see illustration).

9 Slacken the swingarm pivot clamp bolt in

the rider's right-hand footrest bracket (see illustration).

10 Unscrew the nut on the left-hand end of the pivot bolt and remove the washer and the bush (see illustrations).

11 Remove the shock absorbers (see Section 11).

12 Support the swingarm then withdraw the pivot bolt along with the bush from the right-hand side (see illustration). Manoeuvre the swingarm back and remove it (see illustration). Note the spacer in each side of the left-hand pivot and take care not to lose them as they could drop out (see illustration). Also note the sleeve in the right-hand pivot (see illustration).

13 If required, undo the screw and remove the washer securing the chain slider and remove it, noting how it fits, again referring to Step 3 (see illustration). If badly worn or damaged, the slider should be replaced with a new one.

13.12a Withdraw the pivot along with its bush (arrowed) . . .

13.12b . . . and remove the swingarm

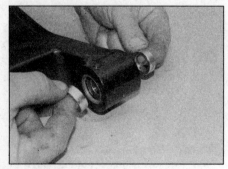

13.12c Take care not to lose the spacers . . .

13.12d . . . or the sleeve

13.13 Chain slider screw (arrowed)

13.23 Install the front sprocket cover

14 Clean, inspect and re-grease all pivot components as described in Section 14.

Installation

15 If removed install the chain slider, smearing the screw threads with copper grease, and not forgetting the washer **(see illustration 13.13)**.

16 Smear the pivot bolt with multi-purpose grease, then slide the right-hand bush onto it with the wider end facing the bolt head. Make sure the spacer is correctly located in each side of the left-hand pivot, and the sleeve is in the right-hand pivot **(see illustrations 13.12c and d)**.

17 Offer up the swingarm, making sure the drive chain is correctly routed, and if available have an assistant hold it in place **(see illustration 13.12b)**. Slide the pivot bolt in from the right-hand side and push it all the way through, locating the bush against the swingarm **(see illustration 13.12a)**.

18 If the rider's right-hand footrest bracket has been removed (for example if the engine was removed, temporarily install it now and tighten its mounting bolts to centralise the bush, then remove it again after the pivot bolt nut has been tightened for installation of the exhaust **(see illustrations 3.5d and c)**.

19 Fit the bush onto the left-hand end of the pivot bolt and fit it against the swingarm **(see illustration 13.10b)**. Install the shock absorbers (see Section 11). Install the rider's left-hand footrest bracket and tighten its mounting bolts to the torque setting specified at the beginning of the Chapter **(see illustrations 13.8c and b)**.

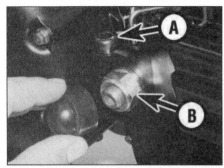

13.37 Remove the cap, then slacken the clamp bolt (A) on each side, then unscrew the nut (B)

13.35 Unscrew the bolts (arrowed) and remove the cover

20 Fit the pivot bolt nut with its washer and tighten it finger-tight, then counter-hold the head of the bolt and tighten the nut to the specified torque setting **(see illustration 13.10a)**. Check that the swingarm moves freely up and down.

21 Tighten the swingarm pivot clamp bolt in each footrest bracket to the specified torque setting, not forgetting the wiring guide on the left-hand side **(see illustration 13.8b)**. Fit the cap onto the left-hand end of the pivot bolt **(see illustration 13.8a)**.

22 On Thruxton, slide the gearchange linkage arm onto the shaft aligning the punch marks and tighten the pinch bolt **(see illustration 13.7)**.

23 Install the front sprocket cover and tighten the bolts to the specified torque **(see illustration)**.

24 If removed install the chainguard, smearing the screw threads with copper grease **(see illustration 13.6)**.

25 Smear the slot in the caliper bracket with some grease **(see illustration 13.4)**. Locate the bracket on the swingarm.

26 Install the rear wheel (see Chapter 6).

27 Fit the brake hose guide, smearing the bolt threads with copper grease **(see illustration 13.3)**.

28 Install the exhaust silencers (see Chapter 3A or 3B).

29 Check and adjust the drive chain slack (see Chapter 1). Check the operation of the rear suspension and brake before taking the machine on the road.

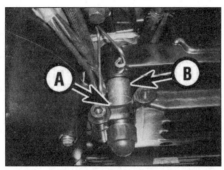

13.40 On each side slide the pivot spacer (A) into the frame and remove the inner spacer (B)

America and Speedmaster

Removal

30 Support the motorcycle on an auxiliary stand that does not take the weight through any part of the rear suspension, or by using a hoist.

31 Remove the exhaust silencers (including the footrest plates on models up to 2010) as described in Chapter 3A or 3B.

32 Remove the battery and its holder (see Chapter 8).

33 Unscrew the bolt securing the brake hose guide to the top of the swingarm and detach the guide **(see illustration 13.3)** – if the bolt is corroded or seized spray it liberally with penetrating fluid, then tap it on the head with a hammer, otherwise it may shear off.

34 Remove the rear wheel (see Chapter 6). Remove the brake caliper bracket from the swingarm, noting how it locates.

35 Undo the front sprocket cover bolts and remove the cover, noting the wiring guide secured by the two front bolts **(see illustration)**.

36 If required, undo the screws securing the chainguard, bearing in mind the information in Step 3 regarding seized bolts/screws **(see illustration 13.6)**. Remove the guard, noting how it fits.

37 Remove the cap from the left-hand end of the swingarm pivot bolt **(see illustration)**. Slacken the swingarm pivot clamp bolt in each side of the frame.

38 Unscrew the nut on the left-hand end of the pivot bolt **(see illustration 13.37)**.

39 Remove the shock absorbers (see Section 11).

40 Support the swingarm then withdraw the pivot bolt. Slide the spacer in each pivot clamp in the frame away from the swingarm, using a drift if necessary, and on the left-hand side remove the inner spacer **(see illustration)**. Manoeuvre the swingarm back and remove it. Note the spacer in the inside of the left-hand pivot and take care not to lose it as it could drop out. Also note the sleeve in the right-hand pivot.

41 If required, undo the screw and remove the washer securing the chain slider and remove it, noting how it fits, again referring to Step 3 **(see illustration 13.13)**. If badly worn or damaged the slider should be replaced with a new one.

42 Clean, inspect and re-grease all pivot components as described in Section 14.

Installation

43 If removed install the chain slider, smearing the screw threads with copper grease, and not forgetting the washer **(see illustration 13.13)**.

44 Smear the pivot bolt with multi-purpose grease. Make sure the spacer is correctly located in the inside of the left-hand pivot, and the sleeve is in the right-hand pivot. Make sure the spacers in the frame clamps are pushed well out.

45 Offer up the swingarm, making sure the

drive chain is correctly routed, and if available have an assistant hold it in place. Slide the pivot bolt in from the right-hand side and push it through, locating the inner spacer onto the left-hand end as it appears **(see illustration 13.40)**. Drift the spacers in the frame clamps against the inner spacer on the left-hand side and the sleeve on the right-hand side, making sure they are set evenly.

46 Fit the pivot bolt nut and tighten it finger-tight, then counter-hold the head of the bolt and tighten the nut to the specified torque setting **(see illustration13.37)**. Check that the swingarm moves freely up and down.

47 Install the shock absorbers (see Section 11).

48 Tighten the swingarm pivot clamp bolt in each side of the frame to the specified torque setting **(see illustration 13.37)**. Fit the cap onto the left-hand end of the pivot bolt.

49 Install the front sprocket cover, not forgetting the wiring guide, and tighten the bolts to the specified torque **(see illustration 13.35)**.

50 If removed install the chainguard, smearing the screw threads with copper grease **(see illustration 13.6)**.

51 Smear the slot in the caliper bracket with some grease. Locate the bracket on the swingarm.

52 Install the rear wheel (see Chapter 6).

53 Fit the brake hose guide, smearing the bolt threads with copper grease **(see illustration 13.3)**.

54 Install the exhaust silencers (see Chapter 3A or 3B).

55 Install the battery holder and the battery (see Chapter 8).

56 Check and adjust the drive chain slack (see Chapter 1). Check the operation of the rear suspension and brake before taking the machine on the road.

14 Swingarm inspection, bearing check and renewal

Inspection

1 Remove the swingarm (see Section 13).

2 Thoroughly clean the swingarm, removing all traces of dirt, corrosion and grease.

3 Inspect the swingarm closely, looking for obvious signs of wear such as heavy scoring, and cracks or distortion due to accident damage. Any damaged or worn component must be replaced with a new one.

4 Check the swingarm pivot bolt is straight by rolling it on a flat surface such as a piece of plate glass (first wipe off all old grease and remove any corrosion using wire wool). If it is bent replace it with a new one.

Bearing check and renewal

5 On Bonneville, T100 and Thruxton models remove the spacer from each side of the left-hand pivot **(see illustration 13.12c)**. Withdraw the bearing sleeve from the right-hand pivot **(see illustration 13.12d)**.

6 On America and Speedmaster models remove the spacer from the inside of the left-hand pivot. Withdraw the bearing sleeve from the right-hand pivot.

7 Lever the grease seal out of each side of each pivot, noting which type fits where, and discard them as new ones must be used **(see illustration)**.

8 Clean off all old grease from the bearings spacers and sleeve. Check the condition of the bearings, noting that there are two caged ball bearings secured by a circlip in the left-hand side and a needle roller bearing in the right-hand side. Slip the sleeve back into the needle bearing and the pivot bolt into the ball bearings and check that there is not an excessive amount of freeplay between the components. If the bearings do not run smoothly and freely or if there is excessive freeplay, they must be replaced with new ones. Refer to *Tools and Workshop Tips* (Section 5) in the Reference section for more information on bearings.

9 Worn bearings can be drifted out of their bores, but note that removal will destroy them; new bearings should be obtained before work commences. Do not forget to remove the circlip before trying to remove the ball bearings. The new bearings should be pressed or drawn into their bores rather than driven into position. In the absence of a press, a suitable drawbolt tool can be made up as described in *Tools and Workshop Tips* in the Reference section. In all cases make sure the marked side of the bearing is on the outside.

10 Fit a new grease seal into each side of each pivot **(see illustrations)**.

11 Lubricate the bearings, seals and all other pivot components with multi-purpose grease.

12 Slide the sleeve into the needle bearing in the right-hand pivot and the spacer(s) into the left-hand pivot **(see illustrations 13.12d and c)**.

15 Drive chain removal and installation

1 Position the bike upright on an auxiliary stand. Rotate the drive chain through one complete rotation to check whether it has a soft 'joining' link – the soft link can be recognised by its identification marks (and usually its different colour), as well as by the staked ends of the link's two pins which look as if they have been deeply centre-punched, instead of peened over as with all the other pins. If a soft link is fitted, the chain can either be removed by splitting the soft link and threading the chain off the sprockets or by removing the rear wheel and swingarm. If the chain is of the endless type (does not have a soft link), it will be necessary to remove the rear wheel and swingarm.

Soft link chain

Note: *The Triumph service tool, Pt. No. A3880205, or one of several commercially-available drive chain riveting tools will be required and if re-using the old drive chain, a new soft link will be required.*

Caution: Use ONLY the correct service tools to secure the soft link – if you do not have access to such tools or do not have the skill to operate them correctly, have the chain installed by a dealer to be sure of having it securely installed. NEVER install a drive chain which uses a clip-type master (split) link.

2 Undo the front sprocket cover bolts and remove the cover. If the sprockets are being replaced with new ones, slacken the front sprocket nut before splitting the chain so that the rear brake can be used to stop the sprocket turning (see Section 16).

3 Locate the soft link in a suitable position to work on by rotating the back wheel.

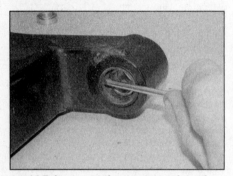

14.7 Lever out the grease seals and discard them

14.10a Fit a new seal into each side . . .

14.10b . . . using a piece of wood to set them in place if necessary

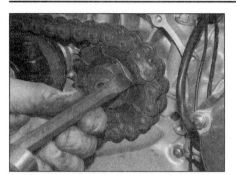

16.2 Bend back the tabs . . .

16.3 . . . then unscrew the nut and remove the washer

16.5 Slide the sprocket off the shaft and remove it

4 Slacken the drive chain as described in Chapter 1, Section 2.

5 Split the chain at the soft link using the tool, following carefully the manufacturer's operating instructions (see also Section 8 in *Tools and Workshop Tips* in the Reference Section). Remove the chain from the bike, noting its routing around the swingarm.

6 Slip the new, or cleaned, drive chain around the front and rear sprockets, leaving the two ends in a convenient position to work on.

7 Referring to Section 8 in *Tools and Workshop Tips* in the Reference Section, install the new soft link from the inside. Fit an O-ring onto each pin, then slide the link through and fit the other two O-rings. Install the new side plate with its identification marks facing out. Stake the new link using the riveting tool, following carefully the instructions provided with the tool. DO NOT re-use old joining link components.

8 After staking, check the soft link and its staked ends for any signs of cracking. If there is any evidence of cracking, the soft link, O-rings and side plate must be replaced with new ones.

9 Fit the sprocket cover and tighten its bolts to the torque setting specified at the beginning of the Chapter.

10 On completion, adjust and lubricate the chain following the procedures described in Chapter 1.

Endless chain

11 Remove the swingarm (see Section 13), then remove the chain.

12 Installation is the reverse of removal. On completion adjust and lubricate the chain following the procedures described in Section 1.

Cleaning

13 If re-using the original chain, clean all road dirt and old lubricant from the chain and sprockets before refitting the chain. Ideally use a proprietary chain cleaner and soft brush to clean the chain – avoid using solvents or other cleaning fluids which might damage the chain's sealing O-rings and do not use jet washers or steam cleaners.

16 Sprockets

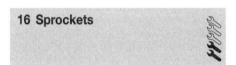

Caution: Renew both sprockets and the chain as a set. It is false economy to renew just one component.

Front sprocket

1 Undo the front sprocket cover bolts and remove the cover **(see illustration 3.5a or 13.35)**.

2 Bend down the tabs on the sprocket nut lockwasher **(see illustration)**.

3 Engage a gear, then have an assistant hold the rear brake on hard. Unscrew the sprocket nut and remove the washer **(see illustration)**. Discard the washer as a new one should be used.

4 Fully slacken the drive chain as described in Chapter 1 – this should provide enough slack to slide the sprocket and chain off the shaft, but if necessary disengage the chain from the rear sprocket to give extra slack. If there is still not enough slack to disengage the chain, either partially or completely remove the rear wheel (see Chapter 6) – partial removal means leaving it between the ends of the swingarm with the chain looped round its sprocket, but the axle needs to be removed and the wheel dropped. If the rear sprocket is being replaced with a new one as well, remove the rear wheel now to give full slack.

5 Slide the front sprocket off the shaft and disengage it from the chain **(see illustration)**.

6 Smear the shaft splines with grease. Fit the new sprocket into the chain and slide it onto the shaft, making sure the marked side is facing out **(see illustration)**. If removed fit the chain onto the rear sprocket or install the rear wheel (see Chapter 6). Take up excess slack in the chain (see Chapter 1, Section 2).

7 Fit the new lockwasher onto the shaft, engaging it with the splines **(see illustration)**. Fit the nut with its shouldered side innermost **(see illustration 16.3)**, and tighten it to the specified torque setting, with the engine in gear and holding the rear brake on hard as before.

8 Bend the rim of the washer up to lock the nut **(see illustration)**. Fit the sprocket cover and tighten its bolts to the specified torque. Adjust the chain so that it has the correct amount of freeplay, then lubricate it (Chapter 1).

16.6 Make sure the sprocket is the correct way round

16.7 Fit a new lockwasher

16.8 Bend the rim of the washer against the flats of the nut

16.10 Rear sprocket nuts (arrowed)

Rear sprocket

9 Remove the rear wheel (see Chapter 6).
10 Unscrew the nuts securing the sprocket **(see illustration)**. Lift the sprocket off the studs.
11 Make sure the studs are tight in the

17.4 Check the rubber dampers

17.3a Lift the sprocket coupling out of the wheel . . .

sprocket coupling. If any are loose remove them, clean their threads, apply a thread locking compound and tighten them to the torque setting specified at the beginning of the Chapter – refer to Tools and Workshop Tips for details on how to tighten studs.
12 Fit the new sprocket with its marked side facing out and tighten the nuts evenly and progressively in a criss-cross pattern to the specified torque setting.
13 Install the rear wheel (see Chapter 6).

17 Rear sprocket coupling/ rubber dampers

1 Remove the rear wheel (see Chapter 6).
Caution: Do not lay the wheel down on the disc as it could become warped. Lay the wheel on wooden blocks so that the disc is off the ground.

17.3b . . . and remove the spacer if loose

2 Grasp the sprocket and twist it back and forth to check for play between the carrier and the rubber dampers. If there is any play new dampers must be installed.
3 Lift the sprocket coupling off the wheel **(see illustration)**. Note the spacer fitted in the bearing on the inside **(see illustration)**. Check the coupling for cracks or any obvious signs of damage.
4 Check the rubber damper segments for cracks, hardening and general deterioration **(see illustration)**. Replace them as a set with new ones if necessary.
5 Procedures for the sprocket coupling bearing are described in Chapter 6.
6 Installation is the reverse of removal. Make sure the spacer is correctly fitted in the bearing on the inside of the sprocket coupling **(see illustration 17.3b)**. Lubricate the damper walls to help them slide into place as you fit the coupling if necessary.
7 Install the rear wheel (see Chapter 6).

Chapter 6
Brakes, wheels and tyres

Contents

Degrees of difficulty

Easy, suitable for novice with little experience	**Fairly easy,** suitable for beginner with some experience	**Fairly difficult,** suitable for competent DIY mechanic 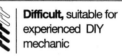	**Difficult,** suitable for experienced DIY mechanic	**Very difficult,** suitable for expert DIY or professional

Specifications

Brakes

	Standard	Service limit
Brake fluid type	DOT 4	
Brake pad minimum thickness...........	1.5 mm	
Front disc thickness – Bonneville, T100 and Scrambler		
790 cc models	5.0 mm	4.5 mm
865 cc models	5.5 mm	5.0 mm
Front disc thickness – Thruxton		
Carburettor models	5.5 mm	5.0 mm
EFI models	5.0 mm	4.5 mm
Front disc thickness – America and Speedmaster models		
Up to VIN 169265	5.0 mm	4.5 mm
From VIN 169266	5.5 mm	5.0 mm
Front disc maximum run-out		
Thruxton...........	0.1 mm	0.3 mm
All other models	0.15 mm	0.3 mm
Rear disc thickness	6.0 mm	5.0 mm
Rear disc maximum run-out...........	0.15 mm	0.3 mm

Wheels

Rim size
Bonneville up to 2008, T100 and Scrambler .... Spoked, front 2.5 x 19 inch, rear 3.5 x 17 inch
Bonneville from 2009 .... Cast, front 3.0 x 17 inch, rear 3.5 x 17 inch
America 2002 to 2006 .... Spoked, front 2.5 x 18 inch, rear 3.5 x 15 inch
America 2007 to 2010 .... Cast, front 2.5 x 18 inch, rear 3.5 x 15 inch
America 2011-on .... Cast, front 3.0 x 16 inch, rear 4.0 x 15 inch
Speedmaster 2003 to 2010 .... Cast, front 2.5 x 18 inch, rear 3.5 x 15 inch
Speedmaster from 2011.......... Cast, front 2.5 x 19 inch, rear 4.0 x 15 inch
Thruxton.......... Spoked, front 2.5 x 18 inch, rear 3.5 x 17 inch
Wheel run-out (max)
Axial (side-to-side) .... 0.6 mm
Radial (out-of-round) .... 0.6 mm

Tyres

Tyre pressures	see *Pre-ride checks*	
Tyre sizes*	**Front**	**Rear**
Bonneville 2001 to 2008, T100 and Scrambler	100/90 19, tubed	130/80 17, tubed
Bonneville 2009-on.	110/70 R17, tubeless	130/80 R17, tubeless
America 2002 to 2006	110/90 18, tubed	170/80 15, tubed
America 2007 to 2010	110/90 18, tubeless	170/80 15, tubeless
America 2011-on	130/90 R16, tubeless	170/80 B15, tubeless
Speedmaster 2003 to 2010	110/90 18, tubeless	170/80 15, tubeless
Speedmaster 2011-on	100/90 R19, tubeless	170/80 B15, tubeless
Thruxton	100/90 18, tubed	130/80 R17, tubed

Refer to the owners handbook, or your dealer for approved tyre brands.

Torque wrench settings

Bleed valves.	6 Nm
Brake hose banjo bolts.	25 Nm
Brake pad retaining pins (front and rear)	18 Nm
Front axle bolt – America and 2003 to 2010 Speedmaster	60 Nm
Front axle – Speedmaster 2011-on	95 Nm
Front axle clamp bolt(s)	
Bonneville, T100, Thruxton and Scrambler	27 Nm
America and Speedmaster.	22 Nm
Front axle nut – Bonneville, T100, Thruxton and Scrambler	60 Nm
Front brake caliper mounting bolts	28 Nm
Front brake disc bolts	22 Nm
Front brake master cylinder clamp bolts	12 Nm
Rear axle nut	
Bonneville, T100, Thruxton and Scrambler	85 Nm
America and Speedmaster.	110 Nm
Rear brake caliper mounting bolts.	40 Nm
Rear brake disc bolts	22 Nm
Rear brake light switch.	15 Nm
Rear brake master cylinder mounting bolts	
Bonneville and T100.	18 Nm
Thruxton, Scrambler, America and Speedmaster	16 Nm

1 General information

Bonneville models up to 2008, all T100, Thruxton and Scrambler models, and 2002 to 2006 America models are fitted with steel-rimmed and spoked wheels and have tubed tyres. All Speedmaster models, 2007-on America models and 2009-on Bonneville models are fitted with cast alloy wheels designed for tubeless tyres only.

Both front and rear brakes are hydraulically-operated disc brakes with twin piston sliding calipers. Speedmaster models from 2003 to 2010 are fitted with twin discs at the front while all other models have a single front disc. *Caution: Disc brake components rarely require disassembly. Do not disassemble components unless absolutely necessary. If a hydraulic brake line is loosened, the entire system must be disassembled, drained, cleaned and then properly filled and bled upon reassembly. Do not use solvents on internal brake components.*

Solvents will cause the seals to swell and distort. Use only clean DOT 4 brake fluid or denatured alcohol for cleaning. Use care when working with brake fluid as it can injure your eyes and it will damage painted surfaces and plastic parts.

2 Front brake pads

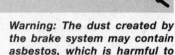

⚠ *Warning: The dust created by the brake system may contain asbestos, which is harmful to your health. Never blow it out with compressed air and don't inhale any of it. An approved filtering mask should be worn when working on the brakes. Do not, under any circumstances, use petroleum-based solvents to clean brake parts. Use a dedicated brake cleaner or denatured alcohol only.*

1 Unscrew the pad retaining pin plug **(see illustration)**. Slacken but do not yet remove the retaining pin **(see illustration)**.

2 Unscrew the caliper mounting bolts and

2.1a Unscrew the plug . . .

2.1b . . . then slacken the pin

2.2a Unscrew the bolts (arrowed) . . .

2.2b . . . and slide the caliper off the disc

2.3 Unscrew and withdraw the pin then remove the pads

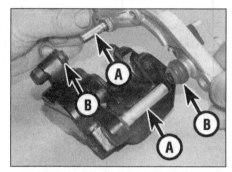

2.9a Slide the caliper and bracket apart and check the pins (A) and boots (B) as described

2.9b Make sure the spring (arrowed) . . .

2.9c . . . and the guide (arrowed) are correctly fitted

slide the caliper off the disc (see illustrations) – there is no need to disconnect the hose.

3 Unscrew and remove the pad pin, noting how it fits (see illustration). Remove the pads from the caliper, noting how they fit (see illustration 2.11a). Note the pad spring in the caliper and the pad guide on the caliper bracket and remove them if required for cleaning or replacement, noting how they fit (see illustrations 2.9b and c).

4 Inspect the surface of each pad for contamination and check that the friction material has not worn beyond its service limit (see Chapter 1, Section 12). If either pad is worn down to or beyond the service limit wear indicator, is fouled with oil or grease, or is heavily scored or damaged by dirt and debris, both pads (in each caliper on Speedmaster models) must be replaced with new ones. Note that it is not possible to degrease the friction material; if the pads are contaminated in any way, new ones must be fitted.

5 If the pads are in good condition clean them carefully, using a fine wire brush which is completely free of oil and grease, to remove all traces of road dirt and corrosion. Using a pointed instrument, clean out the groove in the friction material and dig out any embedded particles of foreign matter. Spray the caliper area with a dedicated brake cleaner to remove any dust and remove and traces of corrosion which might cause sticking of the caliper/pad operation.

6 Check the condition of the brake disc (see Section 4).

7 Remove any traces of corrosion from the

pad pin. Check it for signs of damage and replace it with a new one if necessary.

8 Clean around the exposed section of each piston to remove any dirt or debris that could cause the seals to be damaged. Now push the pistons back into the caliper – if new pads are being fitted you need to push them all the way in to create room for them; if the old pads are still serviceable push them in a little way, not only because it makes installation easier, but also because it serves as a check that neither of the pistons is seized in its bore. To push the pistons back use finger pressure, either on each piston individually or on a piece of wood across both pistons, or use grips and a piece of wood, with rag or card to protect the caliper body (see illustration 3.15b). Alternatively obtain a proper piston-pushing tool from a good tool supplier. It may be necessary to remove the master cylinder reservoir cover or cap and siphon out some fluid. If the pistons are difficult to push back, remove the bleed valve cap, then attach a length of clear hose to the bleed valve and place the open end in a suitable container, then open the valve and try again (see illustrations 11.5a and b). Take great care not to draw any air into the system. If in doubt, bleed the brakes afterwards (see Section 11). If either of the pistons appears seized, block the other piston so all pressure is applied to the one being checked, then apply the brake lever and check whether the piston moves at all. If it moves out but can't be pushed back in the chances are there is some hidden corrosion stopping it. If it is completely seized you will have to overhaul the caliper (see Section 3).

9 Slide the caliper and bracket apart (see illustration). Clean off all old grease and any

signs of corrosion from the slider pins. Check the condition of the rubber boot for each slider pin and make sure they are correctly fitted – they are not listed as being available separately so if they are damaged a new caliper should be considered. Make sure the pad spring is correctly fitted in the caliper and the guide is correctly fitted on the bracket (see illustrations). Apply fresh silicone based grease to each pin and boot, then slide the caliper and bracket together (see illustration 3.16).

10 Lightly smear the backs and sides of the pad backing material and the shank and threads of the pad pin with copper-based grease, making sure that none gets on the friction material.

11 Fit the outer pad into the caliper with the back of the pad against the pistons and seat it against the guide on the bracket (see illustration). Press the pad down against

2.11a Fit the outer pad, making sure it locates correctly against the guide (arrowed) . . .

2.11b . . . then insert the pin

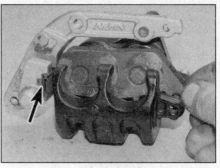

2.11c Fit the inner pad, making sure it locates correctly against the guide (arrowed)

2.12 Fit the caliper and tighten its bolts

the spring and insert the pad pin part-way to locate the pad **(see illustration)**. Fit the inner pad so its friction material faces the outer pad, locating it in the same way **(see illustration)**. Press its end down, slide the pin through and thread it into the caliper tightening it lightly **(see illustration 2.3)**.

12 Slide the caliper onto the disc, making sure the pads locate correctly on each side **(see illustration 2.2b)**. Install the mounting bolts and tighten them to the torque setting specified at the beginning of the Chapter **(see illustration)**.

13 Now tighten the pad pin to the specified torque setting **(see illustration 2.1b)**. Smear some copper grease onto the plug and tighten it **(see illustration 2.1a)**.

14 Top up the master cylinder reservoir if necessary (see *Pre-ride checks*), and refit the diaphragm, plate and reservoir cap. Operate the brake lever several times to bring the pads into contact with the disc. Check the operation of the brake before riding the motorcycle and

3.3 Brake hose banjo bolt (arrowed)

remember that new pads will take a while to bed in; Triumph recommend a break-in mileage of 200m (300km).

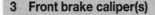

3 Front brake caliper(s)

> **Warning: The dust created by the brake pads may contain asbestos, which is harmful to your health.** Never blow it out with compressed air and don't inhale any of it. An approved filtering mask should be worn when working on the brakes. If a new caliper is being installed all old brake fluid should be flushed from the system. Do not, under any circumstances, use petroleum-based solvents to clean internal brake parts – use new DOT 4 brake fluid only. Use care when working with brake fluid as it can injure your eyes and it will damage painted surfaces and plastic parts – cover these with rag.

Note: *If the entire front brake system is being removed (i.e. master cylinder as well as caliper(s)), or if you intend to change the brake fluid, drain the brake fluid completely from the system (see Section 11), as opposed to retaining the old fluid within it by blocking the hose as described (Step 3).*

1 If the caliper is leaking fluid, or if the brake pads are wearing unevenly, or the pistons do not move smoothly or are tight or stuck in their bores, then caliper overhaul is required – seal kits with or without pistons are both available as required.

2 If you are completely removing the caliper

rather than just displacing it, you will need some new DOT 4 brake fluid and some clean rags.

Removal

3 If the caliper is just being displaced and not completely removed or overhauled, do not disconnect the brake hose. If the caliper is being completely removed or overhauled, unscrew the brake hose banjo bolt and detach the hose(s), noting the alignment with the caliper **(see illustration)**. On Speedmaster models take note of the double hose arrangement on the left-hand caliper **(see illustration 3.4b)**. Discard the sealing washers as new ones must be used on installation. To retain the fluid in the hose either plug the hose using another suitable short piece of hose fitted through the eye of the banjo union (it must be a fairly tight fit to seal it properly), block it using a suitable bolt with sealing washers and a capped (domed) nut, or wrap some plastic foodwrap tightly around (a finger cut off a latex glove also works well), the object being to minimise fluid loss and prevent dirt entering the system. Whatever you do, also cover the end of the hose in rag, just in case. Similarly block or cover the caliper where the hose connects. Alternatively place the hose end into a jar or other suitable container to collect the fluid – make sure the container is properly supported and do not knock it over.

4 If the caliper is just being displaced, on Bonneville, T100 and Scrambler models free the brake hose from its guide **(see illustration)**. On Thruxton, America and Speedmaster models unscrew the bolt securing the brake hose holder **(see illustration)**. On Speedmaster models free the hose from its clips on the mudguard **(see illustration)**.

3.4a Slip the hose out of its guide

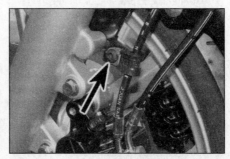

3.4b Unscrew the bolt (arrowed) and detach the guide

3.4c Free the hose from its clips (arrowed)

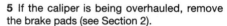

3.8a Position the wood as shown . . .

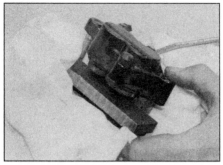

3.8b . . . then apply compressed air . . .

3.8c . . . until both pistons are displaced . . .

5 If the caliper is being overhauled, remove the brake pads (see Section 2).

6 If the caliper is just being displaced, unscrew the caliper mounting bolts and slide the caliper off the disc **(see illustrations 2.2a and b)**.

Overhaul

7 Slide the caliper and bracket apart **(see illustration 2.9a)**. Clean of all old grease from the slider pins. Clean the exterior of the caliper with denatured alcohol or brake system cleaner.

8 Place a piece of wood in the caliper to protect the pistons and caliper and to prevent the pistons from completely leaving their bores – the wood needs to be the thickness shown **(see illustration)**. Displace the pistons using compressed air directed into the banjo bolt bore **(see illustration)**. Use only low pressure to ease the pistons out – do not worry if one comes out before

the other, the other will come out when the first one contacts the wood and can go no further **(see illustration)**. Remove the wood, then remove the pistons **(see illustration)**. Mark each piston head and caliper body with a felt marker to ensure that the pistons can be matched to their original bores on reassembly.

 Warning: Never place your fingers in front of the pistons in an attempt to catch or protect them when applying compressed air, as serious injury could result.
Caution: Do not try to remove the pistons by levering them out, or by using pliers or any other grips.

9 Remove the dust seal from each caliper bore using a wooden or plastic tool **(see illustration)**. Discard them as new ones must be used on installation. If a metal tool is being used, take great care not to damage the bores.

10 Remove and discard the piston seals in the same way **(see illustration)**.

11 Clean the pistons and bores with new brake fluid of the specified type.
Caution: Do not, under any circumstances, use a petroleum-based solvent to clean brake parts.

12 Inspect the caliper bores and pistons for signs of corrosion, nicks and burrs and loss of plating. If surface defects are present, the caliper and/or pistons must be replaced with new ones. If the caliper is in bad shape the master cylinder should also be checked.

13 Lubricate the new piston seals with clean brake fluid or brake grease and fit them into their grooves in the caliper bores **(see illustrations)**.

14 Lubricate the new dust seals and fit them into their grooves in the caliper bores **(see illustration)**.

15 Lubricate the pistons and fit them

3.8d . . . then remove the wood and withdraw the pistons

3.9 Remove the dust seal . . .

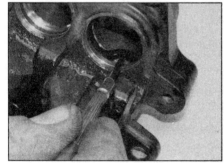

3.10 . . . and the fluid seal from each bore

3.13a Lubricate each piston seal . . .

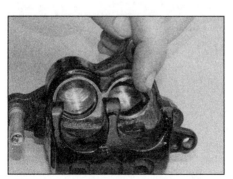

3.13b . . . before fitting it into its groove

3.14 Fit each dust seal in the same way

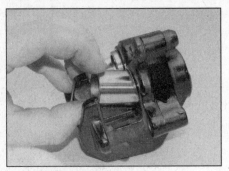

3.15a Fit each piston into its bore . . .

3.15b . . . and push them all the way in

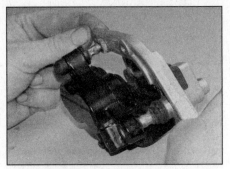

3.16 Grease the pins and boots then join the caliper and bracket

closed-end first into the caliper bores **(see illustration)**. Using your thumbs, push the pistons all the way in, making sure they enter the bore squarely **(see illustration)**.

16 Make sure the pad spring is correctly fitted in the caliper and the guide is correctly fitted on the bracket **(see illustrations 2.9b and c)**. Apply fresh silicone based grease to each slider pin and rubber boot, then slide the caliper and bracket together **(see illustration)**.

Installation

17 If removed, install the brake pads (see Section 2).

18 Slide the caliper onto the disc, making sure the pads sit squarely on either side **(see illustration 2.2b)**. If the caliper doesn't slide on easily, push the pistons a little way back into the caliper using hand pressure on the pads or a piece of wood as leverage. Install the caliper mounting bolts and tighten them to the torque setting specified at the beginning of the Chapter **(see illustration 2.12)**.

19 On Bonneville, T100 and Scrambler models fit the brake hose into its guide **(see illustration 3.4a)**. On Thruxton, America and Speedmaster models fit the brake hose holder **(see illustration 3.4b)**. On Speedmaster models fit the hose into its clips on the mudguard **(see illustration 3.4c)**.

20 If removed, connect the brake hose(s) to the caliper, using new sealing washers on each side of the fitting, noting that on Speedmaster models the left-hand caliper requires three washers for the double hose union **(see illustration)**. Align the hose(s)

as noted on removal **(see illustration 3.3 or 3.4b)**. Tighten the banjo bolt to the torque setting specified at the beginning of the Chapter. Top up the master cylinder reservoir with DOT 4 brake fluid (see *Pre-ride checks*) and bleed the hydraulic system as described in Section 11.

21 Check for leaks and thoroughly test the operation of the brake before riding the motorcycle.

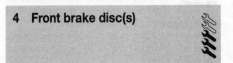

| 4 | Front brake disc(s) |

Inspection

1 Visually inspect the surface of the disc(s) for score marks and other damage. Light scratches are normal after use and will not affect brake operation, but deep grooves and heavy score marks will reduce braking efficiency and accelerate pad wear. If a disc is badly grooved a new one must be fitted.

2 To check disc run-out, position the bike on an auxiliary stand and support it so that the front wheel is raised off the ground. Mount a dial gauge to a fork leg, with the plunger on the gauge touching the surface of the disc about 10 mm (1/2 in) from the outer edge. Rotate the wheel and watch the gauge needle, comparing the reading with the limit listed in the Specifications at the beginning of the Chapter. If the run-out is greater than the service limit, check the wheel bearings for

play (see Chapter 1). If the bearings are worn, install new ones (see Section 16) and repeat this check. If the disc run-out is still excessive, a new disc will have to be fitted.

3 The disc must not be allowed to wear down to a thickness less than the service limit as listed in this Chapter's Specifications. Check the thickness of the disc with a micrometer or Vernier caliper **(see illustration)**. If the thickness of the disc is less than the service limit, a new one must be fitted. On Speedmaster models it is advisable to replace both discs as a set.

4 Always fit new brake pads when a new disc is fitted.

Removal

5 Remove the wheel (see Section 14).

Caution: Do not lay the wheel down and allow it to rest on the disc – the disc could become warped. Set the wheel on wood blocks so the disc does not support the weight of the wheel.

6 Mark the relationship of the disc to the wheel, so that it can be installed in the same position. Where fitted remove the bolt caps **(see illustration)**. Unscrew the disc retaining bolts, loosening them evenly and a little at a time in a criss-cross pattern to avoid distorting the disc, then remove the disc from the wheel.

Installation

7 Before installing the disc, make sure there is no dirt or corrosion where the disc seats on the hub, particularly right in the angle of the

3.20 Always use new sealing washers

4.3 The minimum disc thickness is marked on the disc

4.6 Carefully prise the caps from the bolts

seat, as this will not allow the disc to sit flat when it is bolted down, and it will appear to be warped when checked or when using the brake.

8 Mount the disc on the wheel, making sure any markings are on the outside and any directional arrow is pointing in the direction of normal (i.e. forward) rotation. Align the previously applied match marks (if you're reinstalling the original disc).

9 Clean the threads of the disc mounting bolts, then apply a suitable non-permanent thread locking compound. Install the bolts and tighten them evenly and a little at a time in a criss-cross pattern to the torque setting specified at the beginning of the Chapter. Fit the bolt caps, where applicable.

10 If a new brake disc has been installed, remove any protective coating from its working surfaces. Thoroughly clean the disc using acetone or brake system cleaner.

11 Install the wheel (see Section 14).

12 Operate the brake lever several times to bring the pads into contact with the disc. Check the operation of the brake carefully before riding the bike and remember that new discs and pads will take a while to bed in; Triumph recommend a break-in mileage of 200m (300km).

5 Front brake master cylinder

⚠️ *Warning: Do not, under any circumstances, use petroleum-based solvents to clean internal brake parts. Use new DOT 4 brake fluid only. Use care when working with brake fluid as it can injure your eyes and it will damage painted surfaces and plastic parts – cover these with rag.*

Note: *If the entire front brake system is being removed (i.e. caliper(s) as well as master cylinder), or if you intend to change the brake fluid, drain the brake fluid completely from the system (see Section 11), as opposed to retaining the old fluid within it by blocking the hose as described (Step 8).*

1 If the master cylinder is leaking fluid, or if the lever does not produce a firm feel when the brake is applied, and bleeding the brakes does not help (see Section 11), and the hydraulic hose(s) and the brake caliper(s) is/are all in good condition, then master cylinder overhaul is recommended.

2 Before disassembling the master cylinder, read through the entire procedure and make sure that you have the correct rebuild kit. Also, you will need some new DOT 4 brake fluid, some clean rags and internal circlip pliers.

Note: *To prevent damage to the paint from spilled brake fluid, always cover the fuel tank when working on the master cylinder.*

Caution: *Disassembly, overhaul and reassembly of the brake master cylinder must be done in a spotlessly clean work*

5.5 Pull the wiring connectors (arrowed) off the terminals

area to avoid contamination and possible failure of the brake hydraulic system components.

Removal

Bonneville up to VIN 380776, T100, Thruxton with one-piece handlebars, America and Speedmaster models

Note: *If the master cylinder is being displaced from the handlebar and not being removed completely or overhauled, follow Steps 5, 6 and 9 only.*

3 Remove the rear view mirror (see Chapter 7).

4 Remove the front brake lever (see Chapter 5).

5 Disconnect the electrical connectors from the brake light switch **(see illustration)**.

6 Refer to Chapter 1 and create maximum freeplay in the throttle cables using the adjusters at the handlebar end. Detach the throttle cables from the twistgrip (See Chapter 3) – you may have to also free them from the bracket on the carburettors to get enough slack, but there will be no need to detach the cable ends from the carburettors themselves.

7 Loosen, but do not remove, the screws holding the reservoir cover in place **(see illustration)**.

8 Unscrew the brake hose banjo bolt and separate the hose from the master cylinder, noting its alignment, catching any fluid with a rag **(see illustration)**. Discard the sealing washers as they must be replaced with new ones. Either plug the hose using another suitable short piece of hose fitted through the eye of the banjo union (a fairly tight fit is necessary for a

5.8 Brake hose banjo bolt (arrowed)

5.7 Slacken the reservoir cover screws

good seal), block it using a suitable bolt with sealing washers and a capped (domed) nut, or wrap some plastic foodwrap tightly around (a finger cut off a latex glove also works well), the object being to minimise fluid loss and prevent dirt entering the system. Whatever you do, also cover the end of the hose in rag, just in case. Similarly block or cover the master cylinder where the hose connects.

9 Unscrew the master cylinder clamp bolts, then lift the master cylinder and reservoir away **(see illustration)**.

Caution: *Do not tip the master cylinder upside down or brake fluid will run out.*

10 Remove the reservoir cover, diaphragm plate and rubber diaphragm. Drain the brake fluid from the reservoir into a suitable container. Wipe any remaining fluid out of the reservoir with a clean rag.

11 If required undo the brake light switch screw and remove the switch, noting how it fits **(see illustration 5.5)**.

Bonneville from VIN 380777, Thruxton with clip-on handlebars and Scrambler models

Note: *If the master cylinder is being displaced from the handlebar and not being removed completely or overhauled, follow Steps 14, 15 and 17 only.*

12 Remove the rear view mirror (see Chapter 7).

13 Remove the front brake lever (see Chapter 5).

14 Disconnect the electrical connectors from the brake light switch **(see illustration 5.5)**.

15 Undo the reservoir cap clamp bolt

5.9 Master cylinder clamp bolts (arrowed)

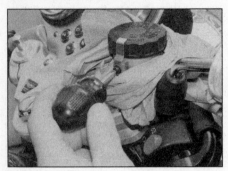

5.15a Undo the screw to release the clamp

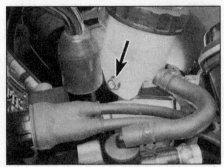

5.15b Reservoir mounting bolt (arrowed)

5.17 Master cylinder clamp bolts (arrowed)

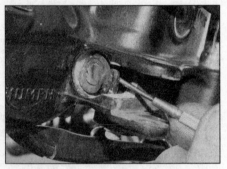

5.20 Remove the boot, noting how it locates

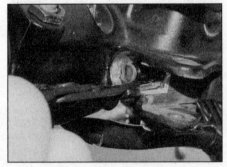

5.21a Remove the circlip . . .

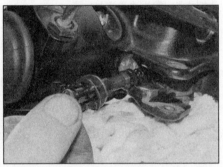

5.21b . . . and withdraw the piston and spring assembly

and remove the clamp (see illustration). Unscrew the reservoir mounting bolt (see illustration).

16 Unscrew the brake hose banjo bolt and separate the hose from the master cylinder, noting its alignment. Discard the sealing washers as they must be replaced with new ones. Seal the hose as described in Step 8.

17 Unscrew the master cylinder clamp bolts, then lift the master cylinder and reservoir away (see illustration).

18 Remove the reservoir cap, diaphragm plate and diaphragm and tip the fluid out into a suitable container. Wipe any remaining fluid out of the reservoir with a clean rag. If required release the clamp securing the hose to the master cylinder and detach it, catching any fluid drops with a rag.

19 If required undo the brake light switch

screw and remove the switch, noting how it fits (see illustration 5.5).

Overhaul

Note: *If the piston assembly is removed from the master cylinder do not re-use it – always obtain a rebuild kit and install the new components.*

20 Carefully remove the dust boot from the master cylinder (see illustration).

21 Using circlip pliers, remove the circlip and slide out the piston assembly and the spring, noting how they fit, and being prepared with the rag to catch the fluid (see illustrations). Lay the parts out in the proper order to prevent confusion during reassembly.

22 Clean out the master cylinder bore with new brake fluid of the specified type.

Caution: Do not, under any circumstances,

use a petroleum-based solvent to clean brake parts.

23 Check the master cylinder bore for corrosion, scratches, nicks and score marks. If damage or wear is evident, the master cylinder must be replaced with a new one. If the master cylinder is in poor condition, then the caliper(s) should be checked as well. Check that the fluid inlet and outlet ports in the master cylinder are clear.

24 Use all of the new parts in the rebuild kit and assemble them all according to the layout of the old ones (see illustration). Lubricate the seal and cup well with brake grease or brake fluid when fitting them.

25 Lubricate the assembly with clean brake fluid. Fit it into the master cylinder, making sure it is the correct way round (see illustration). Make sure the lips on the cup and seal do not

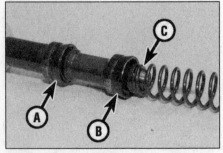

5.24 Make sure the seal (A), cup (B), and spring (C) are correctly fitted – Bonneville, T100, America and Speedmaster type shown

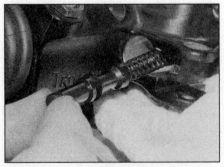

5.25a Slide the piston/spring assembly into the bore

5.25b Fit the washer . . .

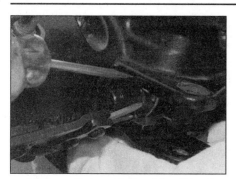

5.25c ... then push the piston in and secure it with the circlip, locating it in the groove

5.26a Fit the boot ...

5.26b ... locating it as shown

turn inside out when they enter the bore. Fit the washer then depress the piston and install the new circlip, making sure that it locates in the groove – use circlip pliers to manoeuvre the circlip into position, then push it into its groove using a small screwdriver if the pliers are too big for the bore **(see illustrations)**.

26 Install the rubber dust boot, making sure the inner lip locates in the groove in the end of the piston, and carefully push the outer lip into the cylinder until it seats **(see illustrations)**.

27 Inspect the reservoir cap rubber diaphragm and replace it with a new one it if it is damaged or deteriorated.

Installation

Bonneville up to VIN 380776, T100, Thruxton with one-piece handlebars, America and Speedmaster models

28 If removed, install the brake light switch **(see illustration 5.5)**.

29 Attach the master cylinder to the handlebar and fit the clamp, aligning the mating surfaces with the punch mark on the handlebar **(see illustration 5.9)**. Tighten the bolts evenly to the torque setting specified at the beginning of the Chapter.

30 If detached, connect the brake hose to the master cylinder, using new sealing washers on each side of the union, and aligning the hose as noted on removal **(see illustration 5.8)**. Tighten the banjo bolt to the torque setting specified at the beginning of the Chapter.

31 Connect the throttle cables (see Chapter 3).

32 Connect the brake light switch wiring connectors **(see illustration 5.5)**.

33 If removed, install the brake lever (see Chapter 5).

34 Fill the reservoir with new DOT 4 brake fluid as described in *Pre-ride checks*. Refer to Section 11 of this Chapter and bleed the air from the system.

35 Fit the rubber diaphragm, making sure it is correctly seated, and the diaphragm plate onto the reservoir, then fit the cover and tighten its screws **(see illustration)**.

36 Install the rear view mirror (see Chapter 7).

37 Check the operation of the front brake and the brake light before riding the motorcycle.

Bonneville from VIN 380777, Thruxton with clip-on handlebars and Scrambler models

38 If removed, install the brake light switch **(see illustration 5.5)**.

39 Attach the master cylinder to the handlebar and fit the clamp with its 'UP' mark facing up, aligning the mating surfaces with the punch mark on the handlebar **(see illustration 5.17)**. Tighten the upper bolt first then the lower bolt to the torque setting specified at the beginning of the Chapter.

40 If detached, connect the brake hose to the master cylinder, using new sealing washers on each side of the unions, and aligning the hoses as noted on removal. Tighten the banjo bolt to the torque setting specified at the beginning of this Chapter.

41 Fit the reservoir onto its bracket and tighten the bolt **(see illustration 5.15b)**. If detached connect the hose to its union and secure it with its clamp.

42 Connect the brake light switch wiring connectors **(see illustration 5.5)**.

43 If removed, install the brake lever (see Chapter 5).

44 Fill the fluid reservoir with new DOT 4 brake fluid as described in *Pre-ride checks*. Refer to Section 11 of this Chapter and bleed the air from the system.

45 Fit the rubber diaphragm, making sure it is correctly seated, the diaphragm plate and the cap onto the master cylinder reservoir **(see illustration)**. Fit the cap clamp **(see illustration 5.15a)**.

46 Install the rear view mirror (see Chapter 7).

47 Check the operation of the front brake before riding the motorcycle.

6 Rear brake pads

 Warning: The dust created by the brake system may contain asbestos, which is harmful to your health. Never blow it out with compressed air and don't inhale any of it. An approved filtering mask should be worn when working on the brakes. Do not, under any circumstances, use petroleum-based solvents to clean brake parts. Use a dedicated brake cleaner or denatured alcohol only.

1 Slacken but do not yet remove the pad retaining pins **(see illustration)**. If necessary, particularly on Bonneville, T100, Thruxton and

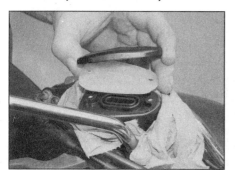

5.35 Seat the diaphragm then fit the plate and cover

5.45 Seat the diaphragm then fit the plate and cover

6.1 Slacken the pins (arrowed)

6.2a Unscrew the bolts (arrowed) . . .

6.2b . . . and slide the caliper off the disc

6.3a Unscrew and withdraw the pins . . .

Scrambler models due to their underslung position, apply some penetrating fluid, making sure none gets on the pads or disc, and give them a tap to free them up.

2 Unscrew the caliper mounting bolts and slide the caliper off the disc **(see illustrations)** – there is no need to disconnect the hose.

3 Unscrew and remove the pad pins, noting how they fit **(see illustration)**. Remove the pads from the caliper, noting how they fit **(see illustration)**. Note the pad spring in the caliper and remove it if required for cleaning or replacement, noting how it fits **(see illustration 6.9)**.

4 Inspect the surface of each pad for contamination and check that the friction material has not worn beyond its service limit (see Chapter 1, Section 12). If either pad is worn down to or beyond the service limit wear indicator, is fouled with oil or grease, or is heavily scored or damaged by dirt and debris, both pads must be replaced with new ones. Note that it is not possible to degrease the friction material; if the pads are contaminated in any way, new ones must be fitted.

5 If the pads are in good condition clean them carefully, using a fine wire brush which is completely free of oil and grease, to remove all traces of road dirt and corrosion. Using a pointed instrument, clean out the groove in the friction material and dig out any embedded particles of foreign matter. Spray the caliper area with a dedicated brake cleaner to remove any dust and remove and traces of corrosion which might cause sticking of the caliper/pad operation.

6 Check the condition of the brake disc (see Section 8).

7 Remove any traces of corrosion from the pad pins. Check them for signs of damage and replace them with new ones if necessary.

8 Clean around the exposed section of each piston to remove any dirt or debris that could cause the seals to be damaged. Now push the pistons back into the caliper – if new pads are being fitted you need to push them all the way in to create room for them; if the old pads are still serviceable push them in a little way, not only because it makes installation easier, but also because it serves as a check that neither of the pistons are seized in their bores. To push the pistons back use finger pressure, either on each piston individually or on a piece of wood across both pistons, or use grips and a piece of wood, with rag or card to protect the caliper body, **(see illustration 3.15b)**. Alternatively obtain a proper piston-pushing tool from a good tool supplier. It may be necessary to remove the master cylinder reservoir cover or cap and siphon out some fluid (see *Pre-ride checks)*. If the pistons are difficult to push back, remove the bleed valve cap, then attach a length of clear hose to the bleed valve and place the open end in a suitable container, then open the valve and try again **(see illustrations 11.5a and b)**. Take great care not to draw any air into the system. If in doubt, bleed the brakes afterwards (see Section 11). If either of the pistons appears seized, block the other piston so all pressure is applied to the one being checked, then apply the brake pedal and check whether the piston moves at all. If it moves out

but can't be pushed back in the chances are there is some hidden corrosion stopping it. If it is completely seized you will have to overhaul the caliper (see Section 7).

9 Slide the caliper and bracket apart **(see illustration 2.9a)** Clean of all old grease and any signs of corrosion from the slider pins. Check the condition of the rubber boot for each slider pin and make sure they are correctly fitted – they are not listed as being available separately so if they are damaged a new caliper should be considered. Make sure the pad spring is correctly fitted in the caliper **(see illustration)**. Apply fresh silicone based grease to each pin and boot, then slide the caliper and bracket together **(see illustration 3.16)**.

10 Lightly smear the backs and sides of the pad backing material and the shanks and threads of the pad pins with copper-based grease, making sure that none gets on the friction material.

11 Fit the outer pad into the caliper with the back of the pad against the pistons **(see illustration 6.3b)**. Fit the inner pad so its friction material faces the outer pad, locating it's curved end against the post on the bracket **(see illustration)**. Press the pads down against the spring then insert the pad pins and thread them into the caliper tightening them lightly **(see illustration 6.3a)**.

12 Slide the caliper onto the disc, making sure the pads locate correctly on each side **(see illustration 6.2b)**. Install the mounting bolts and tighten them to the torque setting specified at the beginning of the Chapter **(see illustration 6.2a)**.

6.3b . . . then remove the pads

6.9 Make sure the spring (arrowed) is correctly fitted

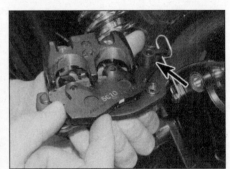

6.11 Make sure the pad locates correctly against the post (arrowed)

13 Now tighten the pad pins to the specified torque setting **(see illustration 6.1)**.

14 Top up the master cylinder reservoir if necessary (see *Pre-ride checks*), and refit the diaphragm, plate and reservoir cap. Operate the brake pedal several times to bring the pads into contact with the disc. Check the operation of the brake before riding the motorcycle and remember that new pads will take a while to bed in; Triumph recommend a break-in mileage of 200m (300km).

7 Rear brake caliper

 Warning: The dust created by the brake pads may contain asbestos, which is harmful to your health. Never blow it out with compressed air and don't inhale any of it. An approved filtering mask should be worn when working on the brakes. If a new caliper is being installed all old brake fluid should be flushed from the system. Do not, under any circumstances, use petroleum-based solvents to clean internal brake parts. Use new DOT 4 brake fluid only. Use care when working with brake fluid as it can injure your eyes and it will damage painted surfaces and plastic parts – cover these with rag.

Note: *If the entire rear brake system is being removed (i.e. master cylinder as well as caliper), or if you intend to change the brake fluid, drain the brake fluid completely from the system (see Section 11), as opposed to retaining the old fluid within it by blocking the hose as described (Step 3).*

1 If the caliper is leaking fluid, or if the brake pads are wearing unevenly, or the pistons do not move smoothly or are tight or stuck in their bores, then caliper overhaul is required – seal kits with or without pistons are both available as required.

2 If you are completely removing the caliper rather than just displacing it, you will need some new DOT 4 brake fluid and some clean rags.

Removal

3 If the caliper is just being displaced and not completely removed or overhauled, do not disconnect the brake hose. If the caliper

7.3 Brake hose banjo bolt (arrowed)

is being completely removed or overhauled, unscrew the brake hose banjo bolt and detach the hose, noting its alignment with the caliper **(see illustration)**. Discard the sealing washers as new ones must be used on installation. To retain the fluid in the hose either plug the hose using another suitable short piece of hose fitted through the eye of the banjo union (it must be a fairly tight fit to seal it properly), block it using a suitable bolt with sealing washers and a capped (domed) nut, or wrap some plastic foodwrap tightly around (a finger cut off a latex glove also works well), the object being to minimise fluid loss and prevent dirt entering the system. Whatever you do, also cover the end of the hose in rag, just in case. Similarly block or cover the caliper where the hose connects. Alternatively place the hose end into a jar or other suitable container to collect the fluid – make sure the container is properly supported and do not knock it over.

4 On America and Speedmaster models free the brake hose from its guide. On all models, if required unscrew the bolt securing the brake hose holder and detach it from the swingarm.

5 If the caliper is being overhauled, remove the brake pads (see Section 6).

6 If the caliper is just being displaced unscrew the caliper mounting bolts and slide the caliper off the disc **(see illustrations 6.2a and b)**.

Overhaul

7 Slide the caliper and bracket apart **(see illustration 2.9a)**. Clean off all old grease from the slider pins. Clean the exterior of the caliper with denatured alcohol or brake system cleaner.

8 Place a piece of wood in the caliper as shown to protect the pistons and caliper and to prevent the pistons from completely leaving their bores – the wood needs to be the thickness shown **(see illustration 3.8a)**. Displace the pistons using compressed air directed into the banjo bolt bore **(see illustration 3.8b)**. Use only low pressure to ease the pistons out – do not worry if one comes out before the other, the other will come out when the first one contacts the wood and can go no further **(see illustration 3.8c)**. Remove the wood, then remove the pistons **(see illustration 3.8d)**. Mark each piston head and caliper body with a felt marker to ensure that the pistons can be matched to their original bores on reassembly.

 Warning: Never place your fingers in front of the pistons in an attempt to catch or protect them when applying compressed air, as serious injury could result.

Caution: Do not try to remove the pistons by levering them out, or by using pliers or any other grips.

9 Remove the dust seal from each caliper bore using a wooden or plastic tool **(see illustration 3.9)**. Discard them as new ones must be used on installation. If a metal tool is being used, take great care not to damage the bores.

10 Remove and discard the piston seals in the same way **(see illustration 3.10)**.

11 Clean the pistons and bores with new DOT 4 brake fluid.

Caution: Do not, under any circumstances, use a petroleum-based solvent to clean brake parts.

12 Inspect the caliper bores and pistons for signs of corrosion, nicks and burrs and loss of plating. If surface defects are present, the caliper and/or pistons must be replaced with new ones. If the caliper is in bad shape the master cylinder should also be checked.

13 Lubricate the new piston seals with clean brake fluid or brake grease and fit them into their grooves in the caliper bores **(see illustrations 3.13a and b)**.

14 Lubricate the new dust seals and fit them into their grooves in the caliper bores **(see illustration 3.14)**.

15 Lubricate the pistons and fit them closed-end first into the caliper bores **(see illustration 3.15a)**. Using your thumbs, push the pistons all the way in, making sure they enter the bore squarely **(see illustration 3.15b)**.

16 Make sure the spring is correctly fitted in the caliper **(see illustration 6.9)**. Apply fresh silicone based grease to each slider pin and rubber boot, then slide the caliper and bracket together.

Installation

17 If removed, install the brake pads (see Section 6).

18 Slide the caliper onto the disc, making sure the pads sit squarely on either side **(see illustration 6.2b)**. If the caliper doesn't slide on easily, push the pistons a little way back into the caliper using hand pressure on the pads or a piece of wood as leverage. Install the caliper mounting bolts and tighten them to the torque setting specified at the beginning of the Chapter **(see illustration 6.2a)**.

19 On America and Speedmaster models fit the brake hose into its guide. On all models if detached fit the brake hose holder onto the swingarm.

20 If removed, connect the brake hose to the caliper, using new sealing washers on each side of the fitting **(see illustration 7.3)**. Align the hose as noted on removal. Tighten the banjo bolt to the torque setting specified at the beginning of the Chapter. Top up the master cylinder reservoir with DOT 4 brake fluid (see *Pre-ride checks*) and bleed the hydraulic system as described in Section 11.

21 Check for leaks and thoroughly test the operation of the brake before riding the motorcycle.

8 Rear brake disc

Inspection

1 Visually inspect the surface of the disc for score marks and other damage. Light scratches are normal after use and will not

8.3 The minimum disc thickness is marked on the disc

8.6 Brake disc bolts (arrowed)

affect brake operation, but deep grooves and heavy score marks will reduce braking efficiency and accelerate pad wear. If a disc is badly grooved a new one must be fitted.

2 To check disc run-out, position the bike on an auxiliary stand and support it so that the rear wheel is raised off the ground. Mount a dial gauge to swingarm, with the plunger on the gauge touching the surface of the disc about 10 mm (1/2 in) from the outer edge. Rotate the wheel and watch the gauge needle, comparing the reading with the limit listed in the Specifications at the beginning of the Chapter. If the run-out is greater than the service limit, check the wheel bearings for play (see Chapter 1). If the bearings are worn, install new ones (see Section 16) and repeat this check. If the disc run-out is still excessive, a new disc will have to be fitted.

3 The disc must not be allowed to wear down to a thickness less than the service limit as listed in this Chapter's Specifications. Check the thickness of the disc with a micrometer or any other measuring tool (see illustration). If the thickness of the disc is less than the service limit, a new one must be fitted.

4 Always fit new brake pads when a new disc is fitted.

Removal

5 Remove the wheel (see Section 15).
Caution: Do not lay the wheel down and allow it to rest on the disc – the disc could become warped. Set the wheel on wood blocks so the disc does not support the weight of the wheel.

6 Mark the relationship of the disc to the wheel, so that it can be installed in the same position. Where fitted remove the bolt caps. Unscrew the disc retaining bolts, loosening them evenly and a little at a time in a criss-cross pattern to avoid distorting the disc, then remove the disc from the wheel (see illustration).

Installation

7 Before installing the disc, make sure there is no dirt or corrosion where the disc seats on the hub, particularly right in the angle of the

seat, as this will not allow the disc to sit flat when it is bolted down, and it will appear to be warped when checked or when using the brake.

8 Mount the disc on the wheel, making sure any markings are on the outside and any directional arrow is pointing in the direction of normal (i.e. forward) rotation. Align the previously applied match marks (if you're reinstalling the original disc).

9 Clean the threads of the disc mounting bolts, then apply a suitable non-permanent thread locking compound. Install the bolts and tighten them evenly and a little at a time in a criss-cross pattern to the torque setting specified at the beginning of the Chapter. Where removed fit the bolt caps.

10 If a new brake disc has been installed, remove any protective coating from its working surfaces. Thoroughly clean the disc using acetone or brake system cleaner.

11 Install the wheel (see Section 15).

12 Operate the brake pedal several times to bring the pads into contact with the disc. Check the operation of the brake carefully before riding the bike and remember that new discs and pads will take a while to bed in; Triumph recommend a break-in mileage of 200m (300km).

9 Rear brake master cylinder

⚠ *Warning: Do not, under any circumstances, use petroleum-based solvents to clean internal brake parts. Use new DOT 4 brake fluid only. Use care when working with brake fluid as it can injure your eyes and it will damage painted surfaces and plastic parts – cover these with rag.*

Note: *If the entire rear brake system is being removed (i.e. caliper as well as master cylinder), or if you intend to change the brake fluid, drain the brake fluid completely from*

the system (see Section 11), as opposed to retaining the old fluid within it by blocking the hose as described (Step 6).

1 If the master cylinder is leaking fluid, or if the pedal does not produce a firm feel when the brake is applied, and bleeding the brakes does not help (see Section 11), and the hydraulic pipe, hose and brake caliper are in good condition, then master cylinder overhaul is recommended.

2 Before disassembling the master cylinder, read through the entire procedure and make sure that you have the correct rebuild kit. Also, you will need some new DOT 4 brake fluid, some clean rags and internal circlip pliers. **Note:** *To prevent damage to the paint from spilled brake fluid, always cover the surrounding components when working on the master cylinder.*

Caution: Disassembly, overhaul and reassembly of the brake master cylinder must be done in a spotlessly clean work area to avoid contamination and possible failure of the brake hydraulic system components.

Removal

3 On Bonneville, T100 and Thruxton models remove the right-hand side panel (see Chapter 7). On Scrambler models, undo the bolts securing the reservoir cover and lift the cover off (see illustration).

9.3 Remove the reservoir cover – Scrambler models

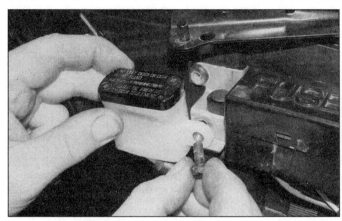

9.4a Displacing the reservoir – Bonneville, T100 and Thruxton

9.4b Displacing the reservoir – America and Speedmaster

9.6a Brake hose banjo bolt (arrowed) - Thruxton

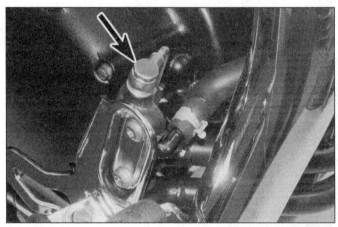

9.6b Brake hose banjo bolt (arrowed) – America and Speedmaster

4 Remove the screw securing the master cylinder fluid reservoir to the frame, then on America and Speedmaster models remove the shroud, and on all models remove the cap, diaphragm plate and diaphragm, and pour the fluid into a container **(see illustrations)**. Replace the cap assembly afterwards.

5 On Bonneville and T100 models remove the rear brake light switch (see Chapter 8).

6 On Thruxton, America, Speedmaster and Scrambler models unscrew the brake pipe banjo bolt and separate the hose from the master cylinder, noting its alignment **(see illustrations)**. Discard the sealing washers as they must be replaced with new ones. Either plug the pipe using another suitable short piece of hose fitted through the eye of the banjo union (a fairly tight fit is necessary for a good seal), block it using a suitable bolt with sealing washers and a capped (domed) nut, or wrap some plastic foodwrap tightly around (a finger cut off a latex glove also works well), the object being to minimise fluid loss and prevent dirt entering the system. Whatever you do, also cover the end of the hose in rag, just in case.

7 Remove the clip and withdraw the pin securing the master cylinder pushrod to the brake pedal **(see illustrations)**.

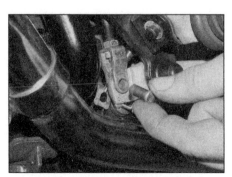

9.7a Remove the pin and detach the rod – Bonneville and T100 shown

9.7b Remove the pin (arrowed) and detach the rod – Thruxton shown

9.7c Remove the pin (arrowed) and detach the rod – America and Speedmaster

9.8a Unscrew the bolts . . .

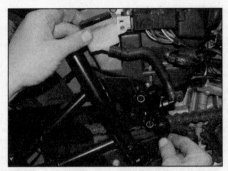

9.8b . . . and remove the master cylinder and reservoir - Bonneville and T100 shown

9.8c Master cylinder bolts (arrowed) - Thruxton shown

9.8d Master cylinder bolts (arrowed) – America and Speedmaster shown

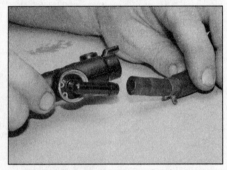

9.9 Release the clamp and detach the hose

9.10a Remove the boot, noting how it locates

8 Unscrew the two bolts securing the master cylinder and remove the master cylinder and reservoir (see illustrations). On Thruxton models note the fitting of the heel guard.

Overhaul

9 If required, release the clamp securing the reservoir hose to the union on the master cylinder and detach the hose and reservoir, being prepared to catch any residual fluid (see illustration).

10 Dislodge the rubber dust boot from the base of the master cylinder and the pushrod and slide it down the rod out of the way (see illustration). Depress the pushrod, then remove the circlip and withdraw the pushrod (see illustration).

11 Slide out the piston assembly and spring (see illustrations 9.16b and 9.17b). Lay the parts out in the proper order to prevent confusion during reassembly (see illustration).

12 Clean out the master cylinder bore with new brake fluid of the specified type.

Caution: Do not, under any circumstances, use a petroleum-based solvent to clean brake parts.

13 Check the master cylinder bore for corrosion, scratches, nicks and score marks. If damage is evident, the master cylinder must be replaced with a new one. If the master cylinder is in poor condition, then the caliper should be checked as well.

14 Inspect the reservoir hose for cracks or splits and replace it with a new one, if necessary. If required, remove the union from the master cylinder by releasing the circlip, but note that the O-ring that seals it is not available separately and so a new union set should be fitted (see illustration).

15 The pushrod assembly and dust boot are available as one kit, and the piston assembly, cup seal and spring are available as another kit. Use all of the new parts, regardless of the apparent condition of the old ones. The circlip must be obtained separately if a new one is needed.

9.10b Release the circlip and remove the pushrod

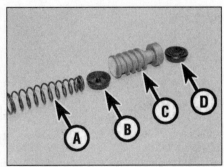

9.11 Spring (A), cup (B), piston (C), seal (D)

9.14 Remove the circlip (arrowed) to release the union

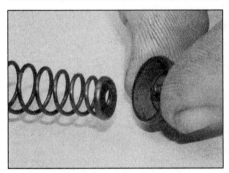

9.16a Fit the cup onto the spring . . .

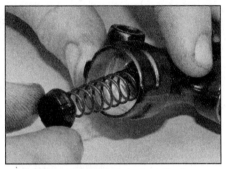

9.16b . . . then fit them into the bore

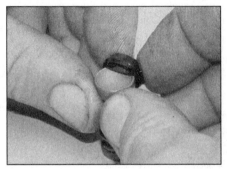

9.17a Fit the seal onto the piston . . .

9.17b . . . locating it in the groove as shown

9.17c Fit the piston into the bore . . .

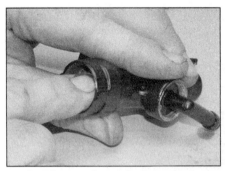

9.17d . . . and push it all the way in

16 Fit the cup onto the end of the spring, locating its peg in the hole (see illustration). Fit the spring wide end first into the master cylinder and push the cup in, making sure its lips do not turn inside out (see illustration).
17 Lubricate the seal with brake grease or clean brake fluid and fit it onto the piston as shown (see illustrations). Lubricate the piston assembly with clean brake fluid. Fit the assembly into the master cylinder, making sure the lips on the seal do not turn inside out when you push it in (see illustrations).
18 Fit the rubber boot onto the pushrod and peel it back so it is inside out as shown and slide it towards the clevis so it is out of the way (see illustration). Fit the circlip around the pushrod. Locate the pushrod end against the piston, then push the piston in until the washer on the pushrod is past the circlip groove, then

fit the circlip into the groove, making sure it is properly seated (see illustrations).
19 Fit the rubber dust boot, making sure

the inner lip is located in the groove in the pushrod, and carefully push the outer lip into the cylinder until it seats (see illustrations).

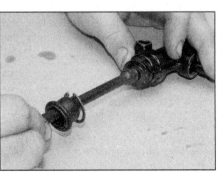

9.18a Insert the pushrod . . .

9.18b . . . and secure it in place with the circlip . . .

9.18c . . . pushing it into place with a small screwdriver

9.19a Slide the boot down . . .

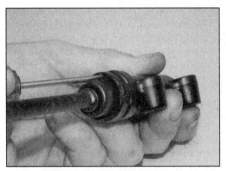

9.19b . . . and push it into place

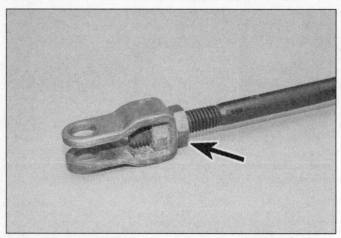

9.21 Check the position of the clevis and adjust it by slackening the locknut (arrowed) and turning it as required

9.21b Check the distance between the centre of the lower mounting bolt hole and the centre of the pin hole in the clevis

20 If removed, fit the reservoir hose union using a new O-ring and secure it with the circlip **(see illustration 9.14)**. Fit the reservoir hose onto the union and secure it with the clamp **(see illustration 9.9)**. Check that the hose is secure and clamped at the reservoir end as well.

Installation

21 Check that the position of the clevis on the pushrod is set correctly **(see illustration)**. The distance between the centre of the lower mounting bolt hole on the master cylinder and the centre of the pin hole in the clevis should be 200.6 mm on Bonneville and T100 models, 82 mm on Thruxton models, 80 mm on Scrambler models and 96 mm on America and Speedmaster models **(see illustration)**. If not, slacken the clevis locknut and thread the clevis up or down as required, then tighten the locknut.
22 Fit the master cylinder onto the footrest bracket, on Thruxton models along with the heel guard, and tighten its mounting bolts to the torque setting specified at the beginning of the Chapter **(see illustrations 9.8d, c, b and a)**.
23 Align the brake pedal with the master cylinder pushrod clevis, then slide in the pin and secure it with the clip **(see illustrations 9.7c, b and a)**.
24 On Bonneville and T100 models install the rear brake light switch (see Chapter 8).
25 On Thruxton, America, Speedmaster and Scrambler models connect the brake pipe to the master cylinder, using a new sealing washer on each side of the banjo union. Ensure that the pipe is positioned so that it butts against the lug and tighten the banjo bolt to the specified torque setting **(see illustrations 9.6a and b)**. On machines fitted with a rigid brake pipe, ensure that the pipe is not bent or kinked during installation.
26 Make sure the reservoir hose is securely clamped at each end. Install the reservoir and tighten the screw **(see illustrations 9.4a and b)**. Fill the fluid reservoir with new DOT 4 brake fluid (see *Pre-ride checks*) and bleed the

system following the procedure in Section 11.
27 Check the operation of the brake and brake light carefully before riding the motorcycle.
28 On Bonneville, T100 and Thruxton models install the right-hand side panel (see Chapter 7). On Scrambler models, install the reservoir cover and tighten the bolts securely **(see illustration 9.3)**.

10 Brake hoses, pipes and unions

Inspection

1 Check brake hose condition regularly and replace the hoses at the specified interval (see Chapter 1).
2 Twist and flex the hoses while looking for cracks, bulges and seeping fluid. Check extra carefully around the areas where the hoses connect with the banjo fittings, as these are common areas for hose failure.
3 Inspect the banjo union fittings connected to the brake hoses and pipe. If the fittings or pipe are rusted, scratched or cracked, replace them with new ones.

Renewal

4 The brake hoses and pipe have banjo union fittings on each end. Cover the surrounding area with plenty of rags and unscrew the banjo bolt at each end of the hose or pipe, noting its alignment, and referring to Chapter 8 for removal of the brake light switch when working on the rear brake system **(see illustrations 3.3, 5.8, 7.3 and 9.6a and b)**. Free the hoses/pipe from any clips or guides and remove them. Discard the sealing washers as new ones must be used.
5 Position the new hose or pipe, making sure it isn't twisted or otherwise strained, and abut the tab on the union with the lug on the component casting, where present. Otherwise align the hose as noted on removal. Install the

banjo bolts (or brake light switch) using new sealing washers on both sides of the unions **(see illustration 3.20)**. Tighten the banjo bolts to the torque setting specified at the beginning of this Chapter. On machines fitted with a rigid brake pipe, ensure that the pipe is not bent or kinked during installation. Note that on the double hose union on the left-hand front caliper on Speedmaster models three new sealing washers are needed.
6 Make sure the hoses/pipe are correctly aligned and routed clear of all moving components. Flush the old brake fluid from the system, refill with new DOT 4 brake fluid (see *Pre-ride checks*) and bleed the air from the system (see Section 11). Check the operation of the brakes carefully before riding the motorcycle.

11 Brake system bleeding

 Warning: Use care when working with brake fluid as it can injure your eyes and it will damage painted surfaces and plastic parts.

Bleeding

1 Bleeding the brakes is simply the process of removing all the air bubbles from the brake fluid reservoir and master cylinder, the hoses and the brake caliper(s). Bleeding is necessary whenever a brake system hydraulic connection is loosened, when a component or hose is replaced, or when a master cylinder or caliper is overhauled. Leaks in the system may also allow air to enter, but leaking brake fluid will reveal their presence and warn you of the need for repair.
2 To bleed the brakes, you will need some new DOT 4 brake fluid, a length of clear vinyl or plastic tubing, a small container partially filled with clean brake fluid, some rags and a ring spanner to fit the brake caliper bleed valve. For

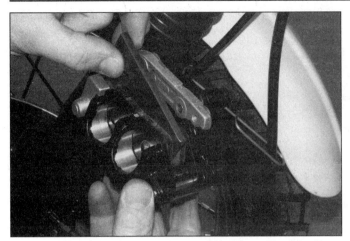

11.8 Insert the metal plate between the brake pads

11.9a Remove the dust cap from the bleed valve (arrowed) - front caliper shown

the front brake you will also need a piece of flat metal plate, approximately 2 mm thick, that will fit between the pads in the front brake caliper once the caliper has been displaced.

3 Cover any painted components as required to prevent damage in the event that brake fluid is spilled.

4 Support the bike securely in an upright position so that the appropriate brake fluid reservoir remains level throughout the procedure.

Front brake

5 On Speedmaster models, bleed one front brake at a time.

6 Loosen the caliper mounting bolts. On machines fitted with an adjustable span brake lever, set the adjuster to position No.1.

7 Ensure that the reservoir is still level, then remove the reservoir cover, diaphragm plate, and diaphragm (see *Pre-ride checks*) and top the fluid up to the UPPER mark.

8 Undo the caliper mounting bolts and slide the caliper off the disc. Fit the metal plate between the pads, then pump the brake lever a few times until the pads grip the plate **(see illustration)**.

9 Pull the dust cap off the bleed valve on the caliper **(see illustration)**. If you are using a ring spanner to slacken and tighten the valve (which is preferable to an open-ended

spanner as it keeps itself in place) fit it over the valve now. Attach one end of the clear vinyl or plastic tubing to the valve and submerge the other end in the brake fluid in the container **(see illustration)**.

10 Support the caliper with the bleed valve uppermost and open the valve, then have an assistant slowly pull the brake lever to the handlebar. With the lever held against the handlebar, close the valve, then release the lever.

11 When the lever is pulled, brake fluid will flow from the caliper into the clear tubing and any air in the system will be visible as bubbles in the fluid.

12 Check the fluid level in the reservoir – do not allow it to drop below the LOWER mark during the bleeding process.

13 Ensure that the bleed valve remains uppermost and rock the caliper gently to ensure no air remains trapped inside. Repeat the process until no air bubbles are visible in the brake fluid leaving the caliper.

14 Ensure that the bleed valve is closed, then disconnect the tubing. Ease the metal plate out from between the brake pads and install the caliper onto the disc. Tighten the caliper mounting bolts to the torque setting specified at the beginning of the Chapter.

15 Pull the brake lever to bring the pads into contact with the disc.

16 Fit the spanner and tubing back onto the bleed valve and submerge the other end of the tubing in the brake fluid in the container.

17 Open the valve, then have an assistant slowly pull the brake lever to the handlebar. With the lever held against the handlebar, close the valve, then release the lever. If no bubbles are visible in the fluid leaving the caliper the process is complete, otherwise repeat the process.

18 On completion, disconnect the tubing, tighten the bleed valve to the torque setting specified at the beginning of the Chapter and install the dust cap.

19 On Speedmaster models, repeat the procedure for the remaining front caliper.

20 Check the fluid level in the reservoir and top-up as necessary, then install the diaphragm, diaphragm plate and reservoir cover (see *Pre-ride checks*). On machines fitted with an adjustable span brake lever, reset the adjuster.

21 Wipe up any spilled brake fluid and check the entire system for leaks.

22 Check the operation of the front brake before riding the motorcycle.

Rear brake

23 Pull the dust cap off the bleed valve on the caliper. If you are using a ring spanner to slacken and tighten the valve (which is preferable to an open-ended spanner as it keeps itself in place) fit it over the valve now. Attach one end of the clear vinyl or plastic tubing to the valve and submerge the other end in the brake fluid in the container **(see illustration)**.

24 Remove the fluid reservoir cover, diaphragm plate, and diaphragm (see *Pre-ride checks*). Ensure that the reservoir is level and top the fluid up to the UPPER mark.

25 Have an assistant apply gentle pressure on the brake pedal, then open the bleed valve until brake fluid flows from the caliper into the clear tubing. Pump the pedal slowly a few times, then hold it down and tighten the valve. Release the pedal slowly.

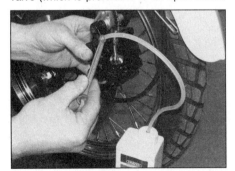

11.9b Set-up for bleeding the front brake

11.23 Set-up for bleeding the rear brake

26 Any air in the system will be visible as bubbles in the fluid leaving the caliper.
27 Check the fluid level in the reservoir – do not allow it to drop below the LOWER mark during the bleeding process.
28 Repeat the process until no air bubbles are visible in the brake fluid leaving the caliper.
29 On completion, disconnect the tubing, tighten the bleed valve to the torque setting specified at the beginning of the Chapter and install the dust cap.
30 Check the fluid level in the reservoir and top-up as necessary, then install the diaphragm, diaphragm plate and reservoir cover (see *Pre-ride checks*).
31 Wipe up any spilled brake fluid and check the entire system for leaks.
32 Install the remaining components in the reverse order of removal.
33 Check the operation of the rear brake before riding the motorcycle.

Changing the fluid

34 Changing the brake fluid is a similar process to bleeding the brakes and requires the same materials and set-up. Note that when changing the fluid on the front brake, unless there is evidence of air in the system, it is not necessary to displace the caliper.
35 First remove the reservoir cover, diaphragm plate, and diaphragm (see *Pre-ride checks*) and siphon the old fluid out of the reservoir, then fill the reservoir to the UPPER mark with new brake fluid.
36 Pull the dust cap off the bleed valve on the caliper and attach the tubing as described above, then have an assistant apply the appropriate brake while you open the valve to expel the old fluid from the system. Retighten the bleed valve when the brake lever or pedal has reached the end of its travel, then release the lever or pedal gradually.
37 Keep the reservoir topped-up with new fluid at all times or air may enter the system. Repeat the process until new fluid can be seen emerging from the bleed valve.

 Old brake fluid is invariably much darker in colour than new fluid, making it easy to see when all old fluid has been expelled from the system.

38 Disconnect the hose, then tighten the bleed valve to the specified torque setting and install the dust cap.
39 On Speedmaster models, don't forget to repeat the procedure for the remaining front caliper.
40 Top-up the reservoir, install the diaphragm, plate, and cover. Wipe up any spilled brake fluid and check the entire system for leaks.
41 Check the operation of the brakes before riding the motorcycle.

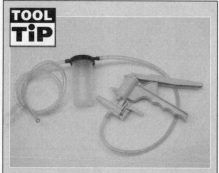

If bleeding the system using the conventional method (or a one-man tool) does not work sufficiently well, try a vacuum brake bleeding kit – follow the instructions supplied with the kit.

Draining the system for overhaul

42 Draining the brake fluid is again a similar process to bleeding the brakes. The quickest and easiest way is to use a commercially available vacuum-type brake bleeding tool (see **Tip**) – follow the manufacturer's instructions. Otherwise follow the procedure described above for changing the fluid, but quite simply do not put any new fluid into the reservoir – the system fills itself with air instead.

12 Wheel inspection and repair

1 In order to carry out a proper inspection of the wheels, it is necessary to support the bike upright so that the wheel being inspected is raised off the ground. Position the motorcycle on an auxiliary stand. Clean the wheels thoroughly to remove mud and dirt that may interfere with the inspection procedure or mask defects. Make

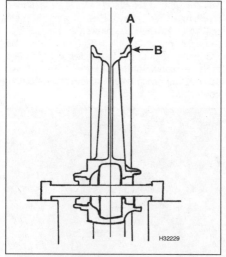

12.2 Check the wheel for radial (out-of-round) runout (A) and axial (side-to-side) runout (B)

a general check of the wheels (see Chapter 1) and tyres (see *Pre-ride checks*).
2 In order to accurately check wheel runout, the wheel must be removed from the machine and the tyre removed from the rim. This allows the runout measurement to be made against the inner, machined, surfaces of the wheel **(see illustration)**. To carry this out successfully, the wheel must be supported centrally on a jig to allow it to be rotated whilst the readings are taken. In view of the equipment required and carefully set-up, it is advised that wheel runout is checked by a Triumph dealer or wheel building specialist.
3 On Speedmaster and America models with cast wheels, inspect the wheels for cracks, flat spots on the rim and other damage. Look very closely for dents in the area where the tyre bead contacts the rim. Dents in this area may prevent complete sealing of the tyre against the rim, which leads to deflation of the tyre over a period of time. If damage is evident the wheel will have to be replaced with a new one. Never attempt to repair a damaged cast alloy wheel.
4 On all other models with spoked wheels, regularly check the spokes as described in Chapter 1. Wheel rebuilding or spoke replacement must be left to a Triumph dealer or wheel building specialist. A great deal of skill and equipment is required, and given the potential for poor handling and machine instability that could result from a poorly-built wheel, it is essential that owners do not attempt repairs themselves.

13 Wheel alignment check

1 Misalignment of the wheels, which may be due to a cocked rear wheel or a bent frame or fork yokes, can cause strange and possibly serious handling problems. If the frame or yokes are at fault, repair by a frame specialist or replacement with new parts are the only alternatives.
2 To check the alignment you will need an assistant, a length of string or a perfectly straight piece of wood and a ruler. A plumb bob or other suitable weight will also be required.
3 Place the bike on an auxiliary stand so that it is upright. Measure the width of both tyres at their widest points. Subtract the smaller measurement from the larger measurement, then divide the difference by two. The result is the amount of offset that should exist between the front and rear tyres on both sides. Note that on America models from VIN 468424 (plus those with VINs 466346, 466437, 467061, 467542 and 468420) the front wheel centreline is offset to the left of the motorcycle's centreline by 2.75 mm; take this into account when checking wheel alignment.
4 If a string is used, have your assistant hold one end of it about halfway between the floor and the rear axle, touching the rear sidewall of the tyre.

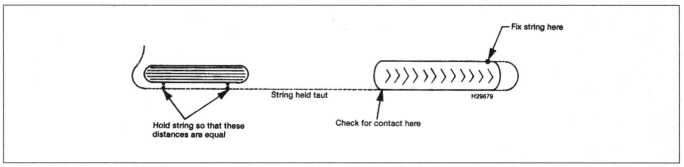

13.5 Wheel alignment check using string

5 Run the other end of the string forward and pull it tight so that it is roughly parallel to the floor **(see illustration)**. Slowly bring the string into contact with the front sidewall of the rear tyre, then turn the front wheel until it is parallel with the string. Measure the distance from the front tyre sidewall to the string.

6 Repeat the procedure on the other side of the motorcycle. The distance from the front

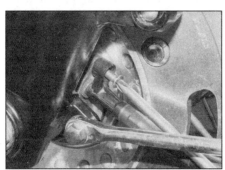

13.7 Wheel alignment check using a straight-edge

tyre sidewall to the string should be equal on both sides.

7 As previously mentioned, a perfectly straight length of wood or metal bar may be substituted for the string **(see illustration)**. The procedure is the same.

8 If the distance between the string and tyre is greater on one side, or if the rear wheel appears to be cocked, refer to Chapter 1, Section 2 and check that the chain adjuster markings coincide on each side of the swingarm.

9 If the front-to-back alignment is correct, the wheels still may be out of alignment vertically.

10 Using a plumb bob, or other suitable weight and a length of string, check the rear wheel to make sure it is vertical. To do this, hold the string against the tyre upper sidewall and allow the weight to settle just off the floor. When the string touches both the upper and lower tyre sidewalls and is perfectly straight,

14.3 Undo the screw and detach the cable

14.4a Unscrew the nut (arrowed) and remove the washer

the wheel is vertical. If it is not, place thin spacers under one leg of the stand until it is.

11 Once the rear wheel is vertical, check the front wheel in the same manner. If both wheels are not perfectly vertical, the frame and/or major suspension components are bent.

14 Front wheel

Removal

Bonneville, T100, Thruxton and Scrambler

1 Support the motorcycle on an auxiliary stand so that the front wheel is off the ground. Always make sure the motorcycle is properly supported.

2 Displace the front brake caliper (see Section 3). Support the caliper with a piece of wire or a bungee cord so that no strain is placed on the hydraulic hose. There is no need to disconnect the hose from the caliper. **Note:** *Do not operate the front brake lever with the caliper removed.*

3 On models with a cable driven speedometer, undo the screw which retains the cable in its housing and draw the cable out **(see illustration)**.

4 Unscrew and remove the axle nut and its washer **(see illustration)**. Slacken the axle clamp bolt on the bottom of the right-hand fork **(see illustration)**.

14.4b Slacken the clamp bolt (arrowed)

14.5 Withdraw the axle and remove the wheel

14.6a Remove the spacer . . .

14.6b . . . and the drive housing – models with cable-driven speedo

5 Support the wheel, then withdraw the axle from the right-hand side and remove the wheel **(see illustration)**. Remove the rubber bung and use a drift to drive out the axle if required, making sure you don't damage the threads. Alternatively a socket on the bolt head and a twisting motion will help it come out.
6 Remove the spacer from the right-hand side of the wheel and the speedometer drive housing from the left on models with a cable driven speedometer **(see illustrations)**. On models with an electronic speedometer, remove the spacers from each side of the wheel **(see illustrations)**.
Caution: Don't lay the wheel down and allow it to rest on a disc – the disc could become warped. Set the wheel on wood blocks so the disc does not support the weight of the wheel, or keep it upright.

America and Speedmaster

7 Support the motorcycle on an auxiliary stand so that the front wheel is off the ground. Always make sure the motorcycle is properly supported.
8 Displace the front brake caliper(s) (see Section 3). Support the caliper(s) with a piece of wire or a bungee cord so that no strain is placed on the hydraulic hose(s). There is no need to disconnect the hose(s) from the calipers. **Note:** *Do not operate the front brake lever with the calipers removed.*
9 On models with a cable-operated speedometer, undo the screw and pull the

14.6c Remove the spacer from the right side . . .

cable out of the drive housing **(see illustration 14.3)**.
10 On all America models and 2003 to 2010 Speedmaster models, unscrew the bolt from the right-hand end of the axle **(see illustration)**. Slacken the axle clamp bolts on the bottom of each fork. Support the wheel, then withdraw the axle from the left-hand side and remove the wheel; use a drift to drive out the axle if it is stuck. Alternatively remove the rubber bung from the axle head and use a large hex key inserted in the head and apply a twisting motion to ease it out **(see illustration)**.
11 On 2011-on Speedmaster models the axle threads directly into the left fork leg. Slacken the axle clamp bolts in the right-hand fork, then unscrew the axle; support the wheel as the axle is withdrawn.

14.6d . . . and left side – Bonneville SE with electronically driven speedo shown

12 Remove the spacer from the right-hand side of the wheel and the speedometer drive housing from the left **(see illustrations 14.6a and b)**. On models with an electronic speedometer, remove the spacers from each side of the wheel.
Caution: Don't lay the wheel down and allow it to rest on a disc – the disc could become warped. Set the wheel on wood blocks so the disc does not support the weight of the wheel, or keep it upright.

All models

13 Check the axle is straight by rolling it on a flat surface such as a piece of plate glass (first wipe off all old grease and remove any corrosion using wire wool). If the axle is bent, replace it with a new one.
14 Check the condition of the wheel bearings (see Section 16).

Installation

Bonneville, T100, Thruxton and Scrambler

15 Apply lithium-based grease to the lips of the bearing seals, to the spacer and to the speedometer drive housing. Fit the spacer into the right-hand side of the wheel, with the wider end facing in **(see illustration 14.6a)**. Fit the speedometer drive housing (spacer on later models) into the left-hand side of the wheel aligning the cut-outs in the drive gear with the tabs on the drive plate **(see illustration 14.6b)**.

14.10a Unscrew the bolt (A) from the axle, then slacken the clamp bolts (B) on each side

14.10b Remove the bung so a large hex key can be used in the axle head

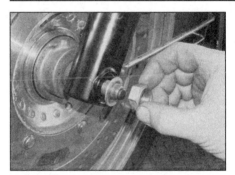

14.17 Fit the washer and tighten the nut finger-tight

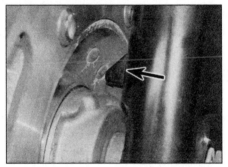

14.19a Butt the housing against the lug (arrowed)

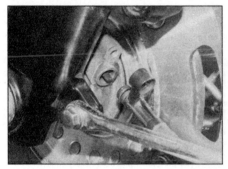

14.19b Locate the drive tab in the slot in the cable end

16 Manoeuvre the wheel into position, making sure it is the correct way round with the speedometer drive housing or spacer on the left and the arrow on the tyre pointing in the direction of forward motion. Apply a smear of grease to the axle.

17 Lift the wheel into place between the forks, making sure the spacer and speedo drive remain in position, and slide the axle in from the right-hand side (see illustration 14.5). Fit the washer and nut and tighten the nut finger-tight (see illustration).

18 Install the brake caliper, making sure the pads sit squarely on each side of the disc (see Section 3). Apply the front brake a few times to bring the pads back into contact with the disc. Take the bike off the stand and support it on the sidestand.

19 Where applicable, turn the speedometer drive housing so the cable socket points back and the housing butts against the lug on the fork (see illustration). Tighten the axle nut to the torque setting specified at the beginning of the Chapter, counter-holding the axle head if necessary. Connect the speedometer cable, making sure it engages correctly over the drive tab, and tighten its screw (see illustration).

20 Take the bike off the sidestand, apply the front brake and pump the front forks a few times to settle all components in position. Now tighten the axle clamp bolt on the bottom of the right-hand fork to the specified torque setting (see illustration 14.4b).

21 Fit the rubber bung into each end of the axle if removed. Check the operation of the front brake carefully before riding the bike.

America and Speedmaster

22 Apply lithium-based grease to the lips of the bearing seals, to the spacer and to the speedometer drive housing. Fit the spacer into the right-hand side of the wheel (see illustration 14.6a). Fit the speedometer drive housing or spacer into the left-hand side of the wheel aligning the cut-outs in the drive gear with the tabs on the drive plate (see illustration 14.6b).

23 On all America models and 2003 to 2010

Speedmaster models, manoeuvre the wheel into position, making sure it is the correct way round with the speedometer drive (spacer on later models) on the left and the arrow on the tyre pointing in the direction of forward motion. Apply a smear of grease to the axle, then lift the wheel into place making sure the spacer(s) and speedo drive remain in position and slide the axle in from the left side. Where applicable, turn the speedo drive housing so the cable socket points back and the housing butts against the lug on the fork (see illustration 14.19a). Fit the axle bolt and tighten it to the specified torque setting.

24 On 2011-on Speedmaster models, manoeuvre the wheel into position, making sure it is the correct way round with the arrow on the tyre pointing in the direction of forward motion. Apply a smear of grease to the axle, then lift the wheel into place making sure the spacers remain in position and slide the axle in from the right side. Tighten the axle to the specified torque setting.

25 Install the brake caliper(s), making sure the pads sit squarely on each side of the disc(s) (see Section 3). Apply the front brake a few times to bring the pads back into contact with the disc(s). Take the bike off the stand and support it on the sidestand.

26 Where applicable, connect the speedometer cable, making sure it engages correctly over the drive tab, and tighten its screw (see illustration 14.19b).

27 Take the bike off the sidestand, apply the

front brake and pump the front forks a few times to settle all components in position. Now tighten the axle clamp bolts on the bottom of each fork (right-hand fork only on 2011-on Speedmaster) to the specified torque setting (see illustration 14.10a).

28 Fit the rubber bung into the left-hand end of the axle if removed (see illustration 14.11). Check the operation of the front brake carefully before riding the bike.

15 Rear wheel

Removal

1 Support the motorcycle on an auxiliary stand so that the rear wheel is off the ground. Always make sure the motorcycle is properly supported.

2 On Bonneville and T100 models remove the exhaust silencers (see Chapter 3A or 3B).

3 Displace the rear brake caliper (see Section 7).

4 Unscrew the axle nut and where fitted remove the washer (see illustration). Turn the chain adjusters in to provide some slack in the chain.

5 Support the wheel then withdraw the axle and lower the wheel to the ground (see illustration). Disengage the chain from the sprocket and hang it over the end

15.4 Unscrew the axle nut and remove the washer if fitted

15.5a Withdraw the axle from the left and lower the wheel . . .

15.5b ... then disengage the chain and manoeuvre the wheel out

15.6 Displace the caliper bracket, noting how it locates on the lug (arrowed)

15.7a Remove the right-hand spacer ...

of the swingarm, then remove the wheel from between the swingarm ends **(see illustration)**.

6 Note how the caliper bracket fits between the wheel and the swingarm, and displace it from the swingarm if required, noting how it locates **(see illustration)**. Note: *Do not operate the brake pedal with the caliper removed.*
Caution: Do not lay the wheel down and allow it to rest on the disc or the sprocket – they could become warped. Set the wheel on wood blocks so the disc or the sprocket does not support the weight of the wheel. Do not operate the brake pedal with the wheel removed.

7 Remove the spacer from each side of the wheel, noting which fits where and which way round **(see illustrations)**.

8 Check the axle is straight by rolling it on a flat surface such as a piece of plate glass (first wipe off all old grease and remove any corrosion using wire wool). If the axle is bent, replace it with a new one.

9 Check the condition of the bearing seals and wheel bearings (see Section 16).

Installation

10 Apply a thin coat of lithium-based grease to the lips of each grease seal, and also to the spacers and the axle.

11 Fit the spacer into each side of the wheel, making sure they are the correct way round **(see illustrations 15.7a and b)**.

12 Locate the slot in the caliper bracket onto the lug on the swingarm **(see illustration 15.6)**.

Manoeuvre the wheel into place between the ends of the swingarm and engage the drive chain with the sprocket **(see illustration 15.5b)**.

13 Lift the wheel into position, making sure the spacers remain in place and the caliper bracket remains aligned, and slide the axle through from the left-hand side **(see illustration 15.5a)**. Make sure it passes through the caliper bracket. Where removed fit the axle washer. On all models fit the axle nut and tighten it finger-tight **(see illustration 15.4)**.

14 Install the brake caliper, making sure the pads sit squarely on each side of the disc (see Section 7). Apply the brake a few times to bring the pads back into contact with the disc. Take the bike off the stand and support it on the sidestand.

15 Adjust the chain slack as described in Chapter 1, then tighten the axle nut to the torque setting specified at the beginning of the Chapter.

16 On Bonneville and T100 models install the silencers (see Chapter 3A or 3B).

17 Check the operation of the rear brake carefully before riding the bike.

16 Wheel bearing replacement

Note: *Before removing the bearings (but having removed the seals etc as required to access the bearings), refer to **Tools and Workshop Tips** in the Reference Section and check them to see if new ones are needed –*

however good their apparent condition, once the bearings have been removed from the wheel they should be replaced with new ones rather than being reused, as the impact on removal could damage them. Always replace the wheel bearings in sets. Never replace the bearings individually. Avoid using a high pressure cleaner on the wheel bearing area.

Front wheel bearings

Note: *Always replace the wheel bearings in pairs, never individually. Avoid using a high pressure cleaner on the wheel bearing area.*

1 Remove the wheel (see Section 14). A caged ball bearing is fitted in each side of the wheel.

2 Set the wheel on blocks so as not to allow the weight of the wheel to rest on the brake disc.

3 Lever out the grease seal on each side of the wheel using a seal hook or a large flat-bladed screwdriver, taking care not to damage the rim **(see illustration)**. Discard the seals. Remove the speedometer drive plate (where applicable) from the left-hand side, noting how it fits **(see illustration)**.

> **HAYNES HINT** *Position a piece of wood against the wheel to prevent the screwdriver shaft damaging it when levering the grease seal out.*

4 Refer to *Tools and Workshop Tips* (Section 5 in the Reference Section) and check the bearings as described. If worn, replace them with new ones as follows.

15.7b ... and the left-hand spacer –
Bonneville, T100, Thruxton and Scrambler type shown

16.3a Remove the seal from each side ...

16.3b ... and remove the drive plate from the left-hand side

16.5a Release the circlip (arrowed) from the right-hand side

16.5b If necessary remove the bearings using a drift as described

16.6 A socket can be used to drive in the bearing

5 Remove the circlip from the right-hand side (both sides on 2011-on Speedmaster) of the wheel **(see illustration)**. Remove the bearing on one side preferably using a commercially available bearing puller, referring to Tools and Workshop tips in the reference Section for details on its use. Alternatively use a metal rod (preferably a brass drift) inserted through the centre of one bearing, pushing the spacer to one side so the drift locates on the inner race of the other bearing, and tapping evenly around it to drive it from the hub **(see illustration)**. Remove the bearing spacer, then turn the wheel over and remove the other bearing.

6 Thoroughly clean the hub area of the wheel. Install a new bearing into the right-hand side with the marked or sealed side of the bearing facing outwards. Using the old bearing, a bearing driver or a socket large enough to contact the outer race of the bearing only, drive it in until it is fully seated **(see illustration)**. Do not drive the bearing in against its inner race. Fit the bearing circlip **(see illustration 16.5a)**.

7 Turn the wheel over and install the bearing spacer. Drive a new bearing into the left-hand side of the hub as described above.

8 Fit the circlip into the left-hand side of the wheel on 2011-on Speedmaster models, making sure it locates in its groove. Fit the speedometer drive plate (where applicable)

16.8a Press the new seals into the hub . . .

into the left-hand side, locating the tabs on the outer rim in the cut-outs in the hub **(see illustration 16.3b)**. Apply a smear of lithium-based grease to the lips of the seals, then press them into the wheel, setting them flush with their housing, using a seal or bearing driver or a suitable socket or piece of wood to drive them into place **(see illustrations)**.

9 Clean off all grease from the brake disc(s) using acetone or brake system cleaner then install the wheel (see Section 14).

Rear wheel bearings

10 Remove the wheel (see Section 15).

16.8b . . . using a piece of wood as shown sets them flush with the rim

Lift the sprocket coupling out of the wheel, noting how it fits **(see illustration)**. A caged ball bearing is fitted in each side of the wheel.

11 Set the wheel on blocks with the disc facing up.

12 Lever out the grease seal on the left-hand side of the wheel using a seal hook or a large flat-bladed screwdriver, taking care not to damage the rim of the hub **(see illustration)**. Discard the seal.

13 Refer to *Tools and Workshop Tips* (Section 5 in the Reference Section) and check the bearings as described. If worn, replace them with new ones as follows.

16.10 Lift the sprocket coupling out of the wheel

16.12 Lever out the grease seal

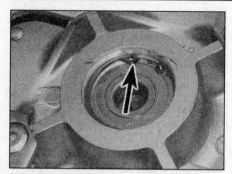

16.14a Release the circlip (arrowed) from the left-hand side

16.14b If necessary remove the bearings using a drift as described

16.16a Press the new seal into the hub . . .

16.16b . . . using a piece of wood as shown sets it flush with the rim

16.18 Remove the spacer from the inside

16.19 Lever out the grease seal

14 Remove the circlip from the left-hand side of the wheel **(see illustration)**. Remove the bearing on one side preferably using a commercially available bearing puller, referring to Tools and Workshop tips in the reference Section for details on its use. Alternatively use a metal rod (preferably a brass drift) inserted through the centre of one bearing, pushing the spacer to one side so the drift locates on the inner race of the other bearing, and tapping evenly around it to drive it from the hub **(see illustration)**. Remove the bearing spacer, then turn the wheel over and remove the other bearing.

15 Thoroughly clean the hub area of the wheel. Install a new bearing into the left-hand side with the marked or sealed side of the bearing facing outwards. Using the old bearing, a bearing driver or a socket large enough to contact the outer race of the bearing only, drive it in until it is fully seated **(see illustration 16.6)**. Do not drive the bearing in against its inner race. Fit the bearing circlip **(see illustration 16.14a)**.

Turn the wheel over and install the bearing spacer. Drive a new bearing into the right-hand side of the hub as described.

16 Apply a smear of lithium-based grease to the lips of the new seal, then press it into the left-hand side of the hub, setting it flush with its housing using a seal or bearing driver or a suitable socket or piece of wood to drive it into place if necessary **(see illustrations)**.

17 Clean off all grease from the brake disc using acetone or brake system cleaner. Install the sprocket coupling assembly **(see illustration 16.10)**. Install the wheel (see Section 15).

Sprocket coupling bearing

18 Remove the rear wheel (see Section 15). Lift the sprocket coupling out of the wheel, noting how it fits **(see illustration 16.10)**. Remove the sprocket coupling spacer from inside the bearing **(see illustration)**.

19 Using a seal hook or a large flat-bladed screwdriver lever out the grease seal from the outside of the coupling, taking care not to damage the rim of the coupling **(see illustration)**. Discard the seal if it is damaged or deteriorated.

20 Refer to *Tools and Workshop Tips* (Section 5 in the Reference Section) and check the bearing as described. If worn, replace it with a new one as follows.

21 Remove the circlip from the outside of the coupling **(see illustration)**. Support the coupling on blocks of wood and drive the bearing out from the inside using a bearing driver or socket **(see illustration)**.

22 Thoroughly clean the bearing recess in the coupling. Drive the bearing in from the outside of the coupling, with the marked or sealed side facing out, using the old bearing (if a new one is being fitted), a bearing driver or a socket large enough to contact the outer race of the bearing, until it is completely seated **(see illustration)**.

16.21a Remove the circlip (arrowed) . . .

16.21b . . . then drive the bearing out from the inside

16.22 A socket can be used to drive in the bearing

16.23 Press the new seal into the housing

23 Fit the circlip into the outside of the coupling, making sure it locates in its groove **(see illustration 16.21a)**. Apply a smear of grease to the lips of the new seal, and press it into the coupling, setting it flush with the rim of its housing, using a seal or bearing driver or a suitable socket if necessary **(see illustration)**.

24 Check the sprocket coupling/rubber dampers (see Chapter 5, Section 17).

25 Clean off all grease from the brake disc using acetone or brake system cleaner. Fit the sprocket coupling into the wheel **(see illustration 16.10)**, then install the wheel (see Section 15).

17 Tyres

General information

1 The wheels fitted on models with spoked wheels are designed to take tubed tyres and those on models with cast wheels are designed to take tubeless tyres. Tyre sizes are given in the Specifications at the beginning of this Chapter and will be listed in the owner's manual together with recommended brands and pressures.

2 Refer to *Pre-ride checks* at the beginning of this manual for tyre maintenance.

Fitting new tyres

3 When selecting new tyres, refer to the tyre options listed in the Owner's Handbook. Ensure that front and rear tyre types are compatible, and of the correct size and speed rating; if necessary, seek advice from a Triumph dealer or tyre fitting specialist **(see illustration)**.

4 It is recommended that tyres are fitted by a motorcycle tyre specialist and that this is not attempted in the home workshop. This is particularly relevant in the case of tubeless tyres because the force required to break the seal between the wheel rim and tyre bead is substantial, and is usually beyond the capabilities of an individual working with normal tyre levers. Additionally, the specialist will be able to balance the wheels after tyre fitting.

5 Repair a punctured tubed tyre by fitting a new inner tube, and ensure that the item which caused the puncture is removed from the tyre tread. Note that punctured tubeless tyres can in some cases be repaired. Seek the advice of a Triumph dealer or a motorcycle tyre fitting specialist concerning tyre repairs.

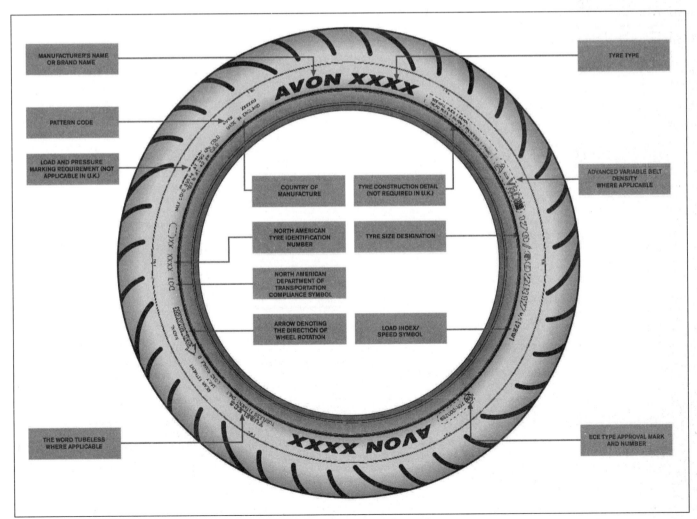

17.3 Common tyre sidewall markings

Chapter 7
Bodywork

Contents

Degrees of difficulty

Easy, suitable for novice with little experience	**Fairly easy,** suitable for beginner with some experience	**Fairly difficult,** suitable for competent DIY mechanic	**Difficult,** suitable for experienced DIY mechanic	**Very difficult,** suitable for expert DIY or professional

1 General information

When attempting to remove any body panel, first study it closely, noting any fasteners and associated fittings, to be sure of returning everything to its correct place on installation. Once the evident fasteners have been removed, try to remove the panel as described but DO NOT FORCE IT – if it will not release, check that all fasteners have been removed and try again.

When installing a body panel, first study it closely, noting any fasteners and associated fittings removed with it, to be sure of returning everything to its correct place. Check that all fasteners are in good condition, including all trim nuts or clips and damping/rubber mounts; any of these must be replaced if faulty before the panel is installed. Check also that all mounting brackets are straight and repair or replace them if necessary before attempting to install the panel. Tighten the fasteners securely, but be careful not to overtighten any of them as the panel may break (not always immediately) due to the uneven stress.

In the case of damage to plastic components, it is usually necessary to remove the broken component and replace it with a new (or used) one. Plastic panels can be repaired by 'plastic welding', so it may be worthwhile seeking the advice of one of these specialists before consigning an expensive component to the bin. Alternatively, for cracks in panels and small areas of damage, repairs can be made using DIY kits.

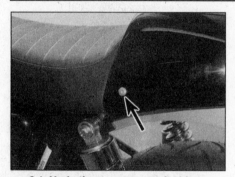

2.1 Undo the screw on each side to release the seat cowl

2.2a Unscrew the bolts (arrowed) . . .

2.2b . . . and remove the seat . . .

2.2c . . . noting how the hooks and tab (arrowed) locate

2.2d Location of the seat bolt Allen key – Scrambler models

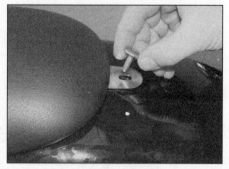

2.5a Unscrew the bolt . . .

2 Seat

Removal

Bonneville, T100, Thruxton and Scrambler

1 On Thruxton models, where fitted, first remove the seat cowl by removing the screw on each side and lifting it off the seat **(see illustration)**. Retrieve the washers

2 Unscrew the bolts at the back of the seat, then draw the seat back and up and lift it off the frame **(see illustrations)**. Note how the tab at the front locates under the fuel tank bracket and how the hook on each side locates under the frame **(see illustration)**. Note that on Scrambler models, a suitable Allen key for unscrewing the seat bolts is located behind the left-hand side panel **(see illustration)**.

America up to 2010

3 To remove the passenger seat unscrew the bolt at the back, then move the seat forwards to release the bracket at the front from the bolt securing the rider's seat.

4 To remove the rider's seat first remove the passenger seat. Unscrew the bolt securing the back of the rider's seat and lift it away, noting how it locates at the front.

Speedmaster and 2011-on America

5 Unscrew the bolt securing the back of the seat **(see illustration)**. Pull the release ring and lift the seat off the mudguard and the frame, noting how the latch engages over its post, and how the tab at the front locates **(see illustrations)**.

Installation

6 Installation is the reverse of removal. Make sure the seat locates correctly. On Speedmaster models, push down on the centre of the seat to engage the latch.

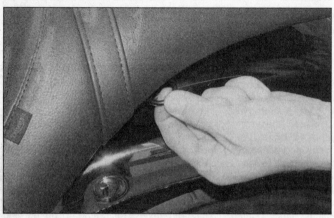

2.5b . . . then pull the ring to release the latch . . .

2.5c . . . and remove the seat, noting how the tab and the post (arrowed) locate

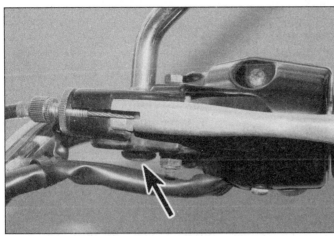

3.1 Unscrew the bolt (arrowed) to release the mirror

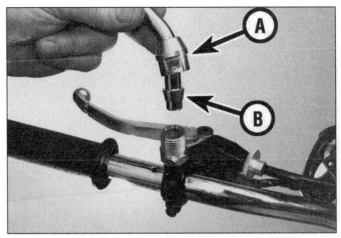

3.2 Mirror retainer (A) and compression ring (B)

3 Mirrors

1 On Bonneville models up to VIN 380776, T100, America and Speedmaster models, unscrew the bolt **(see illustration)** and remove the wave washer from the bottom of the mirror stem. Draw the mirror out of its holder, noting the spacer inside, which should stay in place.

2 On Thruxton models up to 2007, all Scrambler models and Bonneville models from VIN 380777, pull the boot up off the base of the mirror stem. Unscrew the mirror retainer and ease the stem out from the holder, noting the location of the compression ring **(see illustration)**. If the mirror is a loose fit in the holder, fit a new compression ring.

3 On Thruxton models from 2008, handlebar-end mirrors are fitted. Unscrew the retaining bolt, noting its washer and detach the mirror. Note the location of the spacer and bush.

4 Install the mirrors in a reverse of the removal sequence.

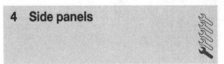

4 Side panels

Bonneville, T100 and Thruxton

1 Undo the screw securing the bottom of the panel, noting the collar **(see illustrations)**. Lift the panel off its upper mounting lugs **(see illustration)**.

2 Installation is the reverse of removal. Make sure the rubber grommets are in good condition and the collar is fitted with the screw.

America and Speedmaster

3 To remove the right-hand panel simply pull it away to release the pegs from the grommets **(see illustration)**.

4.1a Undo the screw (arrowed) . . .

4.1b . . . and remove the collar . . .

4.1c . . . then lift the panel off its top mounts

4.3 Pull the panel away to free the pegs from their grommets

4.5a Undo the screw (arrowed) . . .

4.5b . . . and remove the outer cover . . .

4.5c . . . then undo the screws (arrowed) . . .

4.5d . . . and release the peg from its grommet

4 To remove the right-hand air duct cover undo its screw **(see illustrations 4.5a and b)**.
5 To remove the left-hand air duct covers undo the screw securing the outer cover and remove it noting how it locates **(see illustrations)**. Undo the screws securing the inner cover then pull it away to release the peg from the grommet **(see illustrations)**.
6 Installation is the reverse of removal. Make sure the rubber grommets are in good condition.

Note that a small amount of lubricant (liquid soap or similar) applied to rubber mounting grommets will assist the side panel pegs to engage without the need for undue pressure.

Scrambler

7 To remove and install the left-hand panel, follow the procedure in Steps 1 and 2.
8 To remove the right-hand panel, first pull

the top edge away to release it from the grommets **(see illustration)**.
9 Ease the panel back, then pull it up to release the tabs on the bottom edge from the holes in the air filter housing **(see illustration)**.
10 Installation is the reverse of removal. Make sure the rubber grommets are in good condition.

4.8 Pull the top edge away to release it from the grommets (arrowed) . . .

5 Front mudguard

Bonneville up to 2008 and T100

1 Remove the front wheel (see Chapter 6).

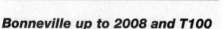

4.9 . . . then lift the panel to release the tabs (arrowed)

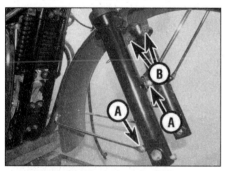

5.3 Unscrew the stay bolts (A) and the mudguard bolts (B) on each side . . .

5.4 . . . and draw the mudguard forwards from between the forks

5.9a Remove the two mounting bolts on each side . . .

2 Draw the speedometer cable out of its guides.

3 Unscrew the bolts securing the mudguard stays to the forks **(see illustration)**.

4 Unscrew the bolts securing each side of the mudguard itself to the forks, then draw the assembly forwards, and remove it **(see illustrations)**.

5 If required separate the mudguard from its stays by unscrewing the bolts, noting the nylon protection washers that fit between them.

6 Installation is the reverse of removal.

Bonneville 2009-on, Thruxton and Scrambler

7 Remove the front wheel (see Chapter 6).

8 Draw the speedometer cable out of its guide – early models.

9 Unscrew the bolts securing each side of the mudguard bracket to the forks, then draw the assembly forwards, and remove it **(see illustrations)**.

10 If required separate the mudguard from its bracket by undoing the four screws.

11 Installation is the reverse of removal.

America and Speedmaster

12 Remove the front wheel (see Chapter 6).

13 Draw the speedometer cable out of its guide (early models). On Speedmaster

models free the brake hose from its clips if not already done **(see illustration)**.

14 Unscrew the bolts securing each side of the mudguard bracket to the inside of each, then draw the assembly forwards, and remove it. Note the brake hose holder secured by the rear bolt on the left-hand side.

15 If required separate the mudguard from its bracket by undoing the two screws on each side.

16 Installation is the reverse of removal.

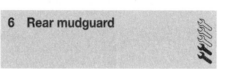

6   Rear mudguard

Bonneville, T100, Thruxton and Scrambler

1 Remove the seat (see Section 2).

2 Disconnect the tail light assembly wiring connector **(see illustration)**.

3 Support the mudguard and undo the four screws securing it to the frame, and remove the mudguard when free. Note the washers with the screws.

4 If required remove the tail light assembly (see Chapter 8).

5 Installation is the reverse of removal.

5.9b . . . and withdraw the mudguard from the forks

America and Speedmaster

6 Remove the seat(s) (see Section 2).

7 Undo the screw and release the wiring connector cover from the top of the air filter housing **(see illustration)**. Disconnect the tail light and rear turn signal wiring connectors.

8 Unscrew the two rear bolts securing each side of the mudguard to the frame brackets and the two bolts at the front securing the mudguard to the frame cross-piece and remove the mudguard.

9 If required remove the tail light and turn signal assemblies (see Chapter 8).

10 Installation is the reverse of removal.

5.13 Free the brake hose from its clips (arrowed)

6.2 Disconnect the wiring connector

6.7 Remove the connector cover

Chapter 8
Electrical system

Contents

Degrees of difficulty

Easy, suitable for novice with little experience	**Fairly easy,** suitable for beginner with some experience	**Fairly difficult,** suitable for competent DIY mechanic	**Difficult,** suitable for experienced DIY mechanic	**Very difficult,** suitable for expert DIY or professional

Specifications

Battery

Capacity	12V, 10 Ah
Charging time	
Normal	5 hours @ 1.2A
Quick	1 hour @ 4A

Charging system

Alternator output	
Carburettor models	27A
EFI models	24A @ 2000 rpm, 26A @ 4000 rpm
Current leakage	1 mA (max)
Alternator stator coil winding	0.3 to 0.6 ohm

Fuses – Bonneville, T100, Thruxton and Scrambler with carburettor engine

1 – Not used . . . . -
2 – Ignition switch main feed 30A
3 – Accessory socket 10A
4 – Alarm 5A
5 – Instruments, ignition control unit, starter relay 15A
6 – Not used . . . . -
7 – Turn signals, brake light, horn 10A
8 – Instrument illumination 5A
9 – Headlight beams 10A
10 – Position/parking lights 5A
11 – Main 30A

Fuses – Bonneville, T100, Thruxton and Scrambler with EFI engine and cable-operated speedometer

1 – Not used . . . . –
2 – Alarm, diagnostic connector 10A
3 – Accessory socket 10A
4 – Ignition switch main feed 10A
5 – EFI system 20A
6 – Not used . . . . –
7 – Turn signals, brake light, horn 10A
8 – Instrument illumination, position/parking lights 5A
9 – Headlight beams 10A
10 – Position/parking lights 5A
11 – Main 30A

Fuses – Bonneville, T100, Thruxton and Scrambler with EFI engine and electronic speedometer

1 – Not used . . . . –
2 – Alarm, diagnostic connector 10A
3 – Accessory socket, GPS 10A
4 – Not used . . . . –
5 – EFI system 20A
6 – Ignition switch main feed 10A
7 – Turn signals, brake light, horn 10A
8 – Position/parking lights 5A
9 – Headlight beams 10A
10 – Position/parking lights 5A
11 – Main 30A

Fuses – America and Speedmaster with carburettor engine

1 – Accessory lights 10A
2 – Ignition switch main feed 30A
3 – Accessory socket 10A
4 – Alarm 10A
5 – Instruments, ignition control unit, starter relay 15A
6 – Not used . . . . -
7 – Turn signals, brake light, horn 10A
8 – Instrument illumination 5A
9 – Headlight beams 10A
10 – Position/Parking lights 5A
11 – Main 30A

Fuses – America and Speedmaster with EFI engine

1 – Accessory lights 10A
2 – Alarm, clock (alarm and GPS on models
with electronic speedometer) 10A
3 – Accessory socket, diagnostic connector 10A
4 – Ignition switch main feed 10A
5 – EFI system 20A
6 – Not used . . . . –
7 – Turn signals, brake light, horn 10A
8 – Accessory lights (headlight), instrument illumination 5A
9 – Headlight beams 10A
10 – Position/parking lights 5A
11 – Main 30A

Bulbs

Headlight	60/55W H4
Parking/position light	4W
Brake/tail light	21/5W
Turn signal	
Bonneville, T100, Thruxton and Scrambler	10W
America and Speedmaster – 2002 to 2010	21W
America and Speedmaster – 2011-on	10W
Warning and instrument lights	1.7W or LED

Torque settings

Alternator cover bolts.	9 Nm
Alternator rotor bolt	
M10 bolt	98 Nm
M12 bolt	120 Nm
Alternator stator and wiring clamp bolts	12 Nm
Front footrest mounting bracket bolts – America and Speedmaster . . .	27 Nm
Neutral switch.	10 Nm
Oil pressure switch.	13 Nm
Rear brake light switch.	15 Nm
Starter motor mounting bolts	10 Nm

1 General information

All models have a 12-volt electrical system charged by a three-phase alternator with a separate regulator/rectifier.

The regulator maintains the charging system output within the specified range to prevent overcharging, and the rectifier converts the ac (alternating current) output of the alternator to dc (direct current) to power the lights and other components and to charge the battery. The alternator rotor is mounted on the left-hand end of the crankshaft.

The starter motor is mounted on the front of the engine. The starting system includes the battery, the starter relay, the starter motor, and the various switches and wires. Some of the switches (sidestand switch, clutch switch and neutral switch) are part of the safety interlock circuit, which cuts the ignition if the sidestand is extended whilst the engine is running and in gear, or if a gear is selected whilst the engine is running and the sidestand is extended. It also prevents the engine from being started if the engine is in gear while the sidestand is down.

Note: *Keep in mind that electrical parts, once purchased, cannot be returned. To avoid unnecessary expense, make very sure the faulty component has been positively identified before buying a replacement part.*

2 Electrical system fault finding

 Warning: To prevent the risk of short circuits, the ignition (main) switch must always be OFF and the battery negative (–) terminal should be disconnected before any of the bike's other electrical components are disturbed. Don't forget to reconnect the terminal securely once work is finished or if battery power is needed for circuit testing.

1 A typical electrical circuit consists of an electrical component, the switches, relays, etc. related to that component and the wiring and connectors that link the component to the battery and the frame. To aid in locating a problem in any electrical circuit, and to guide you with the wiring colour codes and connectors, refer to the *Wiring Diagram* for you model at the end of this Chapter.

2 Before tackling any troublesome electrical circuit, first study the wiring diagram (see end of Chapter) thoroughly to get a complete picture of what makes up that individual circuit. Trouble spots, for instance, can often be narrowed down by noting if other components related to that circuit are operating properly or not. If several components or circuits fail at one time, chances are the fault lies in the fuse or earth (ground) connection, as several circuits often are routed through the same fuse and earth (ground) connections.

3 Electrical problems often stem from simple causes, such as loose or corroded connections or a blown fuse. Prior to any electrical fault finding, always visually check the condition of the fuse, wires and connections in the problem circuit. Intermittent failures can be especially frustrating, since you can't always duplicate the failure when it's convenient to test. In such situations, a good practice is to clean all connections in the affected circuit, whether or not they appear to be good. All of the connections and wires should also be wiggled to check for looseness which can cause intermittent failure.

4 If testing instruments are going to be used, use the wiring diagram to plan where you will make the necessary connections in order to accurately pinpoint the trouble spot.

5 The basic tools needed for electrical fault finding include a battery and bulb test circuit or a continuity tester, a test light, and a jumper wire. A multimeter capable of reading volts, ohms and amps is a very useful and inexpensive alternative and performs the functions of all of the above, and is necessary for performing more extensive tests and checks where specific voltage, current or resistance values are needed.

 Refer to Fault Finding Equipment in the Reference section for details of how to use electrical test equipment.

3 Battery removal and maintenance

Caution: Be extremely careful when handling or working around the battery. The electrolyte is very caustic and an explosive gas (hydrogen) is given off when the battery is charging.

Removal and installation

Bonneville, T100, Thruxton and Scrambler

1 Make sure the ignition is OFF. Remove the seat (see Chapter 7).

2 Unscrew the negative (–) terminal bolt and disconnect the lead from the battery **(see illustration)**.

3.2 Disconnect the negative terminal first, then the positive terminal (arrowed)

3.4 Unclip the strap . . .

3.5 . . . then carefully lift the battery out of the bike

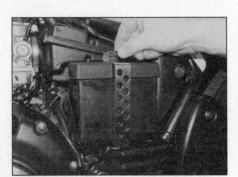

3.9a Remove the clamp . . .

3.9b . . . followed by the cover

3 Lift the insulating cover off the positive (+) terminal, then unscrew the bolt and disconnect the lead.

4 Unclip the battery strap **(see illustration)**.

5 Remove the battery from the bike **(see illustration)**. Note that the ECM unit on EFI

(fuel injected) models is located behind the battery; refer to Chapter 3B, Section 8 for battery removal on EFI models.

6 Before installing the battery, clean the terminals and lead ends with a wire brush or knife, and emery paper.

3.12 Remove the battery from its holder

3.13a Remove the connector cover . . .

7 Installation is the reverse of removal. When you reconnect the leads, connect the positive (+) terminal first.

 Battery corrosion can be kept to a minimum by applying a layer of petroleum jelly or battery terminal (dielectric) grease to the terminals after the cables have been connected. DO NOT use normal lubricating grease.

America and Speedmaster

8 Make sure the ignition is OFF. Remove the left-hand air duct covers (see Chapter 7, Section 4).

9 Undo the battery clamp screw and remove the clamp **(see illustration)**. Remove the battery cover **(see illustration)**.

10 Unscrew the negative (−) terminal bolt and disconnect the lead from the battery.

11 Lift the insulating over off the positive (+) terminal, then unscrew the bolt and disconnect the lead.

12 Tilt the battery out and remove it from the holder **(see illustration)**. Note that the ECM unit on 2008 to 2010 EFI models is located behind the battery.

13 To remove the battery holder, remove the seat(s) (see Chapter 7). Undo the screw securing the wiring connector cover and lift it off the air filter housing **(see illustration)**. Trace the wiring from ignition switch and disconnect it at the connector **(see illustration)**. Release the wiring from any clips and ties and feed it through to the switch, noting its routing. Remove the ignition switch cover by pulling it away at the bottom to release the peg from the grommet, then release the clip at the top and remove it **(see illustration)**. Remove the fusebox lid. Undo the screws and bolts securing the holder and displace it, noting how the lower front bolt secures the wiring guide and the bottom bolt secures the brake light switch and pipe union bracket **(see illustrations)**. Free the fusebox by pushing the clips out from the back, and feed the fusebox through the back **(see illustration)**. If required remove the switch from the holder (see Section 18).

3.13b . . . then disconnect the ignition switch connector

3.13c Remove the switch cover then the fusebox lid (arrowed)

3.13d Undo the three top screws/bolts (arrowed) . . .

3.13e ... and the two bottom bolts ...

3.13f ... then displace the holder, release the fusebox and feed it out the back, and remove the holder

14 Before installing the battery, clean the terminals and lead ends with a wire brush or knife, and emery paper.
15 Installation is the reverse of removal. When you reconnect the leads, connect the positive (+) terminal first.

Inspection and maintenance

16 All models are fitted with a sealed MF (maintenance free) battery. **Note:** *Do not attempt to remove the battery cap(s) to check the electrolyte level or battery specific gravity. Removal will damage the caps, resulting in electrolyte leakage and battery damage.* However the following checks should be regularly performed – remove the battery first (see above).
17 Check that the battery terminals and leads are clean. If corrosion is evident, clean the terminals and lead ends with a wire brush or knife, and emery paper. On installation apply a thin coat of petroleum jelly or battery terminal grease to the connections to slow further corrosion.
18 Keep the battery case clean to prevent current leakage, which can discharge the battery over a period of time (especially when it sits unused). Wash the outside of the case with a solution of baking soda and water. Rinse the battery thoroughly, then dry it.
19 Look for cracks in the case and replace the battery with a new one if any are found. If acid has been spilled on the frame or battery box, neutralise it with a baking soda and

water solution, dry it thoroughly, then touch up any damaged paint.
20 If the motorcycle sits unused for long periods of time, refer to Section 4 and charge the battery once every month to six weeks.
21 Assess the condition of the battery by measuring the voltage across the battery terminals – connect the voltmeter positive (+) probe to the battery positive (+) terminal, and the negative (–) probe to the battery negative (–) terminal. When fully charged there should be 12.6 volts (or more) present. If the voltage falls below 12.0 volts remove the battery (see above) and recharge it as described in Section 4.

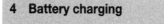

4 Battery charging

Caution: Be extremely careful when handling or working around the battery. The electrolyte is very caustic and an explosive gas (hydrogen) is given off when the battery is charging.

1 Your charger must be rated for 12 volts. Remove the battery (see Section 3). If not already done, refer to Section 3, Step 21, and check the open circuit voltage of the battery.
2 Connect the charger to the battery, making sure that the positive (+) lead on the charger is connected to the positive (+) terminal on the battery, and the negative (–) lead is connected to the negative (–) terminal. The battery should be charged at the rate and for the time specified at the beginning of the Chapter, or until the voltage

across the terminals reaches 12.8V (allow the battery to stabilise for 30 minutes after charging before taking a voltage reading). Exceeding this can cause the battery to overheat, buckling the plates and rendering it useless. Few owners will have access to an expensive current controlled charger, so if a normal domestic charger is used check that after a possible initial peak, the charge rate falls to a reasonable level – if that level is more than specified, then reduce the charging time accordingly **(see illustration)**. If the battery becomes hot during charging **stop**. Further charging will cause damage. **Note:** *In emergencies the battery can be charged at a higher rate of around 4.0 amps for a period of 1 hour. However, this is not recommended and the low amp charge is by far the safer method of charging the battery.*
3 If the recharged battery discharges rapidly when left disconnected it is likely that an internal short caused by physical damage or sulphation has occurred. A new battery will be required. A sound item will tend to lose its charge at about 1% per day.
4 Install the battery (see Section 3).
5 If the motorcycle sits unused for long periods of time, charge the battery once every month to six weeks and leave it disconnected.

5 Fuses

1 The electrical system is protected by fuses of different ratings. The fuses are housed in the fusebox, which on Bonneville, T100, Thruxton and Scrambler models is mounted behind the right-hand side panel (see Chapter 7 for removal if required), and on America and Speedmaster models is behind the fusebox cover on the left-hand side, just to the rear of the battery – remove the cover by pulling it away at the bottom to release the peg from the grommet, then release the clip at the top **(see illustration 3.13c)**.
2 Remove the fusebox lid **(see illustration)**. Each fuse is clearly marked with its rating and must only be replaced by a fuse of the same rating. The circuits relating to the fuses are marked on a label in the fusebox lid, and are listed in the Specifications at the beginning of the Chapter **(see illustration)**. There are

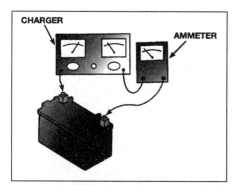

4.2 If the charger doesn't have ammeter built in, connect one in series as shown. DO NOT connect the ammeter between the battery terminals or it will be ruined

5.2a Release the lid to access the fuses

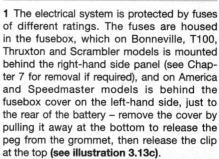

5.2b The fuse identity is marked on a label in the lid

a couple of spare fuses in the fusebox, but not all ratings are included. If a spare is used, always replace it with a new one.

3 The fuses can be removed and checked visually. There is a fuse removing tool fitted in the fusebox (see illustration). If it isn't there use your fingertips or a suitable pair of pliers. A blown fuse is easily identified by a break in the element (see illustration), or can be tested for continuity using an ohmmeter or continuity tester – if there is no continuity, it has blown.

 Warning: Never put in a fuse of a higher rating or bridge the terminals with any other substitute, however temporary it may be. Serious damage may be done to the circuit, or a fire may start.

4 If a fuse blows, be sure to check the wiring circuit very carefully for evidence of a short-circuit. Look for bare wires and chafed, melted or burned insulation. If the fuse is renewed before the cause is located, the new fuse will blow immediately.

5 Occasionally a fuse will blow or cause an open-circuit for no obvious reason. Corrosion of the fuse ends and fusebox terminals may occur and cause poor fuse contact. If this happens, remove the corrosion with a wire brush or emery paper, then spray the fuse end and terminals with electrical contact cleaner.

6 Lighting system check

1 The battery provides power for operation of the headlight, sidelight, tail light, brake light, turn signals and instrument cluster lights. If none of the lights operate, always check battery voltage before proceeding. Low battery voltage indicates either a faulty battery or a defective charging system. Refer to Section 3 for battery checks and Section 29 for charging system tests. Also check the fuses (see Section 5). When checking for a blown filament in a bulb, it is advisable to back up a visual check with a continuity test of the filament as it is not always apparent that a bulb has blown. When testing for continuity, remember that on some bulbs

5.3a Use the tool provided to remove a fuse

it is the metal body of the bulb which is the ground or earth, and make sure when testing a dual filament tail light bulb that you are testing the correct filament, and if in doubt test them both. A definitive way of testing a bulb is to connect it directly to a fully charged 12 volt battery using suitable jumper wires, and to see whether it comes on or not. Note that if there is more than one problem at the same time, it is likely to be a fault relating to a multi-function component, such as one of the fuses governing more than one circuit, or the ignition switch.

Headlight

2 If the headlight fails to work, check the bulb, the bulb terminals and the wiring connector first (see Section 7), then the fuse (see Section 5).

3 If they are good, check for battery voltage at the blue/white (HI beam) or blue/red (LO beam) wire terminal on the bulb connector with the ignition switch ON, and with the light switch (where fitted) and the dip switch set appropriately. If voltage is present, check the black wire circuit to earth (ground) for an open or poor connection.

4 If no problem is found in the wiring and connectors, check the light switches and the ignition switch (see Sections 19 and 18).

5 If no problem is found, it is possible the headlight cut-out relay in the starter circuit is faulty. Voltage to the headlight during normal use passes through the relay, but is diverted from the headlight to the starter relay when the starter button is pressed. No specific test

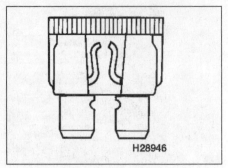

H28946

5.3b A blown fuse can be identified by a break in its element

details are given for the relay so the best way to check it is to substitute it with one that is known to be good and to see if the fault is cured. To access the relay on Bonneville, T100, Thruxton and Scrambler models remove the left-hand side panel (see Chapter 7) (see illustration). To access the relay on America and Speedmaster models remove the fuel tank (see Chapter 3) – the relay is mounted on the right-hand side of the frame on carburettor models and on the left-hand side of the frame on EFI models (see illustration).

6 If a substitute relay is not available, remove the relay and test it as follows: Check for continuity between the blue/yellow and blue wire terminals on the relay – there should be continuity. Apply 12 volts to the white/red (+) and the black/pink (–) terminals on the relay. Now there should be no continuity between the blue/yellow and blue wire terminals, but there should be continuity between the blue/yellow and black wire terminals.

7 If the relay is not faulty, test the wiring to and from it as follows. Disconnect the wiring connector from the relay. Check for battery voltage at the blue/yellow wire terminal on the connector with the ignition ON. Connect the positive (+) probe of the meter to the terminal and the negative (–) to the frame or engine. Also check for voltage at the white/red wire with the ignition ON and the starter button pressed.

8 If no power was present at the relay, check the wiring from the relay to the fuse and then to the ignition switch, and also from the relay to the starter button, for continuity.

9 If power was present at the relay, now

6.5a Headlight cut-out relay (arrowed) – Bonneville, T100, Thruxton and Scrambler

6.5b Headlight cut-out relay (arrowed) – America and Speedmaster carburettor models

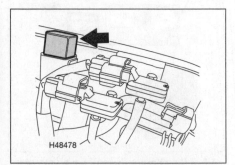

H48478

6.5c Headlight cut-out relay (arrowed) – America and Speedmaster EFI models

7.1 Undo the screws to free the rim . . .

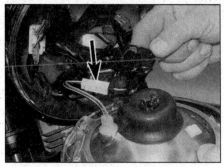

7.2 . . . then disconnect the headlight wiring connector and the sidelight wiring connector (arrowed)

check the blue wire between the relay and the light switch (where fitted) or pass switch and dimmer switch. Also check the black wire from the relay – refer to the wiring diagrams at the end of the Chapter for precise details of the wiring for your model.

Position light/parking lights

10 If the front position/parking light fails to work, check the bulb, the bulb terminals and the wiring connector first (see Section 7), then the fuse (Section 5).

11 If they are good, check for battery voltage at the yellow wire terminal on the supply side of the sidelight wiring connector, with the ignition switch turned to the park position. If voltage is present, with the bulb removed check for continuity between the wiring connector terminals on the sidelight side of the connector and the corresponding terminals in the bulbholder. If there is no continuity replace the sub-loom with a new one or repair the wiring If voltage and continuity are present, check for continuity between the black wire terminal on the supply side of the sidelight wiring connector and earth (ground). If there is no continuity, check the earth (ground) circuit for an open or poor connection. If no voltage is indicated at the yellow wire terminal, check the wiring and connectors between the sidelight and the ignition switch, then check the switch itself. Note that if the light works with the ignition switch ON but not when set to P, or vice versa, the problem lies within the ignition switch.

12 If the tail light fails to work in the park position, check it as described below.

Tail light

13 If the tail light fails to work, check the bulb, the bulb terminals and the wiring connectors first (see Sections 9 and 10), then the fuse (see Section 5).

14 If they are good, check for battery voltage at the yellow wire terminal on the supply side of the tail light main wiring connector, with the ignition switch ON and light switch (where fitted) set appropriately. If voltage is present, with the bulb removed check for continuity in the red and black wires between the wiring connector terminals on the tail light side of the connector and the corresponding terminals in the bulbholder. If voltage and continuity are present, check for continuity between the black wire terminal on the supply side of the tail light wiring connector and earth (ground). If there is no continuity, check the earth (ground) circuit for an open or poor connection.

15 If no voltage is indicated at the yellow wire terminal, check the wiring and connectors between the tail light, the light switch (where fitted) and the ignition switch, then check the switches themselves.

Brake light

16 If the brake light fails to work, check the bulb, the bulb terminals and the wiring connector first (see Section 9), then the fuse.

17 If they are good, check for battery voltage at the green/purple wire terminal on the supply side of the main tail light wiring connector, with the ignition switch ON and the brake lever or pedal applied. If voltage is present, check for continuity in the blue and black wires between

the wiring connector terminals on the tail light side of the connector and the corresponding terminals in the bulbholder. If voltage and continuity are present, check for continuity between the black wire terminal on the supply side of the tail light wiring connector and earth (ground). If there is no continuity, check the earth (ground) circuit for an open or poor connection.

18 If no voltage is indicated at the green/purple wire terminal, check the brake light switches (see Section 14), then the wiring and connectors between the tail light and the switches.

Instrument and warning lights

19 See Section 17.

Turn signal lights

20 If one light fails to work, check the bulb and the bulb terminals first, then the wiring connectors (see Section 12). If none of the turn signals work, first check the turn signal fuse (see Section 5).

21 If the fuse is good, see Section 11 for the turn signal circuit check.

| 7 | Headlight bulb and position/parking light bulb renewal |

Note: The headlight bulb is of the quartz-halogen type. Do not touch the bulb glass as skin acids will shorten the bulb's service life. If the bulb is accidentally touched, it should be wiped carefully when cold with a rag soaked in methylated spirit and dried before fitting.

⚠️ **Warning: Allow the bulb time to cool before removing it if the headlight has just been on.**

Headlight

1 Undo the screw on each side of the headlight and free the rim from the shell, noting how it locates at the top **(see illustration)**.

2 Disconnect the headlight and sidelight wiring connectors **(see illustration)**.

3 Remove the rubber dust cover **(see illustration)**. Release the bulb retaining clip then remove the bulb – to release the clip first release the left-hand outer hook, then release the central rear section, followed by the right-hand outer hook **(see illustrations)**.

7.3a Remove the dust cover . . .

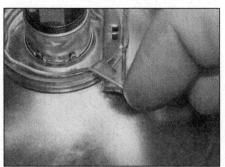

7.3b . . . then release the retaining clip . . .

7.3c . . . and remove the bulb

7.6 Make sure the rim locates correctly

7.10a Pull the bulbholder out . . .

7.10b . . . then carefully pull the bulb out of the holder

8.3 Unscrew the bolt (arrowed) on each side

8.4a Either unscrew the nut (arrowed) and withdraw the bolt to free the shell from its mount . . .

8.4b . . . or unscrew the bolt (arrowed) to free the complete headlight from the yoke

4 Fit the new bulb in a reverse order, bearing in mind the information in the **Note** above. Make sure the bulb and retaining clip locate correctly.
5 Install the dust cover with the TOP mark at the top.
6 Fit the rim onto the shell, making sure it locates correctly, and secure it with the screws (**see illustration**).
7 Check the operation of the headlight.

 HAYNES HiNT *Always use a paper towel or dry cloth when handling new bulbs to prevent injury if the bulb should break and to increase bulb life.*

Position/parking light

8 Undo the screw on each side of the headlight and free the rim from the shell, noting how it locates at the top (**see illustration 7.1**).
9 Disconnect the headlight and sidelight wiring connectors (**see illustration 7.2**).

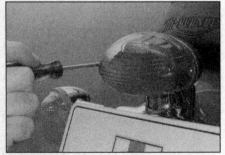

9.1a Undo the screws . . .

10 Pull the bulbholder out of the headlight, then remove the bulb (**see illustrations**). Fit the new bulb in the bulbholder, then fit the bulbholder into the headlight, making sure it correctly seated.
11 Fit the rim onto the shell, making sure it locates correctly, and secure it with the screws (**see illustration 7.6**).
12 Check the operation of the light.

8 Headlight assembly

Removal

1 Undo the screw on each side of the headlight and free the rim from the shell, noting how it locates at the top (**see illustration 7.1**).
2 Disconnect the headlight and sidelight wiring connectors to free the beam unit (**see illustration 7.2**).
3 On Bonneville, T100, Thruxton and

9.1b . . . and remove the lens . . .

Scrambler models unscrew the bolt on each side, noting the washer with the bolt and the rubber damper and plate between the shell and each bracket (**see illustration**). Free the shell from between the brackets and feed all the wiring out through the hole in the back, disconnecting the connectors as required, freeing it from the clips, and noting the routing.
4 On America and Speedmaster models either unscrew the nut, remove the washer and withdraw the bolt securing the shell on its mounting and remove the shell on its own (**see illustration**), or unscrew the mounting bolt on the underside of the bottom yoke and remove the complete assembly, noting the grommet and sleeve (**see illustration**). Feed all the wiring out through the hole in the back, disconnecting the connectors as required, freeing it from the clips, and noting the routing.

Installation

5 Installation is the reverse of removal. Make sure the rubber seal is correctly fitted in the wiring hole in the back. Check the operation of the headlight and sidelight and all the handlebar switch functions, and on Bonneville, T100, Thruxton and Scrambler models the ignition switch functions. Check and adjust the headlight aim (see Chapter 1).

9 Brake/tail light bulb renewal

1 Undo the two lens screws and remove the lens (**see illustrations**).

9.2 . . . and the bulb

10.1 Disconnect the tail light wiring connector

10.6 Unscrew the nuts (arrowed) and remove the tail light

2 Push the bulb into the holder and twist it anti-clockwise to remove it **(see illustration)**.

3 Check the socket terminals for corrosion and clean them if necessary. Line up the pins of the new bulb with the slots in the socket, then push the bulb in and turn it clockwise until it locks into place. **Note:** *The pins on the bulb are offset so it can only be installed one way. It is a good idea to use a paper towel or dry cloth when handling the new bulb to prevent injury if the bulb should break and to increase bulb life.*

4 Install the lens – do not overtighten the screws as it is easy to crack the lens.

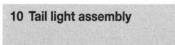

10 Tail light assembly

Removal

Bonneville, T100, Thruxton and Scrambler

1 Remove the seat (see Chapter 7). Trace the wiring from the tail light and disconnect it at the connector **(see illustration)**. Feed the wiring back to the light, noting its routing and freeing it from any ties.

2 Unscrew the three nuts on the underside of the rear mudguard, noting the collars and rubber grommets. Remove the tail light/turn signal assembly and retrieve the rubber pad.

3 To detach the light unit undo the three screws. Disconnect the turn signal wiring connectors and remove the light with the wiring harness.

4 Check the rubber pad and grommets for damage, deformation and deterioration and replace them with new ones if necessary.

America and Speedmaster

5 Remove the seat(s) (see Chapter 7). Undo the screw securing the wiring connector cover and lift it off the air filter housing **(see illustration 3.13a)**. Trace the wiring from the tail light and disconnect it at the connector **(see illustration 3.13b)**. Feed the wiring back to the light, noting its routing and freeing it from any ties.

6 Unscrew the three nuts on the underside of the rear mudguard, noting the collars and rubber grommets **(see illustration)**. Remove the tail light and retrieve the rubber pad.

7 Check the rubber pad and grommets for damage, deformation and deterioration and replace them with new ones if necessary.

Installation

8 Installation is the reverse of removal. Check the operation of the tail light and the brake light.

11 Turn signal circuit check

1 Most turn signal problems are the result of a burned out bulb or a corroded socket. This is especially true when the turn signals function properly in one direction, but fail to flash in the other direction. Check the bulbs and the sockets (see Section 12) and the

wiring connectors. Also, check the fuse (see Section 5) and the switch (see Section 19).

2 The battery provides power for operation of the turn signal lights, so if they do not operate, also check the battery voltage. Low battery voltage indicates either a faulty battery or a defective charging system. Refer to Section 3 for battery checks and Section 29 for charging system tests.

3 If the bulbs, sockets, connectors, fuse, switch and battery are good, the turn signal relay may be faulty – no test details are given for the relay so the best way to check it is to substitute it with one that is known to be good and to see if the fault is cured. To access the relay on Bonneville, T100, Thruxton and Scrambler models remove the left-hand side panel (see Chapter 7) **(see illustration)**. To access the relay on America and Speedmaster models remove the fuel tank (see Chapter 3) – the relay is mounted on the right-hand side of the frame **(see illustration)**.

4 If a substitute relay is not available, or if the relay is not faulty, test the wiring to and from it as follows. Disconnect the wiring connector from the relay. Check for battery voltage at the orange/green wire terminal on the connector with the ignition ON. Connect the positive (+) probe of the meter to the terminal and the negative (–) to the frame or engine.

5 If no power was present at the relay, check the wiring from the relay to the fuse and then to the ignition switch for continuity.

6 If power was present at the relay, now check the light green/brown wire between the relay and the turn signal switch, then check

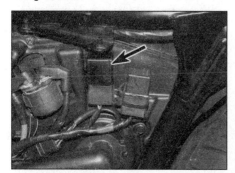

11.3a Turn signal relay (arrowed) – Bonneville, T100 and Thruxton

11.3b Turn signal relay (arrowed) – America and Speedmaster carburettor models

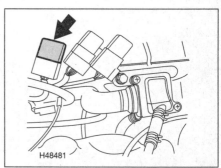

11.3c Turn signal relay (arrowed) – America and Speedmaster EFI models

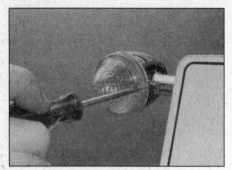

12.1a Undo the screws . . .

12.1b . . . and remove the lens . . .

12.2 . . . and the bulb

the green/red and green/white wires from the switch to the turn signals themselves. Also check for continuity between the black wire from the relay and earth (ground). If there is no continuity, check the earth (ground) circuit for an open or poor connection. If the switch, wiring and connectors are all good replace the relay with a new one.

12 Turn signal bulb renewal

1 Undo the screws securing the lens to the housing and remove it **(see illustrations)**.
2 Push the bulb into the holder and twist it anti-clockwise to remove it **(see illustration)**.
3 Check the socket terminals for corrosion and clean them if necessary.
4 Line up the pins of the new bulb with the slots in the socket, then push the bulb in and

turn it clockwise until it locks into place.
5 Fit the lens, making sure it locates correctly, then install the screws.

13 Turn signal removal

Removal – Bonneville, T100, Thruxton and Scrambler

Front

1 Undo the screw on each side of the headlight and free the rim from the shell, noting how it locates at the top **(see illustration 7.1)**.
2 Disconnect the headlight and sidelight wiring connectors to free the beam unit **(see illustration 7.2)**.
3 Disconnect the turn signal wiring connectors, then draw the wiring out of the back of the shell.

4 On Thruxton and Scrambler models pull the rubber boot off the turn signal mount **(see illustration)**.
5 Unscrew the nut, remove the washers, noting their order, and withdraw the turn signal from the headlight bracket, taking care not to snag the wiring connectors **(see illustration)**.

Rear

6 Remove the tail light (see Section 10, Steps 1, 2 and 3).
7 Unscrew the nut and withdraw the turn signal from the bracket, taking care not to snag the wiring connectors.

Removal – America and Speedmaster

Front

8 On 2002 to 2010 America models and all Speedmaster models, trace the wiring from the turn signal and disconnect it at the connector located inside the handlebar switch housing. Unscrew the bolt and remove the turn signal from the bracket **(see illustration)**.
9 The front turn signals on America models from 2011-on are mounted on the bottom yoke. Release the headlight from its shell (see Section 7) and locate then disconnect the turn signal wiring connector inside the shell (right-hand side wiring has red tape). Remove the two screws from the wiring cover on the front of the bottom yoke and thread the wiring through the cable clip **(see illustration)**. Now unscrew the turn signal retaining nut to free it from the mounting bracket.

Rear

10 Remove the licence plate. Disconnect the turn signal wiring connector **(see illustration)**.

13.4 Pull back the boot to reveal the nut (arrowed) – Thruxton and Scrambler

13.5 Turn signal mounting nut (arrowed) – Bonneville and T100

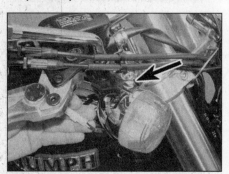

13.8 Disconnect the wiring connector then unscrew the bolt (arrowed)

13.9 Wiring cover screws (arrowed) – 2011-on America

13.10 Disconnect the relevant wiring connector then unscrew the nut

14.2 Pull the front brake switch wiring connectors off their terminals

14.3a Pull the boot off the connector then the connector off the terminals – Bonneville and T100 shown

14.3b Rear brake light switch (arrowed) – America and Speedmaster

11 Unscrew the nut, remove the washers, noting their order, and withdraw the turn signal from the bracket, taking care not to snag the wiring connectors.

Installation

12 Installation is the reverse of removal. Where present set the turn signal locating peg in its hole in the bracket (see illustrations 13.4 and 5). Make sure the wiring is correctly routed and securely connected. Check the operation of the turn signals.

14 Brake light switches

Circuit check

1 Before checking the switches, check the brake light circuit (see Section 6, Steps 16, 17 and 18).
2 The front brake light switch is mounted on the underside of the master cylinder. Disconnect the wiring connectors from the switch (see illustration).
3 The rear brake light switch is mounted behind the right-hand side panel on Bonneville, T100 and Thruxton models, and on the inside of the frame behind the engine on the left-hand side on America and Speedmaster models. The switch is hydraulically actuated by brake fluid pressure when the brake is applied. On Bonneville, T100 and Thruxton models remove the right-hand side panel to access the switch (see Chapter 7). Lift the rubber boot and disconnect the wiring connector from the switch (see illustrations).
4 On Scrambler models, the rear brake light switch is mounted on the inside of the rider's right-hand footrest bracket (see illustration). The switch is connected to the brake pedal by a short spring. Remove the right-hand side panel and trace the wiring from the switch to the connector (see illustration).
5 Using a continuity tester, connect the probes to the terminals on the switch. With the brake lever or pedal at rest, there should be no continuity. With the brake lever or pedal applied, there should be continuity. If the

switch does not behave as described, replace it with a new one.
6 If the switches are good, check for voltage at the black/blue wire (front switch) or orange/green wire in the connector with the ignition switch ON – there should be battery voltage. If there's no voltage present, check the fuse (Section 5) and the wiring between the switch and the fusebox (see the *Wiring Diagrams* at the end of this Chapter). If there is voltage, check the wiring and connectors between the switch and the brake light bulb.

Switch renewal
Front brake light switch

7 The switch is mounted on the underside of the master cylinder. Disconnect the wiring connectors from the switch (see illustration 14.2). Undo the screw and remove the switch (see illustration).

14.4a Rear brake light switch (arrowed) – Scrambler models

14.7 Front brake light switch screw (arrowed)

8 Installation is the reverse of removal. Check the operation of the switch.

Rear brake light switch

9 The rear brake light switch is mounted behind the right-hand side panel on Bonneville, T100 and Thruxton models, and on the inside of the frame behind the engine on the left-hand side on America and Speedmaster models. The switch is hydraulically actuated by brake fluid pressure when the brake is applied. On Bonneville, T100 and Thruxton models remove the right-hand side panel to access the switch (see Chapter 7). Lift the rubber boot and disconnect the wiring connector from the switch (see illustrations 14.3a and b).
10 Unscrew and remove the switch (see illustration). Discard the sealing washers as new ones must be used on installation.

14.4b Location of the rear brake light switch wiring connector

14.10 Unscrew the switch and discard the sealing washers

14.11 Fit the switch using a new sealing washer on each side of the hose union

To retain the fluid in the hose either plug the hose using another suitable short piece of hose fitted through the eye of the banjo union (it must be a fairly tight fit to seal it properly), block it using a suitable bolt with sealing washers and a capped (domed) nut, or wrap some plastic foodwrap tightly around (a finger cut off a latex glove also works well), the object being to minimise fluid loss and prevent dirt entering the system. Whatever you do, also cover the end of the hose in rag, just in case. Similarly block or cover the master cylinder (Bonneville and T100) or the pipe/hose joint piece (Thruxton, America and Speedmaster) that the switch threads into. Alternatively place the hose end into a jar or other suitable container to collect the fluid – make sure the container is properly supported and do not knock it over.

11 Installation is the reverse of removal. Use new sealing washers when installing the rear brake switch and tighten it to the torque setting specified at the beginning of the Chapter **(see illustration)**. Check the operation of the switch.

12 On Scrambler models, the switch is mounted on the inside of the right-hand rider's footrest bracket **(see illustration 14.4a)**. Unhook the return spring from the brake pedal.

13 Remove the right-hand side panel and trace the wiring from the switch to the connector **(see illustration 14.4b)**. Disconnect the connector and release the wiring from any clips or ties.

14 Pull the boot off the lower end of the switch and unscrew the switch from its

15.1 The driven housing is secured by two screws (arrowed)

mounting bracket. If necessary, press the switch sleeve out of the mounting bracket.

15 Installation is the reverse of removal. Make sure the brake light is activated just before the brake takes effect. If adjustment is necessary, hold the switch and turn the adjusting sleeve until the light is activated as required.

---

15 Instrument panel checks

2001 to 2009 models (with cable-operated speedometer)

Speedometer

1 If the speedometer does not work, and it is not due to a broken or seized cable or its drive housing on the front wheel, then it must be replaced with a new one. Note that on America and Speedmaster models the driven housing on the back of the speedo is available as a separate part, so it is worth checking parts availability beforehand **(see illustration)**.

Tachometer – T100, Thruxton and Speedmaster

2 If the tachometer does not work, access the wiring which enters the back of the instrument (see Section 16) and test as follows. Check for continuity in the red wire between the tachometer and the ignition control unit (see Chapter 4 to access it).

Check for continuity between the brown wire and earth (ground). Check for battery voltage in the green/red wire with the ignition ON. If all the wiring and connectors are good substitute the tachometer with one that is known to be good and see if the fault is cured. If not the ignition control unit could be faulty.

2010-on models (with electronic speedometer)

3 The information supply between the ECM and instruments utilises Controlled Area Networking (CAN)-bus technology to create an electronic information network between them. This allows rapid and reliable data transfer around the network. To reduce the amount of wiring in the network, the components are designed to communicate via one or two wires (the red and blue from terminals B28 and B27 of the ECM). These wires are known as a 'data bus'. The instruments have an integral transceiver which receives data 'packets' along the bus.

4 If there is a problem with the can-bus network the MIL (malfunction indicator lamp) in the instruments will come on and the system will display a specific P-code when the fault is downloaded (see Chapter 3B, Section 8).

---

16 Instrument panel and speedometer cable – 2001 to 2009 models

Instrument panel – Bonneville, T100, Thruxton and Scrambler

1 Undo the screw on each side of the headlight and free the rim from the shell, noting how it locates at the top **(see illustration 7.1)**.

2 Disconnect the headlight and sidelight wiring connectors to free the beam unit **(see illustration 7.2)**.

3 Locate the instrument panel wiring connector and disconnect it, noting that EFI models have two connectors. Feed the wiring out of the back of the headlight shell, freeing it from any clips.

4 Unscrew the bolts securing the instrument panel **(see illustrations)**. Displace the panel

16.4a Instrument panel bolts (arrowed) - Bonneville

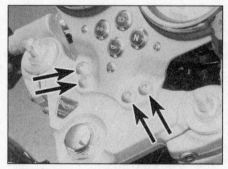

16.4b Instrument panel bolts (arrowed) – Thruxton

16.4c Instrument panel bolts (arrowed) - Scrambler

16.4d Unscrew the ring and detach the cable

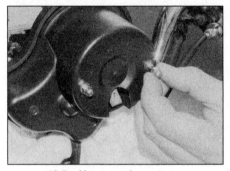

16.5a Unscrew the nuts . . .

16.5b . . . and remove the cover . . .

16.5c . . . and the inner washers

16.5d Use a jewellers screwdriver . . .

16.5e . . . to remove the screw . . .

and unscrew the speedometer cable retaining ring **(see illustration)**.

5 To remove the speedometer, unscrew the nuts and remove the washers securing the cover and draw it off **(see illustrations)**. Remove the inner washers from the studs **(see illustration)**. Undo the small screw in the centre of the trip reset knob and remove the knob **(see illustrations)**. Withdraw the bulbholders, then lift the speedometer out of the panel, noting the rubber damper **(see illustration)**.

6 To remove the tachometer on T100 and Thruxton, unscrew the nuts and remove the washers securing the cover and draw it off **(see illustration)**. Remove the inner washers from the studs. Disconnect the wiring. Withdraw the bulbholders, then lift the tachometer out of the panel, noting the rubber damper.

7 Assembly and installation are the reverse of removal.

Speedometer – America and Speedmaster

8 Undo the screw on each side of the headlight and free the rim from the shell, noting how it locates at the top.

9 Disconnect the headlight and sidelight wiring connectors to free the beam unit.

10 Locate the speedometer wiring connector and disconnect it, noting that EFI models have two connectors. Feed the wiring out of the back of the headlight shell, freeing it from any clips.

11 Unscrew the cable retaining ring **(see illustration)**. Unscrew the bolts securing the speedometer bracket to the top yoke and remove the speedometer.

12 To disassemble the speedometer, undo the screws securing the driven housing to the back of the cover and detach the housing **(see illustration 15.1)**. Undo the small screw in the centre of the trip reset knob and remove the knob **(see illustration)**. Undo the

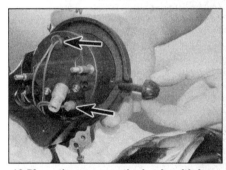

16.5f . . . then remove the knob, withdraw the bulbholders (arrowed) and remove the speedometer

screws securing the cover and draw it off. Withdraw the bulbholders from the speedo, then unscrew the nuts, remove the washers and lift the speedo off its bracket, noting the rubber dampers.

13 Installation is the reverse of removal.

16.6 Tachometer cover nuts (arrowed)

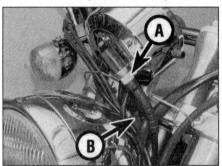

16.11 Cable retaining ring (A) and speedometer bracket bolts (B)

16.12 Undo the screw (arrowed) in the centre of the knob

16.14a Undo the screws (arrowed) . . .

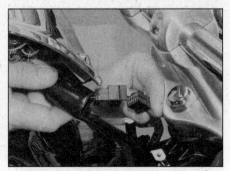

16.14b . . . then displace the panel and disconnect the wiring connector

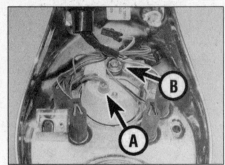

16.15 Tachometer bulbholder (A) and mounting nut (B)

Tachometer – Speedmaster

14 Undo the screws securing the instrument panel to the fuel tank (see illustration). Lift the panel and disconnect the main wiring connector (see illustration).

15 Disconnect the tachometer wiring and pull the bulbholder out (see illustration).

16 Unscrew the nut securing the tachometer to the bracket and draw the tacho out of the top of the panel.

17 Installation is the reverse of removal.

Speedometer cable

18 On Bonneville, T100, Thruxton and Scrambler models unscrew the instrument panel bolts and displace the panel from the top yoke (see illustration 16.4a, b or c).

19 Unscrew the cable retaining ring from the rear of the instrument cluster and detach the cable (see illustration 16.4c or 16.11).

20 Undo the screw securing the lower end of the cable to the drive housing on the left-hand side of the front wheel (see illustration).

21 Withdraw the cable from the guide(s) and remove it from the bike, noting its routing.

22 Route the cable correctly through its guide(s).

23 Connect the cable upper end to the instrument cluster and tighten the retaining ring. On Bonneville, T100, Thruxton and Scrambler models, install the instrument panel in the reverse order of removal.

24 Connect the cable lower end to the drive housing, aligning the slot in the cable end with the drive tab, and secure it with its screw (see illustration).

25 Check that the cable doesn't restrict steering movement or interfere with any other components.

Instrument panel bulbs – all models

26 To access the instrument illumination bulbs refer to the appropriate Steps in Section 16 and either remove the cover from the back of the speedometer or, on Speedmaster models, displace the panel on the fuel tank. Draw the bulbholder out of the instrument, then pull the bulb out of the holder (see illustrations).

16.20 Undo the screw and detach the cable

27 To access the warning light bulbs on Bonneville, T100, Thruxton and Scrambler models, unscrew the instrument panel bolts and displace the panel from the top yoke (see illustration 16.4a, b or c). On

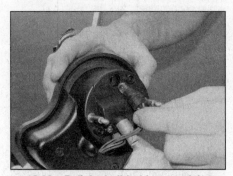

16.26a Pull the bulbholder out of the instrument . . .

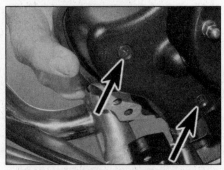

16.27a Undo the screws (arrowed) . . .

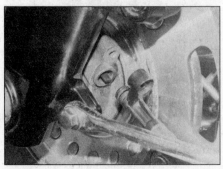

16.24 Locate the drive tab in the slot in the end of the cable

Bonneville, T100 and Thruxton models, undo the warning light cover screws on the back of the instrument cluster and remove the cover (see illustrations). On Scrambler models, unscrew the nuts and remove the cover from

16.26b . . . then pull the bulb out of the holder

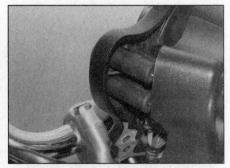

16.27b . . . and remove the cover – Bonneville, T100 and Thruxton

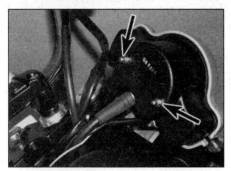

16.27c Undo the nuts (arrowed) . . .

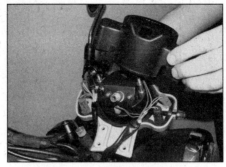

16.27d . . . and remove the cover –
Scrambler models

16.29a Push the bulbholder out of the top
of the panel and remove the lens . . .

16.29b . . . then draw the bulbholder back
out . . .

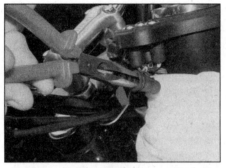

16.29c . . . and carefully remove the bulb
using pliers to grip it if necessary

16.30 Make sure the tabs and slots (arrowed)
are aligned so everything locates correctly

the back of the speedometer (see illustrations).

28 To access the warning light bulbs on America and Speedmaster models, undo the screws securing the instrument panel to the fuel tank (see illustration 16.14a). Lift the panel and disconnect the main wiring connector (see illustrations 16.14b).

29 Push the relevant bulbholder out of the front of the panel, then carefully prise the lens out of the top of the holder (see illustration). Carefully remove the bulb, peeling the rubber boot back to grip it or using pliers carefully if required (see illustration).

30 Fit the new bulb into the holder, then fit the holder back into the panel, making sure the locating tabs and slots align when fitting the warning light lens into the top of the holder (see illustration).

31 Check the operation of the bulb when reassembly is complete.

17 Instrument panel – 2010-on models

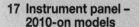

1 Before disturbing the instruments, disconnect the battery negative terminal as described in Section 3.

Bonneville, T100, Scrambler, Thruxton

2 To remove an individual instrument from the panel, unscrew the two domed nuts from the base of the instrument cover and withdraw the cover from the mounting studs

(see illustrations). Disconnect the wiring connector and lift the instrument out of the bracket (see illustrations).

3 Certain Bonneville models (not the SE) may be fitted with a speedometer and warning light panel as shown in Section 16. Access

17.2a Two domed nuts (arrowed) . . .

17.2c Squeeze in its tabs and pull off the
connector . . .

the speedometer as described in the previous paragraph. To access the LED warning light unit, remove the two long screws to release the cover from its base. Disconnect the wire connector, then remove the two screws to free the warning light unit from the instrument bracket.

17.2b . . . retain the instrument cover

17.2d . . . then lift the instrument out of its
bracket

17.4 Speedometer cover screw – America and Speedmaster

America and Speedmaster

Speedometer

4 Remove the single screw from the base of the speedometer cover and withdraw the cover (see illustration). Disconnect the wiring connector.

5 Remove the two screws to free the cover mounting bracket, noting how the screws thread into the speedometer retaining bolts below them. Remove these bolts to free the speedometer from its mounting bracket, taking note of the position of the damping rubbers and plate.

Instrument panel (inc. Tachometer on Speedmaster)

6 Refer to the procedure in Section 16, Steps 14 to 16, noting that the warning lights and instrument illumination are LEDs.

All models

7 Further dismantling of the instruments is not possible and they can be regarded as sealed units. All instrument illumination and warning lights are LEDs.

18 Ignition (main) switch

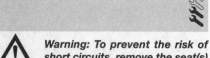

⚠ *Warning: To prevent the risk of short circuits, remove the seat(s) and disconnect the battery negative (–) lead before making any ignition (main) switch checks.*

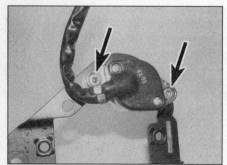

18.7 Ignition switch bolts (arrowed) – America and Speedmaster

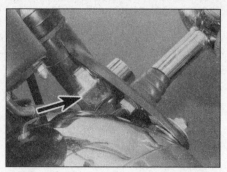

18.6 Ignition switch (arrowed) – Bonneville, T100 and Thruxton

Check

1 On Bonneville, T100 and Thruxton models, undo the screw on each side of the headlight and free the rim from the shell, noting how it locates at the top (see illustration 7.1). Disconnect the headlight and sidelight wiring connectors to free the beam unit (see illustration 7.2).

2 On America and Speedmaster models remove the seat(s) (see Chapter 7). Undo the screw securing the wiring connector cover and lift it off the air filter housing (see illustration 3.13a and b).

3 Trace the wiring from the ignition switch and disconnect it at the connector.

4 Using an ohmmeter or a continuity tester and making the checks on the switch side of the connector, check the continuity of the connector terminal pairs (see the *Wiring Diagrams* at the end of this Chapter). Continuity should exist between the terminals connected by a solid line on the diagram when the switch key is turned to the indicated position.

5 If the switch fails any of the tests, replace it with a new one.

Removal and installation

6 On Bonneville, T100 and Thruxton models, remove the headlight assembly (see Section 8) – the switch is bolted to the inside of the left-hand bracket (see illustration).

7 On America and Speedmaster models remove the battery and its holder (See Section 3) – the switch is bolted to the back of the holder (see illustration).

8 On Scrambler models, the switch is bolted

18.8 Ignition switch (arrowed) – Scrambler models

to the back of the left-hand headlight bracket (see illustration).

9 If not already done, follow the procedure above and disconnect the switch wiring connector, then unscrew the bolts securing the switch and remove it.

10 Installation is the reverse of removal. Check the operation of the switch.

19 Handlebar switches

Check

1 Generally speaking, the switches are reliable and trouble-free. Most troubles, when they do occur, are caused by dirty or corroded contacts, but wear and breakage of internal parts is a possibility that should not be overlooked. If breakage does occur, the entire switch and related wiring harness will have to be replaced with a new one, as individual parts are not available.

2 The switches can be checked for continuity using an ohmmeter or a continuity test light. Make sure the ignition is switched OFF.

3 Undo the screw on each side of the headlight and free the rim from the shell, noting how it locates at the top (see illustration 7.1).

4 Disconnect the headlight and sidelight wiring connectors to free the beam unit (see illustration 7.2).

5 Trace the wiring from the switch housing being checked and disconnect it at the connector inside the headlight shell. Make the checks on the switch side of the connector.

6 Check for continuity between the relevant terminals of the connector with the relevant switch or button in its different positions (i.e. switch off/button released – no continuity, switch on/button pushed – continuity) – see the *wiring diagrams* at the end of this Chapter. Continuity should exist between the terminals connected by a solid line on the diagram when the switch is in its on position or the button is pressed.

7 If the continuity check indicates a problem exists, displace the switch housing (see below) and spray the switch contacts with electrical contact cleaner (there is no need to remove the switch completely). If they are accessible, the contacts can be scraped clean with a knife or polished with crocus cloth. If switch components are damaged or broken, it should be obvious when the switch is disassembled.

Removal

8 If the switch is to be removed from the bike, rather than just displaced from the handlebar, undo the screw on each side of the headlight and free the rim from the shell, noting how it locates at the top (see illustration 7.1). Disconnect the headlight and sidelight

19.10a Undo the screws (arrowed) . . .

19.10b . . . and detach the switch housing

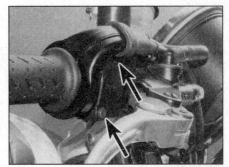

19.11a Right-hand switch housing screws (arrowed) – Thruxton and Scrambler

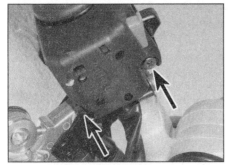

19.11b Left-hand switch housing screws (arrowed) – Thruxton and Scrambler

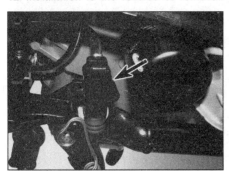

19.12 Ensure pin on switch housing locates in hole (arrowed) – Thruxton and Scrambler

wiring connectors to free the beam unit **(see illustration 7.2)**.

9 Trace the wiring from the switch housing and disconnect it at the connector inside the headlight shell. Work back along the harness, freeing it from all clips and ties, and feed it to the switch, noting its routing. Also disconnect the front brake light switch wiring connectors and/or displace the clutch switch (see Section 14 or 21).

10 On Bonneville, T100, America and Speedmaster models unscrew the handlebar switch housing screws and detach the housing **(see illustrations)**.

11 On Thruxton and Scrambler models unscrew the handlebar switch screws and free the switch by separating the halves **(see illustrations)**.

Installation

12 Installation is the reverse of removal.

Make sure the wiring connectors are correctly routed and securely connected. On Thruxton and Scrambler models when assembling the switch halves locate the pin on the housing into the hole in the handlebar **(see illustration)**.

20 Sidestand switch

Check

1 The sidestand switch is mounted on the frame next to the sidestand pivot **(see illustration)**. The switch is part of the safety circuit which prevents or stops the engine running if the transmission is in gear whilst the sidestand is down, and prevents the engine from being started if the transmission is in

gear unless the sidestand is up and the clutch lever is pulled in.

2 To access the wiring connector on Bonneville, T100, Thruxton and Scrambler models remove the left-hand side panel (see Chapter 7). Trace the wiring from the switch and disconnect it at the connector **(see illustrations)**. If on America and Speedmaster models the connector proves difficult to get at, displace or remove the fuel tank (see Chapter 3A or 3B).

3 Check the operation of the switch using an ohmmeter or continuity test light. Connect the meter between the terminals on the switch side of the connector. With the sidestand down there should be continuity (zero resistance) between the terminals, and with the stand up there should be no continuity (infinite resistance).

4 If the switch does not perform as expected, and the wiring and connectors are good, the switch is defective and must be replaced with a new one.

5 If the switch is good, check the other components in the starter safety circuit (clutch switch, neutral switch and diodes) as described in the relevant sections of this Chapter. If all components are good, check the wiring and connectors between the various components (see the *wiring diagrams* at the end of this book).

Removal and installation

6 Disconnect the switch wiring connector (see Step 2). Feed the wiring back to the switch noting its routing and freeing it from any clips or ties.

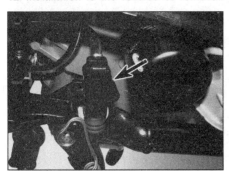

20.1 Location of the sidestand switch (arrowed) – Scrambler models

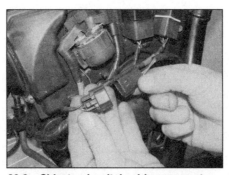

20.2a Sidestand switch wiring connector – Bonneville, T100 and Thruxton

20.2b Sidestand switch wiring connector (arrowed) – America and Speedmaster

20.7a Sidestand switch screws (arrowed) – Bonneville, T100 and Thruxton

20.7b Sidestand switch screws (arrowed) – America and Speedmaster

7 Undo the screws securing the switch and remove it, noting how it locates **(see illustrations)**.

8 Fit the new switch and tighten the screws.

9 Make sure the wiring is correctly routed up to the connector and retained by any clips and ties. Reconnect the wiring connector.

10 Check the operation of the switch.

21 Clutch switch

Check

1 The clutch switch is mounted in the clutch lever bracket. The switch is part of the safety circuit which prevents or stops the engine running if the transmission is in gear whilst the sidestand is down, and prevents the engine from starting if the transmission is in gear unless the sidestand is up and the clutch lever is pulled in. The switch isn't adjustable.

2 To check the switch, ease back the connector retaining ring, then carefully peel back the rubber boot to reveal the connectors **(see illustrations)**. Connect the probes of an ohmmeter or a continuity test light to the two switch terminals. With the clutch lever pulled in, continuity should be indicated. With the clutch lever out, no continuity (infinite resistance) should be indicated.

3 If the switch is good, check the other components in the starter safety circuit (sidestand switch, neutral switch and diodes) as described in the relevant sections of this Chapter. If all components are good, check the wiring and connectors between the various components (see the *wiring diagrams* at the end of this book).

Renewal

4 The switch is mounted in the clutch lever bracket and is an integral component of the left-hand switch assembly.

5 Carefully push up on the catch on the underside of the switch and withdraw it from the lever bracket **(see illustrations)**.

6 Remove the left-hand handlebar switch (see Section 19).

7 Installation is the reverse of removal. Make sure the switch is correctly aligned. Check the operation of the switch.

22 Diodes

1 The diodes are part of the starter lockout circuit which prevents or stops the engine running if the transmission is in gear whilst the sidestand is down, and prevents the engine from starting if the transmission is in gear unless the sidestand is up and the clutch lever is pulled in.

2 Refer to the appropriate wiring diagram at the end of this Chapter to identify the diode unit wire colours. The diodes will only allow current to flow in the direction of the arrowhead.

23 Neutral switch

Check

1 The switch is part of the safety circuit which prevents or stops the engine running if the transmission is in gear whilst the sidestand is down, and prevents the engine from starting

21.2a Ease the retaining ring off . . .

21.2b . . . then pull the boot back to reveal the terminals (arrowed)

21.5a Release the catch using a small screwdriver . . .

21.5b . . . and withdraw the switch from the bracket

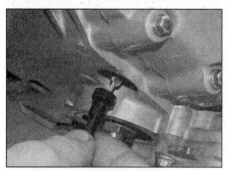

23.3a Pull back the boot . . .

23.3b . . . then pull the connector off the terminal

23.9 Undo the switch and discard the sealing washer

if the transmission is in gear unless the sidestand is up and the clutch lever is pulled in. Before checking the electrical circuit, check the fuse (see Section 5) and the neutral light bulb (see Section 17).
2 The switch is located in the bottom of the engine on the right-hand side near the oil filter.
3 Pull the rubber boot off the switch then pull the wiring connector off the terminal (see illustrations). Make sure the transmission is in neutral. With the connector disconnected and the ignition switch ON, the neutral light should be out. If not, the wire between the connector and instrument cluster must be earthed (grounded) at some point.
4 With the ignition ON check for voltage at the wiring connector. If there is no voltage check the wiring to the switch (see *Wiring Diagrams* at the end of this Chapter). If there is voltage, earth (ground) the connector on the crankcase and check that the neutral light comes on.
5 Check for continuity between the switch terminal and the crankcase. With the transmission in neutral, there should be continuity. With the transmission in gear, there should be no continuity. If the tests prove otherwise, then the switch is faulty.
6 If the switch is good, check the other components in the starter safety circuit (sidestand switch, clutch switch and diodes) as described in the relevant sections of this Chapter. If all components are good, check the wiring and connectors between the various components (see the *wiring diagrams* at the end of this book).

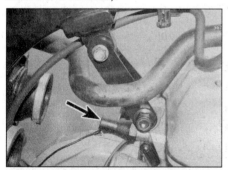

24.3a Oil pressure switch (arrowed) - pull the rubber boot off to access the wiring connector

Removal

7 The switch is located in the bottom of the engine on the right-hand side near the oil filter.
8 Pull the rubber boot off the switch then pull the wiring connector off the terminal (see illustrations 23.3a and b).
9 Clean the area around the switch, then unscrew it from the crankcase (see illustration). Discard the sealing washer.
10 Check the tip of the plunger for wear and damage, and check whether the plunger moves in and out of the body.

Installation

11 Install the switch using a new sealing washer and tighten it to the torque setting specified at the beginning of the Chapter (see illustration 23.9).
12 Connect the wiring connector and fit the rubber boot, then check the operation of the neutral light (see illustrations 23.3b and a).

24 Oil pressure switch

Check

1 When the ignition is first turned ON and before the engine is started, the oil warning light should come on. When the engine is started it should extinguish. If it comes on whilst the engine is running, stop the engine

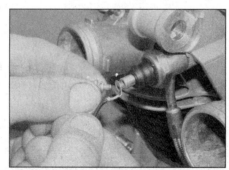

24.3b Undo the screw and detach the wire

immediately and carry out an oil level check. If the oil pressure warning does not come on when the ignition is first turned on, check the bulb (see Section 17), then the fuse (see Section 5).
2 The oil pressure switch is screwed into the back of the cylinder head between the intake ducts (see illustration 24.3a) – depending on the tools you have available (an angled or very short Phillips screwdriver is needed) you may need to remove the carburettors (see Chapter 3 if necessary).
3 Pull the rubber boot off the switch (see illustration). Undo the screw and detach the wiring connector from the switch (see illustration). With the connector disconnected and the ignition switch ON, the oil warning light should be out. If not, the wire between the connector and instrument cluster must be earthed (grounded) at some point.
4 With the ignition ON check for voltage at the wiring connector. If there is no voltage check the wiring to the switch (see *Wiring Diagrams* at the end of this Chapter). If there is voltage, earth (ground) the connector on the crankcase and check that the oil warning light comes on. If it does, the switch is faulty. If not, check the main earth connections between the engine and frame and back to the battery.
5 Now check for continuity between the switch terminal and the hex on the switch body – there should be continuity with the engine at rest and no continuity with the engine running. If the switch does not behave as described a new one must be fitted.

Removal

6 The oil pressure switch is screwed into the back of the cylinder head between the intake ducts (see illustration 24.3a) – depending on the tools you have available (an angled or very short Phillips screwdriver is needed) you may need to remove the carburettors (see Chapter 3 if necessary).
7 Pull the rubber boot off the switch (see illustration 24.3a). Undo the screw and detach the wiring connector from the switch (see illustration 24.3b).
8 Unscrew the switch, making sure the oil pipe union does not turn with it and bend

24.8 Unscrew the switch and discard the sealing washers

25.3 Disconnect the wiring connectors (arrowed) from the horn

25.6 Unscrew the bolt and remove the horn

the pipe, and withdraw the switch from the cylinder head **(see illustration)**. Discard the sealing washers.

Installation

9 Install the switch using new sealing washers on each side of the pipe union and tighten it to the torque setting specified at the beginning of the Chapter **(see illustration 24.8)**.
10 Attach the wiring connector and fit the rubber boot **(see illustrations 24.3b and a)**.
11 Start the engine and check that there are no leaks around the switch. Check the operation of the switch.

25 Horn

Check

1 If the horn doesn't work, first check the fuse (see Section 5) and the battery (see Section 3).
2 The horn is bolted to the front of the frame.
3 Unplug the wiring connectors from the horn **(see illustration)**. Using two jumper wires, apply battery voltage (12 volts) directly to the terminals on the horn. If the horn doesn't sound, replace it with a new one.
4 If the horn sounds, check for battery voltage at the black/blue wire terminal with the ignition ON. If there is voltage check for continuity to earth in the black/purple wire with the button pressed (see *Wiring Diagrams* at the end of this Chapter). If there was no voltage check the black/blue wire between the horn and the fusebox for continuity, then if the wiring is good check the wiring between the switch and the horn button and the button itself (see Section 19).

Renewal

5 The horn is bolted to the front of the frame.
6 Unplug the wiring connectors from the horn **(see illustration 25.3)**. Unscrew the bolt securing the horn and remove it from the bike **(see illustration)**.
7 Install the horn and tighten the bolt. Connect the wiring connectors then check the horn works.

26 Starter relay

Check

1 If the starter circuit is faulty, first check the fuses (see Section 5).
2 To access the relay on Bonneville, T100, Thruxton and Scrambler models remove the left-hand side panel (see Chapter 7). To access the relay on America and Speedmaster models up to 2010, remove the right-hand side panel (see Chapter 7) **(see illustration)**. The starter relay on America and Speedmaster models from 2011-on is located under a rubber cover next to the regulator/rectifier low down just in front of the rear wheel **(see illustration)**.

26.2a Starter relay – America and Speedmaster up to 2010

26.3 Disconnect the starter motor lead from the relay

3 Disconnect the battery negative (–) lead (see Section 3). Lift the rubber terminal cover and unscrew the nut securing the starter motor lead to its terminal and disconnect the lead **(see illustration)**; position the lead away from the relay terminal. Reconnect the battery negative (–) lead. With the ignition switch ON, the engine kill switch in the RUN position, the transmission in neutral, press the starter switch. The relay should be heard to click. If not, switch off the ignition, then remove the relay as described below and test it as follows.
4 Using either a continuity tester or a multimeter set to the ohms x 1 scale, connect to the relay's starter motor and battery lead terminals **(see illustration)**. There should be infinite resistance (no continuity). Using a fully-charged 12 volt battery and two

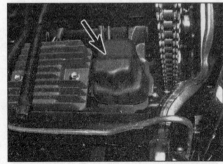

26.2b Starter relay is under rubber cover (arrowed) on America and Speedmaster from 2011

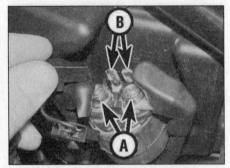

26.4 Connect the meter to the stud terminals (A) and the battery to the blade terminals (B)

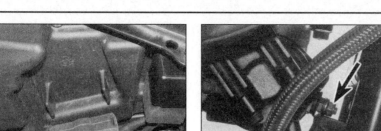

26.8 Slip the relay off its mounts

27.3 Pull back the rubber cover and unscrew the terminal nut (arrowed)

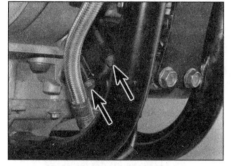

27.4a Unscrew the bolts . . .

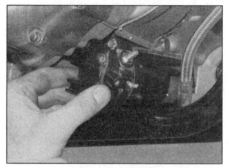

27.4b . . . and remove the starter motor

insulated jumper wires, connect the battery to the blade terminals of the relay. At this point the relay should be heard to click and the multimeter read 0 ohms (continuity). If this is the case the relay is proved good. If the relay does not click when battery voltage is applied and indicates no continuity (infinite resistance) across its terminals, it is faulty and must be replaced with a new one.

5 If the relay is good, check for battery voltage between the wiring connectors with the ignition ON, the transmission in neutral, the kill switch in the RUN position and the starter button pressed. If voltage is present, check the other components in the starter circuit as described in the relevant sections of this Chapter, including the headlight cut-out relay (see Section 6). If no voltage was present or if all components are good, check the wiring and connectors between the various components (see the *wiring diagrams* at the end of this book).

Removal and installation

6 To access the relay on Bonneville, T100, Thruxton and Scrambler models remove the left-hand side panel (see Chapter 7). To access the relay on America and Speedmaster models remove the right-hand side panel (see Chapter 7) **(see illustration 26.2).**
7 Disconnect the battery negative (–) lead (see Section 3).
8 Disconnect the relay wiring connectors **(see illustration 26.4).** Lift the rubber terminal covers and unscrew the nuts securing the

starter motor and battery leads to their terminals. Pull the relay off its mount and slip it out of its rubber sleeve **(see illustration).**
9 Installation is the reverse of removal. Make sure the terminal nuts are tight. Connect the battery negative (–) lead.

27 Starter motor removal and installation

Removal

1 Disconnect the battery negative (–) lead (see Section 3). The starter motor is mounted on the front of the engine.
2 Drain the engine oil (see Chapter 1).
3 Peel back the rubber terminal cover **(see illustration).** Unscrew the nut securing the

27.6 Fit a new O-ring into the groove

lead and detach it.
4 Unscrew the two bolts securing the starter motor **(see illustration).** Draw the starter motor out of the crankcase and remove it from the machine **(see illustration).**
5 Remove the O-ring on the end of the starter motor and discard it as a new one must be used.

Installation

6 Fit a new O-ring onto the end of the starter motor, making sure it is seated in its groove, and smear it and the shaft splines with molybdenum grease **(see illustration).**
7 Manoeuvre the motor into position and slide it into the crankcase **(see illustration 27.4b).** Ensure that the starter motor teeth mesh correctly with those of the starter idle/reduction gear. Install the mounting bolts and tighten them to the torque setting specified at the beginning of the Chapter **(see illustration 27.4a).**
8 Connect the lead to the starter motor and secure it with the nut **(see illustration 27.3).** Make sure the rubber cover is correctly seated over the terminal.
9 Connect the battery negative (–) lead.

28 Starter motor check and overhaul

Check

1 Remove the starter motor (see Section 27). Cushion the motor body with a piece of rag and clamp the motor in a soft-jawed vice – do not overtighten it.
2 Using a fully-charged 12 volt battery and two insulated jumper wires, connect the positive (+) terminal of the battery to the protruding terminal on the rear cover of the starter motor, and the negative (–) terminal to one of the motor's mounting lugs. At this point the starter motor should spin. If this is the case the motor is proved good, though it is worth disassembling it and checking it if you suspect it of not working properly under load. If the motor does not spin, disassemble it for inspection.
3 Check for continuity between the terminal bolt and the rear cover – there should be no continuity (infinite resistance).

Disassembly

Note 1: *Before disassembling the motor, spray some penetrating fluid around the end cover bolt threads and holes – due to the position of the motor on the front of the engine it is possible for the bolt threads to have seized in the cover.*
Note 2: *Triumph do not list replacement parts for the starter motor.*
4 Remove the starter motor (see Section 27).
5 Make some alignment marks between the

28.5 Make some alignment markings between the main housing and end covers

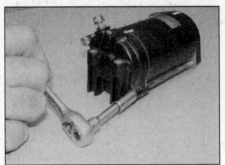

28.6 Unscrew and remove the two long bolts

28.7 Remove the rear cover with the brushplate, then remove the shims (arrowed) from the shaft

28.8 Remove the front cover

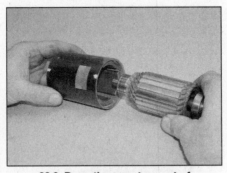

28.9 Draw the armature out of the housing

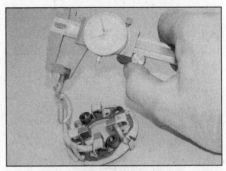

28.11 Measure the length of each brush

main housing and the front and rear covers **(see illustration)**.

6 Unscrew the two long bolts and withdraw them from the starter motor **(see illustration)**.

7 Remove the rear cover from the motor, bringing the brushplate with it **(see illustration)**. Remove the shim(s) from the rear end of the armature shaft or from inside the rear cover. Note the sealing ring around the rim of the cover.

8 Wrap some insulating tape around the teeth on the end of the starter motor shaft – this will protect the oil seal from damage as the front cover is removed. Remove the front cover from the motor **(see illustration)**. Where fitted remove the shim(s) from the front end of the armature shaft or from inside the front cover. Note the sealing ring around the rim of the cover.

9 Withdraw the armature from the main housing, noting that you will have to pull it

out against the attraction of the magnets **(see illustration)**.

10 Unscrew the terminal nut and remove it along with the insulator bush and the O-ring, which you may have to carefully dig out from around the base of the terminal bolt **(see illustrations 28.22d, c, b and a)**. Remove the brushplate from the rear cover, noting how it locates, drawing the terminal bolt out of the cover as you do so **(see illustration 28.21b)**. Remove the insulator piece from the terminal bolt if required **(see illustration 28.21a)**.

Inspection

11 The parts of the starter motor that are most likely to require attention are the brushes. Check their length – no minimum length is specified, but 5 mm or below is considered worn **(see illustration)**.

12 Inspect the commutator bars on the armature for scoring, scratches and

discoloration. The commutator can be cleaned and polished with crocus cloth, but do not use sandpaper or emery paper. After cleaning, wipe away any residue with a cloth soaked in electrical system cleaner or denatured alcohol. Check that the insulating Mica is below the surface of the commutator bars **(see illustration)**. If there is little or no undercut, scrape the Mica away until the undercut is as shown.

13 Using an ohmmeter or a continuity test light, check for continuity between the commutator bars **(see illustration)**. Continuity should exist between each bar and all of the others. Also, check for continuity between the commutator bars and the armature shaft **(see illustration)**. There should be no continuity (infinite resistance) between the commutator and the shaft. If the checks indicate otherwise, replace the starter motor with a new one (the armature is not available separately).

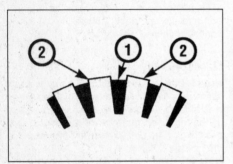

28.12 Check the Mica (1) is below the commutator bars (2)

28.13a Continuity should exist between the commutator bars

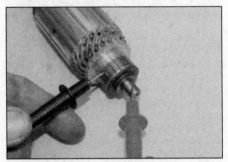

28.13b There should be no continuity between the commutator bars and the armature shaft

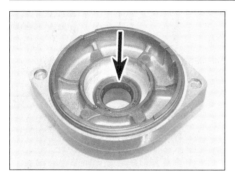

28.15a Check the oil seal (arrowed)

28.15b To remove it push it out using a screwdriver

28.15c Also check the bearing (arrowed)

14 Check the front end of the armature shaft for worn, cracked, chipped and broken teeth.

15 Inspect the front and rear covers for signs of cracks or wear. Check the oil seal in the front cover and the bearing on the shaft for wear and damage **(see illustrations)**. Also check the bush in the rear cover.

16 Inspect the magnets in the main housing and the housing itself for cracks.

17 Inspect the terminal bolt insulator bush, insulator piece and O-ring for signs of damage, deformation and deterioration.

Reassembly

18 Slide the armature into the main housing, noting that the magnets will forcibly draw it in **(see illustration 28.9)**. Grasp each component securely and control the action, taking care not to jam your fingers jammed.

19 Where removed fit the shim(s) onto the front end of the shaft. Make sure the front cover sealing ring is in place. Apply a smear of grease to the lips of the front cover oil seal **(see illustration 28.15a)**. Install the cover, aligning the marks made on removal **(see illustration 28.8)**. Remove the protective tape from the shaft end.

20 Fit the shim(s) onto the rear end of the shaft **(see illustration)**. Press each brush into its housing and lift the spring up off the back of the brush and onto the top of it to keep it in its recessed position **(see illustration)**. Slide the brushplate onto the commutator, aligning the cut-out in the plate rim with the tab on the inside of the housing **(see illustration)**. When the brushplate is in place fit the springs back onto the ends of the brushes **(see**

28.20a Fit the shims onto the shaft

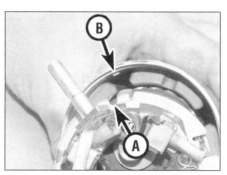

28.20c Fit the brushplate, aligning the cut-out (A) with the tab (B) in the housing

illustration). Check the armature rotates freely in the brushes.

21 Fit the insulator piece onto the terminal bolt **(see illustration)**. Smear the bush in the rear cover with some molybdenum grease. Make sure the rear cover sealing ring is in place.

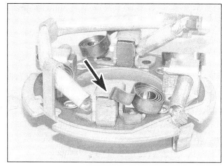

28.20b Fit the end of each spring onto the top of its brush so holding it recessed (arrow)

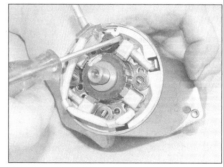

28.20d Relocate each spring end so the brushes are pushed against the armature

Insert the terminal bolt in the cover then locate the cover, aligning the marks made on removal and making sure the shaft enters the bush **(see illustration)**. Check the alignment marks made on removal are correctly aligned, then install the long bolts and tighten them **(see illustration)**.

28.21a Fit the insulator onto the bolt . . .

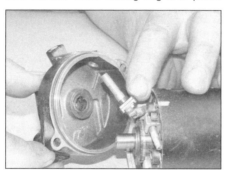

28.21b . . . then fit the bolt into the rear cover, fit the cover . . .

28.21c . . . and install the bolts

22 Fit the O-ring onto the terminal bolt and carefully feed it down so it locates between the bolt and the cover **(see illustrations)**. Fit the bush and the nut **(see illustrations)**.
23 Install the starter motor (see Section 27).

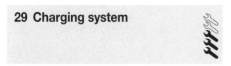

29 Charging system

28.22a Fit the O-ring . . .

28.22b and press it into place . . .

General information and precautions

1 If the performance of the charging system is suspect, the system as a whole should be checked first, followed by testing of the individual components. **Note:** *Before beginning the checks, make sure the battery is fully charged and that all system connections are clean and tight.*
2 Checking the output of the charging system and the performance of the various components within the charging system requires the use of a multimeter (with voltage, current and resistance checking facilities).
3 When making the checks, follow the procedures carefully to prevent incorrect connections or short circuits, as irreparable damage to electrical system components may result if short circuits occur.
4 If a multimeter is not available, the job of checking the charging system should be left to a Triumph dealer or automotive electrician.
5 If the charging system of the machine is thought to be faulty, perform the following checks.

Leakage test

Caution: Always connect an ammeter in series, never in parallel with the battery, otherwise it will be damaged. Do not turn the ignition ON or operate the starter motor when the ammeter is connected – a sudden surge in current will blow the meter's fuse.
6 Disconnect the lead from the battery negative (–) terminal (see Section 3).
7 Set the multimeter to the Amps function and connect its negative (–) probe to the battery negative (–) terminal, and positive (+) probe to the disconnected negative (–) lead **(see illustration)**. Always set the meter to a high amps range initially and then bring it down to the mA (milli Amps) range; if there is a high current flow in the circuit it may blow the meter's fuse.
8 No current flow should be indicated. If current leakage is indicated (generally greater than 1 mA, although more if an alarm or immobiliser is fitted), there is a short circuit in the wiring. Using the wiring diagrams at the end of this Chapter, systematically disconnect individual electrical components, checking the meter each time until the source is identified.

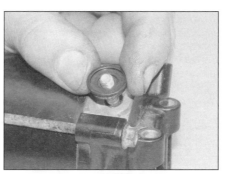

28.22c . . . then fit the bush . . .

28.22d . . . and the nut

9 If no leakage is indicated, disconnect the meter and connect the negative (–) lead to the battery, tightening it securely.

Output test

10 Start the engine and warm it up to normal operating temperature. Refer to Section 3 and access the battery.
11 To check the regulated voltage output, allow the engine to idle and connect a multimeter set to the 0 to 20 volts DC scale (voltmeter) across the terminals of the battery (positive (+) lead to battery positive (+) terminal, negative (–) lead to battery negative

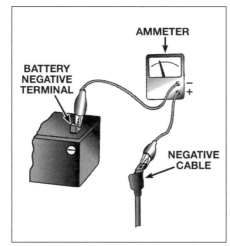

29.7 Checking the charging system leakage rate - connect the meter as shown

(–) terminal). There should be between 13.5 and 15V at 2000 rpm if the charging system is functioning correctly. If voltage is well below this figure, check the alternator stator coils as described in Section 30. If a higher than normal voltage is shown, the regulator function of the regulator/rectifier unit may be at fault.
12 To check the unregulated no-load voltage output disconnect the alternator wiring connector (see Section 30, Steps 2 and 3). Connect a multimeter set to the 0 to 100 volts AC scale (voltmeter) across the black/blue wire terminals in the alternator side of the connector – there are three wires, so connect between each pair in turn, thus taking a total of three readings. Start the engine and slowly increase engine speed to 4000 rpm and note the readings obtained. The unregulated voltage should be around 60 or 70 volts (Triumph do not give a specific figure). If the voltage is much less, check the alternator (see Section 30). If the readings are good, but the charging system is suspect, check the wiring and connectors to the regulator/rectifier and the regulator/rectifier itself (see Section 31).

 HAYNES HINT *Clues to a faulty regulator are constantly blowing bulbs, with brightness varying considerably with engine speed, and battery overheating.*

30.8a Unscrew the two bolts (arrowed), and slacken the two on the left-hand side

30.8b Unscrew the bolts (arrowed) and remove the wiring guide

30.9 Unscrew the bolts and remove the cover

30 Alternator rotor and stator

Check

1 Disconnect the battery negative (–) lead (see Section 3).

2 On Bonneville, T100 and Thruxton models remove the right-hand side panel (see Chapter 7). On Scrambler models, remove the left-hand side panel (see Chapter 7). On America and Speedmaster models remove the seat(s) (see Chapter 7), then undo the screw and release the wiring connector bundle cover **(see illustrations 3.13a and b)**.

3 Trace the wiring back from the alternator cover on the right-hand side of the engine and disconnect it at the connector.

4 Using a multimeter set the ohms x 1 (ohmmeter) scale check that there is a small resistance in the stator coil winding by connecting the probes between each of the black/blue wire terminal pairs on the alternator side of the connector, making a total of three checks. Also check for continuity between each terminal and ground (earth). If the stator coil windings are in good condition the coil resistance readings should be similar to those given in the Specifications at the beginning of this Chapter, and there should be no continuity (infinite resistance) between any of the terminals and ground (earth). If not, check the fault is not due to damaged

wiring or connectors between the connector and stator, which is in the alternator cover on the right-hand side of the engine. If the wiring and connectors are good, the alternator stator coil assembly is at fault and must be replaced with a new one.

Removal

5 Drain the engine oil if required (see Chapter 1), but note that if the bike is on its sidestand there should be no need to drain the oil. Disconnect the battery negative (–) lead (see Section 3).

6 On Bonneville, T100 and Thruxton models remove the right-hand side panel (see Chapter 7). On Scrambler models, remove the left-hand side panel (see Chapter 7). On America and Speedmaster models remove the seat (see Chapter 7), then undo the screw and release the wiring connector bundle cover **(see illustrations 3.13a and b)**.

7 Trace the wiring back from the alternator cover on the right-hand side of the engine and disconnect it at the connector. Feed the wiring back to the coil, noting its routing and releasing it from any clips or ties.

8 On America and Speedmaster models slacken the two left-hand bolts securing the front footrest bracket, and remove the two right-hand bolts, then displace the assembly forwards to give clearance for the alternator cover to be moved past the heel guard **(see illustration)**. Also remove the two bolts on the sprocket cover that secure the wiring guide **(see illustration)**.

9 Working in a criss-cross pattern, unscrew the alternator cover bolts **(see illustration)**. Remove the cover, noting that it will be restrained by the pull of the rotor magnets, and be prepared to catch any residual oil. Discard the gasket as a new one must be used. Remove the dowels for safekeeping if loose.

10 To avoid the possibility of damage remove the ignition pick-up coil (see Chapter 4).

11 Counter-hold the alternator rotor using a rotor strap, making sure it does not damage the pick-up coil triggers, or a suitable holding tool on the flats on the rotor boss and unscrew the rotor bolt **(see illustration)**. Note that the bolt is very tight – if you have difficulty counter-holding the rotor, have an assistant do this for you, or have them engage a gear and apply the rear brake while you counter-hold it. Alternatively use an air wrench if available.

12 To remove the rotor from the shaft it is necessary to use a rotor puller, either the Triumph service tool (Pt. No. T3880203) or a commercial available equivalent from a motorcycle dealer. Thread the rotor puller into the centre of the rotor, making sure if using the Triumph tool that the correct size thread protector button is used according to the size of the rotor bolt, and turn it until the rotor is displaced from the shaft, holding the rotor as described above to prevent the engine turning, and using a mallet if necessary to tap the tool round **(see illustrations)**. Remove the

30.11 Counter-hold the rotor using one of the methods described and unscrew the bolt in its centre

30.12a Thread the puller into the rotor . . .

30.12b . . . and turn it until the rotor is displaced

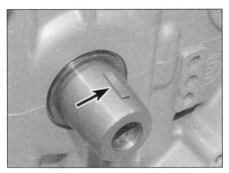

30.12c Remove the Woodruff key (arrowed) if it is loose

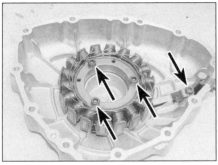

30.13 Unscrew the bolts (arrowed) and remove the stator

30.15 Slide the rotor onto the shaft, aligning the cut-out with the Woodruff key

Woodruff key from its slot in the crankcase if it is loose **(see illustration)**.

13 To remove the stator from the cover, unscrew the bolts securing the stator and the bolt securing the wiring clamp, then free the wiring grommet from its cut-out and remove the stator assembly **(see illustration)**.

Installation

14 Fit the stator into the cover, then route the wiring to the cut-out and fit the wiring clamp **(see illustrations 30.13)**. Apply a suitable non-permanent thread locking compound to the threads of the stator and clamp bolts, and tighten them to the torque setting specified at the beginning of the Chapter.

15 Clean the tapered end of the crankshaft and the corresponding mating surface on the inside of the rotor with a suitable solvent. Fit

the Woodruff key into its slot in the crankshaft if removed **(see illustration 30.12c)**. Make sure that no metal objects have attached themselves to the magnets on the inside of the rotor. Slide the rotor onto the shaft, making sure the groove on the inside is aligned with and fits over the Woodruff key **(see illustration)**. Make sure the Woodruff key does not become dislodged.

16 Measure the rotor bolt width to determine its size – (either 10 mm or 12 mm depending on engine number). Install the rotor bolt with its washer and tighten it to the correct torque setting specified at the beginning of the Chapter for the size of bolt fitted, using the method employed on removal to prevent the rotor from turning **(see illustrations)**.

17 If removed install the ignition pick-up coil (see Chapter 4). Clean any old sealant off the alternator and pick-up coil wiring grommets,

then apply some fresh silicone sealant to them and fit them into their cut-outs.

18 Fit the dowels into the crankcase if removed **(see illustration)**. Install the alternator cover using a new gasket, making sure they locate onto the dowels – take care not to trap your fingers as the cover is drawn into place by the pull of the magnets **(see illustration)**. Tighten the cover bolts evenly in a criss-cross sequence to the specified torque setting.

19 On America and Speedmaster models route the wiring between the covers then secure the guide with the sprocket cover bolts **(see illustration 30.8b)**. Install the two right-hand bolts securing the front footrest bracket and tighten all the bolts to the specified torque setting **(see illustration 30.8a)**.

20 Reconnect the wiring at the connector and secure it with any ties or clips previously released.

21 On Bonneville, T100 and Thruxton models install the right-hand side panel (see Chapter 7). On Scrambler models, install the left-hand side panel (see Chapter 7). On America and Speedmaster models locate the wiring connector bundle cover and tighten its screw **(see illustration 3.13a)**. Install the seat (see Chapter 7).

22 Reconnect the battery lead. If drained, replenish the engine oil (see Chapter 1).

31 Regulator/rectifier

Check

1 No test details are available for the regulator/rectifier. If possible substitute it with one that is known to be good to see if this cures the problem.

2 Check the wiring between the battery, regulator/rectifier and alternator, and the wiring connectors (see *Wiring Diagrams* at the end of this book), and check the alternator and its output if not already done (see Sections 29 and 30).

Removal and installation

3 Disconnect the battery negative (–) lead (see Section 3).

30.16a Install the bolt with its washer. . .

30.16b . . . and tighten it to the specified torque

30.18a Locate the new gasket onto the dowels (arrowed) . . .

30.18b . . . then install the cover

31.6a Regulator/rectifier mounting bolts (arrowed) – Bonneville, T100, Thruxton and Scrambler

31.6b Regulator/rectifier mounting bolts (arrowed) – America and Speedmaster

4 On Bonneville, T100, Thruxton and Scrambler models undo the screw on each side of the headlight and free the rim from the shell, noting how it locates at the top **(see illustration 7.1)**. Disconnect the headlight and sidelight wiring connectors to free the beam unit **(see illustration 7.2)**. Disconnect the regulator/rectifier wiring connector, then draw the wiring out of the back of the shell.

5 On America and Speedmaster models trace the wiring from the regulator/rectifier, which is awkwardly mounted low down ahead of the rear wheel, and disconnect it at the connector, which might on some models be under the carburettors or as on that photographed under the connector cover under the seat – remove the seat(s) (see Chapter 7), then undo the screw and release the wiring connector bundle cover. Disconnect the regulator/rectifier wiring connector **(see illustrations 3.13a and b)**. Feed the wiring down to the regulator/rectifier, noting its routing and releasing it from any ties.

6 Unscrew the two bolts securing the regulator/rectifier and remove it, on Thruxton models supporting the turn signal bracket to avoid straining the wiring **(see illustrations)**.

7 Install the new unit and tighten the bolts. Connect the wiring connector.

8 On Bonneville, T100, Thruxton and Scrambler models install the headlight rim. On America and Speedmaster models if required locate the wiring connector bundle cover and tighten its screw. Install the seat (see Chapter 7).

9 Reconnect the battery negative lead (–) (see Section 3).

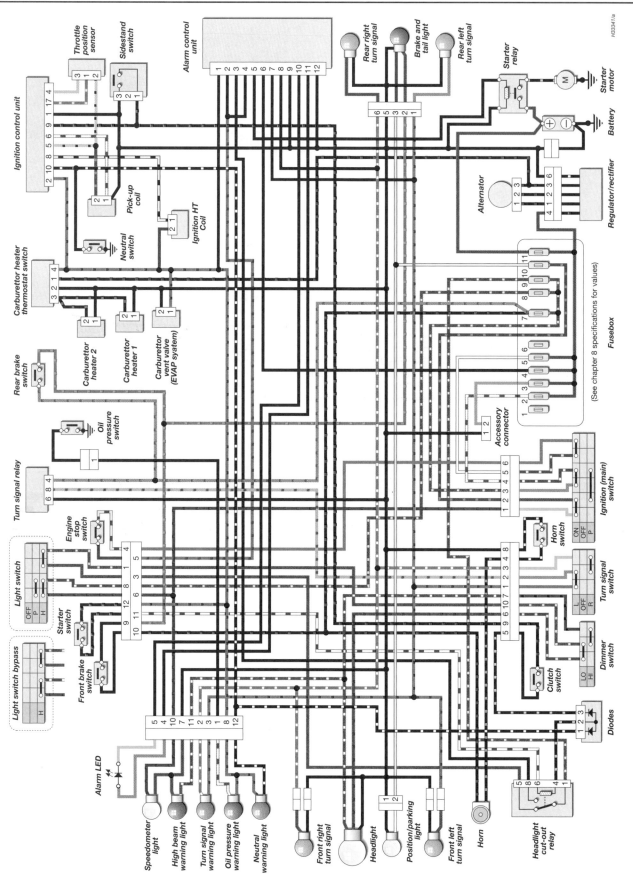

Bonneville - with carburettor engine

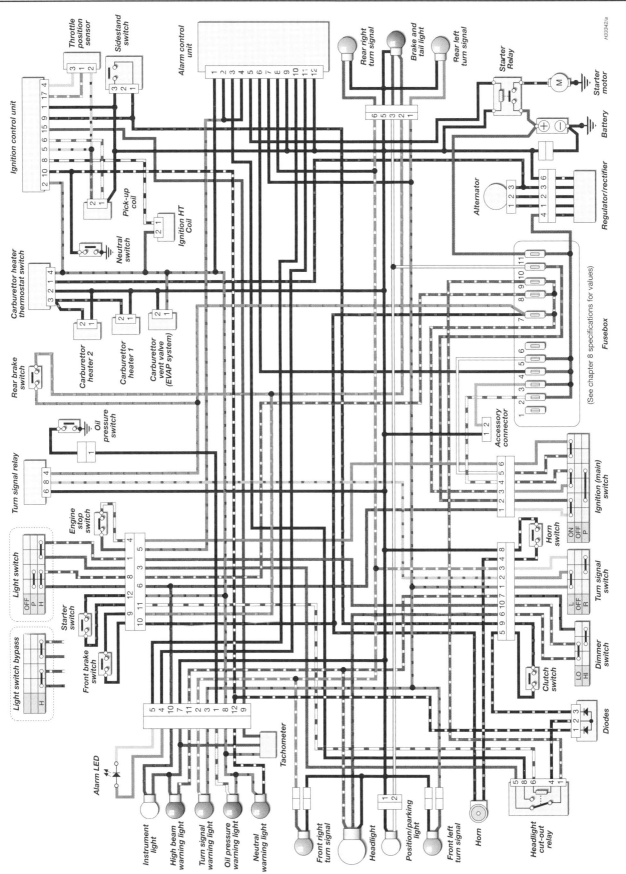

H33342/a

T100 - with carburettor engine

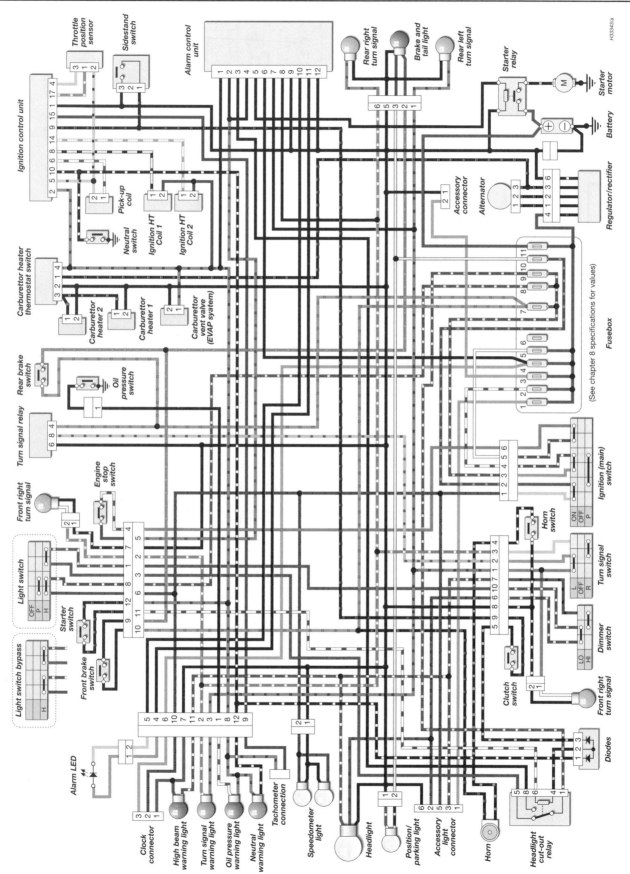

America and Speedmaster - with carburettor engine

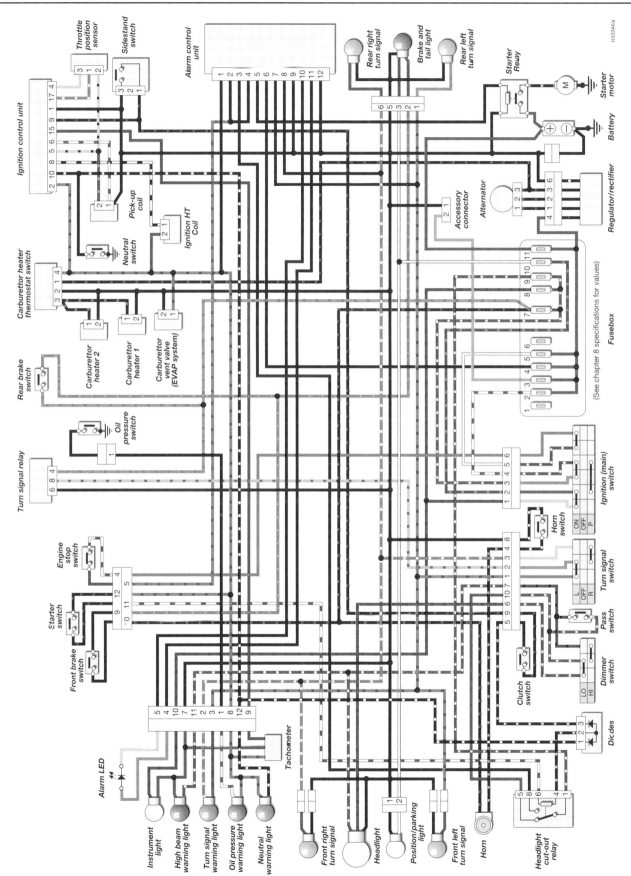

Thruxton and Scrambler - with carburettor engine

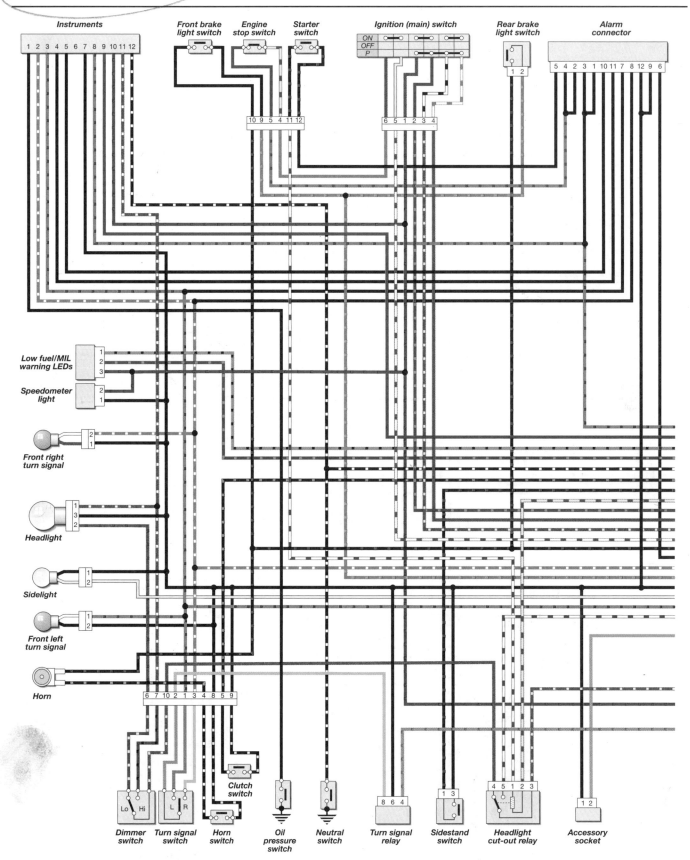

H47405

Bonneville, T100, Thruxton and Scrambler with EFI engine and cable driven speedometer (2008-09)

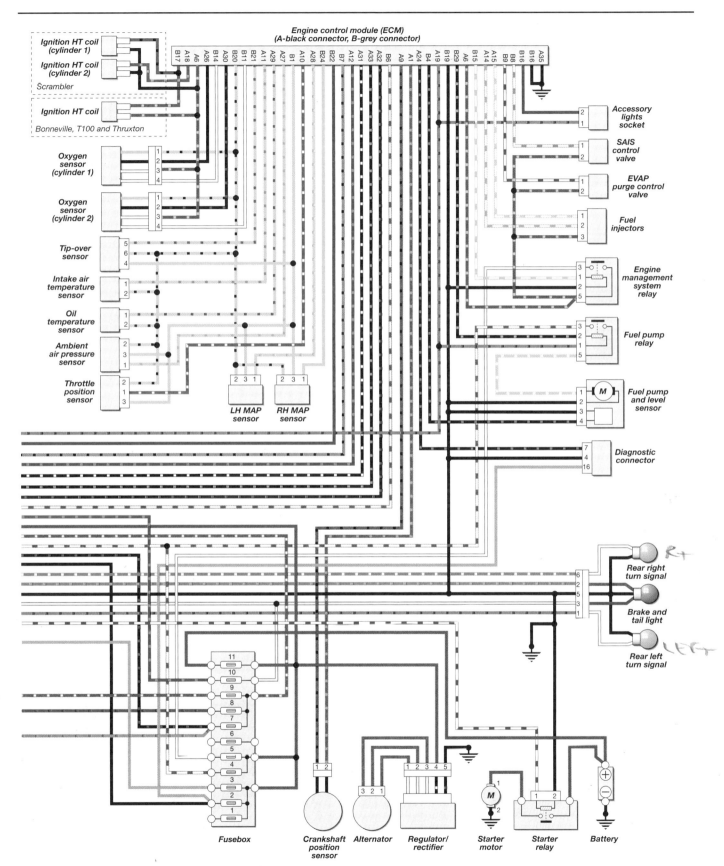

Bonneville, T100, Thruxton and Scrambler with EFI engine and cable driven speedometer (2008-09)

H47406

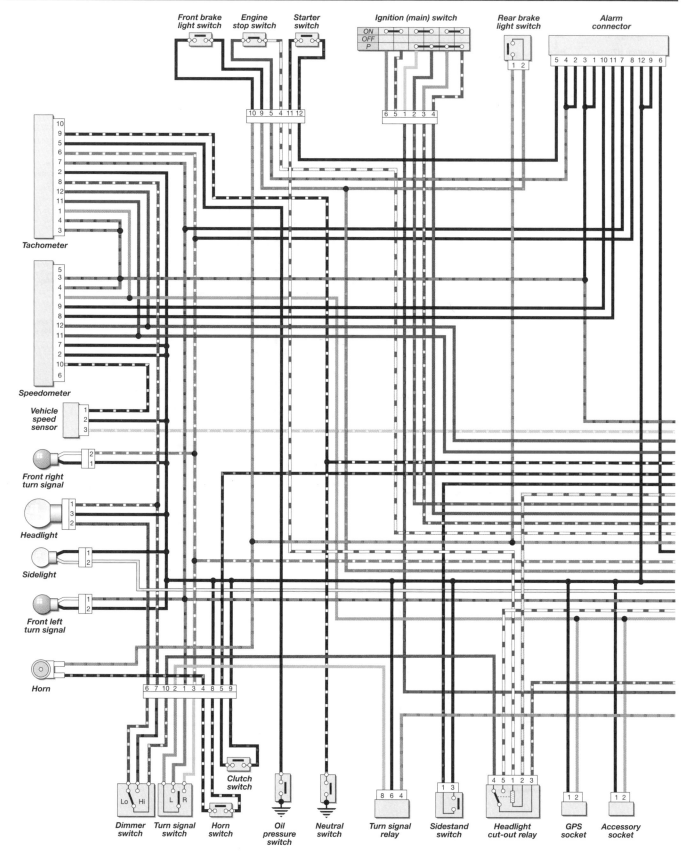

Bonneville, T100, Thruxton and Scrambler with EFI engine and electronic speedometer (2010-on)

H47407

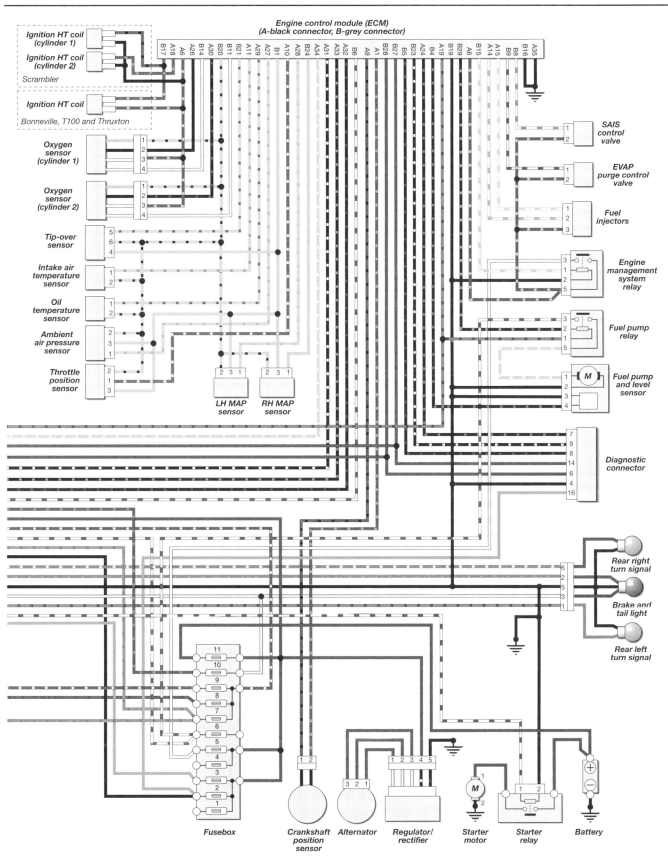

Bonneville, T100, Thruxton and Scrambler with EFI engine and electronic speedometer (2010-on)

H47408

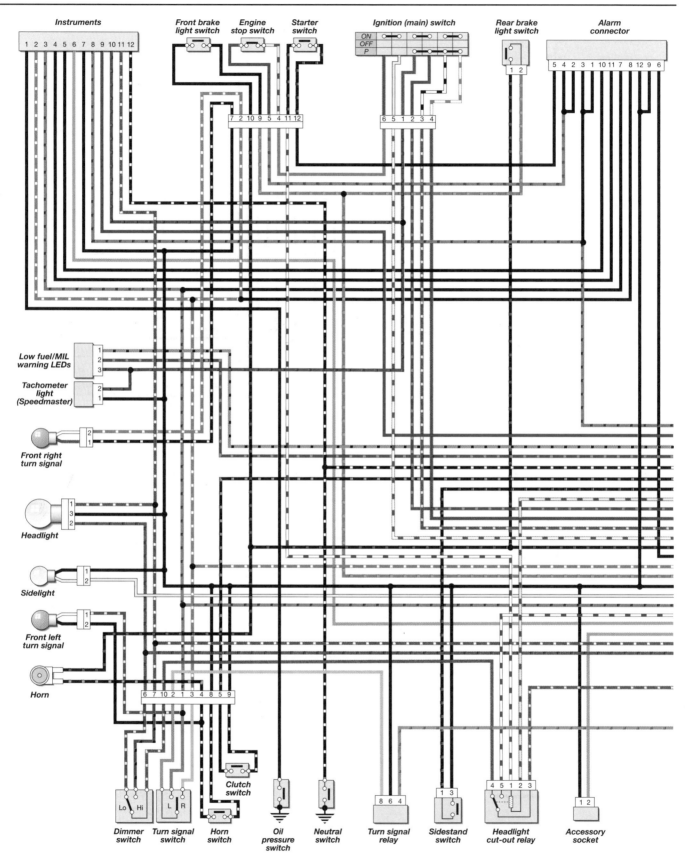

America and Speedmaster with EFI engine and cable driven speedometer (2008-09)

H47409

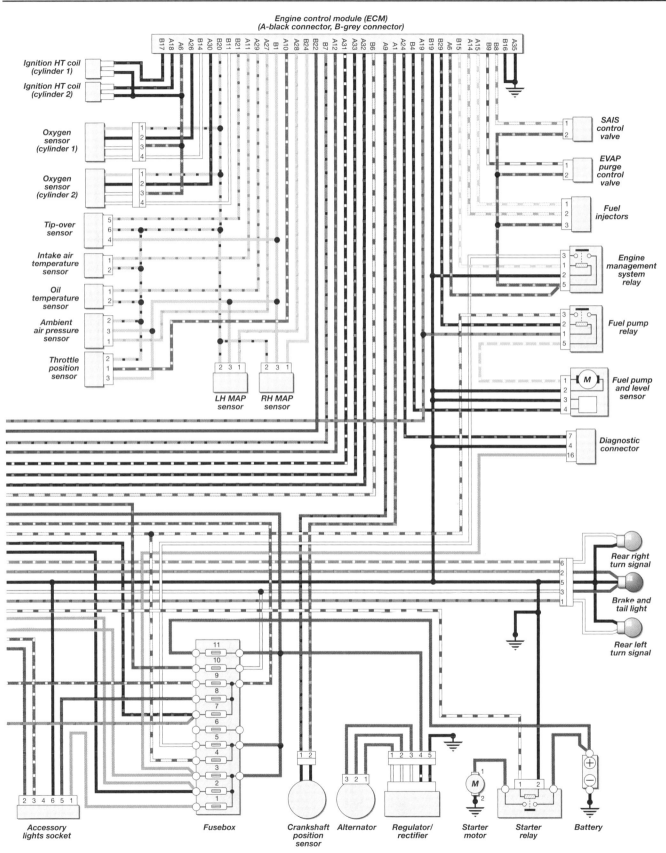

H47410

America and Speedmaster with EFI engine and cable driven speedometer (2008-09)

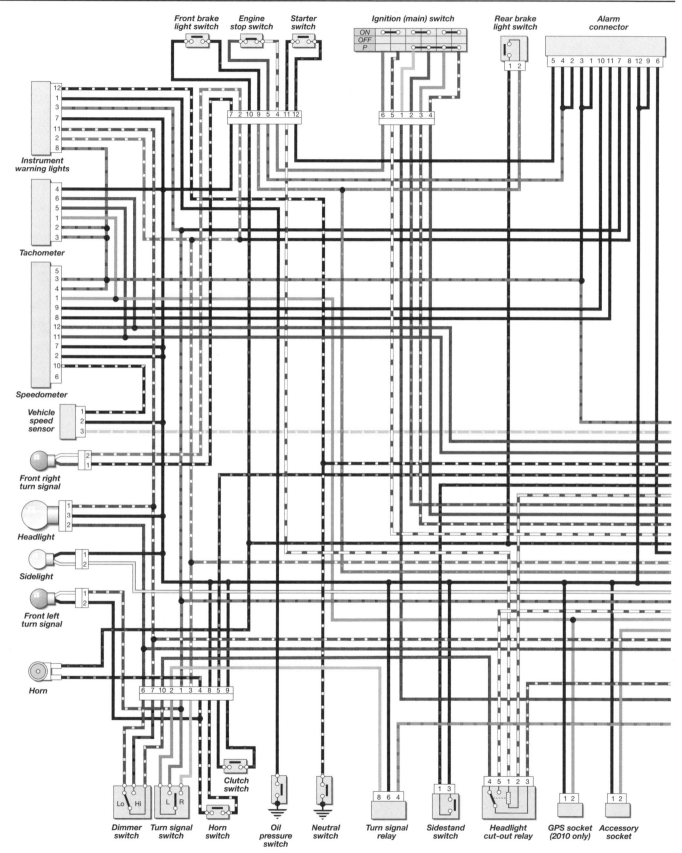

America and Speedmaster with EFI engine and electronic speedometer (2010-on)

H47411

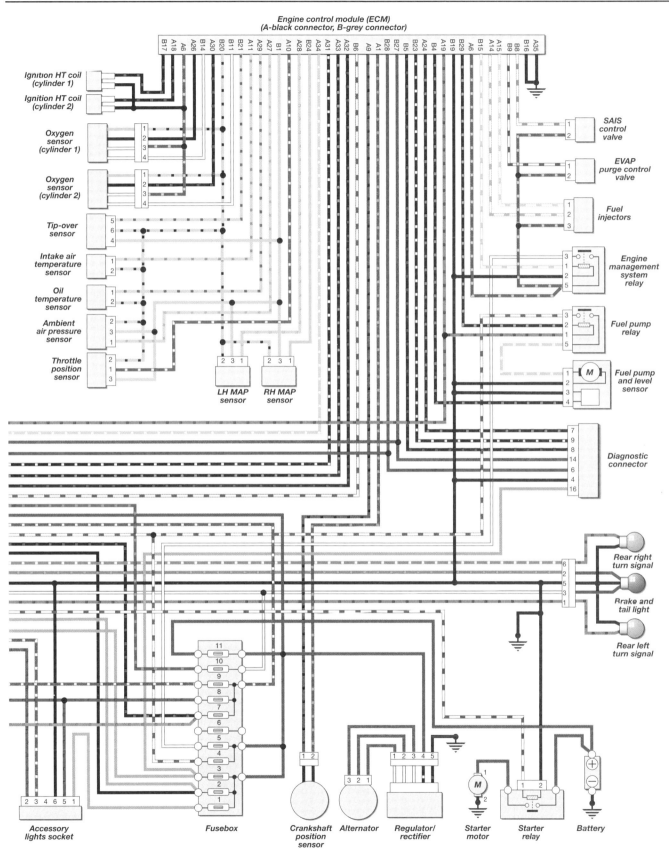

America and Speedmaster with EFI engine and electronic speedometer (2010-on)

H47412

Notes

Reference

Tools and Workshop Tips [REF•2]

- Building up a tool kit and equipping your workshop ● Using tools ● Understanding bearing, seal, fastener and chain sizes and markings ● Repair techniques

Security [REF•20]

- Locks and chains
- U-locks ● Disc locks
- Alarms and immobilisers
- Security marking systems ● Tips on how to prevent bike theft

Lubricants and fluids [REF•23]

- Engine oils
- Transmission (gear) oils
- Coolant/anti-freeze
- Fork oils and suspension fluids ● Brake/clutch fluids
- Spray lubes, degreasers and solvents

Conversion Factors [REF•26]

$$34 \ Nm \times 0.738 = 25 \ lbf \ ft$$

- Formulae for conversion of the metric (SI) units used throughout the manual into Imperial measures

MOT Test Checks [REF•27]

- A guide to the UK MOT test ● Which items are tested ● How to prepare your motorcycle for the test and perform a pre-test check

Storage [REF•32]

- How to prepare your motorcycle for going into storage and protect essential systems ● How to get the motorcycle back on the road

Fault Finding [REF•35]

- Common faults and their likely causes ● How to check engine cylinder compression ● How to make electrical tests and use test meters

Technical Terms Explained [REF•51]

- Component names, technical terms and common abbreviations explained

Index [REF•55]

Buying tools

A toolkit is a fundamental requirement for servicing and repairing a motorcycle. Although there will be an initial expense in building up enough tools for servicing, this will soon be offset by the savings made by doing the job yourself. As experience and confidence grow, additional tools can be added to enable the repair and overhaul of the motorcycle. Many of the specialist tools are expensive and not often used so it may be preferable to hire them, or for a group of friends or motorcycle club to join in the purchase.

As a rule, it is better to buy more expensive, good quality tools. Cheaper tools are likely to wear out faster and need to be renewed more often, nullifying the original saving.

> ⚠️ **Warning: To avoid the risk of a poor quality tool breaking in use, causing injury or damage to the component being worked on, always aim to purchase tools which meet the relevant national safety standards.**

The following lists of tools do not represent the manufacturer's service tools, but serve as a guide to help the owner decide which tools are needed for this level of work. In addition, items such as an electric drill, hacksaw, files, soldering iron and a workbench equipped with a vice, may be needed. Although not classed as tools, a selection of bolts, screws, nuts, washers and pieces of tubing always come in useful.

For more information about tools, refer to the Haynes *Motorcycle Workshop Practice Techbook* (Bk. No. 3470).

Manufacturer's service tools

Inevitably certain tasks require the use of a service tool. Where possible an alternative tool or method of approach is recommended, but sometimes there is no option if personal injury or damage to the component is to be avoided. Where required, service tools are referred to in the relevant procedure.

Service tools can usually only be purchased from a motorcycle dealer and are identified by a part number. Some of the commonly-used tools, such as rotor pullers, are available in aftermarket form from mail-order motorcycle tool and accessory suppliers.

Maintenance and minor repair tools

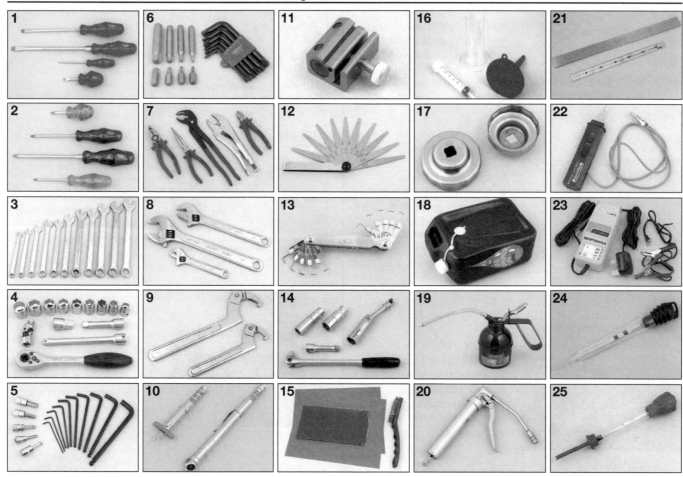

1 Set of flat-bladed screwdrivers
2 Set of Phillips head screwdrivers
3 Combination open-end and ring spanners
4 Socket set (3/8 inch or 1/2 inch drive)
5 Set of Allen keys or bits

6 Set of Torx keys or bits
7 Pliers, cutters and self-locking grips (Mole grips)
8 Adjustable spanners
9 C-spanners
10 Tread depth gauge and tyre pressure gauge

11 Cable oiler clamp
12 Feeler gauges
13 Spark plug gap measuring tool
14 Spark plug spanner or deep plug sockets
15 Wire brush and emery paper

16 Calibrated syringe, measuring vessel and funnel
17 Oil filter adapters
18 Oil drainer can or tray
19 Pump type oil can
20 Grease gun

21 Straight-edge and steel rule
22 Continuity tester
23 Battery charger
24 Hydrometer (for battery specific gravity check)
25 Anti-freeze tester (for liquid-cooled engines)

Repair and overhaul tools

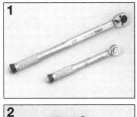

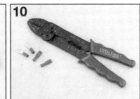

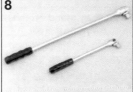

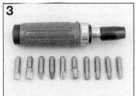

1 *Torque wrench (small and mid-ranges)*
2 *Conventional, plastic or soft-faced hammers*
3 *Impact driver set*

4 *Vernier gauge*
5 *Circlip pliers (internal and external, or combination)*
6 *Set of cold chisels and punches*

7 *Selection of pullers*
8 *Breaker bars*
9 *Chain breaking/ riveting tool set*

10 *Wire stripper and crimper tool*
11 *Multimeter (measures amps, volts and ohms)*
12 *Stroboscope (for dynamic timing checks)*

13 *Hose clamp (wingnut type shown)*
14 *Clutch holding tool*
15 *One-man brake/clutch bleeder kit*

Specialist tools

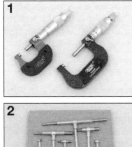
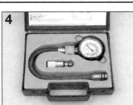

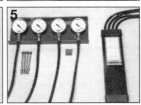
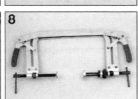
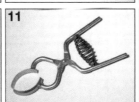

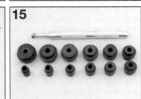
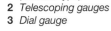

1 *Micrometers (external type)*
2 *Telescoping gauges*
3 *Dial gauge*

4 *Cylinder compression gauge*
5 *Vacuum gauges (left) or manometer (right)*
6 *Oil pressure gauge*

7 *Plastigauge kit*
8 *Valve spring compressor (4-stroke engines)*
9 *Piston pin drawbolt tool*

10 *Piston ring removal and installation tool*
11 *Piston ring clamp*
12 *Cylinder bore hone (stone type shown)*

13 *Stud extractor*
14 *Screw extractor set*
15 *Bearing driver set*

1 Workshop equipment and facilities

The workbench

● Work is made much easier by raising the bike up on a ramp - components are much more accessible if raised to waist level. The hydraulic or pneumatic types seen in the dealer's workshop are a sound investment if you undertake a lot of repairs or overhauls **(see illustration 1.1)**.

1.1 Hydraulic motorcycle ramp

● If raised off ground level, the bike must be supported on the ramp to avoid it falling. Most ramps incorporate a front wheel locating clamp which can be adjusted to suit different diameter wheels. When tightening the clamp, take care not to mark the wheel rim or damage the tyre - use wood blocks on each side to prevent this.
● Secure the bike to the ramp using tie-downs **(see illustration 1.2)**. If the bike has only a sidestand, and hence leans at a dangerous angle when raised, support the bike on an auxiliary stand.

1.2 Tie-downs are used around the passenger footrests to secure the bike

● Auxiliary (paddock) stands are widely available from mail order companies or motorcycle dealers and attach either to the wheel axle or swingarm pivot **(see illustration 1.3)**. If the motorcycle has a centrestand, you can support it under the crankcase to prevent it toppling whilst either wheel is removed **(see illustration 1.4)**.

1.3 This auxiliary stand attaches to the swingarm pivot

1.4 Always use a block of wood between the engine and jack head when supporting the engine in this way

Fumes and fire

● Refer to the Safety first! page at the beginning of the manual for full details. Make sure your workshop is equipped with a fire extinguisher suitable for fuel-related fires (Class B fire - flammable liquids) - it is not sufficient to have a water-filled extinguisher.
● Always ensure adequate ventilation is available. Unless an exhaust gas extraction system is available for use, ensure that the engine is run outside of the workshop.
● If working on the fuel system, make sure the workshop is ventilated to avoid a build-up of fumes. This applies equally to fume build-up when charging a battery. Do not smoke or allow anyone else to smoke in the workshop.

Fluids

● If you need to drain fuel from the tank, store it in an approved container marked as suitable for the storage of petrol (gasoline) **(see illustration 1.5)**. Do not store fuel in glass jars or bottles.

1.5 Use an approved can only for storing petrol (gasoline)

● Use proprietary engine degreasers or solvents which have a high flash-point, such as paraffin (kerosene), for cleaning off oil, grease and dirt - never use petrol (gasoline) for cleaning. Wear rubber gloves when handling solvent and engine degreaser. The fumes from certain solvents can be dangerous - always work in a well-ventilated area.

Dust, eye and hand protection

● Protect your lungs from inhalation of dust particles by wearing a filtering mask over the nose and mouth. Many frictional materials still contain asbestos which is dangerous to your health. Protect your eyes from spouts of liquid and sprung components by wearing a pair of protective goggles **(see illustration 1.6)**.

1.6 A fire extinguisher, goggles, mask and protective gloves should be at hand in the workshop

● Protect your hands from contact with solvents, fuel and oils by wearing rubber gloves. Alternatively apply a barrier cream to your hands before starting work. If handling hot components or fluids, wear suitable gloves to protect your hands from scalding and burns.

What to do with old fluids

● Old cleaning solvent, fuel, coolant and oils should not be poured down domestic drains or onto the ground. Package the fluid up in old oil containers, label it accordingly, and take it to a garage or disposal facility. Contact your local authority for location of such sites or ring the oil care hotline.

OIL CARE

Note: It is illegal and anti-social to dump oil down the drain. To find the location of your local oil recycling bank in the UK, call 08708 506 506 or visit www.oilbankline. org.uk

In the USA, note that any oil supplier must accept used oil for recycling.

2 Fasteners - screws, bolts and nuts

Fastener types and applications

Bolts and screws

● Fastener head types are either of hexagonal, Torx or splined design, with internal and external versions of each type **(see illustrations 2.1 and 2.2)**; splined head fasteners are not in common use on motorcycles. The conventional slotted or Phillips head design is used for certain screws. Bolt or screw length is always measured from the underside of the head to the end of the item **(see illustration 2.11)**.

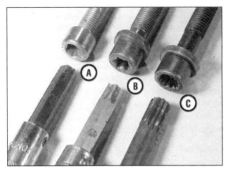

2.1 Internal hexagon/Allen (A), Torx (B) and splined (C) fasteners, with corresponding bits

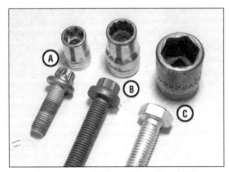

2.2 External Torx (A), splined (B) and hexagon (C) fasteners, with corresponding sockets

● Certain fasteners on the motorcycle have a tensile marking on their heads, the higher the marking the stronger the fastener. High tensile fasteners generally carry a 10 or higher marking. Never replace a high tensile fastener with one of a lower tensile strength.

Washers (see illustration 2.3)

● Plain washers are used between a fastener head and a component to prevent damage to the component or to spread the load when torque is applied. Plain washers can also be used as spacers or shims in certain assemblies. Copper or aluminium plain washers are often used as sealing washers on drain plugs.

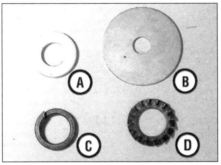

2.3 Plain washer (A), penny washer (B), spring washer (C) and serrated washer (D)

● The split-ring spring washer works by applying axial tension between the fastener head and component. If flattened, it is fatigued and must be renewed. If a plain (flat) washer is used on the fastener, position the spring washer between the fastener and the plain washer.

● Serrated star type washers dig into the fastener and component faces, preventing loosening. They are often used on electrical earth (ground) connections to the frame.

● Cone type washers (sometimes called Belleville) are conical and when tightened apply axial tension between the fastener head and component. They must be installed with the dished side against the component and often carry an OUTSIDE marking on their outer face. If flattened, they are fatigued and must be renewed.

● Tab washers are used to lock plain nuts or bolts on a shaft. A portion of the tab washer is bent up hard against one flat of the nut or bolt to prevent it loosening. Due to the tab washer being deformed in use, a new tab washer should be used every time it is disturbed.

● Wave washers are used to take up endfloat on a shaft. They provide light springing and prevent excessive side-to-side play of a component. Can be found on rocker arm shafts.

Nuts and split pins

● Conventional plain nuts are usually six-sided **(see illustration 2.4)**. They are sized by thread diameter and pitch. High tensile nuts carry a number on one end to denote their tensile strength.

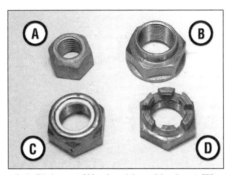

2.4 Plain nut (A), shouldered locknut (B), nylon insert nut (C) and castellated nut (D)

● Self-locking nuts either have a nylon insert, or two spring metal tabs, or a shoulder which is staked into a groove in the shaft - their advantage over conventional plain nuts is a resistance to loosening due to vibration. The nylon insert type can be used a number of times, but must be renewed when the friction of the nylon insert is reduced, ie when the nut spins freely on the shaft. The spring tab type can be reused unless the tabs are damaged. The shouldered type must be renewed every time it is disturbed.

● Split pins (cotter pins) are used to lock a castellated nut to a shaft or to prevent slackening of a plain nut. Common applications are wheel axles and brake torque arms. Because the split pin arms are deformed to lock around the nut a new split pin must always be used on installation - always fit the correct size split pin which will fit snugly in the shaft hole. Make sure the split pin arms are correctly located around the nut **(see illustrations 2.5 and 2.6)**.

2.5 Bend split pin (cotter pin) arms as shown (arrows) to secure a castellated nut

2.6 Bend split pin (cotter pin) arms as shown to secure a plain nut

Caution: If the castellated nut slots do not align with the shaft hole after tightening to the torque setting, tighten the nut until the next slot aligns with the hole - never slacken the nut to align its slot.

● R-pins (shaped like the letter R), or slip pins as they are sometimes called, are sprung and can be reused if they are otherwise in good condition. Always install R-pins with their closed end facing forwards **(see illustration 2.7)**.

2.7 Correct fitting of R-pin. Arrow indicates forward direction

Circlips (see illustration 2.8)

● Circlips (sometimes called snap-rings) are used to retain components on a shaft or in a housing and have corresponding external or internal ears to permit removal. Parallel-sided (machined) circlips can be installed either way round in their groove, whereas stamped circlips (which have a chamfered edge on one face) must be installed with the chamfer facing away from the direction of thrust load **(see illustration 2.9)**.

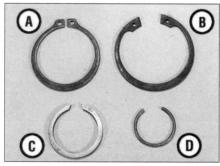

2.8 External stamped circlip (A), internal stamped circlip (B), machined circlip (C) and wire circlip (D)

● Always use circlip pliers to remove and install circlips; expand or compress them just enough to remove them. After installation, rotate the circlip in its groove to ensure it is securely seated. If installing a circlip on a splined shaft, always align its opening with a shaft channel to ensure the circlip ends are well supported and unlikely to catch **(see illustration 2.10)**.

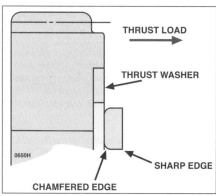

THRUST LOAD

THRUST WASHER

SHARP EDGE

CHAMFERED EDGE

0650H

2.9 Correct fitting of a stamped circlip

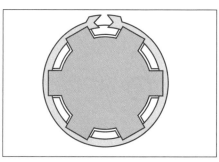

2.10 Align circlip opening with shaft channel

● Circlips can wear due to the thrust of components and become loose in their grooves, with the subsequent danger of becoming dislodged in operation. For this reason, renewal is advised every time a circlip is disturbed.

● Wire circlips are commonly used as piston pin retaining clips. If a removal tang is provided, long-nosed pliers can be used to dislodge them, otherwise careful use of a small flat-bladed screwdriver is necessary. Wire circlips should be renewed every time they are disturbed.

Thread diameter and pitch

● Diameter of a male thread (screw, bolt or stud) is the outside diameter of the threaded portion **(see illustration 2.11)**. Most motorcycle manufacturers use the ISO (International Standards Organisation) metric system expressed in millimetres, eg M6 refers to a 6 mm diameter thread. Sizing is the same for nuts, except that the thread diameter is measured across the valleys of the nut.

● Pitch is the distance between the peaks of the thread **(see illustration 2.11)**. It is expressed in millimetres, thus a common bolt size may be expressed as 6.0 x 1.0 mm (6 mm thread diameter and 1 mm pitch). Generally pitch increases in proportion to thread diameter, although there are always exceptions.

● Thread diameter and pitch are related for conventional fastener applications and the accompanying table can be used as a guide. Additionally, the AF (Across Flats), spanner or socket size dimension of the bolt or nut **(see illustration 2.11)** is linked to thread and pitch specification. Thread pitch can be measured with a thread gauge **(see illustration 2.12)**.

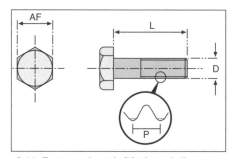

AF

L

D

P

2.11 Fastener length (L), thread diameter (D), thread pitch (P) and head size (AF)

2.12 Using a thread gauge to measure pitch

AF size	Thread diameter x pitch (mm)
8 mm	M5 x 0.8
8 mm	M6 x 1.0
10 mm	M6 x 1.0
12 mm	M8 x 1.25
14 mm	M10 x 1.25
17 mm	M12 x 1.25

● The threads of most fasteners are of the right-hand type, ie they are turned clockwise to tighten and anti-clockwise to loosen. The reverse situation applies to left-hand thread fasteners, which are turned anti-clockwise to tighten and clockwise to loosen. Left-hand threads are used where rotation of a component might loosen a conventional right-hand thread fastener.

Seized fasteners

● Corrosion of external fasteners due to water or reaction between two dissimilar metals can occur over a period of time. It will build up sooner in wet conditions or in countries where salt is used on the roads during the winter. If a fastener is severely corroded it is likely that normal methods of removal will fail and result in its head being ruined. When you attempt removal, the fastener thread should be heard to crack free and unscrew easily - if it doesn't, stop there before damaging something.

● A smart tap on the head of the fastener will often succeed in breaking free corrosion which has occurred in the threads **(see illustration 2.13)**.

● An aerosol penetrating fluid (such as WD-40) applied the night beforehand may work its way down into the thread and ease removal. Depending on the location, you may be able to make up a Plasticine well around the fastener head and fill it with penetrating fluid.

2.13 A sharp tap on the head of a fastener will often break free a corroded thread

● If you are working on an engine internal component, corrosion will most likely not be a problem due to the well lubricated environment. However, components can be very tight and an impact driver is a useful tool in freeing them **(see illustration 2.14)**.

2.14 Using an impact driver to free a fastener

● Where corrosion has occurred between dissimilar metals (eg steel and aluminium alloy), the application of heat to the fastener head will create a disproportionate expansion rate between the two metals and break the seizure caused by the corrosion. Whether heat can be applied depends on the location of the fastener - any surrounding components likely to be damaged must first be removed **(see illustration 2.15)**. Heat can be applied using a paint stripper heat gun or clothes iron, or by immersing the component in boiling water - wear protective gloves to prevent scalding or burns to the hands.

2.15 Using heat to free a seized fastener

● As a last resort, it is possible to use a hammer and cold chisel to work the fastener head unscrewed **(see illustration 2.16)**. This will damage the fastener, but more importantly extreme care must be taken not to damage the surrounding component.

Caution: Remember that the component being secured is generally of more value than the bolt, nut or screw - when the fastener is freed, do not unscrew it with force, instead work the fastener back and forth when resistance is felt to prevent thread damage.

2.16 Using a hammer and chisel to free a seized fastener

Broken fasteners and damaged heads

● If the shank of a broken bolt or screw is accessible you can grip it with self-locking grips. The knurled wheel type stud extractor tool or self-gripping stud puller tool is particularly useful for removing the long studs which screw into the cylinder mouth surface of the crankcase or bolts and screws from which the head has broken off **(see illustration 2.17)**. Studs can also be removed by locking two nuts together on the threaded end of the stud and using a spanner on the lower nut **(see illustration 2.18)**.

2.17 Using a stud extractor tool to remove a broken crankcase stud

2.18 Two nuts can be locked together to unscrew a stud from a component

● A bolt or screw which has broken off below or level with the casing must be extracted using a screw extractor set. Centre punch the fastener to centralise the drill bit, then drill a hole in the fastener **(see illustration 2.19)**. Select a drill bit which is approximately half to three-quarters the

2.19 When using a screw extractor, first drill a hole in the fastener . . .

diameter of the fastener and drill to a depth which will accommodate the extractor. Use the largest size extractor possible, but avoid leaving too small a wall thickness otherwise the extractor will merely force the fastener walls outwards wedging it in the casing thread.

● If a spiral type extractor is used, thread it anti-clockwise into the fastener. As it is screwed in, it will grip the fastener and unscrew it from the casing **(see illustration 2.20)**.

2.20 . . . then thread the extractor anti-clockwise into the fastener

● If a taper type extractor is used, tap it into the fastener so that it is firmly wedged in place. Unscrew the extractor (anti-clockwise) to draw the fastener out.

⚠ **Warning: Stud extractors are very hard and may break off in the fastener if care is not taken - ask an engineer about spark erosion if this happens.**

● Alternatively, the broken bolt/screw can be drilled out and the hole retapped for an oversize bolt/screw or a diamond-section thread insert. It is essential that the drilling is carried out squarely and to the correct depth, otherwise the casing may be ruined - if in doubt, entrust the work to an engineer.

● Bolts and nuts with rounded corners cause the correct size spanner or socket to slip when force is applied. Of the types of spanner/socket available always use a six-point type rather than an eight or twelve-point type - better grip

2.21 Comparison of surface drive ring spanner (left) with 12-point type (right)

is obtained. Surface drive spanners grip the middle of the hex flats, rather than the corners, and are thus good in cases of damaged heads **(see illustration 2.21)**.

● Slotted-head or Phillips-head screws are often damaged by the use of the wrong size screwdriver. Allen-head and Torx-head screws are much less likely to sustain damage. If enough of the screw head is exposed you can use a hacksaw to cut a slot in its head and then use a conventional flat-bladed screwdriver to remove it. Alternatively use a hammer and cold chisel to tap the head of the fastener around to slacken it. Always replace damaged fasteners with new ones, preferably Torx or Allen-head type.

HAYNES HiNT

A dab of valve grinding compound between the screw head and screwdriver tip will often give a good grip.

Thread repair

● Threads (particularly those in aluminium alloy components) can be damaged by overtightening, being assembled with dirt in the threads, or from a component working loose and vibrating. Eventually the thread will fail completely, and it will be impossible to tighten the fastener.

● If a thread is damaged or clogged with old locking compound it can be renovated with a thread repair tool (thread chaser) **(see illustrations 2.22 and 2.23)**; special thread

2.22 A thread repair tool being used to correct an internal thread

2.23 A thread repair tool being used to correct an external thread

chasers are available for spark plug hole threads. The tool will not cut a new thread, but clean and true the original thread. Make sure that you use the correct diameter and pitch tool. Similarly, external threads can be cleaned up with a die or a thread restorer file **(see illustration 2.24)**.

2.24 Using a thread restorer file

● It is possible to drill out the old thread and retap the component to the next thread size. This will work where there is enough surrounding material and a new bolt or screw can be obtained. Sometimes, however, this is not possible - such as where the bolt/screw passes through another component which must also be suitably modified, also in cases where a spark plug or oil drain plug cannot be obtained in a larger diameter thread size.

● The diamond-section thread insert (often known by its popular trade name of Heli-Coil) is a simple and effective method of renewing the thread and retaining the original size. A kit can be purchased which contains the tap, insert and installing tool **(see illustration 2.25)**. Drill out the damaged thread with the size drill specified **(see illustration 2.26)**. Carefully retap the thread **(see illustration 2.27)**. Install the

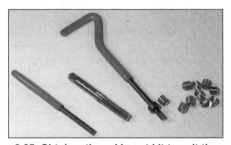

2.25 Obtain a thread insert kit to suit the thread diameter and pitch required

2.26 To install a thread insert, first drill out the original thread . . .

2.27 . . . tap a new thread . . .

2.28 . . . fit insert on the installing tool . . .

2.29 . . . and thread into the component . . .

2.30 . . . break off the tang when complete

insert on the installing tool and thread it slowly into place using a light downward pressure **(see illustrations 2.28 and 2.29)**. When positioned between a 1/4 and 1/2 turn below the surface withdraw the installing tool and use the break-off tool to press down on the tang, breaking it off **(see illustration 2.30)**.

● There are epoxy thread repair kits on the market which can rebuild stripped internal threads, although this repair should not be used on high load-bearing components.

Thread locking and sealing compounds

● Locking compounds are used in locations where the fastener is prone to loosening due to vibration or on important safety-related items which might cause loss of control of the motorcycle if they fail. It is also used where important fasteners cannot be secured by other means such as lockwashers or split pins.

● Before applying locking compound, make sure that the threads (internal and external) are clean and dry with all old compound removed. Select a compound to suit the component being secured - a non-permanent general locking and sealing type is suitable for most applications, but a high strength type is needed for permanent fixing of studs in castings. Apply a drop or two of the compound to the first few threads of the fastener, then thread it into place and tighten to the specified torque. Do not apply excessive thread locking compound otherwise the thread may be damaged on subsequent removal.

● Certain fasteners are impregnated with a dry film type coating of locking compound on their threads. Always renew this type of fastener if disturbed.

● Anti-seize compounds, such as copper-based greases, can be applied to protect threads from seizure due to extreme heat and corrosion. A common instance is spark plug threads and exhaust system fasteners.

3 Measuring tools and gauges

Feeler gauges

● Feeler gauges (or blades) are used for measuring small gaps and clearances (see illustration 3.1). They can also be used to measure endfloat (sideplay) of a component on a shaft where access is not possible with a dial gauge.

● Feeler gauge sets should be treated with care and not bent or damaged. They are etched with their size on one face. Keep them clean and very lightly oiled to prevent corrosion build-up.

3.1 Feeler gauges are used for measuring small gaps and clearances - thickness is marked on one face of gauge

● When measuring a clearance, select a gauge which is a light sliding fit between the two components. You may need to use two gauges together to measure the clearance accurately.

Micrometers

● A micrometer is a precision tool capable of measuring to 0.01 or 0.001 of a millimetre. It should always be stored in its case and not in the general toolbox. It must be kept clean and never dropped, otherwise its frame or measuring anvils could be distorted resulting in inaccurate readings.

● External micrometers are used for measuring outside diameters of components and have many more applications than internal micrometers. Micrometers are available in different size ranges, eg 0 to 25 mm, 25 to 50 mm, and upwards in 25 mm steps; some large micrometers have interchangeable anvils to allow a range of measurements to be taken. Generally the largest precision measurement you are likely to take on a motorcycle is the piston diameter.

● Internal micrometers (or bore micrometers) are used for measuring inside diameters, such as valve guides and cylinder bores. Telescoping gauges and small hole gauges are used in conjunction with an external micrometer, whereas the more expensive internal micrometers have their own measuring device.

External micrometer

Note: *The conventional analogue type instrument is described. Although much easier to read, digital micrometers are considerably more expensive.*

● Always check the calibration of the micrometer before use. With the anvils closed (0 to 25 mm type) or set over a test gauge (for

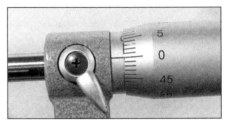

3.2 Check micrometer calibration before use

the larger types) the scale should read zero **(see illustration 3.2)**; make sure that the anvils (and test piece) are clean first. Any discrepancy can be adjusted by referring to the instructions supplied with the tool. Remember that the micrometer is a precision measuring tool - don't force the anvils closed, use the ratchet (4) on the end of the micrometer to close it. In this way, a measured force is always applied.

● To use, first make sure that the item being measured is clean. Place the anvil of the micrometer (1) against the item and use the thimble (2) to bring the spindle (3) lightly into contact with the other side of the item **(see illustration 3.3)**. Don't tighten the thimble down because this will damage the micrometer - instead use the ratchet (4) on the end of the micrometer. The ratchet mechanism applies a measured force preventing damage to the instrument.

● The micrometer is read by referring to the linear scale on the sleeve and the annular scale on the thimble. Read off the sleeve first to obtain the base measurement, then add the fine measurement from the thimble to obtain the overall reading. The linear scale on the sleeve represents the measuring range of the micrometer (eg 0 to 25 mm). The annular scale

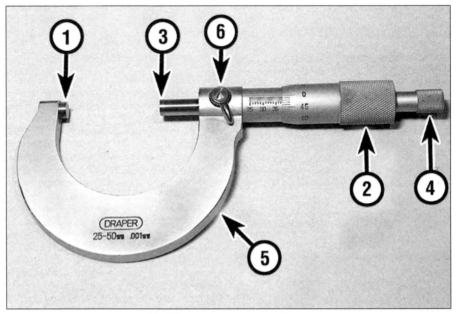

3.3 Micrometer component parts

1 Anvil	3 Spindle	5 Frame
2 Thimble	4 Ratchet	6 Locking lever

on the thimble will be in graduations of 0.01 mm (or as marked on the frame) - one full revolution of the thimble will move 0.5 mm on the linear scale. Take the reading where the datum line on the sleeve intersects the thimble's scale. Always position the eye directly above the scale otherwise an inaccurate reading will result.

In the example shown the item measures 2.95 mm **(see illustration 3.4)**:

Linear scale	2.00 mm
Linear scale	0.50 mm
Annular scale	0.45 mm
Total figure	**2.95 mm**

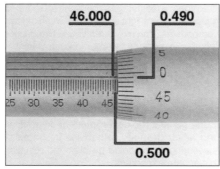

3.5 Micrometer reading of 46.99 mm on linear and annular scales . . .

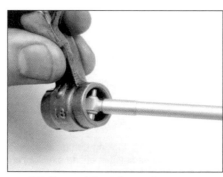

3.7 Expand the telescoping gauge in the bore, lock its position . . .

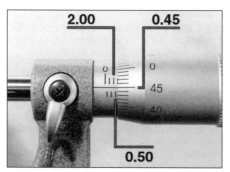

3.4 Micrometer reading of 2.95 mm

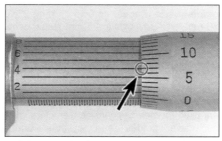

3.6 . . . and 0.004 mm on vernier scale

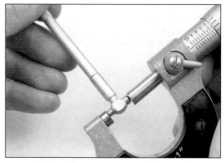

3.8 . . . then measure the gauge with a micrometer

Most micrometers have a locking lever (6) on the frame to hold the setting in place, allowing the item to be removed from the micrometer.

● Some micrometers have a vernier scale on their sleeve, providing an even finer measurement to be taken, in 0.001 increments of a millimetre. Take the sleeve and thimble measurement as described above, then check which graduation on the vernier scale aligns with that of the annular scale on the thimble **Note:** *The eye must be perpendicular to the scale when taking the vernier reading - if necessary rotate the body of the micrometer to ensure this.* Multiply the vernier scale figure by 0.001 and add it to the base and fine measurement figures.

In the example shown the item measures 46.994 mm **(see illustrations 3.5 and 3.6)**:

Linear scale (base)	46.000 mm
Linear scale (base)	00.500 mm
Annular scale (fine)	00.490 mm
Vernier scale	00.004 mm
Total figure	**46.994 mm**

Internal micrometer

● Internal micrometers are available for measuring bore diameters, but are expensive and unlikely to be available for home use. It is suggested that a set of telescoping gauges and small hole gauges, both of which must be used with an external micrometer, will suffice for taking internal measurements on a motorcycle.

● Telescoping gauges can be used to

measure internal diameters of components. Select a gauge with the correct size range, make sure its ends are clean and insert it into the bore. Expand the gauge, then lock its position and withdraw it from the bore **(see illustration 3.7)**. Measure across the gauge ends with a micrometer **(see illustration 3.8)**.

● Very small diameter bores (such as valve guides) are measured with a small hole gauge. Once adjusted to a slip-fit inside the component, its position is locked and the gauge withdrawn for measurement with a micrometer **(see illustrations 3.9 and 3.10)**.

Vernier caliper

Note: *The conventional linear and dial gauge type instruments are described. Digital types are easier to read, but are far more expensive.*

● The vernier caliper does not provide the precision of a micrometer, but is versatile in being able to measure internal and external diameters. Some types also incorporate a depth gauge. It is ideal for measuring clutch plate friction material and spring free lengths.

● To use the conventional linear scale vernier, slacken off the vernier clamp screws (1) and set its jaws over (2), or inside (3), the item to be measured **(see illustration 3.11)**. Slide the jaw into contact, using the thumb-wheel (4) for fine movement of the sliding scale (5) then tighten the clamp screws (1). Read off the main scale (6) where the zero on the sliding scale (5) intersects it, taking the whole number to the left of the zero; this provides the base measurement. View along the sliding scale and select the division which

3.9 Expand the small hole gauge in the bore, lock its position . . .

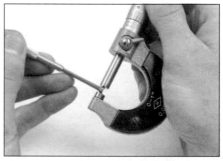

3.10 . . . then measure the gauge with a micrometer

lines up exactly with any of the divisions on the main scale, noting that the divisions usually represents 0.02 of a millimetre. Add this fine measurement to the base measurement to obtain the total reading.

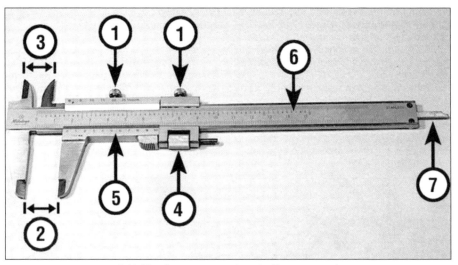

3.11 Vernier component parts (linear gauge)

1 Clamp screws	3 Internal jaws	5 Sliding scale	7 Depth gauge
2 External jaws	4 Thumbwheel	6 Main scale	

In the example shown the item measures 55.92 mm **(see illustration 3.12)**:

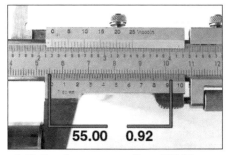

3.12 Vernier gauge reading of 55.92 mm

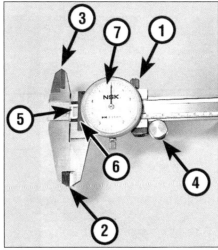

3.13 Vernier component parts (dial gauge)

1 Clamp screw	5 Main scale
2 External jaws	6 Sliding scale
3 Internal jaws	7 Dial gauge
4 Thumbwheel	

Base measurement	55.00 mm
Fine measurement	00.92 mm
Total figure	**55.92 mm**

● Some vernier calipers are equipped with a dial gauge for fine measurement. Before use, check that the jaws are clean, then close them fully and check that the dial gauge reads zero. If necessary adjust the gauge ring accordingly. Slacken the vernier clamp screw (1) and set its jaws over (2), or inside (3), the item to be measured **(see illustration 3.13)**. Slide the jaws into contact, using the thumbwheel (4) for fine movement. Read off the main scale (5) where the edge of the sliding scale (6) intersects it, taking the whole number to the left of the zero; this provides the base measurement. Read off the needle position on the dial gauge (7) scale to provide the fine measurement; each division represents 0.05 of a millimetre. Add this fine measurement to the base measurement to obtain the total reading.

In the example shown the item measures 55.95 mm **(see illustration 3.14)**:

Base measurement	55.00 mm
Fine measurement	00.95 mm
Total figure	**55.95 mm**

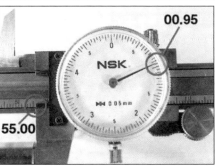

3.14 Vernier gauge reading of 55.95 mm

Plastigauge

● Plastigauge is a plastic material which can be compressed between two surfaces to measure the oil clearance between them. The width of the compressed Plastigauge is measured against a calibrated scale to determine the clearance.

● Common uses of Plastigauge are for measuring the clearance between crankshaft journal and main bearing inserts, between crankshaft journal and big-end bearing inserts, and between camshaft and bearing surfaces. The following example describes big-end oil clearance measurement.

● Handle the Plastigauge material carefully to prevent distortion. Using a sharp knife, cut a length which corresponds with the width of the bearing being measured and place it carefully across the journal so that it is parallel with the shaft **(see illustration 3.15)**. Carefully install both bearing shells and the connecting rod. Without rotating the rod on the journal tighten its bolts or nuts (as applicable) to the specified torque. The connecting rod and bearings are then disassembled and the crushed Plastigauge examined.

3.15 Plastigauge placed across shaft journal

● Using the scale provided in the Plastigauge kit, measure the width of the material to determine the oil clearance **(see illustration 3.16)**. Always remove all traces of Plastigauge after use using your fingernails.

Caution: Arriving at the correct clearance demands that the assembly is torqued correctly, according to the settings and sequence (where applicable) provided by the motorcycle manufacturer.

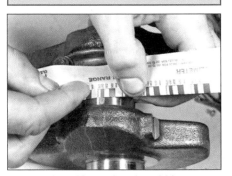

3.16 Measuring the width of the crushed Plastigauge

Dial gauge or DTI (Dial Test Indicator)

● A dial gauge can be used to accurately measure small amounts of movement. Typical uses are measuring shaft runout or shaft endfloat (sideplay) and setting piston position for ignition timing on two-strokes. A dial gauge set usually comes with a range of different probes and adapters and mounting equipment.

● The gauge needle must point to zero when at rest. Rotate the ring around its periphery to zero the gauge.

● Check that the gauge is capable of reading the extent of movement in the work. Most gauges have a small dial set in the face which records whole millimetres of movement as well as the fine scale around the face periphery which is calibrated in 0.01 mm divisions. Read off the small dial first to obtain the base measurement, then add the measurement from the fine scale to obtain the total reading.

In the example shown the gauge reads 1.48 mm **(see illustration 3.17)**:

Base measurement	1.00 mm
Fine measurement	0.48 mm
Total figure	**1.48 mm**

3.17 Dial gauge reading of 1.48 mm

● If measuring shaft runout, the shaft must be supported in vee-blocks and the gauge mounted on a stand perpendicular to the shaft. Rest the tip of the gauge against the centre of the shaft and rotate the shaft slowly whilst watching the gauge reading **(see illustration 3.18)**. Take several measurements along the length of the shaft and record the

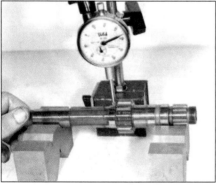

3.18 Using a dial gauge to measure shaft runout

maximum gauge reading as the amount of runout in the shaft. **Note:** *The reading obtained will be total runout at that point - some manufacturers specify that the runout figure is halved to compare with their specified runout limit.*

● Endfloat (sideplay) measurement requires that the gauge is mounted securely to the surrounding component with its probe touching the end of the shaft. Using hand pressure, push and pull on the shaft noting the maximum endfloat recorded on the gauge **(see illustration 3.19)**.

3.19 Using a dial gauge to measure shaft endfloat

● A dial gauge with suitable adapters can be used to determine piston position BTDC on two-stroke engines for the purposes of ignition timing. The gauge, adapter and suitable length probe are installed in the place of the spark plug and the gauge zeroed at TDC. If the piston position is specified as 1.14 mm BTDC, rotate the engine back to 2.00 mm BTDC, then slowly forwards to 1.14 mm BTDC.

Cylinder compression gauges

● A compression gauge is used for measuring cylinder compression. Either the rubber-cone type or the threaded adapter type can be used. The latter is preferred to ensure a perfect seal against the cylinder head. A 0 to 300 psi (0 to 20 Bar) type gauge (for petrol/gasoline engines) will be suitable for motorcycles.

● The spark plug is removed and the gauge either held hard against the cylinder head (cone type) or the gauge adapter screwed into the cylinder head (threaded type) **(see illustration 3.20)**. Cylinder compression is measured with the engine turning over, but not running - carry out the compression test as described in

3.20 Using a rubber-cone type cylinder compression gauge

Fault Finding Equipment. The gauge will hold the reading until manually released.

Oil pressure gauge

● An oil pressure gauge is used for measuring engine oil pressure. Most gauges come with a set of adapters to fit the thread of the take-off point **(see illustration 3.21)**. If the take-off point specified by the motorcycle manufacturer is an external oil pipe union, make sure that the specified replacement union is used to prevent oil starvation.

3.21 Oil pressure gauge and take-off point adapter (arrow)

● Oil pressure is measured with the engine running (at a specific rpm) and often the manufacturer will specify pressure limits for a cold and hot engine.

Straight-edge and surface plate

● If checking the gasket face of a component for warpage, place a steel rule or precision straight-edge across the gasket face and measure any gap between the straight-edge and component with feeler gauges **(see illustration 3.22)**. Check diagonally across the component and between mounting holes **(see illustration 3.23)**.

3.22 Use a straight-edge and feeler gauges to check for warpage

3.23 Check for warpage in these directions

● Checking individual components for warpage, such as clutch plain (metal) plates, requires a perfectly flat plate or piece or plate glass and feeler gauges.

4 Torque and leverage

What is torque?

● Torque describes the twisting force about a shaft. The amount of torque applied is determined by the distance from the centre of the shaft to the end of the lever and the amount of force being applied to the end of the lever; distance multiplied by force equals torque.

● The manufacturer applies a measured torque to a bolt or nut to ensure that it will not slacken in use and to hold two components securely together without movement in the joint. The actual torque setting depends on the thread size, bolt or nut material and the composition of the components being held.

● Too little torque may cause the fastener to loosen due to vibration, whereas too much torque will distort the joint faces of the component or cause the fastener to shear off. Always stick to the specified torque setting.

Using a torque wrench

● Check the calibration of the torque wrench and make sure it has a suitable range for the job. Torque wrenches are available in Nm (Newton-metres), kgf m (kilograms-force metre), lbf ft (pounds-feet), lbf in (inch-pounds). Do not confuse lbf ft with lbf in.

● Adjust the tool to the desired torque on the scale (see illustration 4.1). If your torque wrench is not calibrated in the units specified, carefully convert the figure (see *Conversion Factors*). A manufacturer sometimes gives a torque setting as a range (8 to 10 Nm) rather than a single figure - in this case set the tool midway between the two settings. The same torque may be expressed as 9 Nm ± 1 Nm. Some torque wrenches have a method of locking the setting so that it isn't inadvertently altered during use.

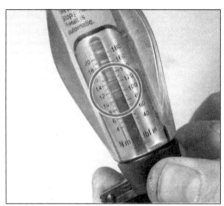

4.1 Set the torque wrench index mark to the setting required, in this case 12 Nm

● Install the bolts/nuts in their correct location and secure them lightly. Their threads must be clean and free of any old locking compound. Unless specified the threads and flange should be dry - oiled threads are necessary in certain circumstances and the manufacturer will take this into account in the specified torque figure. Similarly, the manufacturer may also specify the application of thread-locking compound.

● Tighten the fasteners in the specified sequence until the torque wrench clicks, indicating that the torque setting has been reached. Apply the torque again to double-check the setting. Where different thread diameter fasteners secure the component, as a rule tighten the larger diameter ones first.

● When the torque wrench has been finished with, release the lock (where applicable) and fully back off its setting to zero - do not leave the torque wrench tensioned. Also, do not use a torque wrench for slackening a fastener.

Angle-tightening

● Manufacturers often specify a figure in degrees for final tightening of a fastener. This usually follows tightening to a specific torque setting.

● A degree disc can be set and attached to the socket (see illustration 4.2) or a protractor can be used to mark the angle of movement on the bolt/nut head and the surrounding casting (see illustration 4.3).

4.2 Angle tightening can be accomplished with a torque-angle gauge . . .

4.3 . . . or by marking the angle on the surrounding component

Loosening sequences

● Where more than one bolt/nut secures a component, loosen each fastener evenly a little at a time. In this way, not all the stress of the joint is held by one fastener and the components are not likely to distort.

● If a tightening sequence is provided, work in the REVERSE of this, but if not, work from the outside in, in a criss-cross sequence (see illustration 4.4).

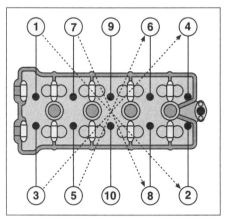

4.4 When slackening, work from the outside inwards

Tightening sequences

● If a component is held by more than one fastener it is important that the retaining bolts/nuts are tightened evenly to prevent uneven stress build-up and distortion of sealing faces. This is especially important on high-compression joints such as the cylinder head.

● A sequence is usually provided by the manufacturer, either in a diagram or actually marked in the casting. If not, always start in the centre and work outwards in a criss-cross pattern (see illustration 4.5). Start off by securing all bolts/nuts finger-tight, then set the torque wrench and tighten each fastener by a small amount in sequence until the final torque is reached. By following this practice,

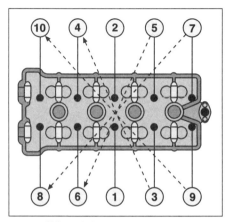

4.5 When tightening, work from the inside outwards

the joint will be held evenly and will not be distorted. Important joints, such as the cylinder head and big-end fasteners often have two- or three-stage torque settings.

Applying leverage

● Use tools at the correct angle. Position a socket wrench or spanner on the bolt/nut so that you pull it towards you when loosening. If this can't be done, push the spanner without curling your fingers around it **(see illustration 4.6)** - the spanner may slip or the fastener loosen suddenly, resulting in your fingers being crushed against a component.

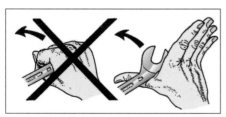

4.6 If you can't pull on the spanner to loosen a fastener, push with your hand open

● Additional leverage is gained by extending the length of the lever. The best way to do this is to use a breaker bar instead of the regular length tool, or to slip a length of tubing over the end of the spanner or socket wrench.
● If additional leverage will not work, the fastener head is either damaged or firmly corroded in place (see *Fasteners*).

5 Bearings

Bearing removal and installation

Drivers and sockets

● Before removing a bearing, always inspect the casing to see which way it must be driven out - some casings will have retaining plates or a cast step. Also check for any identifying markings on the bearing and if installed to a certain depth, measure this at this stage. Some roller bearings are sealed on one side - take note of the original fitted position.
● Bearings can be driven out of a casing using a bearing driver tool (with the correct size head) or a socket of the correct diameter. Select the driver head or socket so that it contacts the outer race of the bearing, not the balls/rollers or inner race. Always support the casing around the bearing housing with wood blocks, otherwise there is a risk of fracture. The bearing is driven out with a few blows on the driver or socket from a heavy mallet. Unless access is severely restricted (as with wheel bearings), a pin-punch is not recommended unless it is moved around the bearing to keep it square in its housing.

● The same equipment can be used to install bearings. Make sure the bearing housing is supported on wood blocks and line up the bearing in its housing. Fit the bearing as noted on removal - generally they are installed with their marked side facing outwards. Tap the bearing squarely into its housing using a driver or socket which bears only on the bearing's outer race - contact with the bearing balls/rollers or inner race will destroy it **(see illustrations 5.1 and 5.2)**.
● Check that the bearing inner race and balls/rollers rotate freely.

5.1 Using a bearing driver against the bearing's outer race

5.2 Using a large socket against the bearing's outer race

Pullers and slide-hammers

● Where a bearing is pressed on a shaft a puller will be required to extract it **(see illustration 5.3)**. Make sure that the puller clamp or legs fit securely behind the bearing and are unlikely to slip out. If pulling a bearing

5.3 This bearing puller clamps behind the bearing and pressure is applied to the shaft end to draw the bearing off

off a gear shaft for example, you may have to locate the puller behind a gear pinion if there is no access to the race and draw the gear pinion off the shaft as well **(see illustration 5.4)**.

> **Caution: Ensure that the puller's centre bolt locates securely against the end of the shaft and will not slip when pressure is applied. Also ensure that puller does not damage the shaft end.**

5.4 Where no access is available to the rear of the bearing, it is sometimes possible to draw off the adjacent component

● Operate the puller so that its centre bolt exerts pressure on the shaft end and draws the bearing off the shaft.
● When installing the bearing on the shaft, tap only on the bearing's inner race - contact with the balls/rollers or outer race with destroy the bearing. Use a socket or length of tubing as a drift which fits over the shaft end **(see illustration 5.5)**.

5.5 When installing a bearing on a shaft use a piece of tubing which bears only on the bearing's inner race

● Where a bearing locates in a blind hole in a casing, it cannot be driven or pulled out as described above. A slide-hammer with knife-edged bearing puller attachment will be required. The puller attachment passes through the bearing and when tightened expands to fit firmly behind the bearing **(see illustration 5.6)**. By operating the slide-hammer part of the tool the bearing is jarred out of its housing **(see illustration 5.7)**.
● It is possible, if the bearing is of reasonable weight, for it to drop out of its housing if the casing is heated as described opposite. If this

5.6 Expand the bearing puller so that it locks behind the bearing . . .

5.7 . . . attach the slide hammer to the bearing puller

method is attempted, first prepare a work surface which will enable the casing to be tapped face down to help dislodge the bearing - a wood surface is ideal since it will not damage the casing's gasket surface. Wearing protective gloves, tap the heated casing several times against the work surface to dislodge the bearing under its own weight **(see illustration 5.8)**.

5.8 Tapping a casing face down on wood blocks can often dislodge a bearing

● Bearings can be installed in blind holes using the driver or socket method described above.

Drawbolts

● Where a bearing or bush is set in the eye of a component, such as a suspension linkage arm or connecting rod small-end, removal by drift may damage the component. Furthermore, a rubber bushing in a shock absorber eye cannot successfully be driven out of position. If access is available to a engineering press, the task is straightforward. If not, a drawbolt can be fabricated to extract the bearing or bush.

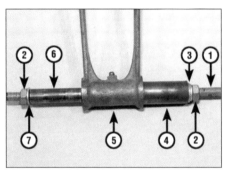

5.9 Drawbolt component parts assembled on a suspension arm

1 Bolt or length of threaded bar
2 Nuts
3 Washer (external diameter greater than tubing internal diameter)
4 Tubing (internal diameter sufficient to accommodate bearing)
5 Suspension arm with bearing
6 Tubing (external diameter slightly smaller than bearing)
7 Washer (external diameter slightly smaller than bearing)

5.10 Drawing the bearing out of the suspension arm

● To extract the bearing/bush you will need a long bolt with nut (or piece of threaded bar with two nuts), a piece of tubing which has an internal diameter larger than the bearing/bush, another piece of tubing which has an external diameter slightly smaller than the bearing/ bush, and a selection of washers **(see illustrations 5.9 and 5.10)**. Note that the pieces of tubing must be of the same length, or longer, than the bearing/bush.
● The same kit (without the pieces of tubing) can be used to draw the new bearing/bush back into place **(see illustration 5.11)**.

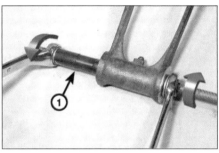

5.11 Installing a new bearing (1) in the suspension arm

Temperature change

● If the bearing's outer race is a tight fit in the casing, the aluminium casing can be heated to release its grip on the bearing. Aluminium will expand at a greater rate than the steel bearing outer race. There are several ways to do this, but avoid any localised extreme heat (such as a blow torch) - aluminium alloy has a low melting point.
● Approved methods of heating a casing are using a domestic oven (heated to 100°C) or immersing the casing in boiling water **(see illustration 5.12)**. Low temperature range localised heat sources such as a paint stripper heat gun or clothes iron can also be used **(see illustration 5.13)**. Alternatively, soak a rag in boiling water, wring it out and wrap it around the bearing housing.

> ⚠ *Warning: All of these methods require care in use to prevent scalding and burns to the hands. Wear protective gloves when handling hot components.*

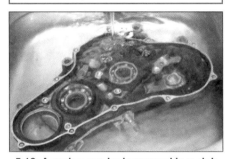

5.12 A casing can be immersed in a sink of boiling water to aid bearing removal

5.13 Using a localised heat source to aid bearing removal

● If heating the whole casing note that plastic components, such as the neutral switch, may suffer - remove them beforehand.
● After heating, remove the bearing as described above. You may find that the expansion is sufficient for the bearing to fall out of the casing under its own weight or with a light tap on the driver or socket.
● If necessary, the casing can be heated to aid bearing installation, and this is sometimes the recommended procedure if the motorcycle manufacturer has designed the housing and bearing fit with this intention.

● Installation of bearings can be eased by placing them in a freezer the night before installation. The steel bearing will contract slightly, allowing easy insertion in its housing. This is often useful when installing steering head outer races in the frame.

Bearing types and markings

● Plain shell bearings, ball bearings, needle roller bearings and tapered roller bearings will all be found on motorcycles (see illustrations 5.14 and 5.15). The ball and roller types are usually caged between an inner and outer race, but uncaged variations may be found.

5.14 Shell bearings are either plain or grooved. They are usually identified by colour code (arrow)

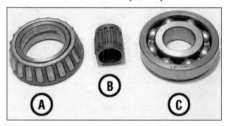

5.15 Tapered roller bearing (A), needle roller bearing (B) and ball journal bearing (C)

● Shell bearings (often called inserts) are usually found at the crankshaft main and connecting rod big-end where they are good at coping with high loads. They are made of a phosphor-bronze material and are impregnated with self-lubricating properties.
● Ball bearings and needle roller bearings consist of a steel inner and outer race with the balls or rollers between the races. They require constant lubrication by oil or grease and are good at coping with axial loads. Taper roller bearings consist of rollers set in a tapered cage set on the inner race; the outer race is separate. They are good at coping with axial loads and prevent movement along the shaft - a typical application is in the steering head.
● Bearing manufacturers produce bearings to ISO size standards and stamp one face of the bearing to indicate its internal and external diameter, load capacity and type (see illustration 5.16).
● Metal bushes are usually of phosphor-bronze material. Rubber bushes are used in suspension mounting eyes. Fibre bushes have also been used in suspension pivots.

5.16 Typical bearing marking

Bearing fault finding

● If a bearing outer race has spun in its housing, the housing material will be damaged. You can use a bearing locking compound to bond the outer race in place if damage is not too severe.
● Shell bearings will fail due to damage of their working surface, as a result of lack of lubrication, corrosion or abrasive particles in the oil (see illustration 5.17). Small particles of dirt in the oil may embed in the bearing material whereas larger particles will score the bearing and shaft journal. If a number of short journeys are made, insufficient heat will be generated to drive off condensation which has built up on the bearings.

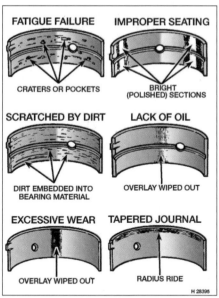

5.17 Typical bearing failures

● Ball and roller bearings will fail due to lack of lubrication or damage to the balls or rollers. Tapered-roller bearings can be damaged by overloading them. Unless the bearing is sealed on both sides, wash it in paraffin (kerosene) to remove all old grease then allow it to dry. Make a visual inspection looking to dented balls or rollers, damaged cages and worn or pitted races (see illustration 5.18).
● A ball bearing can be checked for wear by listening to it when spun. Apply a film of light oil to the bearing and hold it close to the ear - hold the outer race with one hand and spin the inner

5.18 Example of ball journal bearing with damaged balls and cages

5.19 Hold outer race and listen to inner race when spun

race with the other hand (see illustration 5.19). The bearing should be almost silent when spun; if it grates or rattles it is worn.

6 Oil seals

Oil seal removal and installation

● Oil seals should be renewed every time a component is dismantled. This is because the seal lips will become set to the sealing surface and will not necessarily reseal.
● Oil seals can be prised out of position using a large flat-bladed screwdriver (see illustration 6.1). In the case of crankcase seals, check first that the seal is not lipped on the inside, preventing its removal with the crankcases joined.

6.1 Prise out oil seals with a large flat-bladed screwdriver

● New seals are usually installed with their marked face (containing the seal reference code) outwards and the spring side towards the fluid being retained. In certain cases, such as a two-stroke engine crankshaft seal, a double lipped seal may be used due to there being fluid or gas on each side of the joint.

● Use a bearing driver or socket which bears only on the outer hard edge of the seal to install it in the casing - tapping on the inner edge will damage the sealing lip.

Oil seal types and markings

● Oil seals are usually of the single-lipped type. Double-lipped seals are found where a liquid or gas is on both sides of the joint.
● Oil seals can harden and lose their sealing ability if the motorcycle has been in storage for a long period - renewal is the only solution.
● Oil seal manufacturers also conform to the ISO markings for seal size - these are moulded into the outer face of the seal **(see illustration 6.2)**.

6.2 These oil seal markings indicate inside diameter, outside diameter and seal thickness

7 Gaskets and sealants

Types of gasket and sealant

● Gaskets are used to seal the mating surfaces between components and keep lubricants, fluids, vacuum or pressure contained within the assembly. Aluminium gaskets are sometimes found at the cylinder joints, but most gaskets are paper-based. If the mating surfaces of the components being joined are undamaged the gasket can be installed dry, although a dab of sealant or grease will be useful to hold it in place during assembly.
● RTV (Room Temperature Vulcanising) silicone rubber sealants cure when exposed to moisture in the atmosphere. These sealants are good at filling pits or irregular gasket faces, but will tend to be forced out of the joint under very high torque. They can be used to replace a paper gasket, but first make sure that the width of the paper gasket is not essential to the shimming of internal components. RTV sealants should not be used on components containing petrol (gasoline).
● Non-hardening, semi-hardening and hard setting liquid gasket compounds can be used with a gasket or between a metal-to-metal joint. Select the sealant to suit the application: universal non-hardening sealant can be used on virtually all joints; semi-hardening on joint faces which are rough or damaged; hard setting sealant on joints which require a permanent bond and are subjected to high temperature and pressure. **Note:** *Check first if the paper gasket has a bead of sealant*

impregnated in its surface before applying additional sealant.
● When choosing a sealant, make sure it is suitable for the application, particularly if being applied in a high-temperature area or in the vicinity of fuel. Certain manufacturers produce sealants in either clear, silver or black colours to match the finish of the engine. This has a particular application on motorcycles where much of the engine is exposed.
● Do not over-apply sealant. That which is squeezed out on the outside of the joint can be wiped off, whereas an excess of sealant on the inside can break off and clog oilways.

Breaking a sealed joint

● Age, heat, pressure and the use of hard setting sealant can cause two components to stick together so tightly that they are difficult to separate using finger pressure alone. Do not resort to using levers unless there is a pry point provided for this purpose **(see illustration 7.1)** or else the gasket surfaces will be damaged.
● Use a soft-faced hammer **(see illustration 7.2)** or a wood block and conventional hammer to strike the component near the mating surface. Avoid hammering against cast extremities since they may break off. If this method fails, try using a wood wedge between the two components.

Caution: If the joint will not separate, double-check that you have removed all the fasteners.

7.1 If a pry point is provided, apply gently pressure with a flat-bladed screwdriver

7.2 Tap around the joint with a soft-faced mallet if necessary - don't strike cooling fins

Removal of old gasket and sealant

● Paper gaskets will most likely come away complete, leaving only a few traces stuck on

Most components have one or two hollow locating dowels between the two gasket faces. If a dowel cannot be removed, do not resort to gripping it with pliers - it will almost certainly be distorted. Install a close-fitting socket or Phillips screwdriver into the dowel and then grip the outer edge of the dowel to free it.

the sealing faces of the components. It is imperative that all traces are removed to ensure correct sealing of the new gasket.
● Very carefully scrape all traces of gasket away making sure that the sealing surfaces are not gouged or scored by the scraper **(see illustrations 7.3, 7.4 and 7.5)**. Stubborn deposits can be removed by spraying with an aerosol gasket remover. Final preparation of

7.3 Paper gaskets can be scraped off with a gasket scraper tool . . .

7.4 . . . a knife blade . . .

7.5 . . . or a household scraper

7.6 Fine abrasive paper is wrapped around a flat file to clean up the gasket face

7.7 A kitchen scourer can be used on stubborn deposits

the gasket surface can be made with very fine abrasive paper or a plastic kitchen scourer **(see illustrations 7.6 and 7.7)**.

● Old sealant can be scraped or peeled off components, depending on the type originally used. Note that gasket removal compounds are available to avoid scraping the components clean; make sure the gasket remover suits the type of sealant used.

8 Chains

Breaking and joining final drive chains

● Drive chains for all but small bikes are continuous and do not have a clip-type connecting link. The chain must be broken using a chain breaker tool and the new chain securely riveted together using a new soft rivet-type link. Never use a clip-type connecting link instead of a rivet-type link, except in an emergency. Various chain breaking and riveting tools are available, either as separate tools or combined as illustrated in the accompanying photographs - read the instructions supplied with the tool carefully.

> ⚠ **Warning: The need to rivet the new link pins correctly cannot be overstressed - loss of control of the motorcycle is very likely to result if the chain breaks in use.**

● Rotate the chain and look for the soft link. The soft link pins look like they have been

8.1 Tighten the chain breaker to push the pin out of the link . . .

8.2 . . . withdraw the pin, remove the tool . . .

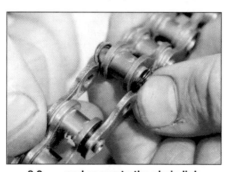

8.3 . . . and separate the chain link

deeply centre-punched instead of peened over like all the other pins **(see illustration 8.9)** and its sideplate may be a different colour. Position the soft link midway between the sprockets and assemble the chain breaker tool over one of the soft link pins **(see illustration 8.1)**. Operate the tool to push the pin out through the chain **(see illustration 8.2)**. On an O-ring chain, remove the O-rings **(see illustration 8.3)**. Carry out the same procedure on the other soft link pin.

> *Caution: Certain soft link pins (particularly on the larger chains) may require their ends to be filed or ground off before they can be pressed out using the tool.*

● Check that you have the correct size and strength (standard or heavy duty) new soft link - do not reuse the old link. Look for the size marking on the chain sideplates **(see illustration 8.10)**.

● Position the chain ends so that they are engaged over the rear sprocket. On an O-ring

8.4 Insert the new soft link, with O-rings, through the chain ends . . .

8.5 . . . install the O-rings over the pin ends . . .

8.6 . . . followed by the sideplate

chain, install a new O-ring over each pin of the link and insert the link through the two chain ends **(see illustration 8.4)**. Install a new O-ring over the end of each pin, followed by the sideplate (with the chain manufacturer's marking facing outwards) **(see illustrations 8.5 and 8.6)**. On an unsealed chain, insert the link through the two chain ends, then install the sideplate with the chain manufacturer's marking facing outwards.

● Note that it may not be possible to install the sideplate using finger pressure alone. If using a joining tool, assemble it so that the plates of the tool clamp the link and press the sideplate over the pins **(see illustration 8.7)**. Otherwise, use two small sockets placed over

8.7 Push the sideplate into position using a clamp

8.8 Assemble the chain riveting tool over one pin at a time and tighten it fully

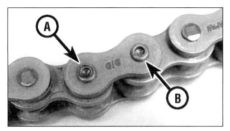

8.9 Pin end correctly riveted (A), pin end unriveted (B)

the rivet ends and two pieces of the wood between a G-clamp. Operate the clamp to press the sideplate over the pins.

● Assemble the joining tool over one pin (following the maker's instructions) and tighten the tool down to spread the pin end securely **(see illustrations 8.8 and 8.9)**. Do the same on the other pin.

 Warning: Check that the pin ends are secure and that there is no danger of the sideplate coming loose. If the pin ends are cracked the soft link must be renewed.

Final drive chain sizing

● Chains are sized using a three digit number, followed by a suffix to denote the chain type **(see illustration 8.10)**. Chain type is either standard or heavy duty (thicker sideplates), and also unsealed or O-ring/X-ring type.

● The first digit of the number relates to the pitch of the chain, ie the distance from the centre of one pin to the centre of the next pin **(see illustration 8.11)**. Pitch is expressed in eighths of an inch, as follows:

8.10 Typical chain size and type marking

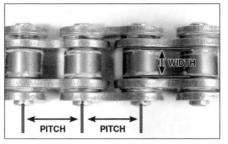

8.11 Chain dimensions

Sizes commencing with a 4 (eg 428) have a pitch of 1/2 inch (12.7 mm)
Sizes commencing with a 5 (eg 520) have a pitch of 5/8 inch (15.9 mm)
Sizes commencing with a 6 (eg 630) have a pitch of 3/4 inch (19.1 mm)

● The second and third digits of the chain size relate to the width of the rollers, again in imperial units, eg the 525 shown has 5/16 inch (7.94 mm) rollers **(see illustration 8.11)**.

9 Hoses

Clamping to prevent flow

● Small-bore flexible hoses can be clamped to prevent fluid flow whilst a component is worked on. Whichever method is used, ensure that the hose material is not permanently distorted or damaged by the clamp.

a) A brake hose clamp available from auto accessory shops **(see illustration 9.1)**.
b) A wingnut type hose clamp **(see illustration 9.2)**.

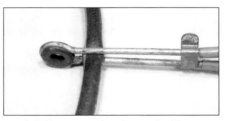

9.1 Hoses can be clamped with an automotive brake hose clamp . . .

9.2 . . . a wingnut type hose clamp . . .

c) Two sockets placed each side of the hose and held with straight-jawed self-locking grips **(see illustration 9.3)**.
d) Thick card each side of the hose held between straight-jawed self-locking grips **(see illustration 9.4)**.

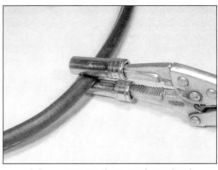

9.3 . . . two sockets and a pair of self-locking grips . . .

9.4 . . . or thick card and self-locking grips

Freeing and fitting hoses

● Always make sure the hose clamp is moved well clear of the hose end. Grip the hose with your hand and rotate it whilst pulling it off the union. If the hose has hardened due to age and will not move, slit it with a sharp knife and peel its ends off the union **(see illustration 9.5)**.

● Resist the temptation to use grease or soap on the unions to aid installation; although it helps the hose slip over the union it will equally aid the escape of fluid from the joint. It is preferable to soften the hose ends in hot water and wet the inside surface of the hose with water or a fluid which will evaporate.

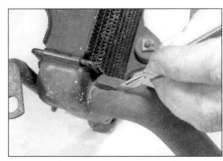

9.5 Cutting a coolant hose free with a sharp knife

Introduction

In less time than it takes to read this introduction, a thief could steal your motorcycle. Returning only to find your bike has gone is one of the worst feelings in the world. Even if the motorcycle is insured against theft, once you've got over the initial shock, you will have the inconvenience of dealing with the police and your insurance company.

The motorcycle is an easy target for the professional thief and the joyrider alike and the official figures on motorcycle theft make for depressing reading; on average a motorcycle is stolen every 16 minutes in the UK!

Motorcycle thefts fall into two categories, those stolen 'to order' and those taken by opportunists. The thief stealing to order will be on the look out for a specific make and model and will go to extraordinary lengths to obtain that motorcycle. The opportunist thief on the other hand will look for easy targets which can be stolen with the minimum of effort and risk.

Whilst it is never going to be possible to make your machine 100% secure, it is estimated that around half of all stolen motorcycles are taken by opportunist thieves. Remember that the opportunist thief is always on the look out for the easy option: if there are two similar motorcycles parked side-by-side, they will target the one with the lowest level of security. By taking a few precautions, you can reduce the chances of your motorcycle being stolen.

Security equipment

There are many specialised motorcycle security devices available and the following text summarises their applications and their good and bad points.

Once you have decided on the type of security equipment which best suits your needs, we recommended that you read one of the many equipment tests regularly carried

Ensure the lock and chain you buy is of good quality and long enough to shackle your bike to a solid object

out by the motorcycle press. These tests compare the products from all the major manufacturers and give impartial ratings on their effectiveness, value-for-money and ease of use.

No one item of security equipment can provide complete protection. It is highly recommended that two or more of the items described below are combined to increase the security of your motorcycle (a lock and chain plus an alarm system is just about ideal). The more security measures fitted to the bike, the less likely it is to be stolen.

Lock and chain

Pros: *Very flexible to use; can be used to secure the motorcycle to almost any immovable object. On some locks and chains, the lock can be used on its own as a disc lock (see below).*

Cons: *Can be very heavy and awkward to carry on the motorcycle, although some types will be supplied with a carry bag which can be strapped to the pillion seat.*

● Heavy-duty chains and locks are an excellent security measure **(see illustration 1)**. Whenever the motorcycle is parked, use the lock and chain to secure the machine to a solid, immovable object such as a post or railings. This will prevent the machine from being ridden away or being lifted into the back of a van.

● When fitting the chain, always ensure the chain is routed around the motorcycle frame or swingarm **(see illustrations 2 and 3)**. Never merely pass the chain around one of the wheel rims; a thief may unbolt the wheel and lift the rest of the machine into a van, leaving you with just the wheel! Try to avoid having excess chain free, thus making it difficult to use cutting tools, and keep the chain and lock off the ground to prevent thieves attacking it with a cold chisel. Position the lock so that its lock barrel is facing downwards; this will make it harder for the thief to attack the lock mechanism.

Pass the chain through the bike's frame, rather than just through a wheel . . .

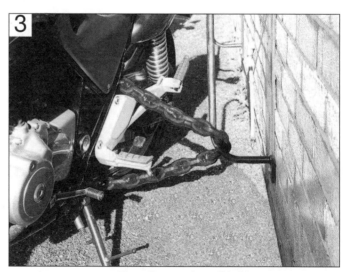

. . . and loop it around a solid object

U-locks

Pros: Highly effective deterrent which can be used to secure the bike to a post or railings. Most U-locks come with a carrier which allows the lock to be easily carried on the bike.

Cons: Not as flexible to use as a lock and chain.

● These are solid locks which are similar in use to a lock and chain. U-locks are lighter than a lock and chain but not so flexible to use. The length and shape of the lock shackle limit the objects to which the bike can be secured **(see illustration 4)**.

Disc locks

Pros: Small, light and very easy to carry; most can be stored underneath the seat.

Cons: Does not prevent the motorcycle being lifted into a van. Can be very embarrassing if you

U-locks can be used to secure the bike to a solid object – ensure you purchase one which is long enough

forget to remove the lock before attempting to ride off!

● Disc locks are designed to be attached to the front brake disc. The lock passes through one of the holes in the disc and prevents the wheel rotating by jamming against the fork/brake caliper **(see illustration 5)**. Some are equipped with an alarm siren which sounds if the disc lock is moved; this not only acts as a theft deterrent but also as a handy reminder if you try to move the bike with the lock still fitted.

● Combining the disc lock with a length of cable which can be looped around a post or railings provides an additional measure of security **(see illustration 6)**.

Alarms and immobilisers

Pros: Once installed it is completely hassle-free to use. If the system is 'Thatcham' or 'Sold Secure-approved', insurance companies may give you a discount.

Cons: Can be expensive to buy and complex to install. No system will prevent the motorcycle from being lifted into a van and taken away.

● Electronic alarms and immobilisers are available to suit a variety of budgets. There are three different types of system available: pure alarms, pure immobilisers, and the more expensive systems which are combined alarm/immobilisers **(see illustration 7)**.
● An alarm system is designed to emit an audible warning if the motorcycle is being tampered with.
● An immobiliser prevents the motorcycle being started and ridden away by disabling its electrical systems.
● When purchasing an alarm/immobiliser system, check the cost of installing the system unless you are able to do it yourself. If the motorcycle is not used regularly, another consideration is the current drain of the system. All alarm/immobiliser systems are powered by the motorcycle's battery; purchasing a system with a very low current drain could prevent the battery losing its charge whilst the motorcycle is not being used.

A typical disc lock attached through one of the holes in the disc

A disc lock combined with a security cable provides additional protection

A typical alarm/immobiliser system

Indelible markings can be applied to most areas of the bike – always apply the manufacturer's sticker to warn off thieves

Chemically-etched code numbers can be applied to main body panels . . .

. . . again, always ensure that the kit manufacturer's sticker is applied in a prominent position

Security marking kits

Pros: *Very cheap and effective deterrent. Many insurance companies will give you a discount on your insurance premium if a recognised security marking kit is used on your motorcycle.*

Cons: *Does not prevent the motorcycle being stolen by joyriders.*

● There are many different types of security marking kits available. The idea is to mark as many parts of the motorcycle as possible with a unique security number **(see illustrations 8, 9 and 10)**. A form will be included with the kit to register your personal details and those of the motorcycle with the kit manufacturer. This register is made available to the police to help them trace the rightful owner of any motorcycle or components which they recover should all other forms of identification have been removed. Always apply the warning stickers provided with the kit to deter thieves.

Ground anchors, wheel clamps and security posts

Pros: *An excellent form of security which will deter all but the most determined of thieves.*

Cons: *Awkward to install and can be expensive.*

Permanent ground anchors provide an excellent level of security when the bike is at home

● Whilst the motorcycle is at home, it is a good idea to attach it securely to the floor or a solid wall, even if it is kept in a securely locked garage. Various types of ground anchors, security posts and wheel clamps are available for this purpose **(see illustration 11)**. These security devices are either bolted to a solid concrete or brick structure or can be cemented into the ground.

Security at home

A high percentage of motorcycle thefts are from the owner's home. Here are some things to consider whenever your motorcycle is at home:

✔ Where possible, always keep the motorcycle in a securely locked garage. Never rely solely on the standard lock on the garage door, these are usual hopelessly inadequate. Fit an additional locking mechanism to the door and consider having the garage alarmed. A security light, activated by a movement sensor, is also a good investment.

✔ Always secure the motorcycle to the ground or a wall, even if it is inside a securely locked garage.
✔ Do not regularly leave the motorcycle outside your home, try to keep it out of sight wherever possible. If a garage is not available, fit a motorcycle cover over the bike to disguise its true identity.
✔ It is not uncommon for thieves to follow a motorcyclist home to find out where the bike is kept. They will then return at a later date. Be aware of this whenever you are returning

home on your motorcycle. If you suspect you are being followed, do not return home, instead ride to a garage or shop and stop as a precaution.
✔ When selling a motorcycle, do not provide your home address or the location where the bike is normally kept. Arrange to meet the buyer at a location away from your home. Thieves have been known to pose as potential buyers to find out where motorcycles are kept and then return later to steal them.

Security away from the home

As well as fitting security equipment to your motorcycle here are a few general rules to follow whenever you park your motorcycle.
✔ Park in a busy, public place.
✔ Use car parks which incorporate security features, such as CCTV.

✔ At night, park in a well-lit area, preferably directly underneath a street light.
✔ Engage the steering lock.
✔ Secure the motorcycle to a solid, immovable object such as a post or railings with an additional lock. If this is not possible,

secure the bike to a friend's motorcycle. Some public parking places provide security loops for motorcycles.
✔ Never leave your helmet or luggage attached to the motorcycle. Take them with you at all times.

Lubricants and fluids

A wide range of lubricants, fluids and cleaning agents is available for motor-cycles. This is a guide as to what is available, its applications and properties.

Four-stroke engine oil

● Engine oil is without doubt the most important component of any four-stroke engine. Modern motorcycle engines place a lot of demands on their oil and choosing the right type is essential. Using an unsuitable oil will lead to an increased rate of engine wear and could result in serious engine damage. Before purchasing oil, always check the recommended oil specification given by the manufacturer. The manufacturer will state a recommended 'type or classification' and also a specific 'viscosity' range for engine oil.

● The oil 'type or classification' is identified by its API (American Petroleum Institute) rating. The API rating will be in the form of two letters, e.g. SG. The S identifies the oil as being suitable for use in a petrol (gasoline) engine (S stands for spark ignition) and the second letter, ranging from A to J, identifies the oil's performance rating. The later this letter, the higher the specification of the oil; for example API SG oil exceeds the requirements of API SF oil. **Note:** *On some oils there may also be a second rating consisting of another two letters, the first letter being C, e.g. API SF/CD. This rating indicates the oil is also suitable for use in a diesel engines (the C stands for compression ignition) and is thus of no relevance for motorcycle use.*

● The 'viscosity' of the oil is identified by its SAE (Society of Automotive Engineers) rating. All modern engines require multigrade oils and the SAE rating will consist of two numbers, the first followed by a W, e.g. 10W/40. The first number indicates the viscosity rating of the oil at low temperatures (W stands for winter – tested at –20°C) and the second number represents the viscosity of the oil at high temperatures (tested at 100°C). The lower the number, the thinner the oil. For example an oil with an SAE 10W/40 rating will give better cold starting and running than an SAE 15W/40 oil.

● As well as ensuring the 'type' and 'viscosity' of the oil match the recommendations, another consideration to make when buying engine oil is whether to purchase a standard mineral-based oil, a semi-synthetic oil (also known as a synthetic blend or synthetic-based oil) or a fully-synthetic oil. Although all oils will have a similar rating and viscosity, their cost will vary considerably; mineral-based oils are the cheapest, the fully-synthetic oils the most expensive with the semi-synthetic oils falling somewhere in-between. This decision is very much up to the owner, but it should be noted that modern synthetic oils have far better lubricating and cleaning qualities than traditional mineral-based oils and tend to retain these properties for far longer. Bearing in mind the operating conditions inside a modern, high-revving motorcycle engine it is highly recommended that a fully synthetic oil is used. The extra expense at each service could save you money in the long term by preventing premature engine wear.

● As a final note always ensure that the oil is specifically designed for use in motorcycle engines. Engine oils designed primarily for use in car engines sometimes contain additives or friction modifiers which could cause clutch slip on a motorcycle fitted with a wet-clutch.

Two-stroke engine oil

● Modern two-stroke engines, with their high power outputs, place high demands on their oil. If engine seizure is to be avoided it is essential that a high-quality oil is used. Two-stroke oils differ hugely from four-stroke oils. The oil lubricates only the crankshaft and piston(s) (the transmission has its own lubricating oil) and is used on a total-loss basis where it is burnt completely during the combustion process.

● The Japanese have recently introduced a classification system for two-stroke oils, the JASO rating. This rating is in the form of two letters, either FA, FB or FC – FA is the lowest classification and FC the highest. Ensure the oil being used meets or exceeds the recommended rating specified by the manufacturer.

● As well as ensuring the oil rating matches the recommendation, another consideration to make when buying engine oil is whether to purchase a standard mineral-based oil, a semi-synthetic oil (also known as a synthetic blend or synthetic-based oil) or a fully-synthetic oil. The cost of each type of oil varies considerably; mineral-based oils are the cheapest, the fully-synthetic oils the most expensive with the semi-synthetic oils falling somewhere in-between. This decision is very much up to the owner, but it should be noted that modern synthetic oils have far better lubricating properties and burn cleaner than traditional mineral-based oils. It is therefore recommended that a fully synthetic oil is used. The extra expense could save you money in the long term by preventing premature engine wear, engine performance will be improved, carbon deposits and exhaust smoke will be reduced.

● Always ensure that the oil is specifically designed for use in an injector system. Many high quality two-stroke oils are designed for competition use and need to be pre-mixed with fuel. These oils are of a much higher viscosity and are not designed to flow through the injector pumps used on road-going two-stroke motorcycles.

Transmission (gear) oil

● On a two-stroke engine, the transmission and clutch are lubricated by their own separate oil bath which must be changed in accordance with the Maintenance Schedule.
● Although the engine and transmission units of most four-strokes use a common lubrication supply, there are some exceptions where the engine and gearbox have separate oil reservoirs and a dry clutch is used.
● Motorcycle manufacturers will either recommend a monograde transmission oil or a four-stroke multigrade engine oil to lubricate the transmission.
● Transmission oils, or gear oils as they are often called, are designed specifically for use in transmission systems. The viscosity of these oils is represented by an SAE number, but the scale of measurement applied is different to that used to grade engine oils. As a rough guide a SAE90 gear oil will be of the same viscosity as an SAE50 engine oil.

Shaft drive oil

● On models equipped with shaft final drive, the shaft drive gears are will have their own oil supply. The manufacturer will state a recommended 'type or classification' and also a specific 'viscosity' range in the same manner as for four-stroke engine oil.
● Gear oil classification is given by the number which follows the API GL (GL standing for gear lubricant) rating, the higher the number, the higher the specification of the oil, e.g. API GL5 oil is a higher specification than API GL4 oil. Ensure the oil meets or

exceeds the classification specified and is of the correct viscosity. The viscosity of gear oils is also represented by an SAE number but the scale of measurement used is different to that used to grade engine oils. As a rough guide an SAE90 gear oil will be of the same viscosity as an SAE50 engine oil.
● If the use of an EP (Extreme Pressure) gear oil is specified, ensure the oil purchased is suitable.

Fork oil and suspension fluid

● Conventional telescopic front forks are hydraulic and require fork oil to work. To ensure the forks function correctly, the fork oil must be changed in accordance with the Maintenance Schedule.
● Fork oil is available in a variety of viscosities, identified by their SAE rating; fork oil ratings vary from light (SAE 5) to heavy (SAE 30). When purchasing fork oil, ensure the viscosity rating matches that specified by the manufacturer.
● Some lubricant manufacturers also produce a range of high-quality suspension fluids which are very similar to fork oil but are designed mainly for competition use. These fluids may have a different viscosity rating system which is not to be confused with the SAE rating of normal fork oil. Refer to the manufacturer's instructions if in any doubt.

Brake and clutch fluid

● All disc brake systems and some clutch systems are hydraulically operated. To ensure correct operation, the hydraulic fluid must be changed in accordance with the Maintenance Schedule.
● Brake and clutch fluid is classified by its DOT rating with most motorcycle manufacturers specifying DOT 3 or 4 fluid. Both fluid types are glycol-based and can be mixed together without adverse effect; DOT 4 fluid exceeds the requirements of DOT 3

fluid. Although it is safe to use DOT 4 fluid in a system designed for use with DOT 3 fluid, never use DOT 3 fluid in a system which specifies the use of DOT 4 as this will adversely affect the system's performance. The type required for the system will be marked on the fluid reservoir cap.
● Some manufacturers also produce a DOT 5 hydraulic fluid. DOT 5 hydraulic fluid is silicone-based and is not compatible with the glycol-based DOT 3 and 4 fluids. Never mix DOT 5 fluid with DOT 3 or 4 fluid as this will seriously affect the performance of the hydraulic system.

Coolant/antifreeze

● When purchasing coolant/antifreeze, always ensure it is suitable for use in an aluminium engine and contains corrosion inhibitors to prevent possible blockages of the internal coolant passages of the system. As a general rule, most coolants are designed to be used neat and should not be diluted whereas antifreeze can be mixed with distilled water to provide a coolant solution of the required strength. Refer to the manufacturer's instructions on the bottle.
● Ensure the coolant is changed in accordance with the Maintenance Schedule.

Chain lube

● Chain lube is an aerosol-type spray lubricant specifically designed for use on motorcycle final drive chains. Chain lube has two functions, to minimise friction between the final drive chain and sprockets and to prevent corrosion of the chain. Regular use of a good-quality chain lube will extend the life of the drive chain and sprockets and thus maximise the power being transmitted from the transmission to the rear wheel.
● When using chain lube, always allow some time for the solvents in the lube to evaporate before riding the motorcycle. This will minimise the amount of lube which will

'fling' off from the chain when the motorcycle is used. If the motorcycle is equipped with an 'O-ring' chain, ensure the chain lube is labelled as being suitable for use on 'O-ring' chains.

Degreasers and solvents

● There are many different types of solvents and degreasers available to remove the grime and grease which accumulate around the motorcycle during normal use. Degreasers and solvents are usually available as an aerosol-type spray or as a liquid which you apply with a brush. Always closely follow the manufacturer's instructions and wear eye protection during use. Be aware that many solvents are flammable and may give off noxious fumes; take adequate precautions when using them (see Safety First!).

● For general cleaning, use one of the many solvents or degreasers available from most motorcycle accessory shops. These solvents are usually applied then left for a certain time before being washed off with water.

Brake cleaner is a solvent specifically designed to remove all traces of oil, grease and dust from braking system components. Brake cleaner is designed to evaporate quickly and leaves behind no residue.

Carburettor cleaner is an aerosol-type solvent specifically designed to clear carburettor blockages and break down the hard deposits and gum often found inside carburettors during overhaul.

Contact cleaner is an aerosol-type solvent designed for cleaning electrical components. The cleaner will remove all traces of oil and dirt from components such as switch contacts or fouled spark plugs and then dry, leaving behind no residue.

Gasket remover is an aerosol-type solvent designed for removing stubborn gaskets from engine components during overhaul. Gasket remover will minimise the amount of scraping required to remove the gasket and therefore reduce the risk of damage to the mating surface.

Spray lubricants

● Aerosol-based spray lubricants are widely available and are excellent for lubricating lever pivots and exposed cables and switches. Try to use a lubricant which is of the dry-film type as the fluid evaporates, leaving behind a dry-film of lubricant. Lubricants which leave behind an oily residue will attract dust and dirt which will increase the rate of wear of the cable/lever.

● Most lubricants also act as a moisture dispersant and a penetrating fluid. This means they can also be used to 'dry out' electrical components such as wiring connectors or switches as well as helping to free seized fasteners.

Greases

● Grease is used to lubricate many of the pivot-points. A good-quality multi-purpose grease is suitable for most applications but some manufacturers will specify the use of specialist greases for use on components such as swingarm and suspension linkage bushes. These specialist greases can be purchased from most motorcycle (or car) accessory shops; commonly specified types include molybdenum disulphide grease, lithium-based grease, graphite-based grease, silicone-based grease and high-temperature copper-based grease.

Gasket sealing compounds

● Gasket sealing compounds can be used in conjunction with gaskets, to improve their sealing capabilities, or on their own to seal metal-to-metal joints. Depending on their type, sealing compounds either set hard or stay relatively soft and pliable.

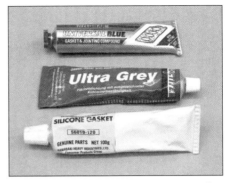

● When purchasing a gasket sealing compound, ensure that it is designed specifically for use on an internal combustion engine. General multi-purpose sealants available from DIY stores may appear visibly similar but they are not designed to withstand the extreme heat or contact with fuel and oil encountered when used on an engine (see 'Tools and Workshop Tips' for further information).

Thread locking compound

● Thread locking compounds are used to secure certain threaded fasteners in position to prevent them from loosening due to vibration. Thread locking compounds can be purchased from most motorcycle (and car) accessory shops. Ensure the threads of the both components are completely clean and dry before sparingly applying the locking compound (see 'Tools and Workshop Tips' for further information).

Fuel additives

● Fuel additives which protect and clean the fuel system components are widely available. These additives are designed to remove all traces of deposits that build up on the carburettors/injectors and prevent wear, helping the fuel system to operate more efficiently. If a fuel additive is being used, check that it is suitable for use with your motorcycle, especially if your motorcycle is equipped with a catalytic converter.

● Octane boosters are also available. These additives are designed to improve the performance of highly-tuned engines being run on normal pump-fuel and are of no real use on standard motorcycles.

Length (distance)

Inches (in)	x 25.4	= Millimetres (mm)	x 0.0394	= Inches (in)
Feet (ft)	x 0.305	= Metres (m)	x 3.281	= Feet (ft)
Miles	x 1.609	= Kilometres (km)	x 0.621	= Miles

Volume (capacity)

Cubic inches (cu in; in³)	x 16.387	= Cubic centimetres (cc; cm³)	x 0.061	= Cubic inches (cu in; in³)
Imperial pints (Imp pt)	x 0.568	= Litres (l)	x 1.76	= Imperial pints (Imp pt)
Imperial quarts (Imp qt)	x 1.137	= Litres (l)	x 0.88	= Imperial quarts (Imp qt)
Imperial quarts (Imp qt)	x 1.201	= US quarts (US qt)	x 0.833	= Imperial quarts (Imp qt)
US quarts (US qt)	x 0.946	= Litres (l)	x 1.057	= US quarts (US qt)
Imperial gallons (Imp gal)	x 4.546	= Litres (l)	x 0.22	= Imperial gallons (Imp gal)
Imperial gallons (Imp gal)	x 1.201	= US gallons (US gal)	x 0.833	= Imperial gallons (Imp gal)
US gallons (US gal)	x 3.785	= Litres (l)	x 0.264	= US gallons (US gal)

Mass (weight)

Ounces (oz)	x 28.35	= Grams (g)	x 0.035	= Ounces (oz)
Pounds (lb)	x 0.454	= Kilograms (kg)	x 2.205	= Pounds (lb)

Force

Ounces-force (ozf; oz)	x 0.278	= Newtons (N)	x 3.6	= Ounces-force (ozf; oz)
Pounds-force (lbf; lb)	x 4.448	= Newtons (N)	x 0.225	= Pounds-force (lbf; lb)
Newtons (N)	x 0.1	= Kilograms-force (kgf; kg)	x 9.81	= Newtons (N)

Pressure

Pounds-force per square inch (psi; lbf/in²; lb/in²)	x 0.070	= Kilograms-force per square centimetre (kgf/cm²; kg/cm²)	x 14.223	= Pounds-force per square inch (psi; lbf/in²; lb/in²)
Pounds-force per square inch (psi; lbf/in²; lb/in²)	x 0.068	= Atmospheres (atm)	x 14.696	= Pounds-force per square inch (psi; lbf/in²; lb/in²)
Pounds-force per square inch (psi; lbf/in²; lb/in²)	x 0.069	= Bars	x 14.5	= Pounds-force per square inch (psi; lbf/in²; lb/in²)
Pounds-force per square inch (psi; lbf/in²; lb/in²)	x 6.895	= Kilopascals (kPa)	x 0.145	= Pounds-force per square inch (psi; lbf/in²; lb/in²)
Kilopascals (kPa)	x 0.01	= Kilograms-force per square centimetre (kgf/cm²; kg/cm²)	x 98.1	= Kilopascals (kPa)
Millibar (mbar)	x 100	= Pascals (Pa)	x 0.01	= Millibar (mbar)
Millibar (mbar)	x 0.0145	= Pounds-force per square inch (psi; lbf/in²; lb/in²)	x 68.947	= Millibar (mbar)
Millibar (mbar)	x 0.75	= Millimetres of mercury (mmHg)	x 1.333	= Millibar (mbar)
Millibar (mbar)	x 0.401	= Inches of water (inH₂O)	x 2.491	= Millibar (mbar)
Millimetres of mercury (mmHg)	x 0.535	= Inches of water (inH₂O)	x 1.868	= Millimetres of mercury (mmHg)
Inches of water (inH₂O)	x 0.036	= Pounds-force per square inch (psi; lbf/in²; lb/in²)	x 27.68	= Inches of water (inH₂O)

Torque (moment of force)

Pounds-force inches (lbf in; lb in)	x 1.152	= Kilograms-force centimetre (kgf cm; kg cm)	x 0.868	= Pounds-force inches (lbf in; lb in)
Pounds-force inches (lbf in; lb in)	x 0.113	= Newton metres (Nm)	x 8.85	= Pounds-force inches (lbf in; lb in)
Pounds-force inches (lbf in; lb in)	x 0.083	= Pounds-force feet (lbf ft; lb ft)	x 12	= Pounds-force inches (lbf in; lb in)
Pounds-force feet (lbf ft; lb ft)	x 0.138	= Kilograms-force metres (kgf m; kg m)	x 7.233	= Pounds-force feet (lbf ft; lb ft)
Pounds-force feet (lbf ft; lb ft)	x 1.356	= Newton metres (Nm)	x 0.738	= Pounds-force feet (lbf ft; lb ft)
Newton metres (Nm)	x 0.102	= Kilograms-force metres (kgf m; kg m)	x 9.804	= Newton metres (Nm)

Power

Horsepower (hp)	x 745.7	= Watts (W)	x 0.0013	= Horsepower (hp)

Velocity (speed)

Miles per hour (miles/hr; mph)	x 1.609	= Kilometres per hour (km/hr; kph)	x 0.621	= Miles per hour (miles/hr; mph)

Fuel consumption*

Miles per gallon (mpg)	x 0.354	= Kilometres per litre (km/l)	x 2.825	= Miles per gallon (mpg)

Temperature

Degrees Fahrenheit = (°C x 1.8) + 32

Degrees Celsius (Degrees Centigrade; °C) = (°F - 32) x 0.56

It is common practice to convert from miles per gallon (mpg) to litres/100 kilometres (l/100km), where mpg x l/100 km = 282

About the MOT Test

In the UK, all vehicles more than three years old are subject to an annual test to ensure that they meet minimum safety requirements. A current test certificate must be issued before a machine can be used on public roads, and is required before a road fund licence can be issued. Riding without a current test certificate will also invalidate your insurance.

For most owners, the MOT test is an annual cause for anxiety, and this is largely due to owners not being sure what needs to be checked prior to submitting the motorcycle for testing. The simple answer is that a fully roadworthy motorcycle will have no difficulty in passing the test.

This is a guide to getting your motorcycle through the MOT test. Obviously it will not be possible to examine the motorcycle to the same standard as the professional MOT tester, particularly in view of the equipment required for some of the checks. However, working through the following procedures will enable you to identify any problem areas before submitting the motorcycle for the test.

It has only been possible to summarise the test requirements here, based on the regulations in force at the time of printing. Test standards are becoming increasingly stringent, although there are some exemptions for older vehicles. More information about the MOT test can be obtained from the TSO publications, *How Safe is your Motorcycle* and *The MOT Inspection Manual for Motorcycle Testing.*

Many of the checks require that one of the wheels is raised off the ground. If the motorcycle doesn't have a centre stand, note that an auxiliary stand will be required. Additionally, the help of an assistant may prove useful.

Certain exceptions apply to machines under 50 cc, machines without a lighting system, and Classic bikes - if in doubt about any of the requirements listed below seek confirmation from an MOT tester prior to submitting the motorcycle for the test.

Check that the frame number is clearly visible.

Electrical System

Lights, turn signals, horn and reflector

✔ With the ignition on, check the operation of the following electrical components. **Note:** *The electrical components on certain small-capacity machines are powered by the generator, requiring that the engine is run for this check.*

a) *Headlight and tail light. Check that both illuminate in the low and high beam switch positions.*

b) *Position lights. Check that the front position (or sidelight) and tail light illuminate in this switch position.*

c) *Turn signals. Check that all flash at the correct rate, and that the warning light(s) function correctly. Check that the turn signal switch works correctly.*

d) *Hazard warning system (where fitted). Check that all four turn signals flash in this switch position.*

e) *Brake stop light. Check that the light comes on when the front and rear brakes are independently applied. Models first used on or after 1st April 1986 must have a brake light switch on each brake.*

f) *Horn. Check that the sound is continuous and of reasonable volume.*

✔ Check that there is a red reflector on the rear of the machine, either mounted separately or as part of the tail light lens.

✔ Check the condition of the headlight, tail light and turn signal lenses.

Headlight beam height

✔ The MOT tester will perform a headlight beam height check using specialised beam setting equipment **(see illustration 1)**. This equipment will not be available to the home mechanic, but if you suspect that the headlight is incorrectly set or may have been maladjusted in the past, you can perform a rough test as follows.

✔ Position the bike in a straight line facing a brick wall. The bike must be off its stand, upright and with a rider seated. Measure the height from the ground to the centre of the headlight and mark a horizontal line on the wall at this height. Position the motorcycle 3.8 metres from the wall and draw a vertical

Headlight beam height checking equipment

line up the wall central to the centreline of the motorcycle. Switch to dipped beam and check that the beam pattern falls slightly lower than the horizontal line and to the left of the vertical line **(see illustration 2)**.

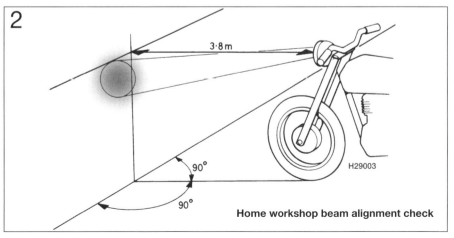

Home workshop beam alignment check

Exhaust System and Final Drive

Exhaust

✔ Check that the exhaust mountings are secure and that the system does not foul any of the rear suspension components.

✔ Start the motorcycle. When the revs are increased, check that the exhaust is neither holed nor leaking from any of its joints. On a linked system, check that the collector box is not leaking due to corrosion.

✔ Note that the exhaust decibel level ("loudness" of the exhaust) is assessed at the discretion of the tester. If the motorcycle was first used on or after 1st January 1985 the silencer must carry the BSAU 193 stamp, or a marking relating to its make and model, or be of OE (original equipment) manufacture. If the silencer is marked NOT FOR ROAD USE, RACING USE ONLY or similar, it will fail the MOT.

Final drive

✔ On chain or belt drive machines, check that the chain/belt is in good condition and does not have excessive slack. Also check that the sprocket is securely mounted on the rear wheel hub. Check that the chain/belt guard is in place.

✔ On shaft drive bikes, check for oil leaking from the drive unit and fouling the rear tyre.

Steering and Suspension

Steering

✔ With the front wheel raised off the ground, rotate the steering from lock to lock. The handlebar or switches must not contact the fuel tank or be close enough to trap the rider's hand. Problems can be caused by damaged lock stops on the lower yoke and frame, or by the fitting of non-standard handlebars.

✔ When performing the lock to lock check, also ensure that the steering moves freely without drag or notchiness. Steering movement can be impaired by poorly routed cables, or by overtight head bearings or worn bearings. The tester will perform a check of the steering head bearing lower race by mounting the front wheel on a surface plate, then performing a lock to lock check with the weight of the machine on the lower bearing (see illustration 3).

✔ Grasp the fork sliders (lower legs) and attempt to push and pull on the forks (see

Front wheel mounted on a surface plate for steering head bearing lower race check

illustration 4). Any play in the steering head bearings will be felt. Note that in extreme cases, wear of the front fork bushes can be misinterpreted for head bearing play.

✔ Check that the handlebars are securely mounted.

✔ Check that the handlebar grip rubbers are secure. They should by bonded to the bar left end and to the throttle cable pulley on the right end.

Front suspension

✔ With the motorcycle off the stand, hold the front brake on and pump the front forks up and down (see illustration 5). Check that they are adequately damped.

Checking the steering head bearings for freeplay

Hold the front brake on and pump the front forks up and down to check operation

6

Inspect the area around the fork dust seal for oil leakage (arrow)

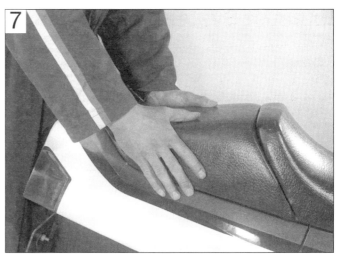

7

Bounce the rear of the motorcycle to check rear suspension operation

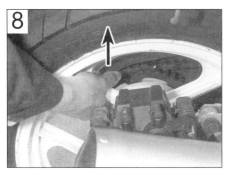

8

Checking for rear suspension linkage play

✔ Inspect the area above and around the front fork oil seals **(see illustration 6)**. There should be no sign of oil on the fork tube (stanchion) nor leaking down the slider (lower leg). On models so equipped, check that there is no oil leaking from the anti-dive units.

✔ On models with swingarm front suspension, check that there is no freeplay in the linkage when moved from side to side.

Rear suspension

✔ With the motorcycle off the stand and an assistant supporting the motorcycle by its handlebars, bounce the rear suspension **(see illustration 7)**. Check that the suspension components do not foul on any of the cycle parts and check that the shock absorber(s) provide adequate damping.

✔ Visually inspect the shock absorber(s) and check that there is no sign of oil leakage from its damper. This is somewhat restricted on certain single shock models due to the location of the shock absorber.

✔ With the rear wheel raised off the ground, grasp the wheel at the highest point and attempt to pull it up **(see illustration 8)**. Any play in the swingarm pivot or suspension linkage bearings will be felt as movement. **Note:** *Do not confuse play with actual suspension movement.* Failure to lubricate suspension linkage bearings can lead to bearing failure **(see illustration 9)**.

✔ With the rear wheel raised off the ground, grasp the swingarm ends and attempt to move the swingarm from side to side and forwards and backwards - any play indicates wear of the swingarm pivot bearings **(see illustration 10)**.

9

Worn suspension linkage pivots (arrows) are usually the cause of play in the rear suspension

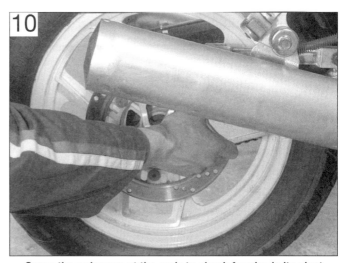

10

Grasp the swingarm at the ends to check for play in its pivot bearings

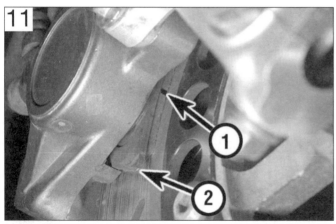

Brake pad wear can usually be viewed without removing the caliper. Most pads have wear indicator grooves (1) and some also have indicator tangs (2)

On drum brakes, check the angle of the operating lever with the brake fully applied. Most drum brakes have a wear indicator pointer and scale.

Brakes, Wheels and Tyres

Brakes

✔ With the wheel raised off the ground, apply the brake then free it off, and check that the wheel is about to revolve freely without brake drag.

✔ On disc brakes, examine the disc itself. Check that it is securely mounted and not cracked.

✔ On disc brakes, view the pad material through the caliper mouth and check that the pads are not worn down beyond the limit **(see illustration 11)**.

✔ On drum brakes, check that when the brake is applied the angle between the operating lever and cable or rod is not too great **(see illustration 12)**. Check also that the operating lever doesn't foul any other components.

✔ On disc brakes, examine the flexible hoses from top to bottom. Have an assistant hold the brake on so that the fluid in the hose is under pressure, and check that there is no sign of fluid leakage, bulges or cracking. If there are any metal brake pipes or unions, check that these are free from corrosion and damage. Where a brake-linked anti-dive system is fitted, check the hoses to the anti-dive in a similar manner.

✔ Check that the rear brake torque arm is secure and that its fasteners are secured by self-locking nuts or castellated nuts with split-pins or R-pins **(see illustration 13)**.

✔ On models with ABS, check that the self-check warning light in the instrument panel works.

✔ The MOT tester will perform a test of the motorcycle's braking efficiency based on a calculation of rider and motorcycle weight. Although this cannot be carried out at home, you can at least ensure that the braking systems are properly maintained. For hydraulic disc brakes, check the fluid level, lever/pedal feel (bleed of air if its spongy) and pad material. For drum brakes, check adjustment, cable or rod operation and shoe lining thickness.

Wheels and tyres

✔ Check the wheel condition. Cast wheels should be free from cracks and if of the built-up design, all fasteners should be secure. Spoked wheels should be checked for broken, corroded, loose or bent spokes.

✔ With the wheel raised off the ground, spin the wheel and visually check that the tyre and wheel run true. Check that the tyre does not foul the suspension or mudguards.

✔ With the wheel raised off the ground, grasp the wheel and attempt to move it about the axle (spindle) **(see illustration 14)**. Any play felt here indicates wheel bearing failure.

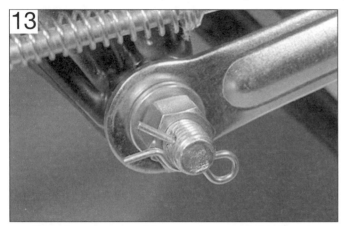

Brake torque arm must be properly secured at both ends

Check for wheel bearing play by trying to move the wheel about the axle (spindle)

Checking the tyre tread depth

Tyre direction of rotation arrow can be found on tyre sidewall

Castellated type wheel axle (spindle) nut must be secured by a split pin or R-pin

Two straightedges are used to check wheel alignment

✔ Check the tyre tread depth, tread condition and sidewall condition **(see illustration 15)**.
✔ Check the tyre type. Front and rear tyre types must be compatible and be suitable for road use. Tyres marked NOT FOR ROAD USE, COMPETITION USE ONLY or similar, will fail the MOT.

✔ If the tyre sidewall carries a direction of rotation arrow, this must be pointing in the direction of normal wheel rotation **(see illustration 16)**.
✔ Check that the wheel axle (spindle) nuts (where applicable) are properly secured. A self-locking nut or castellated nut with a split-pin or R-pin can be used **(see illustration 17)**.
✔ Wheel alignment is checked with the motorcycle off the stand and a rider seated. With the front wheel pointing straight ahead, two perfectly straight lengths of metal or wood and placed against the sidewalls of both tyres **(see illustration 18)**. The gap each side of the front tyre must be equidistant on both sides. Incorrect wheel alignment may be due to a cocked rear wheel (often as the result of poor chain adjustment) or in extreme cases, a bent frame.

General checks and condition

✔ Check the security of all major fasteners, bodypanels, seat, fairings (where fitted) and mudguards.

✔ Check that the rider and pillion footrests, handlebar levers and brake pedal are securely mounted.

✔ Check for corrosion on the frame or any load-bearing components. If severe, this may affect the structure, particularly under stress.

Sidecars

A motorcycle fitted with a sidecar requires additional checks relating to the stability of the machine and security of attachment and swivel joints, plus specific wheel alignment (toe-in) requirements. Additionally, tyre and lighting requirements differ from conventional motorcycle use. Owners are advised to check MOT test requirements with an official test centre.

Preparing for storage

Before you start

If repairs or an overhaul is needed, see that this is carried out now rather than left until you want to ride the bike again.

Give the bike a good wash and scrub all dirt from its underside. Make sure the bike dries completely before preparing for storage.

Engine

● Remove the spark plug(s) and lubricate the cylinder bores with approximately a teaspoon of motor oil using a spout-type oil can (see illustration 1). Reinstall the spark plug(s). Crank the engine over a couple of times to coat the piston rings and bores with oil. If the bike has a kickstart, use this to turn the engine over. If not, flick the kill switch to the OFF position and crank the engine over on the starter (see illustration 2). If the nature on the ignition system prevents the starter operating with the kill switch in the OFF position,

remove the spark plugs and fit them back in their caps; ensure that the plugs are earthed (grounded) against the cylinder head when the starter is operated (see illustration 3).

⚠ **Warning: It is important that the plugs are earthed (grounded) away from the spark plug holes otherwise there is a risk of atomised fuel from the cylinders igniting.**

HAYNES HiNT *On a single cylinder four-stroke engine, you can seal the combustion chamber completely by positioning the piston at TDC on the compression stroke.*

● Drain the carburettor(s) otherwise there is a risk of jets becoming blocked by gum deposits from the fuel (see illustration 4).

● If the bike is going into long-term storage, consider adding a fuel stabiliser to the fuel in the tank. If the tank is drained completely, corrosion of its internal surfaces may occur if left unprotected for a long period. The tank can be treated with a rust preventative especially for this purpose. Alternatively, remove the tank and pour half a litre of motor oil into it, install the filler cap and shake the tank to coat its internals with oil before draining off the excess. The same effect can also be achieved by spraying WD40 or a similar water-dispersant around the inside of the tank via its flexible nozzle.

● Make sure the cooling system contains the correct mix of antifreeze. Antifreeze also contains important corrosion inhibitors.

● The air intakes and exhaust can be sealed off by covering or plugging the openings. Ensure that you do not seal in any condensation; run the engine until it is hot,

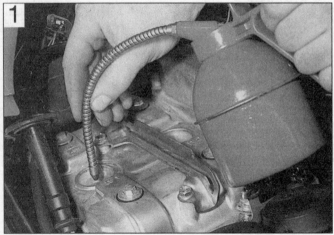

Squirt a drop of motor oil into each cylinder

Flick the kill switch to OFF . . .

. . . and ensure that the metal bodies of the plugs (arrows) are earthed against the cylinder head

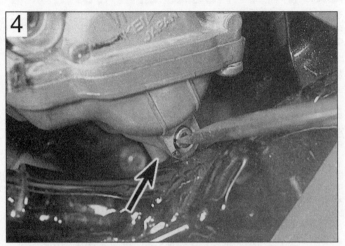

Connect a hose to the carburettor float chamber drain stub (arrow) and unscrew the drain screw

Exhausts can be sealed off with a plastic bag

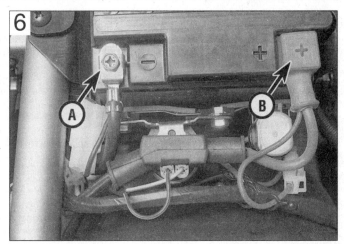

Disconnect the negative lead (A) first, followed by the positive lead (B)

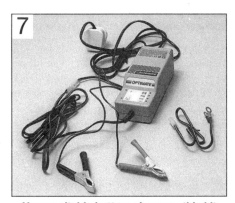

Use a suitable battery charger - this kit also assess battery condition

then switch off and allow to cool. Tape a piece of thick plastic over the silencer end(s) **(see illustration 5)**. Note that some advocate pouring a tablespoon of motor oil into the silencer(s) before sealing them off.

Battery

● Remove it from the bike - in extreme cases of cold the battery may freeze and crack its case **(see illustration 6)**.

● Check the electrolyte level and top up if necessary (conventional refillable batteries). Clean the terminals.
● Store the battery off the motorcycle and away from any sources of fire. Position a wooden block under the battery if it is to sit on the ground.
● Give the battery a trickle charge for a few hours every month **(see illustration 7)**.

Tyres

● Place the bike on its centrestand or an auxiliary stand which will support the motorcycle in an upright position. Position wood blocks under the tyres to keep them off the ground and to provide insulation from damp. If the bike is being put into long-term storage, ideally both tyres should be off the ground; not only will this protect the tyres, but will also ensure that no load is placed on the steering head or wheel bearings.
● Deflate each tyre by 5 to 10 psi, no more or the beads may unseat from the rim, making subsequent inflation difficult on tubeless tyres.

Pivots and controls

● Lubricate all lever, pedal, stand and

footrest pivot points. If grease nipples are fitted to the rear suspension components, apply lubricant to the pivots.
● Lubricate all control cables.

Cycle components

● Apply a wax protectant to all painted and plastic components. Wipe off any excess, but don't polish to a shine. Where fitted, clean the screen with soap and water.
● Coat metal parts with Vaseline (petroleum jelly). When applying this to the fork tubes, do not compress the forks otherwise the seals will rot from contact with the Vaseline.
● Apply a vinyl cleaner to the seat.

Storage conditions

● Aim to store the bike in a shed or garage which does not leak and is free from damp.
● Drape an old blanket or bedspread over the bike to protect it from dust and direct contact with sunlight (which will fade paint). This also hides the bike from prying eyes. Beware of tight-fitting plastic covers which may allow condensation to form and settle on the bike.

Getting back on the road

Engine and transmission

● Change the oil and replace the oil filter. If this was done prior to storage, check that the oil hasn't emulsified - a thick whitish substance which occurs through condensation.
● Remove the spark plugs. Using a spout-type oil can, squirt a few drops of oil into the cylinder(s). This will provide initial lubrication as the piston rings and bores comes back into contact. Service the spark plugs, or fit new ones, and install them in the engine.

● Check that the clutch isn't stuck on. The plates can stick together if left standing for some time, preventing clutch operation. Engage a gear and try rocking the bike back and forth with the clutch lever held against the handlebar. If this doesn't work on cable-operated clutches, hold the clutch lever back against the handlebar with a strong elastic band or cable tie for a couple of hours **(see illustration 8)**.
● If the air intakes or silencer end(s) were blocked off, remove the bung or cover used.
● If the fuel tank was coated with a rust

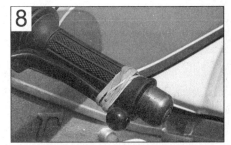

Hold clutch lever back against the handlebar with elastic bands or a cable tie

preventative, oil or a stabiliser added to the fuel, drain and flush the tank and dispose of the fuel sensibly. If no action was taken with the fuel tank prior to storage, it is advised that the old fuel is disposed of since it will go off over a period of time. Refill the fuel tank with fresh fuel.

Frame and running gear

● Oil all pivot points and cables.
● Check the tyre pressures. They will definitely need inflating if pressures were reduced for storage.
● Lubricate the final drive chain (where applicable).
● Remove any protective coating applied to the fork tubes (stanchions) since this may well destroy the fork seals. If the fork tubes weren't protected and have picked up rust spots, remove them with very fine abrasive paper and refinish with metal polish.
● Check that both brakes operate correctly. Apply each brake hard and check that it's not possible to move the motorcycle forwards, then check that the brake frees off again once released. Brake caliper pistons can stick due to corrosion around the piston head, or on the sliding caliper types, due to corrosion of the slider pins. If the brake doesn't free after repeated operation, take the caliper off for examination. Similarly drum brakes can stick due to a seized operating cam, cable or rod linkage.
● If the motorcycle has been in long-term storage, renew the brake fluid and clutch fluid (where applicable).
● Depending on where the bike has been stored, the wiring, cables and hoses may have been nibbled by rodents. Make a visual check and investigate disturbed wiring loom tape.

Battery

● If the battery has been previously removal and given top up charges it can simply be reconnected. Remember to connect the positive cable first and the negative cable last.
● On conventional refillable batteries, if the battery has not received any attention, remove it from the motorcycle and check its electrolyte level. Top up if necessary then charge the battery. If the battery fails to hold a charge and a visual checks show heavy white sulphation of the plates, the battery is probably defective and must be renewed. This is particularly likely if the battery is old. Confirm battery condition with a specific gravity check.
● On sealed (MF) batteries, if the battery has not received any attention, remove it from the motorcycle and charge it according to the information on the battery case - if the battery fails to hold a charge it must be renewed.

Starting procedure

● If a kickstart is fitted, turn the engine over a couple of times with the ignition OFF to distribute oil around the engine. If no kickstart is fitted, flick the engine kill switch OFF and the ignition ON and crank the engine over a couple of times to work oil around the upper cylinder components. If the nature of the ignition system is such that the starter won't work with the kill switch OFF, remove the spark plugs, fit them back into their caps and earth (ground) their bodies on the cylinder head. Reinstall the spark plugs afterwards.
● Switch the kill switch to RUN, operate the choke and start the engine. If the engine won't start don't continue cranking the engine - not only will this flatten the battery, but the starter motor will overheat. Switch the ignition off and try again later. If the engine refuses to start, go through the fault finding procedures in this manual. **Note:** *If the bike has been in storage for a long time, old fuel or a carburettor blockage may be the problem. Gum deposits in carburettors can block jets - if a carburettor cleaner doesn't prove successful the carburettors must be dismantled for cleaning.*
● Once the engine has started, check that the lights, turn signals and horn work properly.
● Treat the bike gently for the first ride and check all fluid levels on completion. Settle the bike back into the maintenance schedule.

This Section provides an easy reference-guide to the more common faults that are likely to afflict your machine. Obviously, the opportunities are almost limitless for faults to occur as a result of obscure failures, and to try and cover all eventualities would require a book. Indeed, a number have been written on the subject.

Successful troubleshooting is not a mysterious 'black art' but the application of a bit of knowledge combined with a systematic and logical approach to the problem. Approach any troubleshooting by first accurately identifying the symptom and then checking through the list of possible causes, starting with the simplest or most obvious and progressing in stages to the most complex.

Take nothing for granted, but above all apply liberal quantities of common sense.

The main symptom of a fault is given in the text as a major heading below which are listed the various systems or areas which may contain the fault. Details of each possible cause for a fault and the remedial action to be taken are given, in brief, in the paragraphs below each heading. Further information should be sought in the relevant Chapter.

1 Engine doesn't start or is difficult to start

- [ ] Starter motor doesn't rotate
- [ ] Starter motor rotates but engine does not turn over
- [ ] Starter works but engine won't turn over (seized
- [ ] No fuel flow
- [ ] Engine flooded
- [ ] No spark or weak spark
- [ ] Compression low
- [ ] Stalls after starting
- [ ] Rough idle

2 Poor running at low speed

- [ ] Spark weak
- [ ] Fuel/air mixture incorrect
- [ ] Compression low
- [ ] Poor acceleration

3 Poor running or no power at high speed

- [ ] Firing incorrect
- [ ] Fuel/air mixture incorrect
- [ ] Compression low
- [ ] Knocking or pinking
- [ ] Miscellaneous causes

4 Overheating

- [ ] Engine overheats
- [ ] Firing incorrect
- [ ] Fuel/air mixture incorrect
- [ ] Compression too high
- [ ] Engine load excessive
- [ ] Lubrication inadequate
- [ ] Miscellaneous causes

5 Clutch problems

- [ ] Clutch slipping
- [ ] Clutch not disengaging completely

6 Gearchange problems

- [ ] Doesn't go into gear, or lever doesn't return
- [ ] Jumps out of gear
- [ ] Overselects

7 Abnormal engine noise

- [ ] Knocking or pinking
- [ ] Piston slap or rattling
- [ ] Valve noise
- [ ] Other noise

8 Abnormal driveline noise

- [ ] Clutch noise
- [ ] Transmission noise
- [ ] Final drive noise

9 Abnormal frame and suspension noise

- [ ] Front end noise
- [ ] Shock absorber noise
- [ ] Brake noise

10 Oil pressure warning light comes on

- [ ] Engine lubrication system
- [ ] Electrical system

11 Excessive exhaust smoke

- [ ] White smoke
- [ ] Black smoke
- [ ] Brown smoke

12 Poor handling or stability

- [ ] Handlebar hard to turn
- [ ] Handlebar shakes or vibrates excessively
- [ ] Handlebar pulls to one side
- [ ] Poor shock absorbing qualities

13 Braking problems

- [ ] Brakes are spongy, don't hold
- [ ] Brake lever or pedal pulsates
- [ ] Brakes drag

14 Electrical problems

- [ ] Battery dead or weak
- [ ] Battery overcharged

1 Engine doesn't start or is difficult to start

Starter motor doesn't rotate

☐ Engine kill switch OFF.

☐ Fuse blown. Check fuse (Chapter 8).

☐ Battery voltage low. Check and recharge battery (Chapter 8).

☐ Starter motor defective. Make sure the wiring to the starter is secure. Make sure the starter relay clicks when the start button is pushed. If the relay clicks, then the fault is in the wiring or motor.

☐ Starter relay faulty. Check if according to the procedure in Chapter 8.

☐ Starter switch not contacting. The contacts could be wet, corroded or dirty. Disassemble and clean the switch (Chapter 8).

☐ Wiring open or shorted. Check all wiring connections and harnesses to make sure that they are dry, tight and not corroded. Also check for broken or frayed wires that can cause a short to ground (earth) (see wiring diagram, Chapter 8).

☐ Ignition (main) switch defective. Check the switch according to the procedure in Chapter 8. Replace the switch with a new one if it is defective.

☐ Engine kill switch defective. Check for wet, dirty or corroded contacts. Clean or replace the switch as necessary (Chapter 8).

☐ Faulty neutral, clutch or sidestand switch. Check the wiring to each switch and the switch itself according to the procedures in Chapter 8.

☐ Faulty headlight cut-out relay. Check according to the procedure in Chapter 8.

☐ Faulty engine management system relay (EFI models). Check according to the procedure in Chapter 3B.

Starter motor rotates but engine does not turn over

☐ Starter clutch defective. Inspect and repair or replace (Chapter 2).

☐ Damaged idle/reduction gear or starter gears. Inspect and replace the damaged parts (Chapter 2).

Starter works but engine won't turn over (seized)

☐ Seized engine caused by one or more internally damaged components. Failure due to wear, abuse or lack of lubrication. Damage can include seized valves, followers, camshafts, pistons, crankshaft, connecting rod bearings, or transmission gears or bearings. Refer to Chapter 2 for engine disassembly.

No fuel flow – carburettor models

☐ No fuel in tank.

☐ Fuel tap strainer clogged. Remove the fuel tap and clean the strainer (Chapter 1 and 3A).

☐ Fuel line clogged. Pull the fuel line loose and carefully blow through it.

☐ Float needle valve clogged. For both of the valves to be clogged, either a very bad batch of fuel with an unusual additive has been used, or some other foreign material has entered the tank. Many times after a machine has been stored for many months without running, the fuel turns to a varnish-like liquid and forms deposits on the inlet needle valves and jets. The carburettors should be removed and overhauled if draining the float chambers doesn't solve the problem (Chapter 3A).

No fuel flow – EFI models

☐ No fuel in tank.

☐ Fuel filter clogged. Drain tank and remove fuel pump assembly for access to filter (Chapter 3B).

☐ Fuel pump relay or pump pressure regulator faulty. Check as described in Chapter 3B.

Engine flooded – carburettor models

☐ Float height incorrect. Check the fuel level and adjust as necessary (Chapter 3A).

☐ Float needle valve worn or stuck open. A piece of dirt, rust or other debris can cause the valve to seat improperly, causing excess fuel to be admitted to the float chamber. In this case, the float chamber should be cleaned and the needle valve and seat inspected. If the needle and seat are worn, then the leaking will persist and the parts should be replaced with new ones (Chapter 3A).

☐ Starting technique incorrect. Under normal circumstances (i.e., if all the carburettor functions are sound) the machine should start with little or no throttle. When the engine is cold, the choke should be operated and the engine started without opening the throttle. When the engine is at operating temperature, only a very slight amount of throttle should be necessary. If the engine is flooded hold the throttle open while cranking the engine. This will allow additional air to reach the cylinders.

Engine flooded – EFI models

☐ Fuel injector stuck open. Check the injectors (see Chapter 3B).

☐ Starting technique incorrect. Under normal circumstances the engine should start with no throttle. In cold weather, operate the choke.

No spark or weak spark

☐ Ignition switch OFF.

☐ Engine kill switch turned to the OFF position.

☐ Battery voltage low. Check and recharge the battery as necessary (Chapter 8).

☐ Spark plugs dirty, defective or worn out. Locate reason for fouled plugs using the spark plug condition chart on the inside rear cover of this manual and follow the plug maintenance procedures in Chapter 1.

☐ Spark plug caps or secondary (HT) wiring faulty. Check condition. Replace either or both components if cracks or deterioration are evident (Chapter 4).

☐ Spark plug caps not making good contact. Make sure that the plug caps fit snugly over the plug ends.

☐ Ignition control unit/ECM defective (Chapter 4).

☐ Pick-up coil/crankshaft position sensor defective. Check the coil referring to Chapter 4 for details.

☐ Ignition HT coil(s) defective. Check the coil(s), referring to Chapter 4 for details.

☐ Ignition or kill switch shorted. This is usually caused by water, corrosion, damage or excessive wear. The switches can be disassembled and cleaned with electrical contact cleaner. If cleaning does not help, replace the switches (Chapter 8).

☐ Wiring shorted or broken between:
   a) Ignition (main) switch and engine kill switch (or blown fuse)
   b) Ignition control unit/ECM and engine kill switch
   c) Ignition control unit/ECM and ignition HT coil(s)
   d) Ignition HT coil(s) and spark plugs
   e) Ignition control unit/ECM and pick-up coil/crankshaft position sensor

☐ Make sure that all wiring connections are clean, dry and tight. Look for chafed and broken wires (Chapters 4 and 8).

1 Engine doesn't start or is difficult to start (continued)

Compression low

☐ Spark plugs loose. Remove the plugs and inspect their threads. Reinstall and tighten to the specified torque (Chapter 1).

☐ Cylinder head not sufficiently tightened down. If the cylinder head is suspected of being loose, then there's a chance that the gasket or head is damaged if the problem has persisted for any length of time. The head nuts should be tightened to the proper torque in the correct sequence (Chapter 2).

☐ Improper valve clearance. This means that the valve is not closing completely and compression pressure is leaking past the valve. Check and adjust the valve clearances (Chapter 1).

☐ Cylinder and/or piston worn. Excessive wear will cause compression pressure to leak past the rings. This is usually accompanied by worn rings as well. A top-end overhaul is necessary (Chapter 2).

☐ Piston rings worn, weak, broken, or sticking. Broken or sticking piston rings usually indicate a lubrication or carburation problem that causes excess carbon deposits or seizures to form on the pistons and rings. Top-end overhaul is necessary (Chapter 2).

☐ Piston ring-to-groove clearance excessive. This is caused by excessive wear of the piston ring lands. Piston replacement is necessary (Chapter 2).

☐ Cylinder head gasket damaged. If the head is allowed to become loose, or if excessive carbon build-up on the piston crown and combustion chamber causes extremely high compression, the head gasket may leak. Retorquing the head is not always sufficient to restore the seal, so gasket replacement is necessary (Chapter 2).

☐ Cylinder head warped. This is caused by overheating or improperly tightened head nuts. Machine shop resurfacing or head replacement is necessary (Chapter 2).

☐ Valve spring broken or weak. Caused by component failure or wear; the springs must be replaced (Chapter 2).

☐ Valve not seating properly. This is caused by a bent valve (from over-revving or improper valve adjustment), burned valve or seat (improper carburation) or an accumulation of carbon deposits on the seat (from carburation or lubrication problems). The valves must be cleaned and/or replaced and the seats serviced if possible (Chapter 2).

Stalls after starting – carburettor models

☐ Improper choke action. Make sure the choke linkage shaft is getting a full stroke and staying in the out position (Chapter 3).

☐ Ignition malfunction (Chapter 4).

☐ Carburettor malfunction (Chapter 3).

☐ Fuel contaminated. The fuel can be contaminated with either dirt or water, or can change chemically if the machine is allowed to sit for several months or more. Drain the tank and float chambers (Chapter 3).

☐ Intake air leak. Check for loose or missing vacuum take-off point blanking cap or hose on the intake adapter on the cylinder head, or loose carburettor tops (Chapter 3).

☐ Intake air leak. Carburettor intake adapters loose, or the O-rings between them and the cylinder head, or on 865 cc engines between them and the insulators and/or between the insulators and the cylinder head, are not seated. Also check for cracks, breaks, tears or loose clamps on the rubbers. Replace the rubber intake manifold joints if split or perished (Chapter 3).

☐ Engine idle speed incorrect. Turn idle adjusting screw until the engine idles at the specified rpm (Chapter 1).

☐ On some America models (VIN range 139158 to 148655) a faulty

ignition control unit could be the problem, if all other possible causes (idle CO levels, carburettor synchronisation, intake air leaks etc) have been eliminated.

Stalls after starting – EFI models

☐ Improper choke action. Make sure the choke linkage shaft is getting a full stroke and staying in the out position (Chapter 3B).

☐ Ignition malfunction. See Chapter 4.

☐ Fuel injection system malfunction. See Chapter 3B.

☐ Fuel contaminated. The fuel can be contaminated with either dirt or water, or can change chemically if the machine is allowed to sit for several months or more. Drain the tank, fuel hoses and fuel rails (Chapter 3B).

☐ Intake air leak. Check for loose throttle body-to-intake manifold connections or a leaking gasket (Chapter 3B).

☐ Throttle bodies out of balance. This will require setting up using the Triumph diagnostic tester.

☐ Engine idle speed too low. Idle speed can be adjusted as described in Chapter 1, but note that Triumph advise it should be set using the diagnostic tester.

☐ Low fuel pressure (see Chapter 3B).

Rough idle – carburettor models

☐ Ignition malfunction (Chapter 4).

☐ Idle speed incorrect (Chapter 1).

☐ Carburettors not synchronised. Adjust carburettors with vacuum gauge or manometer set (Chapter 1).

☐ Carburettor malfunction (Chapter 3A).

☐ Fuel contaminated. The fuel can be contaminated with either dirt or water, or can change chemically if the machine is allowed to sit for several months or more. Drain the tank and float chambers (Chapter 3A).

☐ Intake air leak. Check for loose or missing vacuum take-off point blanking cap or hose on the intake adapter on the cylinder head, or loose carburettor tops (Chapter 3A).

☐ Intake air leak. Carburettor intake adapters loose, or the O-rings between them and the cylinder head, or on 865 cc engines between them and the insulators and/or between the insulators and the cylinder head, are not seated. Also check for cracks, breaks, tears or loose clamps on the rubbers. Replace the rubber intake manifold joints if split or perished (Chapter 3A).

☐ Air filter clogged. Replace the air filter element (Chapter 1).

☐ Fuel tank or carburettor breather/vent pipes pinched, blocked, or incorrectly routed. Check the pipes and replace, re-route and if necessary shorten (on Bonneville some pipes were too long – they should be 360 mm) as required (Chapter 3A).

Rough idle – EFI models

☐ Ignition malfunction. See Chapter 4.

☐ Engine idle speed too low. Idle speed can be adjusted as described in Chapter 1, but note that Triumph advise it should be set using the diagnostic tester.

☐ Throttle bodies out of balance. This will require setting up using the Triumph diagnostic tester.

☐ Fuel injection system malfunction. See Chapter 3B.

☐ Fuel contaminated. The fuel can be contaminated with either dirt or water, or can change chemically if the machine is allowed to sit for several months or more. Drain the tank, fuel hoses and fuel rails (Chapter 3B).

☐ Intake air leak. Check for loose throttle body-to-intake duct connections or loose duct bolts or failed O-ring (Chapter 3B).

☐ Air filter clogged. Fit a new air filter element (Chapter 1).

2 Poor running at low speeds

Spark weak

- [ ] Battery voltage low. Check and recharge battery (Chapter 8).
- [ ] Spark plugs fouled, defective or worn out (Chapter 1)
- [ ] Spark plug cap or HT wiring defective (Chapters 1 and 4).
- [ ] Spark plug caps not making contact. Make sure they are properly connected.
- [ ] Incorrect spark plugs. Wrong type, heat range or cap configuration. Check and install correct plugs (Chapter 1).
- [ ] Ignition control unit/ECM defective (Chapter 4).
- [ ] Pick-up coil defective – carburettor models (Chapter 4). Pulse generator coil defective – EFI models (Chapter 3B).
- [ ] Ignition HT coil(s) defective (Chapter 4).

Fuel/air mixture incorrect – carburettor models

- [ ] Pilot screws out of adjustment (Chapter 3A).
- [ ] Pilot jet or air passage clogged. Remove and overhaul the carburettors (Chapter 3A).
- [ ] Air bleed holes clogged. Remove carburettors and blow out all passages (Chapter 3A).
- [ ] Air filter clogged, poorly sealed or missing (Chapter 1).
- [ ] Air filter housing poorly sealed. Look for cracks, holes or loose clamps and replace or repair defective parts (Chapter 3A).
- [ ] Fuel level too high or too low. Check the float height (Chapter 3A).
- [ ] Intake air leak. Check for loose or missing vacuum take-off point blanking cap or hose on the intake adapter on the cylinder head, or loose carburettor tops (Chapter 3A).
- [ ] Intake air leak. Carburettor intake adapters loose, or the O-rings between them and the cylinder head, or on 865 cc engines between them and the insulators and/or between the insulators and the cylinder head, are not seated. Also check for cracks, breaks, tears or loose clamps on the rubbers. Replace the rubber intake manifold joints if split or perished (Chapter 3A).
- [ ] Fuel tank or carburettor breather/vent pipes pinched, blocked, or incorrectly routed. Check the pipes and replace, re-route and if necessary shorten (on Bonneville some pipes were too long – they should be 360 mm) as required (Chapter 3A).

Fuel/air mixture incorrect – EFI models

- [ ] Fuel injector clogged or fuel injection system malfunction (see Chapter 3B).
- [ ] Air filter clogged, poorly sealed or missing (Chapter 1).
- [ ] Fuel tank breather hose obstructed.
- [ ] Intake air leak. Check for loose throttle body-to-intake duct connections or loose duct bolts or failed O-ring (Chapter 3B).
- [ ] Fuel injection system malfunction. See Chapter 3B.

Compression low

- [ ] Spark plugs loose. Remove the plugs and inspect their threads. Reinstall and tighten to the specified torque (Chapter 1).
- [ ] Cylinder head not sufficiently tightened down. If the cylinder head is suspected of being loose, then there's a chance that the gasket or head is damaged if the problem has persisted for any length of time. The head nuts should be tightened to the proper torque in the correct sequence (Chapter 2).
- [ ] Improper valve clearance. This means that the valve is not closing completely and compression pressure is leaking past the valve. Check and adjust the valve clearances (Chapter 1).
- [ ] Cylinder and/or piston worn. Excessive wear will cause compression pressure to leak past the rings. This is usually accompanied by worn rings as well. A top-end overhaul is necessary (Chapter 2).
- [ ] Piston rings worn, weak, broken, or sticking. Broken or sticking piston rings usually indicate a lubrication or carburation problem that causes excess carbon deposits or seizures to form on the pistons and rings. Top-end overhaul is necessary (Chapter 2).
- [ ] Piston ring-to-groove clearance excessive. This is caused by excessive wear of the piston ring lands. Piston replacement is necessary (Chapter 2).
- [ ] Cylinder head gasket damaged. If the head is allowed to become loose, or if excessive carbon build-up on the piston crown and combustion chamber causes extremely high compression, the head gasket may leak. Retorquing the head is not always sufficient to restore the seal, so gasket replacement is necessary (Chapter 2).
- [ ] Cylinder head warped. This is caused by overheating or improperly tightened head nuts. Machine shop resurfacing or head replacement is necessary (Chapter 2).
- [ ] Valve spring broken or weak. Caused by component failure or wear; the springs must be replaced (Chapter 2).
- [ ] Valve not seating properly. This is caused by a bent valve (from over-revving or improper valve adjustment), burned valve or seat (improper carburation) or an accumulation of carbon deposits on the seat (from carburation or lubrication problems). The valves must be cleaned and/or replaced and the seats serviced if possible (Chapter 2).

Poor acceleration – carburettor models

- [ ] Carburettors leaking or dirty. Overhaul the carburettors (Chapter 3A).
- [ ] Timing not advancing. Faulty pick-up coil or ignition control unit (Chapter 4).
- [ ] Carburettors not synchronised. Adjust them with a vacuum gauge set or manometer (Chapter 1).
- [ ] Brakes dragging. Usually caused by debris which has entered the brake piston seals, or from a warped disc or bent axle. Repair as necessary (Chapter 6).

Poor acceleration – EFI models

- [ ] Intake air leak. Check for loose throttle body-to-intake duct connections or loose duct bolts or failed O-ring (Chapter 3B).
- [ ] Timing not advancing. The ECM or a sensor in the fuel injection system may be defective. If so, they must be renewed as they can't be repaired. The system can only be checked using the Triumph diagnostic tool – see Chapter 3B for details.
- [ ] Throttle bodies not synchronised.
- [ ] Low fuel pressure (Chapter 3B).
- [ ] Brakes dragging. Usually caused by debris which has entered the brake piston seals, or from a warped disc or bent axle. Repair as necessary (Chapter 6).

3 Poor running or no power at high speed

Firing incorrect

☐ Air filter restricted. Clean or replace filter (Chapter 1).
☐ Spark plugs fouled, defective or worn out (Chapter 1).
☐ Spark plug cap or HT wiring defective (Chapters 1 and 4).
☐ Spark plug caps not making contact. Make sure they are properly connected.
☐ Incorrect spark plugs. Wrong type, heat range or cap configuration. Check and install correct plugs (Chapter 1).
☐ Ignition control unit/ECM defective (Chapter 4).
☐ Pick-up coil defective – carburettor models (Chapter 4). Pulse generator coil defective – EFI models (Chapter 3B).
☐ Ignition HT coil(s) defective (Chapter 4).

Fuel/air mixture incorrect – carburettor models

☐ Air bleed holes clogged. Remove carburettors and blow out all passages (Chapter 3A).
☐ Air filter clogged, poorly sealed or missing (Chapter 1).
☐ Air filter housing poorly sealed. Look for cracks, holes or loose clamps and replace or repair defective parts (Chapter 3A).
☐ Fuel level too high or too low. Check the float height (Chapter 3A).
☐ Intake air leak. Check for loose or missing vacuum take-off point blanking cap or hose on the intake adapter on the cylinder head, or loose carburettor tops (Chapter 3A).
☐ Intake air leak. Carburettor intake adapters loose, or the O-rings between them and the cylinder head, or on 865 cc engines between them and the insulators and/or between the insulators and the cylinder head, are not seated. Also check for cracks, breaks, tears or loose clamps on the rubbers. Replace the rubber intake manifold joints if split or perished (Chapter 3A).
☐ Needle incorrectly positioned or worn. Check and adjust or replace (Chapter 3A).
☐ Main jet clogged. Dirt, water or other contaminants can clog the main jets. Clean the fuel tap filter, the float chamber area, and the jets and carburettor orifices (Chapter 3A).
☐ Main jet wrong size. The standard jetting is for sea level atmospheric pressure and oxygen content. Check jet size (Chapter 3A).
☐ Throttle shaft-to-carburettor body clearance excessive. Overhaul carburettors, replacing worn parts or complete carburettor if necessary (Chapter 3A).

Fuel/air mixture incorrect – EFI models

☐ Fuel injector clogged or fuel injection system malfunction (see Chapter 3B).
☐ Air filter clogged, poorly sealed or missing (Chapter 1).
☐ Fuel tank breather hose obstructed.
☐ Intake air leak. Check for loose throttle body-to-intake duct connections or loose duct bolts or failed O-ring (Chapter 3B).
☐ Fuel injection system malfunction. See Chapter 3B.

Compression low

☐ Spark plugs loose. Remove the plugs and inspect their threads. Reinstall and tighten to the specified torque (Chapter 1).
☐ Cylinder head not sufficiently tightened down. If the cylinder head is suspected of being loose, then there's a chance that the gasket or head is damaged if the problem has persisted for any length of time. The head nuts should be tightened to the proper torque in the correct sequence (Chapter 2).
☐ Improper valve clearance. This means that the valve is not closing completely and compression pressure is leaking past the valve. Check and adjust the valve clearances (Chapter 1).

☐ Cylinder and/or piston worn. Excessive wear will cause compression pressure to leak past the rings. This is usually accompanied by worn rings as well. A top-end overhaul is necessary (Chapter 2).
☐ Piston rings worn, weak, broken, or sticking. Broken or sticking piston rings usually indicate a lubrication or carburation problem that causes excess carbon deposits or seizures to form on the pistons and rings. Top-end overhaul is necessary (Chapter 2).
☐ Piston ring-to-groove clearance excessive. This is caused by excessive wear of the piston ring lands. Piston replacement is necessary (Chapter 2).
☐ Cylinder head gasket damaged. If the head is allowed to become loose, or if excessive carbon build-up on the piston crown and combustion chamber causes extremely high compression, the head gasket may leak. Retorquing the head is not always sufficient to restore the seal, so gasket replacement is necessary (Chapter 2).
☐ Cylinder head warped. This is caused by overheating or improperly tightened head nuts. Machine shop resurfacing or head replacement is necessary (Chapter 2).
☐ Valve spring broken or weak. Caused by component failure or wear; the springs must be replaced (Chapter 2).
☐ Valve not seating properly. This is caused by a bent valve (from over-revving or improper valve adjustment), burned valve or seat (improper carburation) or an accumulation of carbon deposits on the seat (from carburation or lubrication problems). The valves must be cleaned and/or replaced and the seats serviced if possible (Chapter 2).

Knocking or pinking

☐ Carbon build-up in combustion chamber. Use of a fuel additive that will dissolve the adhesive bonding the carbon particles to the crown and chamber is the easiest way to remove the build-up. Otherwise, the cylinder head will have to be removed and decarbonised (Chapter 2).
☐ Incorrect or poor quality fuel. Old or a low octane grade of fuel can cause detonation. This causes the piston to rattle, thus the knocking or pinking sound. Drain old fuel and always use the recommended fuel grade (Chapter 3A or 3B).
☐ Spark plug heat range incorrect. Uncontrolled detonation indicates the plug heat range is too hot. The plug in effect becomes a glow plug, raising cylinder temperatures. Install the proper heat range plug (Chapter 1).
☐ Improper air/fuel mixture. This will cause the cylinder to run hot, which leads to detonation. See under relevant heading above for possible causes.

Miscellaneous causes

☐ Throttle valve doesn't open fully. Adjust the throttle grip freeplay (Chapter 1).
☐ Clutch slipping. May be caused by loose or worn clutch components. Overhaul clutch (Chapter 2).
☐ Timing not advancing. Ignition control unit/ECM faulty (Chapter 4).
☐ Engine oil viscosity too high. Using a heavier oil than the one recommended in Chapter 1 can damage the oil pump or lubrication system and cause drag on the engine.
☐ Brakes dragging. Usually caused by debris which has entered the brake piston seals, or from a warped disc or bent axle. Repair as necessary.
☐ Fuel tank or carburettor/throttle body breather pipes pinched, blocked, or incorrectly routed. Check the pipes and replace, re-route and if necessary shorten (on Bonneville some pipes were too long – they should be 360 mm) as required (Chapter 3A or 3B).

4 Overheating

Firing incorrect

☐ Spark plugs fouled, defective or worn out (Chapter 1).
☐ Incorrect spark plugs (Chapter 1).
☐ Faulty ignition HT coil(s) (Chapter 4).

Fuel/air mixture incorrect – carburettor models

☐ Main jet clogged. Dirt, water and other contaminants can clog the main jets. Clean the fuel tap filter, the float chamber area and the jets and carburettor orifices (Chapter 3A).
☐ Main jet wrong size. The standard jetting is for sea level atmospheric pressure and oxygen content. Check jet size (Chapter 3A).
☐ Air filter clogged, poorly sealed or missing (Chapter 1).
☐ Air filter housing poorly sealed. Look for cracks, holes or loose clamps and replace or repair (Chapter 3A).
☐ Fuel level too low. Check float height (Chapter 3A).
☐ Carburettor intake adapters loose. Check for cracks, breaks, tears or loose clamps. Replace the rubber intake adapter joints if split or perished (Chapter 3A).

Fuel/air mixture incorrect – EFI models

☐ Fuel injector clogged (see Chapter 3B).
☐ Air filter clogged, poorly sealed or missing (Chapter 1).
☐ Fuel tank breather hose obstructed.
☐ Intake air leak. Check for loose throttle body-to-intake duct connections or loose duct bolts or failed O-ring (Chapter 3B).
☐ Fuel injection system malfunction. See Chapter 3B.

Compression too high

☐ Carbon build-up in combustion chamber. Use of a fuel additive that will dissolve the adhesive bonding the carbon particles to the piston crown and chamber is the easiest way to remove the build-up. Otherwise, the cylinder head will have to be removed and decarbonised (Chapter 2).

☐ Improperly machined head surface or installation of incorrect gasket during engine assembly (Chapter 2).

Engine load excessive

☐ Clutch slipping. Can be caused by damaged, loose or worn clutch components. Overhaul clutch (Chapter 2).
☐ Engine oil level too high. The addition of too much oil will cause pressurisation of the crankcase and inefficient engine operation. Check Specifications and drain to proper level (Chapter 1 and *Pre-ride checks*).
☐ Engine oil viscosity too high. Using a heavier oil than the one recommended in Chapter 1 can damage the oil pump or lubrication system as well as cause drag on the engine.
☐ Brakes dragging. Usually caused by debris which has entered the brake piston seals, or from a warped disc or bent axle. Repair as necessary.
☐ Excessive friction in moving engine parts due to inadequate lubrication, worn bearings or incorrect assembly. Overhaul engine (Chapter 2).

Lubrication inadequate

☐ Engine oil level too low. Friction caused by intermittent lack of lubrication or from oil that is overworked can cause overheating. The oil provides a definite cooling function in the engine. Check the oil level (see *Pre-ride checks*).
☐ Poor quality engine oil or incorrect viscosity or type. Oil is rated not only according to viscosity but also according to type. Some oils are not rated high enough for use in this engine. Check the Specifications section and change to the correct oil (Chapter 1).
☐ Worn oil pump or clogged oil passages. Check oil pumps and clean passages (Chapter 2).

Miscellaneous causes

☐ Engine cooling fins and/or oil cooler clogged with debris.

5 Clutch problems

Clutch slipping

- [ ] Cable freeplay insufficient. Check and adjust cable (Chapter 1).
- [ ] Friction plates worn or warped. Overhaul the clutch assembly (Chapter 2).
- [ ] Plain plates warped (Chapter 2).
- [ ] Clutch springs broken or weak. Old or heat-damaged (from slipping clutch) springs should be replaced with new ones (Chapter 2).
- [ ] Clutch release mechanism defective. Replace any defective parts (Chapter 2).
- [ ] Clutch centre or housing unevenly worn. This causes improper engagement of the plates. Replace the damaged or worn parts (Chapter 2).

Clutch not disengaging completely

- [ ] Cable freeplay excessive. Check and adjust cable (Chapter 1).
- [ ] Clutch plates warped or damaged. This will cause clutch drag, which in turn will cause the machine to creep. Overhaul the clutch assembly (Chapter 2).
- [ ] On some early Bonneville models (up to VIN 123933) difficulty in engaging gears, or clutch drag/transmission noise when stopped and in gear with the clutch pulled in, is caused by the anti-judder spring, which should be removed along with the spring seat – refer to a Triumph dealer for details.
- [ ] Clutch spring tension uneven. Usually caused by a sagged or broken spring. Check and replace the springs as a set (Chapter 2).

- [ ] Engine oil deteriorated. Old, thin, worn out oil will not provide proper lubrication for the plates, causing the clutch to drag. Replace the oil and filter (Chapter 1).
- [ ] Engine oil viscosity too high. Using a heavier oil than recommended in Chapter 1 can cause the plates to stick together, putting a drag on the engine. Change to the correct weight oil (Chapter 1).
- [ ] Clutch housing seized on input shaft. Lack of lubrication, severe wear or damage can cause the bush to seize on the shaft. Overhaul of the clutch, and perhaps transmission, may be necessary to repair the damage (Chapter 2).
- [ ] Clutch release mechanism defective (Chapter 2).
- [ ] Loose clutch centre nut. Causes drum and centre misalignment putting a drag on the engine. Engagement adjustment continually varies. Overhaul the clutch assembly (Chapter 2).

Clutch noise or vibration

- [ ] Clutch lifter plate not properly centred. Triumph recommend the use of an alignment mandrel when assembling the clutch following overhaul or the fitting of new plates. In practice this is not essential, though if it isn't used great care must be taken to follow the text in Chapter 2 precisely. Remove the clutch cover and check that the pushrod seat slides easily in and out of the transmission input shaft and the bearing in the lifter plate – if it is tight or does not move at all the lifter plate is out of alignment and must be removed and reinstalled correctly.

6 Gearchange problems

Doesn't go into gear or lever doesn't return

- [ ] Clutch not disengaging. See above.
- [ ] Selector fork(s) bent or seized. Often caused by dropping the machine or from lack of lubrication. Overhaul the transmission (Chapter 2).
- [ ] Gear(s) stuck on shaft. Most often caused by a lack of lubrication or excessive wear in transmission bearings and bushes. Overhaul the transmission (Chapter 2).
- [ ] Gear selector drum binding. Caused by lubrication failure or excessive wear. Replace the drum and bearing (Chapter 2).
- [ ] Gearchange shaft centralising spring weak or broken (Chapter 2).
- [ ] Gearchange lever broken. Splines stripped out of lever or shaft, caused by allowing the lever to get loose or from dropping the machine. Replace necessary parts (Chapter 2).

- [ ] Gearchange mechanism stopper arm broken or worn. Replace the arm (Chapter 2).
- [ ] Stopper arm spring broken. Allows arm to float, causing sporadic selector operation. Replace spring (Chapter 2).

Jumps out of gear

- [ ] Selector fork(s) worn. Overhaul the transmission (Chapter 2).
- [ ] Gear groove(s) worn. Overhaul the transmission (Chapter 2).
- [ ] Gear dogs or dog slots worn or damaged. The gears should be inspected and replaced. No attempt should be made to build up the worn parts (Chapter 2).

Overselects

- [ ] Stopper arm spring weak or broken (Chapter 2).
- [ ] Gearchange shaft centralising spring or its post broken or distorted (Chapter 2).

7 Abnormal engine noise

Knocking or pinking

☐ Carbon build-up in combustion chamber. Use of a fuel additive that will dissolve the adhesive bonding the carbon particles to the piston crown and chamber is the easiest way to remove the build-up. Otherwise, the cylinder head will have to be removed and decarbonised (Chapter 2).

☐ Incorrect or poor quality fuel. Old or improper fuel can cause detonation. This causes the pistons to rattle, thus the knocking or pinking sound. Drain the old fuel and always use the recommended grade fuel (Chapter 3A or 3B).

☐ Spark plug heat range incorrect. Uncontrolled detonation indicates that the plug heat range is too hot. The plug in effect becomes a glow plug, raising cylinder temperatures. Install the proper heat range plug (Chapter 1).

☐ Improper air/fuel mixture. This will cause the cylinders to run hot and lead to detonation. Clogged jets (carburettor models) or a clogged injector (EFI models) can cause this imbalance, or an air leak (Chapter 3A or 3B).

Piston slap or rattling

☐ Cylinder-to-piston clearance excessive. Caused by improper assembly. Inspect and overhaul top-end parts (Chapter 2).

☐ Connecting rod bent. Caused by over-revving, trying to start a badly flooded engine or from ingesting a foreign object into the combustion chamber. Replace the damaged parts (Chapter 2).

☐ Piston pin or piston pin bore worn or seized from wear or lack of lubrication. Replace damaged parts (Chapter 2).

☐ Piston ring(s) worn, broken or sticking. Overhaul the top-end (Chapter 2).

☐ Piston seizure damage. Usually from lack of lubrication or overheating. Replace the pistons and cylinder block, as necessary (Chapter 2).

☐ Connecting rod upper or lower end clearance excessive. Caused by excessive wear or lack of lubrication. Replace worn parts (Chapter 2).

Valve noise

☐ Incorrect valve clearances. Adjust the clearances (Chapter 1).

☐ Valve spring broken or weak. Check and replace weak valve springs (Chapter 2).

☐ Camshaft or cylinder head worn or damaged. Lack of lubrication at high rpm is usually the cause of damage. Insufficient oil or failure to change the oil at the recommended intervals are the chief causes. Since there are no replaceable bearings in the head, the head itself will have to be replaced if there is excessive wear or damage (Chapter 2).

Other noise

☐ Cylinder head gasket leaking (Chapter 2).

☐ Exhaust pipe leaking at cylinder head connection. Caused by improper fit of pipe(s) or loose exhaust flange. All exhaust fasteners should be tightened evenly and carefully. Failure to do this will lead to a leak (Chapter 3A or 3B).

☐ Crankshaft runout excessive. Caused by a bent crankshaft (from over-revving) or damage from an upper cylinder component failure.

☐ Engine mounting bolts loose. Tighten all engine mounting bolts (Chapter 2).

☐ Crankshaft bearings worn (Chapter 2).

☐ Camchain tensioner defective. Replace (Chapter 2).

☐ Camchain, drive gear, sprockets or guides worn (Chapter 2).

8 Abnormal transmission noise

Clutch noise

☐ Clutch housing/friction plate clearance excessive (Chapter 2).

☐ Loose or damaged clutch pressure plate and/or bolts (Chapter 2).

☐ Clutch lifter plate not properly centred. Triumph recommend the use of an alignment mandrel when assembling the clutch following overhaul or the fitting of new plates. In practice this is not essential, though if it isn't used great care must be taken to follow the text in Chapter 2 precisely. Remove the clutch cover and check that the pushrod seat slides easily in and out of the transmission input shaft and the bearing in the lifter plate – if it is tight or does not move at all the lifter plate is out of alignment and must be removed and reinstalled correctly.

Transmission noise

☐ Bearings worn. Also includes the possibility that the shafts are worn. Overhaul the transmission (Chapter 2).

☐ Gears worn or chipped (Chapter 2).

☐ Metal chips jammed in gear teeth. Probably pieces from a broken clutch, gear or selector mechanism that were picked up by the gears. This will cause early bearing failure (Chapter 2).

☐ Engine oil level too low. Causes a howl from transmission. Also affects engine power and clutch operation (see Pre-ride checks).

Final drive noise

☐ Chain not adjusted properly (Chapter 1).

☐ Front or rear sprocket loose. Tighten fasteners (Chapter 5).

☐ Sprockets worn. Replace sprockets (Chapter 5).

☐ Rear sprocket warped. Replace sprockets (Chapter 5).

☐ Wheel coupling damper worn. Replace damper (Chapter 5).

9 Abnormal frame and suspension noise

Front end noise

☐ Low fluid level or improper viscosity oil in forks. This can sound like spurting and is usually accompanied by irregular fork action (Chapter 5).

☐ Spring weak or broken. Makes a clicking or scraping sound. Fork oil, when drained, will have a lot of metal particles in it (Chapter 5).

☐ Steering head bearings loose or damaged. Clicks when braking. Check and adjust or replace as necessary (Chapters 1 and 5).

☐ Fork yokes loose. Make sure all clamp pinch bolts are tight (Chapter 5).

☐ Fork tube bent. Good possibility if machine has been dropped. Replace tube with a new one (Chapter 5).

☐ Front axle or axle clamp bolt loose. Tighten them to the specified torque (Chapter 6).

Shock absorber noise

☐ Fluid leak caused by defective seal. Shock will be covered with oil. Replace shocks with new ones (Chapter 5).

☐ Defective shock absorber(s) with internal damage. This is in the body of the shock and can't be remedied. The shocks must be replaced with new ones (Chapter 5).

☐ Bent or damaged shock body. Replace the shocks with new ones (Chapter 5).

Brake noise

☐ Squeal caused by dust on brake pads. Usually found in combination with glazed pads. Clean using brake cleaning solvent (Chapter 6).

☐ Contamination of brake pads. Oil, brake fluid or dirt causing brake to chatter or squeal. Clean or replace pads (Chapter 6).

☐ Pads glazed. Caused by excessive heat from prolonged use or from contamination. Do not use sandpaper, emery cloth, carborundum cloth or any other abrasive to roughen the pad surfaces as abrasives will stay in the pad material and damage the disc. A very fine flat file can be used, but fitting new pads is the best cure (Chapter 6).

☐ Disc(s) warped. Can cause a chattering, clicking or intermittent squeal. Usually accompanied by a pulsating lever and uneven braking. Replace the disc(s) (Chapter 6).

☐ Loose or worn wheel bearings. Check and replace as needed (Chapter 6).

10 Oil pressure warning light comes on

Engine lubrication system

☐ Engine oil pump(s) defective, blocked oil strainer gauze or failed relief valve. Carry out oil pressure check (Chapter 2).

☐ Engine oil level low. Inspect for leak or other problem causing low oil level and add recommended oil (see Pre-ride checks).

☐ Engine oil viscosity too low. Very old, thin oil or an improper weight of oil used in the engine. Change to correct oil (Chapter 1).

☐ Camshaft or journals worn. Excessive wear causing drop in oil pressure. Replace cam and/or cylinder head. Abnormal wear could be caused by oil starvation at high rpm from low oil level or improper weight or type of oil (Chapter 1).

☐ Crankshaft and/or bearings worn. Same problems as above. Check and replace crankshaft and/or bearings (Chapter 2).

Electrical system

☐ Oil pressure switch defective. Check the switch according to the procedure in Chapter 8. Replace it if it is defective.

☐ Oil pressure warning light circuit defective. Check for pinched, shorted, disconnected or damaged wiring (Chapter 8).

11 Excessive exhaust smoke

White smoke

☐ Piston oil ring worn. The ring may be broken or damaged, causing oil from the crankcase to be pulled past the piston into the combustion chamber. Replace the rings with new ones (Chapter 2).

☐ Cylinders worn, cracked, or scored. Caused by overheating or oil starvation. A new cylinder block must be fitted and new pistons installed (Chapter 2).

☐ Valve oil seal damaged or worn. Replace oil seals with new ones (Chapter 2).

☐ Valve guide worn. Perform a complete valve job (Chapter 2).

☐ Engine oil level too high, which causes the oil to be forced past the rings. Drain oil to the proper level (Chapter 1 and *Pre-ride checks*).

☐ Head gasket broken between oil return and cylinder. Causes oil to be pulled into the combustion chamber. Replace the head gasket and check the head for warpage (Chapter 2).

☐ Abnormal crankcase pressurisation, which forces oil past the rings. Clogged ventilation system or breather hose (Chapter 2).

Black smoke – carburettor models

☐ Air filter clogged. Clean or replace the element (Chapter 1).

☐ Main jet too large or loose. Compare the jet size to the Specifications (Chapter 3A).

☐ Choke linkage shaft stuck, causing fuel to be pulled through choke circuit (Chapter 3A).

☐ Fuel level too high. Check and adjust the float height(s) as necessary (Chapter 3A).

☐ Float needle valve held off needle seat. Clean the float chambers and fuel line and replace the needles and seats if necessary (Chapter 3A).

Black smoke – EFI models

☐ Air filter clogged. Clean or renew the element (Chapter 1).

☐ Fuel injection system malfunction (Chapter 4). These system can only be checked using the Triumph diagnostic tool. Refer to Chapter 3B for further information.

☐ Fuel pressure too high due to faulty pressure regulator. Check the fuel pressure (Chapter 3B).

Brown smoke – carburettor models

☐ Main jet too small or clogged. Lean condition caused by wrong size main jet or by a restricted orifice. Clean float chambers and jets and compare jet size to Specifications (Chapter 3A).

☐ Fuel flow insufficient. Float needle valve stuck closed due to chemical reaction with old fuel. Float height incorrect. Restricted fuel line. Clean line and float chamber and adjust floats if necessary (Chapter 3A).

☐ Carburettor intake adapter clamps loose (Chapter 3A).

☐ Air filter poorly sealed or not installed (Chapter 1).

Brown smoke – EFI models

☐ Fuel pump faulty or pressure regulator stuck open (Chapter 3B).

☐ Throttle body-to-intake manifold bolts loose or gasket broken (Chapter 3B).

☐ Air filter poorly sealed or not installed (Chapter 1).

☐ Fuel injection system malfunction (Chapter 3B).

12 Poor handling or stability

Handlebar hard to turn

☐ Steering head bearing adjuster nut too tight. Check adjustment (Chapter 1).

☐ Bearings damaged. Roughness can be felt as the bars are turned from side-to-side. Replace bearings and races (Chapter 5).

☐ Races dented or worn. Denting results from wear in only one position (e.g., straight ahead), from a collision or hitting a pothole or from dropping the machine. Replace races and bearings (Chapter 5).

☐ Steering stem lubrication inadequate. Causes are grease getting hard from age or being washed out by high pressure car washes. Disassemble steering head and repack bearings (Chapter 5).

☐ Steering stem bent. Caused by a collision, hitting a pothole or by dropping the machine. Replace damaged part. Don't try to straighten the steering stem (Chapter 5).

☐ Front tyre air pressure too low (see *Pre-ride checks*).

Handlebar shakes or vibrates excessively

☐ Tyres worn or out of balance (see *Pre-ride checks* and Chapter 6).

☐ Swingarm bearings worn. Replace worn bearings (Chapter 5).

☐ Rim(s) warped or damaged. Inspect wheels for runout (Chapter 6).

☐ Wheel bearings worn. Worn front or rear wheel bearings can cause poor tracking. Worn front bearings will cause wobble (Chapter 6).

☐ Handlebar clamp bolts loose (Chapter 5).

☐ Fork yoke bolts loose. Tighten them to the specified torque (Chapter 5).

☐ Engine mounting bolts loose. Will cause excessive vibration with increased engine rpm (Chapter 2).

Handlebar pulls to one side

☐ Frame bent. Definitely suspect this if the machine has been dropped. May or may not be accompanied by cracking near the bend. Replace the frame (Chapter 5).

☐ Wheels out of alignment. Caused by improper location of axle spacers or from bent steering stem or frame (Chapter 5).

☐ Swingarm bent or twisted. Caused by age (metal fatigue) or impact damage. Replace the swingarm (Chapter 5).

☐ Steering stem bent. Caused by impact damage or by dropping the motorcycle. Replace the steering stem (Chapter 5).

☐ Fork tube bent. Disassemble the forks and replace the damaged parts (Chapter 5).

☐ Fork oil level uneven. Check and add or drain as necessary (Chapter 5).

Poor shock absorbing qualities

☐ Too hard:
   a) *Fork oil level excessive (Chapter 5).*
   b) *Fork oil viscosity too high. Use a lighter oil (see the Specifications in Chapter 5).*
   c) *Fork tube bent. Causes a harsh, sticking feeling (Chapter 5).*
   d) *Shock shaft or body bent or damaged (Chapter 5).*
   e) *Fork internal damage (Chapter 5).*
   f) *Shock internal damage.*
   g) *Tyre pressure too high (Pre-ride checks).*

☐ Too soft:
   a) *Fork or shock oil insufficient and/or leaking (Chapter 5).*
   b) *Fork oil level too low (Chapter 5).*
   c) *Fork oil viscosity too light (Chapter 5).*
   d) *Fork springs weak or broken (Chapter 5).*
   e) *Shock internal damage or leakage (Chapter 5).*

13 Braking problems

Brakes are spongy, don't hold

☐ Air in brake line. Caused by inattention to master cylinder fluid level or by leakage. Locate problem and bleed brakes (Chapter 6).

☐ Pads or disc worn (Chapters 1 and 6).

☐ Brake fluid leak. Causes air in brake line. Locate problem and bleed brakes (Chapter 6).

☐ Contaminated pads. Caused by contamination with oil, grease, brake fluid, etc. Clean or replace pads. Clean disc thoroughly with brake cleaner (Chapter 6).

☐ Brake fluid deteriorated. Fluid is old or contaminated. Drain system, replenish with new fluid and bleed the system (Chapter 6).

☐ Master cylinder internal parts worn or damaged causing fluid to bypass (Chapter 6).

☐ Master cylinder bore scratched by foreign material or broken spring. Repair or replace master cylinder (Chapter 6).

☐ Disc warped. Replace disc (Chapter 6).

Brake lever or pedal pulsates

☐ Disc(s) warped. Replace disc(s) (Chapter 6).

☐ Axle bent. Replace axle (Chapter 6).

☐ Brake caliper bolts loose (Chapter 6).

☐ Brake caliper sliders damaged or sticking, causing caliper to bind. Lubricate the sliders or replace them if they are corroded or bent (Chapter 6).

☐ Wheel warped or otherwise damaged (Chapter 6).

☐ Wheel bearings damaged or worn (Chapter 6).

Brakes drag

☐ Master cylinder piston seized. Caused by wear or damage to piston or cylinder bore (Chapter 6).

☐ Lever balky or stuck. Check pivot and lubricate (Chapter 6).

☐ Brake caliper binds. Caused by inadequate lubrication or damage to caliper sliders (Chapter 6).

☐ Brake caliper piston seized in bore. Caused by wear or ingestion of dirt past deteriorated seal (Chapter 6).

☐ Brake pad damaged. Pad material separated from backing plate. Usually caused by faulty manufacturing process or from contact with chemicals. Replace pads (Chapter 6).

☐ Pads improperly installed (Chapter 6).

14 Electrical problems

Battery dead or weak

☐ Battery charge unable to recover from excessive short journey use. Recharge regularly using a dedicated motorcycle battery charger.

☐ Battery faulty. Caused by sulphated plates which are shorted through sedimentation. Also, broken battery terminal making only occasional contact (Chapter 8).

☐ Battery cables making poor contact (Chapter 1).

☐ Load excessive. Caused by addition of high wattage lights or other electrical accessories.

☐ Ignition (main) switch defective. Switch either grounds (earths) internally or fails to shut off system. Replace the switch (Chapter 8).

☐ Regulator/rectifier defective (Chapter 8).

☐ Alternator stator coil open or shorted (Chapter 8).

☐ Wiring faulty. Wiring grounded (earthed) or connections loose in ignition, charging or lighting circuits (Chapter 8).

Battery overcharged

☐ Regulator/rectifier defective. Overcharging is noticed when battery gets excessively warm (Chapter 8).

☐ Battery defective. Replace battery with a new one (Chapter 8).

☐ Battery amperage too low, wrong type or size. Install manufacturer's specified amp-hour battery to handle charging load (Chapter 8).

Checking engine compression

● Low compression will result in exhaust smoke, heavy oil consumption, poor starting and poor performance. A compression test will provide useful information about an engine's condition and if performed regularly, can give warning of trouble before any other symptoms become apparent.

● A compression gauge will be required, along with an adapter to suit the spark plug hole thread size. Note that the screw-in type gauge/adapter set up is preferable to the rubber cone type.

● Before carrying out the test, first check the valve clearances as described in Chapter 1.

1 Run the engine until it reaches normal operating temperature, then stop it and remove the spark plug(s), taking care not to scald your hands on the hot components.

2 Install the gauge adapter and compression gauge in No. 1 cylinder spark plug hole **(see illustration 1)**.

Screw the compression gauge adapter into the spark plug hole, then screw the gauge into the adapter

3 On kickstart-equipped motorcycles, make sure the ignition switch is OFF, then open the throttle fully and kick the engine over a couple of times until the gauge reading stabilises.

4 On motorcycles with electric start only, the procedure will differ depending on the nature of the ignition system. Flick the engine kill switch (engine stop switch) to OFF and turn the ignition switch ON; open the throttle fully and crank the engine over on the starter motor for a couple of revolutions until the gauge reading stabilises. If the starter will not operate with the kill switch OFF, turn the ignition switch OFF and refer to the next paragraph.

5 Install the plugs back in their caps and arrange the plug electrodes so that their metal bodies are earthed (grounded) against the cylinder head; this is essential to prevent damage to the ignition system **(see illustration 2)**. Position the plugs well away

All spark plugs must be earthed (grounded) against the cylinder head

from the plug holes otherwise there is a risk of atomised fuel escaping from the plug holes and igniting. As a safety precaution, cover the cylinder head cover with rag. Turn the ignition switch and kill switch ON, open the throttle fully and crank the engine over on the starter motor for a couple of revolutions until the gauge reading stabilises.

6 After one or two revolutions the pressure should build up to a maximum figure and then stabilise. Take a note of this reading and on multi-cylinder engines repeat the test on the remaining cylinders.

7 Typical pressures are given in Chapter 1. If the results fall within the specified range and are relatively equal, the engine is in good condition. If there is a marked difference between the readings, or if the readings are lower than specified, inspection of the top-end components will be required.

8 Low compression pressure may be due to worn cylinder bores, pistons or rings, failure of the cylinder head gasket, worn valve seals, or poor valve seating.

9 To distinguish between cylinder/piston wear and valve leakage, pour a small quantity of oil into the bore to temporarily seal the piston rings, then repeat the compression tests **(see illustration 3)**. If the readings show

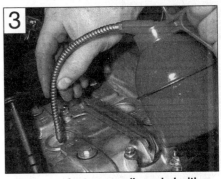

Bores can be temporarily sealed with a squirt of motor oil

a noticeable increase in pressure this confirms that the cylinder bore, piston, or rings are worn. If, however, no change is indicated, the cylinder head gasket or valves should be examined.

10 High compression pressure indicates excessive carbon build-up in the combustion chamber and on the piston crown. If this is the case the cylinder head should be removed and the deposits removed. Note that excessive carbon build-up is less likely with the used on modern fuels.

Checking battery open-circuit voltage

 Warning: The gases produced by the battery are explosive - never smoke or create any sparks in the vicinity of the battery. Never allow the electrolyte to contact your skin or clothing - if it does, wash it off and seek immediate medical attention.

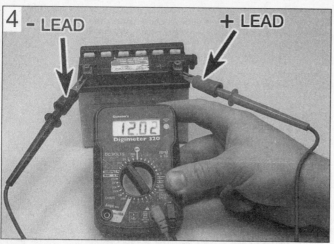

Measuring open-circuit battery voltage

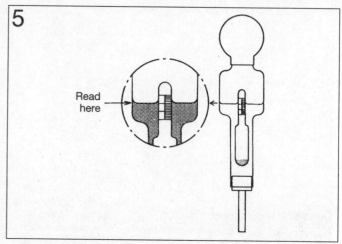

Float-type hydrometer for measuring battery specific gravity

● Before any electrical fault is investigated the battery should be checked.

● You'll need a dc voltmeter or multimeter to check battery voltage. Check that the leads are inserted in the correct terminals on the meter, red lead to positive (+ve), black lead to negative (-ve). Incorrect connections can damage the meter.

● A sound fully-charged 12 volt battery should produce between 12.3 and 12.6 volts across its terminals (12.8 volts for a maintenance-free battery). On machines with a 6 volt battery, voltage should be between 6.1 and 6.3 volts.

1 Set a multimeter to the 0 to 20 volts dc range and connect its probes across the battery terminals. Connect the meter's positive (+ve) probe, usually red, to the battery positive (+ve) terminal, followed by the meter's negative (-ve) probe, usually black, to the battery negative terminal (-ve) **(see illustration 4)**.

2 If battery voltage is low (below 10 volts on a 12 volt battery or below 4 volts on a six volt battery), charge the battery and test the voltage again. If the battery repeatedly goes flat, investigate the motorcycle's charging system.

Checking battery specific gravity (SG)

⚠ *Warning: The gases produced by the battery are explosive - never smoke or create any sparks in the vicinity of the battery. Never allow the electrolyte to contact your skin or clothing - if it does, wash it off and seek immediate medical attention.*

● The specific gravity check gives an indication of a battery's state of charge.

● A hydrometer is used for measuring specific gravity. Make sure you purchase one which has a small enough hose to insert in the aperture of a motorcycle battery.

● Specific gravity is simply a measure of the electrolyte's density compared with that of water. Water has an SG of 1.000 and fully-charged battery electrolyte is about 26% heavier, at 1.260.

● Specific gravity checks are not possible on maintenance-free batteries. Testing the open-circuit voltage is the only means of determining their state of charge.

1 To measure SG, remove the battery from the motorcycle and remove the first cell cap. Draw

Digital multimeter can be used for all electrical tests

some electrolyte into the hydrometer and note the reading **(see illustration 5)**. Return the electrolyte to the cell and install the cap.

2 The reading should be in the region of 1.260 to 1.280. If SG is below 1.200 the battery needs charging. Note that SG will vary with temperature; it should be measured at 20°C (68°F). Add 0.007 to the reading for every 10°C above 20°C, and subtract 0.007 from the reading for every 10°C below 20°C. Add 0.004 to the reading for every 10°F above 68°F, and subtract 0.004 from the reading for every 10°F below 68°F.

3 When the check is complete, rinse the hydrometer thoroughly with clean water.

Checking for continuity

● The term continuity describes the uninterrupted flow of electricity through an electrical circuit. A continuity check will determine whether an **open-circuit** situation exists.

● Continuity can be checked with an ohmmeter, multimeter, continuity tester or battery and bulb test circuit **(see illustrations 6, 7 and 8)**.

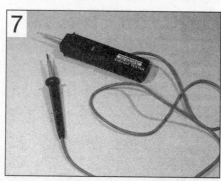

Battery-powered continuity tester

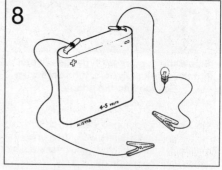

Battery and bulb test circuit

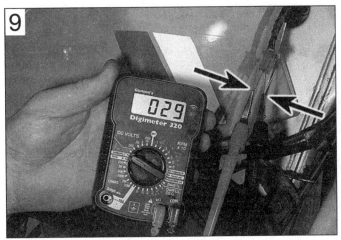

Continuity check of front brake light switch using a meter - note split pins used to access connector terminals

Continuity check of rear brake light switch using a continuity tester

● All of these instruments are self-powered by a battery, therefore the checks are made with the ignition OFF.

● As a safety precaution, always disconnect the battery negative (-ve) lead before making checks, particularly if ignition switch checks are being made.

● If using a meter, select the appropriate ohms scale and check that the meter reads infinity (∞). Touch the meter probes together and check that meter reads zero; where necessary adjust the meter so that it reads zero.

● After using a meter, always switch it OFF to conserve its battery.

Switch checks

1 If a switch is at fault, trace its wiring up to the wiring connectors. Separate the wire connectors and inspect them for security and condition. A build-up of dirt or corrosion here will most likely be the cause of the problem - clean up and apply a water dispersant such as WD40.

2 If using a test meter, set the meter to the ohms x 10 scale and connect its probes across the wires from the switch **(see illustration 9)**. Simple ON/OFF type switches, such as brake light switches, only have two wires whereas combination switches, like the

ignition switch, have many internal links. Study the wiring diagram to ensure that you are connecting across the correct pair of wires. Continuity (low or no measurable resistance - 0 ohms) should be indicated with the switch ON and no continuity (high resistance) with it OFF.

3 Note that the polarity of the test probes doesn't matter for continuity checks, although care should be taken to follow specific test procedures if a diode or solid-state component is being checked.

4 A continuity tester or battery and bulb circuit can be used in the same way. Connect its probes as described above **(see illustration 10)**. The light should come on to indicate continuity in the ON switch position, but should extinguish in the OFF position.

Wiring checks

● Many electrical faults are caused by damaged wiring, often due to incorrect routing or chaffing on frame components.

● Loose, wet or corroded wire connectors can also be the cause of electrical problems, especially in exposed locations.

1 A continuity check can be made on a single length of wire by disconnecting it at each end and connecting a meter or continuity tester

across both ends of the wire **(see illustration 11)**.

2 Continuity (low or no resistance - 0 ohms) should be indicated if the wire is good. If no continuity (high resistance) is shown, suspect a broken wire.

Checking for voltage

● A voltage check can determine whether current is reaching a component.

● Voltage can be checked with a dc voltmeter, multimeter set on the dc volts scale, test light or buzzer **(see illustrations 12 and 13)**. A meter has the advantage of being able to measure actual voltage.

● When using a meter, check that its leads are inserted in the correct terminals on the meter, red to positive (+ve), black to negative (-ve). Incorrect connections can damage the meter.

● A voltmeter (or multimeter set to the dc volts scale) should always be connected in parallel (across the load). Connecting it in series will not harm the meter, but the reading will not be meaningful.

● Voltage checks are made with the ignition ON.

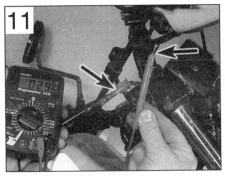

Continuity check of front brake light switch sub-harness

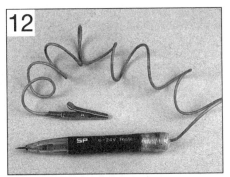

A simple test light can be used for voltage checks

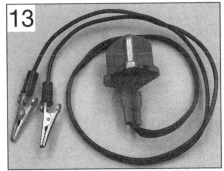

A buzzer is useful for voltage checks

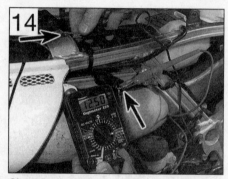

Checking for voltage at the rear brake light power supply wire using a meter . . .

1 First identify the relevant wiring circuit by referring to the wiring diagram at the end of this manual. If other electrical components share the same power supply (ie are fed from the same fuse), take note whether they are working correctly - this is useful information in deciding where to start checking the circuit.

2 If using a meter, check first that the meter leads are plugged into the correct terminals on the meter (see above). Set the meter to the dc volts function, at a range suitable for the battery voltage. Connect the meter red probe (+ve) to the power supply wire and the black probe to a good metal earth (ground) on the motorcycle's frame or directly to the battery negative (-ve) terminal **(see illustration 14)**. Battery voltage should be shown on the meter

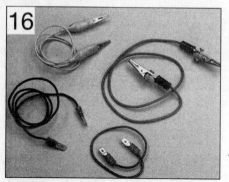

A selection of jumper wires for making earth (ground) checks

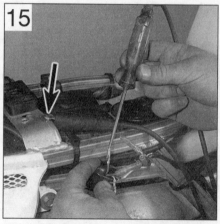

. . . or a test light - note the earth connection to the frame (arrow)

with the ignition switched ON.

3 If using a test light or buzzer, connect its positive (+ve) probe to the power supply terminal and its negative (-ve) probe to a good earth (ground) on the motorcycle's frame or directly to the battery negative (-ve) terminal **(see illustration 15)**. With the ignition ON, the test light should illuminate or the buzzer sound.

4 If no voltage is indicated, work back towards the fuse continuing to check for voltage. When you reach a point where there is voltage, you know the problem lies between that point and your last check point.

Checking the earth (ground)

● Earth connections are made either directly to the engine or frame (such as sensors, neutral switch etc. which only have a positive feed) or by a separate wire into the earth circuit of the wiring harness. Alternatively a short earth wire is sometimes run directly from the component to the motorcycle's frame.
● Corrosion is often the cause of a poor earth connection.
● If total failure is experienced, check the security of the main earth lead from the

negative (-ve) terminal of the battery and also the main earth (ground) point on the wiring harness. If corroded, dismantle the connection and clean all surfaces back to bare metal.

1 To check the earth on a component, use an insulated jumper wire to temporarily bypass its earth connection **(see illustration 16)**. Connect one end of the jumper wire between the earth terminal or metal body of the component and the other end to the motorcycle's frame.

2 If the circuit works with the jumper wire installed, the original earth circuit is faulty. Check the wiring for open-circuits or poor connections. Clean up direct earth connections, removing all traces of corrosion and remake the joint. Apply petroleum jelly to the joint to prevent future corrosion.

Tracing a short-circuit

● A short-circuit occurs where current shorts to earth (ground) bypassing the circuit components. This usually results in a blown fuse.

● A short-circuit is most likely to occur where the insulation has worn through due to wiring chafing on a component, allowing a direct path to earth (ground) on the frame.

1 Remove any bodypanels necessary to access the circuit wiring.

2 Check that all electrical switches in the circuit are OFF, then remove the circuit fuse and connect a test light, buzzer or voltmeter (set to the dc scale) across the fuse terminals. No voltage should be shown.

3 Move the wiring from side to side whilst observing the test light or meter. When the test light comes on, buzzer sounds or meter shows voltage, you have found the cause of the short. It will usually shown up as damaged or burned insulation.

4 Note that the same test can be performed on each component in the circuit, even the switch.

A

ABS (Anti-lock braking system) A system, usually electronically controlled, that senses incipient wheel lockup during braking and relieves hydraulic pressure at wheel which is about to skid.

Aftermarket Components suitable for the motorcycle, but not produced by the motorcycle manufacturer.

Allen key A hexagonal wrench which fits into a recessed hexagonal hole.

Alternating current (ac) Current produced by an alternator. Requires converting to direct current by a rectifier for charging purposes.

Alternator Converts mechanical energy from the engine into electrical energy to charge the battery and power the electrical system.

Ampere (amp) A unit of measurement for the flow of electrical current. Current = Volts ÷ Ohms.

Ampere-hour (Ah) Measure of battery capacity.

Angle-tightening A torque expressed in degrees. Often follows a conventional tightening torque for cylinder head or main bearing fasteners **(see illustration)**.

Angle-tightening cylinder head bolts

Antifreeze A substance (usually ethylene glycol) mixed with water, and added to the cooling system, to prevent freezing of the coolant in winter. Antifreeze also contains chemicals to inhibit corrosion and the formation of rust and other deposits that would tend to clog the radiator and coolant passages and reduce cooling efficiency.

Anti-dive System attached to the fork lower leg (slider) to prevent fork dive when braking hard.

Anti-seize compound A coating that reduces the risk of seizing on fasteners that are subjected to high temperatures, such as exhaust clamp bolts and nuts.

API American Petroleum Institute. A quality standard for 4-stroke motor oils.

Asbestos A natural fibrous mineral with great heat resistance, commonly used in the composition of brake friction materials. Asbestos is a health hazard and the dust created by brake systems should never be inhaled or ingested.

ATF Automatic Transmission Fluid. Often used in front forks.

ATU Automatic Timing Unit. Mechanical device for advancing the ignition timing on early engines.

ATV All Terrain Vehicle. Often called a Quad.

Axial play Side-to-side movement.

Axle A shaft on which a wheel revolves. Also known as a spindle.

B

Backlash The amount of movement between meshed components when one component is held still. Usually applies to gear teeth.

Ball bearing A bearing consisting of a hardened inner and outer race with hardened steel balls between the two races.

Bearings Used between two working surfaces to prevent wear of the components and a build-up of heat. Four types of bearing are commonly used on motorcycles: plain shell bearings, ball bearings, tapered roller bearings and needle roller bearings.

Bevel gears Used to turn the drive through 90°. Typical applications are shaft final drive and camshaft drive **(see illustration)**.

Bevel gears are used to turn the drive through 90°

BHP Brake Horsepower. The British measurement for engine power output. Power output is now usually expressed in kilowatts (kW).

Bias-belted tyre Similar construction to radial tyre, but with outer belt running at an angle to the wheel rim.

Big-end bearing The bearing in the end of the connecting rod that's attached to the crankshaft.

Bleeding The process of removing air from an hydraulic system via a bleed nipple or bleed screw.

Bottom-end A description of an engine's crankcase components and all components contained there-in.

BTDC Before Top Dead Centre in terms of piston position. Ignition timing is often expressed in terms of degrees or millimetres BTDC.

Bush A cylindrical metal or rubber component used between two moving parts.

Burr Rough edge left on a component after machining or as a result of excessive wear.

C

Cam chain The chain which takes drive from the crankshaft to the camshaft(s).

Canister The main component in an evaporative emission control system (California market only); contains activated charcoal granules to trap vapours from the fuel system rather than allowing them to vent to the atmosphere.

Castellated Resembling the parapets along the top of a castle wall. For example, a castellated wheel axle or spindle nut.

Catalytic converter A device in the exhaust system of some machines which converts certain pollutants in the exhaust gases into less harmful substances.

Charging system Description of the components which charge the battery, ie the alternator, rectifier and regulator.

Circlip A ring-shaped clip used to prevent endwise movement of cylindrical parts and shafts. An internal circlip is installed in a groove in a housing; an external circlip fits into a groove on the outside of a cylindrical piece such as a shaft. Also known as a snap-ring.

Clearance The amount of space between two parts. For example, between a piston and a cylinder, between a bearing and a journal, etc.

Coil spring A spiral of elastic steel found in various sizes throughout a vehicle, for example as a springing medium in the suspension and in the valve train.

Compression Reduction in volume, and increase in pressure and temperature, of a gas, caused by squeezing it into a smaller space.

Compression damping Controls the speed the suspension compresses when hitting a bump.

Compression ratio The relationship between cylinder volume when the piston is at top dead centre and cylinder volume when the piston is at bottom dead centre.

Continuity The uninterrupted path in the flow of electricity. Little or no measurable resistance.

Continuity tester Self-powered bleeper or test light which indicates continuity.

Cp Candlepower. Bulb rating commonly found on US motorcycles.

Crossply tyre Tyre plies arranged in a criss-cross pattern. Usually four or six plies used, hence 4PR or 6PR in tyre size codes.

Cush drive Rubber damper segments fitted between the rear wheel and final drive sprocket to absorb transmission shocks **(see illustration)**.

Cush drive rubbers dampen out transmission shocks

D

Degree disc Calibrated disc for measuring piston position. Expressed in degrees.

Dial gauge Clock-type gauge with adapters for measuring runout and piston position. Expressed in mm or inches.

Diaphragm The rubber membrane in a master cylinder or carburettor which seals the upper chamber.

Diaphragm spring A single sprung plate often used in clutches.

Direct current (dc) Current produced by a dc generator.

Decarbonisation The process of removing carbon deposits - typically from the combustion chamber, valves and exhaust port/system.

Detonation Destructive and damaging explosion of fuel/air mixture in combustion chamber instead of controlled burning.

Diode An electrical valve which only allows current to flow in one direction. Commonly used in rectifiers and starter interlock systems.

Disc valve (or rotary valve) A induction system used on some two-stroke engines.

Double-overhead camshaft (DOHC) An engine that uses two overhead camshafts, one for the intake valves and one for the exhaust valves.

Drivebelt A toothed belt used to transmit drive to the rear wheel on some motorcycles. A drivebelt has also been used to drive the camshafts. Drivebelts are usually made of Kevlar.

Driveshaft Any shaft used to transmit motion. Commonly used when referring to the final driveshaft on shaft drive motorcycles.

E

Earth return The return path of an electrical circuit, utilising the motorcycle's frame.

ECU (Electronic Control Unit) A computer which controls (for instance) an ignition system, or an anti-lock braking system.

EGO Exhaust Gas Oxygen sensor. Sometimes called a Lambda sensor.

Electrolyte The fluid in a lead-acid battery.

EMS (Engine Management System) A computer controlled system which manages the fuel injection and the ignition systems in an integrated fashion.

Endfloat The amount of lengthways movement between two parts. As applied to a crankshaft, the distance that the crankshaft can move side-to-side in the crankcase.

Endless chain A chain having no joining link. Common use for cam chains and final drive chains.

EP (Extreme Pressure) Oil type used in locations where high loads are applied, such as between gear teeth.

Evaporative emission control system Describes a charcoal filled canister which stores fuel vapours from the tank rather than allowing them to vent to the atmosphere. Usually only fitted to California models and referred to as an EVAP system.

Expansion chamber Section of two-stroke engine exhaust system so designed to improve engine efficiency and boost power.

F

Feeler blade or gauge A thin strip or blade of hardened steel, ground to an exact thickness, used to check or measure clearances between parts.

Final drive Description of the drive from the transmission to the rear wheel. Usually by chain or shaft, but sometimes by belt.

Firing order The order in which the engine cylinders fire, or deliver their power strokes, beginning with the number one cylinder.

Flooding Term used to describe a high fuel level in the carburettor float chambers, leading to fuel overflow. Also refers to excess fuel in the combustion chamber due to incorrect starting technique.

Free length The no-load state of a component when measured. Clutch, valve and fork spring lengths are measured at rest, without any preload.

Freeplay The amount of travel before any action takes place. The looseness in a linkage, or an assembly of parts, between the initial application of force and actual movement. For example, the distance the rear brake pedal moves before the rear brake is actuated.

Fuel injection The fuel/air mixture is metered electronically and directed into the engine intake ports (indirect injection) or into the cylinders (direct injection). Sensors supply information on engine speed and conditions.

Fuel/air mixture The charge of fuel and air going into the engine. See **Stoichiometric ratio**.

Fuse An electrical device which protects a circuit against accidental overload. The typical fuse contains a soft piece of metal which is calibrated to melt at a predetermined current flow (expressed as amps) and break the circuit.

G

Gap The distance the spark must travel in jumping from the centre electrode to the side electrode in a spark plug. Also refers to the distance between the ignition rotor and the pickup coil in an electronic ignition system.

Gasket Any thin, soft material - usually cork, cardboard, asbestos or soft metal - installed between two metal surfaces to ensure a good seal. For instance, the cylinder head gasket seals the joint between the block and the cylinder head.

Gauge An instrument panel display used to monitor engine conditions. A gauge with a movable pointer on a dial or a fixed scale is an analogue gauge. A gauge with a numerical readout is called a digital gauge.

Gear ratios The drive ratio of a pair of gears in a gearbox, calculated on their number of teeth.

Glaze-busting see **Honing**

Grinding Process for renovating the valve face and valve seat contact area in the cylinder head.

Gudgeon pin The shaft which connects the connecting rod small-end with the piston. Often called a piston pin or wrist pin.

H

Helical gears Gear teeth are slightly curved and produce less gear noise that straight-cut gears. Often used for primary drives.

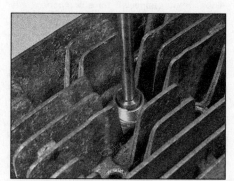

Installing a Helicoil thread insert in a cylinder head

Helicoil A thread insert repair system. Commonly used as a repair for stripped spark plug threads **(see illustration)**.

Honing A process used to break down the glaze on a cylinder bore (also called glaze-busting). Can also be carried out to roughen a rebored cylinder to aid ring bedding-in.

HT (High Tension) Description of the electrical circuit from the secondary winding of the ignition coil to the spark plug.

Hydraulic A liquid filled system used to transmit pressure from one component to another. Common uses on motorcycles are brakes and clutches.

Hydrometer An instrument for measuring the specific gravity of a lead-acid battery.

Hygroscopic Water absorbing. In motorcycle applications, braking efficiency will be reduced if DOT 3 or 4 hydraulic fluid absorbs water from the air - care must be taken to keep new brake fluid in tightly sealed containers.

I

lbf ft Pounds-force feet. An imperial unit of torque. Sometimes written as ft-lbs.

lbf in Pound-force inch. An imperial unit of torque, applied to components where a very low torque is required. Sometimes written as in-lbs.

IC Abbreviation for Integrated Circuit.

Ignition advance Means of increasing the timing of the spark at higher engine speeds. Done by mechanical means (ATU) on early engines or electronically by the ignition control unit on later engines.

Ignition timing The moment at which the spark plug fires, expressed in the number of crankshaft degrees before the piston reaches the top of its stroke, or in the number of millimetres before the piston reaches the top of its stroke.

Infinity (∞) Description of an open-circuit electrical state, where no continuity exists.

Inverted forks (upside down forks) The sliders or lower legs are held in the yokes and the fork tubes or stanchions are connected to the wheel axle (spindle). Less unsprung weight and stiffer construction than conventional forks.

J

JASO Quality standard for 2-stroke oils.

Joule The unit of electrical energy.

Journal The bearing surface of a shaft.

K

Kickstart Mechanical means of turning the engine over for starting purposes. Only usually fitted to mopeds, small capacity motorcycles and off-road motorcycles.

Kill switch Handebar-mounted switch for emergency ignition cut-out. Cuts the ignition circuit on all models, and additionally prevent starter motor operation on others.

km Symbol for kilometre.

kmh Abbreviation for kilometres per hour.

L

Lambda (λ) sensor A sensor fitted in the exhaust system to measure the exhaust gas oxygen content (excess air factor).

Lapping see **Grinding**.
LCD Abbreviation for Liquid Crystal Display.
LED Abbreviation for Light Emitting Diode.
Liner A steel cylinder liner inserted in a aluminium alloy cylinder block.
Locknut A nut used to lock an adjustment nut, or other threaded component, in place.
Lockstops The lugs on the lower triple clamp (yoke) which abut those on the frame, preventing handlebar-to-fuel tank contact.
Lockwasher A form of washer designed to prevent an attaching nut from working loose.
LT Low Tension Description of the electrical circuit from the power supply to the primary winding of the ignition coil.

M

Main bearings The bearings between the crankshaft and crankcase.
Maintenance-free (MF) battery A sealed battery which cannot be topped up.
Manometer Mercury-filled calibrated tubes used to measure intake tract vacuum. Used to synchronise carburettors on multi-cylinder engines.
Micrometer A precision measuring instrument that measures component outside diameters **(see illustration)**.

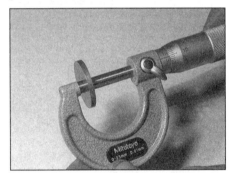

Tappet shims are measured with a micrometer

MON (Motor Octane Number) A measure of a fuel's resistance to knock.
Monograde oil An oil with a single viscosity, eg SAE80W.
Monoshock A single suspension unit linking the swingarm or suspension linkage to the frame.
mph Abbreviation for miles per hour.
Multigrade oil Having a wide viscosity range (eg 10W40). The W stands for Winter, thus the viscosity ranges from SAE10 when cold to SAE40 when hot.
Multimeter An electrical test instrument with the capability to measure voltage, current and resistance. Some meters also incorporate a continuity tester and buzzer.

N

Needle roller bearing Inner race of caged needle rollers and hardened outer race. Examples of uncaged needle rollers can be found on some engines. Commonly used in rear suspension applications and in two-stroke engines.
Nm Newton metres.
NOx Oxides of Nitrogen. A common toxic pollutant emitted by petrol engines at higher temperatures.

O

Octane The measure of a fuel's resistance to knock.
OE (Original Equipment) Relates to components fitted to a motorcycle as standard or replacement parts supplied by the motorcycle manufacturer.
Ohm The unit of electrical resistance. Ohms = Volts ÷ Current.
Ohmmeter An instrument for measuring electrical resistance.
Oil cooler System for diverting engine oil outside of the engine to a radiator for cooling purposes.
Oil injection A system of two-stroke engine lubrication where oil is pump-fed to the engine in accordance with throttle position.
Open-circuit An electrical condition where there is a break in the flow of electricity - no continuity (high resistance).
O-ring A type of sealing ring made of a special rubber-like material; in use, the O-ring is compressed into a groove to provide the sealing action.
Oversize (OS) Term used for piston and ring size options fitted to a rebored cylinder.
Overhead cam (sohc) engine An engine with single camshaft located on top of the cylinder head.
Overhead valve (ohv) engine An engine with the valves located in the cylinder head, but with the camshaft located in the engine block or crankcase.
Oxygen sensor A device installed in the exhaust system which senses the oxygen content in the exhaust and converts this information into an electric current. Also called a Lambda sensor.

P

Plastigauge A thin strip of plastic thread, available in different sizes, used for measuring clearances. For example, a strip of Plastigauge is laid across a bearing journal. The parts are assembled and dismantled; the width of the crushed strip indicates the clearance between journal and bearing.
Polarity Either negative or positive earth (ground), determined by which battery lead is connected to the frame (earth return). Modern motorcycles are usually negative earth.
Pre-ignition A situation where the fuel/air mixture ignites before the spark plug fires. Often due to a hot spot in the combustion chamber caused by carbon build-up. Engine has a tendency to 'run-on'.
Pre-load (suspension) The amount a spring is compressed when in the unloaded state. Preload can be applied by gas, spacer or mechanical adjuster.
Premix The method of engine lubrication on older two-stroke engines. Engine oil is mixed with the petrol in the fuel tank in a specific ratio. The fuel/oil mix is sometimes referred to as "petroil".
Primary drive Description of the drive from the crankshaft to the clutch. Usually by gear or chain.
PS Pfedestärke - a German interpretation of BHP.
PSI Pounds-force per square inch. Imperial measurement of tyre pressure and cylinder pressure measurement.
PTFE Polytetrafluroethylene. A low friction substance.

Pulse secondary air injection system A process of promoting the burning of excess fuel present in the exhaust gases by routing fresh air into the exhaust ports.

Q

Quartz halogen bulb Tungsten filament surrounded by a halogen gas. Typically used for the headlight **(see illustration)**.

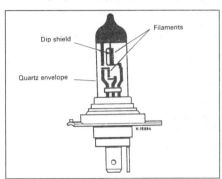

Quartz halogen headlight bulb construction

R

Rack-and-pinion A pinion gear on the end of a shaft that mates with a rack (think of a geared wheel opened up and laid flat). Sometimes used in clutch operating systems.
Radial play Up and down movement about a shaft.
Radial ply tyres Tyre plies run across the tyre (from bead to bead) and around the circumference of the tyre. Less resistant to tread distortion than other tyre types.
Radiator A liquid-to-air heat transfer device designed to reduce the temperature of the coolant in a liquid cooled engine.
Rake A feature of steering geometry - the angle of the steering head in relation to the vertical **(see illustration)**.

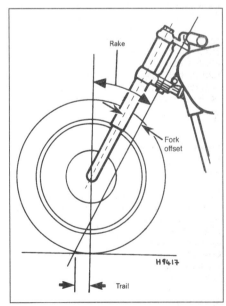

Steering geometry

Rebore Providing a new working surface to the cylinder bore by boring out the old surface. Necessitates the use of oversize piston and rings.

Rebound damping A means of controlling the oscillation of a suspension unit spring after it has been compressed. Resists the spring's natural tendency to bounce back after being compressed.

Rectifier Device for converting the ac output of an alternator into dc for battery charging.

Reed valve An induction system commonly used on two-stroke engines.

Regulator Device for maintaining the charging voltage from the generator or alternator within a specified range.

Relay A electrical device used to switch heavy current on and off by using a low current auxiliary circuit.

Resistance Measured in ohms. An electrical component's ability to pass electrical current.

RON (Research Octane Number) A measure of a fuel's resistance to knock.

rpm revolutions per minute.

Runout The amount of wobble (in-and-out movement) of a wheel or shaft as it's rotated. The amount a shaft rotates 'out-of-true'. The out-of-round condition of a rotating part.

S

SAE (Society of Automotive Engineers) A standard for the viscosity of a fluid.

Sealant A liquid or paste used to prevent leakage at a joint. Sometimes used in conjunction with a gasket.

Service limit Term for the point where a component is no longer useable and must be renewed.

Shaft drive A method of transmitting drive from the transmission to the rear wheel.

Shell bearings Plain bearings consisting of two shell halves. Most often used as big-end and main bearings in a four-stroke engine. Often called bearing inserts.

Shim Thin spacer, commonly used to adjust the clearance or relative positions between two parts. For example, shims inserted into or under tappets or followers to control valve clearances. Clearance is adjusted by changing the thickness of the shim.

Short-circuit An electrical condition where current shorts to earth (ground) bypassing the circuit components.

Skimming Process to correct warpage or repair a damaged surface, eg on brake discs or drums.

Slide-hammer A special puller that screws into or hooks onto a component such as a shaft or bearing; a heavy sliding handle on the shaft bottoms against the end of the shaft to knock the component free.

Small-end bearing The bearing in the upper end of the connecting rod at its joint with the gudgeon pin.

Spalling Damage to camshaft lobes or bearing journals shown as pitting of the working surface.

Specific gravity (SG) The state of charge of the electrolyte in a lead-acid battery. A measure of the electrolyte's density compared with water.

Straight-cut gears Common type gear used on gearbox shafts and for oil pump and water pump drives.

Stanchion The inner sliding part of the front forks, held by the yokes. Often called a fork tube.

Stoichiometric ratio The optimum chemical air/fuel ratio for a petrol engine, said to be 14.7 parts of air to 1 part of fuel.

Sulphuric acid The liquid (electrolyte) used in a lead-acid battery. Poisonous and extremely corrosive.

Surface grinding (lapping) Process to correct a warped gasket face, commonly used on cylinder heads.

T

Tapered-roller bearing Tapered inner race of caged needle rollers and separate tapered outer race. Examples of taper roller bearings can be found on steering heads.

Tappet A cylindrical component which transmits motion from the cam to the valve stem, either directly or via a pushrod and rocker arm. Also called a cam follower.

TCS Traction Control System. An electronically-controlled system which senses wheel spin and reduces engine speed accordingly.

TDC Top Dead Centre denotes that the piston is at its highest point in the cylinder.

Thread-locking compound Solution applied to fastener threads to prevent slackening. Select type to suit application.

Thrust washer A washer positioned between two moving components on a shaft. For example, between gear pinions on gearshaft.

Timing chain See **Cam Chain**.

Timing light Stroboscopic lamp for carrying out ignition timing checks with the engine running.

Top-end A description of an engine's cylinder block, head and valve gear components.

Torque Turning or twisting force about a shaft.

Torque setting A prescribed tightness specified by the motorcycle manufacturer to ensure that the bolt or nut is secured correctly. Undertightening can result in the bolt or nut coming loose or a surface not being sealed. Overtightening can result in stripped threads, distortion or damage to the component being retained.

Torx key A six-point wrench.

Tracer A stripe of a second colour applied to a wire insulator to distinguish that wire from another one with the same colour insulator. For example, Br/W is often used to denote a brown insulator with a white tracer.

Trail A feature of steering geometry. Distance from the steering head axis to the tyre's central contact point.

Triple clamps The cast components which extend from the steering head and support the fork stanchions or tubes. Often called fork yokes.

Turbocharger A centrifugal device, driven by exhaust gases, that pressurises the intake air. Normally used to increase the power output from a given engine displacement.

TWI Abbreviation for Tyre Wear Indicator. Indicates the location of the tread depth indicator bars on tyres.

U

Universal joint or U-joint (UJ) A double-pivoted connection for transmitting power from a driving to a driven shaft through an angle. Typically found in shaft drive assemblies.

Unsprung weight Anything not supported by the bike's suspension (ie the wheel, tyres, brakes, final drive and bottom (moving) part of the suspension).

V

Vacuum gauges Clock-type gauges for measuring intake tract vacuum. Used for carburettor synchronisation on multi-cylinder engines.

Valve A device through which the flow of liquid, gas or vacuum may be stopped, started or regulated by a moveable part that opens, shuts or partially obstructs one or more ports or passageways. The intake and exhaust valves in the cylinder head are of the poppet type.

Valve clearance The clearance between the valve tip (the end of the valve stem) and the rocker arm or tappet/follower. The valve clearance is measured when the valve is closed. The correct clearance is important - if too small the valve won't close fully and will burn out, whereas if too large noisy operation will result.

Valve lift The amount a valve is lifted off its seat by the camshaft lobe.

Valve timing The exact setting for the opening and closing of the valves in relation to piston position.

Vernier caliper A precision measuring instrument that measures inside and outside dimensions. Not quite as accurate as a micrometer, but more convenient.

VIN Vehicle Identification Number. Term for the bike's engine and frame numbers.

Viscosity The thickness of a liquid or its resistance to flow.

Volt A unit for expressing electrical "pressure" in a circuit. Volts = current x ohms.

W

Water pump A mechanically-driven device for moving coolant around the engine.

Watt A unit for expressing electrical power. Watts = volts x current.

Wear limit see **Service limit**

Wet liner A liquid-cooled engine design where the pistons run in liners which are directly surrounded by coolant **(see illustration)**.

Wet liner arrangement

Wheelbase Distance from the centre of the front wheel to the centre of the rear wheel.

Wiring harness or loom Describes the electrical wires running the length of the motorcycle and enclosed in tape or plastic sheathing. Wiring coming off the main harness is usually referred to as a sub harness.

Woodruff key A key of semi-circular or square section used to locate a gear to a shaft. Often used to locate the alternator rotor on the crankshaft.

Wrist pin Another name for gudgeon or piston pin.

Haynes Motorcycle Manuals – The Complete List

Title	Book No
APRILIA RS50 (99 - 06) & RS125 (93 - 06)	4298
Aprilia RSV1000 Mille (98 - 03)	♦ 4255
Aprilia SR50	4755
BMW 2-valve Twins (70 - 96)	♦ 0249
BMW F650	♦ 4761
BMW K100 & 75 2-valve Models (83 - 96)	♦ 1373
BMW R850, 1100 & 1150 4-valve Twins (93 - 04)	♦ 3466
BMW R1200 (04 - 06)	♦ 4598
BSA Bantam (48 - 71)	0117
BSA Unit Singles (58 - 72)	0127
BSA Pre-unit Singles (54 - 61)	0326
BSA A7 & A10 Twins (47 - 62)	0121
BSA A50 & A65 Twins (62 - 73)	0155
Chinese Scooters	4768
DUCATI 600, 620, 750 and 900 2-valve V-Twins (91 - 05)	♦ 3290
Ducati MK III & Desmo Singles (69 - 76)	◇ 0445
Ducati 748, 916 & 996 4-valve V-Twins (94 - 01)	♦ 3756
GILERA Runner, DNA, Ice & SKP/Stalker (97 - 07)	4163
HARLEY-DAVIDSON Sportsters (70 - 08)	♦ 2534
Harley-Davidson Shovelhead and Evolution Big Twins (70 - 99)	♦ 2536
Harley-Davidson Twin Cam 88 (99 - 03)	♦ 2478
HONDA NB, ND, NP & NS50 Melody (81 - 85)	◇ 0622
Honda NE/NB50 Vision & SA50 Vision Met-in (85 - 95)	◇ 1278
Honda MB, MBX, MT & MTX50 (80 - 93)	0731
Honda C50, C70 & C90 (67 - 03)	0324
Honda XR80/100R & CRF80/100F (85 - 04)	2218
Honda XL/XR 80, 100, 125, 185 & 200 2-valve Models (78 - 87)	0566
Honda H100 & H100S Singles (80 - 92)	◇ 0734
Honda CB/CD125T & CM125C Twins (77 - 88)	◇ 0571
Honda CG125 (76 - 07)	◇ 0433
Honda NS125 (86 - 93)	◇ 3056
Honda CBR125R (04 - 07)	4620
Honda MBX/MTX125 & MTX200 (83 - 93)	◇ 1132
Honda CD/CM185 200T & CM250C 2-valve Twins (77 - 85)	0572
Honda XL/XR 250 & 500 (78 - 84)	0567
Honda XR250L, XR250R & XR400R (86 - 03)	2219
Honda CB250 & CB400N Super Dreams (78 - 84)	◇ 0540
Honda CR Motocross Bikes (86 - 01)	2222
Honda CRF250 & CRF450 (02 - 06)	2630
Honda CBR400RR Fours (88 - 99)	◇ ♦ 3552
Honda VFR400 (NC30) & RVF400 (NC35) V-Fours (89 - 98)	◇ ♦ 3496
Honda CB500 (93 - 02) & CBF500 03 - 08	◇ 3753
Honda CB400 & CB550 Fours (73 - 77)	0262
Honda CX/GL500 & 650 V-Twins (78 - 86)	0442
Honda CBX550 Four (82 - 86)	◇ 0940
Honda XL600R & XR600R (83 - 08)	♦ 2183
Honda XL600/650V Transalp & XRV750 Africa Twin (87 to 07)	♦ 3919
Honda CBR600F1 & 1000F Fours (87 - 96)	♦ 1730
Honda CBR600F2 & F3 Fours (91 - 98)	♦ 2070
Honda CBR600F4 (99 - 06)	♦ 3911
Honda CB600F Hornet & CBF600 (98 - 06)	◇ ♦ 3915
Honda CBR600RR (03 - 06)	♦ 4590
Honda CB650 sohc Fours (78 - 84)	0665
Honda NTV600 Revere, NTV650 and NT650V Deauville (88 - 05)	◇ 3243
Honda Shadow VT600 & 750 (USA) (88 - 03)	2312
Honda CB750 sohc Four (69 - 79)	0131
Honda V45/65 Sabre & Magna (82 - 88)	0820
Honda VFR750 & 700 V-Fours (86 - 97)	♦ 2101
Honda VFR800 V-Fours (97 - 01)	♦ 3703
Honda VFR800 V-Tec V-Fours (02 - 05)	♦ 4196
Honda CB750 & CB900 dohc Fours (78 - 84)	0535
Honda VTR1000 (FireStorm, Super Hawk) & XL1000V (Varadero) (97 - 08)	♦ 3744
Honda CBR900RR FireBlade (92 - 99)	♦ 2161
Honda CBR900RR FireBlade (00 - 03)	♦ 4060
Honda CBR1000RR Fireblade (04 - 07)	♦ 4604
Honda CBR1100XX Super Blackbird (97 - 07)	♦ 3901
Honda ST1100 Pan European V-Fours (90 - 02)	♦ 3384
Honda Shadow VT1100 (USA) (85 - 98)	2313
Honda GL1000 Gold Wing (75 - 79)	0309

Title	Book No
Honda GL1100 Gold Wing (79 - 81)	0669
Honda Gold Wing 1200 (USA) (84 - 87)	2199
Honda Gold Wing 1500 (USA) (88 - 00)	2225
KAWASAKI AE/AR 50 & 80 (81 - 95)	1007
Kawasaki KC, KE & KH100 (75 - 99)	1371
Kawasaki KMX125 & 200 (86 - 02)	◇ 3046
Kawasaki 250, 350 & 400 Triples (72 - 79)	0134
Kawasaki 400 & 440 Twins (74 - 81)	0281
Kawasaki 400, 500 & 550 Fours (79 - 91)	0910
Kawasaki EN450 & 500 Twins (Ltd/Vulcan) (85 - 07)	2053
Kawasaki EX500 (GPZ500S) & ER500 (ER-5) (87 - 08)	♦ 2052
Kawasaki ZX600 (ZZ-R600 & Ninja ZX-6) (90 - 06)	♦ 2146
Kawasaki ZX-6R Ninja Fours (95 - 02)	♦ 3541
Kawasaki ZX-6R (03 - 06)	♦ 4742
Kawasaki ZX600 (GPZ600R, GPX600R, Ninja 600R & RX) & ZX750 (GPX750R, Ninja 750R)	♦ 1780
Kawasaki 650 Four (76 - 78)	0373
Kawasaki Vulcan 700/750 & 800 (85 - 04)	♦ 2457
Kawasaki 750 Air-cooled Fours (80 - 91)	0574
Kawasaki ZR550 & 750 Zephyr Fours (90 - 97)	♦ 3382
Kawasaki Z750 & Z1000 (03 - 08)	♦ 4762
Kawasaki ZX750 (Ninja ZX-7 & ZXR750) Fours (89 - 96)	♦ 2054
Kawasaki Ninja ZX-7R & ZX-9R (94 - 04)	♦ 3721
Kawasaki 900 & 1000 Fours (73 - 77)	0222
Kawasaki ZX900, 1000 & 1100 Liquid-cooled Fours (83 - 97)	♦ 1681
KTM EXC Enduro & SX Motocross (00 - 07)	♦ 4629
MOTO GUZZI 750, 850 & 1000 V-Twins (74 - 78)	0339
MZ ETZ Models (81 - 95)	◇ 1680
NORTON 500, 600, 650 & 750 Twins (57 - 70)	0187
Norton Commando (68 - 77)	0125
PEUGEOT Speedfight, Trekker & Vivacity Scooters (96 - 08)	◇ 3920
PIAGGIO (Vespa) Scooters (91 - 06)	◇ 3492
SUZUKI GT, ZR & TS50 (77 - 90)	◇ 0799
Suzuki TS50X (84 - 00)	◇ 1599
Suzuki 100, 125, 185 & 250 Air-cooled Trail bikes (79 - 89)	0797
Suzuki GP100 & 125 Singles (78 - 93)	◇ 0576
Suzuki GS, GN, GZ & DR125 Singles (82 - 05)	◇ 0888
Suzuki GSX-R600/750 (06 - 09)	♦ 4790
Suzuki 250 & 350 Twins (68 - 78)	0120
Suzuki GT250X7, GT200X5 & SB200 Twins (78 - 83)	◇ 0469
Suzuki GS/GSX250, 400 & 450 Twins (79 - 85)	0736
Suzuki GS500 Twin (89 - 06)	♦ 3238
Suzuki GS550 (77 - 82) & GS750 Fours (76 - 79)	0363
Suzuki GS/GSX550 4-valve Fours (83 - 88)	1133
Suzuki SV650 & SV650S (99 - 08)	♦ 3912
Suzuki GSX-R600 & 750 (96 - 00)	♦ 3553
Suzuki GSX-R600 (01 - 03), GSX-R750 (00 - 03) & GSX-R1000 (01 - 02)	♦ 3986
Suzuki GSX-R600/750 (04 - 05) & GSX-R1000 (03 - 06)	♦ 4382
Suzuki GSF600, 650 & 1200 Bandit Fours (95 - 06)	♦ 3367
Suzuki Intruder, Marauder, Volusia & Boulevard (85 - 06)	♦ 2618
Suzuki GS850 Fours (78 - 88)	0536
Suzuki GS1000 Four (77 - 79)	0484
Suzuki GSX-R750, GSX-R1100 (85 - 92), GSX600F, GSX750F, GSX1100F (Katana) Fours	♦ 2055
Suzuki GSX600/750F & GSX750 (98 - 02)	♦ 3987
Suzuki GS/GSX1000, 1100 & 1150 4-valve Fours (79 - 88)	0737
Suzuki TL1000S/R & DL1000 V-Strom (97 - 04)	♦ 4083
Suzuki GSF650/1250 (05 - 09)	♦ 4798
Suzuki GSX1300R Hayabusa (99 - 04)	♦ 4184
Suzuki GSX1400 (02 - 07)	♦ 4758
TRIUMPH Tiger Cub & Terrier (52 - 68)	0414
Triumph 350 & 500 Unit Twins (58 - 73)	0137
Triumph Pre-Unit Twins (47 - 62)	0251
Triumph 650 & 750 2-valve Unit Twins (63 - 83)	0122
Triumph Trident & BSA Rocket 3 (69 - 75)	0136
Triumph Bonneville (01 - 07)	♦ 4364
Triumph Daytona, Speed Triple, Sprint & Tiger (97 - 05)	♦ 3755
Triumph Triples and Fours (carburettor engines) (91 - 04)	♦ 2162
VESPA P/PX125, 150 & 200 Scooters (78 - 06)	0707
Vespa Scooters (59 - 78)	0126
YAMAHA DT50 & 80 Trail Bikes (78 - 95)	◇ 0800
Yamaha T50 & 80 Townmate (83 - 95)	◇ 1247

Title	Book No
Yamaha YB100 Singles (73 - 91)	◇ 0474
Yamaha RS/RXS100 & 125 Singles (74 - 95)	0331
Yamaha RD & DT125LC (82 - 95)	◇ 0887
Yamaha TZR125 (87 - 93) & DT125R (88 - 07)	◇ 1655
Yamaha TY50, 80, 125 & 175 (74 - 84)	◇ 0464
Yamaha XT & SR125 (82 - 03)	◇ 1021
Yamaha YBR125	4797
Yamaha Trail Bikes (81 - 00)	2350
Yamaha 2-stroke Motocross Bikes 1986 - 2006	2662
Yamaha YZ & WR 4-stroke Motocross Bikes (98 - 08)	2689
Yamaha 250 & 350 Twins (70 - 79)	0040
Yamaha XS250, 360 & 400 sohc Twins (75 - 84)	0378
Yamaha RD250 & 350LC Twins (80 - 82)	0803
Yamaha RD350 YPVS Twins (83 - 95)	1158
Yamaha RD400 Twin (75 - 79)	0333
Yamaha XT, TT & SR500 Singles (75 - 83)	0342
Yamaha XZ550 Vision V-Twins (82 - 85)	0821
Yamaha FJ, FZ, XJ & YX600 Radian (84 - 92)	2100
Yamaha XJ600S (Diversion, Seca II) & XJ600N Fours (92 - 03)	♦ 2145
Yamaha YZF600R Thundercat & FZS600 Fazer (96 - 03)	♦ 3702
Yamaha FZ-6 Fazer (04 - 07)	♦ 4751
Yamaha YZF-R6 (99 - 02)	♦ 3900
Yamaha YZF-R6 (03 - 06)	♦ 4601
Yamaha 650 Twins (70 - 83)	0341
Yamaha XJ650 & 750 Fours (80 - 84)	0738
Yamaha XS750 & 850 Triples (76 - 85)	0340
Yamaha TDM850, TRX850 & XTZ750 (89 - 99)	◇ ♦ 3540
Yamaha YZF750R & YZF1000R Thunderace (93 - 00)	♦ 3720
Yamaha FZR600, 750 & 1000 Fours (87 - 96)	♦ 2056
Yamaha XV (Virago) V-Twins (81 - 03)	♦ 0802
Yamaha XVS650 & 1100 Drag Star/V-Star (97 - 05)	♦ 4195
Yamaha XJ900F Fours (83 - 94)	♦ 3239
Yamaha XJ900S Diversion (94 - 01)	♦ 3739
Yamaha YZF-R1 (98 - 03)	♦ 3754
Yamaha YZF-R1 (04 - 06)	♦ 4605
Yamaha FZS1000 Fazer (01 - 05)	♦ 4287
Yamaha FJ1100 & 1200 Fours (84 - 96)	♦ 2057
Yamaha XJR1200 & 1300 (95 - 06)	♦ 3981
Yamaha V-Max (85 - 03)	♦ 4072

ATVs

Title	Book No
Honda ATC70, 90, 110, 185 & 200 (71 - 85)	0565
Honda Rancher, Recon & TRX250EX ATVs	2553
Honda TRX300 Shaft Drive ATVs (88 - 00)	2125
Honda Foreman (95 - 07)	2465
Honda TRX300EX, TRX400EX & TRX450R/ER ATVs (93 - 06)	2318
Kawasaki Bayou 220/250/300 & Prairie 300 ATVs (86 - 03)	2351
Polaris ATVs (85 - 97)	2302
Polaris ATVs (98 - 06)	2508
Yamaha YFS200 Blaster ATV (88 - 06)	2317
Yamaha YFB250 Timberwolf ATVs (92 - 00)	2217
Yamaha YFM350 & YFM400 (ER and Big Bear) ATVs (87 - 03)	2126
Yamaha Banshee and Warrior ATVs (87 - 03)	2314
Yamaha Kodiak and Grizzly ATVs (93 - 05)	2567
ATV Basics	10450

TECHBOOK SERIES

Title	Book No
Twist and Go (automatic transmission) Scooters Service and Repair Manual	4082
Motorcycle Basics TechBook (2nd Edition)	3515
Motorcycle Electrical TechBook (3rd Edition)	3471
Motorcycle Fuel Systems TechBook	3514
Motorcycle Maintenance TechBook	4071
Motorcycle Modifying	4272
Motorcycle Workshop Practice TechBook (2nd Edition)	3470

◇ = not available in the USA   ♦ = Superbike

The manuals on this page are available through good motorcycle dealers and accessory shops.
In case of difficulty, contact: **Haynes Publishing**
(UK) **+44 1963 442030**   (USA) **+1 805 498 6703**
(SV) **+46 18 124016**
(Australia/New Zealand) **+61 3 9763 8100**

MCL24.08/09

Haynes Automotive Manuals

NOTE: If you do not see a listing for your vehicle, consult your local Haynes dealer for the latest product information.

ACURA
- 12020 Integra '86 thru '89 & Legend '86 thru '90
- 12021 Integra '90 thru '93 & Legend '91 thru '95
- Integra '94 thru '00 - see HONDA Civic (42025)
- MDX '01 thru '07 - see HONDA Pilot (42037)
- 12050 Acura TL all models '99 thru '08

AMC
- Jeep CJ - see JEEP (50020)
- 14020 Mid-size models '70 thru '83
- 14025 (Renault) Alliance & Encore '83 thru '87

AUDI
- 15020 4000 all models '80 thru '87
- 15025 5000 all models '77 thru '83
- 15026 5000 all models '84 thru '88
- Audi A4 '96 thru '01 - see VW Passat (96023)
- 15030 Audi A4 '02 thru '08

AUSTIN-HEALEY
- Sprite - see MG Midget (66015)

BMW
- 18020 3/5 Series '82 thru '92
- 18021 3-Series incl. Z3 models '92 thru '98
- 18022 3-Series incl. Z4 models '99 thru '05
- 18023 3-Series '06 thru '10
- 18025 320i all 4 cyl models '75 thru '83
- 18050 1500 thru 2002 except Turbo '59 thru '77

BUICK
- 19010 Buick Century '97 thru '05
- Century (front-wheel drive) - see GM (38005)
- 19020 Buick, Oldsmobile & Pontiac Full-size (Front-wheel drive) '85 thru '05
  Buick Electra, LeSabre and Park Avenue; Oldsmobile Delta 88 Royale, Ninety Eight and Regency; Pontiac Bonneville
- 19025 Buick, Oldsmobile & Pontiac Full-size (Rear wheel drive) '70 thru '90
  Buick Estate, Electra, LeSabre, Limited, Oldsmobile Custom Cruiser, Delta 88, Ninety-eight, Pontiac Bonneville, Catalina, Grandville, Parisienne
- 19030 Mid-size Regal & Century all rear-drive models with V6, V8 and Turbo '74 thru '87
  Regal - see GENERAL MOTORS (38010)
  Riviera - see GENERAL MOTORS (38030)
  Roadmaster - see CHEVROLET (24046)
  Skyhawk - see GENERAL MOTORS (38015)
  Skylark - see GM (38020, 38025)
  Somerset - see GENERAL MOTORS (38025)

CADILLAC
- 21015 CTS & CTS-V '03 thru '12
- 21030 Cadillac Rear Wheel Drive '70 thru '93
  Cimarron - see GENERAL MOTORS (38015)
  DeVille - see GM (38031 & 38032)
  Eldorado - see GM (38030 & 38031)
  Fleetwood - see GM (38031)
  Seville - see GM (38030, 38031 & 38032)

CHEVROLET
- 10305 Chevrolet Engine Overhaul Manual
- 24010 Astro & GMC Safari Mini-vans '85 thru '05
- 24015 Camaro V8 all models '70 thru '81
- 24016 Camaro all models '82 thru '92
- 24017 Camaro & Firebird '93 thru '02
  Cavalier - see GENERAL MOTORS (38016)
  Celebrity - see GENERAL MOTORS (38005)
- 24020 Chevelle, Malibu & El Camino '69 thru '87
- 24024 Chevette & Pontiac T1000 '76 thru '87
  Citation - see GENERAL MOTORS (38020)
- 24027 Colorado & GMC Canyon '04 thru '10
- 24032 Corsica/Beretta all models '87 thru '96
- 24040 Corvette all V8 models '68 thru '82
- 24041 Corvette all models '84 thru '96
- 24045 Full-size Sedans Caprice, Impala, Biscayne, Bel Air & Wagons '69 thru '90
- 24046 Impala SS & Caprice and Buick Roadmaster '91 thru '96
  Impala '00 thru '05 - see LUMINA (24048)
- 24047 Impala & Monte Carlo all models '06 thru '11
  Lumina '90 thru '94 - see GM (38010)
- 24048 Lumina & Monte Carlo '95 thru '05
  Lumina APV - see GM (38035)
- 24050 Luv Pick-up all 2WD & 4WD '72 thru '82
  Malibu '97 thru '00 - see GM (38026)
- 24055 Monte Carlo all models '70 thru '88
  Monte Carlo '95 thru '01 - see LUMINA (24048)
- 24059 Nova all V8 models '69 thru '79
- 24060 Nova and Geo Prizm '85 thru '92
- 24064 Pick-ups '67 thru '87 - Chevrolet & GMC
- 24065 Pick-ups '88 thru '98 - Chevrolet & GMC

- 24066 Pick-ups '99 thru '06 - Chevrolet & GMC
- 24067 Chevrolet Silverado & GMC Sierra '07 thru '12
- 24070 S-10 & S-15 Pick-ups '82 thru '93, Blazer & Jimmy '83 thru '94,
- 24071 S-10 & Sonoma Pick-ups '94 thru '04, including Blazer, Jimmy & Hombre
- 24072 Chevrolet TrailBlazer, GMC Envoy & Oldsmobile Bravada '02 thru '09
- 24075 Sprint '85 thru '88 & Geo Metro '89 thru '01
- 24080 Vans - Chevrolet & GMC '68 thru '96
- 24081 Chevrolet Express & GMC Savana Full-size Vans '96 thru '10

CHRYSLER
- 10310 Chrysler Engine Overhaul Manual
- 25015 Chrysler Cirrus, Dodge Stratus, Plymouth Breeze '95 thru '00
- 25020 Full-size Front-Wheel Drive '88 thru '93
  K-Cars - see DODGE Aries (30008)
  Laser - see DODGE Daytona (30030)
- 25025 Chrysler LHS, Concorde, New Yorker, Dodge Intrepid, Eagle Vision, '93 thru '97
- 25026 Chrysler LHS, Concorde, 300M, Dodge Intrepid, '98 thru '04
- 25027 Chrysler 300, Dodge Charger & Magnum '05 thru '09
- 25030 Chrysler & Plymouth Mid-size front wheel drive '82 thru '95
  Rear-wheel Drive - see Dodge (30050)
- 25035 PT Cruiser all models '01 thru '10
- 25040 Chrysler Sebring '95 thru '06, Dodge Stratus '01 thru '06, Dodge Avenger '95 thru '00

DATSUN
- 28005 200SX all models '80 thru '83
- 28007 B-210 all models '73 thru '78
- 28009 210 all models '79 thru '82
- 28012 240Z, 260Z & 280Z Coupe '70 thru '78
- 28014 280ZX Coupe & 2+2 '79 thru '83
  300ZX - see NISSAN (72010)
- 28018 510 & PL521 Pick-up '68 thru '73
- 28020 510 all models '78 thru '81
- 28022 620 Series Pick-up all models '73 thru '79
  720 Series Pick-up - see NISSAN (72030)
- 28025 810/Maxima all gasoline models '77 thru '84

DODGE
- 400 & 600 - see CHRYSLER (25030)
- 30008 Aries & Plymouth Reliant '81 thru '89
- 30010 Caravan & Plymouth Voyager '84 thru '95
- 30011 Caravan & Plymouth Voyager '96 thru '02
- 30012 Challenger/Plymouth Saporro '78 thru '83
- 30013 Caravan, Chrysler Voyager, Town & Country '03 thru '07
- 30016 Colt & Plymouth Champ '78 thru '87
- 30020 Dakota Pick-ups all models '87 thru '96
- 30021 Durango '98 & '99, Dakota '97 thru '99
- 30022 Durango '00 thru '03 Dakota '00 thru '04
- 30023 Durango '04 thru '09, Dakota '05 thru '11
- 30025 Dart, Demon, Plymouth Barracuda, Duster & Valiant 6 cyl models '67 thru '76
- 30030 Daytona & Chrysler Laser '84 thru '89
  Intrepid - see CHRYSLER (25025, 25026)
- 30034 Neon all models '95 thru '99
- 30035 Omni & Plymouth Horizon '78 thru '90
- 30036 Dodge and Plymouth Neon '00 thru '05
- 30040 Pick-ups all full-size models '74 thru '93
- 30041 Pick-ups all full-size models '94 thru '01
- 30042 Pick-ups full-size models '02 thru '08
- 30045 Ram 50/D50 Pick-ups & Raider and Plymouth Arrow Pick-ups '79 thru '93
- 30050 Dodge/Plymouth/Chrysler RWD '71 thru '89
- 30055 Shadow & Plymouth Sundance '87 thru '94
- 30060 Spirit & Plymouth Acclaim '89 thru '95
- 30065 Vans - Dodge & Plymouth '71 thru '03

EAGLE
- Talon - see MITSUBISHI (68030, 68031)
- Vision - see CHRYSLER (25025)

FIAT
- 34010 124 Sport Coupe & Spider '68 thru '78
- 34025 X1/9 all models '74 thru '80

FORD
- 10320 Ford Engine Overhaul Manual
- 10355 Ford Automatic Transmission Overhaul
- 11500 Mustang '64-1/2 thru '70 Restoration Guide
- 36004 Aerostar Mini-vans all models '86 thru '97
- 36006 Contour & Mercury Mystique '95 thru '00
- 36008 Courier Pick-up all models '72 thru '82
- 36012 Crown Victoria & Mercury Grand Marquis '88 thru '10
- 36016 Escort/Mercury Lynx all models '81 thru '90
- 36020 Escort/Mercury Tracer '91 thru '02

- 36022 Escape & Mazda Tribute '01 thru '11
- 36024 Explorer & Mazda Navajo '91 thru '01
- 36025 Explorer/Mercury Mountaineer '02 thru '10
- 36028 Fairmont & Mercury Zephyr '78 thru '83
- 36030 Festiva & Aspire '88 thru '97
- 36032 Fiesta all models '77 thru '80
- 36034 Focus all models '00 thru '11
- 36036 Ford & Mercury Full-size '75 thru '87
- 36044 Ford & Mercury Mid-size '75 thru '86
- 36045 Fusion & Mercury Milan '06 thru '10
- 36048 Mustang V8 all models '64-1/2 thru '73
- 36049 Mustang II 4 cyl, V6 & V8 models '74 thru '78
- 36050 Mustang & Mercury Capri '79 thru '93
- 36051 Mustang all models '94 thru '04
- 36052 Mustang '05 thru '10
- 36054 Pick-ups & Bronco '73 thru '79
- 36058 Pick-ups & Bronco '80 thru '96
- 36059 F-150 & Expedition '97 thru '09, F-250 '97 thru '99 & Lincoln Navigator '98 thru '09
- 36060 Super Duty Pick-ups, Excursion '99 thru '10
- 36061 F-150 full-size '04 thru '10
- 36062 Pinto & Mercury Bobcat '75 thru '80
- 36066 Probe all models '89 thru '92
  Probe '93 thru '97 - see MAZDA 626 (61042)
- 36070 Ranger/Bronco II gasoline models '83 thru '92
- 36071 Ranger '93 thru '10 & Mazda Pick-ups '94 thru '09
- 36074 Taurus & Mercury Sable '86 thru '95
- 36075 Taurus & Mercury Sable '96 thru '05
- 36078 Tempo & Mercury Topaz '84 thru '94
- 36082 Thunderbird/Mercury Cougar '83 thru '88
- 36086 Thunderbird/Mercury Cougar '89 thru '97
- 36090 Vans all V8 Econoline models '69 thru '91
- 36094 Vans full size '92 thru '10
- 36097 Windstar Mini-van '95 thru '07

GENERAL MOTORS
- 10360 GM Automatic Transmission Overhaul
- 38005 Buick Century, Chevrolet Celebrity, Oldsmobile Cutlass Ciera & Pontiac 6000 all models '82 thru '96
- 38010 Buick Regal, Chevrolet Lumina, Oldsmobile Cutlass Supreme & Pontiac Grand Prix (FWD) '88 thru '07
- 38015 Buick Skyhawk, Cadillac Cimarron, Chevrolet Cavalier, Oldsmobile Firenza & Pontiac J-2000 & Sunbird '82 thru '94
- 38016 Chevrolet Cavalier & Pontiac Sunfire '95 thru '05
- 38017 Chevrolet Cobalt & Pontiac G5 '05 thru '11
- 38020 Buick Skylark, Chevrolet Citation, Olds Omega, Pontiac Phoenix '80 thru '85
- 38025 Buick Skylark & Somerset, Oldsmobile Achieva & Calais and Pontiac Grand Am all models '85 thru '98
- 38026 Chevrolet Malibu, Olds Alero & Cutlass, Pontiac Grand Am '97 thru '03
- 38027 Chevrolet Malibu '04 thru '10
- 38030 Cadillac Eldorado, Seville, Oldsmobile Toronado, Buick Riviera '71 thru '85
- 38031 Cadillac Eldorado & Seville, DeVille, Fleetwood & Olds Toronado, Buick Riviera '86 thru '93
- 38032 Cadillac DeVille '94 thru '05 & Seville '92 thru '04 Cadillac DTS '06 thru '10
- 38035 Chevrolet Lumina APV, Olds Silhouette & Pontiac Trans Sport all models '90 thru '96
- 38036 Chevrolet Venture, Olds Silhouette, Pontiac Trans Sport & Montana '97 thru '05
  General Motors Full-size Rear-wheel Drive - see BUICK (19025)
- 38040 Chevrolet Equinox '05 thru '09 Pontiac Torrent '06 thru '09
- 38070 Chevrolet HHR '06 thru '11

GEO
- Metro - see CHEVROLET Sprint (24075)
- Prizm - '85 thru '92 see CHEVY (24060), '93 thru '02 see TOYOTA Corolla (92036)
- 40030 Storm all models '90 thru '93
  Tracker - see SUZUKI Samurai (90010)

GMC
- Vans & Pick-ups - see CHEVROLET

HONDA
- 42010 Accord CVCC all models '76 thru '83
- 42011 Accord all models '84 thru '89
- 42012 Accord all models '90 thru '93
- 42013 Accord all models '94 thru '97
- 42014 Accord all models '98 thru '02
- 42015 Accord '03 thru '07
- 42020 Civic 1200 all models '73 thru '79
- 42021 Civic 1300 & 1500 CVCC '80 thru '83
- 42022 Civic 1500 CVCC all models '75 thru '79

(Continued on other side)

Haynes North America, Inc., 861 Lawrence Drive, Newbury Park, CA 91320-1514 • (805) 498-6703 • http://www.haynes.com

Haynes Automotive Manuals (continued)

NOTE: If you do not see a listing for your vehicle, consult your local Haynes dealer for the latest product information.

42023 **Civic** all models '84 thru '91
42024 **Civic & del Sol** '92 thru '95
42025 **Civic** '96 thru '00, **CR-V** '97 thru '01, **Acura Integra** '94 thru '00
42026 **Civic** '01 thru '10, **CR-V** '02 thru '09
42035 **Odyssey** all models '99 thru '10
  Passport - *see ISUZU Rodeo (47017)*
42037 **Honda Pilot** '03 thru '07, **Acura MDX** '01 thru '07
42040 **Prelude CVCC** all models '79 thru '89

HYUNDAI
43010 **Elantra** all models '96 thru '10
43015 **Excel & Accent** all models '86 thru '09
43050 **Santa Fe** all models '01 thru '06
43055 **Sonata** all models '99 thru '08

INFINITI
  G35 '03 thru '08 - *see NISSAN 350Z (72011)*

ISUZU
  Hombre - *see CHEVROLET S-10 (24071)*
47017 **Rodeo, Amigo & Honda Passport** '89 thru '02
47020 **Trooper & Pick-up** '81 thru '93

JAGUAR
49010 **XJ6** all 6 cyl models '68 thru '86
49011 **XJ6** all models '88 thru '94
49015 **XJ12 & XJS** all 12 cyl models '72 thru '85

JEEP
50010 **Cherokee, Comanche & Wagoneer Limited** all models '84 thru '01
50020 **CJ** all models '49 thru '86
50025 **Grand Cherokee** all models '93 thru '04
50026 **Grand Cherokee** '05 thru '09
50029 **Grand Wagoneer & Pick-up** '72 thru '91 Grand Wagoneer '84 thru '91, Cherokee & Wagoneer '72 thru '83, Pick-up '72 thru '88
50030 **Wrangler** all models '87 thru '11
50035 **Liberty** '02 thru '07

KIA
54050 **Optima** '01 thru '10
54070 **Sephia** '94 thru '01, **Spectra** '00 thru '09, **Sportage** '05 thru '10

LEXUS
  ES 300/330 - *see TOYOTA Camry (92007) (92008)*
  RX 330 - *see TOYOTA Highlander (92095)*

LINCOLN
  Navigator - *see FORD Pick-up (36059)*
59010 **Rear-Wheel Drive** all models '70 thru '10

MAZDA
61010 **GLC Hatchback (rear-wheel drive)** '77 thru '83
61011 **GLC (front-wheel drive)** '81 thru '85
61012 **Mazda3** '04 thru '11
61015 **323 & Protegé** '90 thru '03
61016 **MX-5 Miata** '90 thru '09
61020 **MPV** all models '89 thru '98
  Navajo - *see Ford Explorer (36024)*
61030 **Pick-ups** '72 thru '93
  Pick-ups '94 thru '00 - *see Ford Ranger (36071)*
61035 **RX-7** all models '79 thru '85
61036 **RX-7** all models '86 thru '91
61040 **626 (rear-wheel drive)** all models '79 thru '82
61041 **626/MX-6 (front-wheel drive)** '83 thru '92
61042 **626, MX-6/Ford Probe** '93 thru '02
61043 **Mazda6** '03 thru '11

MERCEDES-BENZ
63012 **123 Series Diesel** '76 thru '85
63015 **190 Series** four-cyl gas models, '84 thru '88
63020 **230/250/280** 6 cyl sohc models '68 thru '72
63025 **280 123 Series** gasoline models '77 thru '81
63030 **350 & 450** all models '71 thru '80
63040 **C-Class:** C230/C240/C280/C320/C350 '01 thru '07

MERCURY
64200 **Villager & Nissan Quest** '93 thru '01
  All other titles, see FORD Listing.

MG
66010 **MGB** Roadster & GT Coupe '62 thru '80
66015 **MG Midget, Austin Healey Sprite** '58 thru '80

MINI
67020 **Mini** '02 thru '11

MITSUBISHI
68020 **Cordia, Tredia, Galant, Precis & Mirage** '83 thru '93
68030 **Eclipse, Eagle Talon & Ply. Laser** '90 thru '94
68031 **Eclipse** '95 thru '05, **Eagle Talon** '95 thru '98
68035 **Galant** '94 thru '10
68040 **Pick-up** '83 thru '96 & **Montero** '83 thru '93

NISSAN
72010 **300ZX** all models including Turbo '84 thru '89
72011 **350Z & Infiniti G35** all models '03 thru '08
72015 **Altima** all models '93 thru '06
72016 **Altima** '07 thru '10
72020 **Maxima** all models '85 thru '92
72021 **Maxima** all models '93 thru '04
72025 **Murano** '03 thru '10
72030 **Pick-ups** '80 thru '97 **Pathfinder** '87 thru '95
72031 **Frontier Pick-up, Xterra, Pathfinder** '96 thru '04
72032 **Frontier & Xterra** '05 thru '11
72040 **Pulsar** all models '83 thru '86
  Quest - *see MERCURY Villager (64200)*
72050 **Sentra** all models '82 thru '94
72051 **Sentra & 200SX** all models '95 thru '06
72060 **Stanza** all models '82 thru '90
72070 **Titan pick-ups** '04 thru '10 **Armada** '05 thru '10

OLDSMOBILE
73015 **Cutlass** V6 & V8 gas models '74 thru '88
  For other OLDSMOBILE titles, see BUICK, CHEVROLET or GENERAL MOTORS listing.

PLYMOUTH
  For PLYMOUTH titles, see DODGE listing.

PONTIAC
79008 **Fiero** all models '84 thru '88
79018 **Firebird** V8 models except Turbo '70 thru '81
79019 **Firebird** all models '82 thru '92
79025 **G6** all models '05 thru '09
79040 **Mid-size Rear-wheel Drive** '70 thru '87
  Vibe '03 thru '11 - *see TOYOTA Matrix (92060)*
  For other PONTIAC titles, see BUICK, CHEVROLET or GENERAL MOTORS listing.

PORSCHE
80020 **911** except Turbo & Carrera 4 '65 thru '89
80025 **914** all 4 cyl models '69 thru '76
80030 **924** all models including Turbo '76 thru '82
80035 **944** all models including Turbo '83 thru '89

RENAULT
  Alliance & Encore - *see AMC (14020)*

SAAB
84010 **900** all models including Turbo '79 thru '88

SATURN
87010 **Saturn** all S-series models '91 thru '02
87011 **Saturn Ion** '03 thru '07
87020 **Saturn** all L-series models '00 thru '04
87040 **Saturn VUE** '02 thru '07

SUBARU
89002 **1100, 1300, 1400 & 1600** '71 thru '79
89003 **1600 & 1800** 2WD & 4WD '80 thru '94
89100 **Legacy** all models '90 thru '99
89101 **Legacy & Forester** '00 thru '06

SUZUKI
90010 **Samurai/Sidekick & Geo Tracker** '86 thru '01

TOYOTA
92005 **Camry** all models '83 thru '91
92006 **Camry** all models '92 thru '96
92007 **Camry, Avalon, Solara, Lexus ES 300** '97 thru '01
92008 **Toyota Camry, Avalon and Solara and Lexus ES 300/330** all models '02 thru '06
92009 **Camry** '07 thru '11
92015 **Celica Rear Wheel Drive** '71 thru '85
92020 **Celica Front Wheel Drive** '86 thru '99
92025 **Celica Supra** all models '79 thru '92
92030 **Corolla** all models '75 thru '79
92032 **Corolla** all rear wheel drive models '80 thru '87
92035 **Corolla** all front wheel drive models '84 thru '92
92036 **Corolla & Geo Prizm** '93 thru '02
92037 **Corolla** models '03 thru '11
92040 **Corolla Tercel** all models '80 thru '82
92045 **Corona** all models '74 thru '82
92050 **Cressida** all models '78 thru '82
92055 **Land Cruiser** FJ40, 43, 45, 55 '68 thru '82
92056 **Land Cruiser** FJ60, 62, 80, FZJ80 '80 thru '96
92060 **Matrix & Pontiac Vibe** '03 thru '11
92065 **MR2** all models '85 thru '87
92070 **Pick-up** all models '69 thru '78
92075 **Pick-up** all models '79 thru '95
92076 **Tacoma, 4Runner, & T100** '93 thru '04
92077 **Tacoma** all models '05 thru '09
92078 **Tundra** '00 thru '06 & **Sequoia** '01 thru '07
92079 **4Runner** all models '03 thru '09
92080 **Previa** all models '91 thru '95
92081 **Prius** all models '01 thru '08
92082 **RAV4** all models '96 thru '10
92085 **Tercel** all models '87 thru '94
92090 **Sienna** all models '98 thru '09
92095 **Highlander & Lexus RX-330** '99 thru '07

TRIUMPH
94007 **Spitfire** all models '62 thru '81
94010 **TR7** all models '75 thru '81

VW
96008 **Beetle & Karmann Ghia** '54 thru '79
96009 **New Beetle** '98 thru '11
96016 **Rabbit, Jetta, Scirocco & Pick-up** gas models '75 thru '92 & Convertible '80 thru '92
96017 **Golf, GTI & Jetta** '93 thru '98, **Cabrio** '95 thru '02
96018 **Golf, GTI, Jetta** '99 thru '05
96019 **Jetta, Rabbit, GTI & Golf** '05 thru '11
96020 **Rabbit, Jetta & Pick-up** diesel '77 thru '84
96023 **Passat** '98 thru '05, **Audi A4** '96 thru '01
96030 **Transporter 1600** all models '68 thru '79
96035 **Transporter 1700, 1800 & 2000** '72 thru '79
96040 **Type 3 1500 & 1600** all models '63 thru '73
96045 **Vanagon** all air-cooled models '80 thru '83

VOLVO
97010 **120, 130 Series & 1800 Sports** '61 thru '73
97015 **140 Series** all models '66 thru '74
97020 **240 Series** all models '76 thru '93
97040 **740 & 760 Series** all models '82 thru '88
97050 **850 Series** all models '93 thru '97

TECHBOOK MANUALS
10205 **Automotive Computer Codes**
10206 **OBD-II & Electronic Engine Management**
10210 **Automotive Emissions Control Manual**
10215 **Fuel Injection Manual** '78 thru '85
10220 **Fuel Injection Manual** '86 thru '99
10225 **Holley Carburetor Manual**
10230 **Rochester Carburetor Manual**
10240 **Weber/Zenith/Stromberg/SU Carburetors**
10305 **Chevrolet Engine Overhaul Manual**
10310 **Chrysler Engine Overhaul Manual**
10320 **Ford Engine Overhaul Manual**
10330 **GM and Ford Diesel Engine Repair Manual**
10333 **Engine Performance Manual**
10340 **Small Engine Repair Manual, 5 HP & Less**
10341 **Small Engine Repair Manual, 5.5 - 20 HP**
10345 **Suspension, Steering & Driveline Manual**
10355 **Ford Automatic Transmission Overhaul**
10360 **GM Automatic Transmission Overhaul**
10405 **Automotive Body Repair & Painting**
10410 **Automotive Brake Manual**
10411 **Automotive Anti-lock Brake (ABS) Systems**
10415 **Automotive Detailing Manual**
10420 **Automotive Electrical Manual**
10425 **Automotive Heating & Air Conditioning**
10430 **Automotive Reference Manual & Dictionary**
10435 **Automotive Tools Manual**
10440 **Used Car Buying Guide**
10445 **Welding Manual**
10450 **ATV Basics**
10452 **Scooters 50cc to 250cc**

SPANISH MANUALS
98903 **Reparación de Carrocería & Pintura**
98904 **Manual de Carburador Modelos Holley & Rochester**
98905 **Códigos Automotrices de la Computadora**
98906 **OBD-II & Sistemas de Control Electrónico del Motor**
98910 **Frenos Automotriz**
98913 **Electricidad Automotriz**
98915 **Inyección de Combustible** '86 al '99
99040 **Chevrolet & GMC Camionetas** '67 al '87
99041 **Chevrolet & GMC Camionetas** '88 al '98
99042 **Chevrolet & GMC Camionetas Cerradas** '68 al '95
99043 **Chevrolet/GMC Camionetas** '94 al '04
99048 **Chevrolet/GMC Camionetas** '99 al '06
99055 **Dodge Caravan & Plymouth Voyager** '84 al '95
99075 **Ford Camionetas y Bronco** '80 al '94
99076 **Ford F-150** '97 al '09
99077 **Ford Camionetas Cerradas** '69 al '91
99088 **Ford Modelos de Tamaño Mediano** '75 al '86
99089 **Ford Camionetas Ranger** '93 al '10
99091 **Ford Taurus & Mercury Sable** '86 al '95
99095 **GM Modelos de Tamaño Grande** '70 al '90
99100 **GM Modelos de Tamaño Mediano** '70 al '88
99106 **Jeep Cherokee, Wagoneer & Comanche** '84 al '00
99110 **Nissan Camioneta** '80 al '96, **Pathfinder** '87 al '95
99118 **Nissan Sentra** '82 al '94
99125 **Toyota Camionetas y 4Runner** '79 al '95

Over 100 Haynes motorcycle manuals also available

7-12

Haynes North America, Inc., 861 Lawrence Drive, Newbury Park, CA 91320-1514 • (805) 498-6703 • http://www.haynes.com

Preserving Our Motoring Heritage

< The Model J Duesenberg Derham Tourster. Only eight of these magnificent cars were ever built – this is the only example to be found outside the United States of America

Almost every car you've ever loved, loathed or desired is gathered under one roof at the Haynes Motor Museum. Over 300 immaculately presented cars and motorbikes represent every aspect of our motoring heritage, from elegant reminders of bygone days, such as the superb Model J Duesenberg to curiosities like the bug-eyed BMW Isetta. There are also many old friends and flames. Perhaps you remember the 1959 Ford Popular that you did your courting in? The magnificent 'Red Collection' is a spectacle of classic sports cars including AC, Alfa Romeo, Austin Healey, Ferrari, Lamborghini, Maserati, MG, Riley, Porsche and Triumph.

A Perfect Day Out

Each and every vehicle at the Haynes Motor Museum has played its part in the history and culture of Motoring. Today, they make a wonderful spectacle and a great day out for all the family. Bring the kids, bring Mum and Dad, but above all bring your camera to capture those golden memories for ever. You will also find an impressive array of motoring memorabilia, a comfortable 70 seat video cinema and one of the most extensive transport book shops in Britain. The Pit Stop Cafe serves everything from a cup of tea to wholesome, home-made meals or, if you prefer, you can enjoy the large picnic area nestled in the beautiful rural surroundings of Somerset.

> John Haynes O.B.E., Founder and Chairman of the museum at the wheel of a Haynes Light 12.

< The 1936 490cc sohc-engined International Norton – well known for its racing success

The Museum is situated on the A359 Yeovil to Frome road at Sparkford, just off the A303 in Somerset. It is about 40 miles south of Bristol, and 25 minutes drive from the M5 intersection at Taunton.
Open 9.30am - 5.30pm (10.00am - 4.00pm Winter) 7 days a week, *except Christmas Day, Boxing Day and New Years Day*
Special rates available for schools, coach parties and outings Charitable Trust No. 292048